Electronic
Media
Criticism

LEA'S COMMUNICATION SERIES

Jennings Bryant/Dolf Zillmann, General Editors

For a complete list of titles in LEA's Communication Series, please contact Lawrence Erlbaum Associates, Publishers

Electronic Media Criticism

Applied Perspectives

Second Edition

Peter B. Orlik
Central Michigan University

LAWRENCE ERLBAUM ASSOCIATES, PUBLISHERS
2001   Mahwah, New Jersey   London

Lawrence Erlbaum Associates, Inc., Publishers
10 Industrial Avenue
Mahwah, New Jersey 07430

Library of Congress Cataloging-in-Publication Data

Orlik, Peter B.
    Electronic media criticism : applied perspectives / Peter B. Orlik. — 2nd ed.
        p.   cm.
    Includes bibliographical references and index.
    ISBN 0-8058-3641-1 (pbk. : alk. paper)
    1. Mass media criticism.   I. Title.

P96.C76 O76   2000
302.23'7—dc21   00-039324
                                                                          CIP

Books published by Lawrence Erlbaum Associates are printed on acid-free paper,
and their bindings are chosen for strength and durability.

Printed in the United States of America
10 9 8 7 6 5 4 3 2 1

To Chris:

In deepest gratitude for the unwavering music of your support and encouragement

"Always a Franklin"

Brief Contents

Contents

List of Illustrations

List of Critiques

Preface

Electronic Media Criticism, Second Edition, takes the position that radio, television, and emerging on-line programming can be analyzed as art. Therefore, the material heard and seen over the electronic media is worthy of *serious* critical consideration by both industry professionals and the consumers they seek to serve. If you are a media practitioner or practitioner-in-training, *Electronic Media Criticism* offers you theoretically sound and realistic measures by which you can evaluate your own content as well as that of your competitors. These measures are also useful defensively in coping with the charges and challenges frequently hurled at media agencies by other segments of society. On the other hand, even if you are not pursuing a media career, this volume can help improve what critic David Bianculli calls your 'teleliteracy.' The chapters that follow will aid you, as a consumer, in making more beneficial and enjoyable program choices.

Electronic Media Criticism, Second Edition, is not intended to proliferate criticism. Indeed, the electronic media already are critiqued more broadly and enthusiastically than is almost any other area of human endeavor. This is because virtually every consumer has access to several 'receiving sets': radio, television, and computer. With programming delivered to these sets via the publicly owned spectrum, municipally granted right-of-way, or universally accessible ethernet, every member of society takes a proprietary interest in electronic media products. Furthermore, because most people have listened and watched since birth, they believe themselves to be expert judges of media content.

No, the need is not for more criticism, but rather for criticism *refinement*. Refinement is necessary because the fishbowl environment in which media professionals must function has given rise to almost as many haphazard gauges for evaluation as there are programmatic fishes to be scrutinized. And unfortunately, some of these gauges are so specialized or, what is worse, so *biased* as to be applicable to only one program type and/or single special-interest perspective.

The problem is compounded by the fact that media criticism has largely been ignored by the more established evaluative systems common to the literary, dramatic, musical and visual arts. It therefore lacks the respect automatically accorded to criticism affiliated with these allegedly more legitimate disciplines.

Some theorists argue that the shortage of refined media criticism is also due to the relative youth of the enterprise on which it focuses. Because even radio as an expressive medium is less than a century old, goes this argument, there has been comparatively little time for the electronic arts to establish comprehensive assessment standards of their own. Such a view, however, assumes that these electronic arts are so divorced from other creative enterprises that critical procedures common to older disciplines cannot be enlisted for the purpose of audio/video evaluation.

Electronic Media Criticism, Second Edition, adopts a much different orientation. This book argues that principles of criticism developed for more 'mature' artistic enterprises are equally adaptable to, and beneficial for, the tools and products of electronic expression. We also borrow from philosophy, psychology, economics, sociology, and linguistics in suggesting a variety of critical perspectives that, despite their divergence, still can be mutually supportive in evaluating multifaceted media products.

Unlike many other volumes on the topic, this book sees the subject's horizon as stretching far beyond the world of prime-time television. Thus, our purview includes nonprime as well as prime-time content, the aural as well as the visual medium, commercials as well as full-length programs, and "reality" as well as news and scripted entertainment shows. Emerging implications for on-line criticism are also explored as these implications relate to programming intended for broad consumption.

It is not the delivery system but the content it carries that presents the critical challenge. Consumers listen to, watch, and respond to *output*. The particular technology that happens to deliver this output is unimportant to them—at least, until it technically malfunctions! Of course, for the media professional, different delivery systems involve different regulatory, business, and therefore, *content* challenges. These distinctions are highlighted as we proceed.

On the other hand, *Electronic Media Criticism*, Second Edition, does not seek to contribute cutting-edge research in semiotics or quantitative methodologies. Nor is it intended to enhance the graduate school education of communication theorists, despite the worthiness of that aim. Instead, this book gives students interested in media careers (as well as people whose careers are already in progress) an understanding of the program-relevant issues, content, structures, and practices that shape our profession. Simultaneously, *Electronic Media Criticism*, Second Edition, serves as a creator/consumer training manual in how to dissect and cope with programming on a practical, day-to-day basis. Consequently, this volume is a blending of the insights of both industry and academic authorities. Trade publications are cited as frequently as are scholarly monographs. Both perspectives are essential in a broad-ranging art such as ours if we are to develop a valid and viable critical outlook.

Likewise, instead of presenting one way to assess one genre of electronic media content, we explore several procedures that might be used to understand and legitimately evaluate a wide spectrum of projects. In lieu of advocating a single critical approach or methodology, therefore, *Electronic Media Criticism*, Second Edition, illuminates several such systems, each of which can be independently pursued or abandoned as the reader's interest, philosophy, and occupational experience determine.

Along the way, it is hoped that your personal critical sense will be stimulated or, in the words of eminent broadcast critic Robert Lewis Shayon, "revved up" to the enormously important practice of electronic media analysis:

The critical faculty, though apparently inactive in many individuals, is actually quietly idling, like a motor. It needs to be revved up, to accelerate critically, and to fire other idling motors. . . . Once revved up, they can hopefully take off to make their own critical contacts.[1]

To lead you toward this point of combustion, *Electronic Media Criticism*, Second Edition, begins with four chapters that define the critical arena. Chapter 1 delineates the role of criticism, why *legitimate* media criticism is especially needed and how it has evolved in our profession. Chapter 2 isolates key critic functions, responsibilities, and values. This is followed, in Chapter 3, by an examination of how comprehensive criticism implicates the entire communication process. Finally, Chapter 4 explores how human beings acquire and manipulate the knowledge that is the source of both program content and our assessment of it.

The next three chapters cover nuts-and-bolts concerns. They probe the instruments and techniques from which electronic media product is fashioned (Chapters 5 and 6) and the business objectives that motivate this fashioning (Chapter 7).

With this groundwork laid, the book's last eight chapters introduce more specific critical orientations and applications. Chapter 8 explores the audience uses-and-gratifications approach, Chapter 9 focuses on a sociological "depiction" schema, and Chapter 10 pursues a literary/structuralist point of view. In Chapter 11, we examine the philosophical ethics and values orientation before delving into broad-ranging aesthetics perspectives in Chapters 12 and 13. Chapter 14 isolates "reality" programming's special appeals and volatile issues before the concluding section on composite criticism (Chapter 15) demonstrates how these various outlooks can be collectively incorporated to accomplish the critical task.

The three complete sitcom scripts in Appendix A provide specimens for practice in applying several of the methodologies presented in earlier chapters. By design, *The Cosby Show* script precedes those from *The Newsroom* and *The Simpsons* by more than a decade, *The Newsroom* is a Canadian rather than U.S. product, and *The Simpsons* is an animated rather than live-action show. We can thereby experiment with the effects of time, origin, and production genre as critical variables.

Appendix B offers suggested exercises generated from individual chapter discussions as well as from Appendix A's three series scripts. These exercises can be equally beneficial for the independent reader or the student using this book as part of a class.

Whether *your* exposure to this volume is voluntary or class-assigned, you should feel much more comfortable and self-assured in making program content judgments by the time you get to the back cover. As a media professional, it is essential that you learn to make such judgments to improve your profession and your own career prospects. As a literate consumer, the same judgments are required to get the most out of your personal listening/viewing experiences.

Make no mistake about it. Electronic media criticism is a vital ingredient in the betterment of not just its industry, but of the culture as well. *New York Post* critic David Bianculli declares "those who dismiss this mass medium as a crass medium are missing the point. Television is our culture's most common language, its basic point of reference; it is also where our children are first exposed to allusion, satire and other 'literary' concepts."[2] The electronic media are just as important to those children later in their educational life. As Professor Robert Thompson reminds faculty colleagues,

for most college students, television is the culture of choice. They watch it because they want to, and they have been doing so for their entire lives. Instead of knocking TV, why not help them, through careful analysis of the programs, make the significant amount of time they spend watching it more meaningful, more intellectual, and more fun than before? After all, isn't that a principal function of criticism?[3]

Professors Richard Breyer and Peter Moller support this position when they add:

All students, not just those pursuing a career in television, should learn how "television language" contributes to their impressions of the events, products, and personalities that appear on their television screens; . . . it will help them begin to appreciate the sources of the power and magic of the images that play such an important part in their lives.[4]

What Thompson, Breyer, and Moller wrote of television at the end of the 1980s may now increasingly be applied to the on-line world as well.

As we begin our investigation of how to decode and evaluate this old and new media "magic," the key is not to be intimidated by the seeming complexity and vastness of the electronic enterprise, not to be scared off like the title character from *Leave It to Beaver* who confessed to his big brother, "Ya know, Wally, I'm glad I don't know as much about life as you do, otherwise I'd be the biggest chicken in the whole world."[5]

Be reassured. Competent practitioners *can* fearlessly appraise their industry if they combine their practical knowledge of its workings with a supplementary understanding of human perception and human nature. As Robert Lewis Shayon advocated more than a quarter-century ago,

mass media criticism must, with modesty but with courage and daring, touch all the human bases that it can possibly use. For television and radio today everywhere in the world are the total human environment, the mental ecological field where mankind's destiny is being shaped. Let the intellectual who despises and scorns television and radio as the pablum of the comic-strip masses ignore them as he will and fix his gaze on more noble objects of attention—yet the commonalities as well as the peculiarities of his life are impinged upon by the mercurial power of these media.[6]

If you are a media practitioner required to understand and harness this power, you owe it to yourself and your profession to learn to use the tools of criticism for the betterment of everyone concerned.

Valid standards of criticism are essential to any profession's achievement of beneficial change. But these standards can have impact only if new professionals know how to use them. As media research consultant James Fletcher warns, "It is impossible for an industry to change beyond the capacity of its incoming employee pool."[7]

ACKNOWLEDGMENTS

Appreciation is extended to Linda Bathgate, Communications Editor at Lawrence Erlbaum Associates, for her enthusiastic support and promotion of this second edition of

Electronic Media Criticism. Thanks also to Grace Sheldrick, Wordsworth Associates, for her expert copyediting of a complicated manuscript. I am also indebted to Antonia Kaufman of *The Simpsons*, Ken Finkleman, creator of *The Newsroom*, and Kim Tinsley, director of public affairs for *The Cosby Show* for their kindness in providing masterpiece scripts for our analysis and enjoyment. Special mention also must be made of Dr. Thomas O. Olson. His inspiring teaching at Wayne State University imparted to me a respect for media criticism and aesthetics that has found an outlet in this project. In addition, I am grateful to saxophone professor John Nichol who, in teaching an old clarinetist a new instrument, imparted a special aesthetic sensitivity that proved a valuable inspiration for several parts of this manuscript.

Finally, I extend deep gratitude to my wife, Chris, and our two children, Darcy and Blaine, who have patiently endured and supported this project over its fifteen-year progression.

Recognition is also given the following sources for special permission to use key materials throughout this text.

John Fiske and John Hartley, *Reading Television*. Copyright 1978 by Methuen and Company, publishers.

Frye, Northrop; *Anatomy of Criticism: Four Essays*. Copyright 1957 by Princeton University Press. Scattered quotes reprinted by permission of Princeton University Press. Renewed 1985.

Carl Grabo, *The Creative Critic*. Copyright 1948 by The University of Chicago. All rights reserved. Published 1948. Composed and printed by The University of Chicago Press, Chicago, Illinois, U.S.A.

Greene, Theodore Meyer; *The Arts and the Art of Criticism*. Copyright 1940 by Princeton University Press. Scattered quotes reprinted by permission of Princeton University Press. Renewed 1968.

DeWitt Parker, *The Principles of Aesthetics*, second edition. Greenwood Press, 1976. Used with permission of G. Vaughan Parker.

Robert Lewis Shayon, *Open to Criticism*. Beacon Press, 1971. Used by permission of Robert Lewis Shayon.

Jerome Stolnitz, *Aesthetics and Philosophy of Art Criticism*. Copyright 1960, Houghton-Mifflin Company. Used by permission of the publisher.

ENDNOTES

1. Robert Lewis Shayon, *Open to Criticism* (Boston: Beacon Press, 1971), 6.
2. David Bianculli, "Teleliteracy," *TAXI Magazine* (November 1989), 98.
3. Robert Thompson, "The 'Garbage' on Television Is Worth Including in the College Curriculum," *The Chronicle of Higher Education* (October 26, 1988), B3.
4. Richard Breyer and Peter Moller, "The Liberal Arts Curriculum Should Include a Requirement to Study Television and Its Special Language," *The Chronicle of Higher Education* (February 1, 1989), B2–B3.
5. Irwyn Applebaum, *The World According to Beaver* (New York: Bantam Books, 1984), 48.
6. Shayon, 47–48.
7. James Fletcher, remarks to the Broadcast Education Association Convention, April 27, 1989 (Las Vegas).

1 The Essence of Criticism

Every profession has the responsibility to derive methods for assessing the performance of its members. And the professionals themselves must understand and apply those methods to their own works as well as to the works of their colleagues and competitors. This is no less true in the media profession.

Such assessments and appraisals collectively constitute the practice of *criticism*. But, unfortunately, when the term *criticism* is used in common conversation, its implications are often misunderstood. So before we, as electronic media professionals, can learn to use critical methodologies within the context of our field, we first must accurately isolate criticism's essential ingredients and procedures.

WHAT IS CRITICISM?

In everyday speech, when people mention *criticism*, or the act of being *criticized*, they usually mean an unpleasant, negative event. Criticism is assumed to be a destructive weapon rather than a constructive tool. Its sole purpose seems to be the extermination of the object or practice at which this verbal weapon is hurled. Taken in this context, criticism makes an impact only at the expense of its subject. If this really were criticism's main goal, there would be little point in embracing it to help us understand our profession. Rather, we would only be using criticism counterproductively—to destroy electronic media content and/or institutions. Pushed to the extreme, such counterfeit criticism becomes the pursuit of boycotts and bookburnings, in which something is deleted but nothing is created.

Fortunately, legitimate criticism is a more beneficial activity. Certainly, it can point out defects. This, however, is little more than name-calling unless it also explains *why* these elements are defective and suggests what can be done to rectify such flaws. This *rectification*, this suggestion for improve-

ment, is essential in the media profession if its products are to survive and prosper. In a sense, valid criticism is like remodeling a building. In the remodeling process some features must be dismantled or demolished before the improved edifice can be built. This tearing down is never devastation for its own sake, but a necessary stage in the structure's refinement.

If, on the other hand, no suggested plan for improvement (no rectification) is presented, this implies one of two things. Either the program is already perfect (an unlikely possibility in any human creation), or the alleged critic doesn't know enough about the field to fashion a workable recommendation.

The original Greek word for criticism, *krinein*, means to comprehend or to judge. Clearly, both comprehension and judgment are essential tasks in the critical process. The person who does not understand the subject matter and its format cannot be trusted as a critic. An umpire who has never played baseball may make astute judgments if he has attentively watched many games and mastered the league's rule book. An umpire who has never seen a game or read the rules, however, would cause the contest to degenerate into chaos. Similarly, a critic of the electronic media need not actually have worked in our profession as long as he or she has extensively studied our industry's workings (operational rules) and products as well as the specific programmatic product under discussion.

In theory, this obligation applies as much to critics within the government as it does to critics from the general public. However, politicians often ignore the need to experience media content before commenting on it. "I wish more people in Congress would watch our shows before they criticize," laments studio executive Greg Meidel. "In most cases, in meetings I have attended in Washington that have included the President, I was overwhelmed that they tended to criticize when they don't watch the product."[1]

Legitimate criticism, on the other hand, results from conscientious comprehension leading to an informed judgment that includes the responsibility to formulate *positive* as well as negative commentary. As Jerry McNeeley discovered, "Criticism is a carefully considered judgment of the merits and faults of a work of art with the purpose of improving and stimulating interest."[2] In Chapter 12, we discuss at length the concept of electronic media content as art. For now, our point is that "carefully considered judgment" of the work's effective *and* defective properties is the hallmark of valid and professionally helpful criticism. Further, genuine criticism has a goal of expanding and upgrading audience attentiveness ("improving and stimulating interest") to the medium under scrutiny. Thus, it enhances the potential market for our programmatic products and our own career prospects!

But Jerome Stolnitz has pointed out that "we analyze works of art not only in order to understand them better, but also to pass judgment on their *value*."[3] This concept of valuation is especially important because you cannot appraise something that you believe has no worth. Consequently, criticism that is solely negative cannot be criticism at all because it refuses to acknowledge any value in the work it's attacking. Many alleged radio/television critics fail this crucial test when their disdain for the electronic media surfaces. Their comments are not balanced assessments of our industry but are one-sided arguments; they are disparagements that contribute to neither audience understanding of our media nor the comparative valuation of the program under examination. When seen in this light, the pronouncements of such myopic critics are revealed as unreasonable. As Caren Deming counsels, "critics must demonstrate the willingness to meet works and their audiences on their own terms: the willingness to fully understand the forces that compel creators and gatekeepers to make decisions."[4]

Certainly, it is reasonable to assume that nothing created by human beings—radio/television content included—can be all good. But, as Figure 1-1 also argues, it is just as reasonable to conclude that no human

FIGURE 1-1
Constructive criticism perches between these extremes. (Illustration by Scott Huver)

product or medium of expression can be all bad, even if a show's virtue, at first glance, seems to be only that it was properly timed so as not to run into the next program. Legitimate electronic media criticism keeps this criterion of reasonableness in mind while compiling the evaluative *balance sheet* for a particular media product.

The balance sheet analogy must not be taken too literally, however. Seldom, if ever, are the strengths and weaknesses of a particular show exactly equal. Inevitably, there is a tilt toward a positive or negative conclusion. But by inventorying all the benefits and drawbacks, we can understand the properties of this particular program and also, in Stolnitz's words, "understand them *better*" in future listening/viewing decisions and experiences.

Profession-building criticism, then, is knowledgeable comprehension, positive/ negative ascertainment, and resulting "carefully considered judgment" as a means of reasonably estimating the value of a particular work. Through this process, we and our audiences become more sensitive to similar value, or its absence, in other electronic media content.

The *critique* is the vehicle that carries this criticism from its author to media decision-makers and/or media audiences. To be properly focused, the critique uses what Monroe Beardsley calls "a kind of method or principled procedure, by which proposed interpretations can be tested."[5] A wide variety of such methods is available in electronic media criticism. Some of the major ones are sampled in subsequent chapters. Whatever the procedure used, however, a critique should encompass each of the five basic steps that constitute what S. Stephenson Smith calls the *critical process*:[6]

1. Apprehension of the work by means of sense impressions.
2. Analysis of the work which puts it in perspective and corrects unbridled impressionism.
3. Interpretation of the work to the reader of the criticism.
4. Orientation of the work to its place in the history of similar works.
5. Valuation or the determination of the peculiar as well as the general essence of the work.

Our discussion already has touched on several of these aspects. We know that the critic (whether inside or outside the media profession) must have actually listened to or watched the material in question. This is what Smith refers to as "apprehension." The critic cannot simply have learned about its content from someone else or only read about it in a studio press release! Next, by using what Beardsley referred to as "a kind of method or principled procedure," the critic should inventory the components of the work. This step moves us beyond a superficial, initial reaction in order to properly decipher the media product for ourselves so that we then can interpret it for others.

Because no piece of programmatic content exists in isolation, part of this deciphering entails comparing this electronic creation with current or past program ventures of a similar type. You can, for example, look at *Frasier* either in terms of contemporary situation comedies with which it must compete, or in terms of past shows that have helped define the category or *genre*. Finally, the particular worth of the program must be determined by weighing its individual merits and flaws so that the creation's individual significance and its significance for the medium both become clear.

For a specific example of how Smith's five-step *critical process* works, read the preview by *Variety*'s Tony Scott of the made-for-TV movie *Dead Silence*.

This preview clearly demonstrates that Tony Scott has watched the entire "vidpic" and has gathered a number of sense impressions from it (chief come-on; cowed expression; oaths of loyalty and continuing traumas; goes through her motions without much conviction; blatant direction; irritating music; abrupt editing).

Second, the critic puts the work in perspective by indicating that "the production plays basically to the upper teens." This core audience must be kept in mind in analyzing the show as a whole. Third, Scott's interpretation of the TV movie includes a thorough discussion of the plot action and the role of the principal characters within it. He delineates specific weaknesses in story development (nothing's said about the fingerprints; her knowledge of legal procedure makes it clear why she was rejected by Columbia Law School) but he also isolates merits (scene . . . at a graduation party has strength; Nevins lends authenticity to the story).

Fourth, the *Variety* writer orients his readers to the fact that the show is a "drama"

DEAD SILENCE

by Tony Scott

The adventures of three college women who run into a jam during a Palm Springs spring break suggests that writer J. David Miles had a solid idea about moral dilemma, contemporary mores and delineation of characters. Trouble is, the execution of Dead Silence under Peter O'Fallon's blatant direction draws out little of the drama's potential.

Pushy pre-law student Zanna (Renee Estevez), uncertain Joan (Lisanna Falk, chief come-on in the vidpic), and Sunnie (Carrie Mitchum) who's snagged a job at a local TV station (how she keeps it with her tardiness and cowed expression isn't clear), hit the desert community during its spring frenzy.

They don't have time to meet fellas because boozed-up Sunnie, driving Zanna and Joan in their rented car on their first excursion, hits and kills a wayfarer they leave out in the desert. The telefilm involves their reactions, oaths of loyalty and continuing traumas.

Nothing's said about the fingerprints that Zanna's left on the man's golf bag, and her knowledge of legal procedure makes it clear why she was rejected by Columbia Law School. Joan begins coming apart almost immediately. And while the others return to college up north, Sunnie goes through her motions without much conviction.

However, there are some good touches. A scene between Joan and her wealthy Dad (Al Ruscio) at a graduation party has strength and Claudette Nevins lends authenticity to the story as the strict TV station owner.

The three actresses involved in the homicide are acceptable, but the production plays basically to upper teens.

With irritating music by Tim Truman, abrupt editing by Joanna Cappuccilli and routine camerawork by Ernest Holzman, Dead Silence will hardly egg folks on to visit Palm Springs during school break. But it does have an important story to tell about guilt and its ramifications; too bad the vidpic's execution isn't up to the premise.

(Courtesy of George Russell, *Variety*)

that flows from an idea about "contemporary mores" with "an important story to tell about guilt and its ramifications." Due perhaps to the space limitations common to *Variety*'s 'shorthand' industry previews he does not, however, manage to compare the program with other shows sharing similar themes or explore attributes shared by "vidpics" in general.

Fifth, Mr. Scott also presents his specific valuation of *Dead Silence*. He accomplishes this by a contention at the beginning (solid idea about moral dilemma . . . Trouble is, the execution . . . draws out little of the drama's potential), which he repeats at the critique's conclusion (too bad the vidpic's execution isn't up to the premise). Between these valuation *bookends*, the critic has arranged all of the sense impressions, analysis, interpretation, and orientation that lead to his overall appraisal.

Though this *Variety* critique is quite brief, Tony Scott still was able to combine elements of the critical process in achieving reputable criticism as we have defined it:

knowledgeable comprehension, positive/negative ascertainment, and resulting carefully considered judgment as a means of reasonably estimating the value of the particular work under scrutiny.

WHY IS ELECTRONIC MEDIA CRITICISM NEEDED?

Now that we have defined criticism in general and have demonstrated its applicability to radio/television, we need to address the issue of why the practice of legitimate criticism is so important for our profession. Some cynics claim that the very pervasiveness of the electronic media makes systematic criticism of them unnecessary. Broadcasting, cable, and the Internet come directly and continuously into the home, argue media criticism's detractors. This differentiates them from the "real" arts, where criticism is needed to guide people to the appropriate concert hall, theater, gallery, movie house, or bookstore. Media audiences, it is claimed, can make personal and uninstructed content choices without risk or effort in the privacy and convenience of their own dwellings. All that is needed is some sort of printed or electronic listing to serve as a menu from which to choose.

Admittedly, electronic media are readily available to virtually everyone. There is also no debating that each listener and viewer makes thousands of programming choices every year on whim or with out the influence of any outside analyst. Yet, it is this very availability and ever-increasing number of media channels that amplify the need for critical guidance. Former Federal Communications Commissioner Lee Loevinger once observed that "Broadcasting is popular and universal because it is elemental, responsive to popular taste, and gives the audience a sense of contact with the world around it which is greater than that provided by any other medium."[7] This sense of contact, however, becomes a mirage if consumers lack the information and perceptual training necessary to (1) perceive the full range of their options, and then (2) evaluate the appropriateness of their subsequent choices in terms of the program content to which they were, as a result, exposed.

Advocating that the public needs some sort of advice in media selection and interpretation may sound elitist if not downright dictatorial. Yet, we must recognize how ill-prepared most people are to be self-sufficient media consumers as compared to consumers of other goods, services, and literary products. In 1962, when television was still in its adolescence, Moses Hadas pointed out that

in literature . . . there is a tangible critical climate, guided and made articulate by professional critics, perhaps, but shaped by all who take books seriously and write about them. The critical climate, in turn, determines what books are made available; no writer who wishes to be heard and no sane publisher will fly in the face of it. A similar critical climate must be

created for television; all who take education seriously in its larger sense—and not the professed critics alone—should talk and write about television as they do about books.[8]

This condition has not yet come to pass. Certainly our educational system prides itself on its ability to turn out citizens who have learned how to earn a wage, evaluate a retail purchase, balance a checkbook, and make some sense out of the printed word. But the "purchase" of electronic media content through the prioritized expenditure of one's precious time, and the absorption and evaluation of that content in terms of one's own interests and expectations, are issues seldom, if ever, raised in the standard school curriculum. Instead, observes Elayne Rapping, our educational system

subtly instills in us a disdain for "mass culture," for the culture with which we grew up and know most deeply. This is one of the most subtle methods by which our dominant institutions keep most of us—*perhaps most significantly those destined to be the future interpreters of society and culture*—ignorant of the forces and values governing our lives. The Humanities, according to academic wisdom, encompass only those forms created by dead people to interpret past eras.[9] [Italics added.]

Even when electronic media content is touched on in the curriculum, adds Professor Mary Kupiec Cayton, "academic literature focuses on problems and rarely acknowledges the benign, the merely pleasant, and the reassuring aspects of television."[10]

Nevertheless, television and the other electronic media are what constitute the most broadly consulted index of what our society is all about. "Even the most successful paperback book published in any given year has perhaps only a third of the audience of the least popular television show of that same season," points out commentator Ed Weiner. "And although not everyone who watches TV buys books, almost everyone who buys books watches TV."[11]

How many book reports, for example, did you have to complete before finishing high school? On the other hand, how many electronic media listening or viewing reports were assigned? While the decline of the printed word's penetration into our society is nothing to rejoice about, it signals a shift that must be addressed both by the educational establishment and our own profession. Once they leave secondary school, many students will seldom, if ever, read a book again. But all former students will absorb the disjointed equivalent of thousands of book-length narratives that they string together through continuous selection, re-selection and consumption of radio, television, and on-line messages.

"Despite the media's overwhelming influence," Professor J. Robert Craig points out, "serious study of how media messages are researched, produced, and delivered has received little more than cursory attention in our public schools and gone ignored by the educational reform movement."[12] This striking mismatch between classroom exercises and real-world behavior exists at the college level as well. "To say that the communications media are central to the functioning of our society is to state the obvious," affirms Professor Everette Dennis. "However, American undergraduate education almost completely ignores the study of mass communication. Unless students major in communications, journalism, or media studies, they can go through college without acquiring more than fragmentary knowledge about mass communication."[13] Recently, computer literacy has pushed its way onto the educational agenda—proving that curricular change is possible and providing a boost to Internet penetration.

Meanwhile, the continuing resistance to admitting broadcast/cable studies to the curriculum comes from academics who fail to recognize the contradiction between their attitudes and their behaviors. As philosophy professor Alan Olson observes,

We find ourselves in the somewhat curious situation where, on the one hand, intellectuals find it possible, even chic, to say nasty things about television anywhere, anytime, without fear of reprisal. One may even be congratulated for attacking something as allegedly banal as the pop culture that television both spews out and stimulates with abandon. On the other hand, indignant critics of the medium will usually appear on television at a moment's notice if asked to do so. . . . TV bashing, therefore, is a manifestly unconstructive and frequently dishonest activity, particularly in the academy where both the assets and liabilities of the medium and its messages have such far-reaching consequences.[14]

As we discuss in the previous section of this chapter, "indignant critics" are incapable of serving as critics at all because they lack the willingness (or the insight) to perceive any value in their subject.

People who would never dare to assess a sonnet or dissect a sonata feel comfortable making broad, unequivocal pronouncements about radio and television's output. Gene Jankowski, then president of the CBS Broadcast Group, observed that we are "living in a country where it is popular to criticize television. Indeed, I often think that some of the more active critics of our medium don't even own sets, because their letter and oral diatribes are occasionally difficult to match with programs. We very often receive mail before the program appears on the air."[15]

Robert Batscha, president of the Museum of Radio and Television, advances an historical explanation for the discrepancy between the way the older forms of artistic expression and television are treated when he points out:

You know, snapshots became photography because people began to focus on what was really excellent and what was creative. And television is in very much the same early mode. When you think about it, it's one of the few modes of creative expression where people focus on what's bad as opposed to what's good.

I mean, if 10 percent of the books published each year are good, we're lucky. But nobody questions whether or not the book is a creative form. At best, 10 percent of the plays written each year are good, but nobody questions whether theater is a creative form, or a vital form, or a great form of expression. Or that it isn't going to have a great creative future. Yet in television, most of the critics, the press and society focus on the 90 percent that's terrible, not on the 10 percent that's excellent.[16]

Similarly, because of their newness, "we shouldn't be surprised that the Internet and computers in general are being attacked," Professor Mitchell Stephens observes. "Indeed, we should expect more of it. We might expect to hear more people complain of 'drowning in a sea of useless, unedited information,' of 'virtual life,' and an even larger chorus of people proclaiming that these machines 'will never wean me from the portability and smell of my magazines and books.' "[17]

The more longstanding compulsion to berate radio and television stems from the fact that, to some legally arguable extent, broadcasting and cablecasting use a public resource and therefore (like the public schools) must be subject to an especially intense scrutiny by the citizenry. Granted, the public right of way on which a cable franchise depends differs in kind and legal precedent from the spectrum space for which a broadcaster is licensed. But most people assume that both broadcasters and cablecasters are public trustees (or even servants). The channel's contractual dependence on its audience is taken to justify even the most misinformed commentary.

Because a print publisher owns or leases its presses and delivery mechanisms, and because a film studio exhibits its products via the private property of movie houses (and video marts), these media enterprises escape much of the constant buffeting that is the broadcaster's and, to a lesser extent, the cablecaster's lot. Besides, the First Amendment to the U.S. Constitution forbids only "abridging the freedom of speech, or of the press." It says nothing about broadcasting, cablecasting, or, for that matter, the Internet. As historically ridiculous as that strict interpretation seems, it has served as the underpinning for several judicial decisions and as the belief structure for many pressure groups.

The more popular media enterprises become, the more scrutiny and criticism media professionals must expect and be prepared to rebut. In a very real sense, the technological success of radio/television seems to endow them with more power and capabilities than these media actually possess. As network consultant Barbara Lee theorizes, "it may be that new technologies simply provide a ready point of departure to express wistful desires for panaceas for intractable social problems or human frailties. A common approach is to diagnose a problem as one that television has created or, at least, exacerbated, and provide formulas for ways with a little tinkering, television could fix it."[18]

In summary, knowledgeable and reputable electronic media criticism is essential because of these four factors:

1. The pervasiveness and popularity of electronic programming
2. The absence of media literacy from the school curriculum
3. The electronic media's status as a public resource
4. The media's technological success, which makes them appear all-powerful.

As media professionals, it is easy for us to respond to these conditions by promoting criticism that is solely *defensive*. Or, we can attempt to develop content codes (or technical fixes like the V-chip) that serve as convenient "supercensors" to which we and our competitors can passively adhere.

Such actions, however, are the way to professional stagnation rather than continued improvement. Effective electronic media criticism is not an *apology for* the profession but a *refiner* of that profession through the encouragement of what *New York Times* critic Jack Gould once identified as "an alert, critical, articulate audience."[19] Like any art form, electronic programming can only be expected to advance with—not in opposition to—its audiences. "What does improve in the arts," maintained eminent literary critic Northrop Frye, "is the comprehension of them, and the refining of society which results from it. It is the consumer, not the producer, who benefits by culture, the consumer who becomes humanized and liberally educated."[20]

Comprehension-building in the audience also can be advantageous to the media professional. This was recognized even in the early days of our enterprise. In 1930, Leslie Allen of *The Christian Science Monitor* told his readers: "The leaven of intelligent criticism can eventually leaven the whole radiocasting lump."[21] Sixteen years later, CBS founder and board chairman William Paley stated the matter less antagonistically when he asserted that, as far as genuine criticism was concerned, "I believe all broadcasters should welcome it. It is desirable that radio should receive the same sort of intelligent reviewing which books, plays, movies, concerts and so on receive. Formal published criticism of individual radio programs promotes better artistic standards all around."[22]

In the final analysis, the question is not whether there should be electronic media criticism. Such criticism—especially as a negative veneer—is inevitable and unavoidable. Rather, the issue revolves around the need for literate, reasonable analysis by both enlightened consumers outside, and astute professionals inside, the electronic media enterprise. The carping, special-interest preachment will always be with us. However, because it only publicizes problems rather than offering solutions, such censure results in media retrenchment rather than refinement. Knowledgeable comprehension, ascertainment, and judgment of value, on the other hand, serve the needs of public and programmer alike. As art historian Arnold Hauser affirms, "The problem is not to confine art to the present-day horizon of the broad masses, but to extend the horizon of the masses as much as possible. The way to genuine appreciation of art is through education."[23] And much of that educative task, as far as the electronic media are concerned, seems likely to continue to fall to media "artists" themselves.

BRIEF HISTORY OF ELECTRONIC MEDIA CRITICISM

As compared to the other arts, formal critiquing of electronic content is a fledgling activity. Its history seems even shorter when we discover that for the first three decades of the twentieth century what would become electronic media criticism largely restricted itself to an analysis of delivery system hardware. In the early 1920s, *Radio Broadcast* and *Radio News*, the field's two major publications, "appealed primarily to amateurs who constructed and used radio," writes Professor Michael Brown. "As a result, a substantial percentage of the content of both magazines was technical. The early articles provided technical information and training for all levels of skill and interest, promoted a common language for the standardization and exchange of technical information, and provided a site where the information could be shared."[24]

This orientation extended to general publications, too, as evidenced by this 1923 newspaper critique of a radio address by its nation's prime minister:

The voice of General Smuts . . . was loud and clear in tone but unintelligible in speech as a thunderstorm affected the transmission.[25]

At about the same time in the United States, writer Perce Collison was taking a similar approach. Program content, it seemed, existed to serve the purpose of signal clarity rather than the other way around:

As a general rule a single voice gives much better results than a chorus. Likewise a few stringed instruments sound better than an entire symphony orchestra. Jazz bands are an abomination and should be absolutely eliminated not because the public does not like jazz but because the scrambled mess of disjointed harmony that is jazz cannot crowd into a telephone transmitter.[26]

As Ralph Smith recounts in his landmark study of U.S. broadcast criticism's first thirty-five years, "It was unfortunate for the development of criticism that the scientific journalist seemed interested only in opinions about the electronic functioning of a program and was unable to cope with non-technical criticism."[27] This mechanical orientation (promoted by the fact that pre-assembled receiving sets did not even begin to be available until 1920) contributed to the feeling of many intellectuals that broadcasting was at best applied science and at worst, gritty hobbycraft that lacked any tinge of artistic legitimacy (see Figure 1-2). Thus, the crystal-and-wire preoccupations of those early broadcast reviewers set a pattern that later had to be reversed rather than built on.

The nuts-and-bolts view of the medium began to subside only after factory-built radio sets substantially supplanted do-it-yourself kits. At about the same time, radio's newly discovered commercial possibilities attracted famous (or fame-seeking) personalities to the airwaves. Their presence helped replace circuitry conversation with publicist gossip. The explosive popularity of the sound medium, combined with the advertising revenues it was beginning to generate, made radio a prime exposure-builder for rising (or falling) stars. These stars' press agents were happy to provide copy to the print journalists who now found themselves covering broadcasting.

Such gossipy bits of filler usually were printed beside the newspaper's radio schedule—and at a discrete distance from *legitimate* literary, drama and music criticism. Consequently, the trend away from science to celebrities did little to improve the stature of the print media's broadcast coverage. As Smith observes, "The dealer in chit-chat emphasized only the 'personalities' appearing in a show and was inept at any more profound

FIGURE 1-2
Like other endeavors
in the low-tech
1920s, early radio
listening was more
manual dexterity
than content aes-
thetics. (Courtesy of
the Library of Con-
gress)

analysis of it."[28] Even movie criticism enjoyed more stature than what passed for radio analysis. An editorial in a 1937 issue of *Scribner's Magazine* justified the situation this way:

Radio reviewing is not taken more seriously because on the surface there is hardly any need for it. It is not like a moving picture which the reviewer can recommend to his readers, or against which he may warn them. There is a second point: sponsors of the great commercial programs are also advertisers in the newspapers and they may resent unfavorable criticism of their offerings.[29]

A final barrier to meaningful broadcast analysis was that most of the so-called radio columnists knew nothing about the medium, having been assigned to that beat as an add-on to more respected chores. These journalists therefore were content to print what the publicists were happy to provide. As late as 1946 (just before the mushrooming of commercial television) a *Variety* study of radio critics found that almost 85 percent of them were, in the words of Llewellyn White, "mostly office boys or 'old men' who simply print the radio logs, now and then 'highlighting' a few programs in boxes, and for the rest, relying on broadcasters' 'handouts' for filler."[30]

Two keen exceptions to the otherwise blunted state of broadcast criticism during this period were the early 1930s' columns of Volney Hurd and his subordinate, Leslie Allen, in *The Christian Science Monitor*. Although

Hurd was primarily a scientific journalist, he was astute enough to move beyond a strictly technical analysis of radio. And he paid freelance writer Allen to do likewise. In commentary such as the following, which appeared in 1931, Hurd helped his readers put radio's practices and potentials into a larger perspective:

As an advertising medium, it is less than half a dozen years old. Another year or two may bring about needful changes in present practices, voluntarily. If it doesn't, an uprising is inevitable among radio listeners. With the dial tuned elsewhere, the offending broadcaster loses his audience to the unoffending. With the switch turned off, a radio receiver is useful to nobody.[31]

Notice that Hurd did not succumb to the temptation to treat broadcasting as a single lump (a sin of oversimplification some enemies of television still commit today). Instead, he was willing to differentiate between "offending" and "unoffending" stations. Unfortunately, such a discriminating approach to broadcast criticism was rare in the pre–World War II years. But the onset of that conflict, and the accompanying prominence, especially in Europe, of radio as a news and propaganda vehicle demonstrated the fundamental importance of the medium. Robert Landry, radio editor of *Variety* (the entertainment industry's trade publication) was motivated by these global events to make this 1940 appeal:

I urge the point that radio channels are so important to democracy that as a nation we would be much better off to have, rather than not have, a widespread corps of professional radio watchmen.[32]

With the U.S. entry into the war the following year, however, there was little interest in radio introspection. From 1941 to 1945, the medium focused its considerable talents on war-bond selling, morale building, and war news as cleared by the Office of War Information. That the OWI's censorship did not generate substantial and long-term critical commentary was due in large part to its director, Elmer Davis (see Figure 1-3). A former CBS news commentator, Davis possessed substantial credibility and continuously strived to provide journalists with as much information as possible without compromising essential national security.

A new and much more substantive attention to broadcast criticism emerged in 1946—not from journalists or scholars but from the federal government. In that year, the Federal Communications Commission (FCC) released its bombshell "Blue Book." Officially known as *The Report on Public Service Responsibility of Broadcast Licensees*, the study surveyed the discrepancy between what broadcasters had promised the FCC they would do to serve the public interest and their subsequent programming performance. The Blue Book (named for the color of its cover) documented instances of blatant overcommercialization and a lack of both local and public affairs programming. Its effect likely would have been profound were it not that one of the principal authors was Charles Siepmann, a former programming executive for the British Broadcasting Corporation (BBC). Siepmann's alien noncommercial background was exploited by industry apologists in a successful effort to demonstrate that the Blue Book was con-

FIGURE 1-3
OWI director Elmer Davis makes one of his weekly broadcasts to the nation in March 1943. (Photo by Office of War Information)

taminated by foreign ideas (and ideals). Nevertheless, if it did nothing else, the Blue Book raised a storm of public controversy about U.S. broadcasting. This storm raised widespread interest in more, and in more comprehensive, critiquing of radio and the then-emerging television.

Just months after the Blue Book's release, John Crosby wrote his first daily radio column for the New York *Herald Tribune*, an event Ralph Smith lauds as "the beginning of a new era of criticism."[33] As *Newsweek* magazine affirmed a year later,

Previous radio editors were inclined to use their columns for a display of corny and irrelevant wit. But Crosby's followers were learning fast that radio deserved the same adult criticism as music or theatre.[34]

The recognition of radio's importance to the war effort, the debate over the Blue Book, the advent of the substantive Crosby column, and the simultaneous sprouting of television all combined to pave the way for the much more robust electronic media criticism of the 1950s. (It must be noted, however, that this new criticism did not supplant the old publicist/gossip approach but had to share the spotlight with it.)

Less in the public eye than the columns found in mass-circulation newspapers and magazines, a new phenomenon—*academic criticism*—now began to emerge among scholars. Some of this criticism, unfortunately, issued from disgruntled educators who felt that television was not being allowed to reach its potential as an instructional vehicle. In the foreword to his 1956 collection of essays entitled *Television's Impact on American Culture*, for example, William Eliot warned that "A nation that has ceased to read or that has become merely passive in its absorption of entertainment and education by way of a medium like television will have lost the true range of possibilities."[35]

Meanwhile, scholars from the social sciences began to probe the dimensions of the electronic media in the creation and promotion of mass culture, and academics from the humanities explored broadcast programming's aesthetic implications and structures. Sad to say, much of this scholarship was negative; it painted radio and television as instruments for the elite's continued control of the masses through a narcotic progression of programmatic junk. In contrast, Gilbert Seldes (respected as both a journalistic and academic critic) "dared to offer thick readings of television programs at a time when such material was considered beneath the contempt of educated people."[36] In Seldes's balanced view, any art form—television included—was capable of producing excellence. The key standard was not whether this art was generated by or through an electronic medium but instead

whatever engages more of the interests of the individual, whatever tends to enlarge his understanding of life, whatever makes him use more of his faculties and to "live more abundantly" is good; and whatever limits, restricts and diminishes is bad.[37]

By the 1960s, such qualitative commentaries were being joined by an increasing number of *quantitative* works that used the statistical research procedures of modern social science. Funded by CBS, Joseph Klapper's *The Effects of Mass Communication* (1960) attempted to place the influence of the medium within a constellation of additional forces that shape society and social action. Klapper "distinguished between the potential for instantaneous and strong influence of media over individuals and the notion that the effects of media are likely to take time, be very subtle, and that they are mediated by a host of other variables."[38]

In contrast, other quantitative works, like Eron, Walder, and Lefkowitz's *Learning of Aggression in Children* (1971) attributed greater and more negative impact to television programming itself. Meanwhile, in a defiantly nonquantitative manner, Canadian literature professor Marshall McLuhan bridged the gap between journalistic and academic criticism. His widely read volumes asserted that it was the *form* rather than the *content* of television that precipitated changes in human behavior.

In the following two decades, electronic media criticism became even more diversified. Journalistic critics like Robert Lewis Shayon, Jack Gould, Lawrence Laurent, Les Brown, Tom Shales, John J. O'Connor, Jeff Greenfield, David Bianculli, and Merrill Panitt (writing under the pen name Don Merrill) became accessible to wide audiences.

Meanwhile, further removed from the public eye, academic criticism explored a number of new or extended avenues. Among these writings were Northrop Frye's work on genre study, Christian Metz's probing of semiotics (sign systems), Claude Levi-Strauss's applications of structural linguistics, Vladimer Propp's outline of narrative theory, and the labors of a number of other scholars who analyzed texts from cultural, feminist, psychoanalytical, cognitive, mythic, or Marxist perspectives. All of these academics followed in the footsteps of pioneering writers such as Harry Skornia, Wilbur Schramm, Paul Lazarsfeld, Charles Siepmann, and Llewellyn White in using university-level theories and research techniques to decipher and discuss the electronic media's meaning and impact.

A few of these scholars' works have become popular in their own right. Like cutting-edge research in most fields, however, a large portion of academic electronic media criticism remains accessible only to other academics and their students. In some cases, this is probably just as well. As Professor Lawrence Wenner testifies,

In particular, academic critics sometimes feel compelled to show how smart they are. Generally this is done by immersing one's criticism in an entanglement of jargon and speaking to theoretical issues that only cohorts fond of using a similar approach might appreciate.[39]

In contrast, the more focused and lucid elements of academic criticism eventually do filter out to the public at large. This occurs in two ways: through their influence on younger media professionals who have studied these theories during their college years, or in the commentaries of the more adventurous journalistic critics. As early as 1968, Gilbert Seldes detected that

in many colleges, courses in the communications arts have been established in the past ten years, and in some of these the habit of observing popular entertainment is being instilled. The new effort is to give students an intelligent outlook on the mass media, not to make them experts in either the aesthetic or sociological aspects, but to inform their judgment, to make them more selective in their own choices.[40]

More recently, observers like Robert Stengel have remarked on what they perceive to be "the evolution of television criticism into something approaching social and cultural commentary. . . . More critics, particularly the newer ones, say they are less interested in simply previewing a single program. Often a program preview is only a vehicle for a broader commentary on the state of television or more."[41] If this trend is significant, and if it continues, there will be more borrowing of insights among academic and journalist/industry critics, with more eclectic styles of traditional and new media criticism emerging. Some critical approaches most ripe for such sharing are explored later in this book.

ENDNOTES

1. Lynette Rice, "Greg Meidel: The Universal Programmer," *Broadcasting & Cable* (March 24, 1997), 34.
2. Jerry McNeely, "The Criticism and Reviewing of Brooks Atkinson." Unpublished Ph.D. dissertation, University of Wisconsin (1956, 2).
3. Jerome Stolnitz, *Aesthetics and Philosophy of Art Criticism* (Boston: Houghton Mifflin, 1960), 188.
4. Caren Deming, "On the Becoming of Television Criticism," *Critical Studies in Mass Communication* (September 1984), 325.
5. Monroe Beardsley, *The Possibility of Criticism* (Detroit: Wayne State University Press, 1970), 57.
6. S. Stephenson Smith, *The Craft of the Critic*, quoted in Ralph Smith, *A Study of the Professional Criticism of Broadcasting in the United States 1920–1955* (New York: Arno Press, 1979), 113.
7. Lee Loevinger, "The Ambiguous Mirror: The Reflective-Projective Theory of Broadcasting and Mass Communications," *Journal of Broadcasting* (Spring 1968), 110–111.
8. Moses Hadas, "Climates of Criticism," in Robert Lewis Shayon (ed.), *The Eighth Art* (New York: Holt, Rinehart & Winston, 1962), 20.
9. Elayne Rapping, *The Looking Glass of Nonfiction TV* (Boston: South End Press, 1987), 6.
10. Mary Kupiec Cayton, "Lessons from a Course on Television and American Culture," *The Chronicle of Higher Education* (January 26, 1994), A52.
11. Ed Weiner, "You've Seen the TV Show—Now Read the Book," *TV Guide* (October 27, 1990), 15.
12. J. Robert Craig, "Curricular Reform's Missing Link," *Feedback* (Spring 1990), 20.
13. Everette Dennis, "Undergraduate Education Should Stop Ignoring the Importance of the Media," *Chronicle of Higher Education* (February 4, 1987), 36.
14. Alan Olson, quoted in "Melange," *Chronicle of Higher Education* (February 13, 1991), B3.

15. Gene Jankowski, "The Golden Age Revisited." Speech presented to the International Radio and Television Society, March 19, 1979 (New York).

16. Don West, "MT&R in Beverly Hills: An Attic to Die For," *Broadcasting & Cable* (March 11, 1996), 24.

17. Mitchell Stephens, "Which Communication Revolution Is It, Anyway?" *Journalism & Mass Communication Quarterly* (Spring 1998), 11.

18. Barbara Lee, "Taking Television Too Seriously—and Not Seriously Enough," in Katherine Henderson and Joseph Mazzeo (eds.), *Meanings of the Medium* (New York: Praeger, 1990), 151.

19. Jack Gould, "Television: Boon or Bane?" *Public Opinion Quarterly* (Fall 1946), 320.

20. Northrop Frye, *Anatomy of Criticism* (Princeton, NJ: Princeton University Press, 1957), 344.

21. Leslie Allen, *Christian Science Monitor*, May 31, 1930.

22. William Paley, quoted in Ned Midgley, *The Advertising and Business Side of Radio* (New York: Prentice-Hall, 1948), 318–319.

23. Arnold Hauser, *The Social History of Art*, Vol. IV, *Naturalism, Impressionism, The Film Age* (New York: Vintage Books, 1958), 259.

24. Michael Brown, "Radio Magazines and the Development of Broadcasting: *Radio Broadcast and Radio News*, 1922–1930," *Journal of Radio Studies*, Vol. 5, No.1 (1998), 79.

25. Gideon Roos, "Broadcasting in South Africa," *Finance and Trade Review* (July 1954), 38.

26. Perce Collison, "Shall We Have Music or Noise?" *Radio Broadcast* (September 1922), 434–435.

27. Ralph Lewis Smith, *A Study of the Professional Criticism of Broadcasting in the United States 1920–1955* (New York: Arno Press, 1979), 9.

28. Ibid.

29. "Criticism," *Scribner's Magazine* (October 1937), 63.

30. Llewellyn White, *The American Radio* (Chicago: University of Chicago Press, 1947), 123.

31. Volney Hurd, "Too Brief to Tune Off," *Christian Science Monitor* (March 28, 1931).

32. Robert Landry, "Wanted: Radio Critics," *Public Opinion Quarterly* (December 1940), 621.

33. R. Smith, *Professional Criticism*, 45.

34. "Crosby's First Birthday," *Newsweek* (May 19, 1947), 66.

35. William Eliot, *Television's Impact on American Culture* (East Lansing: Michigan State University Press, 1956), xvi.

36. David Marc, "Mass Culture, Class Culture, Democracy, and Prime-Time: Television Criticism and the Question of Quality," in Henderson and Mazzeo, *Meanings of the Medium*, 161.

37. Gilbert Seldes, "Media Managers, Critics and Audiences," in David Manning White and Richard Averson (eds.), *Sight, Sound, and Society* (Boston: Beacon Press, 1968), 48.

38. Robert Wicks, "Joseph Klapper and *The Effects of Mass Communication*: A Retrospective," *Journal of Broadcasting & Electronic Media* (Fall 1996), 564.

39. Lawrence Wenner, "One Part Alcohol, One Part Sport, One Part Dirt, Stir Gently: Beer Commercials and Television Sports," in Leah Vande Berg and Lawrence Wenner (eds.), *Television Culture: Approaches and Applications* (New York: Longman, 1991), 389.

40. Gilbert Seldes, *The New Mass Media: Challenge to a Free Society* (Washington, DC: Public Affairs Press, 1968), 98.

41. Robert Stengel, "Television in Print: The Critic's Choice," *Watch Magazine* (December 1979), 121.

2 Critical Functions

In the previous chapter, we discuss the components of legitimate criticism, why it is needed to advance our electronic media profession, and the uneven historical attempts to meet those needs. Now, it is important to clarify the critic's function. Whether we ourselves perform this evaluative job or it is performed by someone outside our industry, we must identify what critics do and what they value.

First and foremost, we should not allow electronic media criticism to be regarded as inferior to criticism of the more established art forms. Therefore, because *every* critic has the same fundamental responsibilities, this chapter begins with an analysis of the expectations first established by and for the critics of the more traditional arts.

THE CRITIC AS GUIDE

A common thread found in much of the writing about the more conventional forms of criticism is the concept of the critic as a *guide*. Aesthetics scholar Stephen Pepper asserts, for example, that

the critic is like the helpful guide who shows you just where you can get the best view of the object. . . . You would, in fact, find it for yourself if your interest persisted, but if you follow the directions of the experienced guide it will save you some trouble and pains.[1]

Certainly, this is an apt task for a media critic, particularly in preventing the "trouble and pains" we encounter when forced to graze through a thicket of uncharted programs. But the pains are especially acute when watching a show *we* created and seeing the flaws we missed prior to airing!

Similarly, in referring to literary reviewers, Monroe Beardsley affirms that

a critic who offers to improve our acquaintance with literary works by giving interpretations of

them takes on the character of a guide. And if he is a discriminating guide, capable of helping us choose best where to spend our limited time, he cannot avoid evaluations.[2]

Certainly, the escalating number of viewing, listening, and delivery-system choices makes it impossible for any consumer to explore even a fraction of program options. And the less time consumers have, the more essential a good guide (via inside critics' accurate "promos" or outside critics' honest commentaries) becomes in providing audiences with helpful advice.

In formulating this guidance, Professor F. V. N. Painter observed a century ago that "the critic ought to be a person of sound judgment. . . . The critic should have the power to divest himself of prejudice; and like a judge upon the bench, should decide every question by law and evidence."[3] Although the courtroom analogy may be a bit somber when referring, for example, to a situation comedy critique, Painter's emphasis on the need for factual impartiality is relevant. A journalistic critic who believes that all sitcoms are inherently silly and time-wasting has no right to evaluate one. As aesthetics authority Theodore Meyer Greene stresses, the true critic "must be able to apprehend with sympathetic insight both the trivial and the profound."[4] Just as important, producer-critics who fail to objectively assess weaknesses in their comedy series will create business-damaging disappointments for client stations and their audiences.

The critic's role therefore requires the *careful* surveillance of the artistic landscape—the *total* landscape—if the guidance function is to be fulfilled. This entails looking not just at unfamiliar/unique program properties, but at familiar/common ones as well. Any media professional should be able to perform this surveillance. M. S. Piccirillo, in fact, defines critics as "ordinary people with access to tools that enable them to examine the ordinariness of their experience."[5]

Eminent poet/critic T. S. Eliot extends this modest analysis further, reflecting that "the critic to whom I am most grateful is the one who can make me look at something I have never looked at before, or looked at only with eyes clouded by prejudice, set me face to face with it and then leave me alone with it."[6]

Unquestionably, our eyes are most clouded when evaluating our own media creations. Thoughtful criticism by our colleagues often is needed to dissipate that cloud. "A critic's job," concurs media professor Michael Porter, "is to help the viewers [professionals and consumers alike] open their eyes and see a familiar program from a different perspective—to gain some new insight into what this thing we call television is all about."[7]

T. S. Eliot's comment about being *left alone* with the art form is also especially appropriate for the media given the usually solitary act of radio listening, television watching, and on-line exploring. Further, Eliot seems to recognize that criticism's "guide" function embraces a concern for the known as well as the unknown. Thus, even though it is more invigorating to dissect a blockbuster miniseries than a daytime game show, conscientious media professionals take neither at face value when orienting clients and consumers to the full range of their options.

This is not to imply that all electronic content must be found to be of equal worth. As Beardsley mentioned, the process of criticism "cannot avoid evaluations." Appraisal is, after all, a central component of criticism as we define it in Chapter 1. Carrying out this appraisal, however, requires the critic to, in Jerome Stolnitz's words, "make explicit the criteria or yardsticks of value in the light of which he arrived at his judgment. If he fails to do so, his criticism is hopelessly vague and we literally do not know what he is talking about."[8] Terse descriptions in a printed program listing fail to convey value—and so do the cryptic comments that media professionals frequently exchange. Dramas with "chemistry," commercials with "sizzle," and newscasts with "heat" are a few of the pseudo-value statements that have no critical meaning.

It doesn't matter whether our yardstick is aesthetic (How pleasurable is it?), sociological (What social lessons does it teach?), utilitarian (Is this the most appropriate way for our target audience to spend their time at this time?), or a combination of these and other approaches. What *does* matter is that the specific criterion for evaluation is *revealed* so that the people we are addressing can determine that criterion's relevance or irrelevance to their personal (Should I watch it?) or professional (Will it get us an audience?) priorities.

In his *Dead Silence* piece reprinted in Chapter 1, Tony Scott tells us which viewers should like the show ("plays basically to upper teens") and lists some elements that might contribute to this liking (adventures of three college women; contemporary mores; an important story to tell about guilt and its ramifications). He also isolates a number of intrusive factors (blatant direction; irritating music; abrupt editing) that mar the program's execution. Thus, potential viewers, as well as programmers who later might consider re-airing *Dead Silence*, are given key guidance that will help them formulate their decisions about it. Scott thereby has met the critic's obligation to serve as a guide—not as a dictator.

OTHER CRITIC RESPONSIBILITIES

As we have just established, whether we take on the job of critiquing our own media products or those of others, we assume the obligation to serve as a guide. In addition to this fundamental guidance task there are at least five other duties a critic may be called on to perform—depending on the position the critic holds and what is being critiqued. Specifically, these chores might include:

1. Bridge building
2. Suggesting new directions
3. Proposing system-cognizant change
4. Serving as a proxy or watchdog
5. Entertaining

Bridge Building

In many of the arts (such as sculpture), creation is accomplished by one person whose labors are subsequently exposed to relatively small groups of consumers *over an extended period of time*. In the case of the electronic media, however, the creative process is often divided among dozens if not hundreds of people who may be working in several separate organizations to construct a product capable of reception by perhaps millions of consumers *simultaneously*. Given the complexity of the electronic dissemination process, misunderstanding (and even antagonism) can arise between (or among) creators and consumers. Therefore, it is the electronic media critic's responsibility, in Richard Blackmur's words, "to make bridges between the society and the arts." Blackmur signals both the difficulty and importance of this job by labeling it "the critic's burden."[9]

By opening up lines of communication and understanding between creator and consumer (media professional and audience), the critic makes it easier for each to comprehend the needs of the other. The public must understand the constraints to which programming professionals are subject. At the same time, media professionals need to be sensitive to the public's program opinions and preferences. This is part of what MTV's founder, Robert Pittman, means when he stresses that "A programmer is really a sociologist—a reader of the trends in society."[10]

Suggesting New Directions

Literary critic Carl Grabo believed this task, which he labeled *creative criticism*, to be crucial. He argued that "the justification of criticism must largely be the stimulus which it provides for original works."[11] "Creative criticism," Grabo added, "can aid in the dissemination of knowledge, in pointing out to the novelist or dramatist new subjects for his consideration and even, possibly, new techniques with which to experiment."[12]

We seldom think of the proposing of new directions as a key aspect of criticism. Yet such criticism can provide a television script author, radio copywriter, or on-line producer with encouragement and stimulation. This is why electronic media writers scrutinize reels of award-winning commercials and take note of Emmy-achieving programs. And it is in the service of this critic responsibility that *TV Guide's* Matt Roush wrote the following about *The Sopranos* soon after that series debuted in late 1998:

If Martin Scorsese were to collaborate with a suburban-angst guru like John Updike, the result might be an ironic masterpiece on the order of *The Sopranos*, a subtle, droll and utterly original mob drama. . . . Despite seemingly familiar terrain, this is a fresh and unusually realistic yarn, avoiding caricature even in its more outrageous moments. . . . After watching four episodes, I still haven't figured out these goodfellas, which may be the greatest compliment you can pay any TV show these days.[13]

Suggesting and praising new directions yield another benefit for program creators by leading the audience, in the words of Jerome Stolnitz, "to master the work's complexity. Critical analysis can show us formal interrelationships which bind the work together, meanings which make up its truth, expressive significance which gives it resonance and depth."[14] This is precisely the service that key critics (both within and outside the electronic media) performed in their assessment of such breakthrough series as *All in the Family*, *Hill Street Blues*, and *The Simpsons*. These commentators were able to sensitize viewers to the "expressive significance" of Archie Bunker's bigotry, the "formal interrelationships" that cross-stitched *Hill Street's* seeming chaos, and the "resonance and depth" of the simply drawn *Simpsons'* social discourse.

Despite their brevity, commercials also can possess innovative "resonance" that, when given critical notice, inspires new approaches. The 1983 television spot in Figure 2-1 had such unique impact that its "Customer #3" (played by retired manicurist Clara Peller) became a cult figure and her "Where's the Beef?" battlecry was enlisted by presidential candidate Walter Mondale to hobble the credibility of handsome primary opponent Gary Hart. "Where's the Beef" did as much to shape electorate wariness as it did to inspire advertising to pursue a more homespun directness.

Proposing System-Cognizant Change

In exploring critic responsibilities, we have so far relied heavily on the testimony of experts in literary and aesthetic criticism. Their perspectives, after all, are what shaped the artistic domain to which radio/television criticism only recently was admitted. Now, however, the electronic media are mature enough to have acquired reputable critics of their own, some of the most important of whom have been mentioned. While still

CUST. #1: It certainly is a big bun.
CUST. #2: It's a very big bun.

CUST. #1: A big fluffy bun.

CUST. #2: It's a very...big...fluffy... bun.

CUST. #3: Where's the beef?
ANNCR: Some hamburger places give you a lot less beef on a lot of bun.

CUST. #3: Where's the beef?

ANNCR: At Wendy's, we serve a hamburger we modestly call a "Single"— and Wendy's Single has more beef than the Whopper or Big Mac. At Wendy's, you get more beef and less bun.

CUST. #3: Hey, where's the beef? I don't think there's anybody back there!

ANNCR: You want something better, you're Wendy's Kind of People.

faithful to the core traditions of literary and aesthetic criticism, electronic media critics have formulated additional ideas as to what constitute important functions of criticism.

The first of these additional functions, *proposing system-cognizant change*, is broader than our previously discussed task of suggesting new directions. *Change* entails going beyond a programmatic technique to advocate a modification of actual system operations or priorities. Gilbert Seldes believed that it was the duty of electronic media critics to propose change. But he stipulated that

"the changes they suggest should all be workable within that [the capitalist] system. This would be more intellectually honest and would also save a lot of time."[15]

As a former executive in the system (the capitalist system in general and the broadcasting system in particular), Seldes realized that radio and television's substantial operating costs require their allegiance to the power structure that funds them. "The institutional needs and purposes of the television industry," John Hartley amplifies, "are survival and profitability, to be achieved (hope-

FIGURE 2-1
Expressive innovations often are derived from articulate advertising. (Courtesy of Linn Nash, Dancer Fitzgerald Sample, Inc.)

fully) by audience maximization and by minimizing risks and uncertainties."[16] The U.S. critic who ignores this fundamentally capitalist condition when formulating recommendations thus embarks on a futile and probably hostility-producing course of action. The same could be said of a critic who doesn't consider governmental influences when evaluating an overseas state-owned broadcast monopoly.

Inherent in change-proposal, then, is the ability to recognize the parameters within which change is possible. But because any electronic media system is a product of its social and political environment, it will reflect what David Thorburn calls *consensus narrative*: "the ambition or desire to speak for and to the whole of its culture, or as much of 'the whole' as society will permit."[17] Both the critic and the program producer must develop an understanding of what that consensus is before attempting to restructure or extend it. As Professor Mimi White testifies,

there is a range of intersecting, and at times even contradictory, meanings through the course of programming offering some things for most people, a regulated latitude of ideological positions meeting the interests and needs of a range of potential viewers.

But, she continues,

this regulated latitude does not encompass extreme positions and is offered with a strong emphasis on balance and even-handedness to hedge against offending any moderate position.[18]

Probing the boundaries of the acceptable as a means of escaping the trite has always been the preoccupation of the successful artist. Electronic media creators are no different than painters, musicians, or dramatists in this regard. "Nevertheless," cautions Professor Louis Day, "producers of mass entertainment are in a particularly precarious position, because they must entertain and accommodate the needs of the creative community while at the same time being sensitive to the value-laden messages being communicated to a diverse audience."[19]

Despite such formidable pressures, our profession cannot continue to advance if we and outside critics do not continue to push for *system-cognizant* change, change that recognizes situational constraints but seeks a

fresh response to them. As Giles Fowler declares, "one purpose stands above all. The critic states the opening argument in the robust public interplay of ideas and opinions without which the arts can ossify into lifeless museum pieces."[20]

Sometimes, this critic responsibility entails the marshalling of *opposition* to change—proposing a *change to the change*! Many people see television program content ratings, for example, as a positive system innovation designed to make the medium more conscientious and child-friendly. But in his critique below, Jim Sollisch argues that reliance on this change is inherently flawed because any rating scheme lacks a moral point of view. Instead, he advocates replacing the industry labeling of programs with a rededication to the concept of the parent as the ultimate rater.

One can debate Sollisch's contentions and argue with his solution. But the critical value of his piece does not hinge on whether we support what he advocates. Instead, his column has critical merit because he has fashioned his own change proposal that challenges industry and lawmaker assumptions and forces the reader to examine these assumptions more deeply. Film critic John Simon would say that Sollisch's approach thereby constitutes *good criticism* as he defines it:

Good criticism of any kind—of movies, ballet, architecture or whatever—makes us think, feel, respond; if we then agree or disagree is less important than the fact that our faculties have been engaged or stretched. Good criticism informs, interprets, and raises the ultimate questions, the unanswerable ones that everyone must try to answer nonetheless.[21]

Serving as a Proxy or Watchdog

Critical professionals inside or outside the electronic media usually are in a much better position to propose change than are members of the public. That is because consumers seldom have the contacts and never have the time to acquire in-depth comprehension of media workings for themselves. Consequently, it is the critic who must provide this knowledge for listeners and viewers. As former *New York Times* media commentator Jack Gould put it, "Critics in a sense are the proxies of the viewers. This

THE KEY TO TV RATINGS: "P" IS FOR PARENTS

By Jim Sollisch

I was watching television with my kids the other night, something I try not to do very often because, quite frankly, my kids have horrible taste in TV shows. This should come as no big surprise considering my kids' taste in music, food and books. Left to their own devices, kids just can't be trusted to listen to Beethoven, eat tofu or read Shakespeare. So we try to guide then. But when it comes to TV, most of us just bail out, waiting for someone else to devise a rating system we can trust.

So there I was watching a made-for-TV movie with my kids. If it had been rated, it would have been PG, maybe even G. The movie was about a college football star battling alcohol abuse and a distant father. I was lulled almost to sleep by its predictability when suddenly a girl is being assaulted at a party by the handsome football star. Classic date rape scenario. They kiss. She's quite willing. He goes further. She says no. He throws her on the bed. It's clear he's going to rape her. She screams. Finally some guys drag him off. The scene is quite powerful. You can feel her terror.

I turned off the set so I could discuss this with my kids who are ages 6 and 11. One of the boys said "What's the big deal? Nothing happened." The networks that devise the ratings apparently would agree. No nudity. No profanity. No sex. Just simple dating procedure.

I launched into a lecture on date rape. I asked my kids, especially the boys, to imagine how the girl must have felt. How long she might be traumatized by those events. Finally they agreed that something had happened. Something much worse than a four-letter word or a passionate love scene.

The problem with any rating system is that, like my kids, it lacks a moral point of view. If my kids had known that something serious had indeed happened on that screen, then I wouldn't have minded them watching it so much. Content isn't the real problem. Which is why the current push to go beyond age-based ratings to a code that describes content as containing violence, nudity, profanity or sexual situations isn't a substitute for parental guidance.

A system that plops letters on the screen would have to include the same "N" for nudity in a documentary on an artist who painted nudes as it would for a Playboy Channel show on strippers. There's no code letter that can distinguish a tender love scene from an S&M encounter. The violence in a war movie is the same "V" as the Freddy Krueger kind.

Moral point of view is everything. And yet most kids think "if it's rated G or PG, then it's OK." They assume that if we let them watch the show, then the program *and* the behaviors it contains must be OK. It's all morally neutral to them, implicitly endorsed by those who let them watch: their parents.

That's why parents have to see more of the TV their kids are watching and decide what's appropriate and what's not. We are the only raters who matter. And most of us are asleep at the remote.

(Jim Sollisch, a copywriter and creative director at a Cleveland advertising agency, is a commentator on National Public Radio's "Morning Edition" and writes essays for magazines and newspapers. Used with permission of the author.)

does not mean that viewers necessarily will agree with reviewers. But it does mean that there is the common bond of an independent opinion."[22]

Gould's *Chicago Tribune* counterpart, Larry Wolters, stated at about the same time that "the critic alone can serve as a watchdog for the viewer who cannot always speak effectively for himself."[23] For electronic media commentators, then, the critical task goes beyond guiding, bridge-building, suggesting, and proposing. It also embraces an interest in serving as *protector* of the audience when that course of action becomes necessary. Both principled and manipulative critics outside the electronic media wear this protector designation proudly. Thus, when external commentators attempt to crusade against radio/television, professionals *within* the media must also perform the proxy/ watchdog functions. By showing a willingness to fairly describe their own operations and spotlight mistakes when they occur, electronic media practitioners become trusted partners with the public. This makes our profession much less susceptible to attacks from self-styled keepers of the public good who only have axes to grind. The best insurance for our license or franchise resides in an audience who accurately understands what we do.

Because what we do in our complex industry takes on so many dimensions, a media professional faces a variety of subjects to monitor, explain, and redress. Thus, our proxy/watchdog task goes beyond the content in our shows. It also encompasses the many other ways our high-profile enterprise interacts in society. Electronic media executives therefore are often called on to be *complete critics*. As former *Washington Post* writer Lawrence Laurent explained, "This complete critic must be something of an electronics engineer, an expert on our governmental processes, and an electrician. He must have a grasp of advertising and marketing principles. He must be able to evaluate all of the art forms; to comprehend each of the messages conveyed, on every subject under the sun."[24]

Complete critics are best able to exercise the audience's proxy interests. And media executives who can function as such complete critics are crucial instruments in building and maintaining credibility with that audience.

Entertaining

We cannot ignore the fact that the electronic media are seen primarily as entertainment enterprises. Consequently, our public pronouncements about them must also be entertaining. Otherwise, even the most perceptive critical commentary may go unheeded. The breadth and diversity of our public (as compared, for example, to the ballet public) require that electronic media criticism be expressed in a manner that is interesting, concise, and even fun to absorb. The *Minneapolis Tribune*'s Will Jones candidly admitted to this aspect of his work when he wrote that his columns were supposed "to serve as an entertainment feature for the paper."[25] More than three decades ago, the trade publication *Television Age* editorialized that "the critic's function today seems to be to amuse and entertain viewers prospective and actual with wit, if not malice."[26] And P. J. Bednarski of the *Chicago Sun-Times* illustrated that this requirement was still relevant in the 1980s, when he confessed to a National Association of Television Program Executives (NATPE) gathering, "If I wrote about issues all week, I would have no readers."[27]

Having readers is of obvious importance to Bednarski and his newspaper, which has a substantive financial stake in keeping those readers satisfied. The electronic media are just as concerned with audience servicing. It is difficult to imagine, therefore, that the entertainment aspect of a radio/television critique will ever cease to be an important component—at least as far as nonacademic criticism is concerned. The media commentary is rarely a self-standing entity. Rather, it is usually one ingredient of a product (newspaper, magazine, radio/television program, or on-line site) that is being commercially marketed for audience consumption. Given this packaging, entertaining the public is an inevitable if less profound function of electronic media criticism.

In this section, we have examined five sometimes overlapping critic responsibilities: (1) bridge-building, (2) suggesting new directions, (3) proposing system-cognizant change, (4) serving as a proxy or watchdog, and (5) entertaining. It is doubtful that any single piece of criticism will fulfill all of these functions. The length of the critique, the medium in which it appears, and the unique orientation of each critic all influence which of these tasks are emphasized. Still, together with the undelegatable *guidance* responsibility (discussed in this chapter's first section), our five-point inventory stakes out the parameters and the possibilities inherent in electronic media criticism. At the least, this critic responsibility list should undercut the notion that critics are merely, as Neil Hickey jested, "like people who come down from the hills after the battle to shoot the wounded."[28]

WHAT CRITICS VALUE

As just mentioned, all critics bring their own orientation (and perhaps that of their employing agency) to the task of criticism. This orientation is itself inevitably shaped by the values each critic has absorbed over the years. Criticism is, after all, a *human* creation, and every maturing human being assimilates a certain value structure as an inevitable part of growing up. However, if the critical function is to remain open and honest, two things are essential:

1. Critics must be sensitive to the values that they bring to their evaluative task.
2. Audiences must be assisted, through a critic's own candid expression, in detecting that critic's particular value bias so that they can consider it when determining the relevance and worth of the critique.

As Professor Robert Smith reminds us,

critics, like other persons, may wear blinders, which may be ideological (Marxism or conservatism), psychological (a preference for certain kinds of concerns), or expedient (a desire to get by-lines and be quoted). These private commitments of critics may give depth to their writing or may limit their vision.[29]

Audiences have every right to expect that any commentator addressing them will reveal his or her own set of blinders (or, in Marshall McLuhan's words, "goggles") as a credibility prerequisite.

Back in 1959, in his landmark analysis of broadcast criticism, Ralph Smith discovered that practicing critics collectively reflected six value clusters in their commentaries.[30] Specifically, Smith found that critics prized:

1. Honesty/sincerity in terms of the work's purpose and execution
   2. Program variety
   3. Maintenance of human dignity
   4. Diligence in writing and production
   5. Relaxation and informality
   6. Strong sense of responsibility

Though additional qualities have occasionally been mentioned in the intervening decades, even a skimming of contemporary electronic media commentary suggests that these same half-dozen criteria remain core concerns of today's critics.

Honesty/Sincerity in Purpose and Execution

It is not unreasonable to expect a commercial to be packaged as a commercial and not disguised like program content. It also is not unreasonable to demand, as have critics, children's protection groups, and media professionals, that a character in a kid-appeal show refrain from suddenly shifting into the role of product pitchman. Back in the 1950s, puppet Howdy Doody's adult foil, Buffalo Bob, frequently segued into commercial delivery, as did the featured talent in many other shows. This blurring of entertainment and advertising was known as the *integrated commercial.* Its regulatory demise was a triumph of definitional honesty over program-packaging deception.

The issue is not that the actual content of children's (or adult) commercials is fraudulent but that their execution as program matter makes the spots appear to be something they are not. In 1990, for example, actor Wilford Brimley appeared in commercials for hot Quaker Oats cereal promoting it as "the right thing to do." The pitch was clearly a commercial and straightforward in its execution. At the same time, Brimley was featured in a cancer-prevention public service announcement (PSA). No honesty problem existed here, either. The PSA addressed a significant public health concern and did not mention any product. But an honesty issue lurked behind the scenes. Quaker Oats conditioned its purchase of station advertising time on each outlet's promise also to carry the Brimley PSAs. Apparently, the company hoped that the mix of paid and free messages featuring Brimley would cause the public to link cancer prevention with the consumption of Quaker Oats. Some stations approved the contract. But at others, self-critiquing executives decided that the off-air business deal compromised the contextual honesty of the on-air messages and turned the offer down. (Tax preparer H&R Block has used a related method on radio; their purchase of advertising time promoting the firm has been conditioned on the free carriage of Block's "tax tips" PSAs.)

A similar honesty/sincerity question is raised in relation to self-standing program-length commercials (*infomercials*) when they are produced to appear like conventional talk-shows—complete with enthusiastic studio audiences. Again, what media professionals are concerned with is not the right to sell reputable products in long-form but our responsibility to the audience to *tell* them when a sales pitch is a sales pitch.

Honesty disputes also draw critical attention in several areas of news programming. Promos (promotional announcements) for on-air news personnel have been accused of using staged, prescripted events to artificially enhance a newsperson's credibility. Anchor Ann Bishop describes one such promo in which she was required to appear:

It had me in a helicopter, on the radio, giving a description of a boat on fire to my co-anchor. In fact, there was no boat on fire; they dropped a smoke flare, which missed the boat by a mile. The spot was ludicrous. We told them it looked ridiculous. They said we were being difficult. Eventually they saw: it did look idiotic.[31]

Note especially that Bishop, like any conscientious media professional, took on the responsibility to critique her own outlet's performance; she did not abdicate this responsibility to outside critics.

The source and sponsorship of news are also major honesty issues and pose difficult self-critiquing decisions for journalists. In 1995, for example, award-winning Chicago anchor Carol Marin was suspended by her general manager for three days when she "refused to participate in a report about fire safety after learning one of the broadcast's advertisers was a smoke-detector company."[32] In Marin's view, this sponsorship at least raised the appearance that the journalistic integrity of the piece—and therefore her own integrity—had been compromised.

Video news releases (VNRs) constitute a broader honesty question. VNRs are promotion pieces constructed to look like news stories. They are circulated by public relations operatives to television news departments in the hopes their clients thereby will receive free exposure in station newscasts. The practice of VNR use becomes suspect when viewers are not informed of the source of this potentially self-serving footage. "It is considered good public relations practice for VNRs to identify who issued the release as well as the client on whose behalf it was produced," says Rosalee Roberts, former president of the Public Relations Society of America. "It is then up to the TV news organization to identify the source of the video footage used."[33]

Some news departments never use VNRs. Others, particularly smaller, budget-strapped units, find the often-compelling VNR footage irresistible. Honesty simply requires that viewers be informed about who provided the footage so they can factor this into their evaluation of the story's worth. Continuous self-critiquing of VNR use becomes even more important for professionals whose news packages are likely to be picked up by other organizations. "Should a station select a piece coming from a news source such as CNN, an on-air identifier is not required," asserts news critic George Glazer. "The rub comes if CNN used a VNR as the original source, and the station doesn't know it—but CNN has already made an editorial judgment by retransmitting the piece."[34]

Reenactments and simulations in news programs also ignite honesty/sincerity debates as to their purpose and execution. A few years ago, CBS News's short-lived *Saturday Night with Connie Chung* used several unrevealed re-creations. Among these was an actress playing a teenager seeking permission for an abortion. Viewers were misled into believing they were watching an actual event unfold. In November 1992, *Dateline NBC* experienced its own simulation fiasco when, in a story on liability lawsuits against General Motors, it used undisclosed sparking devices to stimulate the explosion of GM trucks in a videotaped "crash test." When the rigging came to light, NBC was forced to settle with GM for $2 million and to issue a lengthy on-air apology. Reacting to such practices, former NBC News President Larry Grossman declared: "In the traditional news operation, any idea of faking to suit a particular need was just unthinkable. What has happened is that management hasn't held people accountable."[35] In other words, internal critiquing of the honesty of a productional practice lapsed—paving the way for much more public and much more negative external critiquing later.

Docudramas (dramatic fiction based on major historical events) raise even more complex honesty/sincerity issues. Even though the docudrama takes its inspiration from actual people and happenings of the past, it is not history but a fictional packaging that can distort reality and harm reputations when the audience perceives it as literal truth. Whether the misinterpretation is unanticipated or encouraged by a docudrama's uncritical producer is not important. What matters is that a deception *does* take place. This is the same sort of deception that occurs when careless newsroom editing makes an interview subject's position seem substantially different from what he or she actually stated.

Even seemingly straight documentaries raise unavoidable honesty implications when their subject matter overflows the time allotted to cover it. The preview by *Variety*'s Van Gordon Sauter (a former network news executive), carefully delineates the worthiness of the intent of a Discovery Channel documentary while pointing out its length-related oversimplifications. Sauter thus differentiates the honesty of creator intent from the distortive elements arising from the program's time constraints.

Electronic media professionals also must wrestle with honesty/sincerity concerns in entirely fictional programs. This is especially true in the matter of *stereotyped* character portrayals. "The term 'stereotype,'" points out Professor George Rodman, "comes from the Greek *stereos*, meaning firm and *typos*, meaning model or type. A stereotype is therefore a fixed impression; its dictionary definition is, 'a fixed or conventional notion or conception, as of a person or group, held by a number of people, and allowing for no individuality, or critical judgment.'"[36] "Stereotypes are oversimplified images of a group," adds the Institute for Mental Health Initiatives, "that are applied to its members with little regard for their individual differences. They are a cultural shorthand, a quick way of characterizing how 'our' group is similar to or different from 'theirs.'"[37]

When ages, occupations, genders, religions, or racial groups are represented in stereotypical ways, the treatment becomes potentially more dishonest the longer it is allowed to remain on microphone or on camera. All Texans, all Native Americans, all Baptists, or all police officers are not the same; and to depict each member of such groups as exactly the same is to be functionally dishonest and insincere to the concept (and additional critic value) of individual *human dignity*. The creation of stereotypes, however explicable within the forced brevity of the typical series episode, tends to be a shortcut that constructs its own barriers to the development and extendibility of that series. Yet, as scholar T. W. Adorno observed as early as 1954,

the technology of television production makes stereotypy almost inevitable. The short time available for the preparation of scripts and the vast material continuously to be produced calls for certain formulas.... It appears inevitable that the kind of person the audience faces each time should be indicated drastically through red and green lights.... Since stereotypes are an indispensable element of the organization and anticipation of experience, preventing us from falling into mental disorganization and chaos, no art can entirely dispense with them.[38]

The critical task, then, while recognizing the inevitability of stereotypes, is to try to distinguish between those that are honest responses to dramatic constraints and those that are insincere defamations of the people being categorized. "Elimination of all stereotypes," argues Louis Day, "would infringe on artistic freedom and sterilize our vicarious experiences through the media. Nevertheless, efforts should be made to change those that are particularly degrading and prejudicial."[39]

Program Variety

To a significant degree, unwarranted human stereotypes also make a negative contribution to *program variety*, the second critic preference that Ralph Smith identified. By their nature, stereotypes are patterns for assumed commonality rather than actual differentiation. For example, today's television frequently features women in occupational roles formerly reserved for men. Yet, the result often has been the narrowing rather than expanding of characterization variety. Robert Alley charges that this practice "deteriorates into a picturing of women as men

DANGEROUS YEARS: PRESIDENT EISENHOWER AND THE COLD WAR

by Van Gordon Sauter

This revisionist documentary reminds old codgers why they liked Ike in the first place and informs younger generations that there was far more to the '50s than Elvis, the hula-hoop and circular television screens. It forcefully makes the point that the cold war of the '50s was dreadfully hazardous and the nation was fortunate to have an old soldier named Dwight David Eisenhower guiding it through the peril.

Many journalists and intellectuals, bitter that voters twice chose the World War II hero over Adlai Stevenson, came to perceive Eisenhower as a shallow, bumbling president in a sleepy era that bridged the world conflict of the '40s with the social activism of the '60s. Wrong!

This rapid-fire documentary, in which each international crisis of the '50s seems to get 15 seconds of fame, is a crash course in that era's unrelenting, ruthless hostility between the U.S. and [the Soviet Union] and the succession of incidents that kept us near the brink of war.

The events are awesome: a leftist coup in Iran, the Suez crisis, American Marines landing on the beaches of Lebanon, Sputnik, the downing of an American U-2 spy plane, the Hungarian revolution, the Korean War, the military defeat of France in what we came to know as Vietnam, a major crisis in Berlin, a calamitous summit in Paris, China shelling Quemoy and Matsu; and the proliferation of nuclear weapons. The list is actually longer.

In an inevitably superficial fashion, this docu traces Ike as he worked his way through those events. It also introduces us to a fascinating array of supporting players, some of whom deserve their own TV portrayals. An example is Kim Roosevelt, Teddy's grandson, a CIA operative who engineered the cunning counter-coup that returned the shah to Iran's Peacock Throne and thwarted Soviet influence there.

But the hero here is Ike—decisive, idealistic, willing to lead. For instance, when key advisers urged him to send American troops to Vietnam to rescue French colonialism, Ike thought about it overnight and the next morning announced his decision: "I will not put one single foot soldier in those rice paddies 10,000 miles away from home. It is not in the national interest."

With that, Ike went off to play golf. Considering the lethal blunders his successors made in Vietnam, Ike deserved his time on the golf course—and, more important, the current appreciation of his presidency.

As a documentary, it is absurd to represent eight such turbulent years in an hour. But the intent is honorable, the reporting and execution of merit and the subject deserving. This broadcast reflects the growing historical perception that in an era when many Americans were contemplating backyard bomb shelters, having Ike in the White House made a lot of sense.

(Courtesy of George Russell, *Variety*)

think women should act doing men's jobs. And therein lies the problem. The jobs, from lawyer, to police, to dozens of other previously all-male professions, bear the male image. One is reminded of those ludicrous outfits Joan Crawford used to wear in order to qualify as a business woman."[40] What results is not richer character variety but greater sameness via male and pseudomale depictions.

The portrayals of businesspersons in general are particularly prone to predictable uniformity. Their shadowy duplicity (as visualized in Figure 2-2) is colored as buffoonery in sitcoms and cast as the carrier of evil in dramas. Ben Stein believes that this repetitive negative portrayal is the by-product of the bruising encounters that most program creators have with entertainment industry executives. As a result, says Stein,

one of the clearest messages of television is that businessmen are bad, evil people, and that big businessmen are the worst of all. . . . The most succinct summary of the way business-men are shown in TV comedies came from a producer of a successful comedy production company. A writer approached him with an idea: How about a comedy with businessmen who were good guys? The producer's answer was, "Impossible."[41]

Critics prize variety within as well as among characters. This is an area in which cop shows have made the greatest strides. The one-dimensional, job-wrapped, self-as-sured automatons like *Dragnet*'s Sgt. Joe Fri-day and the motorcycle jockeys of *CHiPs*, have been replaced by multidimensional humans such as *Hill Street Blues*' Captain Francis Fur-rillo and *NYPD Blue*'s Detective Andy Sipo-witz. These newer lawmen have their doubts and their demons both on and off the job. They change from episode to episode—some-times for the better and sometimes for the worse. In so doing, they treat the audience to a divergence missing from those simplistic earlier shows—and from several poorly drawn contemporary throwbacks.

Another program variety issue frequently mentioned by inside and outside critics oc-curs in shows aimed at child audiences. Here, the "BAM POW ZAP" of much ani-mated production outstrips other content categories. As advertising director Alan Banks pointed out more than a decade ago, even from a strictly business standpoint, this repetition is *bad* business because the mo-notony of the subject matter drives kids else-where:

The audience sees a lot of sameness—one ro-bot show looks like another. No variety, every-thing is predictable even to the young child audience—which can't be taken for granted. . . . so if ratings are down on the com-mercial over-the-air programs, the kids must be watching something else on television.[42]

Increasingly, that something else has become the somewhat more varied fare found on Nickelodeon—as well as the boundless but often non-kid-appropriate world of the

Internet. Over-the-air broadcasting did not heed the critical advice of experts such as Banks, and the audience migrated accord-ingly.

Meanwhile, on the legislative front, the 1990 Children's Television Act mandated that stations (and cable systems originating their own programming) provide material specifically designed to serve *the educational and informational needs of children* aged sixteen and under. Subsequently, broadcasters' license renewals became conditioned on their providing a minimum of three hours per week of programs specifically identified as meeting these needs. The question is whether the response to this governmental edict will increase variety or will just beget dutiful and unimaginative uniformity.

Some observers argue that as a whole, television program variety for both children and adults has never been greater. "TV is getting better," states Pulitzer Prize winning critic William Henry, "because there is so much more of it. If you get cable, options that were pipe dreams a few years ago—round-the-clock news (CNN), round-the-clock sports (ESPN), live coverage of major Congressional hearings (C-SPAN), huge doses of art movies and the higher culture

FIGURE 2-2
In what way does this visual reflect TV's businessperson stereotype? (Courtesy of Bob Porter, Gumpertz/ Bentley/Fried)

(Arts & Entertainment Network)—are often part of the basic service."[43]

On the other hand, it also can be argued that cable has actually inhibited program variety by constantly recycling its own shows as well as sometimes ancient castoffs from the broadcast networks' schedules. While both cable and DBS have also increased their output of original movie, sports, and adult-series programming, much of this has come as part of add-on "pay" packages—a fact used to bolster some critics' contentions that video variety is based on the consumer's ability to pay. Even PBS has narrowed its programming range, concentrating on shows most likely to appeal to viewers who can donate to station pledge drives.

A central question remains: Is program variety the responsibility of each outlet—or is it enough that "television" as a whole provides it? Some commercial broadcasters, for example, have advocated regulations whereby they could pay their local PBS station to air those three hours of harder-to-sell educational/informational shows for them.

The variety issue has even more importance for radio, where narrow formats, tight playlists, and industry consolidation have made the full-service station virtually extinct. Depending on market size, the same broadcaster can own as many as eight stations in the same geographical area. Some critics charge that this severe compression in ownership variety automatically translates into an equally severe narrowing of program variety. But Mark Mays, president of Clear Channel Communication (operator of hundreds of radio outlets) sees it otherwise:

Without the ability to own multiple stations in a market, Clear Channel would be more likely to program only mainstream formats. Owning more signals in a market, we can take a risk with less popular and more diverse formats. The consolidation of ownership in local radio markets has clearly increased listener choice. When you could own only a couple of signals, the dictates of the business forced programming toward the largest groups. Now we are creating new formats as well as new "flavors" of old formats.[44]

Maintenance of Human Dignity

This third quality valued by electronic media critics appears most directly threatened by game and talk shows in which participants are encouraged to perform or recount all sorts of self-depreciating activities. The specific activities have changed over the years, but they have not become less demeaning, as *TV Guide*'s Merrill Panitt chronicled at the conclusion of his review of *The New Newlywed Game*:

In the early days of television, contestants in audience participation shows submitted to physical gags, were hit in the face with pies, dunked in water or mud. The audience laughed because seeing someone else lose dignity is a basic kind of fun and source of laughter.

For this viewer, watching the naivete of *New Newlywed Game* contestants being exploited was an excruciatingly embarrassing experience.[45]

As for many of the popular talk shows, observes Pannitt's successor Jeff Jarvis, "Sally Jessy, Ricki, Geraldo, Maury, Montel, Richard Bey—the 20-plus monsters of daytime—exploit an endless parade of sick, sad, exhibitionist freaks and fools. They make America look like the dark side of *The Beverly Hillbillies*."[46]

Assaults on human dignity are also mounted by news reporters who intrude on private grief at a moment of tragedy, by commercials that picture product nonusers as mindless nerds, and by situation comedies in which parental figures are saved from their own incompetence-caused catastrophe only through the quick thinking of their children or family pet. Even documentaries intended to illuminate a human problem may end up stripping the dignity from their subjects if the show's basic thrust is ill-conceived. This, summarizes *Variety* critic Tom Bierbaum, is what went wrong in an ABC special entitled *Illiterate in America*:

One has to wonder why the show was built around the issue of illiteracy. Perhaps it was thought to be a more attention-grabbing issue than just general education.

But had the special taken a different tack, we could have been spared the long line of interviews of ineffective silhouetted illiterates. Because there was so little to be proven or learned from these interviews, they turned out to be little more than embarrassing.[47]

Reality shows (see Chapter 14) such as *Cops* can also assault human dignity by depicting the poor as the source of virtually all crime. Obviously, *Cops* videographers choose to ride in police cars patrolling high crime areas because this maximizes their chances of gathering usable footage. But because high crime areas tend also to be low-income areas, the same classes of people tend to be shown over and over as the perpetrators and irresponsible victims of violence. Criminal statistics document that white-collar crime such as embezzlement and fraud is a much more widespread phenomenon than violent crime. But there is little video drama in (or chance of) catching a middle-class professional doctoring financial records. So crime and chaos are shown to be the exclusive province of the same unfortunate underclass as ambush cameras give them little opportunity to marshal their dignity.

Conversely, other news or reality programs preserve human dignity when they conceive of their subjects as individuals rather than as exploitable, generalizable props. Such shows pose questions that reflect a revealing sensitivity that does not demand a dignity-robbing response. Even within the crime beat, asserts Jim Snyder, former news vice-president for the Post-Newsweek stations, "There are other stories that can be done about the dimensions of the problem, what people are doing about it, how it's affecting the community."[48]

In fiction programming, too, insightful portrayals of such subjects as mental retardation, physical disabilities, and personality disorders have become much more numerous. When knowledgeably handled, they not only preserve human dignity but, through their creative commitment, can also amplify the diverse sources from which that dignity is capable of springing. On contemporary U.S. television, "the basic message on the screen is that we are a pluralist society with everyone entitled to a place at the table," applauds William Henry. "To judge from TV, America has become mature and confident enough to look at itself whole."[49]

Diligence in Writing and Production

If human dignity is being affirmed on television, as Henry believes, it is due, at least in part, to media professionals' *diligence in writing and production*—the fourth element Ralph Smith found critics to value. In Chapters 5 and 6, we explore electronic media production elements in detail. Writing, on the other

hand, is so central to most programming considerations that its impact is dealt with throughout the rest of this book.

For the moment, then, we turn to *diligence*, which is defined as painstaking perseverance and industriousness. This quality is best appreciated when we encounter its absence. And in electronic media, the absence of diligence is mechanical indifference. Indifference does not escape the competent media professional's notice any more than a flat orchestral presentation under the baton of an ill-prepared or unmotivated conductor escapes the censure of a music reviewer.

Pride of execution is an essential ingredient in any art or craft. When it is missing, audiences detect the effect even if they cannot isolate precisely what is lacking. The radio format rife with "dead air" rather than anticipatory pause and the television sitcom in which a fanatical laugh track bumpers incoherent scripting are examples of the absence of diligence. Such carelessness can ruin programs, stations, and media careers while rightly drawing critical heat.

For now, you may find it instructive to reread the preview of *Dead Silence* in the previous chapter. How many examples of diligence in writing and production does critic Tony Scott discuss? How many examples of an absence of such diligence does he identify? The answers to these two questions go a long way toward explaining and quantifying his overall evaluation of that program.

Relaxation and Informality

At first glance, this fifth of Smith's critically acclaimed elements would seem the opposite of writing and production diligence. However, astute media professionals realize two things: how hard creators have to work to make radio/television program fare seem effortless, and how important the casual can be to listeners and viewers in seeking relief from both the pressures of real life and the stimulating yet stressful experiences in other programming choices (such as newscasts, action/adventure shows, and dramatic presentations).

Whether it was Garrison Keillor's *A Prairie Home Companion* on radio or Johnny Carson's *Tonight Show* on television, intricately fashioned nonchalance has long provided soothing audience therapy. This soothing quality, however, is dependent on consummate communicators who know how to conceal the intensity of their labors. In fact, the importance of relaxation and informality may be one factor that led to Carson's replacement by the seemingly laid-back Jay Leno rather than the hyperkinetic Joan Rivers. True, Rivers previously had resigned her guest-host role on *Carson* to develop a competing talk show. But even on her own vehicle, Rivers's frenetic enthusiasm clashed with the psychology of the late-night adult audience.

On the other hand, actor James Garner always projects the epitome of relaxation—to the point that his pleasingly casual style is mistaken for effortlessness. "People have often said that Jim Garner makes it look easy, so therefore he can't be working very hard," comments Stephen Cannell, co-creator of *The Rockford Files*, in which Garner had the starring role. "But Jim's talent is that very thing. You have to have a tremendous engine in there to do what he does." Garner himself realizes that "Everybody says I make it look easy, but that's what I'm trying to do, to make the audience think it's the first time I've ever said something. But my mind is going a million miles a minute. Every word, every sentence, every pause, is very well studied."[50] It is the same for popular song lyrics. That is why stellar Broadway lyricist/composer Stephen Sondheim cautions that "Making lyrics feel natural, sit on music in such a way that you don't feel the effort of the author, and so they shine and bubble and rise and fall is very, very, very, very, very hard to do."[51]

Newscasts are not exempt from a critical expectation of studied informality, either. Perhaps that is because portable video has made tragic news so instantaneously graphic that it would be undigestible without calming counterpoints from the anchor. In a review of the Big Three networks' evening news offerings, for example, Marvin Kitman made relaxation a key comparative criterion:

Dan Rather at CBS makes me nervous. I never know when he is going to do something bizarre, like walk off the show. . . . He looked, more relaxed in Saudi Arabia than in the studio. It's as if there are two of them, Dan Rather and Mr. Angry. . . .

Tom Brokaw . . . reads the news like his jaws are wired. . . . He has always been at his most comfortable on the road. Yet covering the war from Saudi Arabia, he has been uncomfortable.

So would you if your replacement in the studio was Jane Pauley, who is only the best straight news reader in the business today. . . .

Peter Jennings is usually first in the ratings for a reason. He is good. Jennings is ahead because he is closest to being easygoing, calm, a natural reader. . . . He is a little too handsome, perhaps a little too smooth sometimes. But Jennings is always comfortable.[52]

The value of relaxation and informality also is recognized in the creation of commercials. This is particularly true when the product benefit can be related to leisure or rest. In the Figure 2-3 photoboard, for instance, the unsettling, tension-building conditions cited in the soundtrack are soothingly overshadowed by the dreamy diversion displayed in the visual.

The ultimate validation of electronic media critics' support of the value of relaxation may be Fish TV. When CableVision of Columbia, South Carolina, found itself with a temporarily vacant channel, the system's marketing manager put a simple fresh-water aquarium in his studio, pointed a fixed-position camera at it, and added a jazz accompaniment soundtrack. The result was Fish TV. A few months later, when Fish TV was discontinued to make way for the Sci-Fi Channel, the phones lit up. After weeks of viewer complaints, Fish TV was restored by the manager who found himself viewing it as an aid to relaxation. As media critic Debra Goldman observed, the executive's "sensation is confirmed by research that shows watching fish lowers people's blood pressure. . . . Television is supposed to be relaxing, although most studies indicate TV induces not relaxation, but a state of passive yearning . . . and advertising has scrambled to satisfy that craving, cramming ads with ever more complex visual and aural information in the hope of keeping viewers' fingers off the zapper. . . . But maybe they just want less. Maybe they just want to watch fish."[53] There may be a lesson here, not only for TV programmers, but for overstimulated website designers as well.

Strong Sense of Responsibility

This final quality that critics value is much more illusive and comprehensive than is relaxation/informality's emotional reward. In

(MUSIC UNDER THROUGHOUT)
VO: 37 YEARS AGO CLUB MED MADE
A SPECIAL ARRANGEMENT WITH
CIVILIZATION.

SEND US YOUR FRAZZLED,...

...YOUR CRAZED,...

FIGURE 2-3
The primacy of Club
Med's informality
appeal is encapsu-
lated in its "Antidote
for Civilization"
theme statement.
(Courtesy of Ann
Milne, Ammirati &
Puris Inc.)

...YOUR BELEAGUERED,...

...YOUR BURNT OUT,...

...YOUR OVERBURDENED,...

...YOUR TENSION RIDDLED,

AND WE'LL SEND YOU BACK

A HUMAN BEING.

essence, a *strong sense of responsibility* reflects the notion that, as their first priority, the electronic media operate in the service of their society rather than to the enrichment of their shareholders. Profit is fine, but not when it is attained to the detriment of the public interest. The belief in radio/television as a social resource is embedded in our communications law and critical commentary. Through their licensing and franchising processes, most broadcasters and cablecasters are aware of this social responsibility expectation—even if they do not all practice it.

A continuing problem that broadcast (and now, on-line) professionals face is that some people construe social responsibility simplistically. These self-appointed public guardians want the electronic media to feature content that presents only the good, the true, and the morally uplifting. And they are willing to define "goodness, truth, and upliftment" in exclusively negative terms—by pointing out when our programming lacks it!

Knowledgeable critics reject this shallow view, of course, because they recognize that in a democratic society, electronic communicators must function as reflective *artists*, not as law-dictating *moralists*. Theodore Meyer Greene draws the artist/moralist distinction this way:

The artist portrays men as they are, with all their virtues and vices, *and* as they ought to be; the moralist is actively concerned to eradicate vice and to foster human virtue. The artist as artist is content to understand human nature with all its potentialities and limitations, and to reveal his insight through his art. . . . Furthermore, the artist's specific insights, as these are expressed in his art, are invaluable to the moral agent, while art in general aids morality in strengthening the imagination.[54]

The socially responsible artist/communicator, then, is right to provide depictions of both good and evil as programmatic case studies through which society's moralists can instruct those people willing to follow their teachings. In fact, by raising an ugly or socially delicate issue, the electronic media can facilitate the audience's coming to grips with that issue in a values-clarifying manner.

Perceptive critics (both inside and outside the media) understand this. They recognize that a media producer's sense of responsibility is shown, not by the chosen subject matter, but by the totality of the approach taken toward that subject matter. As Jerome Stolnitz cautions,

if we consider the subject matter alone, we might just as well be talking about the real life "model," for we ignore all that makes the work a distinctive aesthetic object. It is like saying that *Macbeth* is simply a story about a lot of murders.[55]

DeWitt Parker makes a more extensive case for our moral right (and social responsibility) as artists to portray the perverse as well as the positive when he argues on behalf of any work of art:

Even when it offers suggestions for unwonted acts, it furnishes the spirit and the knowledge requisite for determining whether they will fit into the scheme of life of the spectator. It is characteristic of puritanic critics of art, in their eagerness to find motives for condemnation, to overlook this element of reflection. . . . Only by knowing other ways of life can we be certain of the relative worth of our own way. . . . For morality, to be genuine, must be a choice; the good must know its alternative or it is not good.[56]

In this chapter we have examined the critic as guide, the five additional responsibilities of media criticism, and the six programmatic qualities that critics have especially valued. Though these tasks and attitudes are conducted and reflected by outside commentators, it is essential that professionals *within* the media also take them seriously. If we allow criticism to be the sole province of others, then we become *reactive* pawns instead of *proactive* decision-makers.

Even when they are hostile, outside critics of all persuasions perform an important service in making sure we are aware of those "other ways of life" to which Parker referred. Without such commentators, we lose society's multiple pulse—a pulse that we are *expected* to monitor because of the media placed in our care.

ENDNOTES

1. Stephen Pepper, *The Work of Art* (Bloomington: Indiana University Press, 1955), 58–59.
2. Monroe Beardsley, *The Possibility of Criticism* (Detroit: Wayne State University Press, 1970), 62.
3. F. V. N. Painter, *Elementary Guide to Literary Criticism* (Boston: Ginn and Company, 1903), 4–5.
4. Theodore Meyer Greene, *The Arts and the Art of Criticism* (Princeton, NJ: Princeton University Press, 1952), 468.
5. M. S. Piccirillo, "On the Authenticity of Televisual Experience: A Critical Exploration of Para-Social Closure," *Critical Studies in Mass Communication* (September 1986), 353.
6. T. S. Eliot, "The Frontiers of Criticism," in *On Poetry and Poets* (London: Faber and Faber, 1957), 117.
7. Michael Porter, "Realism versus Discourse Theory: Two Approaches to Reading Character in *thirtysomething*," in Leah Vande Berg and Lawrence Wenner (eds.), *Television Criticism* (New York: Longman, 1991), 129.
8. Jerome Stolnitz, *Aesthetics and Philosophy of Art Criticism* (Boston: Houghton Mifflin, 1960), 11.
9. Richard Blackmur, "A Burden for Critics," in *The Lion and the Honeycomb* (New York: Harcourt, Brace, 1955), 206.
10. Robert Pittman, Luncheon Address to the International Radio & Television Society Faculty/Industry Seminar, February 7, 1991 (New York).
11. Carl Grabo, *The Creative Critic* (Chicago: University of Chicago Press, 1948), 22.
12. Ibid., 39.
13. Matt Roush, "All in the Family: Suburban Monsters," *TV Guide* (January 16, 1999), 44.
14. Stolnitz, 375.
15. Gilbert Seldes, *The Public Arts* (New York: Simon & Schuster, 1964), 211.
16. John Hartley, "Invisible Fictions: Television Audiences, Paedocracy, Pleasure," in Gary Burns and Robert Thompson (eds.), *Television Studies: Textual Analysis* (New York: Praeger, 1989), 230.
17. David Thorburn, "Television as an Aesthetic Medium," in James Carey (ed.), *Media Myths and Narratives: Television and the Press* (Newbury Park, CA: Sage, 1988), 56.
18. Mimi White, "Ideological Analysis and Television," in Robert Allen (ed.), *Channels of Discourse* (Chapel Hill: University of North Carolina Press, 1987), 160–161.

19. Louis Day, *Ethics in Media Communications: Cases and Controversies* (Belmont, CA: Wadsworth, 1991), 211.
20. Giles Fowler, "Reviewing Course Focuses on Logical Analysis of the Arts," *Journalism Educator* (Spring 1988), 19.
21. John Simon, *Private Screenings* (New York: Macmillan, 1967), 4.
22. Jack Gould, "A Critical Reply," *New York Times* (May 26, 1957).
23. Larry Wolters, quoted in George Brandenburg, "TV Critic's Role Is Middleman—Wolters," *Editor and Publisher* (December 23, 1961), 39.
24. Lawrence Laurent, "Wanted: The Complete Television Critic," in Robert Lewis Shayon (ed.), *The Eighth Art* (New York: Holt, Rinehart and Winston, 1962), 156.
25. Will Jones, quoted in George Condon, "Critic's Choice," *Television Quarterly* (November 1962), 27.
26. "But Who Listens?" *Television Age* (September 27, 1965), 19.
27. "TV Critics Take the Stand," *Broadcasting* (January 21, 1985), 72.
28. Ibid.
29. Robert Smith, *Beyond the Wasteland: The Criticism of Broadcasting*, rev. ed. (Annandale, VA: Speech Communication Association, 1980), 5.
30. Ralph Smith, *A Study of the Professional Criticism of Broadcasting in the United States 1920–1955* (New York: Arno Press, 1979), 483–490.
31. Eric Mankin, "Newsman or Make-Believe Poker Player: I Can't Be Both," *TV Guide* (November 26, 1988), 54.
32. J. Max Robins, "Tabloid Host on the Hot Seat in Chicago," *TV Guide* (May 17, 1997), 49.
33. Adam Shell, "VNRs in the News," *Public Relations Journal* (December 1992), 20–23.
34. George Glazer, "Let's Settle the Question on VNRs," *Public Relations Quarterly* (Spring 1993), 43–46.
35. Geoffrey Foisie and Sharon Moshavi, "NBC Story Goes Up in Flames," *Broadcasting* (February 15, 1993), 8.
36. George Rodman, *Mass Media Issues*, 3rd ed. (Dubuque, IA: Kendall/Hunt, 1989), 268.
37. "Stereotyping and Hate," *Dialogue* (Fall 1994), 1–2.
38. T. W. Adorno, "Television and the Patterns of Mass Culture," in Bernard Rosenberg and David Manning White (eds.), *Mass Culture: The Popular Arts in America* (New York: The Free Press, 1957), 483–484.
39. Day, 286.
40. Robert Alley, "Values on View: A Moral Myopia?" *Critical Studies in Mass Communication* (December 1985), 405.
41. Ben Stein, *The View from Sunset Boulevard* (New York: Basic Books, 1979), 15–17.
42. Allen Banks, "The Problem with Kids These Days Is Programmers," *Broadcasting* (March 9, 1987), 22.
43. William Henry, "Is TV Getting Better or Worse?" *TV Guide* (March 12, 1988), 3–4.
44. Michael Keith, "*JRS* Forum," *Journal of Radio Studies*, Vol. 5, No.1 (1998), 4–5.
45. Merrill Panitt, "The New Newlywed Game," *TV Guide* (February 28, 1987), 40.
46. Jeff Jarvis, "The War on Talk Shows," *TV Guide* (January 13, 1996), 11.
47. Tom Bierbaum, "At a Loss for Words—Illiterate in America," *Variety* (September 10, 1986).
48. Peter Viles, "News Execs Grumble about Tabloid TV," *Broadcasting & Cable* (September 27, 1993), 43.
49. Henry, 4.
50. Steve Pond, "The Garner Files," *TV Guide* (November 26, 1994), 20–21.
51. Lynn Elber, "Send in Sondheim: Bravo Salutes Musical Theatre Master," (Mt. Pleasant, MI) *Morning Sun* (June 6, 1995), 10.
52. Marvin Kitman, "Three Men and a Maybe," *TV Guide* (March 16, 1991), 16.
53. Debra Goldman, "Gone Fishin'," *ADWEEK* (May 3, 1993), 21.
54. Greene, 266.
55. Stolnitz, 356.
56. DeWitt Parker, *The Principles of Aesthetics*, 2nd ed. (Westport, CT: Greenwood Press, 1976), 273–275.

3 Criticism and the Communication Process

Up to this point, we have established a definitional framework for what criticism is, why criticism is needed, and how it has evolved as a tool for electronic media analysis. We have also inventoried the functions of criticism and isolated the programmatic qualities that critics have emphasized. We now are ready to look in more detail at the various orientations that media criticism can take. Even though the range of approaches is wide, it is possible to get a grasp of the subject by seeing how our critical activities revolve around the fundamental components of the communication process.

PROCESS PERSPECTIVE

In its most elemental state the communication process consists of what we refer to as (1) *originator*, (2) *message*, (3) *medium*, and (4) *receiver*. This process thus is the carrier of all human interaction. Harold Lasswell verbally modeled it in 1948 as:

Who
Says What
In Which Channel
To Whom
With What Effect[1]

Lasswell's model, Severin and Tankard point out, "has been called oversimplified, but, as with any good model, it focused attention on important aspects of communication."[2] It also served as the basis for more sophisticated and special-purpose models that other theorists developed in subsequent years. Whatever the model we use to conceptualize it, the communication process serves as the framework for the profession in which we work; it also is the vehicle by which the actual critiques of our profession's output are transported.

As Figure 3-1 illustrates, criticism can focus on any of the four communication-process components. (For the purposes of criticism, we are treating Lasswell's fifth component—"with what effect"—as the debatable outcome or end result of the other four.) Sometimes, a person assuming the role of critic may concentrate his or her commentary on just one of these components and deemphasize discussion of the others. This practice, however, may seriously undermine that critique's accuracy. Because communication-process elements are so intertwined, accentuating one to the exclusion of the others invites distortion. It is difficult to gauge the "with what effect" of a *message*, for instance, without some comprehension of its *originator*'s identity and purpose, the nature and impact of the *medium* by which that originator chose to transmit it, and the attributes and characteristics of its *receiver(s)*.

This process-centered approach to communication certainly did not begin with Lasswell or with the advent of the electronic media. In fact, in his *Rhetoric*, the Greek philosopher Aristotle recognized it more than 2,000 years ago. As Howard Ziff points out, Aristotle revealed "that the motives of the speaker and psychology of the audience are equally as important as the message itself, that the message is shaped not only by its end and intention but also by its very rhetorical structure, its verbal medium."[3] As electronic communicators, all we have done is apply some wonderous technological tools to broaden that verbal (and later, visual) medium's reach and richness.

Anybody expecting to construct usable criticism must be aware of the multifaceted communication perspective that such criticism demands. This is true whether we are media professionals looking out, or journalists, academics, and "just-plain-consumer"

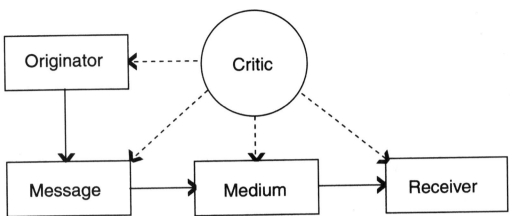

FIGURE 3-1
Basic model of communication and the critical perspective.

critics looking in. And because the electronic media are such public rhetorical instruments, everyone can have their say. Robert Lewis Shayon, a pioneer in comprehensive electronic media criticism, recognized that "All people are critical, at different levels of intensity, insight, and awareness. All of us are truly critics-in-being, some more awakened than others. Some don't even know that they are critics; some critics of a higher order would benefit from a reevaluation of their competency."[4] The meaningfulness of each individual's critical contribution must not be judged on his or her occupation, but on whether they have considered the full process implications of the communication event.

Certainly, each critic's unique background will play a significant role in the *emphasis* that critic places on each communication process element. As professional insiders, there is a natural tendency for us to concentrate on message or medium aspects. Thus, the advertising copywriter is fixated on how his or her words and ideas have been selected and packaged (the *message*). The media buyer is immersed in choosing which stations and networks to use and the schedule through which this commercial will run (the *medium*). But if the needs of the client/*originator* and the interests of the audience/*receiver* get submerged in the search for fine words and cunning time buys, we lose sight of our critical and communicative purpose.

ORIGINATOR CRITICISM

In examining the *originator* of the electronic media message, you are seldom looking at a single individual. Instead, you are usually assessing a group or groups of people gathered into corporate structures such as marketing divisions, stations, news departments, production studios, advertising agencies, cable systems, and networks. Originators can be subdivided into two groups: those who *commission* the work (such as clients, news directors, and programmers) and those who *create* the work in response to such orders. This latter group may include, among others, art directors and copywriters, reporters and videographers, scriptwriters and directors, and website creator/developers. Taken together, as Figure 3-2 depicts, the two groups comprise the twin originator attributes—the initiation, and the design—of media content.

A broadcast or cable network constitutes an *originator* when it produces a program itself. But it is solely a *medium* when it transmits content prepared by others. In practice, these two enterprises are sometimes difficult to separate. However, this lack of separation can constitute a potent topic for critical attention. Did that new action/adventure

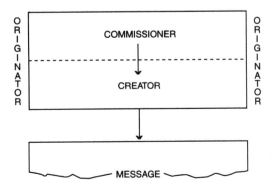

FIGURE 3-2
Subdividing the originator function.

drama fail because it was poorly produced by a California studio or because the commissioning network kept interfering in decisions about casting and storyline development? If the latter scenario was the case, it was the fault of the network *as originator*. If, on the other hand, the program died because the network was unable to convince enough of its affiliated stations to "clear" (agree to air) it, or because the network scheduled it against a competitor's blockbuster, the blame must be attributed to the network's role as a *medium*. (A studio can also blunder in the capacity of medium, of course, by failing to garner the support of enough large-market stations to make possible the distribution of a new first-run game show.)

This distinction has been further blurred following the October 1995 sunset of the FCC's *financial interest and syndication* (fin-syn) *rules* that largely had prevented broadcast networks from owning and subsequently syndicating (selling) their prime-time programs after these shows' network runs. The death of fin-syn, and the studio/network mergers and co-productions thereby made possible, put newly combined companies like Disney/ABC in a powerfully amalgamated originator/medium position.

Such convergence notwithstanding, it is still important to examine critically and separately the seminal role played by content originators—regardless of whether their parent companies exercise other process functions. In addressing this task, British sociologist Jeremy Tunstall uses the term *communicators* instead of originators, and he defines them as

non-clerical workers within communications organizations—people who work on selecting, shaping and packaging of programmes, "stories" and other messages for transmissions to the ultimate audience.[5]

Notice that Tunstall's communicators are responsible for preparing content for transmission; they do not carry out the transmission themselves. Note also that their tasks are not mere transcribing (clerical) functions but involve the actual gleaning and honing of the creative message product. By virtue of this decision-making status, such professionals become the people whose performance is monitored through *originator* criticism.

Contributions these originators make usually are evaluated as a group product (Carsey-Werner Productions; DDB Advertising; the CBS News Division) rather than assessed as individually attributed labors. This is to be expected. In the words of sociologist Charles Wright, "the production of mass communications is an organized social activity, rarely the direct handiwork of a single creative artist."[6]

A partial exception to the "originator as group" approach is recognized in *auteur* criticism. This orientation began in the 1950s when a group of French film critics argued that some Hollywood film directors had managed to forge unique styles in their films—despite the corporate constraints of the studios for which they worked. Auteur criticism was later applied to television; here, the *executive producer* exercises the responsibilities that the motion picture industry vests in the director. Thus, the distinctive stamp of such executive producers as Aaron Spelling (*The Love Boat, Beverly Hills 90210*), Gary David Goldberg (*Family Ties, Spin City*), Stephen Cannell (*The Rockford Files, Wiseguy*), Matt Groening (*The Simpsons, Futurama*), and Steven Bochco (*L.A. Law, NYPD Blue*) came to be recognized and discussed as auteur commentary.

Despite these and a handful of other possible auteur exceptions, such as Norman Lear, Hugh Wilson, and Diane English, electronic media originator criticism still focuses primarily on ensembles rather than on virtuosos. Either way, originator criticism has one overriding purpose. According to Eliseo Vivas, it should "enlighten the artist on the true nature and meaning of his created object, since the artist may do better or worse or quite differently than he intends."[7] As this variance between artistic intent and artistic result is probably greater for group than for individual efforts (given the fact that it *is* a group doing the creating), the exercise of originator criticism in electronic media is particularly important. A perceptive critic is invaluable in detecting when a program's focus has been lost in "group-think."

For two reasons, this is a critical task that we in the media should try to perform for ourselves. First, we are usually more attuned to the specifics of the production process and its pitfalls. Second, our in-house critiques can be done outside the public eye—weaknesses can be addressed before audience attention need be called to them.

In a more long-term way, aesthetics authority Theodore Meyer Greene considers the exploration of artistic intent to be a key element of what he calls *historical criticism*.

The special task of historical criticism, Greene asserts, "is that of determining the nature and intent of works of art in their historical context . . . we can hope to understand, so far as lies in our power, what it was that authors or makers of works of art intended to express, and to interpret this intention in the light of *their* interests and cultural background."[8] (To put this in extreme perspective: It is doubtful you'd want a college English professor to grade your abilities based on essays you wrote for sixth-grade assignments!)

Obviously, the history of a situation comedy series or a syndicated radio feature will be considerably more contemporary and informal than a discussion of Michelangelo's development of the Sistine Chapel ceiling. However, understanding the cultural context that spawned each of these enterprises is equally important if the critic is to probe for the originator's real motivation, the motivation beyond the simple completion of a contract. Ben Stein's *The View from Sunset Boulevard*, for instance, explored how the insular world in which the Los Angeles creative community resides influences the composition of television programming digested by nationwide audiences. That these creators often were unaware of the impact of their residency on the character of their program output illustrates just how important the analysis of the originator function can be.

Television creator/originators vehemently disagreed with some of Stein's theses about them. Such a difference of opinion between critics (especially those outside the media) and originators always is to be expected. This does not mean that *hostility* between the two need result. But it does affirm criticism professor Hilary Cohen's observation that

the relationship between artist and critic has always been a love-hate affair. It's not surprising that artists loathe being publicly damned as much as they love being publicly praised. . . . Artists are uneasy in a relationship they can't quite dismiss because they recognize their dependency on the critics to make their work known, whether or not they recognize their desire for the critic's validation.[9]

As mentioned earlier, we in the electronic media may enjoy an advantage in pursuing originator criticism, precisely because our internal 'praising' and 'damning' is *not* done publicly. Our analysis can be accepted or rejected without damaging the public's perception of the originators or their projects.

Nevertheless, despite the capacity to publicly harm, the *outside* critic's legal right to conduct appraisals of electronic media originators was expressly recognized in a 1987 U.S. Supreme Court decision. The high court let stand a California tribunal's determination that an allegedly libelous evaluation of a television producer by a newspaper writer was a constitutionally protected statement of opinion. Specifically, the case involved a sex-education documentary produced by KHJ-TV (Los Angeles) under the supervision of Walter Baker, the station's programming vice-president. In reviewing the program, *Los Angeles Herald Examiner* critic Peter Bunzel wrote,

My impression is that executive producer Walt Baker . . . told his writer . . . We've got a hot potato here—let's pour on titillating innuendo and as much bare flesh as we can get away with. Viewers will eat it up.[10]

For his part, Baker maintained that a reviewer "has a right to attack the show but not me when [his remarks are] not true."[11] The Supreme Court felt otherwise. Thus, whether one agrees with reviewer Bunzel's mode of expression, the court's finding on his behalf clearly affirms a critic's right to make comments that focus on the creator/originator as well as on the content/message.

Of course, originator criticism seldom degenerates into judicial skirmishing. That is fortunate because legal proceedings, even when critics triumph, have a tendency to inhibit the overall expression of criticism and to make critic/creator relations unnecessarily antagonistic. As we have discussed, analysis of the originator function is important not only to consumer media understanding but also to sensitizing creators to new possibilities and existing problems. "The biggest complaint of disc jockeys around the country is that they don't get enough feedback," reports *Radio and Records* columnist Dan O'Day. "They want critiquing—even if it's negative."[12]

On the television side, too, concerned originators appreciate competent critiquing. "I think that TV critics have risen in status over the years," observes the *Washington Post*'s Pulitzer Prize–winning television editor Tom

Shales. "We're not dismissed as much as we were; some of what we write is taken to heart. I think some of the better executives read TV critics and care what they say."[13] Actions on the part of either originator or critic that constrict such feedback will only lessen the chance for electronic media improvement.

The following radio personality profile by Dan Kening of the *Chicago Tribune* demonstrates that originator criticism need not be negative to be revealing. It also reflects the fact that the smaller number of people required to mount an aural compared to a visual production probably makes it easier to conduct an originator-focused critique of radio than of television. Still, the rationale for originator analysis remains the same in both media. The critical purpose is to help audiences as well as creators better understand the dynamics of content conception.

Mr. Kening's piece delineates the originator function clearly. It also provides the public with important revelations as to how this function is apportioned among on-air and management personnel. Kening further conveys the insecurity and "mentally draining" aspects that can accompany and inhibit an on-air career. Though he is focusing on Bubba the Love Sponge, the critic paints a picture that seems to include much of radio as its backdrop. We thus learn something about Bubba's *messages*—and about the *medium* that alternately promotes and rejects them. In this way, potential *receivers* have been given a frame of reference as to whether they might like or dislike the Love Sponge's current style.

MESSAGE CRITICISM

Message evaluation is the primary thing many people think of when the subject of criticism is mentioned—often to the exclusion of the other three communication process components. Certainly, message content is what most obviously distinguishes one electronic media enterprise from another. But what we need to examine here is beyond what the producer put into the message. We must realize that electronic media messages are subject to *external* definition—with a broad range of meanings potentially emerging.

One way to calculate this potential is with *re-creative criticism*. In the same way he used the term *historical criticism* to encompass originator-aimed analytical activity, Theodore Meyer Greene attaches the label *re-creative criticism* to the procedure of examining messages. To Greene,

the special task of re-creative criticism is that of apprehending imaginatively, through sensitive artistic response, what the artist has actually succeeded in expressing in a specific work of art . . . to *re*-create a work of art is to apprehend the content which its author actually expressed in it, i.e., to interpret it correctly as a vehicle of communication.[14]

In other words, our critique of a program—whether that critique is delivered internally to our professional colleagues or externally to the public at large—needs to reveal the central communication content that the project's producers have ended up packaging for audience reception.

However, modern mass communication theorists argue that revealing "author expression" is only one part of message analysis. What is more important, they assert, are the meanings that *audiences* subsequently invest in those messages. "Audiences do not simply receive messages," explains Celeste Condit, "they decode texts."[15] And since different audiences—or even different members of the same audience—bring different backgrounds to this decoding process, a variety of meanings may result. A media message is therefore considered to be *polysemic*—it possesses multiple (even contradictory) significances. Simply stated, *polysemy* denotes that meanings do not repose in messages but in receivers.

A leading proponent of this approach, John Fiske, maintains that the success of a program may depend on how polysemic its creators have been able to make it. "To be popular," says Fiske, "a television program must be polysemic so that different subcultures can find in it different meanings that correspond to their differing social relationships."[16] Thus, young viewers may enjoy *The Simpsons* because of Bart's outrageous rejection and sabotaging of authority. At the same time, older audiences can take pleasure in the animated program's social satire and multiple references to historic political figures and movie devices. To the producer's benefit, viewers from both perspectives can

WYTZ'S LOVE SPONGE

by Dan Kening

In sports, sometimes the addition of one key player can turn a team's fortunes around. Ailing contemporary hit station WYTZ-FM 94.7 is hoping that the return of Bubba the Love Sponge to Chicago's airwaves will change its luck.

What's a Bubba the Love Sponge, you ask? The man with that unlikely moniker—an appellation bestowed upon him six years ago by a fellow disc jockey—joined "Hot 94.7" last month in morning drive, replacing the hapless team of Welch and Woody.

This is the second tour of duty in Chicago for Bubba (a k a Todd Clem, from Warsaw, Ind.), who's only 25, and in his seventh station change in three years.

In his relatively brief career, Bubba has carved out a reputation as one of radio's more colorful and outrageous characters.

How outrageous? An article in the Orlando Sentinel described him as "one who makes New York disc jockey Howard Stern look like Marie Osmond."

But if you listen to Bubba on WYTZ, you'll hear a streetwise, high-energy radio persona rapping with "homeboys" and "girlfriends" on the phones, but little of what was perceived as so "controversial" at his two most recent stops: Philadelphia and Orlando.

"I think I really had to tone things down from what I was doing," said Bubba, who did evenings at WYTZ's archrival, WBBM-FM 96.3, two years ago and readily admits to being influenced by WLUP-AM's Steve Dahl.

"But once we get the snowball rolling a little faster here, I think I'll be able to let loose a little more. Right now I'm very much under the microscope, and every word I say is being analyzed. It's frustrating, but at the same time I'm very grateful for the opportunity I've been given here. At this point, not being so nasty and controversial might make me a better disc jockey."

The Love Sponge was hired at WYTZ by program director Gregg Cassidy, who once fired him from a station in Grand Rapids, Mich. "There are lots of reasons why he's been blown out in other cities, and some were valid and some were not," Cassidy said. "But Bubba's a natural 'street' person, and we badly needed to get some street back on this radio station."

It's no secret that the ABC/Capital Cities-owned station desperately needs fresh blood. In Arbitron's last radio ratings, WYTZ ranked 23rd with a 1.3 audience share, compared with 5.8 at No.3 "B-96."

Bubba admits that there's an element of revenge in being pitted against his old station. "I'd like nothing more than for this station to beat them," he said. "Nothing would make me happier than to see their evil empire destroyed."

This is also one Love Sponge who has been wrung dry by his seesaw career. "I'm kind of mentally drained right now from having moved around so much, doing well for a station and then being blown out by a management change. But I also have a lot of confidence in myself and in the people here at this radio station, and I really hope things will work out."

"If not, maybe I'll just go back to Warsaw, Ind., and be a football coach. The most important thing in life is not the W-2 form, but how happy you are."

share the same program and contribute to the sum of its ratings.

Unfortunately, polysemy can also work to the detriment of the electronic communicator's interests. A 1970s Geritol commercial showed a tearful young mother putting her small son on a school bus. She waved as the bus disappeared down the road—to the accompaniment of an announcer voice-over stressing the need for an iron supplement (Geritol) so a woman can cope with her family duties. But in cities as diverse as Boston and Winston-Salem, the poignant scene was often interpreted as Geritol's endorsement of forced busing to achieve racial balance in schools—which federal courts had ordered in those and other locales. Obviously, the polysemic nature of this 'school bus' vignette was not predicted by the advertising agency. And it certainly wasn't to Geritol's market advantage. So media professionals must be vigilant to the divergent decodings that their messages might inspire. "The text can no longer be seen as a self-sufficient entity that bears its own meaning and exerts a similar influence on all its readers," warns Fiske. "Rather, it is seen as a potential of meanings that can be activated in a number of ways."[17] (See Figure 3-3 for one pictorial example of polysemy.)

A growing body of research suggests that the more audiences feel *encouraged* to take part in the message-making, the better received will be the media content. For instance, Auter and Davis conducted a study of television programming in which characters "break the fourth wall" (speak directly to viewers). Academic researchers often label such a technique *self-reflexivity*. Self-reflexive shows examined by the study included historic properties like *Burns and Allen* and *The Dobie Gillis Show* as well as the more contemporary series *Moonlighting* and *It's Garry Shandling's Show*. Among the Auter/Davis findings:

FIGURE 3-3
Even a single frame can be polysemic. How many different 'readings' can you make of this photo? (Photo by Lloyd DeGrane from his photo documentary book, *Tuned In: Television in American Life*)

Clips that broke the fourth wall were rated significantly more entertaining . . . and significantly more sophisticated than were clips that did not break the wall. . . . What the study seems to point to is a generalized liking for the practice of breaking the fourth wall. To some extent this has been ascertained by programmers who use the practice with increasing frequency, as in Fox's instant hit, [*Malcolm in the Middle*]. But the liking for the practice may be even deeper than programmers suspect. . . . The findings suggest that people like to be included in the context of their media. And when message producers make the extra effort to acknowledge their audiences' existence, audience members are ready to take part. Further analysis and careful use of such involving techniques as "fourth wall breaking" may help program producers to achieve the goal of getting audience members to attend to the message.[18]

Professor Jenny Nelson sees this "liking to be included in the context of their media" as an explanation for the popularity of reruns. As she discovered in her interviews with viewers:

Televisual experience is not so much a matter of the amount of time the set stays on but the intensity of a moment of encounter and its quality of human illumination. . . . Thus our fascination with reruns—'not so much a matter of where are they but when is this.' Where was I then? What was I like then? How was I situated and informed? These are the once-lived experiences that come back to us through our own narration of a rerun: we become the medium of communication. As an artifact that speaks, reruns continue to speak to us, but in a speech already spoken. . . . We begin to realize our own hidden contribution to this speaking. Vague memories become clearer and/or more disturbing: so this is how I used to think, how I used to be.[19]

The success of *Nick at Nite*, the cable service that stitches together twenty- and thirty-year-old programs into nostalgia-potent blocks, is a further extension of this principle.

But audiences do not "make their own messages" only from the individual program, or from a single network service. They now possess the technology to create their own message composites from a multitude of sources. Through use of the TV set's remote control and the VCR's fast-forward button, today's viewers graze across multiple program offerings and speed through segments deemed unappealing. Of course,

radio button-pushers have been doing this even longer. Such skipping, zipping, and zapping, John Fiske asserted,

allows the viewer to construct a viewing experience of fragments, a postmodern collage of images whose pleasures lie in their discontinuity, their juxtaposition, and their contradictions. This is segmentation taken to the extreme of fragmentation and makes of television the most open producerly text for it evades all attempts at closure. It is a forum of scratch video that produces an individualized text out of its mass-produced works.[20]

However, Fiske's observation predated the rollout of the Internet—a monumentally more fragmented medium than is conventional television, and a medium in which the individualized text can be click-constructed from one's own surfing as well as one's own website.

We have clearly gone a long way beyond the unidirectional model with which we started this chapter. We now recognize that communication process events—especially in the proliferating world of electronic media—have codings and decodings flying in cross-directions. In a sense, as Figure 3-4 illustrates, we have added a new loop in which Lasswell's "With What Effect" becomes, in part, each receiver's power to go back and polysemically negotiate the message as the process continues.

Lasswell's verbal model and the diagram we originally generated from it are helpful in freeze-framing the essential communication components. But like any static model, they are incapable of accurately conveying the dynamic process of one person interacting with another—let alone the procedure whereby electronic media producers interact with unseen millions. Thoughtful message criticism serves to remind producers that their control over message meaning is fragile at best. Once they determine the meanings they *intend* (no small task in itself), the producers can then attempt to restrict content to only the elements and structures most likely to trigger those meanings *exclusively*.

FIGURE 3-4
The initial reception of a media message is only the starting point for the assignment of meaning through polysemic negotiation.

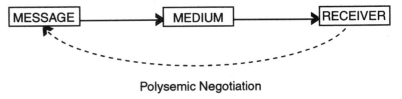

MESSAGE → MEDIUM → RECEIVER

Polysemic Negotiation

Fortunately for electronic media professionals, the possibilities for receiver-constructed meanings of a single message are not limitless. We can narrow meaning options through what we put into our show, site, or commercial, what we leave out, and how we arrange the elements we do choose to include. Then, via *medium* selection (the third element in our basic communication process model), we can target the audience segments (universes) most likely to make a positive response to the content and packaging we have picked.

This is anything but a simple task. What this discussion of message criticism emphasizes is that receivers will not always react to our content package:

as we want,
    or as we expect,
        or even as we fear!

Celeste Condit summarizes the divergency of electronic media message processing this way:

Audience members are neither simply resistive nor dupes. They neither find television [or radio] simply pleasurable, simply an escape, nor simply obnoxious and oppressive. The audience's variability is a consequence of the fact that humans, in their inherent character as audiences, are inevitably situated in a communication *system*, of which they are a part, and hence have some influence within, but by which they are also influenced.[21]

It is this system to which we now turn our attention.

MEDIUM CRITICISM

The ancient royal practice of killing the messenger who brought bad news has been modernized in this century into the pastime of attacking the electronic media when they spotlight society's irritations. Through such devices as TV-set burnings, video abstinence crusades, Surgeon General's reports, and showcase Congressional hearings, the electronic media in general—and television (and now the Internet) in particular—are blamed for all sorts of problems and plagues. Such a blanket indictment results from pseudo-criticism that looks *only* (and negatively) at the medium while completely ignoring the other aspects of the communication process.

An example of medium-bashing commentary is this broad denunciation of television by Michael Parenti that convicts television not for any specific content piece or category, but simply for its technological capabilities:

The most pervasive effect of television—aside from its actual content—may be its very existence, its readily available, commanding, and often addictive presence in everybody's home, its ability to reduce hundreds of millions of citizens to passive spectators for major portions of their lives. Television minimizes personal interactions within families and communities. . . . A single information source can transmit images and viewpoints directly into millions of minds, making it difficult for people to separate the real from the unreal, pacifying and immobilizing them, fragmenting their perceptions, blunting their imaginations and their critical judgments, shortening their attention spans, and diminishing their taste for intelligent public and private discourse.[22]

In similar but more pointed manner, writer Jerry Mander quotes a Native American schoolteacher's lament:

When TV came to my village I saw an immediate change. The kids lost all interest in the native language. They only wanted English. But worst of all is that storytelling has stopped cold. . . . We'd ask our grandparents for the same stories night after night. . . . The old people were windows into the past. . . . We used to honor our old people but that's all going now. The generations are sitting all together now, silently watching television. And on TV it seems like being young is all that matters and that the old have nothing to say.[23]

Criticism like this seems to argue that there is something in the essential nature of the medium that is inherently blameful. However well-intentioned, such an approach is flawed criticism because it allows no possibility of positive valuation or rectification—essential components of criticism as defined in Chapter 1.

Radio also has not escaped such blanket condemnation. We are all familiar with the periodic attacks on radio's record lyrics as the corrupters of our youth. This fear of radio's intrusiveness is not a new concern.

More than four decades ago, German media theorist Gunter Anders charged that

because the receiving sets speak in our place, they gradually deprive us of the power of speech, thus transforming us into passive dependents. . . . The pairs of lovers sauntering along the shores of the Hudson, the Thames or the Danube with a portable radio do not talk to each other but listen to a third person—the public, usually anonymous, voice of the program which they walk like a dog or, more accurately, which walks them like a pair of dogs. . . . Intimate conversation is eliminated in advance; and whatever intimate contacts take place between the lovers are introduced and stimulated not by them, but by that third party—the husky or crowing voice of the program which (for is that not the very meaning of "program"?) tells both lovers what and how to feel or do.[24]

It is frightening to speculate on what Anders might have thought of today's Walkmans!

Similar dread about the electronic media as dangerous presences is periodically expressed or implied in the attitudes of U.S. clergy, members of Congress eager for a safe re-election issue, and earnest citizens groups. This one-track blame-placing is what we might call (with apologies to Meredith Willson, creator of *The Music Man*) the "Trouble-Right-Here-in-River-City" phenomenon. Now, it is not the pool hall on Main Street whose effects parents are supposed to fear, but a multitude of electromagnetic boxes that have insinuated themselves into our homes and cars. (That the enclosed automobile was itself condemned in the 1920s as a vehicle to promote mobile and illicit lovemaking by the nation's youth is a comparable though separate story.)

Even educated human services providers still succumb to the temptation of blaming client ills on the electronic media. In 1992 (not 1922) a home economist wrote a column for a local newspaper in which she asserted that

television watching has reached epidemic proportions among very young children, and in the winter when the weather is bad, television viewing increases even more.

Some of the negative effects heavy television viewing can have on children include loss of imagination, diminished thinking powers, unnatural passivity, verbal logic damage, violence modeling, superimposed values and distortion in perceived reality. Heavy viewing children also seem fearful of the world and are more apt to have bad dreams than kids who saw less television.[25]

Reputable research has yet to validate these charges, of course, but invoking the persistent myth of the evil tube is an easy way to appear to be treating complex problems. What is even more bizarre is that television's dangers somehow are seen as much more ominous than those posed by radio. Thus, this same home economist, after listing a number of ways for reducing children's television viewing, suggests the following antidote:

Use the record player and radio to fill the sound gap when the television goes off.[26]

It is as if she is advocating that children take in less Mr. Rogers and more Howard Stern!

Fear of the on-line medium is engendering similarly one-sided commentary and concern. Congressional attempts to ban pornography from the Internet, the installation of site/subject blocking devices by schools and libraries, and public condemnation of the Web as the trigger for mass murder and mayhem are simply the latest manifestations of criticism that focuses on the medium to the exclusion of the other parts of the communication process. Such medium-fixated concern often results in technological quick-fixes like television's V-chip—where one "machine" is created to hamper or cancel out another—and with no attention to legitimate and laudable message content that may be inhibited along the way.

Why is criticism of only the *medium*—criticism that largely ignores the other components of the communication process—so prevalent? And why is it so negative?

In 1948, just before the emergence of U.S. television, eminent media scholars Paul Lazarsfeld and Robert Merton identified three key reasons that both followers and leaders fear the mass media.[27] In essence, they concluded that

1. The pervasiveness of the media and its consequent power for manipulation lead people to believe they have no way of exercising control or restraint over these media. [This concern differs from earlier fears of pool halls and closed cars only in degree.]

2. Economic interest groups may use the media to ensure continuance of an economic and social status quo that serves their interests. Results of this are the minimizing of social criticism and the deterioration of the audience's critical thinking skills.

3. In catering to large audiences, the media will cause a deterioration of artistic tastes and cultural standards.

Though their purview included all the 1948 mass media, Lazarsfeld and Merton seemed to recognize the special prominence of the *electronic* media by most often citing radio examples to buttress the points of their discussion. It must be emphasized that the two scholars were talking, not about specific *messages*, but about widespread attitudes toward the *media* system that carries these messages. Thus, they were engaging, almost exclusively, in *medium criticism*.

Nothing we have said should be taken to mean that medium criticism is inherently wrong or defective. Our point is that, by itself, medium criticism supplies only one of four critical vantage points necessary to a comprehensive understanding of the communication process. Unfortunately, as just cited, when medium criticism is conducted to the exclusion of the other orientations, it is much more likely to constitute either a weapon to be aimed at our communication vehicles or a platform for the expression of fears about them.

Television (the medium, even more than its messages) is especially vulnerable to such myopic critiquing because of the "pervasiveness" factor that Lazarsfeld and Merton attributed to the pre-TV media of 1948. Thirty years later, Gene Jankowski, then president of the CBS Broadcast Group, asserted that "All the talk, criticism, concern and controversy that surrounds our industry today is taking place because of the important role that television plays every day for more than 200 million Americans."[28]

By the mid-1980s, veteran critic Les Brown was pointing to an intramedia reason for the continued pummeling of television as vehicle: "The press still regards television as the enemy, as its chief competitor, and cannot get around its own bigotry towards this immensely popular medium that can produce, distribute and exhibit in a single process."[29]

Whether or not Brown's observation remains valid today, the reasonable practice of criticism by professionals both inside and outside our industry requires that the critic approach the medium being analyzed with an open mind. As Robert Landry, one of the first true radio critics, once observed, a constructive critic

cannot function in a temper of constant dislike of the medium, the mass mind, and advertising. That way lies the intellectualized wisecrack and the clichés of condescension. Such a critic can have no real contact with the radio audience. He cannot share or interpret its enthusiasms. Indeed one wonders if he can even tolerate these enthusiasms.[30]

Any professional working in the electronic media has to believe that there is much in our industry to be enthusiastic about. Otherwise, coming to work every day would be an increasingly tedious chore. At the same time, enthusiasm does not mean unequivocal cheerleading for everything that our medium—or our own company—dispenses. Instead, perceptive medium critiquing means understanding what is systemically possible given the constraints within which all of us must operate.

In their book *Organizational Life on Television*, Vande Berg and Trujillo categorize these medium constraints into three categories: audience constraints, political constraints, and societal constraints.[31] Though they were primarily discussing network television, these limitations can be applied to all media enterprises.

Audience constraints refer to a medium's need to identify and attract a specified segment of the public in order to justify a program's existence. A schedule of programs possessing that justification provides the station or system that carries it with a reason for being. We discuss this topic in greater detail in Chapter 7. For now, suffice it to say that no mass outlet can long survive without due regard for the quantity and characteristics of the target consumer universe it is trying to assemble.

In the United States *political constraints* on a medium are not imposed from without by the government; they are imposed from within by the various parties and interests involved in program production, distribution, and exhibition. Organization-dwellers colloquially refer to this as 'internal politics.' These partisan relationships, tradeoffs, and turf wars are the stuff of industry gossip and inevitable by-products of expensive enterprises chasing intangible audiences. "Indeed," argues John Hartley, "the real relationships of broadcasters are not with audiences as such but with other professionals in the industry: with advertisers, funding agencies, suppliers and—it's about as close as they get—with audience research organizations."[32] Hartley may be overstating the situation, particularly with regard to local outlets whose pulse-taking of community preferences is a key to competitive success. Still, even at the station or cable-system level, complex business relationships ultimately determine what the public receives and when it receives it.

Societal constraints encompass such factors as public interest (or public pressure) groups whose highly visible actions and pronouncements can have a direct impact on the operating policies of media establishments. These same groups further influence the electronic media indirectly by lobbying the government for regulatory or legislative change.

Professional critics outside our industry can also be considered a societal constraint. As *Washington Post* television critic Tom Shales bluntly puts it, "The one weapon I have is to embarrass the guys when they screw up."[33] In a few instances (such as federal obscenity laws and bans on cigarette advertising) the societal constraints on broadcasting in particular are explicit. More often, however, these constraints only implicitly suggest the boundaries within which media activities are less likely to be considered antagonistic. Depending on your point of view, program projects are either courageous or foolhardy when they move beyond this zone of general acceptance.

The acceptance zone for broadcast television is more narrowly drawn than are zones for media vehicles with more restricted audience access. Everyone can receive over-the-air programming as a virtual birthright. Thus, broad public agreement on that content is an operational given. But cable or satellite material, as well as rented cassettes and Internet service, get into the home only through a receiver's overt action and payment. This allows these media enterprises greater latitude in the shaping of product.

A significant amount of contemporary medium criticism is now devoted to exploring the divergent ways in which these various vehicles serve as communication agents.

"Your television set," declares Michael Schrage, "becomes a computer screen becomes a video games console becomes a VCR becomes a pay-per-view movie conduit becomes an online information retrieval device."[34] In the matter of VCR movie rentals, for instance, Dean Krugman makes the case that the take-out cassettes constitute a discrete medium experience by allowing for more directive or active viewing. Consumers of VCR movies are no longer watching conventional television, Krugman believes, but are participating in an experience more like cinema-going. Thus, they do not engage in the number of competing household activities that are so often permitted during "regular TV."[35]

Conventional research has been slow to recognize what some experts call these new media (and others label as variations on our old media). This analysis lag has inhibited medium criticism and also has retarded the ability of traditional electronic media systems to adapt. For instance, as advertising executives Mark McNeely and Scott Marshall complain to their colleagues,

we've been remarkably pig-headed in trying to ignore this fundamental shift in the way people watch TV. We're all quick to criticize Detroit for its sloth in responding to the Japanese challenge, yet our industry is still plodding along with the programming and advertising equivalents of a fin-bedecked two-ton cruiser.

With remote controls and a multitude of cable channels, if today's viewers are the slightest bit bored . . . they are only an imperceptible thumb twitch away from saying adios. Better to go watch lions cavort or Madonna contort and return when the ads are over. Raise your hand if this is what you do. And you're in the business.[36]

These are the sort of system-based challenges that effective *medium* criticism (rather than senseless media bashing) can explore.

One new approach to medium criticism is suggested by Greg Riker, Microsoft's director of Advanced Consumer Technology. Any communications vehicle, says Riker, can be analysed and categorized on the basis of three characteristics: bandwidth, latency, and storage.[37] *Bandwidth* relates to how much information can be processed at once. *Latency* measures how long it takes to get a response. *Storage* refers to how much information usefully can be retained. Applying this three-part standard to various electronic media gives us an understanding of the comparative capacity of each vehicle and a basis for gauging the potentials and limitations of each.

Bandwidth-rich media, such as cable and satellite, for example, legitimately can be expected to provide more varied and individually tailored program choice than can the more bandwidth-limited broadcast television (even after its digital upgrade). And the storage capability of on-line services deserves to be recognized—even if it usually takes longer (latency) to access events on a computer screen than to switch from one television program to another. (In stressing the importance of these qualities, Riker points out that bandwidth, latency, and storage are central to the measurement of more than just electronic media. Though disguised under different terms, these same attributes are used by supervisors to measure employee performance!)

RECEIVER CRITICISM

Historically, the practice of receiver criticism has tended to focus on the *effect* that an originator's medium-conveyed message has on the audience. As we see in our discussion of message criticism, however, it is now recognized that part of this effect involves the triggering of polysemic reinterpretations of the message by the various constituencies who make up that audience. "We are not all identical empty vessels being filled up with TV content," Elayne Rapping reminds us. "We are active and very diverse human beings, coming to any given TV show with our own histories and experiences, our own ways of understanding and responding to what is shown, our own levels of attention and immediate moods."[38]

Thus, receiver criticism entails speculating about the uses and gratifications that consumers sought to acquire from a given program. It further includes the attempt to assess whether these or other gratifications were achieved. And receiver criticism most obviously encompasses the originator-assisting function of trying to ascertain just who these listeners or viewers are.

From the vantage point of the media producer, the process should begin by determining what specific audience we are striving to reach. Throwing out a randomly selected lure to see what might bite is neither efficient fishing nor efficient message-production technique. Instead, we try to arrange our on-air or on-line elements with the assumed needs and interests of a preselected audience in mind. Who do you suppose is the target universe for the commercial in Figure 3-5? What leads you to this conclusion? What receiver gratifications are built into the commercial and associated with the product?

In the case of program series, the application of receiver criticism can help explain why a seemingly successful property has been terminated. For instance, the CBS detective show *Cannon*, featuring the hefty William Conrad in a title role, went off the air not because its raw ratings were low, but because its increasingly elderly audience skew was unattractive to advertisers. Conrad later returned in *Jake and the Fatman*—a series whose skew was kept more saleable by the presence of virile young costar Joe Penny.

A similar audience composition problem forced *The Lawrence Welk Show* off the commercial networks. But that property was sustained when further analysis of its receiver appeal led to the decision to continue the series for syndication directly to stations. Away from the broad audience-delivery pressures of expensive prime-time, the program thrived in syndication as a tailor-made advertising vehicle for the makers of Polident and Geritol. (Still later, noncommercial stations again revived *Welk* because its senior, yet affluent audience proved likely prospects for pledge drives.) In short, incisive receiver critiquing led to a shift of medium that allowed the same consumers to be reached by other, more appropriate marketers in a cost-effective manner.

Whatever the media project, Professor James Andrews tells us that audience composition best can be understood if we analyze this makeup in terms of three key receiver variables: knowledge, group identification, and receptivity to the topic and purpose.[39]

Knowledge involves our assessment of what the target receivers are familiar with in terms of the subject of our message and/or the people with whom we have populated it. Due to its parent series' devoted and long-

"On Being Big." By 'Rhino' Vincent.

:30 TV

FIGURE 3-5
(Courtesy of Patrick D. Scullin, The Bloom Agency)

RV: I've always been the biggest person in the room. Even when I was born.

Now when you're big, you tend to like things big.

Like this Chicken Big Sandwich from Church's. It's a big piece of crispy chicken served with dressing on a big bun.

And all for only ninety-nine cents.

That means you can have dinner for under ten bucks.

VO: Church's Chicken. Big pieces. Little prices.

Get Church's delicious Chicken Big Sandwich, fries and drink for only one ninety-nine!

(INTERCHANGEABLE FOR DIFFERENT PROMOTIONAL OFFERS)

standing following, syndication's *Star Trek: The Next Generation*, for instance, could assume a deeper and more cohesive knowledge base among its audience than can the producer of a new network sitcom. The sitcom creator, in an attempt to start from a more clearly defined knowledge base, might feature an already-popular actor or actress in the new series. Because the audience feels comfortably acquainted with the star, they may be eager—or at least willing—to learn a new show environment.

Group identification variables traditionally have been expressed by audience measurement companies in terms of age/sex demographic cells: for example, males 18–34, women 55+. This is known as *quantitative* research. But through the computer-activated refinement of research techniques, certain *psychographic* or life-style clusters also have been identified. The most in-depth receiver probing even attempts to isolate audience values and belief structures in an effort to better tailor commercials and programs to activate the so-called hot buttons of consumer interest. This moving beyond the counting of audience members in demographic cells in order to more precisely define consumers by their affiliations and attitudes is known as *qualitative* research. Organizational memberships, political orientations, and periodical subscriptions can all be a part of this data base.

Receptivity to the topic and purpose, Andrews's final receiver variable, is in many ways the product of his other two factors. The knowledge that consumers *bring to* the message and the group identifications and values they use in *negotiating* that message (recall our earlier discussion of polysemy) determine how they rate its appropriateness and relevance. If potential receivers do not assign importance to what we have to say, it doesn't matter how much we have spent to achieve glowing production values or the number of outlets on which our project is carried.

Electronic media professionals now realize that we can't *dictate* audience attention—let alone audience agreement. As John Cawelti observes,

recent mass communication research has shown beyond question that the mass culture model of communication positing a power relationship between an irresistible elite and a helplessly incoherent mass audience is totally inadequate as a description of the real social complexity of relationships between media and their various publics. Recent research stresses the influence of the network of social reference groups which intervene between the media and the audience, shaping the public's perception and reaction to communication in many ways.[40]

It is easy for electronic media professionals to become angry with receivers who fail to respond to the brilliance of the messages on which writers and technicians have so strenuously labored. But astute receiver criticism should never damn the audience for the message/medium choices it makes. Instead, we must try harder to understand and sympathize with how those target receivers are oriented. Only by considering current audience preferences can electronic communicators hope to nudge or shift those preferences to encompass the content they've fashioned.

Likewise, we have every right to expect *outside* critics to accept the public as it is when critiquing our productions. On too many occasions, lamented then-FCC Commissioner Lee Loevinger, "when the public gets what it wants from the mass media this incurs the wrath of an intellectual elite and the slings and arrows of outraged critics who have been demanding service to the public—but who have been expecting their own rather than the public's views and tastes."[41]

On the other hand, electronic media professionals as well as outside critics can also err in the practice of receiver criticism by assuming public taste to be less than it is. Syndicated columnist Ernie Kreiling recognized this when he stated that "most of us critics are guilty of precisely the same sin of which we accuse broadcasting, namely underestimating the American public and catering to a lower common denominator of tastes than we should."[42] Certain writers betray a susceptibility to this attitude when they pander to their audience by callously denying their own expertise. But as Gilbert Seldes declares,

The critic who so earnestly insists that he is no surer in judgment than the untrained public is failing in his job or being patronizing, in a sort of inverse snobbery, and a little hypocritical. He seems at times to be begging people to remain ignorant, threatening them with a loss of aesthetic virginity if they eat of the fruit that grows on the tree of knowledge.[43]

The quality of our professional output improves only as fast as the perceptiveness of our receivers is improved. Respecting an audience does not mean surrendering our chance to stretch their awareness. "Far from being passive dupes, the people are highly discriminatory in the cultural commodities that they choose to make into their popular culture," John Fiske argues. "Far from seeing them as the weakest, most powerless, commodified end of the economic chain, we actually need to see them as the driving force behind the cultural industries. They constitute the force that keeps the industries on their toes, that keeps them uncertain, that keeps them moving."[44]

Before concluding this discussion of receiver criticism, one further caution must be raised about its application. We have stressed that understanding the receiver is of crucial importance in fashioning meaningful programming—and meaningful critiques of that programming. However, such understanding can be corrupted into attempted manipulation when a critic exploits his or her audience relationships for prejudicial attacks on our medium, its messages, and its practitioners. These tirades may enhance the prestige of the alleged critic in certain quarters, but they will never produce media betterment. As Ralph Smith testifies, a reputable critic's "final aim is not to arouse violent antagonistic responses from the industry and strong partisan support from a handful of readers; it is to involve broadcasters and the public in a cooperative critical endeavor."[45]

Of course, neither is it the critic's role to avoid all controversy by continuously and self-servingly echoing majority sentiments. As *Washington Post* TV editor Tom Shales declares, "I don't like critics who try to get some of the refracted popularity of a hit show by overpraising it."[46]

Profession-enhancing criticism does not set the four components of the communication process against each other. Nor does it succeed by concentrating on one element of the process to the total neglect of the other three. All four parts of this systemic quartet are as essential to good criticism as they are to the successful realization of the program which that criticism is monitoring. As aesthetician Eliseo Vivas defines it:

Criticism seeks

to reveal the aesthetic value of an object,	[message criticism]
to relate it to the structure that sustains it,	[medium criticism]
and to relate the object to the traditions to which it belongs,	[receiver criticism]
and to define the intention of the artist.[47]	[originator criticism]

As a concluding illustration of thorough communication-process criticism, read *Vic-*

VICTIM'S RIGHTS

by Debra Goldman

If you're a TV syndicator looking to launch the next talk-show sensation in a market saturated with dysfunctional gladiators a la The Jerry Springer Show, what ploy is most likely to succeed? The anti-Springer, of course. Twentieth Television hopes it has found that very thing with Mother Love, the empathy-oozing hostess of talk-show comer Forgive or Forget.

While Springer and company exploit conflict, Mother Love exploits "healing." Described in a press release as a "unique public forum for those who have wronged [family and friends] to make amends," Forgive or Forget's format brings the repentant sinner before a huge door. The open portal either reveals the injured party (forgiven!) Or yawning emptiness (forget it!). It combines the suspense of The Price Is Right with the satisfactions of The People's Court.

Since it premiered last spring, the show boasts ratings increases of 25 percent to 50 percent in some markets, even knocking off Oprah on oc-

casion in New York. Warm, uplifting and proudly plus-sized, Mother Love possesses the one-of-us appeal of the original Oprah, long before the personal-chef-de-low-fat cuisine and glam-girl Hollywood makeover. A former welfare mother turned bus driver turned drive-time radio-show host, Mother is as effective weeping for guests whose hopes of reconciliation are fulfilled, as she is hugging and comforting those who've been disappointed.

Nor could anyone argue with her common sense counsel: Deal with the past, put it behind you and the lessons you've learned will take you to a brighter day. It's the best, if usually ignored, advice anyone nursing a pain or grievance could hope for. Even apologizer-in-chief Bill Clinton could identify with one Jeff Stewart, who, the announcer intones, "treated his ex-girlfriend like garbage."

Jeff confesses to cheating on her, stealing from her and—most damning in the eyes of the audience—taking the furniture he bought her when he moved out. He'd just finished a four-year prison stint when they met, he explains, and he didn't know how to treat a woman with the respect she deserves. Now he's learned his lesson and wants her back. But there is no Cadillac behind door No. 1; his ex doesn't show. The audience's collective moan is without pity or regret; they clearly think the creep deserves it.

The payoff comes when his girlfriend gets the last word on videotape. "You're ugly, you're nasty, you're dirty, you're filthy, you're a disease that's contagious. I hate you," she declares as the camera stares mercilessly at a rejected Jeff. Chair throwing is wholesome comic relief compared to this kind of psychological violence.

It's little wonder that Jeff was the only guest in the five episodes I watched who actually asked forgiveness for wrongs committed. Most come to Mother Love not to make apologies but to demand them from others. They are sinned against, not sinning. The accused parties are often revealed to be waiting backstage from the start, where they're seen shaking their heads and rolling their eyes at the testimony against them. They come through the door not to forgive, but to continue the fight on TV.

A couple of weeks ago, a program was devoted to a typical talk-show circus act: the tired conflict between Paula Jones' sister and brother-in-law (who debunk Paula's story) and adviser Susan Carpenter-McMillan. Safe to say there were no apologies, but lots of sex talk and name calling. Forgive or Forget is not so much anti-Springer as stealth-Springer.

In the ongoing evolution of the talk show, Forgive or Forget is a telling hybrid. In classic Ricki-Jenny-Sally style, it plays to our Roman-arena lust for conflict as entertainment, then it slaps us upside the head like those superstar super-egos Judge Judy and Dr. Laura. Mother Love is less ringmaster, as Jerry is so aptly described in his upcoming movie, and more strict-but-loving high school principal. When the audience begins to boo, Mother Love cuts them off. Members of the audience are not allowed to point their fingers belligerently at the guests on stage. When a guest begins her tale "Me and my boyfriend," Mother quickly interrupts, "My boyfriend and I." You can wallow in prurient swill, but you've got to speak properly while you do it.

Indeed, it's the discipline the audience loves. When a guest ignores Mother's admonishment to let her opponents speak, the hostess draws up her maternal bulk and informs the cotton-candy-coiffed blonde that Mother Love is running this show. I couldn't help inwardly cheering along with the thrilled studio audience, which is why one admiring critic called the show "nearly guilt-free exploitation TV."

Forgive or Forget allows us to indulge our creepy voyeurism and feel uplifted by it at the same time. In a proudly perverse TV genre, Forgive or Forget may be the most perverse show yet. Just another way of saying it seems destined to be a hit.

tim's Rights by Debra Goldman (see p. 47). *Originator criticism* is covered via revelations about Twentieth Television's strategy in launching *Forgive or Forget,* Mother Love's own background, and the attributes and techniques she brings to the show. Goldman's discussion of the TV syndication market and of the way prominent talk shows have evolved within it provides insights into the genre that constitutes *medium criticism.* The effect on viewers and their likely reactions (indulging creepy voyeurism while feeling uplifted at the same time; "nearly guilt-free exploitation TV") represent *receiver criticism* and also suggest the polysemic nature of this healing/hurting vehicle. The remaining elements of the critique all aggregate *message criticism* by providing a number of specific examples of show content in which Goldman finds both positive and negative attributes.

ENDNOTES

1. Harold Lasswell, "The Structure and Function of Communication in Society," in Lyman Bryson (ed.), *The Communication of Ideas* (New York: Harper and Brothers, 1948).
2. Werner Severin and James Tankard, *Communication Theory: Origins, Methods, Uses* (New York: Hastings House, 1979), 30.
3. Howard Ziff, "The Uses of *Rhetoric*: On Re-reading Aristotle," *Critical Studies in Mass Communication* (March 1986), 112.
4. Robert Lewis Shayon, *Open to Criticism* (Boston: Beacon Press, 1971), 5.
5. Jeremy Tunstall, ed., *Media Sociology: A Reader* (Urbana: University of Illinois Press, 1970), 15.
6. Charles Wright, *Mass Communication: A Sociological Perspective*, 2nd ed. (New York: Random House, 1975), 60.
7. Eliseo Vivas, *Creation and Discovery* (New York: Noonday Press, 1955), 191.
8. Theodore Meyer Greene, *The Arts and the Art of Criticism* (Princeton, NJ: Princeton University Press, 1952), 370.
9. Hilary Cohen, quoted in Mary Ann Watson, "Television Criticism in the Popular Press," *Critical Studies In Mass Communication* (March 1985), 68.
10. "Supreme Court Lets Press Rulings Stand," *Broadcasting* (January 19, 1987), 188.
11. Ibid.
12. Dan O'Day, Luncheon Address to the Great Lakes Radio Conference, April 15, 1989 (Mt. Pleasant, MI).
13. Don West, "A Fan's Notes—and Comment," *Broadcasting & Cable* (September 26, 1994), 40.
14. Greene, 370–371.
15. Celeste Condit, "The Rhetorical Limits of Polysemy," *Critical Studies in Mass Communication* (June 1989), 104.
16. John Fiske, "Television: Polysemy and Popularity," *Critical Studies in Mass Communication* (December 1986), 391.
17. John Fiske, "British Cultural Studies and Television," in Robert Allen (ed.), *Channels of Discourse* (Chapel Hill: University of North Carolina Press, 1987), 269.
18. Philip Auter and Donald Davis, "When Characters Speak Directly to Viewers: Breaking the Fourth Wall in Television," *Journalism Quarterly* (Spring/Summer 1991), 165–170.
19. Jenny Nelson, "Eyes Out of Your Head: On Televisual Experience," *Cultural Studies in Mass Communication* (June 1989), 400.
20. John Fiske, *Television Culture* (London: Methuen, 1987), 105.
21. Condit, 120.
22. Michael Parenti, *Make-Believe Media: The Politics of Entertainment* (New York: St. Martin's, 1992), 11–12.
23. Jerry Mander, from "In the Absence of the Sacred," quoted in "Native Canadians and the End of Storytelling," *Media & Values* (Winter 1993), 5.
24. Gunter Anders, "The Phantom World of TV," in Bernard Rosenberg and David Manning White (eds.), *Mass Culture: The Popular Arts in America* (New York: Free Press, 1957), 361.
25. Cheri Booth, "Offer Children Alternative Activities to Reduce Hours Spent Viewing Television," (Mt. Pleasant, MI) *Morning Sun*, January 21, 1992, 5.
26. Ibid.
27. Paul Lazarsfeld and Robert Merton, "Mass Communication, Popular Taste and Organized Social Action," in Bryson, *Communication of Ideas*.
28. Gene Jankowski, "The Golden Age Revisited." Speech presented at the International Radio and Television Society, March 19, 1979 (New York).
29. Les Brown, "Remarks to the Iowa TV Critics Conference," *Critical Studies in Mass Communication* (December 1985), 393.
30. Robert Landry, "The Improbability of Radio Criticism," *Hollywood Quarterly* (1946–47), 70.
31. Leah Vande Berg and Nick Trujillo, *Organizational Life on Television* (Norwood, NJ: Ablex, 1989), 9–14.
32. John Hartley, "Invisible Fictions: Television Audiences, Paedocracy, Pleasure," in Gary Burns and Robert Thompson (eds.), *Television Studies: Textual Analysis* (New York: Praeger, 1989), 239.
33. "Tom Shales: The Write Stuff," *Broadcasting* (April 11, 1988), 110.
34. Michael Schrage, "Beyond Game Boy," *ADWEEK* (January 27, 1992), 17.
35. Dean Krugman, "An Investigation of the Selection and Viewing Process of New Media Services and Technologies." Paper presented at the Broadcast Education Association Convention, April 29, 1989 (Las Vegas).
36. Mark McNeely and Scott Marshall, "Thumb Wrestling," *ADWEEK* (January 13, 1992), 18.
37. Greg Riker. Presentation at the International Radio and Television Society Faculty/Industry Seminar, February 9, 1996 (New York).
38. Elayne Rapping, *The Looking Glass World of Nonfiction TV* (Boston: South End Press, 1987), 12.
39. James Andrews, *The Practice of Rhetorical Criticism* (New York: Macmillan, 1983).

40. John Cawelti, untitled book review, *American Quarterly* (Summer 1968), 142.

41. Lee Loevinger, "The Ambiguous Mirror: The Reflective-Projective Theory of Broadcasting and Mass Communications," *Journal of Broadcasting* (Spring 1968), 112.

42. Ernie Kreiling, quoted in Gale Adkins, "Radio-Television Criticism in the Newspapers: Reflections on a Deficiency," *Journal of Broadcasting* (Summer 1983), 283.

43. Gilbert Seldes, *The Public Arts* (New York: Simon & Schuster, 1956), 292.

44. John Fiske, "Popular Television and Commercial Culture: Beyond Political Economy," in Burns and Thompson, *Television Studies*, 30–31.

45. Ralph Lewis Smith, *A Study of the Professional Criticism of Broadcasting in the United States 1920–1955* (New York: Arno Press, 1979), 473.

46. West, 35.

47. Vivas, 201.

4 Knowledge Processing

So far, we have examined the key attributes and functions of criticism as well as its application to the various components of the communication process. In this chapter, we further explore electronic media criticism by looking at knowledge acquisition. How do individuals and audiences come to know and understand things? How might their comprehension procedures be categorized? How can media criticism consider these differences in knowledge attainment when appraising the potential of program product? These are the major questions this chapter discusses.

EMPIRICAL AND NORMATIVE OUTLOOKS

In seeking to understand and to judge phenomena—electronic media content included—we must attempt to reconcile two distinct orientations: the empirical and the normative. As we see in this section, empiricism can stand alone as a means of impersonally *understanding* something. But in criticism, normativism then follows up on this initial understanding as a means of qualitatively *judging* whether the programmatic something in question is "good" or "bad."

Empiricism

Empirical methodology is, at its heart, a descriptive two-stage process. Relying on observation, the *empiricist* attempts to gather as much relevant detail as possible and then to explain it by discovering how the details are in harmony.

Let us say, for example, that radio station KURP consistently plays fifty-two minutes of music in an hour. Its closest competitor, airing a similar format, plays only forty-one minutes. Through further monitoring of the two outlets, we ascertain that neither offers any newscast except in morning drivetime and neither uses foreground (talky) disc jockeys. Ultimately, we isolate what seems to be the main source of their numerical music difference: KURP transmits only eight minutes of commercials per hour whereas the competition advertises for *nineteen*!

Having accumulated these facts, we, as empiricists, must then attempt to explain the reason(s) behind them. KURP tells its listeners that it "plays more music because we like to treat you better." To the public, this may seem to be a plausible and congenial explanation. But conscientious empiricists/critics (particularly those at competing facilities) do not accept it at face value; they survey further to find out if other factors might be present.

Through access to ratings books, it comes to light that KURP is able to attract less than one-fourth the target listeners that its prime competitor is drawing. Because of this, even though it charges significantly less for its airtime, KURP is hard pressed to sell even eight minutes per hour. The competition, by contrast, has no difficulty finding advertisers for all nineteen minutes of its "avails." In short, KURP plays more music—not because it has any special affection for its listeners—but because the tunes are filling time the station is unable to sell to sponsors.

As incisive empiricists, we weren't satisfied merely to ascertain what the station was airing. Nor did we accept KURP's public "we like to treat you better" assertion at face value. Instead, we applied more extensive scrutiny in order to comprehend the situation. We gathered the full details (empiricism's first stage) and then set about to explain their relationship to each other (empiricism's second stage).

Any perceptive media professional is, initially, an empiricist who probes below the surface as one means of moving toward the "carefully considered judgment" that good criticism requires. Description of observed occurrences is one part of reaching that judgment. But description alone has little purpose without the subsequent unveiling of the determinant conditions that have caused the described entity to be what it is.

Unequivocal acceptance of KURP's claim that its "more music" is a listener-serving gift will not disclose the reality of the station's continuing unpopularity or enable us to discover what has caused that unpopularity. Is the format poorly executed, with harsh transitions between elements? Is the station signal weak? Is it located on a remote end of the dial ("in the glovebox") or, as is increasingly the case with AM music outlets, on the wrong dial altogether? These and other questions can and *must* be asked by any professional who wants to compete in the market under scrutiny.

As in any profession, this knowledge acquisition inquiry can be brutally hard work. "Knowledge does not come free to any of us; we have to suffer for it," points out *National Journal* editor Jonathan Rauch. "We have to stand naked before the court of critical checkers and watch our most cherished beliefs come under fire. Sometimes we have to watch while our notion of evident truth gets tossed in the gutter."[1]

Thus, if only to protect their own interests, people pursuing an electronic media career must prepare themselves to be industrious and courageous empiricist/critics. Such a critic will, in Robert Lewis Shayon's words, "talk to himself, self-deprecate, needle, challenge, scorn and provoke. He must stimulate, repudiate, query, refuse, oppose—in a phrase, he must continually say to himself:

'So what?'"[2] This is as true in examining our own on-air product as it is in dissecting the product put out by competitors. Even though he was referring to criticism of older art forms, Theodore Meyer Greene was bolstering this point when he observed that

from Greek and Roman times, through the Middle Ages and the Renaissance, and down to the modern period most of the critics who have achieved distinction and whose names have endured have been those who were not content to bask in the pleasing "aesthetic surface" of art, but who sought rather to delve beneath this surface to the interpretations of human life and objective reality.[3]

To apply this to our situation, the "aesthetic surface" of KURP's more-music format may or may not be pleasing in itself; but in either case, we empirically must dig deeper. If the station's sound seems pleasing to an experienced programmer, why do so few listeners select it? And if it is not pleasurable, what needs to be changed? And why hasn't this change been implemented already?

Sustained empirical observation and its second-stage search for explanations must follow in tandem if the critic/professional is to succeed in the knowledge-processing task. This task is as vital to valid external criticism as it is to the critiquing we conduct internal to our industry. For a moment, imagine the disservice that the ill-conceived "kicks" newspaper review would do to listeners and other stations in KURP's market.

Clearly, Mr. Rubato's empiricism ceases at the boundaries of whatever first impres-

---

GET YOUR KICKS ON KURP

by Johnny Rubato

This Radio Ranger has been scouring the local spectrum and has found a real jewel. That gem is KURP. The folks at KURP (rhymes with "burp") should be congratulated for their apparent decision to decommercialize the radio scene. The station is the first in town consistently to deliver 52 minutes of tunes per hour. While other outlets seem to pride themselves on how many advertisements they can fire off, KURP proves that it puts listeners' interests first.

For ears who'd rather hear song than sell in an adult music format, AM 850 is a sure bet. If you're a contemporary music fan of more than pimple-cream mentality, you should check out KURP. When enough listeners do, maybe we'll have fewer commercials and more melodies to enjoy all across those digital dials of ours. As always, the Ranger is riding the radio range rounding up good sounds for you.

J.R.

sion he gathers. He has accepted at face value the station's explanation for its main claim to fame and conveys this claim *un*critically—without searching for other facts or explanations. He unknowingly urges his readers to patronize a station because of a condition that flows from its failure rather than from its success and then tries to inflict that same business-defective procedure on other outlets in the market. Notice, too, that this critic has said nothing *specific* about the selection, arrangement, or flow of the tunes played on KURP. The reader merely learns that there is "more" music in a quantitative sense. (The critic's "pimple-cream" crack does not help in this regard because it pertains more to the demographic skew of KURP's format than to its execution.)

To Rubato, less advertising automatically means better programming. (This is his underlying *normative* belief.) But he has not *empirically* analyzed the KURP situation well enough to ascertain whether its on-air product supports this contention. If, on the other hand, he did conduct such an analysis, Rubato has failed to convey the specifics of his findings to his audience.

Let us assume that Rubato's column has clout in this market. What might be the effects of his piece? First, more people would 'check out' KURP. If the station is slickly programmed and they like what they hear, these people will listen more often. This will boost the station's rating book numbers and cause it to take one of two courses of action: either it will add more commercials per hour, or it will substantially raise its rates for the eight minutes it currently sells. The first approach would cause KURP to abandon the characteristic that initially attracted these new listeners. They, in turn, might abandon the station. On the other hand, raising its rate card to the point at which eight minutes of advertising generate the same revenue as twelve or sixteen minutes on other stations will put KURP's pricing out of reach for many potential advertisers. The time will now be more difficult to sell than it was before! This tactic might also put pressure on other stations to inflate their rates in order to reassert their comparative value to advertisers—a move that could drive some local sponsors out of radio entirely and into competing media.

But what if KURP is *not* skillfully programmed? What if its music selection is hap-

hazard with harsh or dissonant transitions between format elements? In this case, Rubato has guided his public to an event of lesser value for no other reason than that they will experience this poor quality with fewer interruptions! More astute music listeners will detect this bad bargain on their own and will seek out other stations. But the less sophisticated—the people who could benefit the most from a critic's guidance—may accept KURP on its own terms and miss the opportunity for more pleasing service on competing outlets. In summary, Rubato neither fully observed nor fully analyzed his data and thus has failed as a critic in general and as an empiricist in particular.

By definition, empiricism is a scientific enterprise; it is important to our profession in converting the intangibles of our air-time product into salable audiences or pay-per-view responses. As Ien Ang observes of television,

Empirical science, and the authority of the knowledge produced by it, has become indispensable to manage and regulate institutional practices; . . . we can see a growing reliance on empirical stocks of knowledge gathered through scientific methods within television institutions. The ever-increasing importance of audience measurement in almost all television institutions in the world is only one indication for the heightened status of scentifically-based rhetoric.[4]

Whether the subject is audience measurement, station commercial "load," or any other operational aspect of our profession, genuine empiricism leads to the knowledgeable comprehension that is the requisite of true criticism. Superficial empiricism, like Rubato's, however, can produce only "jump-to-conclusion" distortions that deceive the public and inhibit their ability to fashion realistic expectations as to what our media can provide.

The Normative View

Empiricism's counterpart, the *normative* perspective, seeks to erect standards or benchmarks by which to make an evaluation or judgment. Some theorists would say that where empiricism is more scientific and objective, normativism is more humanities-based and subjective. Or, as Stephen Little-john extends the comparison,

Science aims to standardize observation; the humanities seek to create individuality. If the aim of science is to reduce human differences in what is observed, the aim of the humanities is to understand individual human responses.[5]

As we discussed, Rubato implicitly demonstrates the normative perspective with his individual assessment that a radio format's value (the *norm* by which it should be judged) is directly proportional to how few commercials it contains. That Rubato neither states this position directly nor provides rationale for it, however, makes his subjective normative stance as shallow as his objective empirical performance.

As we explore in Chapters 7 through 13, there are many normative standards from which to choose. But whatever standard is used, it can be applied successfully only after we have engaged the empirical perspective in order to sufficiently comprehend the object in question.

In the case of some operational issues, we may decide that normativism isn't applicable. Former FCC Commissioner Lee Loevinger advanced an analogy that illustrates the limits of the normative outlook:

It is silly to condemn a camel for having a hump and praise a horse for having a straight back, or condemn a horse for requiring frequent drinks of water and praise a camel for his ability to travel without water. These characteristics are simple facts of existence and are not rationally the basis for either praise or blame. These are things for which normative standards are irrelevant and the only reasonable course is to observe and understand. Once we observe and understand [empiricism] the nature of camels and horses we can then decide the use to which each is put.[6]

When Rubato demeaned commercial radio for being commercial, he was indulging in the same sort of irrational behavior that Loevinger's example isolates. In effect, Rubato was censuring the camel for its hump despite the fact that it is this advertising revenue hump that allows the commercial camel to survive.

From our discussion in Chapter 1, you may recall that Charles Siepmann's contribution to the FCC's "Blue Book" was at-tacked for the same reason: his prior involvement with the British Broadcasting Corporation's noncommercial "horse" made his critiquing of U.S. commercial radio's "camel" seem irrelevant. At least, that was the argument that U.S. broadcasters successfully raised.

Decades ago, the marketing director for a photocopier manufacturer had a similar, though more positive, encounter with solely normative thinking. His company had sponsored a number of cultural specials on television: documentaries, ballets, and Shakespearean plays. For this action, the company garnered many awards from the intellectual establishment. It also received many unsolicited proposals to sponsor programs on such arcane topics as Lithuanian embroidery. While the marketing executive graciously accepted the awards, he was understandably put off by the proposals because they reflected a belief that his company was so gullible that it would sponsor anything with a narrow, esoteric appeal.

The empirical reality, of course, was that the documentaries and the Shakespearean productions happened to attract the viewers that the marketer was paid to reach: upscale, well-educated decision-makers who, at the stroke of a pen, could lease expensive photocopiers by the dozens. If downscale, mass-appeal shows of the time, such as *The Beverly Hillbillies* or *Petticoat Junction*, were able to deliver this target audience with similar cost-efficiency, the executive would have been just as likely to sponsor them. The failure of the purely normative intellectuals and program proposers to understand this empirical truth made the marketer's job more cluttered.

Certainly, the normative perspective is essential if we are to reasonably estimate a work's value. Valuation can be derived only through the application of some yardstick, be it artistic, philosophical, sociological, or (as in the case of the photocopier marketer) financial. But if we don't empirically examine the property to understand its purpose, our normative valuation is likely to be useless—because we, like the award-givers cited above—don't understand what the endeavor is striving to accomplish.

Johnny Rubato's valuation of KURP was wrong because he believed the station was seeking to diminish commercials when, instead, it was desperately striving for more listeners to make more time sales feasible. The intellectuals' appraisal of the photocopier company's sponsorships was defective because they thought the firm was seeking to raise the cultural level of television. It was, instead, just trying to reach the hottest prospects for machine rentals. In both instances, the norms selected by the outside evaluators were chosen through empirical ignorance of program originator goals. Consequently, all that resulted was misunderstanding.

It is probably true, as Ralph Smith asserts, that outside critics in particular "are inclined to be moralists, unafraid to preach standards, and idealists, untiring in their efforts to bring commercially subsidized mass arts into closer relationship with traditional arts."[7] However, this tendency can be tolerated only to the extent that the standards preached are relevant to the environment within which the media enterprise must exist. In other words, the outside critic's normative conclusions are only as useful and effective as that critic's empirical observation and knowledge of our industry. It must be recognized that, unlike empirical knowing, normative "knowledge," by itself, is unlikely to result in viable determinations. Scientist/poet Miroslav Holub contends, for example, that the difference between scientific and poetic questioning (empiricism and normativism) is that poetry poses unanswerable questions whereas science poses solvable ones.[8]

In summary, both empirical and normative outlooks are indispensable in the promotion and understanding of our profession and its products—but only when the two perspectives are used in a complementary fashion. What effective electronic media critiquing depends on is the careful progression through these three knowledge-processing steps:

1. Here's *what* it is.   [Empiricism Stage One]

2. Here's *why* it is.   [Empiricism Stage Two]

3. Here's whether   [Normativism]
   that's good or
   bad.

THE FOUR WAYS OF KNOWING

All of our knowledge, empirical and normative, is accumulated in a variety of ways. In

his incisive *Beyond the Wasteland*, Robert Rutherford Smith argues that a critic's comprehension is really the amalgamation of three separate orientations. Taken together, this amalgamation and its trio of components make up what he refers to as "the ways of knowing."[9]

The Way of the Scientist

The first of Smith's ways of knowing, the way of the scientist, is entirely empirical; it involves the gathering and explanation of data. A scientist seeks *evidence*—ideally, quantifiable evidence—as a means of establishing fact.

In the electronic media, for instance, a *rating* is supposedly an objective, empirical measurement of program or station popularity at a given time, as distinguished from the popularity of all other life pursuits to which a consumer might otherwise attend. A *share*, however, is a measure of that popularity compared only to competing programs or stations within the same medium. In other words, the share is the portion of the *active* radio or television audience that has chosen your outlet over others. The scientific formulae for ratings and shares are expressed this way:

$$\text{Rating} = \frac{\text{people or homes using your outlet}}{\text{total people or homes in survey}}$$

$$\text{Share} = \frac{\text{people or homes using your outlet}}{\substack{\text{surveyed people or homes using} \\ \text{the medium}}}$$

Currently, radio tends to be measured in terms of individual listeners, or PURs (persons using radio). Television, on the other hand, historically has been concerned with *homes* using television (HUTs). Now, television measurement is moving toward expression of individual rather than household use preferences through application of electronic measurement devices called *people meters*. "The people meter has now, for better or worse," observes Ien Ang, "become the new standard of empirical truth that the industry has to live by; . . . it symbolizes the desire for having ever more complete, objective, accurate, in short, more 'realistic' knowledge on people's viewing behaviour."[10]

Whether gathered by people meters or the more traditional diaries, phone interviews, and household-aggregating electronic boxes, the resulting data are put through the same computations. To illustrate how this scientific knowing scheme functions, assume we have a television sample size of 550 people statistically selected to represent a regional population mass of 7 million.

Through whatever data-gathering means we are using, we find that 396 of the sample are watching TV at the time our game show, *Spittin' Distance*, is aired. Of these 396, exactly 99 indicated they tuned to *Spittin' Distance*. Dividing 99 (the number viewing us) by 550 (the total number of people in the sample) we find that our game show has achieved an 18 rating:

$$\frac{99}{550} \quad .18$$

In other words, assuming our sample size and composition are statistically valid, we can estimate that 18 percent of the population was watching *Spittin' Distance*.

To compute the share, we divide that same 99 by 396 (the sample's total *active* viewing audience). The result shows our program garnered a 25 share:

$$\frac{99}{396} \quad .25$$

Thus, one-quarter (25 percent) of all active viewers in the survey report that they watched *Spittin' Distance*.

Again, assuming that our sample statistically mirrors the makeup of the total area population of 7 million, we infer that 72 percent (396 divided by 550) of our sample is using television at the time; this translates into an active viewership of 5,040,000 (7 million multiplied by .72). We further conclude (and inform our advertisers) that 1,260,000 people (7 million multiplied by our rating of 18, or .18) are reached by our game show.

These advertisers could then divide whatever it costs them for a commercial on *Spittin' Distance* by 1,260,000 to see how much they are spending to reach each viewer. Because this computation results in a tiny decimal, in practice sponsors first divide that total audience by 1,000. They then divide the cost of air time by the result. This calculation derives a CPM or *cost-per-thousand* figure. (The abbreviation is CPM and not CPT because M is the Roman numeral designation for 1,000.)

The bottom line for advertisers on our program thus would be computed as follows, assuming that a thirty-second commercial on *Spittin' Distance* costs $4,600.

$$\frac{1,260,000}{1,000} \quad \begin{array}{l} \text{1,260 groups of one thousand} \\ \text{people each} \end{array}$$

$$\frac{\$4,600}{1,260} \quad \begin{array}{l} \$3.6508, \text{or a CPM of about} \\ \$3.65 \end{array}$$

It thus costs an advertiser approximately $3.65 to reach a thousand people through one commercial on *Spittin' Distance*. In most instances, this cost would be considered a bargain because it is only one-fourth to one-eighth the cost a sponsor typically would expect to incur in buying most broadcast television. As we discuss in Chapter 7, our example has been further oversimplified by not analyzing whether those 1.2 million viewers of *Spittin' Distance* are the kind of people our prospective advertisers are interested in reaching.

Notice, too, that in all of these empirical, scientific calculations, we have not determined *why* those 1.2 million people chose to watch *Spittin' Distance*. We are just inferring that they did watch, based on a massaging of the data from our 550-person sample. In fact, rapidly accumulating scientific evidence shows that ratings-derived audience estimates are not true measures of actual cognition. Back in 1984, M.I.T. researcher Russell Neuman pointed out that "a decade ago, researchers found the average viewer's eyes on the set only 65 percent of the time under normal conditions. More recent research confirms that competing activities— eating, talking on the telephone, reading, playing—go on during 30 to 50 percent of 'viewing' time."[11] Looking at the multichanneled TV environment of the 1990s, researcher Ien Ang put more qualifications on the significance of ratings for advertisers:

In fact, what has become increasingly uncertain in the new television landscape is exactly 'what takes place' in the homes of people when they watch television. No longer can it be conveniently assumed—as traditional ratings discourse does—that having the TV set on equals watching, that watching means paying attention to the screen, that watching a programme implies watching the commercials inserted in it, that watching the commercials leads to actually buying the products being advertised. Thus, 'viewing behaviour' loses its convenient one-dimensionality: measuring 'it' can never be the same anymore.[12]

And with the advent of Internet video streaming, multidimensionality becomes the rule. The electronic media's use of scientific empiricism can generate mounds of quantified conclusions. With newer instruments such as people meters and product package scanners, these mounds of data can become mountains. Yet, as information gathering becomes more refined, our conclusions about what it all means in actual listening, viewing, and marketing behavior become more tentative.

Granted, empirical audience measurement remains an essential ingredient in estimating the financial value (a normative index) of the product that media professionals provide. But it is doubtful that the way of the scientist will ever be able, on its own, to fully explain the complex process of program dissemination and digestion. A family room is not a chemistry laboratory, and a television program is not a test tube. Electronic media absorption by consumers is anything but a controlled and predictable activity. But that is what makes our profession so much more of an adventure!

The Way of the Mystic

The scientific way of knowing proceeds empirically (even though its *findings* can be applied normatively to justify or deplore the object or condition that empiricism has uncovered). In contrast, *the way of the mystic*, Robert Smith's second mode of knowing, operates from a fundamentally normative attitude. To the mystic, *truth*, rather than data assimilation, is all-important. If this truth can be verified by empirical evidence, so much the better. But in the mystic's view, physical data are not superior to such unquantifiable powers as faith, belief, and spiritual vision.

Science, as the FCC has frequently discovered, therefore is incapable of resolving values conflicts. In the 1970s, for example, the commission found itself embroiled in a seemingly endless string of format controversy cases. Typically, a citizen's group protesting a radio station's change in music would attempt to challenge the license or to block the facility's sale to a new owner with different format plans. Is classical music

"better" than alternative rock? Is alternative rock "superior" to country? Is country more or less in the public interest than jazz? Obviously, such questions cannot be resolved empirically. They are value- and taste-laden issues that are impossible to quantify in the arts in general or in electronic media art in particular. Indeed, writes Roger Rollin, past president of the American Culture Association, "Not a single major critical movement in the arts and letters since the Fifties has held up taste as a critical principle—not structuralism, not linguistic analytical philosophy, not feminism and neo-Marxism, not reception theory and its variants, and not deconstructionism. For all of these movements are based more upon reason and empirical data from the social sciences than upon the quasi-religious faith on which traditional humanistic [mystic-oriented] thought tends to be grounded."[13]

It was not surprising, then, that the FCC sought the help of the courts in backing out of the (mystical) format-adjudicating business. As long as a station programmed what it said it would program, the commission let the more tangible financial values of the marketplace decide whether a format change was appropriate.

To return to our original example, Johnny Rubato's mystical belief that KURP was a preferred station because it ran fewer commercials seems to contradict the scientific ratings that showed the station's prime competitor to attract more than four times as many listeners. Rubato's values determination thus clashed with empirical data. On the surface, this does not make him wrong—it just demonstrates that his belief/preference is markedly different from listeners who choose the same music on a different station.

As a critic, however, he should have attempted to ascertain the *reason* for this discrepancy. (Perhaps KURP is suffering from a smaller coverage pattern or an inadequate promotions budget.) But in restricting himself to a mystical viewpoint, Rubato has not searched for any empirical explanations to justify his belief that fewer commercials mean better radio. Consequently, he has failed to gain or communicate a thorough understanding of his subject.

To cite another example, consumer crusaders invoking exclusively the mystical way of knowing would not feel compelled to establish a causal link between television's plot-action use of firearms and the occurrence of armed robberies. They simply "know" that the latter is the result of the former—and no empirical data base could convince them otherwise.

Those of us within the electronic media possess our own mystical sides, of course. Former NBC and CBS newsman Marvin Kalb, for instance, once told a conference of student broadcasters,

I think that television does something very serious to the mind, something bordering on brain damage. I think it affects the way in which we read, how much we read, whether reality is something that can be absorbed through a rectangle, whether it is something far more complicated than that.[14]

Kalb is entitled to his beliefs, and his distinguished background in broadcast journalism invests these beliefs with authority. But as media professionals, we must remind ourselves (and perhaps our public) that such statements remain *personal* visions with which we can freely agree or disagree. They are not, to this point in our research capabilities, anything like verifiable fact.

These examples are not meant to suggest that the mystical perspective is only a destructive thunderbolt that the disenchanted hurl at our enterprise. Actually, electronic media producers and their advertising agency customers frequently exploit the way of the mystic as a means of courting audiences. Thus, the following radio commercial enthusiastically espouses the vision of Old Milwaukee beer as the beverage to be believed in and protected over romantic relationships and kitchenware. Despite the reference to "great price," the spot does not prove much about the product in an empirical sense. Instead, what is articulated is the normative belief structure that prizes the beer on the basis of its visceral male pleasure.

ANNCR: So my girlfriend and I got into this big fight—and yeah, I suppose it was my fault 'cause I went out with another girl. I tried to explain that it doesn't mean I don't care for her. It actually made me appreciate her more. But Geez, did she get mad. Started throwing plates and breakin' stuff. Even threw an Old Milwaukee at me. Good thing I caught it, 'cause Old Milwaukee is a good beer at a great price—it'd be a shame to waste it. Imagine, throwing a perfectly good Old Milwaukee! What's the big deal anyway? You'd think she'd be glad her sister got a date. Old Milwaukee. Available wherever beer is sold.

(Courtesy of Pat Rooker, Ross Roy Communications, Inc.)

Television often mobilizes a mystical response as well. In the Figure 4-1 photoboard, the use of Mr. Turkey is interwoven with the values of family love and parental warmth. The "spiritual vision" projected here is of prolonged nurturing—you secure a long-term, caring impact when you give your offspring Mr. Turkey's nourishment.

The way of the mystic invokes deep-seated personal or philosophical values. That the objective validity of these values cannot be proven in an empirical way makes them no less real or profound for the people who hold them. In fact, subjecting mystical values to enforced empirical certification often leads to disappointment or alienation. When science failed to confirm or reject the image on the Shroud of Turin as that of Jesus Christ, some people were disillusioned with science and others lost their affection for this religious artifact. How much better if the way of the scientist and that of the mystic had not been required to validate each other. They are two fundamentally different procedures for knowing. Human comprehension cannot always expect them to intersect. We explore the mystical dimension more fully in Chapter 11.

The Way of the Rhetorician

As we have seen, the way of the mystic is normative-based, and the way of the scientist is grounded in empiricism. Robert Smith's third knowledge processor, *the way of the rhetorician*, is both normative *and* empirical. It centers on the winning of arguments. These arguments may be won on the basis of a belief structure, by citing the quantified product of scientific research, or through a combination of both of these orientations. When we function as rhetoricians, the important thing is that a decision in our favor is arrived at, presumably by reputable means.

TITLE: "HOLD ONTO SOMETHING GOOD" LENGTH: 30

COMMERCIAL NO.: QBCZ-0535

FIGURE 4-1
(Courtesy of
Campbell-Ewald
Advertising)

(MUSIC UP) SINGERS: NEVER GONNA LET YOU GO . . .

GONNA HOLD YOU IN MY ARMS FOREVER . . .

(MUSIC UNDER) AVO: No one could love our kids more than we do.

We want to nurture them and nourish them forever.

And giving them Mr. Turkey can help . . .

because Mr. Turkey is so deliciously low in fat and

high on taste you might just start a healthy habit they could hold onto for a lifetime.

That way, with great tasting Mr. Turkey . . .

when you're not holding them . . .

they'll still be holding onto . . .

something good . . . Mr. Turkey.

SINGERS: NEVER GONNA LET YOU GO . . . HOLD YOU IN MY ARMS FOREVER.

"Hold Onto Something Good . . . Mr. Turkey."

More specifically, Professors Karen and Donald Rybacki define *rhetorical communication* as "a message with verbal and often visual symbols that are deliberately chosen to influence an audience whose members have the ability to change their beliefs or behaviors as a consequence of experiencing the message."[15] The key word here is *influence*. Unlike the other two ways of knowing so far discussed, rhetoric can *never* be just a static find-

ing or belief. It is always a dynamic attempt to motivate our audience toward adoption of a specific attitude or action. Rhetoric is "a particular kind of knowledge" observes Professor Jay Parini, "knowledge of the most productive ways of 'making' language, of creating meaning, and of eliciting responses within the bounds of predictability."[16]

Professors Young, Becker, and Pike add that the practice of rhetoric is "concerned primarily with a creative process that includes all the choices a writer makes from his earliest tentative explorations of a problem . . . through choices in arrangement and strategy for a particular audience, to the final editing of the final draft."[17] Even though this definition refers to written products, it can also apply to oral/visual communication whether or not that communication passes through an intermediate written form.

The "creative choice process" to which Young, Becker, and Pike refer involves weighing the comparative strengths of scientific and mystical approaches as to which will be more effective in swaying a given audience (a *target universe*, as mass communicators often label it). How these arguments are structured and exhibited is just as important in gaining the decision as is their selection. Thus, the rhetorician is a form-and-content *eclectic* who borrows from the empirical as well as from the normative to package in an imaginative fashion the most advantageous discourse possible.

To Aristotle, the proofs of the rhetorical argument were of three types: *logos, pathos,* and *ethos. Logos* is an appeal to reason and the objective evaluation of information. For our purposes, we can equate *logos* with the way of the scientist. *Pathos*, by comparison, triggers an emotional, often value-laden response in our audience, which can be closely tied to the mystical. *Ethos* meanwhile involves the credibility of the message originator. In the electronic media, this includes the professionalism with which the commercial or program seems to have been produced. Shoddy production values are usually perceived by the audience as the characteristic of a less attractive or less trustworthy enterprise.

Aristotle carefully distinguishes these three proofs, but "he never suggests that they can in any way be thought of as independent of each other," points out Howard Ziff. "All three appeals are present in any rhetoric."[18]

Obviously, commercials, program promos, and public service announcements are prime examples of rhetorical communication. Like the Mr. Turkey advertisement in Figure 4-1, they frequently lean more heavily on *pathos* than *logos*, but both elements are still detectable. The fact that Mr. Turkey is "up to 97 percent fat free" is a quantifiable piece of *logos* immersed in the *pathos* of parental warmth and delivered by the *ethos* of intimate visuals and a well-accepted song lyric.

In other spots, however, rhetorical strategy decrees that *logos* should come to the fore. The Federal Express "Murphy's Victory" treatment in Figure 4-2, for instance, uses the *logos* proof of Ms. Murphy's efficient neutralizing of her cranky boss as documentable evidence of client Federal Express's superior tracking capability. The reasoned practicality of this FedEx benefit is the focus of the demonstration—but it is heightened by the *pathos*-rich applause the product-using Ms. Murphy consequently receives from her fellow subordinates. This response validates her credibility (*ethos*) with her colleagues and, by association, the *ethos* of Federal Express.

Program creators also practice the way of the rhetorician in advancing the themes that hold their stories together. Any meaningful program, like any commercial, holds an implicit or explicit point of view; and rhetorical knowledge processing affords the greatest elasticity as to how that view is promoted.

Ziff again consults Aristotle to demonstrate that there are three major types of persuasive discourse that might be used to reach a program's (or an advertisement's) rhetorical goals: the *forensic or judicial,* the *demonstrative or epideictic,* and the *deliberative or political.*

The *forensic/judicial* discourse encompasses more than the arguments played out on *Law and Order, Judge Judy,* or news stories of important trials. It also, says Ziff, includes "virtually all discourse that directs our attention and establishes our relationship to the past."[19] Historical dramas and documentaries, patriotic specials, and even retrospectives of everything from *The Tonight Show* to *The Brady Bunch* function in this connection. Syndicators exploit the forensic discourse further when they repackage and distribute *evergreens* (old series like *I Love Lucy* or *M*A*S*H*) that command persistent appeal with succeeding generations of viewers.

In comparison, the *demonstrative/epideictic* discourse is present-oriented, "concerned with public occasions of praise and blame, with celebrating or condemning . . . the ritual that confirms daily existence."[20] Electronic media news coverage falls into this rhetorical category. So does the radio format's daypart modifications that blend in

(BKGD MUSIC: DRAMATIC) BOSS: Murphy!! (MS. MURPHY LOOKS STARTLED) That package you sent

to Denver; it never got there!! MS. MURPHY: What?

MALE ANNCR: Introducing, Tracking Software from Federal Express. (SFX: COMPUTER BEEPS)

MS. MURPHY: It was picked up at 5:20 last night, and it was delivered at

9:42 a.m., and signed for by..Kate Donovan.

Should I call for you, sir?

BOSS (MUTTERS): Never mind. ANNCR: Now, you can track packages

right from your computer

on your desk. (SFX: BOSS GOES OUT THE DOOR)

(SFX: THE WHOLE OFFICE APPLAUDES MS. MURPHY)

(SFX CONTINUES)

(MUSIC AND SFX ENDS)

with its listeners' cyclic life-style concerns (morning drive re-orientation to the world, midday aid in getting through work, afternoon drive anticipation of freedom, and evening relaxation). And, with its real-time chat rooms and instantaneous updates of present happenings, the Internet may be the most *demonstrative/epideictic*-rich vehicle of all.

Finally, the *deliberative/political* discourse has as its purpose energizing the audience to undertake a specific course of action or belief. Thus, whereas Aristotle's forensic/judi-

FIGURE 4-2 (Courtesy of Jill Bachenheimer, BBDO Worldwide)

cial procedure focuses on the past, and his demonstrative/epideictic approach deals with the present, deliberative/political rhetoric emphasizes the future. "Aristotelian analysis of a television drama," Ziff points out, "might quickly uncover that rather than being a present-oriented, epideictic celebration of life, it is in fact, political and deliberative, recommending attitudes and actions, a form of subtle exhortation."[21] Commenting on *Star Trek* and its syndicated successor (*Star Trek: The Next Generation*), for example, anthropologist Conrad Kottak argues that the shows go beyond science/fiction entertainment to promote a definite deliberative/political agenda:

One of *Star Trek*'s constant messages is that strangers, even enemies, can become friends. Less obviously, the message is about cultural imperialism, the assumed irresistibility of American culture and institutions. Even communist nationals (Chekhov) can be seduced and captured by an expansive American culture. Spock, although from Vulcan, is half-human, with human qualities. We learn, therefore, that our assimilationist values will eventually not just rule all Earth, but extend to other planets as well. With *The Next Generation*, Klingon culture, yet more alien than Vulcan and personified by Bridge Officer Worf, has joined the melting pot. . . . Inevitably, American culture will triumph over all others—by convincing and assimilating, rather than conquering.[22]

With its three Aristotle-identified types of persuasive discourse, the trio of Aristotelian proofs (*logos, pathos, ethos*), and its embracing of both the scientific and the mystical, the rhetorical approach is significantly more complex than the other two ways of knowing from which it borrows. But it therefore is also more flexible in how best to approach the audience being targeted.

The Way of the Critic

Rhetoricians, however, are not the most active borrowers. That distinction belongs to practitioners of the fourth way of knowing: *the way of the critic*. In arriving at their evaluations, critics (whether inside or outside our profession) are as likely to accept rhetorical argument as they are to prize scientific evidence or embrace mystical truth. As conscientious critics of the electronic media, then, we should consider and exercise all of our

options in attempting to meet the definition of comprehensive criticism arrived at in Chapter 1. "Although," as Robert Smith cautions, "critics should be fair and accurate in using sources, there is no arbitrary limit upon the kinds of support they can use to inform a critical judgment."[23]

The critique by the *Washington Post*'s David Remnick demonstrates how the scientist's search for empirical explanation, the mystic's focus on normative truth, the rhetorician's preference for winnable argument, and the critic's need for comprehensive evaluation can all be intertwined in even a relatively brief analysis.

Remnick has gathered a number of pieces of observable data. We learn that the documentarist "does not use a narrator. Instead he tries to let his pictures and talking heads do all the work." There is further empirical evidence that the featured coach endows the show with a voice of "considerable" timbre though the viewer is unable to measure the impact of this voice because the camera apparently focuses mainly on Coach Hill rather than on his players. The street scenes prove that there is traffic in the neighborhood—but not that there are drugs. In this critique, then, the *way of the scientist* seems to conclude that the data gathered did not explain or validate the program producer's premise for including it.

Remnick clearly retains a *way of the mystic* belief structure that helps orient him to his subject in a normative way. Basketball, he maintains, is something of which children's dreams are made, something that can lead a child "to a few conclusions about life itself." Still, this faith in the activity is qualified by a mystical "sense" that there is "too much stress being placed on the game as a singular alternative to a wasted life." Basketball, in short, is losing its virtue as a teacher because it is forced to assume the role of a savior. Therefore, asserts the critic, we need "to help kids get as enthusiastic about school as they are about sports." These are clearly Remnick's values, and his candid articulation of them helps the reader understand the normative goggles through which he is viewing *Playground Pros*.

Rhetorically, the critique then argues that the program does not live up to its own (or the critic's) values because there seems to be discord between "announced and reannounced" "proper virtues" and the "implicit

MISSING THE TOUGH SHOTS: UNFULFILLED PROMISE OF "PLAYGROUND PROS"
by David Remnick

Playground basketball is a rich subject, for it goes beyond the sport to the dreams of children and adolescents. The game, with its strange combination of subtlety and strength, can take possession of a kid and can lead him or her to a few conclusions about life itself.

David Johnson's documentary, produced locally by the Workshop for the Visual and Performing Arts and airing tonight at 8:30 on Channel 32, focuses on the youth basketball program at the 3rd District Metropolitan Boys and Girls Club at 14th and Clifton streets N.W. Johnson means to talk about the virtues of that program, its emphasis on teamwork, discipline and sportsmanship. One hoped that he could match on video what, say, Pete Axhelm did for New York playgrounds in his book, "The City Game."

But for all its good intentions, "Playground Pros" fails to come alive, visually or even educationally. Johnson does not use a narrator. Instead, he tries to let his pictures and talking heads do all the work, and they are not up to the task.

For minutes at a time we watch Coach Edward Hill shout on the sidelines as his 11-year-olds struggle on the court. "Defense!" he will scream, typically. Or "Pressure!" Or "Where's the Foul?" Other than to measure the timbre of Hill's voice—which is considerable and, by all reports, inspiring—it is hard to see what we are to learn from all the shouting.

The neighborhood the program draws on for its players is, the film says, "a drug corridor," while the basketball court is "an oasis in the desert." But the shots of street life are static, never showing much more than traffic. One is grateful when the film turns back to the court, dribbling guards being more interesting than coasting Buicks.

More troubling than the images, however, are some of the implicit messages of "Playground Pros." Even while the proper virtues are announced and reannounced, there is a disturbing sense that too much air is being pumped into the basketball, too much stress being placed on the game as a singular alternative to a wasted life.

Hill quite properly says that he doesn't want his players to think "that basketball is the be-all and end-all . . . [lest] they become one-dimensional." He says that basketball "gives them that sense of identity . . . they can walk with their chest stuck out." He even admits that he sometimes invites losing so that his kids can learn from it.

And yet, minutes later, there is the same coach telling his players that the upcoming tournament will be "just like a war."

Missing in "Playground Pros" is a point of view, a documentary filmmaker who not only celebrates a world but also asks tough questions of it. Such as: How can we help kids get as enthusiastic about school as they are about sports? Is it possible that there is too much emphasis on sports as an escape hatch from poverty? How do the lessons of the court carry over into the more important realms of life?

The only conclusion of "Playground Pros" is a good luck wish on the team's upcoming tournament. That is just not enough.

(© *The Washington Post*)

messages" the documentarist has allowed to surface. Is basketball something "kids can learn from" or "just like war"? The absence of a clear "point of view" on this central issue is of great concern to Remnick, and he strategically marshalls this concern in the climactic conclusion to his piece.

The ultimate *way of the critic* evaluation that builds on the contributions of the other three knowing processes is this: *Playground*

Pros "fails to come alive, visually or even educationally." The producer's methods are "not up to the task," and we lack "a documentary filmmaker who not only celebrates a world but also asks tough questions about it." "This," in Remnick's final assessment, "is not enough." Thus, his evaluative judgment [the way of the critic] becomes the justified and inevitable result of

- components he observed in the program [the scientist];
- his own triggered values and beliefs [the mystic];
- and the arguments raised not only within the show but also those clashes arising from the differing subject matter visions of producer and critic [the rhetorician].

In summary, the four ways of knowing resemble the points of view that might be found in a courtroom during a murder trial:

1. A forensic pathologist is called on to establish probable time and cause of death. Less unequivocally, one or more psychiatrists might be asked for professional evaluations of the defendant's psychological state and capabilities. Such testimony represents, of course, the way of scientists.

2. The defendant's boss and fourth-grade teacher are character witnesses who profess their belief that the man is incapable of such a heinous crime. Later, the accused's ex-wife asserts he is all too capable of homicide. That these beliefs contradict each other does not make reaching a verdict easier, but it does represent the usually unprovable nature of the way of the mystic.

3. Meanwhile, as well-trained rhetoricians, the prosecuting and defense attorneys do their best to arrange all this fact and faith into patterns that are most advantageous to their respective cases.

4. Finally, as conscientious critics, the judge and jury must structure the ground rules and then weigh evidence, belief, and argument in reaching an evaluative pronouncement that will serve justice and stand the critical scrutiny of possible appeals court review.

In the case of electronic media criticism, such appellate review is ultimately conducted by listeners and viewers, each of whom determines whether the critic's findings fairly judged the program under surveillance.

As a final illustration of how the four ways of knowing combine to help us construct as well as evaluate our media products, study the classic Subaru commercial in Figure 4-3.

First, empirical demonstration (the way of the scientist) totally occupies frames 5–12. Here, we observe the car in action, including its turbo and four-wheel-drive capabilities. The son's mystical need for independence, for making a youth-oriented statement in his first car purchase, has been established in the first two frames. But this seems to be contradicted by the dad's more conservative value structure, as revealed in frames 3 and 4—both by his words and the visual of an old, unflashy station wagon. A rhetorical confrontation between the two is set up by frames 13–16 and comes to a head with the dad's expression of betrayal in frame 17—"I thought we agreed . . . you'd buy a Subaru." But suddenly, in frame 18, the two opposing mystical viewpoints converge when the son climactically reveals, "But Dad . . . I did." As punctuated by frame 19's "moo" of revelation, the son has rhetorically won the argument both through his words and his purchase decision—a perfect strategy in a commercial aimed at the young car-buying audience. Finally, in frame 20, we have a way-of-the-critic amalgamation. The son's truth is empirically affirmed in the visual's stylish automobile while the dad's truth is ratified by the value statements supered over it. As we see the physical evidence on the screen, the voiceover reaffirms our *you can have it both ways* rhetorical and critical summation: an exuberant "new" "XT Coupe"—that still epitomizes prudent economy and durability ("Inexpensive. And built to stay that way").

THE PERCEPTUAL TRIAD

Another approach to knowledge processing focuses not on methodologies for critical analysis of a message but on ascertaining the level at which a *receiver* subsequently comes to grips with that message. The celebrated American composer Aaron Copland embraced this receiver-oriented procedure

SBAR 5616

(MUSIC UNDER: SOFT HOMESPUN)
SON: Remember when you were my age Dad?

C'mon Dad, you understand what I mean, it's my first car.

DAD: It's your money, Son, but if you want my advice, buy another Subaru. It's been good to us.

SON: (ASSURINGLY) Sure, Dad.

(MUSIC SHIFTS TO HARD ROCK & ROLL)

(MUSIC)

(MUSIC)

(MUSIC)

TURBO

(MUSIC)

(MUSIC)

(MUSIC)

(MUSIC)

(MUSIC)

(MUSIC)

(MUSIC)

(MUSIC)

(MUSIC STOPS)

DAD: I thought we agreed.. .you'd buy a Subaru.

SON: But Dad. . .I did.

(SFX: COW MOOS)

ANNCR: (VO) The new Subaru XT Coupe. Inexpensive. And built to stay that way.

ALSO AVAILABLE IN :30 NATIONAL AND :25 & :05 DEALER VERSIONS
LEVINE, HUNTLEY, SCHMIDT AND BEAVER, INC.
250 PARK AVENUE
NEW YORK, NEW YORK 10177

FIGURE 4-3
(Courtesy of Harold Levine, Levine, Huntley, Schmidt and Beaver, Inc., Advertising)

in his segmentation of the three musical planes to which a listener might attend: "(1) the sensuous plane, (2) the expressive plane, (3) the sheerly musical plane."[24] If we broaden Copland's perspective to include not just tonal and rhythmic cues but visual and linguistic ones as well, his same three-part system can be used to study how electronic media content is absorbed.

The Sensuous Plane

The sensuous plane involves seeking out a stimulus for the pleasure of the sound, sight, or visceral feeling itself. The receivers lose themselves in the phenomenon "without thinking, without considering it in any way," reports Copland. "One turns on the radio while doing something else and absent-mindedly bathes in the sound. A kind of brainless but attractive state of mind is engendered."[25]

Obviously, the receiver goal associated with attention at this level is to escape, to flee reality and uncritically bask in conscious fantasy or semiconscious reverie. When, for example, we refer to some radio formats as "background," or "wallpaper" music, we are alluding to their tendency to be absorbed as sensuous rather than expressive (meaning-specific) events. However popular such a format might be, it poses special problems for advertising copywriters who must break through this mist to secure fully conscious attention to their product message or station promo. Conversely, "foreground" formats such as "news/talk" or "country" (given its storyline-dominant music lyrics) may more fully engage listener attention but then trigger mental recess when a commercial pod arrives.

Certain television programs are also more likely to be sensuous-plane dominant. The music video genre is mentioned in this regard, as are the action/adventure series in which chase-and-carnage sequences predominate or situation comedies in which visual slapstick supplants character insight. Philosophy professor Mary Sirridge recalls *Miami Vice* as mirroring such limitations:

Novel camera techniques, interposed images, and jarring juxtapositions help to convince the viewer that he is in the presence of something Artistic. The clear indication that this is borrowing, and not genuine art, is that *Miami Vice* strings such elements together undigested, creating the ambiance of art, but no meaning. The water cascade has visual importance, but no meaning; there is really no point in anybody dying in slow motion here—there is nobody whose final moment it is significant to draw out; . . . the viewer is invited to watch the technique, appreciate the artistry, see how smoothly sex and violence can be filmed. . . . The car and boat chases for which *Miami Vice* is famous are narratively fractured by obviously unusual camera angles. Again the same message: think about the camera angle, the space . . . but don't take the story seriously . . . it's all done with surfaces.[26]

Even commercials, where the meaning is supposed to be clear product promotion, can go overboard with sensuous-plane imagery that engulfs or amazes the audience while obscuring the client's selling objective. The bigger the production budget, the more likely this might happen, as Barbara Lippert recounts in critiquing a British Airways spot:

Shot for five weeks on an island off Australia's Great Barrier Reef, it involved 300 actors, 40 boats, numerous helicopters and stunt pilots, and 40,000 square feet of red, white and blue silk. As with some high-concept art project, the actors on land do a running heave-ho, covering an entire island, Christo-style, in bunting. . . . The opening shots, of the helicopters arriving with military precision, are dazzling. It's like a piece of visual algebra, underscored wonderfully by the music (a haunting soprano voice, overdubbed 50 times, backed by strings and percussion). . . . But once the cameras leave the fabulous opener in the heavens, and we get boatloads of actors arriving on land, the spot starts looking smiley and phoney. . . . We can appreciate the money, time and talent it took to create this spectacle, but we really don't understand to what end.[27]

These examples should not be taken to suggest that all sensuous-oriented content is superficial or phony. The near hypnotic appeal of a Balanchine ballet on PBS is, although highly sensuous for dance lovers, certainly neither simplistic nor contrived. Likewise, the power of a televised linebacker colliding with a quarterback or the grace of a hockey goalie sliding across our picture tube to stop a puck are sensuous-dominant but still genuine experiences. And the raving gyrations of Homer Simpson or evocative melodies underscoring *Ally McBeal* and *Homicide: Life on the Street* are no less authentic because they appeal first to the physical pleasure of sight or sound.

The key point of distinction is this: Are the sensuous elements honestly being presented either for themselves or as relevant enhancers of the expressive (meaning) plane? Or, on the other hand, are they being exploited to hide deficient scripting or thematic bankruptcy? Sensuous-level cues candidly selected to heighten our enjoyment of this plane are engaging and legitimate. When forced to masquerade as meaning, however, they lose their legitimacy.

The Expressive Plane

Copland's second plane, the expressive, pertains explicitly to this complex subject of meaning—for him, "the meaning behind the [sensuous] notes." For media practitioners, the expressive embodies the meaning underlying the electronic effects and productional patterns we use. Thus, when we engage the expressive plane, we are moving below the sensuous surface. We want to find out if the program matter offers long-term significance in addition to short-term gratification. To forge successful communicative transactions, media professionals must understand the implications of the content they or their suppliers have constructed. In other words, we cannot afford to be satisfied with first impressions. As aesthetics scholar Theodore Meyer Greene put it,

the less reflective the agent, the more will his evaluations be determined by the poignancy of each immediate experience; the more thoughtful he is, the more will he tend to evaluate his experiences and their objects in a wider frame of reference, i.e., in terms of their more ultimate import for himself and his fellow men. *Both* emotion [the sensuous] and expression [the expressive] are requisite to *adequate* evaluation.[28]

Because of the complexity of the electronic media and their availability to all segments of the population, many people in our audiences will be "less reflective." They lack the training for greater expressive-plane comprehension of our transmitted content. (Recall the discussion of *Why Is Electronic Media Criticism Needed?* in Chapter 1.) Therefore, it is in the media professional's best interest to teach consumers about the expressive plane. The less reflective listeners/viewers need no help in experiencing our programming's sensuous stimuli, but the greatest potential for long-term program loyalty and productive response to commercials resides in the expressive plane.

Film authority Robert Edmonds sees an analogous situation in cinematic creations when he compares the richness of what he labels *intra-artistic* and *extra-artistic* perceptions:

The perceptions of organizational arrangements within the film we can properly call *intra-artistic* because they occur in terms of the aesthetic elements and structures. The additional associations that will be generated in us we can call *extra-artistic* because they are, in a sense, outside the purely aesthetic or dramatic aspects of the film even though they may have

been stimulated by them. It is these associations that provide the basis for what the film "means" to us. The more associations we have the more the film will mean to us.[29]

Similarly, as just mentioned, the more associations—the more *meaning*—that our listeners and viewers can be guided to apprehend in a piece of electronic media content, the longer will that content and its appeal stick with them. This is as true for recalling a commercial's brand and benefits as it is for remembering to "tune in again" to a previously enjoyed radio format, television program, or web destination.

The Productional/Technical Plane

Copland's third plane—the "sheerly musical"—consists, in electronic media, of the productional elements that carry and structure the presentation. As we see in Chapters 5 and 6, these factors include not just the recording and manipulation of sound, illumination, and angle of vision, but also the talents and techniques that writers, actors, directors, and technicians bring to the property. The most skillful of these manipulations will not be noticed by the audience, but their absence or mishandling are widely detected by viewers conditioned to expect 'network quality production values' in everything they watch. As Emmy-winning television editor Philip Sgriccia reveals,

My job . . . is to tell a story in a seamless and entertaining way while keeping my contribution invisible. I think it's a nice compliment when someone tells me they enjoyed the show and didn't notice my editing. If their attention was called to the editing, they are not watching the story [functioning on an expressive plane level] and I haven't done my job properly.[30]

It is the same with commercials. "Advertising agencies should be in the business of selling *ideas*—not production values or the latest executional techniques of a trendy director," avows award-winning creative director Ron Sandilands. "The idea is to develop something substantive that can be stated simply and communicate a strong selling message to the consumer."[31]

But while huddled over a keyboard or an editing machine, or while coping with the chaos of a studio or remote production, it is easy to let form and format overshadow concept and content. We can fall prey to the same occupational hazard as musicians who, Copland laments, "often fall into the error of becoming so engrossed with their arpeggios and staccatos that they forget the deeper aspects of the music."[32] As critic Merrill Panitt once wrote about the deservedly short-lived *USA Today: The Television Show*, "The first few shows were pretty much of a mess, crammed with graphics, gimmicks and glitz that raced by, leaving viewers wondering what on earth was going on."[33]

Therefore, a continuing task of electronic media practitioners—whether working at a local outlet, a network, or on-line—must be to make certain that we and our colleagues are never so beguiled by our techniques that we lose sight of a project's expressive-plane objective.

The Planes Combined

When we assume the task of critic, it is our responsibility to help both our colleagues and their publics achieve a fuller understanding of a work's totality. When we are dealing specifically with consumers, our emphasis needs to be on helping them understand the limitations and challenges we face on the *productional/technical plane*, and sensitizing them to the richness of *expressive plane* meaning that can be present in a well-honed media project.

Conversely, when we are working with professional colleagues and subordinates, it is important to promote greater appreciation for the *sensuous plane* capabilities of their medium, and enhanced attention to the *expressive plane* purpose that should be motivating the message in question. People in our industry frequently must be reminded to take a step back from the nuts and bolts of the process in order to visualize the total creation.

All three planes simultaneously reside in a given programmatic product, of course. But nobody can ever equally absorb all three at the same time. Nevertheless, the astute professional will try to raise the perceptual level both of publics and practitioners so that each group can fully experience each plane—and therefore better understand the other group's perspective.

Professor Jimmie Reeves, for example, has insightfully applied perceptual triad criticism in his analysis of television sports. Although he uses different terminology, Reeves addresses each part of the triad:

The behind-the-scenes labor of producers, directors, sound technicians, video editors, and camera operators is masked, or made invisible, by conventional production techniques. Unless the conventions are violated, either by error or by design, the visual processing [*productional/ technical plane*] of the sporting event generally remains inconspicuous. . . .

While we may not always be aware of how the television production crew frames and focuses our view of the sporting event, we are generally aware of two distinct planes of symbolic action that coexist in sports discourse: the presentational [*expressive*] plane and the performance [*sensuous*] plane. Although athletic figures appearing on the performance plane are the main focus of attention in the sports arena, their actions are interpreted and filtered by broadcast professionals and sports experts speaking on the presentational plane; . . . the sports performance takes on meaning only in relation to other performances . . . athletic performances are converted into records—the most strike outs, the most yards gained, the most passes completed. This statistical conversation, in turn, becomes privileged male knowledge . . . a major component of the "language" of sports narration.[34]

For a final and more message-specific example of perceptual triad decoding, turn to the Friskies commercial in Figure 4-4. There are two main *sensuous* pleasures here: the visual cuteness of the kitten, and the visceral feeling of speed we get as it zooms through the household in frames 1, 2, 4–9, and 13. These two sensations are combined and enhanced by the humorous touch of race-car sound effects in frames 2, 8, and 16.

The sound effects also constitute a clever aspect of the *productional/technical* process, of course, as does the compelling floor-level camera work. In frames 2, 5, 7, 9, and 13 the shots contribute a 'kitten's eye view' to get us further involved in the scene. Meanwhile, in those shots where we actually see the kitten, our cat-lover target audience might be led to speculate on how much footage had to be expended to capture the feline in these poses. ("How much film would I waste trying to get my cat to do this?") Such speculation, in turn, is calculated to elicit greater in-

"ZOOMING KITTEN"

FIGURE 4-4
(Courtesy of Lintas: New York. Creative Director: Ken Musto; Art Director: Dave Mangan; Copywriter: Don Sheehan)

COMMERCIAL NO: CMKF 8013

COMMERCIAL LENGTH: 30 SECONDS

ANNCR: (VO) What does a frisky new kitten need?

(SFX: CAR PEELING OUT.)

New Friskies Kitten Formula.

Cause kittens burn up

three times the energy

and need three times

as much calcium:

(SFX: CAR BRAKES AND CAR CRASH)
as adult cats.

So they need the extra protein and calcium of Friskies Kitten Formula.

It has all the calcium of milk

to build strong bones and teeth.

So, if you want

your frisky kitten to grow into a frisky cat...

get new Friskies Kitten Formula

and bring out the frisky in your Kitty.

(SFX: CAR ZOOMING BY)

volvement in the re-creation of the message by the people the advertiser is most trying to impact.

Expressively, there is a clear demonstration that the effect of this cat food on your pet will mirror the brand name. Even high-energy, out-of-control kittens who 'wipe out' into sewing baskets will get the nutrients they need. The visual shows "frisky," the audio lists the nutritional qualities needed to achieve "frisky," and the final three frames enhance this cumulative meaning as the re-fueled cat now blasts past the package that apparently created his spunk. Finally, the graphic 'super' in frame 15 gives this advertiser-preferred meaning further recognition by casting the benefit into authoritative print. All three planes of the perceptual triad thus mutually support the knowledge result that the commercial's producers sought to achieve.

A KNOWLEDGE EPILOGUE

Copland's three planes, Robert Rutherford Smith's four ways of knowing, and the associated empirical and normative perspectives are protocols that attempt to categorize how knowledge is gathered, decoded, prioritized, and evaluated.

Electronic media professionals who understand the divergent yet complementary ways in which consumers absorb program matter are in a much better position to communicate. Armed with such sensitivity, these professionals can better identify the options open to them in conforming to the differing "knowledge"-intake patterns and preferences of particular audiences. As media scholar Samuel Becker concludes, "Sophistication in more than one approach to knowing can stimulate the development and persuasive testing of imaginative solutions to problems."[35]

ENDNOTES

1. "Melange," *Chronicle of Higher Education* (April 28, 1993), B2.
2. Robert Lewis Shayon, *Open to Criticism* (Boston: Beacon Press, 1971), 33.
3. Theodore Meyer Greene, *The Arts and the Art of Criticism* (Princeton, NJ: Princeton University Press, 1952), 233.
4. Ien Ang, *Desperately Seeking the Audience* (London: Routledge, 1991), 9.
5. Stephen Littlejohn, *Theories of Human Communication*, 3rd ed. (Belmont, CA: Wadsworth, 1989), 7.
6. Lee Loevinger, "The Ambiguous Mirror: The Reflective-Projective Theory of Broadcasting and Mass Communication," *Journal of Broadcasting* (Spring 1968), 113.
7. Ralph Smith, *A Study of the Professional Criticism of Broadcasting in the United States 1920–1955* (New York: Arno Press, 1978), viii.
8. Miroslav Holub, quoted in Lee Edgren, "A Spotlight in Immense Darkness," *Teaching Enrichment* (February 1992), 8.
9. Robert Rutherford Smith, *Beyond the Wasteland: The Criticism of Broadcasting*, rev. ed. (Annandale, VA: Speech Communication Association, 1980), 3–4.
10. Ang, 83.
11. Russell Neuman, "Finding the Quality Time in TV Viewing," *ADWEEK Television 1984 Special Issue* (August 1984), 32.
12. Ang, 92.
13. Roger Rollin, "Popular Culture and the Death of Good Taste," *Phi Kappa Phi Journal* (Fall 1994), 15.
14. Marvin Kalb, "The Role of Media in Society," *College Broadcaster* (February 1989), 15.
15. Karen Rybacki and Dennis Rybacki, *Communication Criticism: Approaches and Genres* (Belmont, CA: Wadsworth, 1991), 2.
16. Jay Parini, "The Theory and Practice of Literature: A New Dialogue?" *Chronicle of Higher Education* (September 9, 1992), B2.
17. Richard Young, Alton Becker, and Kenneth Pike, *Rhetoric: Discovery and Change* (New York: Harcourt, Brace & World, 1970), xii.
18. Howard Ziff, "The Uses of *Rhetoric*: On Rereading Aristotle," *Critical Studies in Mass Communication* (March 1986), 114.
19. Ibid., 113.
20. Ibid.
21. Ibid., 114.
22. Conrad Kottak, *Prime-Time Society* (Belmont, CA: Wadsworth, 1990), 104–105.
23. Robert Smith, 4.
24. Aaron Copland, *What to Listen for in Music*, rev. ed. (New York: Mentor Books, 1957), 18.
25. Ibid.
26. Mary Sirridge, "The Good, the Bad, and the Counterfeit: A Tolstoyan Theory of Narrative," in Katherine Henderson and Joseph Mazzeo (eds.), *Meanings of the Medium* (New York: Praeger, 1990), 116.
27. Barbara Lippert, "Overbooked," *ADWEEK* (April 17, 1995), 54.
28. Greene, 462–463.
29. Robert Edmonds, *The Sights and Sounds of Cinema and Television* (New York: Teachers College Press, 1982), 163.
30. Philip Sgriccia, in Peter Orlik, *The Electronic Media: An Introduction to the Profession*, 2nd ed. (Ames: Iowa State University Press, 1997), 110.
31. Ron Sandilands, "Sandilands' Creative Review," *Winners* (February 1988), 9.
32. Copland, 21.
33. Merrill Panitt, "USA Today: The Television Show," *TV Guide* (November 19, 1988), 39.
34. Jimmie Reeves, "TV's World of Sports: Presenting and Playing the Game," in Gary Burns and Robert Thompson (eds.), *Television Studies: Textual Analysis* (New York: Praeger, 1989), 209.
35. Samuel Becker, "Critical Studies: A Multidimensional Movement," *Feedback* (Fall 1985), 24.

5

Tonal and Talent Ingredients

The previous chapter concludes with a discussion of the last of Aaron Copland's three musically derived perceptual planes—the "sheerly musical" or, as we apply it to electronic media, the "productional/technical" vantage point. This and the next chapter examine productional elements in more detail by dividing them into three categories: musical ingredients, on-stage talent ingredients, and stage-molding ingredients. The first two are the subject of this chapter, and the third comprises Chapter 6. Together, these three elements are the raw material out of which our programmatic creations are constructed. It thus is important to examine them individually before moving on in subsequent chapters to analyze their cumulative results. We begin by looking at *music*, which, for our profession, is an initial component rather than an artistic end goal.

THE MUSICAL INGREDIENT

One difficulty we face in critiquing the use of music *as a programmatic tool* is the same difficulty encountered by people who critique *music itself*. The problem is that music, as composer Richard Wagner observed, "begins where speech leaves off." Therefore, the use of mere words to evaluate tonal progressions seems a questionable enterprise. "To be sure," wrote aesthetics scholar DeWitt Parker, "music is a language which we all understand because it expresses the basic mold of all emotion and striving; yet it is a language which no two people understand in the same way, because each pours into that mold his own unique experience."[1] Roy Dickinson Welch adds, "Though the emotions suggested by a given composition may be apparent to most men, it is well-nigh im-

possible to describe them in words acceptable to all [people]."[2] If aesthetics experts find themselves in this quandary, how can an electronic media professional expect to come to grips with music?

Fortunately, media practitioners need only realize that we are not in the business of critiquing music *for itself*. We are evaluating music in terms of its contextual effectiveness within certain program or system frameworks. Once we have specified the framework, we can try to determine whether a given musical treatment seems to be working, whether another is needed, or if music is even appropriate in this particular situation.

We are not discounting music's power by treating it as only one of many productional tools at our disposal. We are just recognizing that the electronic media are no more analogous to the art of music than they are to the literary, visual, or dramatic arts. Rather, our industry borrows from and amalgamates some or all of these arts in the process of creating programmatic product.

Certainly, music possesses various properties and characteristics that give it a special communicative potency. Recent scientific research suggests, according to William Allman, "that the mental mechanisms that process music are deeply entwined with the brain's other basic functions, including perception, memory and even language."[3] Listening to the intricacies of Mozart's music, for example, now is being advocated as a method for increasing a child's IQ.

Nonetheless, music in and of itself "is the most 'artificial' of the arts," asserts Theodore Meyer Greene, "because its primary medium, i.e., the system of tones based on any given scale, as well as its generic forms, have meaning only in a musical context. That is, this meaning attaches itself to them only by association and convention."[4] This is certainly the case in the electronic communications environment. Music over the media acquires meaning not for itself, but for the "associative" role it plays in conjunction with other productional elements. Even a live-broadcast concert is not the presentation only of music. Instead, it is a remote performance event encased in a series of announcements and spatial perspectives, an event that is generally designed to magnify the star musicians involved—be they the Metropolitan Opera Company or Marilyn Manson. Furthermore, argues *BE Radio*'s editor-in-chief Skip Pizzi, "until audio recording was possible, music was only experienced live, and could only be captured in a written score. This defined what we call the Classical period, when the composer was king. Once the ability to capture a specific *performance* through sound recording [and long-distance transmission] became possible, the performer assumed dominance, and the era of 'popular music' was established."[5]

In our role as media professionals, we do not have to be concerned with whether the music or its interpreter is "king," because we do not have to critique music solely *as music*. Instead, we need to concentrate on whether the musical choices in a given programmatic context are optimal ones. Specifically, this task calls for scrutiny of four interdependent attributes: *clarity, execution, continuity*, and *aptness of task*.

Clarity

Clarity refers to the acoustic integrity of the music's electromechanical capturing and transmission. This is influenced by such technical considerations as the type of microphones, speakers, recorders, mixers, processors, and disc drives and players that pick up, store, manipulate, and reproduce the musical content. If we have control over the performance (as in the commercial 'bed' recording session pictured in Figure 5-1), we then can set up the music's creation and capturing in a way that should eliminate clarity imperfections at the source. However, clarity is further dependent on such hardware-heavy elements as transmitters, towers and antennas, satellite uplinks and downlinks, and ethernet lines. Such equipment and systems affect the quality of any electronic message. But they are vitally important in carriage of the continuous tones and timbres of music where distortion and constriction are much more noticeable than in the conveyance of harmonically forgiving speech.

In recent decades, the superior fidelity of FM over AM radio figured prominently in the clarity issue—as the migration of music-emphasizing formats to the FM band attested. The promise of digital radio—both terrestrial and satellite—will probably put an end to AM/FM distinctions altogether and may further lessen critical issues of musical clarity in

FIGURE 5-1
A carefully sculpted recording of commercial background music. (Courtesy of TM Century, Inc., Dallas, Texas)

the broadcast business. Meanwhile, fiber optic and other broadband technologies are substantially narrowing clarity concerns in the wired electronic media as well.

If our musical concern is *only* one of clarity, we are probably part of the engineering community rather than programmers. In this instance, we would be oriented like the "science" critics of the 1920s mentioned in Chapter 1. However, even engineers now recognize that 'high-tech' clarity in isolation has little merit other than to dress up faulty musical performances. As recording engineer Piper Stevenson admonishes,

we have it all: great equipment with astounding capabilities, proliferating software algorithms to suit even the wildest dreams, all on an ever-expanding technological horizon. . . . What we fail to notice is that while the technology has advanced, the talent who use the gear . . . have not progressed accordingly. In the process of searching for that "perfect piece of gear," we have ended up cheating the listener by placing technology before art. . . . We need people who realize that the artform existed long before the integrated circuit. Until we do this, our technologically over-produced recordings are worthless; they are an engineering experience gone haywire.[6]

Indeed, the clarity of electronic media sound today is so much a given that most listeners and nonengineer media professionals don't stop to think about what might have been lost in the sometimes "over-produced" result. Harkening back to Chapter 2's discussion of honesty as a critic-preferred value, it must be recognized that musical clarity should never be elevated over musical authenticity.

Execution

This second element of electronic media music criticism is concerned with whether the performers and presenters of the music seem to know what they are doing. Listeners and viewers do not need an extensive background in music theory to be sensitive to execution any more than they require classes in playwriting as a prerequisite to understanding dramatic dialogue. The disc jockeys who know little about the *genre* they play and the 'cover versions' of top group hits by low-talent copycat ensembles are executional failures whom we may need to *explain* to consumers—but seldom need to point out.

Certainly, as David Altheide and Robert Snow affirm, "Talent and skill are judged differently by different listeners, but every music aficionado can recognize the presence or absence of those qualities. Radio stations occasionally try to 'hype' a performer of dubious talent, but this is rarely successful. Even established stars who sluff-off or 'lose it' are quickly dropped by the listening audience."[7]

At the other extreme is the media execution that is too immaculate. In the case of musical recordings, veteran reviewer Samuel Singer points out that "the technical perfection achieved through careful editing [video as well as audio] may sometimes rob a performance of spontaneity and urgency."[8] Worse, adds recording engineer Piper Stevenson, "a large percentage of today's musical performances are sub-standard; and the technology used to record these performances is often utilized to correct the deficiencies of the primary art of creating the music [the execution]."[9]

Technical proficiency as a substitute for executional responsiveness is also a factor in the prepackaged music service that, through too much slickness, makes the local radio station carrying it seem mechanistic, bloodless, and remote. Everything is done so flawlessly that the receiver loses any sense of human intimacy. Though hard to achieve, the executional accomplishment of skilled talent/listener interaction is what distinguishes the truly communicative music outlet.

Music programming, therefore, must not sound robotlike either in the musical selections themselves or in the way they are packaged. Skillfully presented music can trigger a greater depth and range of emotional responses in our receivers than can any collection of words no matter how intimate. "Words," points out DeWitt Parker, "are means of communication as well as expression; they therefore embody of any experience only as much as can be passed from speaker to hearer; but in music the full personal resonance of experience is retained. In music we get so close to ourselves that at times it is almost frightening."[10] Well-executed music can be so self-referential for listeners because of "its power to structure our auditory experience and thus to make sense of it," writes clinical psychiatrist Anthony Storr. "This is refreshing, because it permits the same kind of scanning, sorting, and rearrangement of mental contents which takes place in reverie or in sleep."[11] Deftly programmed music radio therefore can be escapist in the most positive sense because it provides an immediate and highly personal means for rejuvenating reflection.

Musical execution is a concern for television as well as radio, of course—especially in music-focused services such as MTV, VH-1, The Nashville Network, and selected programs on PBS and Arts & Entertainment. But once the picture is added, the executional focus is less on the music than on how well that music becomes interwoven with camera shots and visual portrayals. This is especially true of music videos, where, as Charles Turner recalls, "pop musicians and their fans entered the 1980s with a *new perceptual agenda*, a joint readiness for watching instead of listening, for sharing the music in pictorial bits and bytes."[12] Such pictorial sharing works well when the visual performance matches the executional level of the original song. But unfortunately, asserts film critic Kenneth Turan, "most rock videos suffer because either: a) they are stuck with songs that don't particularly lend themselves to visual equivalents or b) all the creativity went into the writing of the song, with the video version being kind of a throwaway afterthought."[13] Even a chart-busting tune can't fully carry a music video if the pictorial execution is haphazard.

The Internet now puts the consumer in this executional driver's seat. Not only does the on-line world provide a sweeping new avenue for music's dissemination, but it also empowers end users to fashion their own pictorial/musical performances from disparate sources. By critically evaluating packages put together by professionals, web-using amateurs draw their own executional lessons about how to marry music and graphics to create new synchronous experiences.

Continuity

The third element of media music criticism is *continuity*. In probing this aspect, we ask, How are the individual musical segments programmed to establish linkages with each other and perhaps (particularly in radio) with the time of day? Obviously, there are infinite numbers of ways to string music videos or audio selections together; but something more than random chance must determine what comes first, what comes last, and the order of the selections in between.

This 'something more' is the planning and artistic skill of the video producer or the radio station's program director. An abrupt clash of musical keys, genres, or stylings may disorient the audience to the extent that their expressive and even sensuous plane pleasures are derailed. What music theorist Leonard Meyer said of individual compositions is just as true of a *progression* of *several* tunes: "The enjoyment of music comes from the subtle interweaving of expectation and surprise. If there is too much surprise in a musical piece, a listener gets lost; if there is too little surprise, the listener becomes bored."[14]

Skillful musical continuity, then, balances predictability with innovation so audience preferences are adhered to at the same time their interest is piqued. Ideally, our programmatic music progression should mesh so well with listener/viewer attention cycles that their ebb and flow are as one. "Life begins," remarked composer Roger Sessions, "with an up-beat, the first breath of the new born child corresponding to the preparatory anacrusis of a musical statement, and ends, like the most natural and satisfying rhythm, with a downbeat."[15]

In the same way, an electronic media program or format will attempt to arrange its musical sequences to match the life beats of its target public. This is most noticeable in foreground music radio, where, as Altheide and Snow discovered, "this rhythmic variation provides a sense of balance within the general tempos of a time segment. Developing this rhythmic balance has become such a sophisticated operation that many stations now employ computer technology to insure appropriate music scheduling."[16]

In more of a background sense, musical continuity is a vital component of dramatic programs, too. Here, the musical stylings flow and shift to match similar shifts and twists in the plot action. This is perhaps most common in crime shows, which, point out researchers Kathleen Turner and Raymond Sprague,

have traditionally used the nineteenth-century idea of thematic transformation: a melody, usually taken from the show's musical theme, undergoes various changes as it is presented in different keys (major and minor), harmonizations, musical textures, rhythmic or metric structures, and timbres to help set moods for the various scenes. The music directors for these shows rely on the fact that as members of a common culture we have learned to attach certain similar meanings to these changes. For example, a shift from a major-mode harmonization to a minor-mode harmonization generally signals a shift from a happy to a more troubled mood. While most audience members do not consciously comment, "Oh, listen to that minor-mode modulation," almost all derive a similar message from such a shift.[17]

Well-crafted musical continuity, in whatever electronic format, services and capitalizes on those shared meanings to help us better attract and hold our target audiences. Once they are engaged by this flow, it should be harder for them to zip, zap, or punch to a competing outlet.

Aptness of Task

Aptness of task is the fourth and final musical attribute that the electronic media professional should be fully prepared to critique. Here, the issue is whether music has been asked to perform functions in keeping with its capabilities.

Giving specific task assignments to music is not a new practice. As perceptual psychologist Rudolf Arnheim discovered, no less a personage than Plato

recommended music for the education of heroes because it made human beings partake in the mathematical order and harmony of the cosmos, located beyond the reach of the senses; whereas the [visual] arts, and particularly painting, were to be treated with caution because they strengthened man's dependence on illusory images.[18]

It thus would seem that Plato might value radio's music more than that of the "illusory-image"-filled music video. (In fact, the philosopher warned that music was capable of performing *negative* as well as positive labors. He thus would allow in to his ideal Republic only "rhythms appropriate to a life of courage and self-control"[19] while barring compositions that expressed "drunkenness, effeminacy, and inactivity."[20]

Plato's musical preferences are not our main concern, of course. As electronic media professionals, we need to evaluate whether a given piece of music is equal to and appropriate for the programmatic chore to which it has been assigned.

Aptness/inaptness of task is easily comprehended in the case of the television program soundtrack. In fulfilling this background function, music can serve as either a legitimate heightener of audience involvement or as a sleazy apologist for dull dialogue or ponderous plot. A good example of the effective use of music can be gleaned from a Tom Shales review of an NBC miniseries called *A Year in the Life*:

Here and there the drama is brightened by a flash of style. A dark night of the soul for young Sam, circa 4:18 A.M., becomes a montage set to the Percy Sledge classic "When a Man Loves a Woman," and does he ever. The n'er-do-well, played believably by Morgan Stevens, does his base running to an infectious, uncredited piano piece.[21]

Conversely, an illumination of music's blatant misuse is revealed in this classic *TV Guide* 'Jeers' citation:

To the nighttime soaps for intrusive background music. ABC's *Dynasty* and CBS's *Knots Landing* and *Dallas* employ scores that are as boisterous as the shouting matches between Krystle and Alexis. As one of our readers points out, it never fails that just as a critical conversation is taking place, the music blares on with greater determination. This does not, as the directors might hope, underscore the plot; it undermines it.[22]

On radio, the requirements of a particular format design set up their own aptness boundaries. The most astute program directors and radio consultants exhibit a keen instinct for knowing how to draw those boundaries to parallel the preferences of a particular target audience. As researchers Irving Rein and Craig Springer affirm,

musical arrangements reflect the aesthetic assumptions of the intended audience; . . . music which ignores the aesthetic standards of intended audiences is denied airplay, media coverage, and sales. Gaining acceptance requires a musician [and subsequently, a program director] to use elements which the intended audience understands as musically valuable.[23]

A tune is 'apt' if that value comes through clearly to whatever audience segment the program director is striving to capture. It is 'inapt' if its appeal falls outside that segment.

Finally, commercials also are heavy users of music—sometimes aptly and sometimes not. In general, when music is called on to enhance a strong, clear creative concept in a way that mirrors the product personality intended by the advertiser, we say that the music's use is appropriate. When, however, the music is expected to cover for imprecise dialogue or substitute for a clear selling benefit, a producer is expecting too much explicitness from an inherently implicit tool.

The television commercial in Figure 5-2 makes no such inapt demands of its music. Sung to the tune "Sugar Pie" by the native Michigan group who made that tune famous, the adapted lyric projects a love for the state while showing appealing summer

scenes calculated to get prospective tourists to love it, too. The creative concept is to position Michigan as a place for summer fun, and the Four Tops' lighthearted hit easily carries this fun theme without changing that "golden oldie's" character. In the process, neither the song nor the product is compromised.

A Musical Summary

Clarity, execution, continuity, and aptness of task constitute a criteria quartet by which even nonmusical media professionals can comprehend, consider, and evaluate the use of music in their projects. To illustrate how these four benchmarks can be interrelated, even in analyzing something as brief as a

FIGURE 5-2
(Courtesy of Marcie
Brogan, Brogan &
Partners)

LYRICS: (Four Tops singing)
Michigan, my home state

You know that I love you

I can't help myself

I love you and nobody else...

VO: (Four Top)
Michigan is tops for summer
excitement

You betcha!

It's as easy as...

LYRICS: (Four Tops singing)
Sugar pie, honey bunch,
You know that we love you...

Say Yes to Michigan.

LADYSMITH BLACK MAMBAZO REFRESHES 7-UP'S RAIN CONCEPT

by Barbara Lippert

Soft-drink advertisers have always used lots of liquid imagery to convey the idea of refreshment: We've seen oceans, waves, falls, ice, fizz, and even the hosing of cars. This is supposed to convey fun, energy, and up times. When The Seven-Up Co. launched a new campaign a few years ago, it fixed on rain, which comes down. There would seem to be a connection: the "uncola" is the color of rain, and the jingle said it "feels so good, comin' down, down, down. . . ."

So they made feel-good, up advertising about rain coming down. But while I know that rain is pure and sometimes mystical, and dramatic and maybe even romantic, the saying "Knowing when to come in out of the rain," comes to mind. These bits of folk wisdom do come in handy.

One of the first commercials showed oldsters sitting on a porch, when a rain shower appears. One would think they would duck for cover. But instead, they get up from their rocking chairs, run out to face the elements, drink 7-Up and do a jig.

The sight of oldsters gamboling is sweet. But the scene appears to be made from the energetic-septuagenarian factory that grew out of the success of the movie Cocoon.

Another spot showed a proud farmer and his wife. With the start of the rain, they do a dignified little proud-farmer dance. Perhaps these two have reasons to dance, but we should give them some more privacy.

More recent spots for 7-Up are vastly improved. They used better music (one spot adapted a Who song, Love, Rain on Me; another, Eric Clapton's Let It Rain), which made better sense of the rain. And the spots had more of a contemporary look and feel.

And now we get this "Beautiful Rain" spot, featuring the music of the South African a cappella group Ladysmith Black Mambazo. They sang and worked with Paul Simon on his Graceland album. The sheer grace and beauty of their voices, and the exactness of their singing, are not easy to describe: The music stopped me cold. The group sings in English and Zulu. Here the agency adapted the group's song Beautiful Rain from its Shaka Zulu album. Although we hear lush, sophisticated harmonies, their sound has an intense emotive power: It is moving, and beautiful, and spiritual, but it is the music of resistance. Sounds that are this naked and powerful are rarely heard in commercials.

One of the lines that the group sings is: "Don't disturb the beautiful rain." The agency seemed to respect that idea and showed admirable restraint in matching the music to images. The pacing is languid, with slow takes and slow drinking. A barechested guy in pajamas lifts a 7-Up to his lips and drinks slowly. Inserted into the song is the line "Feels so good, comin' down." But it doesn't affect the reverie of the music.

There also are shots of rain against a window and over docked boats. A policeman is shown outside dressed in a yellow slicker.

Overall, I don't think the individual images are as strong as the music. But there is a power and grace to the pacing. And I like the way the spot ends cleanly, with the 7-Up logo superimposed in the corner of the image. In all, it works.

(Reprinted with permission of *ADWEEK*)

commercial, read the critique by *ADWEEK*'s Barbara Lippert.

While we expect big-budget, network commercials to be well-produced, Ms. Lippert still covers the issue of musical *clarity* by referring to the "exactness of their singing." "Sounds that are this naked and powerful are rarely heard in commercials," she says, and thereby testifies to clarity's contribution in distinguishing the overall spot.

*Executiona*l questions are interwoven with clarity issues in this critique due to the starkness of the musical soundtrack. It is not multileveled but the product of vocalists singing *a cappella* (unaccompanied). What comes through here are "the sheer grace and beauty of their voices," with "lush, sophisticated harmonies" and a sound possessing "an intense emotive power." Certainly, the performers seem to know what they are doing, as does the agency which "showed admirable restraint in matching the music to images."

Effective musical *continuity* is the outgrowth of the progressive music and image matching. Both visual and musical flow seem to be cooperatively "languid." And even when another lyric segment—"Feels so good, comin' down"—is inserted into *Beautiful Rain*, it "doesn't affect the reverie of the music." Instead, the continuity is preserved: "there is a power and grace to the pacing."

Aptness, meanwhile, is comparatively discussed by contrasting "Beautiful Rain" with previous 7-Up spots. Two earlier ads using music to accompany oldsters dancing seemed much less appropriate to Ms. Lippert. One reminded her more of the movie *Cocoon* than of 7-Up, and the other dance vignette seemed too self-consciously intrusive on the characters. Later spots, in contrast, "used better music . . . which made better sense of the rain." Finally, with the adaptation of the Ladysmith Black Mambazo cut, 7-Up's agency seems to have captured something "moving, and beautiful, and spiritual." However, there is an aptness drawback to music that is so powerful: "Overall," cautions Lippert, "I don't think the individual images are as strong as the music." In other words, the music may overshadow the visual's selling message which is, after all, the whole point of the project.

As electronic media professionals, we must remember that for us, music is a tool. It is just one of several ingredients that we interweave to accomplish our communication objectives. When we allow it to dominate, when we allow musical objectives to overshadow programmatic objectives, we become musicians rather than mass communicators. And we are not being paid to be musicians.

Certainly, music is an extremely potent and personally involving resource. As aesthetics scholar DeWitt Parker recognized,

We fill in the impersonal form of musical feeling with the concrete emotions of our own lives; it is our strivings, our hopes and fears which the music expresses. . . . As we listen to the music, we shall see the things we hope for, or fear or desire; or else transport ourselves among purely fanciful objects and events.[24]

When our audiences are allowed to go off on "purely fanciful" excursions, however, they will not be fully cognizant of our program or our advertisement. To succeed, maintains Kenneth Turan, even sensuous-plane-emphasizing music videos need to project "a synthesis of music, words and images, all elements merging and playing off each other to make the whole more than the parts."[25]

Unquestionably, music is more dominant—more foreground—in some contexts than in others. But it is never our sole ingredient, and its transmission is never our only objective.

THE ON-STAGE TALENT INGREDIENT

Depending on the programmatic context, music's presence can be either overt or subtle. What we call the *on-stage talent ingredient*, however, is always front and center in the audience's perception. This ingredient comprises the announcers, disc jockeys, reporters, hosts, commentators, and actors and actresses who, via electronic media, hope to establish direct consumer contact. The high visibility of these jobs makes their basic functions well recognized. Thus, what we stress in this section are the key *implications* of on-stage performance; these implications need to be the focus of our professional assessment.

Radio People

Looking at the format-driven world of radio first, it is clear that program hosts (most notably disc jockeys and talk show personalities) must accomplish two main objectives: they must establish a sense of personal communication, even personal intimacy with the listener; and they must maximally exploit and blend in with all the elements of the format in which they work. Some hosts, for instance, know a great deal about the subject of their show, be it heavy metal or mental hygiene. But they are unable to generate a sense of conversation between themselves and their listeners. Other hosts possess a keen ability to stimulate a feeling of listener dialogue. Yet, they are so ignorant of their format's mechanics or subject matter that their performance seems all surface and no substance.

For better or worse, in the packaged totality of today's radio service, the communicator and the format content must not be merely compatible but perfectly synchronized. (This is why a station format change usually involves wholesale on-air personnel changes as well.) Nationally prominent radio consultant Tim Moore sees this personality dimension as vital to the successful positioning of a station in its market. He divides it into two fundamental qualities:

1. The correct amount of talk required to "lubricate" the format;
2. The sense of control the on-air host seems to bring to and through the microphone.[26]

In recalling Dan Kening's piece on Bubba the Love Sponge in Chapter 3, for example, Kening observes that

if you listen to Bubba on WYTZ, you'll hear a streetwise, high-energy radio persona rapping with his "homeboys" and "girlfriends" on the phones.

Still, the requirements of his new station's formula require Bubba himself to admit that

"I think I really had to tone things down from what I was doing. . . . But once we get the snowball rolling a little faster here [intensify the format], I think I'll be able to let loose a little more. . . . At this point, not being so nasty and controversial might make me a better disc jockey."

In short, the need to regulate the amount and type of talk to meet formatic requirements is paramount if a host is to stay in appropriate on-air control of the specific situation that station program executives have designed.

Unfortunately, the design can become *too* controlled and predictable, especially if air personalities allow themselves to become merely mindless cogs in it. To avoid this communicative stagnation, "you must always be ready to give an extra effort every day to your show," says veteran radio host Patty Williamson. "Note that it is not a *shift*. A shift is what a lineman at the local automobile factory works. A *show* is your chance to interact with your audience every day. That is quite a bit more difficult than opening the mic and reading liner cards."[27]

Both on-air talent and station management share the responsibility to balance control with spontaneity when it comes to host communication. "Put simply," asserts program consultant Tyree Ford, "it's not just what you say, it's what you say *and* the way you say it. Those stations that are successful have a sense of identity that is stronger than the strongest positioning statement. No collection of words can communicate more strongly than the intent of the individual who speaks them."[28]

Even though he was referring to artists in general, aesthetician DeWitt Parker may have articulated the most incisive description of the aural on-stage performer when he wrote: "The artist must be able to create, in the external world, something to charm the senses as well as to speak the mind. . . . His work remains a show, a make-believe, to the end; or rather it makes of reality itself a show."[29]

Electronic Newspersons

Packaging reality into digestible shows is exactly what electronic journalism is all about. Consequently, there are obvious similarities between news talent and successful radio entertainment personalities.

Because news is usually subsumed within an entertainment-oriented environment, news presenters have been generally believed to need pleasing visual and/or aural appearances in order to make inherently unpleasant events palatable for the public. In television, this belief has often resulted in the perception that physical comeliness has been prized over journalistic ability. In their study of female anchors, for example, researchers Erika Engstrom and Anthony Ferri found that over the past ten years, there has been no change in these anchors' stated concerns: "(1) how comments made about women anchors by both managers and viewers center on their appearance rather than their competence; (2) the disparity in the importance placed on men and women anchors' appearance; and (3) the constant criticism of women anchors' wardrobe, hair, weight and age." The group of anchor women studied "recognizes this as a challenge they must deal with rather than a *de facto* barrier to career advancement."[30]

While physical appearance continues to be a more important criterion for women then for men, news consultant John Bowen asserts that for all members of the news team, *social* attractiveness is now more highly prized than is *physical* attractiveness. In comparing older, established anchors to more youthful, transient ones, he recounts that

during the 1970s there was a great deal of emphasis on the young, the handsome, the beautiful. But after a lot of moving around, by the end of the '70s it was very clear that the great strength of many stations was these old warhorses, because they were the true authority. They knew their markets, they were well identified in their markets, they had a self confidence on air and they could communicate about their markets as if they really knew and understood.[31]

Clearly, adds veteran news executive Mike Cavender, "On the outside you need an attractive communicator, an effective communicator. But the quality that [stars] share is when the camera goes on and they're telling you a story, that's exactly what they're doing. They're not reading script, they're not reciting from a TelePrompTer. They're telling you a story. That's what people like to hear."[32]

Media scholars Dennis Davis and Stanley Baran isolated this same key component two decades ago when they pointed out that

The informal or happy news format assures us that newscasters are friendly people, that the news genre is especially attractive to those viewers who want to frame the news as they would frame gossip. It assures them that they are getting the news straight from trustworthy friends, not from professional newspeople working for a remote bureaucracy.[33]

As long as the performers and studio set (see Figure 5-3) project the 'trustworthy friend' motif, striking handsomeness is no longer essential. "When television personalities are socially attractive and create the context for interaction, rewarding relationships develop," Professors Rebecca Rubin and Michael McHugh discovered. "This would suggest that viewers are more interested in television personalities who are attractive as social or work partners rather than physically attractive."[34] In his study of anchor longevity, researcher Mark Harmon similarly found that "Regular local television news viewers valued friendly anchors, anchors who were calm in a crisis, and anchors who were involved in the community."[35]

Social attributes probably are most valued over physical ones in the case of weatherpersons. As Elayne Rapping has observed:

Weather people are usually the homiest, wittiest . . . and most informal members of the news team. They are often loved by community members, who will choose a particular news station as much for the weatherperson as anything else. If there is no one at home to commiserate with about the eight days of rain we've just had; no one to complain to about having to cut the grass, miss the softball game, or whatever may happen, we've still got good old Bill What's His Name to share it with. He understands just how we feel. He too forgot his umbrella, or had to shovel his walk four times in one week.[36]

These social attributes are even more important than are the radar and graphic systems that outlets continuously promote. "You can have a weather department with every whiz-bang gizmo out there," says Bryan Busby, chairperson of the American Meteorological Society's Board of Broadcast Meteorology, "but if these guys and gals are perceived as stuffed shirts or not involved in the community, they're probably not going to be as successful as the weather department that came to my kid's school, or that I saw at the Rotary Club, or that hosted a telethon."[37]

Sportscasters also are expected to project more than stats and entertaining subject coverage, writes Professor Michael Seidel. To be successful, on-air sports talent "must perform services that go beyond analysis and amusement; they must, after a fashion, console. . . . You long for the familiar voice of the broadcaster to hint, even if merely by the

FIGURE 5-3
Today's news sets,
like the talent who
inhabit them, tend to
project comfortable,
social relationships.
(Photo courtesy of
Rees Associates, Inc.
Facility Design:
Rees Associates, Inc.
News Set Design:
G&G Designs/
Communications)

soothing assurance of the terms of his employment, that tomorrow is another day."[38]

In short, when it comes to judging on-air newspersons, be they anchors, reporters, weatherpersons, or sportscasters, the central critical standard seems to be whether the talent sympathetically can project a likeable competence that conveys a sense of *involved immediacy*:

It is happening NOW!
Our reporter and anchor friends are
    physically or electronically
    on-scene!
Via their pilotage, WE have been
    transported to experience the
    scene with them!

It is this excitement that makes electronic news different from and, in some people's minds, *superior* to the world of print. Radio learned the audience-holding advantage of involved immediacy as far back as the 1930s, and it is an advantage that on-stage news presenters are constantly striving to exploit.

The resulting reward for audiences (and benefit for the electronic media) has long been recognized by perceptive scholars—even those outside the communication discipline. Half a century ago, for example, aesthetics authority Theodore Meyer Greene fathomed that

in a written description of a contemporary event some time must necessarily elapse between actual occurrence of the event described and its verbal portrayal, and an additional period of time must elapse between the writing of the text and its perusal by the reader. From the reader's point of view, the historical present, as portrayed, has already been pushed back twice over into the historical past, whereas the radio announcer can not only describe what is occurring in his own present, but is able to convey to the listener a vivid sense of actual participation in events which are just as contemporaneous to him.[39]

This vivid sense is all a veneer, of course, if the news staff are not skilled and responsible enough journalists to be capable of comprehensively gathering and accurately weighing relevant information. (See the script of *The Newsroom* in Appendix A for a particularly sardonic vision of news style over substance.) "Listen closely while I let you in on a fraternal secret," whispers former FCC Chairman Alfred Sikes. "Nothing is easier for a public official than bamboozling journalists who don't do their homework, who haven't taken the trouble to master the area on which they've been charged to inform the public."[40] "Ultimately," concludes professor and veteran television newsperson Dow Smith, "reporting skill impacts how well a journalist survives over the years."[41]

Regardless of the delivery system, or the comely or friendly demeanor of the presenter, a foundation of this reporting skill must be effective *writing*. In her study of the attitudes of almost two hundred successful journalists, Judy Polumbaum found a universal belief that writing "remains an imperative skill for all types of media. Even on-line editors who saw digital media as the wave of the future, offering superior delivery and greater accessibility, also made the point that accurate, credible, well-written content remains the key."[42] The capacity of the medium, and the presentational capability of the on-air or on-line talent, are both wasted if the news message they convey is hobbled with jumbled or vacuous prose.

Other Television Personalities

We cannot conclude our scrutiny of the on-stage talent ingredient without an examination of game show hosts and television actors.

Our discussion of game show hosts can be brief—not because there is any shortage of such positions but because the characteristics by which they are critiqued are similar to standards used to evaluate radio talent and news personnel. Thus, contest mentors also must establish a strong sense of friendly communication. In their case, however, this

communication must be attained not only with the at-home viewer, but with on-stage contestants and a studio audience as well.

Game show hosts also must insinuate themselves into the program's fabric and pacing so that context and coordinator accelerate in tandem toward whatever installment climax the game's format entails. These personally winsome M.C.s therefore control the tempo of the game by regulating contestant responses. Above all, they strive to bring that same sense of involved immediacy to their televised tournaments as anchors and reporters inject in their newscasts—and for the same audience-holding reasons. In his review of the immensely popular *Wheel of Fortune, TV Guide*'s Merrill Panitt isolated what he believed to be the perfect attributes for a game show ringmaster when he reported:

> The host is Pat Sajak, a former television weatherman and public-affairs show moderator. A smooth operator, he is pleasant enough, asks the contestants where they're from and what they do without getting in the way of the game. . . . As game-show hosts go, he's as good as they come and well worth the half million a year he is paid.[43]

Sajak later tried his hand as a CBS late-night talk show host—a seemingly similar situation, but one, as he found, in which the central performer must be always prepared to take center stage. When a talk show lags, there are no spinning wheels or neon game boards to pick up the slack. Conversely, *Who Wants to be a Millionaire*'s host Regis Philbin cut his teeth on talk shows before making the shift to the game show world. Despite *Millionaire*'s comparatively minimal set, his previous experience allowed him to successfully carry the contest without appearing to dominate the contestants.

Some television actors can command a good deal more in salary than even a premier game show host like Sajak and Philbin. And actors, unlike game show hosts, don't have to complete multiple episodes in a single shooting day! Still, while the salaries and working conditions may vary, *visual impact* (not necessarily physical beauty) remains of significant importance to actors, contest conductors, and newscasters alike. For actors, the key to this visual impact is emotional and physical believability in terms of the role to be played. Veteran actor Lane Smith, who portrayed Richard Nixon in ABC's *The Final Days*, found that in pursuing this credibility, his back and neck suffered from the continuous hunching of his shoulders for the six weeks of production. "Just doing Nixon's mannerisms," mused Smith, "has enabled me to see how uptight and knotted he must have been."[44]

This sometimes painful attention to detail is much more essential on television than in the theater. The intimate nature of the camera magnifies any awkward contrivance and exposes any slip of characterization. Under such a microscope, wrote Russian filmmaker V. I. Pudovkin, performers would do well "to exercise the finest shading of voice and gesture."[45]

As a film *creator*, Pudovkin's comments have a great deal of relevance to television. For the *actor*, however, there are some differences between the two media. The late actor/director John Houseman, who worked in both, discovered that

television puts more emphasis on the spoken word; it lessens the importance and effectiveness of the reaction shot, which is the most basic element of most film performances; it encourages a more naturalistic mode of acting; its emotional curves tend to be shorter, intended for a more direct and immediate effect on the viewer.[46]

To involve viewers in the doings on the small screen, and to involve them in spite of the distractions of their surroundings and the comparative brevity of most television program segments, presents a tremendous focusing challenge for actors. As media scholar Horace Newcomb observes, "even when landscape and chase become part of the plot, our attention is drawn to the intensely individual problems encountered, and the central issue becomes the relationship among individuals."[47] *X-Files* creator Chris Carter appreciates and revels in this TV challenge because he has found that there "are things that don't work in movies, a kind of exploration of character and stories about small things. . . . The small human stories; on television you can tell those stories. They're beautiful stories—and actually they're extremely important to us and worth telling—but somehow they don't make it to the big screen."[48]

"But paradoxically," add researchers Margaret Duncan and Barry Brummett,

the small screen and limited amount of information would be boring if a still, small face were all that was portrayed. So television must animate its people even as it favors people over action. . . . Television dramas of war will keep turning from vast battle scenes to the worried faces of individual soldiers. Now, a worried, sweaty face on . . . a film screen would be overwhelming. Every unsightly pore and blemish would be visible. But television, because of its small size, is paradoxically able to offer intimate close-ups of actors and to give those actors primacy over other aspects of the drama.[49]

Under such conditions, performer believability becomes a function of not just physical appearance, but also of concentration and controlled nonverbal embellishment.

Concentration is an inherent part of any actor's trade that must be especially tightened in television. Director George Schaefer, for instance, knows that theatrical actors communicate *beyond* the footlights to generate and monitor unanimity of reaction on the part of their audience. In creating television, conversely, Schaefer finds he must convince his actors to ignore what's out there in the darkness if they are to sculpt their performances properly.[50]

Even in the case of live-studio-audience situation comedies, performers cannot play *to* that audience but can only use it as a partial guide in deriving the timing of their delivery for the camera. Add to this the breakneck production schedule of television as opposed to film or stage work, and it becomes clear how rigorously distilled the process of video acting must be. "You don't have time to do your scenes," complains veteran series actor (*Dynasty, The Colbys*) Ken Howard. "You have to be ready in two takes. That can be an incredible burden. I think many good feature-film actors would be crushed on TV."[51] Yet, versatile actress Tracey Ullman prefers television for this very reason: "Film is so slow. It takes three hours to set up a 2-shot. I lose my energy. TV is much more rapid where you can keep your focus."[52]

Nevertheless, a number of major cinematic stars have flopped in the video environment, bolstering the Hollywood adage that 'TV makes stars, but stars don't make TV.' The theory, according to industry observers Mark Christensen and Cameron

Stauth, is that "the twenty-one-inch tube humbled major entertainment deities, just as the large movie screen exploited their glory to its fullest. The small screen thrust actors into a format that rewarded performers the audience felt intimate with, and punished those the audience felt in awe of."[53] (How similar this seems to the way television news personalities are now appraised.)

Controlled nonverbal embellishment, the third component of believability in television acting, is, in a sense, the creation as well as the requisite of video performance. "Until the advent of modern visual and aural recording techniques," suggests John Cawelti, "these [nonverbal] aspects of performance were largely ephemeral. . . . Now, however, performances can be recorded, filmed or taped. Thus, modern communications technology has given the nonverbal aspects of performance an even greater importance."[54]

Though more highly theoretical, the principles of modern Gestalt psychology also help undergird this attention to nonverbal detail. The Gestalt hypothesis, explains Rudolf Arnheim, "means that if the forces that determine bodily behavior are structurally similar to those that characterize the corresponding mental states, it may become understandable why psychical meaning can be read off directly from a person's appearance and conduct."[55] (Recall Lane Smith's earlier comments about what he learned from physically mirroring Richard Nixon.) Whether this Gestalt is fully recognized by television audiences, it is true that the time-constricted productions for the small screen exploit every visual cue they can—even the most intimate—to quickly register and develop a sense of character. The Gestalt of actor believability in the visual medium, in summary, is an interwoven combination of physical appearance, mental concentration, and controlled nonverbal enrichment.

AN ON-STAGE CURTAIN LINE

Throughout our discussion of electronic media performers, two essential criteria for success have constantly surfaced: *intimacy* and *intensity*. Electronic media are in constant and close proximity to the public. People share their cars, their bedrooms, and (in the case of personal media like The Walkman) their very bodies. It is inevitable, then, that the performers who communicate with consumers through these media must generate warm and enveloping recognition if they are to secure favorable responses. "Ours is a business of ratings," radio talk show host Phil Tower reminds us, "and if more people choose your station [or your program] because they feel a kinship with you, then ultimately your position in that market is strengthened because of the bond you have forged between your station and its listeners."[56]

As we have discovered, however, it takes immense skill and effort for performers to achieve pleasing intimacy and focused intensity, to be able to turn a performance on or off at the flick of a switch. Being a "talent" in our profession is anything but easy, although it must *seem* easy if listeners and viewers are to respond favorably.

This projection of ease is especially important to the video talk show host, a role that amalgamates all of the talent attributes we have heretofore discussed. These socially attractive performers can appear passionate about the subject or guest being featured, but they still must be in control of the topic, the situation, and their own nonverbal reaction to it. The audience must believe that the host has just strolled on camera for a spontaneous chat, despite the hours of prepreparation and on-air concentration that go into construction of this spontaneity. And, points out Jim Paratore, president of Telepictures Productions, "for talk/variety and softer forms, the softer the show, the stronger the host has to be."[57] Hard or soft, television hosts, like their radio counterparts, become ratings-successful because they industriously cajole audiences into enjoying them even when audience and host opinions clash. They are like that expansive person at the end of the bar or the adjacent health club machine whom you always disagree with—but genuinely yearn for when he or she isn't around.

Whether it's video talk or any of the other electronic performance venues just discussed, serving as "talent" is usually laborious and sometimes demeaning—as humorist Dave Barry discovered. Asked to host a television series, Barry responded:

"Sounds like fun." And thus I became a talent. That's what TV people call you if you go in front of the camera: a "talent." They call you that right to your face. Only after a while you realize they don't mean that you have any actual *talent*. In fact, it's sort of an insult. In the TV business, "talent" means "not the camera, lighting or sound people, all of whom will do exactly what they're supposed to do every single time, but the bonehead with the pancake makeup who will make us all stay in the studio for two extra hours because he cannot remember that he is supposed to say 'See you next *time*' instead of 'See you next *week*.' " It reminds me of the way people in the computer industry use the word "user," which to them means "idiot."

When you are a TV talent, you are meat. People are always straightening your collar, smearing things on your face, and talking about you in the third person, saying things like: "What if we had him sitting down?" and "Can we make his face look less round?" and "Can we do anything about his nose?"[58]

Glamourous? Hardly. But a brutally accurate depiction of what it's usually like to be a "talent." Whether one becomes a performer or works in some other aspect of the electronic media, success as a professional requires the recognition that on-stage talent, like music, is no more than an *ingredient* of a production. It cannot be an enterprise unto itself. Veteran television actor Peter Michael Goetz puts electronic media performing in realistic perspective when he muses:

If nothing else, there is a certain satisfaction in hitting the exact marks, remembering the precise moment we put the cigarette to our lips for continuity, maintaining the eight-foot distance between the car we are driving and the camera truck, being aware of holding our posture so we don't shadow our fellow actors, not being distracted by the maneuvering crew, and somehow even managing to remember our lines.[59]

ENDNOTES

1. DeWitt Parker, *The Principles of Aesthetics*, 2nd ed. (Westport, CT: Greenwood Press, 1976), 143.
2. Roy Dickinson Welch, "A Discussion of the Expressed Content of Beethoven's Third Symphony," in Theodore Meyer Greene, *The Arts and the Art of Criticism* (Princeton, NJ: Princeton University Press, 1952), 488.
3. William Allman, "The Musical Brain," *U.S. News and World Report* (June 11, 1990), 56.
4. Greene, 322.
5. Skip Pizzi, "Deep Impact," *BE Radio* (July 1998), 6.
6. Piper Stevenson, "What About Art?" *Recording Engineer/Producer* (June 1990), 10.
7. David Altheide and Robert Snow, *Media Logic* (Beverly Hills, CA: Sage, 1979), 29.
8. Samuel Singer, *Reviewing the Performing Arts* (New York: Richards Rosen Press, 1974), 126.
9. Stevenson, 10.
10. Parker, *Principles*, 146.
11. "Melange," *Chronicle of Higher Education* (January 27, 1993), B2.
12. Charles Turner, "Music Videos and the Iconic Data Base," in Gary Gumpert and Robert Cathcart (eds.), *Intermedia*, 3rd ed. (New York: Oxford University Press, 1986), 382.
13. Kenneth Turan, "How to Tell TV's Good Videos from the Bad Ones," *TV Guide* (August 10, 1985), 14.
14. Allman, 60.
15. Roger Sessions, "The Composer and His Message," in Melvin Rader (ed.), *A Modern Book of Esthetics*, 5th ed. (New York: Holt, Rinehart and Winston, 1979), 255.
16. Altheide and Snow, 25–26.
17. Kathleen Turner and Raymond Sprague, "Musical and Visual Invention in *Miami Vice*: Old Genre, New Form," in Leah Vande Berg and Lawrence Wenner (eds.), *Television Criticism: Approaches and Applications* (New York: Longman, 1991), 280.
18. Rudolf Arnheim, *Visual Thinking* (Berkeley: University of California Press, 1969), 2.
19. Plato, *The Republic*, trans. by Francis Cornford (New York: Oxford University Press, 1950), 88.
20. Ibid., 86.
21. Tom Shales, " 'Year': Tried and True Charms," *Washington Post* (December 15, 1986), D1.
22. "Cheers 'N' Jeers," *TV Guide* (July 2, 1988), 23.
23. Irving Rein and Craig Springer, "Where's the Music? The Problems of Lyric Analysis," *Critical Studies in Mass Communication* (June 1986), 253–254.
24. Parker, *Principles*, 143.
25. Turan, 12.
26. Tim Moore, "Producing the Image." Speech presented at the Great Lakes Radio Conference, April 25, 1981 (Mt. Pleasant, MI).
27. Patty Williamson, in Peter Orlik, *The Electronic Media: an Introduction to the Profession*, 2nd ed. (Ames: Iowa State University Press, 1997), 398.
28. Tyree Ford, writing in "Monday Memo," *Broadcasting* (May 11, 1987), 18.
29. DeWitt Parker, *The Analysis of Art* (New Haven, CT: Yale University Press, 1926), 21.
30. Erika Engstrom and Anthony Ferri, "From Barriers to Challenges: Career Perceptions of Women TV News Anchors," *Journalism &*

Mass Communication Quarterly (Winter 1998), 798–799.

31. Doug Hill, "Where Hal Wanzer Is Bigger Than Dan Rather," *TV Guide* (February 13, 1988), 27.

32. Shawn O'Malley, "Star Qualities: How to Spot a Potential Anchor in the Newsroom," *Communicator* (April 1998), 44.

33. Dennis Davis and Stanley Baran, *Mass Communication and Everyday Life* (Belmont, CA: Wadsworth, 1981), 100.

34. Rebecca Rubin and Michael McHugh, "Development of Parasocial Interaction Relationships," *Journal of Broadcasting and Electronic Media* (Summer 1987), 288.

35. Mark Harmon, "Television News Anchor Longevity, Name Recall, Parasocial Interaction, and Paracommunity Orientation," *Feedback* (Spring 1997), 7.

36. Elayne Rapping, *The Looking Glass World of Nonfiction TV* (Boston: South End Press, 1987), 58–59.

37. Andrew Bowser, "Weather Fronts Local News," *Broadcasting & Cable* (October 27, 1997), 66.

38. Michael Seidel, "Field and Screen: Baseball and Television," in Kathleen Henderson and Joseph Mazzeo (eds.), *Meanings of the Medium* (New York: Praeger, 1990), 53.

39. Greene, 187.

40. Alfred Sykes, "The Eight Blindspots of TV News Have Left Us Poorly Informed," *Broadcasting* (May 11, 1992), 63.

41. Dan Trigoboff, "The Gender Trap," *Broadcasting & Cable* (April 5, 1999), 25.

42. Judy Polumbaum, "The School-Workplace Partnership and Conversations in Cyberspace," *Journalism & Mass Communication Educator* (Summer 1999), 79.

43. Merrill Panitt, "Wheel of Fortune," *TV Guide* (October 5, 1985), 1.

44. Michael Leahy, "The Nixon Drama Revisited—Has TV Got It Right?" *TV Guide* (October 28, 1989), 2.

45. V. I. Pudovkin, *Film Production and Film Acting* (New York: Grove Press, 1970), 234.

46. John Houseman, "Is TV-Acting Inferior?" *TV Guide* (September 1, 1979), 25.

47. Horace Newcomb, *TV: The Most Popular Art* (Garden City, NY: Anchor Books, 1974), 249.

48. Cynthia Littleton, "Chris Carter: Serial Thriller," *Broadcasting & Cable* (July 26, 1996), 23.

49. Margaret Duncan and Barry Brummett, "The Mediation of Spectator Sport," in Vande Berg and Wenner, 377.

50. George Schaefer, comments in *Television Makers*, Newton E. Meltzer-produced televised PBS documentary, 1986.

51. Ken Howard, "Why I Left Prime-Time TV for Harvard," *TV Guide* (February 21, 1987), 6.

52. Tracey Ullman, presentation to the National Association of Television Program Executives Convention, January 16, 1997 (New Orleans).

53. Mark Christensen and Cameron Stauth, *The Sweeps* (New York: Bantam Books, 1985), 129.

54. John Cawelti, "With the Benefit of Hindsight: Popular Culture Criticism," *Critical Studies in Mass Communication* (December 1985), 370.

55. Rudolf Arnheim, *Toward a Psychology of Art* (Berkeley: University of California Press, 1967), 58.

56. Phil Tower, in Peter Orlik, *The Electronic Media: An Introduction to the Profession* (Boston: Allyn and Bacon, 1992), 282.

57. David Tobenkin, "Why We Like to Watch Talk TV," *Broadcasting & Cable* (September 28, 1998), 33.

58. Dave Barry, *Dave Barry's Greatest Hits* (New York: Ballantine Books, 1988), 136–137.

59. Peter Michael Goetz, in Orlik, 2nd ed., 433.

6 Stage-Molding Ingredients

The ingredients of the previous chapter—music and talent—are understood by the audience only after they have been filtered through microphone and camera. These technical instruments are the shapers of the audio/visual stage. What the camera sees or the microphone detects is what determines the width, height, and depth of the electronic proscenium (active stage area). This chapter examines these productional properties in detail, beginning with the subject of sound.

AURAL TRANSITIONS AND VOLUME

On radio, how we shift from one sound to another is as important in directing and maintaining audience attention as is shot sequencing in television. A pause between sound elements can create suspense. But too long a pause, or one inappropriately placed, will be perceived as "dead air." This is a blatant invitation to listener tune out or 'punch-thru' to another station. Conversely, a seamless replacement of one aural element with the next may propel the hearer effortlessly along with the flow. But any clash of musical keys or talent voice qualities becomes much more jarring because of this proximity. Fading in one event while fading out another may help redirect audience attention. But the midpoint of this gradation may constitute a listener-disorienting moment in which nothing is distinct.

In short, aural transitions, like visual shot changes, carry both communicative potential and communicative risk. In every audio situation, there are one optimal and several increasingly less advantageous transition choices. The following Mercury Paint radio script, for instance, suggests a number of potent sound elements to enhance the selling picture. For the bulk of the commercial, however, the specific way in which these sounds are to be interwoven with words—the actual transition blueprint—is left up to the expertise of the spot's producer, Chuck Blore & Don Richman Inc. Exactly how and when might that producer insert and delete each sound element called for in the script?

ANNCR: Picture this. A church, hidden down in the valley, where good people go to pray. The color's gone away,
(SFX: RUSTY GATE GROAN FEATURE UNDER NEXT LINE)
ANNCR: the gate is rusting and the bells are peeling. Your job is to dress the church in its Sunday best. And you can do it, with Mercury Paints.
(SFX: FEATURE PAINT CAN BEING OPENED)
ANNCR: Spread it around.
(MUSIC: LOVELY, LIQUID MUSICAL SIMULATION OF A PAINT BRUSH, PAINTING, LITTLE BY LITTLE THROUGHOUT THE REST OF THE SPOT. WE HEAR THE CHURCH COME TO LIFE --- A CHOIR, BELLS, ORGAN, ETC.)
ANNCR: Mercury's been mixin' paints in Michigan longer than church mice have been playing steeple chase. Mercury Paint is made right. Mercury Paint is made right here in Michigan by people who know how to make paint and weather mix. Lord, look at that church. Makes you think you've died and gone to Heaven, doesn't it? Mercury Paints --- like that. Mercury Paints don't cost much at all, and you can get them at all Mercury Paint Stores. They've got all the stuff you need, and they really know their stuff. Mercury

Paints; the paints the professionals use.

(Courtesy of Chuck Blore & Don Richman Incorporated)

To help answer this question, let's define the terminology options available. Sound effects and music are most often instructed to FADE IN or FADE OUT when respectively introduced and removed from the scene. Sound effects and music that are *already present* in the scene may be requested to FADE UP or FADE DOWN in order to enlarge or diminish their part in the total sound picture. We can also use refinements to these general directions, such as ESTABLISH, SNEAK IN/ SNEAK OUT, FEATURE/FEATURE BRIEFLY, or call on hybrid transitions such as FADE UP AND OUT, FADE DOWN AND UNDER, FADE UP AND UNDER, and FADE DOWN AND OUT. We might, in addition, CROSSFADE one music or sound-effect cue to another by *overlapping* the receding element with the incoming source. When both elements are musical in nature, the CROSSFADE is also known as a SEGUE. Now, as an exercise, select from these options to rewrite the Mercury Paint spot's body and conclusion. Do this by interweaving the sound elements clustered in the MUSIC directions block with the copy lines that follow it. Don't forget to indicate where each element enters, how it enters, with what (if any) other elements it is sharing the sound stage, and when and how it exits.

In recent years, audio transitions have taken on greater importance in television as well. It used to be assumed that sound and picture were always faded in and faded out in tandem. But now, producers of dramatic programs sometimes stagger their entry to simulate certain physiological or psychological effects. In its pioneering way, the audio of a *Hill Street Blues* roll call, for instance, typically preceded any visual cue save for a digitalized time indication on a black screen. It was as though we were waking up to the situation, with our ears generally anticipating our eyes in the inadvertent return to consciousness. Similarly, the killing of audio at the end of a newscast while the anchors are still seen conversing seems to suggest that they continue on in their duties even though their sharing with us is temporarily suspended.

Herbert Zettl points out that sound serves three important functions for television: "(1) to supply essential or additional information, (2) to establish mood and aesthetic energy, and (3) to supplement the rhythmic structure of the screen event."[1] Thus, the audio is much more than a bit player to the video's discourse. In fact, Rick Altman maintains that the television soundtrack actually dominates the picture by determining what we choose to look at on the screen. Unlike cinema, the television event exists amidst a myriad of household distractions. The audio thus must both fill in the gaps and lure the *listener* to resume *viewer* status. "The sound," says Altman, "serves a value-laden editing function, identifying better than the image itself the parts of the image that are sufficiently spectacular to merit closer attention by the intermittent viewer."[2]

This is not to suggest that television uses blaring volume to grab our attention back to the screen. That would only encourage viewers to turn down the sound, push the "mute" button, change the channel, or leave the room. Nor can television (or on-line video) subsist with an artificially low volume for long and continue to hold audience attention. Instead, video volume is a relatively level phenomenon, directing in-and-out-of-eye-shot consumers to what mood or subject is important at the moment.

In radio, however, varied volume serves a crucial spotlighting function. Without access to television's close-ups and long shots, radio must manipulate sound intensity to bring us toward or away from the objects of its attention. Gradations in volume are what plot out the action on the radio stage and permit the easily followed shift from one aural scene to the next. This is as true for music or sound effects as it is for words. A fade-out allows one tune to recede while a fade-in rotates the next to the center of our perception like the shift of scenery on a revolving stage. Different formats spin this stage at different speeds, but volume's objective of simultaneously holding and redirecting listener attention is always the same.

THE VIDEO STAGE

As just mentioned, while radio must rely solely on volume manipulation, television can use a number of visual mechanisms to focus audience perception. Shot changes are just one of these. In fact, hundreds of books and articles have been written about the small screen's visual grammar and the wealth of technological devices on which this grammar is built.

We need not all be productional experts. But as competent professionals, we should be familiar enough with the basic sets of visual tools that we can critically detect their use or misuse, their absence or overemphasis, in the video projects with which we are associated.

LIGHT AND SHADOW

Light and shadow are the most primary of television's implements. Without light, we can have no picture. In one sense, then, we can consider light to be just a basic commodity for proper functioning of our cameras. Herbert Zettl refers to this property of lighting as *Notan*, or "lighting for simple visibility. Flat lighting has no particular aesthetic function; its basic function is that of illumination. Flat lighting is emotionally flat, too."[3] Obviously, a solely Notan approach would allow lighting to play only a passive and objective role in a production. Other on-stage and stage-molding elements would have to assume the entire burden of establishing meaning and mood. Further, a lighting design that is exclusively Notan reinforces the two-dimensionality of the video screen, forcing characters and camera shot selection to do all the work of scene sculpting and emphasis.

Fortunately, *chiaroscuro* lighting is also available. Chiaroscuro is concerned not only with simple illumination but also with how light can determine and contrast with shadow. With chiaroscuro, says Zettl, "the basic aim is to articulate space . . . to clarify and intensify the three-dimensional property of things and the space that surrounds them, to give the scene an expressive quality."[4] In the hands of a competent lighting director, chiaroscuro converts illumination into a key element for pictorial composition and enhancement of the mood most appropriate to the program's or commercial's goals. It thus capitalizes on the psychological properties of light and dark, which aesthetician DeWitt Parker compares in these terms:

We know that light has a direct quickening and darkness a direct quieting effect upon mental processes; that in the light men feel relatively secure and at home, while in the dark they are uneasy and afraid; and we know that these feelings vary with the intensity of light or darkness and the time of day.[5]

We can illustrate the discriminating importance of lighting and shadow by examining the Figure 6-1 television commercial that actually promotes illumination's attainment.

After a dim, spooky exterior shot in frame 1, we find the same foreboding chiaroscuro shadows dominating the interior of the cabin, virtually swallowing up the actors in frames 2–5. The momentary contrast of comforting light in frame 6 is only the harbinger of disaster as the overheated bulb plunges our heroes into total and terrifying darkness in frame 7. Then, the illuminative dominance of the Philips light bulb takes over the foreground in frames 8 and 9 to bring a positive reassurance to our—if not the two men's—experience. Were frames 2–5 more fully illuminated (Notan-lit), however, the pseudosinister build-up to the product demonstration/solution would have lacked comparative punch.

Whether working on a commercial, newscast, or entertainment program, it is the lighting director's task "to create imagery through the use of light," says lighting director Bill Holshevnikoff. "Does the feel of the lighting match the mood of the scene or program? Is the quality of the light (hard light vs. soft light) appropriate for the piece? Do the subject and background lighting feel balanced and appropriate? These are the types of questions that go through my mind on every job."[6] When these questions are answered correctly, the viewer is led to assimilate the desired subject and mood without any attention being called to lighting's fundamental contribution.

We cannot leave the subject of lighting without mentioning the more abstract concept of the TV (or computer) screen itself as the source of illumination. Video artist Frank Gillette has pointed out that with television, "you look *into* the source of light, with film you look *with* the source of light. In television, the source of light and the source of information are one."[7] Because of this, infers Peter Crown, sitting in front of a TV set is like sitting in front of a fireplace, and "television's hypnotic effect can create a strange rapport between viewer and screen that is totally unrelated to program content."[8] Certainly, the average viewer will find little reason to explore (or even detect) this speculative prop-

(SFX: GROWLING/RUSTLING NOISES)

1st MAN: What was that?

2nd MAN: The Boogie Man...from the Black Lagoon!

1st MAN: There's something out there.

2nd MAN: Don't worry. As long as the lights are on, we're fine.

(SFX: LIGHT BULB BLOWS)

1st MAN: What do we do now?
(SFX: GROWLING NOISE)
2nd MAN: Run for your life!

ANNCR (VO): It's time to change your light bulb.

Philips Longer Life square bulbs last 33% longer than ordinary round bulbs.

FIGURE 6-1
Lighting to sell lighting. (Courtesy of Arthur Bijur, DFS-Dorland)

erty. But it is an interesting theory for media professionals to consider when thinking about lighting's importance.

HORIZONTAL AND VERTICAL CAMERA PLANES

Video's second stage-molding ingredient consists of the horizontal and vertical camera planes. Because both of these planes are a function of television shots, we first must establish just what a *shot* is.

The Shot Defined

In 1935, film student Raymond Spottis-woode defined a shot as "a portion of film portraying physical objects without visible spatial or temporal discontinuity."[9] Obviously, Spottiswoode's definition poses some problems for us. For one thing, we are concerned with *video* instead of (or in addition to) "film." The greater difficulty with his statement, however, relates to the idea of "spatial discontinuity." Through rapid panning, tilting, or other motions, for instance, today's techniques allow us to achieve spatial discontinuity within the fabric of a single shot.

What can be salvaged from the Spottiswoode definition is the concept of *temporal continuity*. In a single shot, in other words, the continuousness of the camera's viewpoint is not interrupted. Therefore, a more contemporary and usable definition of *shot* for our purposes was proposed in 1987 by Gorham Kindem. He signifies shots as "continuous recordings of actions within a scene made by a single camera."[10]

Horizontal Camera Plane

The term *horizontal camera plane* essentially identifies a given shot's optical span, ranging from the almost microscopic intimacy of the extreme close-up (ECU) to the broad cover shot (CS) or full shot (FS) that surveys the entire scene. In between, as illustrated on the continuum in Figure 6-2, we find several other gradations. Researcher Maria Grabe found that most authorities in the field support the general principle that "the close-up shot commands attention and establishes emotional closeness between television content and viewers, whereas the long shot encourages a certain level of distance and detachment between content and viewers."[11]

Long shots (LS), alternatively identified as *wide* shots (WS) may also, in shooting interior scenes, be interchangeably referred to as *full* shots. (That's right—three different terms for what might be the same vantage point!) In any event, such shots show a character from head to toe, if not an entire scenic stage. Medium shots (MS) can also vary widely depending on the scope of the scene. But in television, they are generally thought of as framing only the upper two-thirds of a standing character with minimal additional revelation of the set behind.

When two or three characters are featured, a medium two-shot (M2S) or medium three-shot (M3S) can be specified. For more definitive designation, the terms *medium long shot* (MLS) and *medium close-up* (MCU) signify each end of the medium shot spectrum. Finally, in the close-up (CU), the specific character or prop fills most of the screen so that, for example, only the head and shoulders of a person is seen. The extension of this, the extreme close-up (ECU) gets in even tighter to devote the entire frame to a nose, mouth, or hand.

To illustrate some of these horizontal camera plane variations further, look again at the Philips commercial in Figure 6-1. Frame 1 is a cover/full shot, frames 2, 3, 5, and 6 are medium two-shots, and frames 4, 8, and 9 are close-ups. (Frame 7 is whatever the viewer conceives it to be, thereby adding to audience involvement in the story-building.)

As Wurtzel and Dominick tell us, this battery of shot types ensures that "the viewer, as represented by the camera, does not remain in one viewing position. He sees the action from both close-range and at a distance, depending on the director."[12] The director's main concern in this regard, maintains Robert Williams, is

how to maximize attention and minimize interference. . . . He is the person who selects the type of shot to which the viewer will be exposed. He may select a close-up which may or may not direct attention. Another possibility is that he may select a loose-shot which may expose extraneous objects or materials to the viewers. This may prove to be a distraction which would serve as interference since the audience would then be required to select and evaluate the entire body of information presented to it.[13]

What viewers are allowed to see and what they are visually prohibited or discouraged from seeing are crucial determiners of the involvement viewers feel with a developing television narrative and the meaning they attach to that narrative. In his book, *Interviews with Film Directors*, critic Andrew Sarris gives this illustration:

If the story of Little Red Riding Hood is told with the Wolf in close-up and Little Red Riding Hood in long-shot, the director is con-

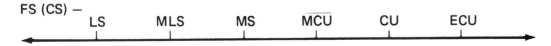

FS (CS) — LS   MLS   MS   MCU   CU   ECU

FIGURE 6-2
The TV Horizontal Plane Continuum.

cerned primarily with the emotional problems of a wolf with a compunction to eat little girls. If Little Red Riding Hood is in close-up and the Wolf is in long-shot, the emphasis is shifted to the emotional problems of vestigial virginity in a wicked world. Thus, two different stories are being told with the same anecdotal material.

Figure 6-3's visual excerpt from a Dr Pepper commercial shows how further refinements in shot framing and character stance can create yet a third twist on the story.

Usually, it is neither essential nor desirable that television's horizontal camera plane shows an audience the whole scene. "Early television mindlessly replicated the depth of space common to a stage play or Renaissance painting," Professor David Miles points out, "rather than taking advantage of its small cube."[14] Such productions therefore lacked the living room (and bedroom) intimacy that the medium later learned to exploit. Even when a full shot *is* used, the viewer is incapa-

ble of perceiving the scene in its entirety; this is a fact that visual artists long have understood. "Literally one can never see the whole picture in all its detail in focus at one time," writes art scholar Stephen Pepper. "But one can feel the whole picture in all its detail in a funded consciousness with certain details in clear focus and the rest fused into these as memories of their character and interrelationships."[15] By encouraging this active and immediate memory-building, a skilled director facilitates more in-depth viewer participation. In the words of respected television analyst Gilbert Seldes, "It is the *mind*, not the eye that creates long shots and medium shots and closeups; and the well-handled camera satisfies us by being true to our thoughts and, when it acts for the heart, to our desires."[16]

Vertical Camera Plane

Especially within the fabric of the horizontal camera plane's tighter (closer) shots, the *ver-*

FIGURE 6-3
Dr Pepper inverted the Little Red Riding Hood legend to promote its sugar-free soft drink. Taken in isolation, what is the implication of this visual point of view? What meaning is the horizontal camera plane suggesting here? (Courtesy of Lee Kovel, Young & Rubicam/New York)

LITTLE RED
Product: SUGAR FREE DR PEPPER

tical camera plane gives the viewer the feeling of looking up at, or down on, a character or object. Most but not all authorities believe these angles thereby confer attributes of dominance or submissiveness on the featured subject. Pioneered in film, this technique is explained by film scholar Donald Livingston:

The angle of a shot has a marked influence on the audience's psychological reaction to the subject matter photographed. As demonstrated in *The Fallen Idol*, angles shooting upward cause the subject matter to appear stronger, more powerful than the audience. Angles shooting downward give the audience a feeling of strength and make the subject appear weaker.[17]

This vertical plane assertion has never been unequivocally proven by communication researchers and is subject to qualifications. McCain, Chilberg, and Wakshlag, for example, found that "high and low angle shots have different effects depending on how they are employed in the context of a sequence of shots."[18] Nonetheless, these researchers did conclude that if the viewer *does* infer dominance from camera angle, a negative implication may result:

A camera shooting upward toward a televised or film performer may increase the perceived power that he or she has over individual audience members. Camera angles which present figures to receivers as bigger than life and wielding some sort of dominance over them are not the types of people with whom audiences can easily relate.[19]

In other words, assuming that upward angles (called *low angle shots*) do confer dominance, viewers may be turned off to the characters so shown. This may be an appropriate reaction to stimulate in the portrayal of fictional villains, but it is not the attitude a station would want directed at its news team. Friendliness (recall our Chapter 5 discussion) and dominance don't mix; so low-angle views of electronic reporters are studiously avoided.

SPATIAL MOBILITY

Because television viewers cannot physically 'move around' in the picture-tube field, our third television stage-molding ingredient, *spatial mobility*, must simulate this effect on the viewer's behalf. Spatial mobility can be achieved by any of three methods: lens motion, camera-head motion, and camera base movement.

Lens Motion

The chief lens motion facilitator is the *zoom*. A zoom lens is a lens whose focal length can be changed during use. Thus, our point of view can be seamlessly propelled from a broad-angle view (up close) to a telephoto view (far away). Such zooming does distort perspective, of course, making for an unnatural change in viewer orientation. Because telephoto (zoom in) shots compress perspective, and broad-angle (zoom out) shots stretch perspective, even a slow-speed zoom can make us feel as though we are being respectively hurled into, or yanked out of, the scene. There seems nothing voluntary about the zoom. We get where we are going—or more precisely, where the director dispatches us. But the ride is not always pleasant. The zoom seems to *force*, rather than *entice* us in or out.

Zooms are not all bad, of course. News actuality and sports coverage (not to mention treasured moments captured by the family camcorder) would be more limited if the camera had to physically move so rapidly over distance. Particularly in the case of prescripted programming and commercials, however, the *lens motion* option should be approached gingerly, lest we seem to grab viewers by the collars and hurl them about.

Camera-Head Motion

With camera-head motion, the base of the camera remains stationary while the actual camera changes orientation on top of this mounting. This motion is analogous to a person standing in one place but changing the position of his or her head to see in different directions and heights. Camera-head motion encompasses both horizontal and vertical plane options.

Panning is camera-head motion on the horizontal plane. The camera is turned left or right to follow an action or provide a *pan*oramic view across a scene. Because the base of the camera does not move, the panning procedure changes the angle of view on our subject in the same way that angle is impacted when our eyes pan back and forth across a football field or race track. We can stay with the action but do not substantially alter our distance from it.

Tilting and *pedding* constitute camera-head motion on the vertical plane. If you focus on an object and raise or lower your head, you are performing the same function as a camera tilt. Some of the same potential vertical plane implications of dominance and submissiveness apply here. We tend to be in awe of a figure or edifice that we have to tilt up to scan but are casual or even condescending to a subject we must tilt down to view. Pedding (pedestaling), by comparison, involves raising or lowering the entire camera on its mounting 'tube' without changing its base location. This is akin to the perspective we get when we stand on tiptoe or squat down to see an object without raising or lowering our heads. We see different parts of the subject but at a constant, level angle that is less likely to trigger the implicit psychological cues occurring with panning and tilting.

Camera-Base Movement

When the camera actually changes location, the spatial relationship among objects in the frame is substantially modified, as is the viewer's relationship to those objects. Camera-base movement seems to put viewers in motion, giving them the feeling that they are much more active participants than is actually the case. As Professor Philip Kipper found in his research, "the moving camera provides viewers with more information about the physical form of objects and about the three-dimensional layout of a television scene. . . . The viewer comes along for the ride, so to speak, entering the physical world on the screen, but also, perhaps penetrating the emotional or dramatic reality as well."[20]

Dollying involves pushing the camera into or out of the scene. Unlike the zoom, the dollying movement is more gradual and gives the viewer a sense of walking, rather than hurtling, into the picture. With the dolly, there is no distortion of perspective. Scenic elements pass into or out of the audience's field of vision exactly as they would in a "real-life" stroll.

Trucking (sometimes called *tracking*) is the moving of the camera parallel to the scene

rather than into or out of it. In a truck shot, viewers perceptually are either walking or riding alongside a scene's actor, vehicle, or other moving subject. Or, the director's focus is on featured scenery past which the audience is traveling. A truck can also involve movement in *opposition* to the direction of the shot's subject, of course. This tends to be jarring and fragmentary because subject and viewer are soon out of each other's frame. But for that reason, an 'opposing motion' truck is effective in suggesting conflict, hurry, or disorientation.

The trio of camera movement designations known as *craning, arcing,* and *booming* are more or less interchangeable. They require that the camera be mounted on a long manual, hydraulic, or electric arm. This arm makes possible shots involving smooth, flowing changes in height and semicircular distance as the camera sweeps toward, through, and away from the scene. The shifts in perspective are dramatic and substantial—so substantial, in fact, that the use of craning is limited primarily to action/adventure projects and outdoor spectacles.

As a summarizing inventory of the various techniques for achieving spatial mobility, examine the Avon commercial in Figure 6-4.

Because a photoboard, by itself, is a series of isolated pictures without movement of their own, let us imagine that this spot in Figure 6-4 used the following list of spatial mobility devices within its various frames. Use this list to capture in your own mind the visual sensation and meaning that these motion options might have projected.

Frame 1	crane down
Frame 2	zoom in
Frames 3 and 4	truck right
Frame 5	tilt up
Frame 6	truck left
Frame 7	dolly in
Frame 8	ped down
Frame 9	zoom in
Frames 10 and 11	pan right
Frame 12	arc out

Were this shot plan actually to have been followed in the Avon spot, of course, the resulting narrative would have been too visually frenetic for the dreamy, nostalgic theme of the piece. This is, after all, a 30-second commercial for beauty-affirming lipstick, not a five-minute climax to an action/adven-

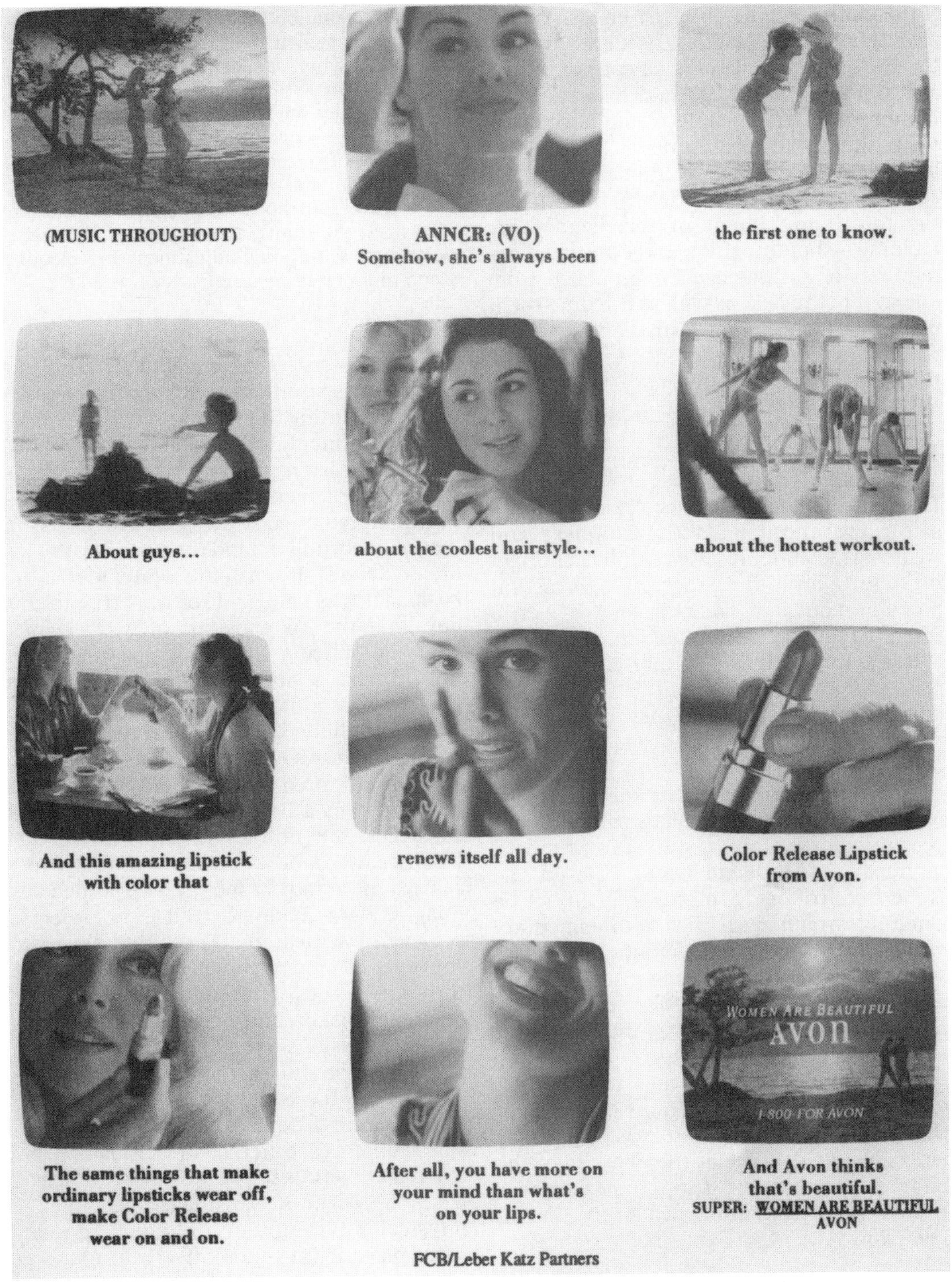
(MUSIC THROUGHOUT)
ANNCR: (VO)
Somehow, she's always been
the first one to know.
About guys...
about the coolest hairstyle...
about the hottest workout.
And this amazing lipstick
with color that
renews itself all day.
Color Release Lipstick
from Avon.
The same things that make
ordinary lipsticks wear off,
make Color Release
wear on and on.
After all, you have more on
your mind than what's
on your lips.
WOMEN ARE BEAUTIFUL
AVON
1-800-FOR AVON
And Avon thinks
that's beautiful.
SUPER: WOMEN ARE BEAUTIFUL
AVON
FCB/Leber Katz Partners

FIGURE 6-4 (Courtesy of Vonda LePage, FCB/Leber Katz Partners)

ture film. Our objective here simply is to provide a point-of-reference exercise in visualizing the various spatial mobility techniques and some of their communicative implications.

SHOT TRANSITION AND DURATION

The techniques of spatial mobility are used within single shots, as the term *shot* is defined earlier in this chapter. (Thus, on the Avon photoboard [Figure 6-4], even though there are separate pictures for each of frames 3/4, and 10/11, the hypothetical spatial mobility devices we specified would have made them single "shots"; frames 3 and 4 combined in a truck right and frames 10 and 11 amalgamated by a pan right.) In contrast, the fourth ingredient of television stage molding—shot transition and duration—determines how the viewer is propelled from one shot to the next as well as the time spent within each shot. Shot transition and duration, more than any other factor, ordains the pacing of a visual sequence.

Transition

The *cut*—the instantaneous 'take' from one picture to another—is the simplest and swiftest transition. A series of quick cuts can make for a rapid-fire progression, which, if properly motivated, compels each viewer to assemble the individual shots into meaning. *Dissolves*, in which one picture gradually replaces another are, by contrast, softer and more fluid. If very slow, they can suggest passage of time or even engagement of remembrance.

Superimpositions freeze the dissolve at its midpoint so that both pictures share our perception, one atop the other. To be meaningful, individual elements in each of the 'super'-contributing pictures need to be carefully arranged so that complementary entities are located in different parts of the screen. *Wipes* occur when one picture pushes another off the screen. *Fades*, finally, are nothing more than dissolves into or out of the limbo of blackness.

Some theorists argue that to maintain viewing within the distractions or inertia of the home environment, television usually embraces the dissolve at the expense of the more dynamic intercutting that film pioneered. As artist/critic David Antin sees it, television's

endless, silken adjustments, encouraged and sometimes specifically called for by the director and usually built into the cameraman's training, tend to blur the edges of what the film director would normally consider a shot. To this we can add the widespread use of fade-ins and fade-outs and dissolves to effect temporal and spatial transitions, and the director's regular habit of cutting on [spatial] movement to cushion the switch from one camera to another. This whole arsenal of techniques has a single function—to soften all shocks of transition. Naturally the different functions of various genres of program or commercial will alter the degree of softening, so a news program will maintain a sense of urgency through its use of cuts, soft though they may be, while the soap opera constantly melts together its various close shots with liquid adjustment and blends scene to scene in recurrent dissolves and fades.[21]

How shots are strung together thus is important in shaping viewers' comprehension and maintaining their attention. In fact, television commentator Michael Arlen argues that in television creation, "the real power is the power of men and women who control the montage effects, the technologists who instinctively understand the truth of [film pioneer Sergei] Eisenstein's statement: 'The basic fact was true, and remains true to this day, that the juxtaposition of two separate shots by splicing them together resembles not so much a simple sum of one shot plus another shot as it does a creation.' "[22]

As just alluded to, *montage* is the name we give to the result of splicing shots together to achieve a desired effect. To V. I. Pudovkin, montage was a linking process that helped construct and unfold the story. In Sergei Eisenstein's hands, however, montage became a more radical tool in which opposing images were made to collide in order to achieve new meaning. These two divergent concepts of montage evolved and competed through decades of international filmmaking before television came on the scene. Film and video professionals then borrowed from this heritage in producing their messages.

Most of these electronic media professionals came to realize, however, that television audiences differed substantially from cinema audiences in psychological attentiveness, the encountered image size, and the physical environment in which viewing takes place. Film's more divergent montage juxtapositions tended therefore to be avoided on television.

Nonetheless, the continuous nature of television programming sometimes makes for some unintentional montage statements. Because of the ethics-protecting separation between news and sales departments, for instance, there is the occasional embarrassment in which a journalistic item and the commercial that follows create an unintended montage discourse.

CBS's acclaimed *Sunday Morning* news show once did a piece on a small ethnic neighborhood about to be bulldozed to make way for a new Cadillac plant. In the last shot of the story, viewers saw the stooped sadness of parishioners and their elderly priest at the steps of their soon-to-be-razed church. The next image on the screen (a commercial) was of happy General Motors workers in a GM factory who were celebrating that, in this company, people come first! Such inadvertent montage fiascos probably are preferable to sales departments dictating story arrangement to newsrooms, of course. And their inadvertence shows that journalistic judgments are not being compromised by time sales considerations.

At other times, however, visual montage is *deliberately* used to make claims or accusations that the message originator would not dare articulate in soundtrack narration. This is often a problem in political commercials (polispots). Professor Paul Messaris cites a classic but by no means the latest example:

An especially disturbing application of this principle occurred in a political ad used by Richard Nixon against Hubert Humphrey in the 1968 presidential campaign. A shot of a smiling Humphrey was juxtaposed with images of death and destruction in Vietnam and rioting in the U.S.[23]

Whether calculated or inadvertent, montage can be a powerful stage-molding ingredient. Prudent professionals thus diligently monitor its use even when, as in most polispots, they cannot legally censor montage defamation.

Duration

Duration, shot transition's counterpart, decrees how *long* a given shot is held. The length of time that should be devoted to a single shot has been at issue almost from television's birth. The two opposing schools of thought on the topic were well sketched by Professor Robert Williams more than three decades ago when he concluded that "One group seems to feel that camera position should not be changed unless there is a reason for it and this reason is usually apart

from that of changing it for the sake of variety and interest. The other group, larger in number, feels that if a shot is held too long, attention will be lost."[24]

Certainly, character blocking has a role to play in this debate. People in motion can be followed by the camera within the confines of a single shot, and that motion will be enough to sustain 'variety and interest.' Therefore, there is no felt need for a shot change. The shooting of a stationary person, however, whether on a newsroom stool, a sitcom sofa, or a soap opera bed, requires the director to face the question of duration head on.

The two contrary orientations Williams mentioned have not merged in the years since this observation. If anything, they have become more distinct as newer rationales for one or the other approach are developed. MTV founder Robert Pittman, for instance, would infer that duration depends on the age of the target audience. To Pittman, the over-fifty generation "thinks of TV as a replacement for other forms of entertainment, such as books, movies or conversation. Therefore, they respond to traditional forms of TV. This one-thing-at-a-time generation (pre-TV adults) grew up on trains of thought that made all the stops—ideas that progress in a sequential mode."[25] It naturally follows that this sequential mode is better served by shot durations that correspond to paragraphs rather than phrases.

The younger generation, on the other hand, "processes information in a nonlinear manner," argues Pittman, so these viewers readily respond to a "quick burst of information format" that moves "very quickly with quick cuts, no transitions."[26] In other words, because TV is TV and not a print substitute as far as these younger viewers are concerned, they have grown up with, understand, and have come to expect movement and brevity in the shots to which they attend.

Advances in switching technology have provided new transition/duration devices to visually speak to the MTV generation and its even more "nonlinear" offspring. *Flash*, for instance, creates an effect reminiscent of video gaming. "Analysis of MTV and news magazine programs such as *Hard Copy, Inside Edition, A Current Affair*, and *American Journal* reveals that approximately five frames of video white are inserted between two shots to create a startling flash," Maria Grabe explains. "This transitional technique mimics the effect of a flash camera."[27] Other key devices calculated to lubricate easily bored eyeballs include, according to Grabe, *slide and peel*, "a sophisticated wipe that mimics the turn of a page in a book"; *rotations and bounces*, which occur "when an image flips (vertical axis) or tumbles (horizontal axis) 360 degrees"; and *fly effect*, which "involves miniaturizing an image and at the same time moving and spinning it into a new position on the screen or moving it off screen."[28]

These and dozens of even more specialized digital shot changes can be called up instantaneously either to improve or confound viewer comprehension. If the transition (and the duration to which it contributes) is appropriate to the programmatic subject matter, audiences acquire a clearer conception of the message. But if transitions are forced or unmotivated, understanding of presentation purpose will be sabotaged. Transition for transition's sake only substitutes artifice for involvement, as sports analyst Phil Mushnick pointed out in a critique of one aspect of contemporary football coverage:

TV doesn't show huddles anymore. The end of every play signals the start of a dizzying tour of every gizmo and gadget at a producer's disposal—and the disposal of many of them is what producers should consider. The huddle has been sacrificed at the altar of TV excesses. The 40 seconds or so between plays are now reserved for taking us here, there and everywhere: shots from blimps, of blimps, shots of bare-chested drunks; network promos, website addresses; misleading graphics that arrive spinning and whirring. . . . Can't we stay on the field once in a while? Can't we provide a tangible sense of continuity to the game for even two consecutive plays?[29]

The collective pacing and progression of video images are as significant to audience attention and apprehension as is the actual content each image contains. An unrelenting, breakneck sequence of exotic picture changes soon becomes as boring as a lockstep, listless dissolve between the same two shots. As award-winning director/cinematographer Bill Miller instructs:

Great symphonies are composed of soft passages, passionate passages, pompous passages, and the like. Videos, too, can have mood swings. Let the substance, audience, creative style, and your own passion dictate. You can cast a spell over your audience with a hypnotic wide shot of the gentle rolling surf and then shock them awake with quick-cutting close-ups of cars, trucks, and buses pounding, banging, and clanging along a metal bridge over an urban waterfront. By choosing the right [transition] style you can alter the mood of the audience, set them up, and then let them down smoothly or with the crash of a grand piano on a cement sidewalk.[30]

CAMERA/CHARACTER ARRANGEMENT

The final television stage-molding ingredient, camera/character arrangement, pertains to the physical relationship of the camera to the performer's and viewer's fields of focus. Does the lens convey a primarily straight-on view of the character? Or does it look in modified profile, from behind, or even through the eyes of, that character? Some action/drama programs and film commercials place the viewer within the psychological fabric of events by showing characters and their encounters from a variety of vantage points. This is essentially "one-camera Hollywood-style" production. The scene is shot in segments from several angles by a single camera. Then the most effective shots and their arrangement are determined in post-production editing. Using this technique, the camera can move right into the proscenium of the scene because the director needn't worry about getting in the way of other cameras or assembling the final sequence 'in real time' (at the moment of production).

One-camera style can provide advantages to the performers as well, especially when the camera used is hand-held rather than tripod-mounted. In *Homicide: Life on the Street*, for example, critic Stephanie Williams observed that "the hand-held Minicams have allowed actors with a wide range of styles, from André Braugher's swagger to Clark Johnson's regular-guy rap, plenty of breathing room. 'The camera is moving as much as the actors are, so the actors forget the camera's even there,' says executive producer Tom Fontana."[31] Often referred to as *shaky-cam*, this highly intrusive portable camera technique "can suggest a variety of situational and affective states—spontaneity, naivete, confusion, improvisation, instability, even chaos," states Professor Gregory Gutenko. However, like any professional productional tool, shakycam's use must be deliberate rather than random. Therefore, Gutenko adds, "Since the body has specific points of pivot and leverage, the 'authenticity' of camera shake corresponds to moves that a body in motion will produce. Bad shakycam will exhibit movement that is entirely arbitrary."[32]

Daytime soap operas and situation comedies, conversely, rely on base-mounted equipment in *three-camera, live-tape,* or *three-camera film* procedures. The whole scene is shot using multiple cameras simultaneously. In "live-tape," the director tries to choose the best shots in 'real-time' by switching back and forth among live cameras. (If the three cameras feed separate recording decks, miscues still can be fixed in postproduction.) In "three-camera, film," the footage is first processed and then edited (usually after being transferred to tape or digital vehicles). Either way, we are much less likely than in one-camera style to obtain views from inside the scene because the cameras would be forced to physically trespass into that scene.

When the chosen production technique does make them feasible, inside-the-scene views generally can be divided into *reaction shots* and *reverse angles.* Reaction shots focus on the nonverbal commentary displayed by one character in response to the words/actions of another character or event that is momentarily off-screen. Thus, they allow the viewer to detect a character attitude that the scriptwriter may not wish revealed to other people in the scene. When carefully planned, reaction shots are as much a part of the narrative as is dialogue and may, in fact, be more revealing of character motivation and frame of mind.

Reverse angles allow viewers to look *with* instead of just *at* a character. They therefore bring the camera directly into the action's proscenium. The audience might, for example, see a character deliver a line and then, through a reverse angle, watch through that same character's eyes as the line makes its impact on someone else. In this case, the reverse angle is a reaction shot, too. (The technique also can be engaged even *before* the other character has a chance to react—while the message-initiating person is still speaking.) Often designated as a POV (point-of-view) shot, the reverse angle implants the audience within a depicted character's mind's eye. When the shot is deliberately defocused or wobbly, it can even convey the feeling of physical or mental infirmity.

When the shot represents the view of a character, it is also known as *subjective camera.* Subjective camera is not usually possible in three-camera productions, however, for the reasons we just mentioned. "Hence," points out Robert Allen, "subjectivity in soap operas is usually rendered aurally rather than visually, by showing a close-up of a character while his or her thoughts are heard on the sound track."[33] In situation comedies, the general absence of subjectivity may be advantageous. The sitcom's essentially detached view reassures viewers that they can eavesdrop on, rather than stumble into, the comedic episode and its often participant-disparaging interactions. The audience enjoys laughing at the situation—but they do not wish visually to feel as though they are its cause or the butt of the joke.

An audience's spatial point-of-view in relation to a visualized subject is, in itself, a key conveyor of meaning. This is true of all the visual arts. Painters, in their creation of what is essentially a one-shot, single-camera experience, have long been sensitive to point-of-view dynamics. As Gilbert Seldes reminds us,

The ways in which the Last Supper has been treated pictorially is a prime example. The earliest representations show the disciples facing us, and the stress is on the sacrament, not the prediction of treachery. In Leonardo the dramatic interaction of all the disciples is conveyed by the direction in which we are looking—at one another or at Jesus, not at us. The lesson is clear: when we want to hypnotize the audience (to sell them something), the direct gaze into the camera is correct; for drama, people face one another, not us.[34]

When television characters "break the fourth wall," when they address us directly rather than another character, they are said to be exhibiting *self-reflexivity.* "This use of self-reflexivity," according to J. P. Williams, "at once breaks up the audience's willing suspension of disbelief by reminding them that they are watching television and reinforces their connection with the show through the feeling that this is a joke being shared by audience and character."[35] In

Seldes's words, the character is still trying 'to sell them something'—but that something is the supposedly audience-friendly nature of the program itself.

Whatever the camera/character arrangement, the ultimate question is whether the production's choices have led the viewer to what aesthetics authority Stephen Pepper calls "the point of optimum receptivity":

Where is the best point to see a picture, or to listen to a piano? One [or one's camera] has to move around in the consummatory area and find out. Nevertheless, that point is settled by the very structure of the field. It is a dispositional property of the situation. For the organism moving about in the field it is the ideal and norm of correctness of all his actions in the field. It is the place where he ought to be.[36]

THE HDTV VARIABLE

For program producers, the issue of where the viewer "ought to be" is compounded as efforts are made to shoot productions for both conventional video and HDTV (high definition television). Because conventional television uses an aspect ratio of 4:3 (four units wide by three units high) and HDTV's ratio is 16:9, issues arise as to how shots should be framed during production. (See Figure 6-5 for a graphic history/comparison of film and television aspect ratio.)

Cinematography critic Bob Fisher reports that "most film producers are now 'future-proofing' their programs, composing in 4:3 format and protecting the edges of the frame for 16:9 in anticipation of eventual DTV [digital television] or HDTV distribution."[37] However, while this practice seems to make production sense, it may get in the way of reaching that *point of optimum receptivity* to which Pepper referred. "Where we place the characters in the frame in relation to each other and the environment is an important part of the story," states International Cinematographers Guild president George Dibie. "If we put someone on the edge of the frame, there is always a reason. Maybe we want them to feel isolated. If you recompose that image for 16:9, the character is no longer on the edge of the frame. That's like changing the words in the script. It changes the meaning."[38]

Pans and zooms in the 4:3 original may also present a problem in the expanded 16:9 version. "There's too much information to process," says Chief Engineer Tom Beauchamp. "It kind of overloads the viewer."[39] On the other hand, this expanded vista can prove advantageous when shooting exclusively for HDTV. The wider screen allows a director—particularly in sports coverage—to stick with one wide shot of the action and let each viewer find her or his own point of optimum receptivity. "The director is not going to have to cut as much as he used to to keep up with the action," says sports producer/director Ken Fouts. "The viewer has a better seat."[40] Vilmos Zsigmond, director of photography on movies including *Deliverance* and *Close Encounters of the Third Kind*, adds that HDTV's wider aspect ratio can fundamentally improve visual drama by simplifying shot progression: "You can tell a story with fewer cuts because you can see backgrounds along with the close-ups. You don't need an establishing shot; you see where you are already."[41]

In characterizations, too, the wide-screen digital format can bring greater subtlety to video drama. "We no longer have to go for broad strokes," affirms film expert Barry Clark. "An actor doesn't have to slam his fist or slam a door to prove he's angry. Maybe he just has to raise an eyebrow. I truly feel that HD will provide for the emancipation of TV from hyperbole and clichés."[42] However, this same graphic clarity also presents new challenges for set designers and make-up artists. When NBC began broadcasting *The Tonight Show with Jay Leno* in HDTV, much more care had to be taken with set preparation. "Things you never think you could see on camera are there," reports NBC Studios executive producer Gary Considine. "For example, in one test shoot you could see three pieces of lint on the guest chair. It's really bizarre, but it's a beautiful picture."[43]

And for news anchors as well as actors, the HDTV camera "is a magnifying glass for detail—every wrinkle, every blemish and every speck of dandruff on a shoulder," cautions industry reporter Jill Geisler. "On-camera talent beware: in a business already cosmetically driven, there's likely to be even more pressure to 'pretty up' for the cameras. Smile—you're on high definition TV, and cosmetic dentistry may be in your future."[44] Fortunately, *skin contouring cameras*, first in-

FIGURE 6-5
The evolution of film and video aspect ratio relationships. (Illustrations by Barbara Miles for S&VC magazine)

The silent film had an aspect ratio of 1.33:1, and migrates naturally to the 4:3 video screen.

The Academy aperture, used in Hollywood's golden age, was 1.37.1, close enough to 4:3 to work with the slightest edge cropping.

Along came CinemaScope, anamorphosed on the film, and cropped-and-panned like crazy for video (or else letterboxed, as shown below.)

Most non-anamorphic Hollywood films drifted to 1.85:1, and the sides had to be cropped less energetically for video.

Today, shoot the film 1:65:1 for European cinemas, crop the top and bottom very slightly for 1.85:1 in American cinemas, and crop very slightly for 16:9 letterbox video.

troduced in 1989, make it possible to digitally remove talent wrinkles while the newscast or drama is being shot. Network anchors Dan Rather, Peter Jennings, and Tom Brokaw have all benefited from this technology, as have innumerable talk show hosts and soap opera stars.[45] Thus, HDTV and associated digital technologies may simultaneously provide viewers with both a truer and more fabricated picture of reality.

A STAGE-MOLDING SYNOPSIS

Aural transition and volume, light and shadow, horizontal and vertical camera planes, spatial mobility, shot transition and duration, and camera/character arrangement are all tools to construct a compelling stage picture out of elusive electromagnetic impulses. When effectively planned and executed, these stage-molding ingredients, in consort with the on-stage skills of performers and the multifaceted benefits of music, can make electronic media consumption an entertaining, involving, and even enlightening experience.

But as media professionals, it is our job to critique the use of these tools carefully so that their potential is neither wasted nor inflated. Video writer/producer Rick Weiss asserts that, in our art as in any other, it all comes down to one fundamental question: "Why do we pick up a brush, a chisel or a camera in the first place? Look at architecture, painting, photography and filmmaking. In any public art form, aesthetic trends emerge only when the mind masters the technology. The first clue of this emergence is when we become blasé about the tools but passionate about the expression."[46]

No matter how slick the cadences, performances, and visual manipulations, they ultimately can be evaluated only in terms of their appropriateness and utility to a given message's purpose. Production is execution, but it is *writing* that usually structures conception. Because production must therefore be judged in terms of the conception that motivated it, we examine extensively the scripted core of electronic media programming in several subsequent chapters.

Tonal, talent, and stage-molding artistry notwithstanding, a media professional must never be distracted from appraising whether a programmatic project's specific objective was attained. In the words of an advertising industry caution, we must see beyond productional technique to determine "whether all that pucker led to a kiss."

ENDNOTES

1. Herbert Zettl, *Sight Sound Motion: Applied Media Aesthetics* (Belmont, CA: Wadsworth, 1973), 330.
2. Rick Altman, "Television/Sound." Paper presented to the Society for Cinema Studies, March 24, 1984 (Madison, WI).
3. Zettl, 44.
4. Ibid., 38.
5. DeWitt Parker, *The Analysis of Art* (New Haven, CT: Yale University Press, 1926), 82.
6. Bill Holshevnikoff, "The Light Side of the News," *Video Systems* (May 1999), 48.
7. Frank Gillette, *Frank Gillette Video: Process and Metaprocess*, Jodson Rosenbush (ed.) (Syracuse, NY: Everson Museum of Art, 1973), 21.
8. Peter Crown, "The Electronic Fireplace," *Videography* (March 1977), 17.
9. Raymond Spottiswoode, *A Grammar of Film* (London: Faber & Faber, 1935), 44.
10. Gorham Kindem, *The Moving Image: Production Principles and Practices* (Glenview, IL: Scott, Foresman, 1987), 103.
11. Maria Grabe, "Explicating Sensationalism in Television News: Content and the Bells and Whistles of Form." Paper presented to the Association for Education in Journalism & Mass Communication Convention, August 1998 (Baltimore).
12. Alan Wurtzel and Joseph Dominick, "Evolution of Television Drama: Interaction of Acting Styles and Shot Selection," *Journal of Broadcasting* (Winter 1971/72), 104.
13. Robert Williams, "On the Value of Varying TV Shots," *Journal of Broadcasting* (Winter 1964/65), 34.
14. David Miles, "Breaking Out of the Gutenberg Galaxy: Volvo Invents Cubist Television." Paper presented to the Speech Communication Association Convention, November 19, 1993 (Miami Beach).
15. Stephen Pepper, *The Work of Art* (Bloomington: Indiana University Press, 1955), 28.
16. Gilbert Seldes, *The Public Arts* (New York: Simon & Schuster, 1956), 12.
17. Donald Livingston, *Film and the Director* (New York: Macmillan, 1958), 52.
18. Thomas McCain, Joseph Chilberg, and Jacob Wakshlag, "The Effect of Camera Angle on Source Credibility and Attraction," *Journal of Broadcasting* (Winter 1977), 43.
19. Ibid., 44.
20. Philip Kipper, "Television Camera Movement As a Source of Perceptual Information," *Journal of Broadcasting & Electronic Media* (Summer 1986), 304–305.
21. David Antin, "Video: The Distinctive Features of the Medium," in John Hanhardt (ed.) *Video Culture: A Critical Investigation* (Rochester, NY: Visual Studies Workshop, 1986), 160.
22. Michael Arlen, *The Camera Age* (New York: Farrar, Straus & Giroux, 1981), 79.
23. Paul Messaris, "Ethics in Visual Communication," *Feedback* (Fall 1990), 5.
24. Robert Williams, "Varying TV Shots," 35.
25. Robert Pittman, "MTV's Lessons: We Want What We Want Immediately," *ADWEEK* (May 27, 1985), 34.
26. Ibid.
27. Grabe, "Explicating Sensationalism."
28. Ibid.
29. Phil Mushnick, "The No-Huddle Broadcast," *TV Guide* (September 19, 1998), 46.
30. Bill Miller, "Shooting with Style," *Video Systems* (December 1998), 80.
31. Stephanie Williams, "Life on the Set," *TV Guide* (December 28, 1996), 38–39.
32. Gregory Gutenko, "Evaluating Shakycam—Possible Criteria," *Feedback* (Winter 1997), 29.
33. Robert Allen, "Reader-Oriented Criticism and Television," in Robert Allen (ed.), *Channels of Discourse* (Chapel Hill: University of North Carolina Press, 1987), 91.
34. Seldes, 187.
35. J. P. Williams, "When You Care Enough to Watch the Very Best: The Mystique of *Moonlighting*," *Journal of Popular Film and Television* 16 (1988), 92.
36. Pepper, 54.
37. Bob Fisher, "Through the Looking Glass," *EMMY* (June 1999), 36.
38. Ibid.
39. Harry Jessell, "A New Ball Game with HDTV," *Broadcasting & Cable* (September 15, 1997), 102.
40. Ibid.
41. James Fadden, "The Aesthetics of HDTV," *Video Systems* (January 1998), 32.
42. Kathleen O'Steen, "Close-Ups," *EMMY* (December 1998), 55.
43. Glen Dickson, "NBC Ready to Go with HD Leno," *Broadcasting & Cable* (April 19, 1999), 4.
44. Jill Geisler, "Digital Dynamics," *Communicator* (April 1999), 31.
45. J. Max Robins, "A New Wrinkle in Video Technology," *TV Guide* (September 28, 1996), 57.
46. Rick Weiss, "Today's Trends Suggest Tomorrow's Reality," *Video Systems* (December 1992), 41.

7

Business Gratifications

In Chapters 5 and 6, we examine the productional ingredients from which the electronic media draw in order to construct the "pucker" that hopefully "leads to a kiss." In this and the following chapter, we dissect the dynamics of that kiss—the goals and satisfactions that originators and receivers seek to derive from embracing media programming. We begin, in this section, by scrutinizing the originator or business side of the courtship, because, in the United States, it is business considerations that initiate the media's sender/receiver flirtation.

COMMERCE AND ART

Some people object to making marketplace considerations a significant factor in the practice of media criticism. But as art critic George Boas observed, "Works of art have always been a commodity and critics would do well to observe not only how artistry changes in response to economic demand but how works of art themselves change."[1] Michelangelo had his Pope Julius and Mozart his Emperor Joseph. Even though each artist was thus creating, in a sense, for a market of one—for a single sponsor/patron—it *was still a market*. Unfortunately, failure to accurately assess their respective markets' less discerning tastes caused both Michelangelo and Mozart great stress.

"The reconciliation of art and business is never an easy thing," advises scholar Carl Grabo, "nor has it been too well achieved in the past."[2] And if reconciliation has been difficult in the traditional 'fine arts,' with their narrow and relatively homogeneous audience, it is certainly a challenge in the electronic arts, with their vast and varied public. Successful producer Garry Marshall (*The Odd Couple, Happy Days, Laverne and Shirley*) once characterized the impact of the commerce/art duality this way: "I'm an artist in a business and since television is the biggest business, it's harder to be an artist. . . . I'm an artist as often as I can be."[3] Two decades later, at his induction into *Broadcasting & Cable* magazine's Hall of Fame, Marshall made his point more explicitly:

People ask me the difference between doing television in the '70s compared to the '90s. I always had a nightmare in the '70s that I was doing The Last Supper as a movie of the week and the network would come to me and say, 'Judas isn't testing well. Could you give him a dog or something?' In the '90s as I direct The Last Supper, for financial reasons two of the disciples have Coca-Cola cans in front of them.[4]

Like any responsible media professional, Marshall is shouldering the task of trying to explain to consumers (and sometimes to colleagues) why his product must constitute a business and how business decision-making impacts that product's form and content. Stations, networks, cable systems, and production houses are such expensive enterprises to build and maintain that in order to fund their continuance, they must rely on either substantial government subsidy or the profit motive. To ignore this fiscal inevitability is to ignore a fundamental reality with which all art, in varying degrees, must come to grips.

Public broadcasting is no more immune to this inevitability than are its commercial cousins. Throughout the 1980s, as federal support for noncommercial radio/television decreased, public broadcasters found themselves turning more and more to commercial underwriters and consumer pledge drives to meet payroll and keep the transmitter warm. Though they don't seek a "profit" per se, noncommercial stations and systems must raise enough money to operate. What doesn't come from government subsidy must come from the private sector. This is as true in European broadcasting's move to 'privatization' (free enterprise media ownership) as it is in U.S. public broadcasting, where the withdrawal of federal dollars demands that stations be more self-sustaining. As Ien Ang asserts:

the trend is unmistakable: more and more have public service organizations developed an explicit interest in ratings, 'audience maximization' and similar concerns that derive from the competitive commercial system. . . . More and more, in other words, is the audience-as-public transformed, at least apparently, into an audience-as-market.[5]

This does not necessarily mean that the electronic media, public or commercial, are identical in character with any other business. As Professor Eileen Meehan argues,

television is not reducible solely to manufacture nor to artifact. Rather, television is a *complex combination of industry and artistry*. . . . Television is always and simultaneously an artifact and a commodity that is both created and manufactured; television always and simultaneously presents a vision for interpretation and an ideology for consumption to a viewership that is always and simultaneously a public celebrating meaning and an audience produced for sale in the marketplace. . . . While we recognize that economics set the parameters, we must also recognize that television is a very peculiar sort of industry—a culture industry that reprocesses the symbolic "stuff" from which dreams and ideologies are made.[6] [italics added]

Though Meehan restricted her comments to the video medium, they could as well be applied to radio, of course. Both media must attempt to reconcile the requirements of business while delivering a product that is expected to be art. This didn't seem that difficult—at first.

BOTTOM-LINE PREEMINENCE

Once upon a time, as all good fairy tales start, U.S. broadcasting was regarded as a pseudo-public service calling that would magically sustain itself simply by offering 'quality' programming in the public interest and over the public airwaves. Everyone's idea of what constituted the public interest (and quality) differed from everyone else's, but a common theme seemed to be that there should be only enough selling to pay the bills incidental to providing this service.

Like mainstream newspapers, stations (and therefore their owners and operators) were seen as serving some calling higher than other business ventures. This demanded a special willingness to forego any commercial excess likely to widen the profit margin. Stations, in fact, were held to even a higher standard than newspapers because they operated on an electromagnetic spectrum that, in theory, belonged to the citizenry at large.

A substantial number of broadcasters did take this responsibility to heart and supported the principle that running a radio or television station was not like running a gas station or a bowling alley. As Thomas Murphy, CEO of ABC Inc., before it was bought by Disney, recalls:

The way I was brought up in the business, the first thing we discussed when we went to the office every day was whether what we were doing was living up to our responsibilities as a broadcaster to our community. And then, after you figured out that you were doing everything you should in that area, you paid attention about what you could do to knock the brains out of the competition, which is what most people do most of the time.[7]

Conscientious broadcasters like Murphy thereby adopted what veteran network news executive Richard Wald[8] called the *bifocal view of broadcasting*:

WHAT YOU SEE UP CLOSE IS PROFIT AND LOSS.

What you see farther away is "doing good."

Even though they were close readers most of the time, electronic media managers needed only to glance up to see the other vision staring them in the face.

If that historic vision is still shimmering on the horizon, it is a horizon that has become more and more distant in the face of corporate takeovers that have brought non-media business interests into control of many broadcast, cable, and studio properties and have forced even media-exclusive corporations to become huge, publicly traded entities locked in a constant struggle to deliver fat dividends to impatient shareholders. Federal loosening of ownership restrictions throughout the 1990s resulted in larger and fewer station groups and cable MSOs (multiple-system owners). To secure business clout and benefit from economies of scale, a company either had to get larger or had to sell out to another chain more financially able to pursue that same goal.

Industry consolidation has taken other forms as well. The sunset of the FCC's *financial interest and syndication* (fin/syn) *rules* in 1995 meant that broadcast networks were now able to take ownership interest in their prime-time programs. By the fall of 1999, the Big Four networks—for the first time ever—owned more than half of the shows on their evening line-ups.[9] Meanwhile, old and new media interests, from broadcasting to telephone companies to Internet players, merged and remerged for survival and profit. As industry analyst Debra Goldman explains it:

The rationale for getting bigger seems simple and necessary. The more the media splinter and take new shapes, the more the big boys need to own all the pieces, from studios to networks to theme parks to magazines to T-shirts. . . . Once they bulk up, the media megaliths become halls of mirrors in which each of their entertainment products can be endlessly reflected. . . . For the basic fact of life in a fractured media environment is that the more pieces there are vying for attention, the more the impact of each piece will depend on its relationship to the other pieces. The World Wide Web is nothing more than that principle brought to digital life.[10]

Amidst all of this media consolidation and financial aggregation, broadcasting's legacy of "doing good" became much more difficult to discern. Veteran radio and television executives looked through their bifocals to find themselves out of the industry entirely or peering upward at new management structures and myopic boards of directors whose sole concern is the quarterly dividend. "I'm having to do weekly rather than monthly P&L's [profit-and-loss statements]!" reports long-time television station executive Jon Bengtson. "The history of your station or your past record means nothing. It's a question of what dollars have you generated today?"[11]

These same fiscal pressures squeeze every segment of the electronic media industry. The quest for the television program/schedule, radio format, cable network, or website concept that will bring monetary success while still doing qualitative "good" is thus more perilous than ever. "I believe in the bottom line," admits independent television

producer Chuck Fries. "But I also think there's a midpoint here. An old producer once said: 'In my drawer are all the projects I want to do. What you see on the screen are the things they'll buy.' "[12] "I would love to put together a schedule that is 100 percent high-quality," states top ABC executive Robert Iger, "but we are in a business to make money. At the same time, I'd love to put on shows that are high-quality and make money, but the two of these aren't necessarily mutually inclusive. It's a balance you have to strike."[13] NBC News producer Brett Holey chimes in, "Being innovative and being commercially successful are sometimes two contradictory goals."[14]

Quality on the Balance Sheet

Given a choice, virtually all media executives would enjoy making or distributing 'quality' programming. Let's assume, for the moment, that there is some general agreement among producers and public as to just what quality is. (We address that question more extensively in Chapters 11 to 13.) Even if we accept this huge assumption, would quality in a program property automatically translate into a fiscal asset? Clearly, the comments from Fries, Iger, and Holey lead us to believe that they would say 'no.' Is there, then, no relationship between the artistry of a show and its profitability?

For one thing, observes advertising executive Paul Schulman, "A quality show will last longer with low ratings than a show without quality. . . . Quality does extend a program's life by allowing it a second or third shot at another time period. But if it misses the mark on a quality basis, it usually doesn't get a second chance."[15]

On the other hand, laments former MTM and NBC executive Grant Tinker, "The pressures that come down from the top make it more difficult for entertainment people than it was for the executives even a few years ago; . . . with the cost pressures today, the networks don't reach out as often for those quality loss-leaders that we'd like to do."[16] And *Brooklyn Bridge*'s creator Gary David Goldberg reveals, "When we decided to do *Brooklyn Bridge*, I decided I didn't want to make any concessions to television and I think its the best work I've ever done. However, somewhere the economic reality will intersect us and at that time the show will have to go off the air because we won't stay on with a lesser product."[17] Of course, Goldberg had the clout to make those decisions because of the huge financial rewards he had reaped from his hit series *Family Ties*, a show in its own right that was frequently recognized as a "quality" product. Nevertheless, *Brooklyn Bridge* lasted less than two full seasons, and a disenchanted Goldberg asserted that he would never "do television again." (Only a few seasons later his production company's *Spin City* had established itself as a mainstay of ABC's prime-time schedule.)

Part of the equation here relates to what it costs to mount a given production. There is obvious incentive for a network to keep a critically acclaimed, less-expensive show on the air even if its audience level is relatively low. For one thing, it will take fewer ratings points to cover the program's licensing costs. For another, its "quality" designation probably will attract a more "upscale" audience that will be appealing to certain 'prestige' advertisers. A big-budget show like *Brooklyn Bridge*, however, does not possess such an advantage. Conversely, points out CBS executive Peter Tortorici, "When [critically acclaimed] *Northern Exposure* got on the air, it did so because it was able to be produced on a lower-than-normal budget for its initial summer run."[18]

Up to this point, we have talked exclusively about quality as reflected in scripted network series. But the qualitative dimension can be applied to syndicated or local programming as well. And however a show is distributed, some executives maintain that a program's quality *must* be a function of cost and audience delivery. According to this school of thought, quality cannot exist independently of budgetary considerations. MCA Television Group president Robert Harris took this position when he asserted that

quality is very subjective. I think some may argue that the highest quality program on American television today is *Wheel of Fortune*: it costs the least to produce, it makes the most money. And a lot of people watch it. Therefore, it's a quality program.[19]

Creators and the Business Process

In light of these divergent criteria that 'quality' is expected to meet, it is not surprising that program creators and the executives who purchase their wares often see the world in conflicting ways. As we mention at the beginning of this chapter, a natural tension between creators and their patrons has always existed. In this regard, Michelangelo and Mozart were no different than the major and minor artists who labor on the precarious scaffolding of today's radio and in television's unstable throne rooms. The intensified bottom-line pressures associated with the takeover, cross-media consolidation, and consequent debt load borne by electronic media enterprises have only heightened, not initiated, the natural creative/commerce strain.

Sometimes this strain can be severe. Based on his study of the Hollywood creative community, for instance, Ben Stein charges that the TV writer

is actually selling his labor to brutally callous businessmen. One actually has to go through the experience of writing for money in Hollywood or anywhere else to realize just how unpleasant it is. Most of the pain comes from dealings with business people, such as agents or business affairs officers of production companies and networks. The number of calamities that can and do happen can hardly be believed unless they are experienced. The TV writer is not an honored guest at the Greenbriar [a posh executive conference center]. He is actually down there in the pit with the clawing agents and businessmen, and he often has reason to feel that he has been shortchanged, to say the least.[20]

Stein's observation is strikingly similar to a complaint Mozart once wrote to his father:

If I have some work printed or engraved, how can I protect myself from being cheated by the engraver? . . . I almost feel inclined not to sell any more of my compositions to any engraver, but to have them printed or engraved by subscription at my own expense.[21]

The creator for today's electronic media faces the same quandary. Unless he or she (like Gary David Goldberg) becomes wealthy enough to own or lease the "engraving company" (production house), there is a hobbling dependency on the people who do possess such an enterprise. Further, the production company's capability to "engrave" on tape or film is useless if the financial interests who control the means of transmission cannot be persuaded to carry that celluloid or digital electromagnetic engraving to the public and pay a fair license fee that will help the producer cover expenses. Even as successful a production company head as Stephen Cannell (*Rockford Files, Baretta, The A-Team, Wiseguy*) unequivocally states that, in negotiating with networks or other distributors,

my formula now is that I will not manufacture a show unless I can make it for a license fee, plus foreign [sales rights], plus overhead. I have to pay that overhead whether I'm making a show or not. That's rent, my payroll department, secretary, the producer contracts that are in place, all that. And whatever the allocation of that overhead is, plus license fees, plus foreign, if I figure I can make the show for that, then it's a go. If I can't then I have to figure out how to either take in a partner or it's off.[22]

Conglomerating ownership trends are making the situation even more constrained as the number of major studio and outlet players is further compressed. The cost of these takeovers (or the expense of fighting them off) puts more and more pressure on the final entry in media businesses' profit-and-loss statements—and thus adds even more tension to the relationship between creators and those who purchase their products. Respected television critic Les Brown sees the effects of these financial changes to be so sweeping as to constitute what he labels a "new morality" in electronic media operations. The "big money" investors who have entered the media are, Brown warns, "coming without any passion for the industry at all, with passion for the bottom line."[23]

This condition, in turn, has precipitated in academic media criticism what Professor Samuel Becker sees as "the growing distrust of big business by many scholars, fueled by the growing dominance of a relatively few transnational telecommunications industries, the continuing conglomerization of the media industries within the United States and, at the same time, the trend within this country to reduce government pressure on the broadcasting industries to serve public as well as shareholder interests."[24]

Media creators and conscientious critics, whether 'outsider' academics or 'insider' media professionals, must recognize this situation but not despair of it. Media enterprises probably are, as Joseph Russin said of

radio stations, "businesses first and beacons of truth and justice second."[25] But this only makes them commercial; it does not make them inevitably evil or valueless. Professor Louis Day summarizes the acceptable limits to bottom-line preeminence this way:

There is nothing *inherently* immoral in the profit motive or the accumulation of wealth. Many wealthy entrepreneurs and philanthropists have used their considerable economic resources to benefit social causes and charity. Likewise, certain businesses and corporations have revealed a sense of social obligation by plowing some of their profits back into the communities they serve. Self-interest *can be* the servant of the public's interest, because the pursuit of profits can work to the benefit of the society at large. Ethical questions do arise, however, when commercial interests are allowed to dominate other social obligations. The issue, in any given situation, is how to *balance* economic pressures against individual or institutional duties to others.[26]

Both in terms of the quality question and the issue of creator clout in the business process, bottom-line preeminence has probably been most constructively visualized by the Washington Post Company's chairman, Katherine Graham. In her keynote speech delivered at a NATPE (National Association of Television Program Executives) Convention, Graham advanced her belief that quality was not necessarily "intellectual or elitist" programming. "I don't believe television should be restricted to *David Brinkley, Masterpiece Theatre*, and *Wall Street Week*," she asserted. Instead, quality results from giving the best people the freedom to do their best, with the management skill to keep them going "in the right direction."[27]

As media professionals, it is up to us to use our sharpest critical tools in striving to determine, in any given case, what that 'right direction' happens to be.

RATINGS, SHARES, AND TONNAGE

In the electronic media, bottom-line concerns translate most directly into how many and what kind of people are reached by a given outlet or show. From a business gratifications standpoint, it is essential to realize that media enterprises ultimately are *not* in operation to select and deliver programs to audiences. Instead, they are in the *audience construction* industry.

Putting it even more bluntly, an electronic media outlet *manufactures* an audience via programming that serves as bait to attract listeners or viewers. Through careful packaging of format and flow, the intent is to capture and hold these consumers so that their eyes and ears can be rented out to advertisers in typical units of fifteen, thirty, or sixty seconds. The size and composition of these rented-out audiences vary widely from situation to situation. But the aim is to sculpt an audience whose characteristics mirror as closely as possible the type of people the outlet's advertisers are striving to reach.

Any marketers, or any station, system, or network executives who do not appreciate this dynamic are doomed to failure. They are like those dinosaur railroad managers who thought they were in the train business rather than the transportation business. And any critical appraisal that misses this reality is bound to mislead the public and be ignored by media professionals. Thus, broadcasters, cablecasters, and other electronic outlet operators have *two* publics: advertisers and consumers. The one public remains the means by which the other's business ends are achieved.

British producer and critic John Ellis, among others, sees this situation in negative terms. Ellis distinguishes between 'viewers' and 'audiences' and chastises broadcasters for preferring the latter over the former:

Broadcasting institutions are not concerned with 'viewers,' but they are with 'audience.' Viewers are individuals, people who use TV within their domestic and group social contexts. Viewers are the few people who ring in to the duty officer, or write to the broadcasters or to newspapers, expressing their opinions. Viewers record programmes on VCRs and use them later, pausing or replaying when attention wanders, shuttling forward when interest fades. Audiences, however, do not have these irritating characteristics. Audiences are bulk agglomerations created by statistical research. They have no voices and the most basic of characteristics, they 'belong' to income groups and are endowed with a few broad educational and cultural features. Audiences do not use TV, they watch it and consume it. Broadcasters do not seek viewers, they seek audiences.[28]

Although it deftly champions the cause of the independent viewer, Ellis's lament does not change the fact that the existence of *audiences* (as he defines them) pays the way for the programs from which those individualistic viewers can select.

The delivery of audience as measured by rating, share, and cost-per-thousand is mathematically deciphered in Chapter 4. The rise and fall of these numbers are specific benchmarks of business gratification or gratification absence; they are the making or breaking of programs, formats, delivery systems, and individual careers. Mal Belville, one of the pioneers of the U.S. audience measurement industry, inventories the impact of 'the ratings':

They determine the price that will be paid for programs and the pay that performers will receive. They govern the rates that advertisers will pay for 60-second or 30-second or smaller units in and around a program. Ratings determine stations' audience and rank order in their market, and to a large degree they dictate the profitability of broadcasting stations and their value when put up for sale. The salary and bonus compensation of key network and station officials are also governed by ratings success. Ratings results ultimately determine whether top management and program and news management in television and radio broadcast organizations will retain their jobs, be promoted, or demoted.[29]

Nowhere is the gratification of *big* numbers more prized than in prime-time network television, where the costs of program creation and delivery still make for a true *tonnage* environment. *Tonnage* is an industry term for the delivery of large, even massive audiences in which the sheer numbers of people reached take on a greater importance than the types of people these are. Thus, the typical daily newspaper is a tonnage (quantity) medium, constantly seeking to increase the numbers of copies sold to whoever will buy them. Most magazines (and websites), on the other hand, are typically nontonnage or *qualitative* media and strive to deliver a precisely defined category of consumers (*target universe*) to their advertisers. Prime-time network television, in this sense, is like the newspaper. Most radio station and many cable channel formats, conversely, attempt the audience delivery precision of a magazine.

A tonnage orientation is most likely to occur *where the number of same-service competitors is low and the cost of production is high*. Daily newspapers are comparatively expensive enterprises to run. However, they are either the only paper in town or face but a single competitor. In fact, most U.S. dailies are territorial monopolies with no significant rival for local print readership or advertising. Even with its system of regional printing plants, *USA Today* cannot directly compete with 'hometown papers' for local news and advertising. Thus, that local newspaper continues in its historic quest to be the omnibus (something for everyone) medium in which how many people in the area are reading becomes much more important than targeting to any single demographic group.

Network television used to enjoy an analogous position. Until the mid-1970s, the local television landscape typically consisted of three network affiliates with perhaps a struggling independent station and a noncompeting public broadcasting outlet thrown in. During evening prime time, when the largest number of homes-using-television (HUTS) was achieved, the combined three-network share of audience was frequently 90 percent or higher. Some 75 to 80 percent of the entire country tuned in to network programming for at least part of the evening. ABC, CBS, and NBC thus benefited from almost the same preeminent position as that enjoyed by the local newspaper. Not surprisingly, this was the era that spawned network executive Paul Klein's *LOP* (Least Objectional Program) *Theory* in which viewers were forced to choose what they least disliked from a three-item menu.

Since that time, of course, the pattern has changed markedly. Cable television brought dozens of new signals to town, including distant television stations and satellite-delivered cable-only networks. This paradoxically stimulated construction of both new conventional and low-power (LPTV) independent stations at the same time it presented these newcomers with a broader range of competitors. A fourth network—Fox—wedged its way into this expanded environment while VCRs enabled viewers to time shift network and cable offerings or become their own programmers via rented video cassettes or material they produced themselves with their own camcorders. "Technology," writes Professor Richard Blake, "has moved in like a greedy landlord and broken the global village into condominiums; . . . the world has become less a tribal village and more an urban apartment building, where people in adjacent flats cannot recognize one another."[30]

In further validation of Blake's observation, more fledgling broadcast networks like The WB and UPN were hatched by the end of the century, DBS (direct broadcast satellite) was packaging and relaying both existing and satellite-exclusive program services, and the World Wide Web was contributing its own means for the ultimate fragmentation of 'audience' into independent consumer/programmers. Nevertheless, the Big Four networks (ABC, CBS, Fox, and NBC) still commanded the majority of television prime-time viewing choices. "Even though broadcast network viewership erosion can't be denied," states media analyst Richard Katz, "the networks are still the only way to reach 10 million to 20 million people with one commercial."[31] However, as broadcast network numbers continue their slow erosion, at some point the decreasing tonnage numbers will cease to be substantial enough to justify the huge costs to advertisers that prime-time, network programming incurs. As early as 1987, CBS chief researcher David Poltrack told an industry/academic seminar that the networks could no longer afford to develop "broad-scale programming to attract everyone. We just can't attract everyone. There are too many alternatives out there."[32]

Unfortunately for the broadcast networks, their structures and procedures, even after painful downsizing, are still geared to a tonnage world. And evening broadcast network viewing levels are still just 'tonnage enough' to reap significant profits when a prime-time show does succeed. It seems as though none of the Big Four wishes to be the first to pull out of the game and seek more precisely drawn universes with more affordable programming.

Despite the problems this scenario poses for the broadcast networks, the post-LOP era offers program creators and viewers new opportunities in the expanded-choice spectrum. If every show is getting lower numbers due to audience fragmentation, perhaps those programs with a small but loyal audience will now be able to remain on somebody's air. "Prime time television, plain and simply, is getting better," critic Les Brown cheered in 1987. "Maybe it's because you don't need as high a rating today to succeed with a television show."[33] If production costs are not contained, however, those lower rating and share numbers will not translate into acceptable financial return for the producers and outlets involved. Advertising agencies buy time to sell their clients' products, not to bankroll expensive, underdelivering shows. "Whether you're network A or network B, or you're cable channel C or cable channel D, the motivation is to provide programing for advertisers so that they can do their job," asserts Television Bureau of Advertising president Ave Butensky. "That's what that's about."[34] Even advertisers in search of an "up-scale audience skew" will not continue to pay tonnage rates to reach non-tonnage-size audiences.

In non-prime time, TV tonnage preoccupations have ebbed much less resistantly and much more gradually. This is due to non-prime's traditionally lower viewing levels and (therefore) their comparatively less intimidating advertising rate-card prices. Network program production budgets have always been modest in lesser-viewed dayparts. Consequently, it is significantly easier for station syndicated programming as well as for cable network offerings to compete outside of prime time with what the Big Four networks are doing.

This keen competition for the smaller, off-prime audiences also makes for more precise audience targeting by everyone. As John Fiske has pointed out, television's "success in the financial economy depends upon its ability to serve and promote the diverse and often oppositional interests of its audiences."[35] This is much easier to accomplish when tonnage expectations are absent.

As a whole, the magazine industry made the shift from tonnage to demographic specifics (what we today call a *niche orientation*) in the 1950s. Once the massively popular television medium had arrived on the scene, advertisers were no longer willing to pay expensive magazine rates to reach smaller but still frustratingly diverse audiences. Many magazines found themselves with too few readers to deliver tonnage but too heterogeneous a readership to provide targeted marketing. General circulation overweights such as *Look, Collier's*, and the original *Saturday Evening Post* thus met their demise, to be replaced by publications that offered much smaller but also much more homogeneous audiences to advertisers in search of precisely drawn demographics.

The same thing was happening to radio as a response to the same video threat. Television preempted network radio's long-standing tonnage expectations and converted the elder electronic medium to a locally programmed entity in which the universe-isolating format became the mark of success. Later, when FM came to parity with and then far surpassed AM's popularity, the number of truly competing stations more than doubled. *Narrowcasting* to population slivers became the only feasible path to survival. In the words of broadcast consultant Charles Warner, "Delineating yourself becomes essential when every station is moving to a 4 share."[36]

Modern radio stations (like many cable networks) are format-specific, whereas television stations are program-specific. That is, people turn to a radio outlet (or The Weather Channel or MTV) for a definite kind of gratification that they expect to be available no matter what the hour. Even though the on-air presenters change, the general nature of the outlet's programming is assumed to remain a predictable constant. "Clearly, the livelihood of radio's future is intertwined with the industry's ability to understand and then attract a specific, targeted demographic," affirms *The Radio World Magazine*'s editor Charles Taylor. "There simply is no such thing as a mainstream station today. To succeed: Niche, then target."[37]

In broadcast television, conversely, consumers tend to move from program to program. They select individual shows rather than specific outlets or methods of transmission. Also, once a coaxial cable is attached to the viewer's set, a UHF superstation four states away or a cable network uplinked from Denver become as easy to tune to as a VHF network affiliate located a mile down the street. How one receives the signal is no longer important (if, indeed, it ever was). The viewer's sole concern is the program to be retrieved. A consumer in search of a sporting event or a sitcom can find it without regard for, or even awareness of, the transmission entity originating it. Everything simply comes from "the cable (or the Direct Broadcast Satellite) company" in one easy-to-tune cluster.

For cable (as contrasted with *broadcast*) networks, the economics of their business now make it possible for such entities as the above-mentioned Weather Channel and

MTV (as well as other services like CNN Headline News, Comedy Central, or various regional sports networks) to take a page out of radio's book and air one format exclusively. As in radio, cable advertisers know precisely what kind of viewer they are getting without *waste circulation*—paying to reach a substantial number of people who do not comprise their target market.

With the coming of digital transmission, in fact, specialized cable networks can subdivide themselves to be even more targeted. Pay-movie services like HBO can offer multiple networks devoted to different film types, and basic cable companies such as Discovery are able to mount four or five variations tailored to more specific science/travel interests. This trend continues to follow the radio model, where "country" has fragmented into such niches as young country, bluegrass, and classic country, while "rhythm-and-blues" audiences can select from subcategory formats such as rhythm CHR, urban classics, jazz, and urban contemporary.

As commerce fine-tunes its marketing strategies to favor more precise demographic and psychographic (life-style) targeting, the trend to more specifically tailored programming and delivery channels seems likely to accelerate. The advertiser's concern for cost-per-thousand gratification remains a constant. But in today's segmented listening and viewing world, raw rating/share numbers—and the tonnage mentality they often signify—are becoming less and less meaningful to all but the most diversified package goods manufacturer.

This can mean new opportunities and can open up new options for program creators and the electronic media that distribute their wares. Provided that the cost of program production or program licensing can be kept in check, a niche service can aggregate an extremely segmented audience on a national basis and can "rent it out" to advertisers whose products match the life-style preferences of that audience sliver exactly. In a complete reversal of Paul Klein's old LOP Theory, this strategy can even result in on-air product that constitutes some non-targeted viewers' MOPs—*most objectional programs*! As Fox executive Carolyn Wall discovered in that network's edgy infancy, "If you've got a market that likes you, it doesn't matter if everyone else hates it—you'll succeed."[38]

QUANTIFYING CONTROVERSY

For a niche service, controversial programming can be a quick way to create a "buzz" and attract the attention of a target audience. For a program deliverer that nurtures some tonnage aspirations, however, controversy can scare off large segments of the population and, simultaneously, the mainstream advertisers who are seeking to speak to them. When Fox decided to broaden the base of its advertising appeal by grabbing expensive program rights like National Football League coverage and by drastically upgrading its affiliate station list, it needed to become comparatively less edgy and to compress the spectrum of the "everyone elses" who hated it. Fox could still afford to be more daring than CBS—but it needed to be less antagonistic than the narrowcasting Comedy Central.

As a business gratification, then, controversial programming's chance of success increases as target audience specifications are narrowed. Usually, the more urban and youth-oriented the target, the better the chance that edgy offerings will attract them and the advertisers for whom they are such a prized commodity. It is much easier for a niche cable service to steer its overall image in this direction than it is for a broadcast network with its broader-demographic tonnage mentality and its hundreds of FCC-licensed affiliates that will bear the brunt of any local viewer revulsion.

As a cable network, Comedy Central could risk airing the raunchy cartoon *South Park* because the network had no local affiliates to placate, an overwhelmingly youth-seeking advertiser base, and a show that cost comparatively little to produce. The program began with few advertisers and a rate card of only $4,000 per 30-second spot. Initially, even many of Comedy Central's usually tolerant clients stayed away from the cartoon's explicitness. Before long, however, the show drew an astonishing 51 share among males ages eighteen to twenty-four in the network's 47-million home universe, a 36 share among women in that same universe, and a 5.4 rating overall—making it the second-highest-rated cable show in the country. Suddenly, spots were going for $45,000, and advertising agencies were encouraging their clients to get aboard. "*South Park* has the buzz right now. And it's got the numbers in the

THINKING ABOUT ADVERTISING ON **ABC**'s "NOTHING SACRED"? THINK AGAIN!

September 18 is the premiere of the ABC show "Nothing Sacred." The folks at Disney and ABC won't reveal who the advertisers are, but that's okay, we'll know soon enough. And when we do we'll mobilize our 350,000 members to conduct a campaign against the sponsors that they won't forget. In addition, we will contact our friends in the Protestant, Jewish and Muslim communities to join the protest.

Quite frankly, we've had it with Disney. First Michael Eisner treats us to the Disney/Miramax movie "Priest" and now he lays "Nothing Sacred" on us. In March 1995 the Catholic League became the first organization in the nation to call for a boycott of Disney. When we did so, few took us seriously. But now—given the large number of organizations that have also called for a boycott of Disney—few don't take us seriously.

A word to the wise: take this campaign seriously and move your ad money to some other show.

Catholic League
For Religious and Civil Rights

**1011 First Avenue, New York, NY 10022
(212) 371-3191, Fax: (212) 371-3334
http://www.catholicleague.org**

FIGURE 7-1
A boycott-promoting layout in *Advertising Age*. (Courtesy of William Donohue, Catholic League)

young men demos to back it up," one agency media buyer remarked. "We've told some of our clients: 'Yes, the material can be questionable. But it's a hot show and the young people are watching. Are you willing to risk it to be seen by your target demo?' "[39] The answer, of course, was a resounding 'Yes!'

Meanwhile, during the same fall season, ABC premiered *Nothing Sacred*, a well-scripted drama promoted by the network as a look deep into the struggles of a Roman Catholic priest "to balance his faith in God with the temptations and troubles of modern life." Even before the show debuted, however, the conservative Catholic League was buying space in advertising trade publications to warn prospective advertisers (see Figure 7-1), and local stations were being served with petitions from irate churchgoers.

Overall ratings for this tonnage medium show languished around 4.5—and were only about 2.1 in the advertiser-coveted eighteen-to-forty-nine-year-old category. At a time when the majority of prime-time shows were selling spots for six figures, ABC began by asking $55,000 for *Nothing Sacred* and soon reduced the price by $20,000, as tonnage-seeking advertisers like K-Mart and Weight Watchers International pulled out. Nowhere near profitability for ABC, the program was pulled after only a few weeks. "Because the show's not a hit or even marginally successful, with just a little pressure from this Catholic group most advertisers say, 'I don't need this aggravation,' " one advertising executive admitted.[40] And the same agency buyer urging his clients into *South Park* on Comedy Central was also encouraging them to stay clear of *Nothing Sacred* on ABC, asserting that "our attitude is we don't need the grief and our clients don't need the grief."[41]

Notice that the boycott of *Nothing Sacred* was launched by people who had yet to see the show, thus ignoring the first step in S. Stephenson, Smith's *critical process* as discussed in Chapter 1. Furthermore, the program's pilot episode had been written under a pen name by a Catholic priest, and the Jesuit publication *America* had run a glowing review. But from a business gratification sense, the damage had already been done. An expensive-to-produce, older-skewing show on a tonnage-dependent medium could not withstand the pressure that a lower-cost property on a youth-oriented niche channel could deflect—or even bask in!

The business gratifications danger in all of this for the broadcast networks is that they can become marginalized; they can become seen as so safe and unchallenging to everyone that they are the prime programming choice of no one. "Cutting edge material has to be presented by ad-supported television networks," warns movie producer Fred Pierce, "if they are going to be able to compete within this framework of an expanding universe of cable channels. If advertisers want the networks to remain viable, they have to support it. Otherwise network TV will end up becoming ineffectual and bland."[42]

AUDIENCE MEASUREMENT UNCERTAINTY

As the discussion above demonstrates, "the ratings" gauge the economic viability of delivery systems and their programming. Indeed, virtually every business gratification in our industry is tied in some way to the data that come from audience measurement services. These data even benchmark advertiser tolerance of controversial program content. "People are not willing to take the heat for a bad number," media buying executive Paul Schulman points out, "but for a good number they'll look the other way."[43] Unfortunately, there is more and more concern about how accurate this measurement has become in the fragmented multichannel world of the twenty-first century. As researcher Ien Ang relates,

This dissolution of "television audience" as a solid entity became historically urgent when "anarchic" viewer practices such as zapping and zipping became visible, when viewing contexts and preferences began to multiply, in short when the industry, because of the diversification of its economic interests, had to come to terms with the irrevocably changeable and capricious nature of "watching television" as an activity.[44]

With its hand-held key pad, the *people meter* was supposed to compensate for these changed audience behaviors. In 1987, Nielsen converted its national television sample from *audimeters*, which recorded only when a set was on and to which channel it was tuned, to people meters. Unlike the old audimeter, which was set/household-based, the people meter strives to be viewer-based by having each member of the household punch in a personal code number when he or she starts and ceases viewing. (See Figure 7-2.)

Unfortunately, this greater involvement on the part of consumers may also inject greater error into the process. Children's viewing patterns in particular seem subject to measurement distortion because kids either neglect to punch in or use incorrect codings. It is hoped that *passive* (advanced) people meters that use infrared devices to automatically identify viewers by their facial characters eventually will rectify these problems. Ultimately, two-way digital delivery may provide the means whereby the viewing selections of every household (if not of every

FIGURE 7-2
On-screen prompts from a people meter. The graphic display confirms that Sue, John, and Mary have all "logged in" that they are watching this set. (Courtesy of Nan Myers, The Arbitron Company)

viewer) will be tallied, making ratings a system of actual counting instead of statistical sampling. Still, "standard measures of audience size make no distinctions between viewers in terms of their involvement with programs (or any advertisements they may carry) because they measure all 'viewing' equally," writes Professor Barrie Gunter. "Indeed, most television ratings systems, technically speaking, measure viewers' presence in the room with the television switched on, rather than actual viewing."[45]

Radio audience measurement similarly is afflicted with doubts. For several years, radio stations and advertising agencies could compare outlet performance from two perspectives. Arbitron used diaries filled out by selected listeners, and Birch/Scarborough relied on telephone interviews. Even though each methodology tended to favor different formats, cross-checking between them helped validate station audience performance. In December 1991, however, the Birch service was discontinued, leaving Arbitron as the only comprehensive provider of radio listenership data. Is this single service enough to ensure accuracy? Some broadcasters have their doubts. "Top-of-mind awareness is what gets you Arbitron numbers," advises Jacor Communications chief executive Randy Michaels, "but this may not replicate actual listening."[46]

Radio and television audience measurement estimates may never approach the tangibility and comprehensiveness of print's 'copies sold' numbers. Yet, the electronic media must compete with print for advertising dollars. They must justify to advertising agencies and their clients that money expended on commercials is money well spent. Ultimately, our profession's business gratifications can be fully satisfied only when there is widely shared faith in what "the numbers" are saying.

That rating/share reports are not deep enough gauges of a program's popularity is sometimes reflected after a show has been canceled. When he was heading NBC's programming efforts, Brandon Tartikoff once observed that "the greatest outpouring of sentiment and passion usually comes after a show is canceled, and I would love as a ratings-monger and programmer, to be aware of that kind of support at the time I am making a decision; . . . sometimes it's hard to put Humpty Dumpty back together again."[47]

If measuring past show performance is difficult, then estimating the future success of program properties in today's fragmented media world is nearly impossible. Advertising analyst Stephen Battaglio reports that "gone are the days when predictions for success could be based on a show's time period or the track record of its star. Competition from cable and the power of the remote control have turned the projections for hits and misses by agency media departments into virtual guesswork."[48]

Thus, in the electronic media, business gratifications are now as difficult to anticipate before the fact as they are to *profitably* document after the fact. Quantitative "information is indispensable for the industry to operate," writes Ang, "but there is constant agony in industry circles about the adequacy of the information they get from audience measurement."[49] This agony has been extended to the on-line world, where disagreements over what to count (site visits, hits, clicks, page views, actual e-commerce purchases) are as vocal as are debates over how to count them. In addition, both advertisers and electronic media outlets now are faced with trying to compare traditional media message impact with that of new media. "What does it mean when 1,000 people visit your site?" asks Farris Kahn, interactive marketing coordinator for GM's Saturn division. "Is it better or worse than 100,000 people seeing your TV commercial?"[50] In today's world, even precise counting of the audience is only a first step in determining whether the needs of the participating businesses thereby have been efficiently served.

SCHEDULING AND FLOW ANALYSIS

Despite the growth of new media, and the business gratification questions these new media raise, television remains the dominant entertainment vehicle. Viewer use of television has changed, however, forcing programmers to refine scheduling strategies. As Battaglio alluded to earlier, "a show's time period" used to be a highly significant factor in predicting and attaining ratings supremacy. But given fickle-fingered remote controls, time-shifting VCRs, and the massive number of channel options, the outlet or network programmer is no longer in complete control of when, and in what order, viewers watch a show.

The programmer's power is likely to decline even more with the coming of PVRs (personal video recorders). Pioneered by companies like TiVo and Replay, PVRs are essentially computer hard drives capable of recording television programs. These set-top devices can automatically capture up to 30 hours of shows while also permitting viewers to pause, rewind, or fast forward past ads while watching TV in real time. A PVR can also be programmed to record any show that corresponds to a particular viewer preference. It could, for example, automatically "grab and store" all documentaries on birds or all telecast movies starring Tom Hanks. "This new generation of set-top boxes takes us to a whole new era of 'appointment TV,'" writes advertising critic Debra Goldman, "except this time, the viewers are scheduling the appointments."[51]

This may not be all bad for advertisers. The modem connection that gives viewers such flexibility also carries back to program sources a report of the choices these viewers have made. Armed with this information, advertisers could substitute precisely targeted commercials for general pitches. Households whose viewing preferences indicate the presence of young children could receive ads promoting an auto maker's family mini-van rather than its luxury sedan. Households whose preferences evidence a more "mature" demographic could be sent laxative rather than pimple-cream pitches.

Until PVR-type devices achieve significant penetration, however, general advertising will still be the rule, and scheduling by professional programmers will remain strategically significant—particularly in the launch of new shows and the nurturing or smothering of struggling ones. What comes before and after, as well as what is simultaneously available from competing services, are still important considerations when large numbers of viewers lack the technology, the expertise, or the will to computerize their show selections. Thus, astute professionals still analyze blocks of television programs in the same way that a radio format is critiqued.

Sometimes referred to as *flow analysis*, this procedure makes the assumption that a program or format segment in isolation is perceived differently than one experienced as part of an extended listening or viewing block. "Programming practice actively discourages the viewer from thinking of the schedule in terms of a sequence of isolated and unrelated programs," points out media professor Robert Allen. "In fact, enormous amounts of energy go into covering over the gaps between programs and stitching each segment into the larger programming fabric."[52] Beginning in 1994, for example, NBC required program suppliers to shorten their end credits, then squeezed these credits into a half-screen to make room for other material that propelled the viewer immediately into the following show. Commercials could come later, once the top- or bottom-of-the-hour break had been seamlessly bridged. Most other programmers soon adopted similar strategies to keep viewers from grazing through options on competing channels.

Contrary to the portrayal in Figure 7-3, the dynamics of managing flow can be bewildering. This is because different parties have different priorities in flow construction. In describing the considerations that NBC's programming head was required to balance in prime-time scheduling, for instance, industry observer Richard Turner reported that "he must consider that NBC's affiliated stations will care most about the shows that lead into their local news, where they make their money, but that his own research department will care most about 8 o'clock (ET) because a strong show kicking off prime time can power the whole night."[53]

A more specific illustration of the difficulties of merging affiliate/network flow (particularly in the case of "live" programming) is contributed by John Sias, then group president for ABC Television. Sias relates the considerations that have gone into how the network's *Monday Night Football* is timetabled. As the Sias example indicates, there usually is no perfect solution when network and affiliate preferences are at cross-purposes. Whether the games start at 8:00 or 9:00 in a given season ultimately depends on which option seems to create the most economically advantageous flow for the network and its station partners—as well as what can be negotiated with the program supplier (in this case, the NFL):

Most of the affiliates in the East—well, all of them in the East and Midwest—want them to start at 8 because of the runovers. As the

FIGURE 7-3
A popular miscon-
ception about the
process and ease of
program scheduling.
(Illustration by
Scott Huver)

games have gotten longer and longer . . .
they're devastating to affiliates' 11 o'clock
news, which is a critical part of their weekly
offering. So the affiliates are more than
aroused on the subject, and very, very distressed with it.

The West Coast has a different problem. If
we start at 8 Eastern time, then they're starting at 5 o'clock, which is right in the middle
of their drive time and at the start of two-
and-a-half hours or three hours of local programming with the exception of network
newscasts.[54]

One advantage cable networks have over
their broadcast counterparts in such situations, of course, is that they can program entire twenty-four-hour periods without worrying about lead in or lead out from a local
affiliate's time.

Radio has its flow quandaries, too. But,
like cable, the network/affiliate issues that
complicate broadcast television are largely
absent. This is because radio *networks* or *syn-*

dicated services (the distinction between the
two is now inconsequential) exist solely to
further their affiliates' flow plans. A station
selects a network/syndicator either for how
well that supplier's individual offerings will
fit in with the local format or for how completely that supplier delivers the *total* format.
In the latter case, it is a question of how
seamlessly local announcements and *stop sets*
(commercial breaks) can be inserted into the
network stream. Whether they are occasional or continuous, if the network or syndicator elements do not smoothly interweave with what the local station wants to
air—the station will find another program
supplier.

Working either at the local station or the
network/syndicator level, radio programmers design elaborate "hot clocks" to specify
what type of element will happen at a given
time within a given hour during a given
daypart. Unfortunately, a format that works
well in audience delivery in one locale can be

a bust in another—even if competing stations in the two cities are closely comparable. The reason for this inconsistency may have nothing to do with the competence of the format developer or the local air personnel. Instead, it is often a function of life-style misflow. The hot clock that succeeds beautifully in a market in which factory shift changes and/or school starting/dismissal times occur on the hour can be completely out of sync with a town in which such events occur at the quarter or half hour. Similarly, a locality in which the average commute is one hour will have substantially divergent format needs from one in which most people can drive to or from work in fifteen minutes. The sensitive media professional will learn to recognize these variables in music or talk segment design—and will exploit them accordingly.

In both radio and television, flow and overall scheduling strategy thus are at least as important as individual program selection in achieving business gratification. In fact, CBS's former programming head, Michael Dann, has frequently maintained that the position a program is assigned still is much more vital to it and its outlet's success than is the content of the program itself.

An interesting ramification of this principle is that rating/share "failures" can nevertheless be bottom-line successes if their scheduling accomplishes a reasonable goal in a cost-effective manner. In early 1987, former NBC News correspondent Lloyd Dobyns made a prediction that illustrates this phenomenon:

In September, ABC News started running *Our World* with Linda Ellerbee and Ray Gandolf in prime time. The new show is up against NBC's *The Cosby Show*, television's monster hit. But *Our World* is cheaper to produce than an entertainment program. If by some miracle *Our World* can succeed against *Cosby*, its return on investment will be enormous. Even if it dies, its failure will cost a lot less than a Hollywood sitcom. Either way, ABC's profit-and-loss sheet will look better.[55]

In a typical week, *Cosby* outdrew *Our World* in audience by a ratio of at least 4 to 1. But the documentary series remained on the air as proof of Dobyns's projection. The show constituted a business success for certain advertisers in search of the older and up-scale male audience that was *Our World*'s primary

constituency. Given the program's nontonnage numbers, these advertisers were able to purchase prime time at bargain-basement rates. At the same time, ABC made a modest profit because of *Our World*'s comparatively meager production costs. Still, after one season, flow considerations forced the show's cancellation as local affiliates would no longer sanction this lightweight start to a prime-time night.

This scenario has been repeated dozens of times since, with ratings potential versus the competition being weighed against program acquisition costs and the appeal to advertisers of the type of viewers likely to be attracted. "It is now more important to be the most profitable, than to be first in the ratings," points out NBC News producer Brett Holey.[56] All of the long-standing program strategies, such as counterprogramming (running a show appealing to a different audience than competing offerings), *hammocking* (putting a new or weak show between two strong ones), or *tentpoling* (placing a strong program between two new or weak ones), are not tools to increase ratings, but mechanisms to enhance profitability.

Ultimately, schedule and flow analysis is reduced to five fundamental questions to which the programmer must prepare critical responses:

1. Is the program/element length appropriate to the subject matter?

2. Is the time of day appropriate to the available and sought-after audience?

3. Is the content choice advantageous in terms of the competition's simultaneous offerings?

4. Does the feature assist audience flow from the event that precedes it to the event that follows it?

5. Is the cost of the programming compatible with the revenues likely to be derived from airing it? (For public broadcasting this entails whether an underwriter can be found to support it and/or whether the program will appeal to consumers most likely to contribute to the station's pledge drives.)

THE FINAL BALANCE SHEET

Bottom-line return, as facilitated by the program creation and scheduling processes that make the construction of audiences possible, is the electronic media's core business gratification. Though it is vital to probe the artistic, symbolic, sociological, and psychological dimensions of program content, our enterprise's economic realities also must be taken into consideration. As Robert Lewis Shayon recognized decades ago,

the creator's view had to be broadened to include the market-place complex in which the creator is the least important element. Talent, however publicized and misrepresented as the *sine qua non* of the game, is really the pawn, disposable, dispensable, and easily replaceable. The man who can choose the winners in the program race has the talent that is truly treasured by the managers behind the scenes.[57]

However essential it is to survival, 'winning' at the profit game is not our *only* concern, of course. The best media professionals, maintains Bernadette McGuire of the National Association of Public Television Stations, "are those who understand the business side of broadcasting and know how to use it for the benefit of society."[58]

As we apply the perspectives of criticism to our profession, business gratification can neither be ignored nor can it become the sole criterion by which our "bi-focal" enterprise is evaluated. "What is called for," in the words of media expert Les Brown, "is a knowledgeable criticism and commentary that accepts the reality of the television [and overall media] system which exists, and that seeks to help it raise its aims—criticism that spurs the industry to self-examination rather than to arguments in self-defense."[59]

ENDNOTES

1. George Boas, *A Primer for Critics* (New York: Greenwood Press, 1968), 124–125.
2. Carl Grabo, *The Creative Critic* (Chicago: University of Chicago Press, 1948), 123.
3. Horace Newcomb and Robert Alley, *The Producer's Medium* (New York: Oxford University Press, 1983), 12.
4. "Hall of Fame: The Class of 1994," *Broadcasting & Cable* (November 14, 1994), 19.
5. Ien Ang, *Desperately Seeking the Audience* (London: Routledge, 1991), 30.
6. Eileen Meehan, "Conceptualizing Culture as Commodity: The Problem of Television," *Critical Studies in Mass Communication* (December 1986), 448–449.
7. Don West, "Broadcaster's Broadcaster," *Broadcasting & Cable* (November 13, 1995), 40.
8. Richard Wald, speech to the International Radio & Television Society Faculty/Industry Seminar, February 22, 1979 (Glen Cove, NY).
9. Eric Schmuckler, "Show Time," *Adweek Upfront Programming* (May 31, 1999), 49.
10. Debra Goldman, "The Shape of Things to Come," *Adweek Media Quarterly* (September 18, 1995), 6.
11. Jon Bengtson, remarks to the Broadcast & Cinematic Arts Department Advisory Board, Central Michigan University, October 26, 1991 (Mt. Pleasant, MI).
12. Steve Coe, "The Quality Controllers," *Broadcasting & Cable* (December 5, 1994), 47.
13. Thomas Tyrer and William Mahoney, "Iger Says Sweeps More Important Than Season." *Electronic Media* (August 19, 1991), 26.
14. Brett Holey, remarks to Broadcast & Cinematic Arts students, Central Michigan University, October 2, 1989 (Mt. Pleasant, MI).
15. Steve Coe, "Quality TV: Hollywood's Elusive Illusions," *Broadcasting* (November 18, 1991), 3, 17.
16. Ibid., 17.
17. Ibid.
18. Ibid., 3.
19. "The Play's Still the Thing," *Broadcasting* (December 14, 1987), 76.
20. Ben Stein, *The View from Sunset Boulevard* (New York: Basic Books, 1979), 27.
21. Wolfgang Amadeus Mozart, letter to his father, February 20, 1784, quoted in Sam Morgenstern (ed.), *Composers on Music* (New York: Pantheon, 1956), 84.
22. "Hollywood's Man of the Hours," *Broadcasting* (November 14, 1988), 46, 48.
23. "Bang-Up NATPE for Action-Adventure Shows," *Broadcasting* (February 2, 1987), 67.
24. Samuel Becker, "Critical Studies: A Multidimensional Movement," *Feedback* (Fall 1985), 24.
25. Joseph Russin, "Confessions of a Rookie Owner," *ADWEEK Radio 1984 Issue* (November 1984), 44.
26. Louis Day, *Ethics in Media Communications: Cases and Controversies* (Belmont, CA: Wadsworth, 1991), 178–179.
27. Katherine Graham, keynote speech to the NATPE Convention, February 23, 1988 (Houston).
28. John Ellis, "Channel 4: Working Notes," *Screen*, Vol. 24, No. 6 (1983), 49.
29. Hugh Belville, *Audience Ratings: Radio, Television, Cable* (Hillsdale, NJ: Lawrence Erlbaum, 1985), xi.
30. Richard Blake, "Condominiums in the Global Village," in Rodman, 131.
31. Richard Katz, "Network TV: Eroding but Not Going Away," *ADWEEK Media Outlook* (September 8, 1997), 8.

32. "Bang-Up NATPE," 69.

33. Les Brown, "Trends in TV Criticism," speech to the Broadcast Education Association Convention, March 28, 1987 (Dallas).

34. "Television from Two Points of View," *Broadcasting & Cable* (January 8, 1996), 36.

35. John Fiske, *Television Culture* (London: Methuen, 1987), 326.

36. Charles Warner, "Selling in the New Competitive Era," speech to the Broadcast Education Association Convention, March 27, 1987 (Dallas).

37. Charles Taylor, "State of the Industry," *ADWEEK Radio Supplement* (September 4, 1995), 5.

38. Carolyn Wall, remarks to the International Radio & Television Society Faculty/Industry Seminar, February 7, 1991 (New York).

39. Chuck Ross, "Advertisers Flock to Comedy Central's Racy 'South Park,' " *Advertising Age* (January 12, 1998), 3, 38.

40. Chuck Ross, " 'Nothing Sacred' Keeps Faith Despite Boycott Push," *Advertising Age* (October 20, 1997), 16.

41. Ross, "Advertisers Flock," 38.

42. Joe Mandese, "Struggling to Stay on the Beat," *Advertising Age* (January 17, 1994), 42.

43. Christopher Stern, "Ad Agencies Still Upbeat on 'NYPD Blue,' " *Broadcasting & Cable* (October 4, 1993), 64.

44. Ang, 154–155.

45. Barrie Gunter, "On the Future of Television Ratings," *Journal of Broadcasting & Electronic Media* (Summer 1993), 360.

46. Randy Michaels, remarks to the Great Lakes Radio Conference, April 6, 1991 (Mt. Pleasant, MI).

47. "Network Programing Chiefs Face Viewers for Quality TV," *Broadcasting* (October 2, 1989), 50.

48. Stephen Battaglio, "Luck of the Draw," *ADWEEK* (January 27, 1992), 20.

49. Ang, 8.

50. Scott Donaton, "Standards Required to Make Next Leap," *Advertising Age* (November 4, 1996), s30.

51. Debra Goldman, "New Digital Recorders Give Power to the People," *ADWEEK* (June 28, 1999), 14.

52. Robert Allen, "Talking about Television," in Robert Allen (ed.), *Channels of Discourse* (Chapel Hill: University of North Carolina Press, 1987), 3.

53. Richard Turner, "Countdown to the Final Choices," *TV Guide* (October 15, 1988), 27.

54. John Sias, quoted in "Life on the Downside at Capcities/ABC," *Broadcasting* (December 22, 1986), 64.

55. Lloyd Dobyns, "Producer to Reporter: 'Think Weird, Think Live, Good Luck,' " *TV Guide* (February 14, 1987), 37.

56. Holey, remarks.

57. Robert Lewis Shayon, *Open to Criticism* (Boston: Beacon Press, 1971), 120.

58. Bernadette McGuire, "Self-Regulation and Government Regulation." Speech to the Broadcast Education Association Convention, March 27, 1987 (Dallas).

59. Les Brown, "Remarks to the Iowa TV Critics Conference," *Critical Studies in Mass Communication* (December 1985), 395.

8

Audience Gratifications

As we explore in the previous chapter, audience research caters to business gratifications by producing mounds of data about who is listening and watching and for how long. Via diaries, telephone interviews, shopping-mall intercept questionnaires, people meters, and on-line registrations, industry decision-makers acquire information to define and divide electronic media patrons into a number of demographic and psychographic (life-style) categories. Yet, while we are gathering ever-more sophisticated documentation of the *who*, the counterpart explanation of the *why* remains much more elusive.

Knowing that a certain number of a given type of people patronized our show is helpful in after-the-fact justification of advertising rates. To a certain extent, this information can also predict who will listen or watch in the upcoming weeks. But Nielsens and Arbitrons do not tell us what brought these consumers to our format, program, or website. The ratings books do not indicate what need(s) these audience members were seeking to satisfy. These needs and their implications are the subjects of this chapter.

A CONSUMER USES OVERVIEW

Establishing that a hit television program garnered an 11 rating and a 19 share is a *quantitative* but not a *qualitative* determination. What did these audiences find enjoyable? Was it the show's locale and basic premise? The script/plot development? The talent who were cast? What, *exactly*, about these factors brought about audience satisfaction? And just what *was* that satisfaction, anyway? Lacking the answers to these and related questions, media professionals cannot predictably duplicate a hit's success in fashioning a subsequent series (or format). In fact, we cannot even ensure that we are emphasizing the proper elements to keep the current show popular in subsequent months. If, however, we have some glimpse of the satisfaction clusters that have drawn audience members to this programming, we can come closer to identifying what we should continue to emphasize in it—as well as what ingredients we might want to include in future projects under development.

What we are pursuing here has come to be known as *uses and gratifications* research. Pioneered by Professor Elihu Katz as early as 1959, "this movement has shifted attention away from questions of media effects toward questions of media use," points out William Evans. "This includes a conceptualization of audience needs that sees gratification as primary in the media effects process. Thus, media consumers were seen as rational agents whose various uses of media offerings depend upon how these offerings serve various social-psychological functions."[1] According to David Swanson:

Uses and gratifications research has made substantial contributions to our understanding of the mass communication process. Important elements and correlates of the psychological context in which exposure to mass media occurs have been brought to light by a great many uses and gratifications studies. . . . Empirical studies have discovered that gratifications take many forms, from learning information that can be instrumental in performing one's role as a citizen to consuming media fare in a relaxing ritual. . . . Audience members exhibit some independence and diversity in linking gratifications to media messages as they creatively use mass communication to try to accomplish their desired ends.[2]

Uses and gratifications research, in other words, rejects the old legacy-of-fear approach, in which the mass media were seen as domineering agents that could easily manipulate the huddled masses thrown together in rapidly industrializing societies. Instead, the modern uses and gratifications orientation "assumes that the audience is powerful, taking an active part in selecting media," writes Professor Joey Reagan. "Those who adhere to 'active audience' perspectives assume that people select media that more closely match their needs and interests."[3] "Succinctly put," adds Professor Carolyn Lin, "The strength of this theory is its ability to allow researchers to study mediated communication situations via single or multiple sets of psychological needs, psychological motives, communication channels, communication content, and psychological gratifications within a particular or cross-cultural context."[4] Relating this to our Chapter 4 discussion of empiricism's two stages, ratings and shares constitute the (Stage One) "what" of audience analysis, but it is uses and gratifications data that attempt to explain the (Stage Two) "why" that audience chose the particular programs they did.

An underlying assumption to the uses and gratifications approach, point out researchers Elizabeth Perse and Alan Rubin, is that "when needs and desires cannot be met in more natural ways, people turn to media."[5] Thus, our programming is seen as performing a *compensatory function*. Rather than adding an entirely new dimension to audience members' lives, electronic media content is sought after because it fills in gratification gaps in people's 'real-world' existence. This may be why some very predictable shows sometimes are much more popular than are highly innovative offerings. Audiences know what to anticipate from the content and how it will serve their need expectations.

Viewed from this perspective, program 'quality' is anything but some high-brow or elitist ingredient. Rather, 'quality' is an extremely functional commodity that audiences actively seek to purchase with an investment of their time. The more accurately the program producer can guess the gratifications that target consumers will seek from the show, the more likely that show will be seen as "good" by those consumers. As Ien Ang cautions us:

'Quality' as formally defined and operationalized by the institutions [studios and media outlets] in their programming decisions may well not at all correspond with what in practical terms counts as 'quality' in the social world of actual audiences. We should realize, as Charlotte Brunsdon has remarked, that people constantly make their own judgements of quality when they watch television, judgements which can vary from situation to situation, depending on the type of satisfaction they look for at any particular time. From this perspective, 'quality' is not a fixed standard of value on which the professional broadcaster holds a patent, but is a radically contingent criterion of judgement to be made by actual audiences in actual situations, 'something [in Brunsdon's words] that we all do whenever we channel hop in search of an image or sound which we can identify as likely, or most likely, to satisfy.'[6]

Media professionals who are ignorant of this uses and gratifications dynamic may totally misread target audiences and thereby misuse their opportunities to connect with those audiences. Such imperceptive professionals will often take pleasure in a programmatic element that escapes consumers entirely. Or, consumers may choose to listen or watch in order to enjoy a component of which even the producer is relatively unaware.

This is one reason that professional critics' pronouncements and documented audience choices are at times so diametrically opposed, with the reviewer praising a series the public avoids or the public flocking to a program the critic despises. It is not necessarily a matter of critic and consumers having *conflicting tastes*, but rather of possessing *different orientations and priorities*.

The following commentary by advertising executive and consumer behavior specialist Susan Small-Weil illustrates just how radically different the appeals that media producers (and critics) invest *in* a message may be from the gratifications that consumers derive *from* it. Though she is focusing on the obvious distinction between adult and toddler expectations, Small-Weil's examples are much more generalizable to media consumers at large than we often want to believe. It is not that listeners and viewers are infantile. Rather, the point is this: What audiences seek to do with our narratives is usually much more straightforward than the devious or super-slick cues we sometimes place in those narratives. When we over-design or "overmediate" our format or program, we may be losing sight of the fundamental purposes that consumers wish our content to serve. And thus, we may lose or confuse them.

A CHILD'S-EYE VIEW

by Susan Small-Weil, Ph.D.

Until my son Cameron was born two-and-a-half years ago, I believed I could repress my "insider" knowledge of the marketplace and be open-minded when I listened to consumers describe how they approach a category, react to a new concept, or become motivated by a test commercial. The only thing I thought of was the last focus group, the most recent segmentation study or the sociologist's definition of my target consumer as "advanced Annie," "wait and watch Wendy," or "status quo Sally."

But raising a 2-year-old changes how you think. It forces you to forget everything you've learned throughout life and view the world fresh and new. That's the joy of being a parent, and the magic of being a child.

I've learned a lot from Cameron. Cameron smashes his Cozy Coupe into his fire engine after viewing a Volvo commercial—to him Volvo is violent, not safe. Cameron refuses to eat eggs because he believes eggs are drugs and will do bad things to his brain. For that matter, Cameron won't drink cherry- or raspberry-flavored seltzer because he believes that someone has doctored the seltzer with cherry-flavored Tylenol. And he rejects grape lollipops because they remind him of having a cold, and having to down grape-flavored Dimetapp.

Cameron won't eat Welch's squeezable jelly because it has a warning symbol on the side telling people how not to squeeze it—a symbol Cameron says is "the same one as [the warning symbol on poisons] in the garage."

Through Cameron I've learned to view symbols, images, shapes, words, even flavors from a truly objective vantage point. In this way, I see something different from what I previously believed I saw. I've learned to open my eyes to see the world the way the consumer sees it.

My new approach is to view advertising as if I were Cameron. Cameron loves Tropicana orange juice. He associates it with fresh oranges; I think that's pretty good imagery. He wants to use Plax mouthwash because he believes his mouth will "have fun"; that should promote share growth.

Cameron calls Merv Griffin "that funny fat man" because of his Resorts International advertising in which he goes from restaurant to restaurant getting fatter and fatter. That's a great image for a hotel or restaurant in a world where Slim-Fast sales just passed $1 billion.

And Cameron is confused by celebrity endorsements for cola beverages. One day he informed me that Kevin (from The Wonder Years) drinks Coke. Then he shook his head and said, "No, no, he drinks Diet Pepsi; no, no, he drinks Coke; no, no. . . ." Clearly Cameron is caught up in the cola wars. Why not? The rest of us are!

As for the basic rules of advertising, Cameron, like the rest of us, falls in Rule 1: He likes advertising that shows babies and puppies. As for the "brand mention rule," Cameron doesn't need to hear the brand name three times, or hear it in the first seven seconds of the commercial. He just needs to see the name and the package. After all, someone isn't saying the name in the store. New York Deli potato chips or Honey Nut Cheerios manage to scream out to him in the store without ever having their name spoken.

And from Cameron's reaction to the Energizer Bunny, I knew that those few bunny skeptics were wrong. The skeptics said that the average consumer could not appreciate the parody commercials interrupted by the intrusion of the bunny. But the look on Cameron's face the very first time the bunny walked across a coffee table was a sure sign that the advertising would achieve broad-scale appeal. The look was one that could only be replicated by a UFO landing in the middle of Cameron's bedroom, delivering Mickey Mouse holding a case of M&Ms. To Cameron, like everyone else, surprise is exciting.

Of course, Cameron spent the entire Christmas season waiting for bunnies to appear in every commercial. The rest of us began to expect the bunny only when we saw an unfamiliar brand name. To Cameron, everything is an unfamiliar brand name (except Coke, Pepsi, Tropicana . . .), so he waits for bunnies to appear in every ad from "The Heartbeat of America" to "Reach Out and Touch Someone." I think viewing the world as Cameron does could save us a lot of money on copy tests or costly on-air mistakes.

Cameron's approach mirrors the charm of the movie Big. Tom Hanks was successful as a marketer of children's toys because he could think like a child—not like we think a child thinks. There's a big difference.

People tell me Cameron watches too much TV. Maybe so. What I say is that we as advertisers probably don't watch enough. Or else we only watch it from our ivory towers. One thing I'm sure of: As much as I try to teach Cameron the things he needs to know, he in turn teaches me. I have a better, more relevant perspective on advertising.

(Reprinted with permission of ADWEEK)

Whether we are dealing with commercials or programs, children or adults, radio, television, or the Internet, finding the likely *audience* gratifications is infinitely more important to communicative success than is inventorying the gratifications we, as media professionals, get from watching or listening to the message. No one is paying us to produce or distribute what we personally enjoy or wish for. What we are employed to do is to resonate with our target audiences by tapping into the gratifications they are most likely to be seeking—via images that most unmistakably service those gratifications.

In several decades of exploring the uses and gratifications goals of media consumers, researchers have evolved a large number of categories and systems for organizing and cataloguing these gratifications. In their 1973 research, for example, Elihu Katz and his associates explored how helpful the media were in satisfying fourteen "important needs" that the researchers further subdivided into no fewer than thirty-five subcategories.[7] Though such comprehensive taxonomies cannot be detailed in this single chapter, we can distill the results of this and a great deal of other uses and gratifications research to derive a manageable list of seven admittedly overlapping use/gratification factors:

1. Entertainment/time punctuation
2. Information/surveillance
3. Escapism/nostalgia
4. Companionship/conversation building
5. Problem solving
6. Personal enrichment and development
7. Catharsis/tension release

While probing these factors, it is necessary to keep three qualifications in mind: (1) listening/viewing searches and choices may often be motivated by a combination of two or more of these gratifications categories; (2) originating media professionals may not be fully aware of the range of gratifications cues that has been encoded into their programming; and (3) consumers may not be able to detect precisely the core gratifications they are seeking and/or absorbing from a given piece of radio/television content.

When *All in the Family* became immensely popular in the early 1970s, for instance, some observers celebrated the event as an affirmation that mainstream America was now ready to reject Archie Bunker–style bigotry. It was assumed that the show's viewers were drawn to it because they appreciated the social satire and its championing of the values of human tolerance (personal enrichment and development). However, uses and gratifications research later uncovered that certain viewers gravitated to *All in the Family* because they identified *with* Archie; they were pleased that television now had the courage to feature people like themselves who 'tell it like it is' (companionship/conversation building.) "The segment of viewers who interpreted Archie as the hero were people who shared Archie's point of view on social and political issues," observe Professors Christine Scodari and Judith Thorpe. "To avoid dissonance, perhaps, they would selectively dismiss those aspects of the text which might indicate to most people that Archie was created to present an unflattering portrait of the political philosophy he embraces."[8] Though it was not creator Norman Lear's intent, *All in the Family* thus served divergent gratifications that combined to consolidate its rating success. Much more recently, NBC research found that there was no unified audience for its monster hit *Seinfeld*. Instead, there were about twenty distinct audiences, each with its own reasons for watching. "From the promotion of the show to scheduling the promotions, we had to take that into account," reveals NBC West Coast president Don Ohlmeyer. "If all you're doing is saying tonight people want to watch *Seinfeld*, you've missed it, there are no 'people.' "[9]

We should also realize that a uses and gratifications approach assumes a different orientation toward a communication transaction than what we allude to at the beginning of the chapter as *media effects* research. Media effects research tries to ascertain how those media influenced, shaped, or even manipulated the citizenry. But in the case of uses and gratifications, asserts former top CBS executive Gene Jankowski,

the real question is not "what does television do to people?" but "what do people do with television?" given the opportunity. . . . If television [or any other medium] is perceived as a force capable of manipulating the individual, without his or her consent, it will be structured one way. If it is seen as a device used by the individual to satisfy his or her needs, it will be structured another way. . . .

This is a distinction in content that derives from a distinction in philosophy. One point of view holds that television is a self-contained and powerful force molding the lives, actions and attitudes of its viewers. Another holds that television is a significant advance in the long history of media development whose value, like that of all its predecessors, comes from *the degree of satisfaction the user derives from it*.[10] [italics added]

Under the uses and gratifications scenario then, we scrutinize the listener or viewer, in the words of British theorists John Fiske and John Hartley, "as an individual with certain psychological needs. He takes these needs

with him to the television screen [or other electronic receiver], and the mass communicator attempts to gratify them."[11] For this mass communicator, of course, the dual trick is in ascertaining which need clusters (such as those we are about to discuss) are most appealing to the target audience and also the type of message most likely to be perceived as addressing those emphasized needs to create the advertisement response or program loyalty we want. As Denis McQuail reminds us, "What is central for mass communication is not message-making or sending and not even the messages themselves, but the choice, reception and manner of response of the audience."[12]

ENTERTAINMENT/TIME PUNCTUATION

Entertainment/time punctuation is the most obvious and most common gratification that the public seeks from the electronic media. "In American society," wrote George Comstock and his colleagues, "the central use and gratification of television is entertainment. Entertainment is not only predominant in content, but the seeking of entertainment is the predominant rationale offered by the public for viewing television."[13] In 1997, a study by Roper Starch Worldwide found that 81 percent of Americans surveyed believed that entertainment was a "very" or "somewhat" important role for television to play.[14]

People have similar attitudes about radio, but often with more emphasis on the *time punctuation* component of this appeal. It is not just that audiences are being entertained, but also that they are being catered to via a predictable schedule that undergirds the rituals of their existence. Radio's portability and ease of intake (one is not required to sit in front of it to fully experience the message) make the medium a prime vehicle for waking up to the day, marking the commute to/from work or school, and setting the stage for break time, meal time, fun time, and bed time. Radio-listening options divide the day into comfortable, bearable units that provide a smoothing continuity to the sometimes erratic rhythms of our lives. "Whether they hear a time check or not, listeners can tell time by fixed features on their favorite station," affirms radio consultant Ed Shane.

"I call these benchmark features 'subliminal timekeepers.' They are radio's equivalent of my neighbor's morning walk to his curb. . . . The most successful radio stations put their features or programs into parallel with their listeners' daily habits in order to reinforce the habit of listening."[15]

With its early morning news magazine staples, its afternoon soaps, its early and late evening newscasts, and the variety of boredom-inhibiting programs in between, broadcast television is also a time bracketer, though on a less unbroken basis than the formatic flow of radio. "Just as the segments of our real day tend to demand different elements of our personalities to emerge," observes Elayne Rapping, "so do the talk and information shows that follow us through out schedules. Television is in that sense a real mirror—translated into media symbols and images—of our daily lives. It makes us at home no matter what we are doing by doing the same things in the same manner."[16]

To a significant degree, many cable channels use their more specialized (niche) role to try to outdo broadcast television as life-style-serving time punctuators. Such tactics have only caused broadcast stations and networks to try even harder to service this gratification. Cable "life-style" channels and programs increasingly are being mirrored by competing syndicated shows on broadcast stations. Meanwhile, broadcast networks are entering into ventures to *repurpose* their daytime soaps, serving the traditional at-home soap audience during the day and then profiting from evening cable repeats of these dramas to mesh with the schedules and diversion requirements of working women. In cable and in broadcast television, it is not just a matter of being entertaining, but also of being entertaining in a way that blends in with the temporal expectations and needs of a given daypart's available audience. Certain shows and personalities transfer well to different dayparts; others do not. "There are some shows we all look forward to watching at particular times on particular days," writes TV critic Joe Queenan. "I'd even go so far as to identify a biorhythmic element here, which is why we like watching Katie Couric at seven in the morning but might not enjoy her at midnight."[17]

Some critics feel that 'mere' entertainment and time-marking programming is inherently frivolous and undeserving of serious attention. Other observers disagree. "One function of mass-communicated entertainment," suggests Charles Wright, "is to provide respite for the individual which, perhaps, permits him to continue to be exposed to mass-communicated news, interpretation, and prescriptions so necessary for his survival in the modern world."[18]

A case in point is how two soft-drink companies handled their 1991 Super Bowl commercials as the onset of the Persian Gulf ground war loomed. Laura Bird recounts that

advertisers were jittery for days before the broadcast, knowing that their most expensive creative blowouts of the year might be overshadowed or pre-empted by live footage from the Gulf War. In a last-minute change of heart, Coca-Cola replaced its comic spots for Diet Coke with a somber salute to the troops. In contrast, Diet Pepsi spots starring Ray Charles aired as scheduled. The theme, "You've Got the Right One Baby, Uh-Huh," caught the attention of the fun-starved masses, and Pepsi became a home-front hero.[19]

Thus, for commercials as well as for programs, entertainment can be a lubricant that makes more 'substantive' gratification-serving elements possible and endurable. David E. Kelley, Emmy-award winning creator of *Picket Fences, Chicago Hope, The Practice*, and *Ally McBeal*, frames the issue this way:

I don't think it's appropriate for the producers ever to say, 'OK, this is my hour to teach you something more and make you aware of a problem. Now take this.' You've got to honor your relationship with your audience—that they sit down because they want to be entertained. And that doesn't mean you can't provoke them and antagonize them and challenge them in the course of the entertainment as long as you keep the entertainment part of the equation alive.[20]

Even in the pre-electronic era of the late nineteenth century, philosopher George Santayana recognized the importance of entertainment-oriented diversions when he proposed that

we may measure the degree of happiness and civilization which any race has attained by the proportion of its energy which is devoted to free and generous pursuits, to the adornment of life and the culture of the imagination. For it is in the spontaneous play of his faculties that man finds himself and his happiness. . . . He is a slave when all his energy is spent in avoiding suffering and death, when all his action is imposed from without, and no breath or strength is left him for free enjoyment.[21]

INFORMATION/SURVEILLANCE

Information/surveillance, our second audience gratifications factor, is (as Charles Wright just pointed out), what entertainment provides a respite from! We still need the information, however, if we are to cope with the complexity of contemporary life. Consequently, our unavoidable reliance on mass-mediated news stimulated DeFleur and Ball-Rokeach's "dependency theory." This theory suggests that "everyone in modern urban industrialized western society is psychologically dependent to a great extent on the mass media for information which enables them to enter into full participation in society."[22] Individuals require media-delivered information to function in modern society," add Rubin and Windahl. "The more salient the information needs, the stronger is the motivation to seek mediated information to meet these needs, the stronger the dependency on the medium, and the greater is the likelihood for the media to affect cognitions, feelings, and behavior."[23]

For decades, a variety of researchers have reported that television is the most popular medium in serving this gratification. In its first (1959) survey commissioned by the television industry, the Roper Organization asked participants where they got most of their news. With multiple responses possible, 57 percent indicated newspapers and 51 percent mentioned television. But by 1963, television topped newspapers by 55 percent to 53 percent, and the margin widened over the next two decades.[24] More significantly, the 1987 Roper study suggested that TV's popularity now had taken on an *exclusionary* power when it reported that

for the first time, a majority of Americans cite *only* television as their main source of news.

For years, television has been the leading source of news, meaning that more people have cited it as a primary source of news than have cited other sources of news. Today, 66 percent of Americans mention television as a main news source, compared to 36 percent

who mention newspapers, 14 percent who cite radio, and 4 percent who say magazines.

But the number of people restricting their response to television *alone* . . . has been steadily increasing—and has hit 50 percent for the first time. This is double the level of twenty years ago and up from 39 percent in 1980.[25]

While subsequent analyses suggest that the Roper reports overstated the situation, there is general agreement that television news in general—and local TV news in particular—continue to outpace newspapers. A 1996 study by Professors Guido Stempel and Thomas Hargrove found that 70.3 percent of those surveyed used local TV news as their primary information source, followed by 67.3 percent for network TV news and 59.3 percent for daily newspapers.[26]

Given the comparative brevity of most television news stories, and the prominence of "if it bleeds it leads" reportage on local stations, such findings have become a focal point for a great deal of critical commentary. Electronic news professionals worry about this situation as much as do outside critics. Even the legendary Walter Cronkite expressed his reservations about the role people are willing to let television play when he told a group of college broadcasters:

The whole thing is a sound bite and we're compressing news to such a degree that, as in compressing any gas, we end up compressing the gas to the point where it creates more heat, explosive heat, frequently than light. I think this is a problem we face. This leads us, of course, to an image-driven information medium, and an image-driven society.[27]

Certainly, there is CNN's more expansive main channel. And the Congress-covering C-SPAN. And special channels for business news. But the people who watch these services are "news junkies," rather than people for whom television is the only news medium. Instead, it is the highly condensed and predigested information of station and broadcast network newscasts (as well as CNN Headline News) that reaches the consumers who *don't reach for* additional information sources. This is not the broadcast journalists' fault, of course. But it presents those journalists with a problem and a responsibility that their constrained format is incapable of substantially addressing.

Consumers who predominately rely on television news—or, in fact, on any mass-mediated news—have made a trade-off. On the one hand, they receive a much wider view of the world (a much more panoramic *surveillance* capability) than they could ever dream of achieving on their own. In the case of electronic media, this view can also be instantaneous. On the other hand, this wider view has been achieved by taking a step back from reality. When one sees or hears a radio/television news event, it is *not* reality but a one-eyed or one-eared electromagnetic reproduction of a tiny piece of reality that has been further processed to conform to short and unyielding time limits. The individual news story can only be a tiny piece of the mosaic—like a single colored cell in a massive stained-glass window. The problem arises when audiences believe—or are led to believe—that this tiny fragment is the totality.

In July 1967, for instance, there was a major civil disturbance in Detroit. Detroiters who were away on summer vacation and saw news footage on television believed that the entire city was a mass of flames. In fact, the week-long torching occurred within an area of approximately 144 square blocks, and primarily in much more circumscribed pockets of that area. Why were even vacationing Detroiters misled? Because they often saw the same burning building from four or five different camera angles on different stations and networks. News crews were dispatched to where "action" was taking place—there was no news value in filming a squirrel crossing a quiet neighborhood street. So the same isolated fire or disturbance, as tragic as it may have been, became magnified by the combination of multiple vantage points into something much greater than it really was.

Conversely, when we see only a *single* mass-mediated view of a subject, that, too, has a tendency to become 'the whole' in audience perceptions. We "saw Kosovo" on television like we "saw Vietnam" and often drew our informational conclusions accordingly, via isolated and precensored video snippets. The same thing can happen in reading print or on-line text reports, of course. But "seeing" appears so much more real and all-encompassing than merely an after-the-fact "reading."

The public will continue to look to television to meet the information/surveillance

gratification. That genie is out of the bottle. But it is incumbent on video professionals to understand the limitations of their brand of surveillance—and to honestly communicate those limitations to their audiences.

Even though far fewer people consider radio as a prime gratifier of the information/surveillance need, it remains the medium of choice in terms of local/instantaneous news. (Where do *you* turn to find out if school has been canceled?) Television still needs a picture to truly *be* television. A TV voice-over announcement to a "Special Bulletin" slide is simply radio on another channel. Even though ENG (electronic newsgathering) units, satellites, and camcorders make news pictures quicker than ever to capture, there is still nothing so rapid as an incoming phone call that is patched onto the air. And the more local we get, the more likely it is—from both a format and economic standpoint—that radio rather than television will cover it and cover it soonest. All-news radio devotes its entire existence to serving the information/surveillance gratification, of course, but any format can contribute to meeting this need via selected newscasts, discussions, or announcements.

The Internet offers tremendous opportunities to extend and combine information sources. Broadcast and cable networks, radio and television stations, and traditional print media are bringing their content to the Web. Some of this content consists of stories they did not have the time or the space to carry on their conventional outlet. Other material is a repurposing of stories that were first reported on their air or published in their pages. But the Internet does not distribute information only from established news sources. Individuals with a modicum of equipment and computer expertise can now be information providers to the world—if the world can somehow be led to find them through the right portals or links. The reliability of this information is uncertified, of course, and its publication may constitute nothing more than erroneous gossip. On the other hand, such Web activities also have the capacity to create the electronic version of the crusading pamphleteer whose accounts provide a fresh alternative to establishment voices and their journalistic preoccupations.

How great a role the on-line medium (and its wide divergency of content providers) will play in meeting the overall information needs of audiences will depend on the way that delivery system, and accessibility to it, evolves. Via both traditional and on-line avenues, the giant and consolidated media corporations will still be major information/surveillance providers. In at least some small way, however, the Web holds out the promise that there will be electronic alternatives that can serve to further democratize the scope and source of information servicing. "From journalism to Wall Street, some of the world's most powerful institutions are reluctantly coming to grips with the Internet's inevitability," writes technology commentator Jon Katz. "They still don't like it very much. They might ache for those recent but happier days when they could set their agendas unmolested, quietly selecting the books that would be big, the ideas Congress would debate, the candidates we would choose between, the hours when they'd rather sell stocks. But those days are gone, almost surely for good."[28]

ESCAPISM/NOSTALGIA

Escapism/nostalgia, our third gratifications cluster, is in many ways the opposite of the information/surveillance need. Even though virtually all people some of the time (and a few infomaniacs all of the time) seek to be informed about the current events and forces of their world, there is also the contrary pressure to flee reality's troubles and data overload through escape to a more pleasing environment. This attitude conforms to Charles Zwingmann's definition of nostalgia as

the individual's response to change and/or an abstraction thereof (anticipated change) by a symbolic return to, or reinstatement of, those features of his past, which are perceived as having (had) the greatest gratification value.[29]

With escapism/nostalgia, it is not simply a need to be entertained, but a desire to *withdraw* (in the case of nostalgia, to withdraw into the past). Unfortunately for the electronic media, this withdrawal may result in a counterproductive consumer retreat from the media themselves. Although "entertainment viewing motivations significantly contribute to substantial amounts of television

viewing and to a felt affinity with the medium," reports researcher Alan Rubin, "escapist viewing—or using the television medium to forget about personal problems and to get away from other people or tasks—results in reduced viewing levels, and does not contribute to a sense of television affinity. . . . In short, other social activities or functional alternatives may be instrumental in gratifying escapist needs or drives."[30] Rubin's findings thus suggest that television encounters greater competition as an escape purveyor than it does as a supplier of entertainment.

Does this mean that the electronic media should avoid appealing to escapism lest we drive consumers to other pastimes? Probably not. As researchers Ronald Lembo and Kenneth Tucker have found,

viewers report using the visual quality or symbolic space as a starting point for thinking and fantasizing about their own lives. For example, the contours or movements of images may evoke thoughts and feelings about themselves, about people they know, past experiences, and so on. Viewers can embark on short, imaginative excursions into their own inner world, and then just as quickly return to programming once again.[31]

Just *how quickly* they return to our programming is a matter of some concern, of course.

In striving to understand escapism as a gratification, it thus is important for media professionals to probe the conditions that prompt a target audience to *seek* escapism and the programmatic elements that allow them to *find* escapism without mentally absenting themselves from the show or commercial in question. Media theorist John Fiske reminds us that "escapism or fantasy necessarily involves both an escape from or evasion of something and an escape to a preferred alternative: dismissing escapism as 'mere fantasy' avoids the vital question of *what* is escaped from, *why* escape is necessary, and *what* is escaped to."[32]

For radio as well as television, nostalgia has become escapism's most important corollary—a trend given further impetus by the baby boomers' shuffle through middle age. Derived, reveals Fred Davis, from the Greek words for "home" and "pain," nostalgia consists of an emotional yearning for or fond remembrance of a better time and place.[33] On radio, this psychological affinity has meshed well with the marketplace need to fashion more distinctly targeted formats. The result is a wealth of program designs ranging from big band 'swing' music to so-called rock oldies formats that draw their selections either from the mid-1960s to 1970s or (in a younger-skewing variation) from the mid-1970s to the late 1980s.

Initially, the oldies formats were especially appealing to stations on the foundering AM band because much of their music did not require state-of-the-art stereo fidelity. In fact, for older nostalgia-seekers who grew up in an AM-dominant world, the use of this medium deepened the escapist experience. Now, however, even forty- or fifty-year-old tunes have been digitally reprocessed into stereo for enjoyment on FM outlets as well. That is because "the nostalgia craze runs deep into every part of American life," says radio programming consultant Jeff Pollack. "Traditional values and good times are back."[34]

Television also directly courts nostalgia in 'look-back' programs. This is most noticeable in the reappearance of the so-called Golden Age television programs of the 1950s and 1960s. Former NBC and CBS programming executive Michael Dann believes that "most people look back on the Golden Age not as a reflection of TV, but as a reflection of their youth. So it's a psychological viewpoint, not a historical or critical one."[35] "By now," adds advertising critic Barbara Lippert, "several generations have come of age with a TV consciousness that has changed the way we perceive everything. We seem to be nostalgic not for any particular time in history, but for the video or filmic innocence that came with that time."[36]

That these vintage evergreen shows are being favored by programmers is due to a number of business as well as audience gratification reasons: (1) the expanding number of outlets in search of reasonably priced product to air; (2) the absence of production costs for old in-the-can shows that have been gathering dust on studio shelves; (3) the shrinkage of the number of available series coming off-network as fewer programs stay on the nets long enough to accumulate enough episodes for stripping (5-day-a-week) scheduling; and (4) the fact that for today's teen viewers, these shows present a "Back-to-the-Future" escape to a less threatening and music-dominant era they did not have the opportunity to experience first-hand.

TV nostalgia is not confined to old evergreen series, of course. A number of contemporary programs also cater to escapism/nostalgia by adopting 'period' settings. What is interesting in vehicles like *The Wonder Years* and *That '70s Show*, however, is that they are created with nostalgia as a prime gratification. Evergreens, in contrast, began as present-tense entertainment that only later became pieces of archival escapism, sometimes, as on the popular *Nick at Nite*, even clustered on their own dedicated services.

Garry Marshall, creator of *Happy Days* and its spin-offs, points out that there are definite business gratifications and safety nets in constructing shows that, from their very inception, blend both entertainment and nostalgia appeals:

ABC asked me to write a show about young people, but to avoid the subject of drugs. In the early '70s, that didn't compute. So I came up with the idea of setting the show in the '50s and that turned out to be a wonderful idea for another reason: nostalgia. People were tired of the uncertainty of the '60s. They loved the idea of innocent kids in a traditional American family. We also knew the reruns wouldn't look dated: this '50s show was already dated.[37]

Happy Days now benefits from a kind of double time warp. Older viewers still use this 1970s show as a gateway back to their youth in the 1950s, while the next generation seeks it out as a reminder of their youth in the 1970s, when they were watching the series' original network run.

In summarizing nostalgia, researchers Lynette Unger, Diane McConocha, and John Faier point out that it can be divided into two categories—public and private:

Private nostalgia, individually experienced, is the reflection on previous personal episodes. Like a scrapbook, the mind holds a collection of fragments of past personal life. These sentimental fragments of positively distorted memory are called up by the individual who seeks continuity in his or her life. . . .

However, not all nostalgic emotions relate to personal or private experience. Feelings of joy, pleasure, and security can be elicited by images that relate to historic events or times that are socially or collectively held to be of value. . . . This form of nostalgia is referred to as public nostalgia.

It is through public nostalgia that society can make the attempt to escape the social worries of the day. It is the positive reflection on the past that provides society with continuity in a changing world. . . .

The interaction between private and public nostalgia is important, particularly in advertising appeals. Many of the symbols and images that convey mainstream public nostalgia are part of private nostalgia. . . . Society can also look back on "happy days" and feel nostalgic about the music, the clothes, or the food from that period. By being nostalgic, both the society and the individual can maintain continuity in a threatening environment.[38]

Escapism in general, and nostalgia in particular, thus seems a very positive force. In fact, English professor Jerry Herron reminds us that all that we call *culture* is nostalgic: "Culture, then, is the finest form of presumptive nostalgia: the longing we imagine others would feel if they only realized the value of things they never knew about, but now seem disastrously to have 'forgotten'."[39] Nevertheless, as media professionals, we need to be alert to excesses in serving escapism/nostalgia, excesses that may cast our programs or commercials in a negative light. Literary critic Carl Grabo once cautioned that "in some literature the real and the imagined worlds are confused and the reader cannot separate the false and the true. . . . Escape purports to be, or is mistaken by its readers to be, an honest picture of life."[40] In speaking of an equally romanticized, yet more historic Golden Age than the one to which Michael Dann earlier alluded, Grabo adds this electronic-media relevant admonition:

In our nostalgia for a better world, a world of justice and goodness, we grasp at the enchanted picture of life as it never was except in the fabled Golden Age, which is no more than our vision of the future given the fixity and immortality of the past. . . . If the past is made to seem better than it was, we are encouraged to turn our backs to the future and desire what is impossible, a return to some state of the past, whether real or imagined. This is true escapism, the living in the past; whereas, it is our greatest, our imperative duty, to live in the present and the future and, by wrestling with the evils which we know, make the future better than the past. By living in and believing in a false past we retard the evolution of life.[41]

Nonnostalgic escapism, of course, places the perceiver in a 'false' present or future. As long as the nature of this falseness is understood, the fantasy can be positive. Occasional indulgence in escapist content is probably a healthy diversion and has been the source of many great artistic products that have brought pleasure both to their creators and to the audiences those creators have strived to reach. But when the search for escapism constantly overshadows all other gratifications, then debilitation can result. Thus, continuous immersion in video gaming and sci-fi sojourns or unbroken absorption with televised sports and talk show soul-barings may be equally dangerous pursuits in their ability not just to temporarily divert, but also to continuously disconnect. Individual media 'programs' do not create escapist harm. It is only the unvaried aggregation of such programs that can turn gratification to dependency. As sociologist Charles Wright warns, "Too much escapism, too many TV [or on-line] circuses at one's fingertips, may distract people from important social issues and divert them from useful social participation and action."[42]

COMPANIONSHIP/ CONVERSATION BUILDING

Companionship/conversation building, our fourth gratification cluster, is partially linked to escapism/nostalgia. This affinity is most graphically illustrated in what is called *retro TV*—the updating of ten- or twenty-year-old television series rather than simply re-airing the original episodes. The aim here is to serve some viewers' wish to escape at the same time as we cater to other viewers' felt need for companionship. "These shows' characters have become part of our lives; they're old friends," comments NBC Senior Vice-President Steve White. "In some ways these familiar characters have become bigger today than ever before."[43] Professor Christopher Geist further observes, "We all grew up letting our favorite TV characters into our living rooms every week. There's a real bond that's developed between these shows and viewers. So it's only natural that we want to see them again twenty years later. We want to check in with them and make sure the characters are turning out all right."[44]

Whether it's a Brady Bunch family reunion or the newest character in a contemporary prime-time hit, an electronic media companion can serve an important consumer need. As Professor Mark Levy discovered,

although the audience cannot communicate directly with the mass media performers, viewers are still said to interact with the personae. Audiences are thought to [in the words of Donald Horton and R. Richard Wohl] "benefit from the persona's wisdom, reflect on his advice, sympathize with him in his difficulties, forgive his mistakes." For most members of the audience, para-social interaction is considered complementary to social communication. However, for people with few or weak social ties, para-social interaction may offer a functional alternative for inadequate interaction opportunities.[45]

Para-social interaction, then, is the label we give to the one-sided interpersonal relationship that audience members establish with electronic media characters. Researcher Michael Antecol fully defines para-social interaction as "a relationship of friendship or intimacy by a television viewer with a remote media character. It is based on affective ties by the viewer with the media character. As such it may take the form of seeking guidance from the characters, making friends with them and imagining being part of the program's social world."[46] Psychologists Horton and Wohl isolated and christened this phenomenon as early as 1956 when they described consumer linkages to media personalities in these terms:

They "know" such a persona in somewhat the same way they know their chosen friends: through direct observation and interpretation of his appearance, his gestures and voice, his conversation and conduct in a variety of situations.[47]

Depending on whether these para-social companions facilitate or inhibit listener/viewer interactions with "real" people, they can be seen as playing either a positive or negative socialization role.

This is why we link the companionship gratification with that of conversation building. A beneficial outgrowth of media acquaintances is that exposure to them gives us the material (and perhaps the models) for communicating more effectively with 'real life' people. "Television is an enormous provoker of conversation, people talk about it endlessly, and through their talk they incor-porate it into the culture of their everyday lives," writes John Fiske. "The meanings of television are not just reference points for comparative judgments, not just shared cultural experience, though they are, of course, both of these; they are as 'real' a part of everyday experience as doing the shopping, playing with the kids, or mowing the lawn."[48]

With its gossipy content as well as its chronological segmentation into daily episodes, the soap opera is especially fertile as a conversation stimulator. As Professor Robert Allen submits,

the day-long, institutionally enforced suspension of those stories increases the viewer's desire to once again join the lives of the characters the viewer has come to know over the course of years of viewing. And, because the viewer cannot induce the text to start up again, some of the energy generated by this protensive tension might get channeled into discourse about the text among fellow viewers.[49]

Though soap operas may be more potent conversation builders than some other genres, any program matter—commercials included—can serve this gratification. Thus, Elayne Rapping reminds us that "ads are the stuff of our common social communication: the small talk of a society filled with strangers and loners; the jokes of a nation eager to forget the many aspects of their lives that are not at all funny, and over which they have no control."[50] For example, in deliberately featuring a now-obscure actor from a breakthrough but long-ago role, the commercial in Figure 8-1 uses renewed companionship to motivate watching and to provide the grist for the payoff punchline. "We were overwhelmed by the response to the campaign," writes David Henthorne, the commercial's creator. "The spots created a strong word-of-mouth 'buzz' for Marsh and have measurably increased cake sales."[51] Meanwhile, viewers got the two-tiered gratification of re-establishing their companionship with Hamill/Skywalker while acquiring a derivative slogan to sweeten conversation with real-life acquaintances.

In our daily interpersonal exchanges we can regale our family or acquaintances with a description of the Energizer Bunny's latest incarnation. We can discuss David Letterman's monologue—and even mimic his mannerisms—as a way of facilitating casual conversation. And we can fume about the callous, manipulative boss on a prime-time drama or console each other about the fourth successive physical attack to which our favorite soap opera heroine fell prey. All of these electronic exposures efficiently motivate discussion with the real-life people around us. If, in real life, we are inspired to behave like that boss or to inflict those soap-opera-depicted injuries on others,

however, the mass-mediated companionship experience becomes a source of concern to Congressional committees and PTAs.

The media present a rich variety of 'virtual' companions; but it ultimately is up to each audience member to choose which of these companions to enjoy recoiling from and which of these to take pleasure in emulating. Our industry's best contribution to

FIGURE 8-1
(Courtesy of David Henthorne, Ron Foth Advertising)

video | audio

OPEN ON
MARK HAMILL IN
KITCHEN.

MARK HAMILL:
WHEN I WANT TO MAKE AN
OCCASION REALLY SPECIAL,
I START WITH A REALLY
SPECIAL CAKE...

WIDE SHOT OF MARK
HAMILL.

FROM MARSH.

THEY'RE DELICIOUS, AND THE
DESIGNS ARE AWESOME.

CUT TO MARK
SHOWING THE
STAR WARS CAKE.

MY...UM...*KIDS* LOVE
THIS ONE.

video   audio

CUT TO MARK.

MARK HAMILL:
THERE'S JUST ONE THING.
MARSH CAKES ARE SO MOIST, I
NEVER KNOW WHETHER TO
SERVE THEM WITH FORKS OR
SPOONS…

CUT TO MARK
THINKING.

FORKS OR SPOONS
HMMMM…

CUT TO MARK'S
REACTION.

MYSTERIOUS VOICE:
USE THE *FORKS*, LUKE.

_____video   audio_____

CUT TO MARK.

7

MARK HAMILL:
I THINK I'LL USE
THE FORKS.

CUT TO MARSH LOGO

SUPER:
WE VALUE YOU.

VISIT US ON THE WEB AT
(www.marsh.net)

8

ANNCR:
MARSH...
YOUR SUPERMARKET FOR
THE NEW MILLENNIUM.

CUT TO MARK.

9

MARK HAMILL:
WHO'S "LUKE"?

the companionship gratification probably is its ability graphically to aggregate a much wider array of human portrayals and human situations than real-life experience has time to provide. "What we can't find in real life, we look for on TV," says media executive and analyst Betsy Frank. "Major network programs showcase universal themes—searching for surrogate family, coping with hard times, acceptance of individuality, the conflict between old and new social roles. And with people feeling more disconnected now than ever before, watching a high-rated program gives us a sense of community."[52]

Thus, even though "there is a kind of knowledge that television can give us about our own personal lives, television's real value is in reminding us that we belong to the public life," asserts commentator/author Richard Rodriguez. "People who are lonely know best that television is their tenuous tie to the civic life. I think of shut-ins and patients in hospitals. The television drones on around and above them as a comforting reminder that they still belong to the world."[53] On the other hand, warns author Louise Bernikow, "the danger television presents to the lonely is that it can keep them passive, reducing whatever stirring they have to bring more people into their lives or to deepen the connections they do have."[54] Seeming to justify Bernikow's concern, a 1998 NFO Research Study commissioned by Ogilvy Public Relations found that 26 percent of Americans spend more time watching television than talking to other people.[55]

The same potentials and perils can be attributed to radio, of course, where the talk format most unequivocally pursues the companionship gratification. As former ABC Radio president and talk format innovator Ben Hoberman describes it,

Talk listening is foreground listening. You have to really listen and become engaged in the conversation. Talk is also personal. In fact, talk is the most intimate of all formats. People reveal their deepest problems and concerns on the air. In a sense, talk radio has become a communal backyard fence over which we chat with our neighbors, share experiences, ask for advice and express our opinions.[56]

Because it reaches its audience through a single, highly focused sense, Marshall McLuhan called radio a "hot" medium in which the personalities are projected much more intensely than in the "cool," multisense arena of television. According to McLuhan's theory, radio talk show hosts like Rush Limbaugh (Figure 8-2) or Howard Stern can become much more dominant media companions than would be the case on television—an argument bolstered by the fact that both Limbaugh and Stern were unable to repeat their highly successful radio shows in a television environment.

The intrusively intimate nature of radio means that companionship/conversation building is not the exclusive province of talk stations. The Reymer & Gershin Associates *Radio Wars II* study, for example, found that the 14 percent of the radio audience whom the researchers labeled as "Friend Seekers,"

FIGURE 8-2
Rush Limbaugh, one of radio's 'high definition' companions. (Photo by EJ Camp/ Outline, Courtesy of Multimedia Entertainment)

and the 22 percent dubbed "Social Followers," turned to *several types* of stations to meet their companionship requirements.[57] The prominence and breadth of this radio gratification cited in the *Radio Wars II* and subsequent research led Heritage Media's radio group president, Paul Fiddick, to argue that companionship has overshadowed all other gratifications in the medium. "People do not listen to radio for entertainment," asserts Fiddick. "They use the radio to fill the holes in their life. In our culture, silence is synonymous with loneliness."[58]

The Internet's chat rooms offer newer and much more interactive electronic companionship opportunities than radio and television can provide. Yet, these personally programmed interchanges are not programming in the sense that they aggregate audiences. Rather, the chat room simply provides the hall (often advertiser-supported) in which a multitude of individual conversations can take place. The only stable structures susceptible to critiquing become the policies governing the chat room's use and the protections these policies may or not provide for the safety and privacy of the companionship/conversation-seeking participants. The Internet serves this gratification in a much broader sense as well by its linkings with the other electronic media. "TV shows such as *The X-Files* have come of age on the World Wide Web," technology writer Jon Katz points out. "Soap operas have their own, wildly popular Websites that archive scripts, keep track of characters and story lines, and make programs continuous and integral parts of fan's lives."[59]

All of this research and commentary notwithstanding, we must recognize that the electronic media still do not have a monopoly on serving the companionship gratification. Nor should the radio, television, or the Internet servicing of this gratification automatically be blamed when certain individuals withdraw from the rest of society. Anthropologist Conrad Kottak, in fact, poses the hypothesis that "in a culture where people like to be alone, TV may contribute to greater isolation [pseudo-companionship]. However, in one where people like to be with others, it may lead to greater social interaction [conversation building]."[60]

Alternatively, it may be that any socially curious individual requires more varied experiences than those available from face-to-face dialogues. Perhaps what DeWitt Parker wrote about prose fiction's role in the 1920s can just as easily apply to electronic media's function in the 1990s:

We read because we are lonely or because our fellow men have become trite and fail to stimulate us sufficiently. If our fellows were not so reticent, if they would talk to us and tell us their stories with the freedom and brightness of a [Robert Louis] Stevenson, or if their lives were so fresh and vivid that we never found them dull, perhaps we should not read at all. But, as it is, we can satisfy our craving or knowledge of life only by extending our social world through fiction. Fiction may teach us, edify us, make us better men—it may serve all these purposes incidently, but its prime purpose as art is to provide us with new objects for social feeling and knowledge.[61]

Because its moving audiovisual image is initially more lifelike than the immobile medium of print, the television version of this gratification may not need to possess the expansive innovation that Parker sought from static prose. Gilbert Seldes recognized the often more conventional nature of TV companionship when he observed that

for millions of people television has the same quality as a conversation with friends, almost the same quality as the mere presence of members of the family who needn't do anything exciting or unusual, so long as they are in the house, but who would be sorely missed if they departed.[62]

As the video-profitting Ronald Reagan told the citizenry during his 1984 re-election campaign, "Television is becoming the American neighbor" by generating "continuity and reassurance in place of the traditional extended family."[63] And Ted Halbert, ABC Entertainment's top executive, adds this footnote: "We don't even know our next door neighbors anymore, so we use television to get our gossip."[64] As we have discovered in our earlier discussion, this same comment could be applied to the radio and on-line substitute neighborhoods as well.

PROBLEM SOLVING

This fifth gratification, problem solving, is most overtly catered to by commercials, public service announcements (PSAs), and program promotional materials (promos). Commercials typically unveil a difficulty or deprivation that their product or service is designed to fix. PSAs sensitize us to social or personal shortcomings and offer suggested solutions, and promos help resolve the uncertainty of what to watch or listen to now, later today, tomorrow, or next week.

In the Figure 8-3 Tio Sancho advertisement, for instance, the questioning consumer's failure to keep taco droppings off his chest in frames 5–7 is contrasted with Tio's (Uncle's) frame 4 success that accrues from using his own brand of shells.

In a similar problem-solving ritual, the following thirty-second radio PSA for the American Red Cross portrays one graphic humanitarian need already being met while raising a further support problem that seemingly can be addressed only by the listener's donation.

FIGURE 8-3
(Courtesy of David Sackey, W. B. Doner and Company, Advertising)

TIO SANCHO

MESS
30 seconds

V/O: Say, Tio Sancho.
TIO: Si.
V/O: What's so special about your taco shells?

TIO: Well, mine don't fall apart so they taste great.
V/O: I don't see the connection.
TIO: Come here. V/O: Okay.

TIO: I'll taste my Tio Sancho taco...you taste that other brand.

SFX: CRUNCH...

SFX: CRUNCH...

TIO: Mmmm. How's yours?

MAN: I don't know, it fell apart.

TIO: Really? Mine is delicious.

ANNCR: Tio Sancho. A man who knows a taco tastes better in your mouth than on your shirt.

TIO: Si.
ANNCR: Si.

(SFX: RUBBLE FALLING)
RESCUE WORKER: Can you hear me?
TRAPPED GIRL: Yes——everything fell on me.
WORKER: Okay, don't worry, we're going to help you.
GIRL: I'm scared.

ANNCR: We hear you. We're the American Red Cross. We help train rescue workers. Provide medical attention, food and shelter. And work to get people's lives back to normal. Last year, millions of people

```
        needed our help. Desperately.
        Now we need yours.
GIRL: Please hurry——
ANNCR: The American Red Cross.⁶⁵
```

Only slightly less obviously, electronic media *programs* also serve as audience problem-solvers. Newscasts and news magazine features now include tips on nutrition, money management, cooking, child-rearing, vegetable purchasing, and a host of other consumer-help topics. Entire cable networks devote themselves to financial matters, weather information, health care, and homemaking. Even fictional series can provide some assistance. By frequenting a doctor, lawyer, or other socially relevant dramatic show, "we turn our personal and social problems over to the characters who can solve them magically in the space of an enclosed hour," Professor Horace Newcomb remarked back in 1974. "Doubtless, one reason for the popularity of these successful series is the way in which they deal with contemporary problems in a self-conscious manner. . . . Always the problems are solved. In most cases they are solved by the heroic qualities of the central characters."[66]

More contemporary dramas, however, are more likely to resist neat fixes. Cutting-edge series such as Barry Levinson's *Homicide*, David E. Kelley's *The Practice*, and Dick Wolf's *Law and Order* steadfastly refuse to solve all the problems they raise. And shows that do oversimplify solutions to difficulties are now likely to merit critical disdain, as in critic Jeff Jarvis's conclusion to a review of *7th Heaven*:

On this show, problems are solved and scars are healed even faster than they are on a sit-com. On *7th Heaven*, everything is made OK in the time it would take to read a greeting card. And the emotions are just as cheap.[67]

For their part, sitcoms and other half-hour shows have always found it much more difficult to raise and resolve significant societal and personal problems while still presenting the required character/plot interaction. It is not merely that sitcoms are supposed to be "funny," but that they have only thirty (actually, twenty-two) minutes to present a reasonable solution. Thus, when a situation comedy portrays a major social quandary, it usually projects a disappointing gratification package. Either the problem (infidelity, child or substance abuse, homophobia, etc.) can't be substantively (yet comedically) packaged in the time available, or the necessarily rapid 'solution' comes across as contrived, simplistic, or even insulting. Nevertheless, some shows have surmounted these obstacles. *Murphy Brown*'s battle with cancer, and *Spin City*'s depiction of the mayor's African-American aide being stopped by police because of his color, are two examples of well-crafted sitcoms that aid in problem-solving by realistically addressing just how confounding some problems can be.

When the problem-solving gratification is able to be feasibly engaged, Americans seem to use radio/television the way the natives of the African nation of Zimbabwe have traditionally used music: to call up and ask advice of ancestors and other sympathetic spirits who could never appear without the medium's assistance. The electronic media bring up issues that audiences are too inept or self-conscious to raise themselves. Thus, the problem-solving art conveyed via these media functions like art in general. Through art, according to Melvin Rader and Bertram Jessup, "Our very defeats in 'real life' become our triumphs in the life of art. Esthetically, we become masters of our troubles, our frustrations, our defeats—by becoming interested in them, by making them into works of art instead of merely suffering them."[68]

PERSONAL ENRICHMENT AND DEVELOPMENT

The sixth gratification construct, personal enrichment and development, comes the closest to the old British Broadcasting Corporation ideal of using the electronic media to uplift public and personal taste. As the BBC's first director general, the legendary Sir John Reith, characterized this mission:

We have tried to found a tradition of public service, and to dedicate the service of broadcasting to the service of humanity in its fullest sense. We believe that a new national asset has been created . . . the asset referred to is of the moral and not the material order—that which, down the years, brings the compound interest of happier homes, broader culture and truer citizenship.[69]

Putting it more bluntly, this means giving the public what it *needs* rather than what it *wants*.

From U.S. broadcasting's beginnings, however, both the culture of the nation and the overwhelmingly commercial nature of the system militated against such an approach. Many members of the audience were not eager to be enriched and developed—especially via a medium that was seen as recreational rather than instructional. Commercial broadcasters realized this. Force-feeding "uplifting" content to an unreceptive public was not the way to maximize audiences in a competitive environment. Let noncommercial (instructional) broadcasters be the overt "enrichers"—even though they were a very minor force in U.S. radio/television until well into the 1960s. It was not that the commercial broadcasting establishment was hostile to enrichment and development as a programmatic outcome. Instead, for the most part, that establishment merely chose to follow—rather than to lead—tonnage audience tastes.

Attempting to decipher the U.S. public's taste is a difficult proposition, of course, because there exist a multitude of publics who often mirror rapidly shifting taste preferences. One pioneering effort in this regard was undertaken by sociologist Herbert Gans. He divided U.S. society into five "taste publics"[70] that exhibit varying affinity for (or tolerance of) the 'enrichment' element in the media content they choose:

1. *High Culture*: the serious and even avant-garde writers, artists, composers and critics.
2. *Upper-Middle Culture*: the better educated and generally affluent professional and managerial class and their families who are the prime consumers, but not the creators, of fine art.
3. *Lower-Middle Culture*: the largest taste public, made up primarily of white-collar people and possessing at least some postsecondary collegiate or technical education.
4. *Low Culture*: blue-collar skilled and semiskilled workers; a taste public that constituted the most numerous group in the 1950s but is constricting as these families send their children to college and as the

number of heavy industrial/manufacturing jobs shrinks.
5. *Quasi-Folk Low Culture*: the very poor and undereducated people with limited job skills and uncertain economic futures who inhabit depressed rural areas as well as big-city ghettoes.

In terms of the gratifications they seek from the electronic media, the Low and Quasi-Folk Low Cultures favor entertainment and escapism. Unfortunately for the Quasi-Folk group, they lack the financial resources to be appealing to, and the educational level to be easily reachable by, most mass marketers. Thus, there is relatively little programming that takes their interests and attitudes into consideration. (In fact, some of the furor caused by the obscenity prosecutions of the musical group 2 Live Crew in the early 1990s came from individuals who charged that the trials were merely an attempt by the dominant power structure to suppress electronic media content that served segments of this taste public in their own vernacular.)

In any event, instead of entertainment/escapism, the High and Upper-Middle Cultures perceive their media use choices to be motivated by a quest for personal enrichment and development. Even though these two groups may, in fact, be *entertained* by the public broadcasting, Arts & Entertainment, and Discovery programs they seek out, they perceive these more as enrichment activities. Critic Robert MacKenzie directly reflects this psychology when he advocates that

the trick, of course, is to watch television on purpose. This means separating the stimulants from the soporifics, finding programs that make you feel more alive rather than less so.[71]

Arts/information cable networks like those mentioned above, classical/easy listening radio formats, traditional news and public affairs programs, and the occasionally "critically acclaimed" broadcast network series are built on these two taste publics. But tonnage or near-tonnage delivery systems generally cannot afford to cater to their rarefied preferences.

In fact, the High Culture group is so small and sophisticated that the radio/television industry can seldom afford to offer anything at all for them—and is usually rebuffed when it tries. In addition, many people in this group, for all their artistic sophistication, are not that well-off financially and so are anything but prime targets for advertisers of pricey products and services.

Finally, the expanding Lower-Middle Culture uses the electronic media for both entertainment/escape *and* enrichment/development gratifications. Programming that can touch these two bases simultaneously thus offers special incentives for this taste public as well as for the advertisers and programmers seeking to shorten the odds of reaching them. More than any other genre, the so-called event program is designed for this purpose, with the miniseries especially appropriate. This multipart treatment of a best-selling novel, famous personage, or historical event begins with a subject with which the core potential audience is already familiar. Its text, at least superficially, holds out a self-improvement excuse for engaging in succeeding nights of recreative viewing. If well scheduled and promoted, the miniseries or similarly derived made-for-TV movie promises to break viewers' mundane routines while offering the parallel pleasures of enrichment and entertainment. It is no accident that PBS's biggest hit to date, Ken Burns's *The Civil War*, constituted this sort of package. The movie *Titanic* also combined these two gratifications and, more important for the electronic media, allowed them to similarly meet entertainment and enrichment appetites in a multitude of related documentaries, news magazine pieces, and Website data banks.

Programming exclusively designed to service personal enrichment and development is inherently limited in its appeal. As the BBC ultimately discovered, attempted force-feeding of this gratification ultimately proves counterproductive. Once multiple-gratification-serving broadcast alternatives became available to the British public (via the Independent Television Authority in 1954 and, initially, the pirate radio vessels of the 1960s), they deserted the BBC in droves. The state-owned Corporation therefore had to diversify its own gratification menu.

Some U.S. commercial broadcasters see a similar scenario being played out in children's television. Regulations put in place in the 1990s now require all commercial television stations to air three hours of programming per week specifically aimed at meeting "the educational and information needs" of children—in other words, the personal enrichment/development gratification.

Some broadcasters feel that creating shows that explicitly meet such a mandate only results in programming that children are likely to avoid. Reduced audiences mean broadcasters take in less money to pay for such programming. Producers are forced to deliver cheaper shows whose lowered production values consequently make them even less appealing to children. As an alternative, various commercial broadcasters ask to be allowed to donate money to public broadcasting. These funds would enable PBS to provide more, higher-quality, and better-promoted children's programming all in one place. This, of course, is the same program variety issue raised in Chapter 2. But it also raises the fundamental question of whether government (or the electronic media) can ever succeed in forcing a particular gratification preference—no matter how ennobling—on a specific audience.

CATHARSIS/TENSION RELEASE

Catharsis/tension release, our seventh and final audience gratification, is also the most controversial. When many theorists and critics use the term *catharsis*, they are referring to a highly debatable theory that centers on violent content carried by the electronic media. In brief, this catharsis theory asserts that media violence can be beneficial because its simulated experiencing relieves people of the tension that might otherwise result in real-life aggression. By vicarious participation in the electronic assault, the need to perpetrate actual violence is diminished. As psychologist Jerome Lopiparo explains it,

within all of us—child and adult alike—there reposes a potential for violence, TV or no TV. Once this is accepted, we may then be more receptive to the notion that the expression of this aggression, whether via fantasy or outright overt behavior, is not only normal, but, in many respects, quite beneficial. What we are then left with is the possibility that the aggressiveness our children watch on TV may actually be *reducing* overt expressions of violence, rather than increasing them as critics would have us believe.[72]

Certainly, there are many variables to a catharsis event, as Professors Gary Copeland and Dan Slater point out. They argue that this often emotionally polluted subject can and should be more rationally and constructively examined once all these variables are taken into account:

A reformulation of the catharsis paradigm to include levels of fantasy ability, the type of mediated message which best triggers fantasies, and the content of the fantasies evoked could provide a resurgence of interest in catharsis as an effect of viewing mediated violence.[73]

When, however, we move beyond the study of catharsis itself and attempt to place the phenomenon within a gratifications context, a thorny list of further questions emerges:

1. When people (especially those Copeland and Slater label "high fantasizers") choose aggression-depicting programs, do they make this selection because:

a. they want to reduce their own levels of aggressive behavior

OR

b. they feel the desire to interact *more* aggressively?

2. Alternatively, when people seek out nonviolent or prosocial programs, do they make this selection because:

a. they wish to show more compassion toward others

OR

b. they want to *reduce* their felt need to engage in 'real-life' compassionate conduct?

Even partial receptivity to the theory of media-induced catharsis as a gratification source unavoidably brings us face-to-face with the reality of human imperfection. In fact, this issue is not restricted to the electronic media. DeWitt Parker applies it to all artistic endeavors when he argues that "art provides a medium through which the more animal side of our nature may receive imaginative satisfaction."[74]

Putting the deliberation in a more classical context, we can return to Aristotle. In his *Poetics*, he first broached the subject of catharsis. To him, catharsis constituted a dramatic blending of fear and pity. This was not pity in the humanitarian sense. Instead, as George Comstock and his colleagues point out, Aristotle's pity-engendering catharsis "seems to be nothing more than a fear that has been evoked by a sense of what today might be called 'identification' or 'empathy with an observed victim'; emotionally it involves caring about oneself much more than it involves caring about the observed victim."[75] In other words, the *better-them-than-me* reaction that we are likely to feel in response to a real tragedy in a newscast or a dramatized tragedy in a scripted series is a natural (if not particularly noble) tension-reliever that has been recognized for more than two thousand years.

Perceptive analysts have recognized that this fundamental attribute of audience psychology is a particularly important ingredient of certain program types. Thus, in speaking of what she labels the "savior" (cop, doctor, rescue team) shows, Rose Goldsen recounts that

the watching nation is nightly asked to share vicariously the attitudes toward death and suffering characteristic of professionals who deal with them daily. Professionals must learn to distance their feeling from sympathy and empathy with the agonies endured by sufferers. It's a way of insulating themselves from what would otherwise be unbearable emotion if they allowed themselves to feel in an "unprofessional" way. The watching nation, now, is invited to pick up the same [tension-relieving] attitudes of distanced uninvolvement.[76]

Consequently, some critics believe a negative result of such programs—whether 'reality' shows like *Cops* or scripted series such as *Law and Order* or *ER*—is that the public is further desensitized to violence and human suffering.

This concern is most worrisome when it comes to childrens' viewing. The electronic media in general—and television in particular—unquestionably play some developmental role in teaching children about their world and how they should respond to it. (We explore this "media-teaching" function more fully in the following chapter.) Therefore, a steady diet of potentially desensitizing programs could make it much more difficult for a child to learn to care about the human tragedies faced by others, particularly when peer pressure further reinforces such a nonreaction. As Judith Myers-Walls, a professor of child development, observes:

Like others their age, my children and their friends do their best to appear unaffected by the media violence they see, so they will not appear weak or prudish. With some children, it can become a contest. The quantity of violent media and the impersonal but graphic way violent content is presented can lead quickly to a tough, unaffected response. Such desensitized children learn to avoid taking responsibility for the violence around them; they may even be able to watch a real life violent event with no emotional response and no sense of personal obligation to react.[77]

Thus, while many strident voices charge that media violence stimulates the young to commit real-world violence, the broader and more sinister threat may be that it covertly innoculates audiences, young and old, against caring or concern. For, while a minority of people actually resort to physical violence, everyone is capable of adopting selfish noninvolvement as a stock tension release.

Despite fears that it triggers imitative physical aggression or dulls sympathetic human response, media violence has proved difficult to regulate. The V-chip allows blanket blocking of programs their producers have labeled as violent, but it cannot take the context of the violence into account. Constitutional protections rightly inhibit most forms of censorship, but they therefore ensure the inevitability that some antisocial behavior will be media-glorified. And, there is the longstanding influence of our own business and psychological motivations with which to contend. As broadcast critic Robert Lewis Shayon recognized three decades ago,

we fear violence and enjoy it with guilt, because it calls to our own deeply latent potential for violence in response to a violent world. With such a sure-fire, instant crowd-catcher providing the essential energy which runs our industries, our networks, our advertising agencies—in short, our style of life—to call for the voluntary or involuntary regulation of violence on TV is to call for instant self-destruction of the system. By "system" I mean TV based on advertiser support.[78]

With such volatile issues involved, it is easy to focus exclusively on the intertwined subjects of catharsis and violence and forget that much of the tension-release gratifica-tion is much more simple and innocuous. Often, it is a need for nothing more than a respite from the draining but undramatic stresses of normal living, where we are never completely in charge of our own destiny. "One of the great things about being able to push a button and turn the TV dial," observes media personality/psychologist Joyce Brothers, "is that it gives us a feeling of control. It allows us to change our world abruptly, and it helps satisfy our conflicting and often contradictory needs for adventure on the one hand and security and safety on the other."[79]

In the case of radio, tension release may be no further away than the next musical 'set.' In referring to the format he markets, for example, Bonneville Broadcasting's James Opsitnik calls *easy listening* "an adult coping mechanism which complements and compensates for busy lives in chaotic urban environments. . . . Listeners use easy listening music as a mood enhancer to reduce tension, relax and to cope with the world (or the traffic) around them."[80] Other listeners may just as likely find their release in the exuberance of heavy metal or the folksy chords of mainstream country. (On the other hand, country music may prove no release at all. In a study of forty-nine metropolitan areas, sociology professor Steven Sack found that "the greater the radio market share of country music, the greater the incidence of suicide. The themes in country music foster a suicidal mood among people already at risk of suicide."[81] This, of course, would be the very antithesis of the tension-release gratification!)

Tension release—with or without catharsis overtones—is a prominent need that contemporary consumers bring with them to the listening or viewing experience. It therefore becomes an important, if volatile, issue that conscientious programmers continuously must confront.

A GRATIFICATIONS CAUTION

In serving catharsis/tension release or any of the other six gratification clusters we have examined, success comes from clearly packaging and promoting our offerings so that potential audiences can make an accurate estimate of what the content could do for (rather than *to*) them. Even a well-executed program may be poorly received if it delivers a gratifications construct that runs counter to what listeners or viewers were led to expect.

ENDNOTES

1. William Evans, "The Interpretive Turn in Media Research: Innovation, Iteration, or Illusion?" *Critical Studies in Mass Communication* (June 1990), 151.
2. David Swanson, "Gratification Seeking, Media Exposure, and Audience Interpretations: Some Directions for Research," *Journal of Broadcasting & Electronic Media* (Summer 1987), 237–238.
3. Joey Reagan, "The 'Repertoire' of Information Sources," *Journal of Broadcasting & Electronic Media* (Winter 1996), 112.
4. Carolyn Lin, "Looking Back: The Contribution of Blumler and Katz's *Uses of Mass Communication* to Communication Research," *Journal of Broadcasting & Electronic Media* (Fall 1996), 574.
5. Elizabeth Perse and Alan Rubin, "Chronic Loneliness and Television Use," *Journal of Broadcasting & Electronic Media* (Winter 1990), 39.
6. Ien Ang, *Desperately Seeking the Audience* (London: Routledge, 1991), 167.
7. Elihu Katz, Michael Gurevitch, and Hadassah Haas, "On the Use of the Mass Media for Important Things," *American Sociological Review* (April 1973), 164–181.
8. Christine Scodari and Judith Thorpe, *Media Criticism: Journeys in Interpretation* (Dubuque, IA: Kendall-Hunt, 1992), 46.
9. Betsy Sharkey, "Master of His Domain," *ADWEEK Upfront* (June 1, 1998), 35.
10. Gene Jankowski, writing in "Monday Memo," *Broadcasting* (December 17, 1990), 30.
11. John Fiske and John Hartley, *Reading Television* (London: Methuen, 1978), 71.
12. Denis McQuail, "With the Benefit of Hindsight: Reflections on Uses and Gratifications Research," *Critical Studies in Mass Communication* (June 1984), 183.
13. George Comstock et al., *Television and Human Behavior* (New York: Columbia University Press, 1978), 11.
14. Don West, "V-Chips, Kids TV Have All-American Appeal," *Broadcasting & Cable* (October 20, 1997), S6.
15. Ed Shane, "Radio and Subliminal Timekeeping," *Feedback* (Winter 1994), 2–3.
16. Elayne Rapping, *The Looking Glass World of Nonfiction TV* (Boston: South End Press, 1987), 132.
17. Joe Queenan, "Justifiable Homicide," *TV Guide* (May 10, 1997), 20.
18. Charles Wright, "Functional Analysis and Mass Communication," in Lewis Dexter and David White (eds.), *People, Society, and Mass Communications* (New York: The Free Press, 1964), 108.
19. Laura Bird, "Lessons from the War," *ADWEEK Superbrands 1991 Issue*, 41.
20. Steve Coe, "The Dramatic License of David Kelley," *Broadcasting & Cable* (June 12, 1995), 16.
21. George Santayana, *The Sense of Beauty* (1896), reprinted in Melvin Rader (ed.), *A Modern Book of Esthetics*, 5th ed. (New York: Holt, Rinehart and Winston, 1979), 168.
22. Fiske and Hartley, 73.
23. Alan Rubin and Sven Windahl, "The Uses and Dependency Model of Mass Communication," *Critical Studies in Mass Communication* (June 1986), 185.
24. Guido Stempel and Thomas Hargrove, "Mass Media Attitudes in a Changing Media Environment," *Journalism & Mass Communication Quarterly* (Autumn 1996), 549.
25. *America's Watching: Public Attitudes toward Television* (New York: Television Information Office, 1987), 4.
26. Stempel and Hargrove, 552.
27. "The Role of Media in Society," *College Broadcaster* (February 1989), 17.
28. Jon Katz, "How the Net Changed America," *Yahoo! Internet Life* (September 1999), 99.
29. Charles Zwingmann," Heimweh or Nostalgic Reaction: A Conceptual Analysis and Interpretation of a Medico-Psychological Phenomenon." Unpublished Ph.D. dissertation, Stanford University (1959), 193.
30. Alan Rubin, "Television Uses and Gratifications: The Interactions of Viewing Patterns and Motivations," *Journal of Broadcasting* (Winter 1983), 49–50.
31. Robert Lembo and Kenneth Tucker, "Culture, Television, and Opposition: Rethinking Cultural Studies," *Critical Studies in Mass Communication* (June 1990), 109.
32. John Fiske, *Television Culture* (London: Methuen, 1987), 317.
33. Fred Davis, *Yearning for Yesterday, A Sociology of Nostalgia* (New York: The Free Press, 1979).
34. "Everything Old Is New Again in Radio," *Broadcasting* (July 28, 1986), 56–57, 64.
35. Michael Dann, "The '50s 'Golden Age'? Today's TV Is Better," *TV Guide* (May 19, 1984), 10.
36. Barbara Lippert, "Mitsubishi: Rapid-Eye Repast for the 'Re' Generation," *ADWEEK* (October 24, 1988), 19.
37. Garry Marshall, "Happy Days Is Here Again," *TV Guide* (February 29, 1992), 12–13.
38. Lynette Unger, Diane McConocha, and John Faier, "The Use of Nostalgia in Television Ad-

vertising: A Content Analysis," *Journalism Quarterly* (Fall 1991), 346.

39. Jerry Herron, quoted in "Melange," *Chronicle of Higher Education* (December 9, 1987), B2.

40. Carl Grabo, *The Creative Critic* (Chicago: University of Chicago Press, 1948), 108.

41. Ibid., 109.

42. Charles Wright, *Mass Communication: A Sociological Perspective*, 3rd ed. (New York: Random House, 1986), 21.

43. Noreen O'Leary, "Networks Get into the Retro Act," *ADWEEK* (March 18, 1986), 20.

44. Ibid.

45. Mark Levy, "Watching TV News as Para-Social Interaction," *Journal of Broadcasting* (Winter 1979), 69–70.

46. Michael Antecol, "Learning from Television: Parasocial Interaction and Affective Learning." Presentation to the Association for Education in Journalism & Mass Communication Convention, August, 1997 (Chicago).

47. Donald Horton and R. Richard Wohl, "Mass Communication and Para-Social Interaction: Observations on Intimacy at a Distance," *Psychiatry* 19 (1956), 216.

48. John Fiske, "Popular Television and Commercial Culture: Beyond Political Economy," in Gary Burns and Robert Thompson (eds.), *Television Studies: Textual Analysis* (New York: Praeger, 1989), 34.

49. Robert Allen, "Reader-Oriented Criticism and Television," in Robert Allen (ed.), *Channels of Discourse* (Chapel Hill: University of North Carolina Press, 1987), 84.

50. Rapping, 171.

51. David Henthorne, letter to Peter Orlik, August 27, 1999.

52. Mary Alice Kellogg, "How America Really Watches TV," *TV Guide* (July 29, 1995), 29.

53. Richard Rodriguez, "LA: Watching the Riots," *TV Guide* (May 23, 1992), 31.

54. Louise Bernikow, "Is TV a Pal—or a Danger for Lonely People?" *TV Guide* (October 25, 1986), 5.

55. "Takes," *ADWEEK* (January 11, 1999), 14.

56. Ben Hoberman, "Take Another Listen to Talk Radio," *Broadcasting* (February 24, 1986), 20.

57. Mark Kassof, "Radio Wars II: How to Push Listeners' Hot Buttons." Speech presented to the National Association of Broadcasters Convention, April 13, 1985 (Las Vegas).

58. "Marketing, Not Programing Will Be the Key to Radio in 90's," *Broadcasting* (May 21, 1990), 63.

59. Katz, 97.

60. Conrad Kottak, *Prime-Time Society* (Belmont, CA: Wadsworth, 1990), 148.

61. DeWitt Parker, *The Principles of Aesthetics*, 2nd ed. (Westport, CT: Greenwood Press, 1976), 189–190.

62. Gilbert Seldes, *The Public Arts* (New York: Simon & Schuster, 1956), 102.

63. David Hoffman, "President Says TV Becomes a Neighbor as Families Change," *Washington Post* (August 28, 1984), 23.

64. Ted Halbert, remarks at the International Radio & Television Society Newsmaker Luncheon, February 19, 1993 (New York).

65. Courtesy of Pam Freeman, The Advertising Council, Inc.

66. Horace Newcomb, *TV: The Most Popular Art* (Garden City, NY: Anchor Books, 1974), 260.

67. Jeff Jarvis, "7th Heaven," *TV Guide* (September 21, 1996), 10.

68. Melvin Rader and Bertram Jessup, "Art in an Age of Science and Technology," in Rader, *Esthetics*, 499.

69. John Reith, quoted in Simon Frith, "The Pleasures of the Hearth: The Making of BBC Light Entertainment," *Formations of Pleasure* (London: Routledge & Kegan Paul, 1983), 108.

70. Summarized from Herbert Gans, *Popular Culture and High Culture* (New York: Basic Books, 1974), 69–94.

71. Robert MacKenzie, "A Busy Person's Guide to TV," *TV Guide* (April 8, 1989), 2.

72. Jerome Lopiparo, "Aggression on TV Could Be Helping Our Children," in George Rodman (ed.), *Mass Media Issues*, 3rd ed. (Dubuque, IA: Kendall/Hunt, 1989), 243.

73. Gary Copeland and Dan Slater, "Television, Fantasy and Vicarious Catharsis," *Critical Studies in Mass Communication* (December, 1985), 359.

74. DeWitt Parker, *The Analysis of Art* (New Haven, CT: Yale University Press, 1926), 108.

75. Comstock et al., 424.

76. Rose Goldsen, *The Show and Tell Machine* (New York: The Dial Press, 1977), 225.

77. Judith Myers-Walls, "Suggestions for Parents: Children Can Unlearn Violence," *Media & Values* (Summer 1993), 19.

78. Robert Lewis Shayon, *Open to Criticism* (Boston: Beacon Press, 1971), 239–240.

79. Joyce Brothers, "The Shows That'll Make You Feel Better," *TV Guide* (July 29, 1989), 14.

80. James Opsitnik, writing in "Monday Memo," *Broadcasting* (November 5, 1990), 24.

81. "Music to Die For," *Wayne State University Alumni News* (Fall 1993), 5.

Depiction Analysis

Every electronic media program, no matter its length or delivery system, unavoidably serves an instructive function. This is as true of commercials, radio lyrics, Web 'events,' and television sitcoms as it is of 'hard news' programs and documentaries. As our twenty-first century perceptual world widens, physical participation in most of it becomes less and less feasible. The electronic media fill in this direct-experience gap with their dynamic and inevitable sound and sight curriculum that teaches us not only about places and events, but also about human interaction. As Professor Mary Strom Larson points out,

All television [and indeed all consumer-focused electronic media] is to some degree educational, inasmuch as it provides a rich source of behaviors and roles to observe and from which to learn. This premise is based on social learning theory which explains that in addition to real-life models, television models are used by viewers to shape behavior and cultivation theory which explains that viewers' expectations of real-life experiences are shaped by the experiences they see depicted on television.[1]

Thus, the impact of such an electronic curriculum can be profound, influencing how people interpret and respond to the reality of which they *are* an actual part. According to Professor Joshua Meyrowitz, this has special implications for young people:

our children, for example, were once isolated from adult life by being physically isolated at home or school. But television now takes children across the globe even before they have permission to cross the street. Child viewers witness war, starvation, brutality, as well as a broad spectrum of everyday adult problems, anxieties, and fears. This does not suggest that children simply imitate what they see on TV, but rather that their image of adults and adulthood has been radically altered. No wonder children now seem older, and have less fear of, and respect for, adults.[2]

Media professionals should probe for the lessons that their programming is imparting to adults as well as to children. Otherwise, we can be caught totally off guard when one of our shows or commercials inadvertently projects a tenet that becomes the center of controversy. *Depiction Analysis* is the process by which we attempt to isolate these sometimes subtle programmatic teachings.

DEPICTION DIVERSITY AND CULTIVATION

Most of the time, electronic media producers do not set out to *instruct* their audience. Rather, their whole focus is on creating a piece of media content that will be attractive enough to the right audience and in the right numbers so that a financial profit will ensue.

An important exception is content created to satisfy the 1990 Children's Television Act mandate that broadcasters provide programming *specifically designed* to serve the educational and informational needs of children. Six years later, an FCC rulemaking sought to clarify Congressional intent. It specified that, effective in September 1997, television stations must air three hours per week of identified "core educational programming" if they wanted to facilitate their license renewals. To avoid raising constitutional issues, the FCC kept the definition of such programming deliberately vague, saying only that an identified show must have education as a significant purpose that "furthers the positive development of children sixteen years of age and under." There also was no mention of what was to be taught. As then-FCC Chairman Reed Hundt wrote, his agency's so-called 'kidvid rule':

pointedly says that nothing in the rule relates to the point of view or opinions of the children's shows at issue. A TV licensee can teach creationism or evolution. The FCC just shouldn't care about viewpoint; we care only that the station try to teach something to kids a certain amount of time a week. So the kidvid rule doesn't reward or punish any broadcaster for its views or opinions.[3]

Studiously imprecise though it is, this rare commercial occurrence of deliberately instructive programming forces media practitioners to carefully consider and focus the lessons conveyed by certain of their shows. Unfortunately, they seldom take the same care in dissecting the by-product teachings found in the rest of the schedule.

All commercials are explicit tutors, of course. However, their clearly identified curriculum strives to limit itself to a single lecture glorifying the product or service being advertised. On the other hand, the lessons conveyed by programs (especially non-kidvid-intended shows) are much more unpredictable and numerous. And the power of such lessons is not diminished simply because they are unintended by-products of the packaging of news and entertainment. *Every* piece of electronic media content that enters the home carries a potential *diversity* of teachings that may take root in the minds of the audience. Every listener or viewer is inevitably a 'student' of media pedagogy—and sometimes (even in the case of the highly focused commercial) those students absorb a lesson that the electronic producer never meant to convey. "All television is to some extent educational television," argue Dennis Lowry and David Towles, "in that attitudes, values and various types of coping behaviors are always being taught."[4] (The same could be said of radio, though in a more diffuse way, given the multitude of elements in a given format hour.)

In some cases, a creator is totally unaware of the lessons that have been embedded in his or her message. What Professor Bruce Gronbeck points out about TV series is fully applicable to all electronic media program matter:

Any messages "communicated" by television series lie not so much "in" the program or "in" the intent of the producers, directors, writers, actors, and editors. Rather, the messages lie in the culture and codes which are shared by all these people—and their viewers. . . . Different groups of viewers, of course, will be engaged on different levels or in different are-

nas-of-meaning, depending upon their sophistication, experiences, and the like.[5]

The *cultivation effect* impacts media consumers who are among the more continuously 'engaged.' In essence, states anthropologist Conrad Kottak, the cultivation effect proposes that "the more time people spend watching television, the more they perceive the real world as being similar to that of television."[6] According to communication theorists Barry Sapolsky and Joseph Tabarlet, cultivation theory further suggests "that television offers a consistent, stable set of messages that serves as a common socializer. Further, heavy consumption of the highly repetitive messages of television can create a distorted picture of social reality."[7]

Despite the significant body of research into the cultivation effect, its validity has yet to be unequivocally established. Professor W. James Potter indicates some obstacles such research faces:

Perhaps, one reason for the consistently weak evidence is the difficulty, which is often ignored, of determining what television world beliefs are. The difficulty can be attributed to several reasons. First, the television [and radio] world is made up of such a large number of mass produced messages and images. . . . The theorists [notably George Gerbner and colleagues] say that "the more we live with television, the more invisible it becomes." So determining what constitutes an effect is not a task that always has a clear answer.

A second reason for the difficulty in determining the television world answer is the degree of interpretation that must be employed in determining what the "television world" answer should be. Even though determining the accurate television world answer is critical to cultivation research, this task is often treated in a superficial manner.[8]

Depiction analysis is one admittedly less scientific response to this challenge. Though it is complementary to the efforts of cultivation research, 'depiction' is not necessarily dependent on them since it does not concern itself only with 'heavy' media users. Instead, the more informal depiction approach attempts to uncover the *most likely* answers that a given program or commercial provides to five fundamental "world view" questions. The assumption is that the more often a given consumer attends the "electronic academy," the more likely he or she is to learn the lessons embedded in the media content. As media professionals, we can then come to some determination as to whether our studio, agency, or outlet wishes to be associated with the catechism that is seemingly being conveyed by the project under scrutiny.

This depictive scrutiny must take into account the audience at whom the program is aimed, of course. The narrower and more defined are our target consumers, the more market research is available to guide us as to the likely response these consumers will implicitly make to depiction's five questions. "Put simply," says John Fiske, "different programs are designed (usually fairly successfully) to attract different audiences,"[9] with each audience perceiving its own discrete, contrasting, or overlapping lessons.

Complications most often arise when an unintended audience is exposed to a media message. Most obviously, this occurs when so-called adult programming is scheduled and transmitted in such a way as to be readily available to children. Numerous studies have found that child-intended programming typically constitutes no more than 10 percent of a child's total television viewing. This percentage may be even lower in the case of Internet use. And relying on parents to moderate this discrepancy is naive. "The notion of parental control is an upper-middle class conceit," Professor George Gerbner asserts, "since one-third of children come home to an empty house."[10] Therefore, a careful depiction analysis conducted from an adult perspective may not prove of much utility when large numbers of young people become part of the audience. For example, consider the little boy who used his allowance to buy a box of feminine hygiene pads because the commercial told him that by owning such things "I get to go swimming and skiing and horseback riding."

With these qualifications in mind, let us now explore in detail each of depiction's five questions. A given program or commercial may implicitly emphasize only one or two of these queries, but cues relating to all five are inevitably present in every electronic media message people hear or see. Specifically, the question quintet from which depiction-derived teachings spring is as follows:

1. What are the characteristics of our physical environment?

2. What is society like?

3. What consequences flow from our actions?

4. What are our responsibilities?

5. What are the standards by which we should evaluate ourselves?

Let's look, in order, at each question, as well as at some of the ways in which each is typically answered.

WHAT ARE THE CHARACTERISTICS OF OUR PHYSICAL ENVIRONMENT?

Electronic media bring us instantaneous and even interplanetary images of the habitat that surrounds us. Even though the media message may not convey the precise locale in which we ourselves live, we can compare our physical conditions with those being portrayed to better assess the quality of our own situation.

Thus, we are grateful that we do not live in the existence-threatening dust of drought-stricken East Africa, the war-ravaged landscapes of Kosovo, or, for that matter, the urban squalor of many of the beats patrolled by *Cops*. On the other hand, we may envy the posh surroundings in which our favorite daytime or prime-time soap opera dwellers cavort. If, through our programming selections, we choose to experience more of the former, we will probably be more self-satisfied than if we select a preponderance of the latter.

As Marshall McLuhan once reminded us, a refrigerator can be a revolutionary symbol of deprivation to people who have no refrigerators. So, the more media images suggest that we are living outside the physical comfort zone of the "good life mainstream," the greater the possibility for anger or self-pity to arise. New York sociologist Terry Williams has found that many poor children learn they *are* poor by watching television. "At first the kids are appalled," he reports. "They're [angry] at the idea of being poor. But what they internalize is, 'How can I get that?' . . . the American way is to take it, to connive and take it any way you can."[11] One associated theory proposes that immigrant tenement dwellers of the 1880s were much more positively motivated to self-improvement than were their successors a century later because they didn't have television pictures constantly mocking them with suburban images of just how far they had to go.

As is the case with any of the depiction lessons, audience perception of mediated physical setting and its furnishings cannot always be predicted. During the depths of the Stalinist era, a minor Soviet bureaucrat thought citizen morale would be substantially boosted if his countryfolk perceived how much better were USSR living conditions than those of the working classes in the United States. So the movie version of novelist John Steinbeck's *The Grapes of Wrath*, starring Henry Fonda, was shown to gatherings of Soviet workers. The bureaucrat expected his fellow citizens to be repelled by the shacks and tents to which Steinbeck's dust-bowl-fleeing Okies were consigned, and therefore to be grateful for their own spartan, state-owned apartments. What the Soviet viewers focused on, however, was not the migratory landlessness of the Okies but the jealousy-producing fact that even these oppressed Americans possessed the mobile comforts of their own automobiles! Clearly, *The Grapes of Wrath* answered a physical condition question for Soviet citizens—but not in the way the bureaucrat had hoped.

This overt and unsuccessful attempt at attitudinal manipulation is a far cry from the U.S. electronic media producer's selection of setting as a mere formula backdrop for character interaction. Still, that backdrop always becomes a depictive factor, nonetheless. And the lessons flowing from it may inadvertently overshadow other aspects of the program.

The repetitive image of the physically pristine yet frustratingly unattainable California life-style (with the apocalyptically portrayed exception of south central L.A.) that blatantly taunts so many viewers, for instance, is not a plot by the Los Angeles Chamber of Commerce. It is simply the by-product of the facts that most television writers live there and that directors still find it financially and climatically easier to shoot there. Yet, this mere convenience is often the teacher of an obtrusive physical environment lesson. After moving to Los Angeles, East Coast lawyer-turned-critic Ben Stein noticed that

the lives of men and women and children on TV shows, so different from any life I had ever seen or participated in, was really the life of

Los Angeles—the clean streets; . . . the shiny new cars issued to everyone over sixteen; . . . the tinkling of glasses around a swimming pool; the pastel hues of storefronts; the dark, richly upholstered restaurant interiors; the squealing of tires along canyon roads; and much more.

To a significant degree, TV-land remains L.A.-land or, at the very least, urban, coastal United States. The thousands of miles and municipalities large and small that separate Los Angeles (and San Francisco) from New York (or Miami or Boston) are something of which most studio producers are aware but do not really comprehend.

For some reason (perhaps because of the weather or the fact that they grew up on the East Coast and fled to the West) writers portray New York, Boston, and (as a generic if geographically mismatched convenience) Chicago as much more grimy and physically constrained environments than the other coast's expansive California cleanliness. The cities at both extremities of the country are depicted as exciting, crime-ridden and trendy, but the East seems more claustrophobically threatening. As a small-town New Mexico student once told a visiting critic, "I've never gone to New York. But you watch *Cagney & Lacey* and its all subways and real dark. Somebody is getting murdered all the time, and it's like you have to get used to it if you want to live there. I don't ever want to go to New York."[13]

Certainly, residents of New York City may, through their *direct* experience, see things much differently—and might harbor their own fears about desert-depicted small-town New Mexico. Yet, because most people do not live in New York, menacing media portrayals of the municipality can have a significant impact. The short-lived show *Brooklyn Bridge* took a much gentler view of the Big Apple, but even the opening credits made clear that this view was the unrecapturable vista of four decades past.

In an opposite yet identical way, the Michigan portrayed in the Figure 9-1 commercial is not the environment experienced by the inner-city dweller in Detroit or Flint. Obviously, this spot seeks to attract summer tourists. It evokes only locales thought to be most pleasing to them. This is a skillful, positive sampling of physical reality in the same way that *Cagney & Lacey* (and many other shows before and since) teach their negative

"I AM MICHIGAN (GULL & PEOPLE)"

FIGURE 9-1
A promotional an-
swer to depiction's
physical environment
question. (Courtesy
of Marcie Brogan,
Brogan & Partners)

SINGERS: I AM MICHIGAN.

V/O: I am vast waters along endless coastlines.

I am deep forests sheltering majestic life.

I am towering cliffs that guard the immensity of the Great Lakes.

And miles of sand gathered by the wind.
SINGERS: THIS IS WHAT I AM.

V/O: I am exuberance.

I am tranquility.

I am moments.

I am memories.

I am rivers that roll and bend and sometimes fall.

I am rich, green meadows.

...and elegant places.

SINGERS: YES, MICHIGAN.
THE FEELING IS FOREVER.
YES, MICHIGAN,
THE FEELING IS FOREVER.

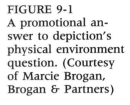

urban-environment lesson as a means of heightening dramatic tension.

Although neither the "I Am Michigan" spot nor any single program can ever reflect an entire environment, each can instruct the viewer, in purposeful or incidental ways, about the characteristics of a particular physical habitat. This lesson will be construed as accurate to the extent that it does not conflict with any past belief or experience the viewer possesses.

Distortion can arise mainly from the total absence of other experience. As Michael Leahy cautions,

perhaps the gritty, urban dramas would pose no hazards at all if there were other dramas that shed a less sensational light on everyday life in cities at once vibrant, troubled, intimidating, exhilarating.[14]

WHAT IS SOCIETY LIKE?

As we have just illustrated, persons can come to fear small towns as well as big cities if they lack first-hand experience and encounter unchallenged and negative media depictions. In fact, Ben Stein found just such a 'Hicksville phobia' to be present in prime-time television and in the minds of the producers whose work is displayed there. This condition is more a *social* teaching than a physical environment one. And it is this teaching Stein attributes to one basic condition:

Most of the writers and producers originally come from large eastern cities or from Los Angeles, and they are uncomfortable with the whole concept of small towns. . . . It is largely *terra incognita*, and like everyone else in the world, TV writers and producers are frightened by what they do not know.

There is also an ethnic difference that frightens some. The Hollywood TV writer tends generally, although not always, to be Jewish or Italian or Irish and he sees people in the small towns as not being ethnic at all. He sees them, moreover, as not being friendly toward ethnics, especially Jews. . . . And, of course, it could hardly be more natural for people who fear they might be 'beat up' in small towns because of their race to feel some anger toward them.[15]

Thus, it did not surprise Stein that in much of the television programming he watched, "Small towns were superficially lovely [physical environment] but under a thin veneer of compose there was lurking, terrifying evil [society] waiting to ensnare the innocent Natty Bumpo [James Fenimore Cooper's woodsman hero] of the big city."[16] *Twin Peaks* later followed this societal form to a tee. Conversely, *Northern Exposure* inverted it by leavening Dr. Fleischman's urban-bred cynicism with an Alaskan hamlet's engaging rustic candor. And *Due South* invested that rustic candor in a Canadian Mountie transplanted to Chicago who won over big-city barbarians with what one critic called "a ceaselessly straight face, a maple-tree spine, and a moral sense that these days is about as extinct as the dodo."[17]

Whatever the pattern a given program follows, its social portrayals represent the most volatile aspects of its content. Media content is almost always an exploration of people, after all. And how these depicted people's heritage and status govern their interactions creates an implicit portrait of how our actual society functions and malfunctions. "Television must be understood, but too seldom is, as part of the process whereby we gain social knowledge," writes Professor Denise Kervin; "that is, knowledge about the beliefs and representations existing in society, thereby perhaps reinforcing the status quo, perhaps questioning it, or perhaps even challenging its premises. Television engages in ideological work in its use of ideas and images."[18]

When this 'ideological work' portrays—as it frequently does—certain people accepting subjugation to the authority of others, the program content has introduced the issue of *hegemony*. "Briefly," explains John Fiske, "hegemony may be defined as that process whereby the subordinate are led to consent to the system that subordinates them. This is achieved when they 'consent' to view the social system and its everyday embodiments as 'common sense.' "[19]

Such *hegemonic* portrayals often present contradictory social lessons depending on which audience is reading the program content. Ronald Lembo and Kenneth Tucker tell us that scholars

who study television argue that people interpret the text of programming in various ways because differing locations in the social structure give rise to distinct material interests, resulting in differing strategies of interpretation. *Oppositional* interpretations of the text depend on people's subordinate status. Through continued "readings" of television texts, oppositional interpretations become a source of cultural resistance and provide a basis for political empowerment."[20]

If, as an individual and a member of a group, we are disturbed by where media depictions place people like us on the social ladder, we will probably decode and respond to a program much differently than will audience members who are comfortable with this societal assumption.

It is more than a matter of liking or disliking. Viewers react to media characters via one of two broad schema: realistic and discursive. According to Fiske, a *realism theory of character* decrees that the audience interprets the media personage solely as an individual and responds entirely on that basis. The character is simply taken at face value. Fiske's *discursive theory of character*, conversely, refers to cases in which viewers see characters not merely as individuals but as symbols or metaphors for social power structures and hierarchies. If they like/approve of the symbol, then their discursive reading of the character is *supportive*. It is when they dislike or disapprove of what the character seems to stand for that Lembo and Tucker's *oppositional* discursive reading takes place.

Programs shift to the discursive arena at their peril. *Ellen* was a reasonably successful ABC sitcom about a young single woman and her friends who worked in a bookstore. Starring stand-up comic Ellen DeGeneres, the show (originally titled *Friends Like These*) featured characters that a mass audience realistically read as likeable pals in lighthearted situations. But in a subsequent season, after several weeks of cryptic gags, an entire episode was devoted to character (and real) Ellen announcing her lesbianism. The show became a discursive lightning rod. Supportive and oppositional readings swirled in the trade and popular press, *Ellen*'s ratings fell off, and chances for lucrative off-network syndication plummeted. This negative result had less to do with audience attitudes toward homosexuality than it did with the fact that viewers could no longer enjoy the show realistically, but rather were forced to digest it discursively. Many members of the existing viewership simply were unwilling to 'read' the show in this radically different way.

The prominence of the *Ellen* example notwithstanding, in the main, discursive readings relate to notions of social class rather than of sexual orientation. These 'class' readings can be no less unsettling to audiences, however, because Americans have preferred to ignore assertions that class structures exist in the United States. There's an absence, "an unbecoming discretion," claims sociologist Todd Gitlin, when it comes to electronic media portrayal of social class. "It's the great taboo of American life."[21] Therefore, it is not surprising that the possibility that unexpected discursive/hegemonic readings of their programs and commercials are taking place makes advertising agencies, studios, and networks very nervous. If even the most entertainment-promoting program or benefit-centered commercial is interpreted as a social statement, what might this do to ratings levels and sales curves?

To Professor Richard Blake, such studied avoidance of 'disruptive' social portrayals has meant only that the portrayals the electronic media do provide have been *that much more* disruptive because they so scrupulously try to ignore class chasms. "Mass communication, as it penetrated the inner cities of the United States in the 1960s and the third world in the next decade," recounts Blake, "brought a sense not of participation but of exclusion. The image of the good life, available so readily to middle-class Americans on the gray-blue screen, was not accessible to everyone, and the result was outrage and violence."[22]

It is no longer a case of television *ignoring* the racial minorities who so often find themselves part of the 'real-life' underclass. Rather, producers frequently have decided to set what they believed to be a noncontroversial and ingratiating course by promoting minority characters to powerful, counter-hegemonic positions. Today, there are shows featuring ethnic minority doctors, lawyers, and entrepreneurs. "I cannot recall a time in TV history when there were so many upscale minority achievers moving into professional ranks," says history professor Carlos Cortez, with the resulting social lesson being "the accessibility of the American dream." Unfortunately, Cortez adds, "most minorities haven't even begun to make contact with the dream, and TV has turned its back on them. . . . It presents an ersatz world, because segregation does exist in massive amounts. In fact, the evidence suggests it's an increasingly *re*-segregated world—along both race and class lines."[23]

Thus, simply elevating minority characters to high-status roles can actually intensify oppositional readings of these programs by people who see no possibility of ever achieving those roles themselves. Though highly successful, *The Cosby Show* of the 1980s often found itself in this quandary. As Professor Lauren Tucker explains:

On the one hand, *Cosby* is lauded as a "revolutionary" moment in the history of Black representation on U.S. television. By recoding the image of Black Americans as socially and economically successful, the series effectively moved the racial discourse of television toward the symbolic construction of racial equality and a colorblind society.

Yet, other critical voices within the commentary argue that *Cosby* may have merely been reformist at best, or perhaps even retrograde, with respect to the series' influence on the public discourse on race. This line of criticism questions the assumption that the positive images of an affluent Black family were necessarily positive in their effect on progress toward racial equality and tolerance. Extolling the rewards of Black, middle-class success, the series promoted individualistic explanations for the persistence of Black inequality and seduced Black and White Americans into believing that those who fail to achieve the American Dream have only themselves to blame. *The Cosby Show* continued television's twin traditions of investing Black characters with the values and mores of White middle-class culture and ignoring the social and economic realities germane to most Black Americans.[24]

It may be instructive at this point to read the script of the "Theo's Holiday" *Cosby Show* episode reprinted in Appendix A. Can you find elements in this episode that support each of these divergent opinions as to the sitcom's societal teachings?

Most economists and sociologists believe that in real life, the gap between rich and poor has widened. Thus, the challenge for the electronic media is to find ways to portray people on both sides of the gap without antagonizing the rich with 'guilt trips' and the poor with images of humiliation. "The goal of TV is to sell goods and services to people with the wherewithal to buy them, not to solve social problems," argues advertising executive Doug Alligood. "The solutions to those problems won't come until someone on the *social* level decides to do something about them. Solutions won't come from advertisers. And so they won't come from television."[25]

While Alligood's point is well taken, it does not change the fact that audience members "read" programmed content from their distinct social vantage points. The electronic media may not be able to solve 'the problem,' but our profession is inevitably held accountable for how that problem is imaged.

Little wonder, then, that some of the most perceptive and relevant social commentary exists in animated programming, from *Tiny Toons* to *The Simpsons* to *Ren & Stimpy* to *South Park*. Whether they are puppets, hunks of clay, movable dolls, or artist sketches, animated characters possess a unique flexibility. As animation authority Leonard Maltin says of cartoon folk:

We get a vicarious kick out of watching them speak the unsayable, do the unthinkable—because they're "only cartoon characters, we can cheer them without seeming antisocial ourselves. . . . Cartoons allow us to indulge our youthful dreams, act out the thoughts society teaches us to inhibit and have a good time in the bargain.[26]

More constructively, author Ella Taylor believes that shows like *The Simpsons* are uniquely capable of reflecting contemporary upheavals in society and in family life. "*The Simpsons*," she says, "goes further in articulating these difficulties than *Roseanne*. But because it's a cartoon, it's safer. It seems less real."[27] (You may wish to read *The Simpsons* script in Appendix A at this point to evaluate this premise for yourself.) Even as an adult-oriented, late-evening show, *South Park* would not long survive if its scurrilous language was seen and heard to come out of the mouths of flesh-and-blood child actors. But voiced by animated characters—graphically rendered with anything but Disney/kid-friendly finesse—*South Park*'s graffitilike guerilla warfare can be enjoyed by grown-ups as deceptively unthreatening satire. Social reality may be no joking matter, but animated characters can make it seem like one while articulating important *and perceptive* societal lessons in the process.

WHAT CONSEQUENCES FLOW FROM OUR ACTIONS?

Whatever their social or family status, listeners and viewers continuously search for ways to cope with their human and physical worlds. As we discuss in Chapter 8, different groups, in their media-use patterns, may lean toward different gratifications clusters as part of this coping strategy. But regardless of the program selection or real-life choices they make, consumers would like the results to be forecastable. Media depictions oblige by teaching a curriculum of prediction. The many media-provided answers to the "What would happen if I . . . ? question range along a continuum from the scrupulously scientific to the most fantastically improbable. Therefore, in our message design, we must always be sure that the public cannot easily confuse one end of this continuum with the other! Children and adults must be able accurately to separate depictive results that are probable (even inevitable) from those that are creative hyperbole or impossible fiction.

Commercials are certainly the most streamlined consequence teachers. They can project audience members into a future that is bright with the product or dismal without it. But the more extreme the claim (particularly in terms of assertions that move beyond the province of the product category) the more likely is this lesson to be counterfeit. Thus, the toothpaste that claims to convert your mouth into a beacon of sexuality is a charlatan tutor because it moves beyond the product's fundamental reason for being.

In contrast, the Figure 9-2 spot for Check-Up Gum restricts itself to the feasible assertion that the confection will help you remove plaque conveniently ("with dignity") when brushing is too awkward. The consequence of doing otherwise is also portrayed to amplify the preferability of the Check-Up Gum solution. This product may not give you a smile that will automatically win presentations, but neither will it sabotage your suit.

Sexual Consequences

In a more serious vein, social psychologists and electronic media critics have been particularly concerned with the program-ming-displayed consequences (or lack of them) associated with sexual portrayals. In 1985, for instance, a task force of the American Academy of Pediatrics charged that television's treatment of sex roles and human sexuality was "unrealistic and misleading." Adolescence is painted as a period of constant sexual crisis, sexual relationships are shown to develop rapidly, and the risk of pregnancy is rarely explicated, stated the task force's report.

Almost fifteen years later, research by the Henry J. Kaiser Family Foundation suggested that the situation had not improved. After analyzing more than 1,300 television shows, the Kaiser study found that while 56 percent of them featured sexual content, just 9 percent of these included any expression of concern about safe-sex practices.[28]

Erroneous teachings about the consequences of sex and love experiences (made worse because of the failure to differentiate between these two interactions) have frequently been carried by television and radio programming. Audio song lyrics seem no less guilty in this regard than do video melodramas. And when sex and love are intermingled as a commodity, the results of both are likely to be misrepresented. In their research on soap operas, for instance, Dennis Lowrey and David Towles discovered that

the transcending message on soap operas concerning sex is that it is primarily for unmarried partners. Yet, though contraception is seldom mentioned, pregnancy is rare. Even though life on most of the soap operas takes place in the sexually fast lane, no one ever comes down with a sexually transmitted disease.[29]

Yet, the greatest distortion in consequences depiction, writes critic William Henry, "is not the prevalent sex outside marriage but rather the scarcity of sex inside marriage that makes TV so prurient. Prime time implies there is no fun without sin, no kiss except a stolen one."[30] Producer Paul Aaron agrees: "To separate out the sex and say 'Oh my gosh, we're showing some kind of forbidden activity' is to deny an extraordinary part of the communication between married people. It seems to me we make a bigger deal out of sex by mystifying it and making it taboo."[31] The result of such misguided mod-

FIGURE 9-2
(Courtesy of Becky
McConnell, Bozell,
Jacobs, Kenyon &
Eckhardt, Inc.,
Advertising)

(MUSIC UNDER & THROUGHOUT)

MAN: Excellent lunch, Mr. Runstead.
RUNSTEAD: Yes, it was.

(TURNS TO BENSON) Benson, I'm
of the understanding your presentation
kicks off this afternoon's session.

BENSON: (MOUTH FULL OF
TOOTHPASTE) Mmmm-hmmm.
(NODS) Mmmm-hmmmm.
RUNSTEAD: I needn't stress the
importance of that presentation,
Benson.

BENSON: (MOUTH STILL FULL OF
TOOTHPASTE) Mmmm-hmmm.
VO: It's not hard to figure out why
people don't always brush after eating.

BENSON: (REACTING TO
STAIN) Uh-oh.
VO: But now, Check-Up
Toothpaste introduces

Check-Up plaque fighting gum. It's
clinically proven

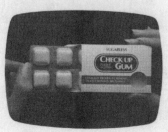

to help remove plaque...with dignity.

Check-Up Gum. When you can't brush,
chew.

esty is to portray the prime consequence of marriage as an end to sexual excitement.

As the influence of religion and the family unit has ebbed, television in particular has become, by default, what researcher E. J. Roberts calls the "electronic sex educator." Even though the medium did not seek such a task, it has been given it nonetheless. Often, programming professionals fail either to realize or to respond responsibly to this assignment. Even in terms of conveying fundamental biological results, sexually oriented programming like soap operas "are not training films on sex," point out researchers Muriel and Joel Cantor. "What teenagers learn are [only] sexual manners and morals, how to initiate relationships with potential sexual partners and what to expect from members of the opposite sex when the relationship becomes intimate."[32]

Prime-time television usually does no better. In her analysis of evening programming, Diana Workman found that "rather than enlightening the audience, television serves to more deeply entrench discomfort about sex and contributes to continued ignorance in society about love, sex, and responsibility."[33] She further discovered that, though sexual intercourse was suggested an average of 2.5 times per hour, and a range of "discouraged sexual practices such as sadomasochism and exhibitionism were suggested at a rate of 6.2 times per hour," educational information about sex was "infrequently presented, occurring at a rate of 1.6 times per hour." Worst of all from an accurate consequences-teaching standpoint, Workman observed that "Rare as they are, TV pregnancies are apt to end in miscarriages and stillbirths, leaving the characters apparently unchanged by the experience. Still more common are sexual relationships untroubled by worries about pregnancy and sexually transmitted diseases, even though safe sex, contraception and sex education are rarely discussed."[34] Meanwhile, the HIV/AIDS crisis is seldom broached outside news and occasional PSA venues.

The electronic media should not strive to avoid all reference to sex and sexual situations. No artistic endeavor that pretends to service and reference humankind could operate under such a constraint. As the Canadian Broadcasting Corporation's *Guidelines on Sex-Role Portrayal* makes clear, there is "nothing reprehensible about on-air representation of tasteful, positive, relevant sexuality, which portrays persons in control of and celebrating their own sexuality."[35]

Once a sexual issue is raised, however, the artist (painter, musician, novelist, TV, or online scriptwriter) assumes a responsibility to treat the subject in a way that does no *consequential* disserve to the likely audience.

Violence Consequences

"Sex-and-violence" almost becomes a single word to the electronic media's most uncompromising detractors. And in one sense, it may be appropriate to lump the two subjects together because distortive treatments of both tend to occur when the consequences of the depicted act are ignored.

Some of the most perceptive concern about media violence has come not from people who wish unrealistically to sanitize its electronic treatment but from critics concerned with the dangerous consequences lesson such sanitization conveys. Physician Mike Oppenheim has framed the issue this way:

Critics of TV violence claim it teaches children sadism and cruelty. I honestly don't know whether or not TV violence is harmful, but if so, the critics have it backward. Children can't learn to enjoy cruelty from the neat, sanitized mayhem on the average series. There isn't any! What they learn is far more malignant: that

guns or fists are clean, efficient, exciting ways to deal with a difficult situation. Bang!—you're dead! Bop!—you're unconscious (temporarily).

. . .

Seriously, real-life violence is dirty, painful, bloody, disgusting. It causes mutilation and misery, and it doesn't solve problems. It makes them worse. If we're genuinely interested in protecting our children, we should stop campaigning to "clean up" TV violence. It's already too antiseptic. Ironically, the problem with TV violence is: it's not violent enough.[36]

Adds Dick Wolf, producer of the critically acclaimed *Law & Order*, "My feeling is, if you're going to show someone being shot, then show them writhing on the ground in pain, see them in a hospital three days later, still writhing in pain. Don't make it glamorous."[37]

One way in which the consequences of violence are made glamorous is having hero figures be violence perpetrators. A 1998 study funded by the National Cable Television Association found that nearly 40 percent of the violent incidents on television were initiated by hero figures who were likely to be positioned as attractive role models. Animated superheroes were particularly likely to commit violent acts with impunity and with no appreciation for the consequences of their actions.[38] Because these cartoon 'good guys' are especially appealing to children, such glamorization is of special concern. "In children's programs I see the good guys win," observed veteran network programming executive Jeff Sagansky, "but by beating the crap out of the bad guys."[39]

To help media producers avoid glamorizing violence and its consequences, the Institute for Mental Health Initiatives has proposed five key suggestions:

Eliminate violent scenes that do not contribute to the plot or character development or to the story in a true crime piece.
Depict violence as a last resort for heroes who have used their wits in encountering danger.
Depict thoughtless violence and the use of weapons as weak and shortsighted; depict the verbalization of anger and fear and the struggle to delay violent action as strong.
Portray the emotional, social and economic impact of violence on perpetrators, victims, families and witnesses.
Avoid portrayals that show violence as socially desirable, thrilling or glamorous, or the only option for dealing with conflict. Do not broad-

cast images of violence excessively, such as in promotions and advertisements. Do not show violence without portraying the tragic consequences of violence.[40]

Notice that these IMHI guidelines do not simplistically seek to "get rid of" media violence. Instead, they attempt to ensure that consequences lessons about violence are accurate and prosocial. This realistic approach to the inevitable depiction of violence mirrors stands taken by responsible industry groups such as the National Cable Television Association, which adopted the following policy statement:

We believe that the depiction of violence is a legitimate dramatic and journalistic representation of an unavoidable part of human existence. We also believe that the gratuitous use of violence depicted as an easy and convenient solution to human problems is harmful to our industry and society. We therefore discourage and will strive to reduce the frequency of such exploitative uses of violence while preserving our right to show programs that convey the real meaning *and consequences of violent behavior.* [italics added][41]

Other Consequence Contexts

As the NCTA policy statement indicates, the consequences of violent and other similarly dynamic events are important concerns, not just in scripted fiction, but also in what NCTA labels "journalistic representations." Unfortunately, the shorter and more entertainment-oriented the news program and its stories become, the more difficult it is to move beyond the event to establish its residual impact. Researchers C. Richard Hofstetter and David Dozier have found, for example, that "non-sensational news is more likely than sensational news to mention political processes explicitly, to provide differing points of view, to describe processes, *to speculate about consequences*, and to employ more than a single attributed source of information." [italics added][42]

Whether woven into a commercial, an entertainment program, or a newscast, consequences lessons reveal life's cause-and-effect relationships. But when producers leave these lessons to chance, the result usually is an improbable commercial, an erroneous drama, or a contextless news show. Worse, if a producer totally ignores the implicit conse-

quences teachings embedded in a program's content, these teachings may later surface as negative and controversial spectres that special interest groups exploit to further their own opportunistic interpretations of what a show 'means.'

No programming genre can avoid consequences conveyance or can escape the possibility that the cumulative impact of these consequence lessons might be negative. For decades, 'animal-hero' shows like *Lassie, My Friend Flicka, Flipper*, and *Gentle Ben* were assumed to represent the best in kid-friendly television programming. However, more careful analysis of these series reveals a common consequence fallacy: when kids get in peril, *relying on an animal friend rather than on an (often inept) adult will result in rescue.* It is unsettling to contemplate the influence a steady diet of such a consequence teaching might have on young children and the strategies they might subsequently adopt to extricate themselves from danger. In seeking aid in real life, one should count on a cop instead of a cat; but that was not the consequence lesson that many of these well-meaning menagerie programs projected.

Because consequence lessons are going to be read into every media portrayal, it is up to content producers to make certain that they have made this lesson as unequivocal, accurate, and audience-appropriate as possible. Leaving consequence lessons to chance is the mark of a hack and not of an artist. As the gentle, perceptive, and award-winning producer Fred Rogers (of *Mister Rogers' Neighborhood*) explains: "What you see in real art is that there are consequences to people's behavior, and that those consequences are dealt with."[43] No media professional should be satisfied to do less.

WHAT ARE OUR RESPONSIBILITIES?

This fourth depiction question can be paraphrased as "What Do Others Expect of Us?" Depending on how the audience member relates to the media situation, this query can also be inverted into the mirror-image question of "What Do We Expect of Others?" In watching a family drama, for example, children can use the kid actors as guides to how they themselves are expected to behave. But just as important, the depicted parents reflect meaty lessons to those viewing children as to what they might anticipate from their own parental figures. For parent viewers, of course, the process works in exactly the opposite manner. (It also *fails to work* to the extent that the show's portrayals are outlandish, simplistic, or mean-spirited.)

However one phrases or uses it, this depiction question normally is answered more by what electronic media characters *do* than by what they *say*. It also encompasses the notion that certain role-model occupations are expected to fulfill certain duties. The obligations of mother, father, lawyer, law enforcement officer, physician, teacher, clergy, and journalist historically were treated with pervasive respect by the electronic media, and depicted characters in these roles who failed to live up to their consequent responsibilities tended to be painted with special scorn. On the other hand, the responsibilities exercised by such groups as politicians and businesspeople typically have been portrayed in negative terms.

Sometimes, the accretion of these mediated obligations makes it difficult for people in real life to live up to the positive expectations and to counteract the negative ones. Many police, for instance, were happy to see *Dragnet* and *Adam-12*-type characters gradually replaced by those of *Hill Street Blues, NYPD Blue,* and *Homicide: Life on the Street*—men and women who were attainably human, not heroically sanctified. In discussing their landmark study of how officers in a selected police department reference TV law enforcement depictions, Professors Michael Pacanowsky and James Anderson reported that their subjects were put off by

the portrayal of policemen as too good and criminals as too bad. One cop complained about the extent to which the media goes "overboard" to really build up the bad guy" as bad. And *Adam-12* [two unflappable and photogenic California squad-car partners] for him, was an example of where the media went "overboard on the good cop thing." There is a certain suspicion among some social commentators and social scientists as well that many cops have an "authoritarian personality" and prefer to see the world in simple good and bad terms. Certainly this cop, and many on the Valley View [fictitious name] force, perceived media representation of cops and robbers in good and bad terms to be askew. In fact, the

cops seemed to prefer that the researchers/ride-alongs not perceive them as "good guys," but just as guys like anybody else doing a job.[44]

Idealized parental figures on the media can present the same expectational problems for mothers and fathers that "overly good cops" cause police. *Leave It to Beaver*'s Ward Cleaver and the Jim Anderson (actor Robert Young) of *Father Knows Best* set perfect paternal standards in an unfortunately imperfect world. As Paul Witt (producer of such series as *The Golden Girls* and *Empty Nest*) recalls of such 'father perfect' shows of his childhood,

It was a sanitized view of American life. It bore no resemblance to anything I knew. I came from a solid family, but I actually began to think we were dysfunctional because on TV no one ever argued the way we did, and no kid ever did anything worse than tell a lie.[45]

As has happened with police portrayals, the pedestals have since been lowered as much by Homer Simpson as by *Home Improvement*. It is not that real-life parental responsibilities have changed—but that media treatment of them now also includes attempts and failures as opposed to an unbroken string of triumphs.

Still, there remain plenty of examples in which the mass-mediated benchmark for parental (and general adult) success continues to be unattainably high. In the case of males, observes educator Ian Harris:

Men in all classes are affected by white collar professional images broadcast through the media and rarely supplemented by images of men in other job categories and occupations. . . . Male sex role standards describe a life where American men are supposed to be good fathers, contribute to their communities and occupy positions of power and wealth. The reality of most men's lives, however, is very different from those media-promoted financial and professional success images.[46]

Subsequent to Harris's writing, characters such as the title role in *Roc* and *Roseanne*'s Dan Connor have proven to be exceptions to the rule—but the rule remains firmly (if less exclusively) in place.

Media-conveyed expectations of women are no less skewed. In many cases, the Donna Reed homebodies have been replaced by females who can do it all and who hold mastery over both the marketplace and the maternal hearth. But this is at best a mixed blessing. As a Connecticut teacher and married mother of two sons recalls,

I was overwhelmed with trying to clean the house and feed the kids and work and have a socially and politically active life. It wasn't working out. And why not? Everyone else, as I saw on TV, had a wonderful house and great kids and everything was hunky-dory. I didn't see any dust in those homes. . . . So what's wrong with me? I was trying to fit in and I couldn't. I felt such stress. And I lived with guilt all the time.[47]

Advertising can be as distortive in setting women's expectations as can programming, of course. Female advertising executives know this better than anyone. Especially offensive to Lubicom Advertising's Pam Newman are the commercial portrayals asserting that women are expected to stay forever young in order to be happy and successful. "It upsets me," testifies Newman, "that everyone has to be seventeen years old and blond. What's wrong with growing old?"[48] It is ironic that, while fiction series like *The Golden Girls* and *Murder, She Wrote* have served to contradict this youth expectation, the allegedly nonfiction worlds of commercials—and newscasts—still very much support it. The only thing scarcer than an older woman in a general-product spot is an older woman behind a local news anchor desk.

If the responsibility to stay youthful seems paramount in media depictions, youth themselves are sometimes shown material suggesting that any responsibility is nonexistent. Nowhere is this more apparent than in music videos. Researchers Vincent, Davis, and Boruszkowski discovered that "the most staggering implication of our study is found in the way rock videos glorify luxury and material wealth. Life is painted as jovial, containing few responsibilities. There are few occupational references in videos yet no one ever addresses the problem of how one gets the money necessary for the luxurious life being portrayed."[49]

In contrast, occupational references that *are* numerous—but numerously negative—occur in the frequent and hostile media depictions of business persons and politicians. Storylines and newsstories concentrate on the *lack* of responsibility exercised by people in these occupations and/or on their failure to live up to public interest expectations.

As pertains to businesspeople, a Media Institute content analysis conducted by R. J. Theberge two decades ago found that in prime time

two out of three businessmen are portrayed as criminal, evil, greedy, or foolish; almost one-half of all work-related activities performed by businessmen involve illegal acts, most big businessmen are portrayed as criminals; and television almost never portrays business as a social or economically useful activity.[50]

Theberge summarized his findings with the observation that "the business world in general is portrayed . . . as the embodiment of all that is wrong with American capitalism. . . . The interests of business are unalterably opposed to those of working people and consumers. What is good for business is not likely to be in the interest of American society."[51] Although the Theberge research has been criticized for its limited scope, it nonetheless signaled a continuing negative business depiction. A 1997 television study by the conservative Media Research Center, for example, found that of the 514 criminal characters found during the survey period, nearly 30 percent were business owners or corporate executives. This 30 percent was also the most likely to commit murder.[52] Thus, in a significant number of media lessons, the responsibility of commerce is taught as the obligation to enrich itself at the expense of the public to the greatest degree possible—and to eliminate those who get in the way.

Portrayals of scientists are often a corollary of this antibusiness syndrome, perhaps because scientists are viewed merely as corporate drones in lab coats. A 1980 University of Michigan study, for instance, concluded that the scientists of fictional programming were usually shown to be threatening, unpleasant, and somewhat unstable.[53] A decade later, Henry Perkinson reemphasized this trend when he observed that

scientists are rarely heroes on television shows. More likely they appear as villains who use their knowledge for evil purposes. If he is not malevolent, the television scientist is cold and unfeeling—like Mr. Spock, the science officer of the space ship *Enterprise*. . . . Usually isolated from the rest of society, the TV scientist spends most of his time seeking the knowledge that will consolidate his dominion over nature and therefore over mankind.[54]

This is hardly a positive recruitment mechanism for the scientific community—or an incentive for the study of science by any but antisocial school children.

For their part, politicians seem, in their media depictions, to fare even worse than do businesspeople and technologists. Such portrayals may occur because businesspeople are private citizens, after all, with no specific mandate to do public good. Public officeholders, on the other hand, have entered an occupation supposedly grounded in public service. Thus, when portrayed politicians behave badly, it seems a deliberate betrayal of the responsibility they voluntarily chose to fulfill.

In 1985, Senators William Cohen and Gary Hart found television's prime-time picture of public servant professional and personal *ir*responsibility to be so blatant that they penned an insiders' bipartisan rejoinder for *TV Guide*. (This proved more than a little ironic given Hart's subsequently exposed infidelities.) The two legislators conceded that some public officials lack competency. But Cohen and Hart also argued that television greatly overstated the problem by depicting 'prime-time' politicians who failed to live up to public expectations as the rule rather than the exception:

They are flat, one dimensional, mildly corrupt, always conniving and driven by a lust for power and personal aggrandizement. In a phrase, television has tended to see Washington's political figures as people made up in equal parts of stupidity and cupidity.[55]

(At least part of *The West Wing*'s critical acclaim and popular approval has resulted from this much more recent drama's refusal to follow such simplistic conventions.)

Electronic journalism, Cohen and Hart felt, presented a much more balanced picture, but its brief snippets of coverage do not possess the scripted determinism of a prime-time melodrama. The examples of individual ignominy that actually were Watergate and Iran/Contra took years to uncover; the foibles of fictitious characters in the made-for-TV *Washington Mistress* could be dramatically exposed in a single night.

This is not to say that political news can't have its tawdry side. Coverage of the Bill Clinton/Monica Lewinsky relationship fermented for months and seemed to confirm fictional TV's sleaziest politician portrayals. But did this depiction prove that real-life politicians were being even less responsible than before? Or was it simply that Bill Clinton has the misfortune to live in an era of continuous, twenty-four-hour television news—whereas John F. Kennedy could philander in a world where even network newscasts were only fifteen minutes in length? Because political journalists are paid to uncover the bad rather than the good, it may be that negative responsibility examples seem more numerous today simply because there is more coverage—not because there is more irresponsibility.

Perhaps the electronic media's contemporary capacity for continuous and instantaneous news carries with it a new burden to use some of this capacity to illuminate positive political role models. Many respected public officials worry that such overwhelmingly negative news and entertainment political depictions can seriously undermine the citizenry's expectations for the system—and discourage dedicated individuals from taking responsibility for it. Veteran public servant Brent Scowcroft, who has been an advisor to several U.S. presidents, once told a Georgetown University audience:

Disdain for Government leads the best people to shun service in that Government; less talented people are even more prone to provide a grist for investigative reporting, which further tarnishes the image of Government and so on.[56]

This, of course, is not to imply that electronic images of our public officials must be uncritically deferential—only that the media accept the possibility of the politically responsible as well as the irresponsible. (For a critique of a TV documentary that demonstrated just such acceptance, review Van Gordon Sauter's assessment of *Dangerous Years: President Eisenhower & the Cold War*, in Chapter 2.)

Whatever the role model being depicted, programming acquires long-term meaning when it satisfyingly documents audience-relatable responsibilities and the successful struggles to meet them. Media content that ignores personal responsibilities, or that focuses solely on those people who disdain them, is much less likely to be remembered—and much more likely to depress. As the Institute for Mental Health Initiatives point out, "Characters who struggle to manage their fears in order to do a job, get out of a tough situation, or heal a damaged relationship provide models of courage for viewers."[57]

WHAT ARE THE STANDARDS BY WHICH WE SHOULD EVALUATE OURSELVES?

For some people, their primary standard for self-evaluation simply replicates the previous depiction answer pertaining to responsibilities. In other words, these persons evaluate themselves positively if they live up to the expectations mandated by their role in life. Yet, for many of us, the occupation in which we toil is not the sole or most prized aspect of our existence. In fact, for some individuals stuck in an unpleasant situation, the tasks they have to perform to ensure the survival of themselves and their family may have little to do with how they appraise themselves.

This final depiction query, then, probes what is most important to you, what your priorities or 'hierarchy of preferences' happen to be, what it is that you most fervently pursue. Every human being needs to answer this question cluster incisively if he or she is to have any hope of making sense out of life. And the more this issue remains open, tentative, or unresolved in a person's own mind, the more prominently media depictions will influence its outcome. Like it or not, electronic media content offers a wealth of self-evaluative teachings that, unfortunately, often shape a conflicting curriculum.

Again, commercials are the most pointed conveyors of these lessons by advocating a standard based on the consumption or acceptance of the commodity they promote. Thus, in the Michelin Tire spot in Figure 9-3, we are encouraged to select our tires based on the safety they provide for our family rather than on their initial cost. We do this by making sure that conserving for long-term goals doesn't compromise immediate protection. In depictive terms, *we should evaluate ourselves as to how well we safeguard our family today*—not on how many pennies we might save for a tenuous tomorrow.

The baby in this Michelin commercial seems contented throughout the spot and is unequivocally happy in frame 3. This is significant. Many electronic media critics have come to the conclusion that *happiness* itself is by far the most frequent and overarching evaluative standard that the electronic media purvey. After all, the U.S. Declaration of Independence is unique in asserting that not just life and liberty, but "the pursuit of happiness" are God-given "inalienable rights." What is more natural, therefore, than the penetration of "the happiness ethic" into the fibre of the country's most popular leisure enterprise?

Yet, this condition is not inevitably beneficial. "What gets my goat about TV," laments veteran actor Jason Robards, "is that everybody has to be *happy* all the time. Rich and happy and thin. If you're not, there's something wrong with you. You need fast-fast-fast relief. It can come from Bufferin, Binaca, or booze, but it's got to be fast. There's no problem that can't be solved in a 30-minute sitcom. Sex is the shortcut to love."[58]

The securing of instant happiness, in other words, is not just presented by the media as an immediate gratification. It is taught, much more importantly, as a long-term model for how well each of us is succeeding as an individual. Hence, Robards's comment on sex as a depicted shortcut to love has a special poignancy because of its self-evaluative implications. As health educator J. L. McCary postulates,

Sex appeal is extolled by the various mass communications media as a means of instant popularity, success, admiration, and security. Young men, whose heightened sex drives are equaled only by their feelings of adolescent insecurity, are particularly susceptible to the idea that their masculinity is measured by the number of women they have seduced. . . . Young women, on the other hand, become indoctrinated by the communications media with the importance of being "sexy."[59]

Visual sexiness as a young female self-evaluative standard is expressly taught in music videos—as well as in the advertisements that bumper them. In their study of commercials on MTV, Nancy Signorielli and her colleagues discovered that

Female characters in these commercials appeared less frequently, had more beautiful bodies, were more physically attractive, wore more

1. (MUSIC) WOMAN: Honey, I think it's time we got a new set of Michelins.

2. MAN: Couldn't we save a little on a cheaper brand?

3. WOMAN: Well, our last set of Michelins got over 60,000 miles.

4. MAN: We've got to watch every penny, now

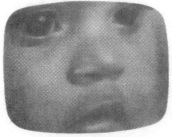

5. that Becky's going away to college.

6. WOMAN: Yeah, but you know, there's one thing more important than putting Becky through college.

7. MAN: Hm, what's that?

8. WOMAN: Making sure she gets there.

9. ANNCR: Michelin. Because so much is riding on your tires. (MUSIC OUT)

sexy and skimpy clothing, and were more often the object of another's gaze than male characters. All of these findings supported the idea that visual attention was highly emphasized for female characters. The portrayals in these commercials reveal a disturbing message: The primary purpose of women's effort is to "look good" and to be the object of visual attention of others.[60]

Not only MTV commercials advance this premise, of course. In an effort to distance themselves from their "housewife as brain-dead drudge" heritage, some package-goods spots also wrap their product in sex, somehow implying that the use of the item makes the user more sexy. Examine the S'wipes commercial in Figure 9-4. On which self-evaluative standard does it concentrate more: (1) the cleanliness of one's kitchen or (2) the sensuality of one's body? Harkening back to Jason Robards's comment, is this shortcut to cleaning also positioned as a shortcut to sexiness?

Of course, sexiness is not the only standard for self-assessment in general, and happiness in particular, that the electronic curriculum teaches. Indeed, for adolescents, no less than for their parents, the wealth and glitter that often accompany sexual depictions present as much of a comparative measure of "how I'm doing" as does one's perceived success with members of the opposite gender. In studying the teen-agers

FIGURE 9-3
(Courtesy of Michelin
Tire Corporation)

FIGURE 9-4
(Courtesy of Laveda
B. Miles, Henderson
Advertising, Inc.)

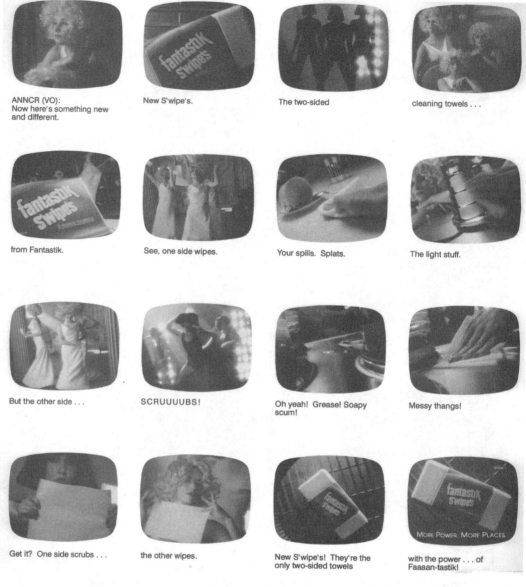

ANNCR (VO):
Now here's something new
and different.

New S'wipe's.

The two-sided

cleaning towels . . .

from Fantastik.

See, one side wipes.

Your spills. Splats.

The light stuff.

But the other side . . .

SCRUUUUBS!

Oh yeah! Grease! Soapy
scum!

Messy thangs!

Get it? One side scrubs . . .

the other wipes.

New S'wipe's! They're the
only two-sided towels

with the power . . . of
Faaaan-tastik!

MORE POWER. MORE PLACES.

growing up in blue-collar Cicero, Illinois, for instance, critic Michael Leahy found that

> *Dallas and Dynasty* offer titillation and glamour for them too, but always, at some point, the moment comes for kids when the wealth and social prowess of the characters remind them of what they aren't, bring them crashing back to these row houses and factories, leaving them feeling trapped.[61]

Television executive Charles Sutton of Inner City Broadcasting amplifies Leahy's observation by asserting that the video medium inevitably, "annoints. It tells you who is important and makes them visible, and it says who isn't important and makes them invisible."[62]

This is why diversified casting is so important an issue and so central to the self-evaluative lessons that programs and commercials teach. The one thing more threatening to audience members' self-esteem than negative visibility for their ethnic group is NO visibility. As NBC West Coast President Scott Sassa, himself Asian American, testifies:

> I've got to tell you, growing up, seeing David Carradine as a Chinese guy pissed you off. I think we get lost in this issue of diversity. . . . There is diversity and there is meaningful diversity. You not only want to see someone that

looks like you on TV, you want to see someone that is a role model, someone that you want to be with, someone that you want to aspire to be.[63]

Do all audience members uncritically accept and defer to all media self-evaluative portrayals (or their absence)? Of course not. Instead, individuals formulate any of three possible responses to the mass-mediated norms they encounter:

1. To the extent that the evaluative standards taught by media portrayals do not significantly clash with our personal and ingrained measures of self-worth, they are likely to be tolerated.

2. Conversely, when media-suggested standards collide with the assessment mechanisms we and our family or peers embrace, the media standards will be summarily rejected.

3. But if we ourselves, due to unformed personal priorities or the absence of a compatible reference group, lack clear self-evaluative standards, the benchmark fostered by electronic media portrayals may be adopted—for better or worse.

This third scenario most concerns social and media critics and constitutes the core of the debate about children and programming. As child psychiatrist Robert Coles warns,

A child who is having a rough time of it personally—whose parents, for instance, are mostly absent, or indifferent to him or her, or unstable—will be much more vulnerable to the emotional and moral power of television. . . . No question, such children can be badly hurt by television, can be persuaded by it to act cruelly, wantonly, irrationally. A stable family, with a vigorous moral life, well and constantly enunciated by parents, will likely provide a persisting immunity to the influence of various shows—whereas a weak and vulnerable family is more likely to fall under the spell of those same programs.[64]

The V-chip is seen by some people as a technological protector for all children regardless of their family situation, as a device that will magically ensure that only positive self-evaluative models pass through the tube and into the youngster. However, researcher Dale Kunkel asserts that "many families will simply never use the V-chip technology. Indeed, it is precisely those children from fam-

ilies with less attentive parents that are at greatest risk from being harmed by TV violence, because their parents may not be present to moderate TV's influence."[65]

The electronic media did not ask to be the prime teacher of juvenile self-evaluative standards any more than they sought to be the main answerer of depiction's other four questions. But where traditional instructive institutions are largely absent, the media curriculum is learned by default. Society "is asking television to do too much," observed ABC Broadcast Group president David Westin. "It comes into our households, it entertains and informs us, but it is not a baby-sitter or a religious educator or a parent. Unfortunately, the pressures in our society have forced the medium into those roles."[66] As media professionals, we can't ignore those roles simply because we didn't seek to fill them in the first place. So, careful depiction analysis, especially of programming to which children are most likely to be exposed, can help us avoid abusing this important—though unsought—assignment.

PRACTICING DEPICTION ANALYSIS

To provide an example of how depiction's five questions can comprise a lesson-probing but still concise critique, examine the following student-composed assessment of an episode of *Homicide: Life on the Street*. For instructive purposes, the program answer/lesson that the student isolated for each of depiction's five questions has been underlined.

The depictive lessons Sarah Adams identifies are not necessarily the only ones in the program, of course. There may be several other more or less prominent answers to each depiction query. While Sarah's assigned task was to find one documentable answer per question, a full-blown depiction analysis would seek to uncover as many plausible answers as possible, thereby anticipating the range of possible audience reactions to the piece of media content under scrutiny.

For another application of depiction analysis, begin by reading *The Newsroom* episode script reprinted in Appendix A. Then compare the following depictive decoding of it with your own impressions.

A DEPICTIVE ANALYSIS OF <u>HOMICIDE: LIFE ON THE STREET</u>

by Sarah Adams

In the world of <u>Homicide: Life on the Street</u>, <u>the big city is a decaying, dangerous place which is either chaotically cluttered or depressingly bare</u>. This episode portrayed a world of rotting corpses (complete with nearby swarms of flies), endless garbage dumpsters, and crumbling row houses. The detectives' desks were strewn with papers and eating utensils while, in the cemetary, the gravestones were nearly atop one another. In contrast, the motel room where the fat man was strangled was devoid of all but the most basic furnishings. There was no happy medium in this physically schizophrenic urban world--the environment was either suffocatingly littered or hollow and empty. The suburban home of the murdered Jenny Goode's parents served as a stark contrast to these city scenes. It was clean, light and roomy; a seemingly far-removed safe haven from the city. Too bad Jenny didn't stay there.

<u>City society includes numerous criminals who prey on often flawed or naive victims.</u> For instance, the young woman with the gunshot wound to the head talks about her Aunt Calpurnia who has had such a tragic life. But the detectives soon learn that the aunt is insurance beneficiary to the "unfortunate" niece who has now survived the third attempt on her life! They also discover that the aunt has "suffered the loss" of five husbands--all of them dying of mysterious causes. The niece cannot even imagine that Aunt Calpurnia would do anything wrong.

Meanwhile, Jenny Goode's parents assure the detectives that they've done their part by "putting the word out" that the police are looking for a blonde-haired man with a woman's sandal in his sportscar. The incredulous detectives try to explain to the well-intentioned parents that spreading such information will only force the killer into hiding. This naive innocence only makes the plight of the victims and their families more tragic. We can tolerate villains being taken advantage of (as in Detective Pembleton's interrogation room trickery); but the naive victim seems pure and likeable. For the viewer, further victimizing the victim is almost unbearable.

These pathetic victims help to drive home the uncompromising consequence that <u>violent death leaves permanent scars on families and society</u>. The best example of this lesson's teaching occurs in the heart-wrenching reality of a suburban kitchen. After nearly half an hour of dead bodies and seemingly callous cops, the viewer sits in as two detectives interview the parents of murdered drug addict Jenny Goode. Suddenly, a little girl appears out of nowhere, and the grandmother shushes her, pointing out that she and grandpa are talking to the police. The little girl fixes somber eyes on the officers and then turns back to her grandmother with the question: "Are they gonna bring my mommy back?" It all suddenly becomes very personal as the viewer realizes that this particular murder harmed a living, breathing daughter and mother as well as the people who loved her. We are hit with the reality that the survivors' grief-stricken lives will never be the same.

Though they almost destroyed the detectives' chances of finding the killer, Jenny's parents help illustrate that <u>it is everyone's responsibility to see that justice is served</u>. Detective John Munch evidenced this same lesson while working on her case. Munch has neglected the Goode murder because forensic analysis ruled her death accidental--she had been run over by a car. Munch's partner doesn't buy that story and Munch angrily retorts: "Don't I have enough to worry about without worrying about her?" His partner replies: "Jenny Goode was murdered, John. Someone has got to speak for her!" Munch begins to feel guilty and gets deeply involved in the case, even staying all night in the squad room going through photos of suspects. His tireless search for justice leads to the killer's arrest and confession. Munch comes to realize, as does the audience, that it is his duty as a human being to see that justice is accomplished.

As Munch also helps to establish, we should evaluate ourselves not on heroic standards, but simply on whether we do what is required of us. Rookie detective Bayliss proved a fascinating character in this regard because he saw the role of a homicide detective through naive eyes similar to those of many viewers. He tells his new commander at the beginning of the episode: "This [homicide detail] is what I've always wanted to do; you know, a 'thinking' cop." His implication is that homicide is much more glamorous and stimulating than the life of the typical officer. But

throughout the episode, Bayliss subsequently is exposed to the homicide detective's distasteful duties: from examining the almost nude body of an overweight, strangled sex pervert, to the intense and manipulative interrogation of the pervert's young, suspected killer. Little by little, his illusions of 'murder police' heroism, praise and glamour are destroyed. At the close of the program, the audience finds the rookie alone on the first case in which he is the 'primary.' It is pouring rain, and the bloody body of a little girl lies nearby. Bayliss's face tells the viewer that the reality--the grinding duty--of his new career has set in. He now understands that he must do his job because it is something he is counted on to perform; not because he will win the support and admiration of others. He realizes this job produces no heroes. With a sickened but determined look, he raises his badge and proclaims the grim career path he has chosen: "Homicide."

(Courtesy of Sarah Adams)

It is important to recognize that a depiction critique is as much a product of its own time and place as is the program it dissects. In examining a 1950s show from a post-2000 prospective, we are likely to detect lessons that appear simplistic, sexist, and/or sociologically abrasive. Yet, none of these may have been detected or learned that way by viewers living in the Eisenhower era. "Take *The Honeymooners*, for example, one of the classics because of the extraordinary performances," writes media historian Mary Ann Watson. "In its first run no one expressed concern about Ralph's threats of physical violence against his wife. Today's

viewers, though, while still touched by the poignancy of the Kramdens' affection for each other, wince to hear, 'One of these days, Alice, one of these days, Pow! Right in the kisser!' "[67]

As novelist David Handler wrote of his once-favorite show, "I stopped loving *Ozzie and Harriet* when I grew up and it didn't. . . . Like a lot of other kids who grew up on it, I denounced it as brainwashing. I rebelled. Yet, years later, Handler revised his assessment and confessed that "as we raise our own kids, we find ourselves glancing back more and more to that '50s *Ozzie and Harriet* world we thought was real. . . . I've let the

A DEPICTIVE ANALYSIS OF THE NEWSROOM

A dark media satire, this Canadian series by actor/writer/director Ken Finkleman teaches some often unpleasant lessons in sardonically funny ways. Finkleman stars as George Find-

lay, an insecure and conniving Toronto news director. Good seldom triumphs here--perhaps because there is very little good that shows up for the battle.

As its name suggests, The Newsroom demonstrates that the corporate/professional environment is made up of sunless, artificially lit cubicles in which struggles for personal dominance are continuously played out. A counterpart lesson is that the outside world is hostile territory that has value only in the exploitable tragedies that it nurtures. Overturned tanker trucks crushing civilians "on the 401," homeless men freezing to death, golfers killed by lightning, and Bangkok conflagrations become mere grist for the inside world's gossip and profit.

That corporate, enclosed habitat shelters a society that is self-centered, duplicitous, and manipulative. Colleagues are important only to the extent that they advance or retard one's own career game plan. As anchorwoman Lindsay encapsulates it: "Personally, I love Jim Walcott and respect his work, but run with him and you're heading for a loss." People use whatever material is available (from intercepted phone calls to distortedly edited videotape) to stay on top in ever-shifting balances of power. No one can fully trust anyone or anything in a society where even the apples in your muffins can be surreptitiously replaced by turnips.

A continuing consequence of existence in such a world is that when you manipulate others, you yourself will be manipulated. Lindsay's attempt to displace Jim and George only gets her banished to Winnipeg. Even her former ally Rani quickly backs away and retreats with a crew to salvage her own career. George's two seemingly trusted assistants, Mark and Jeremy, waste no time in distancing themselves when it looks as if he's been displaced. Even when George rebounds with the creative tape editing that seems to show Lindsay as a drunk, his triumph appears unlikely to be permanent. "Tired and old wins the race," he crows, but his comment also hints that this 'race' will ultimately take its toll. Overseeing all of this, Sid Adilman, the newspaper columnist god of gossip, reigns as both chronicler of and contributor to the latest body count.

By their very nature, dark comedies tend to satirize repulsive behaviors rather than to showcase admirable ones. The Newsroom is no exception. Its lesson seems to be that our sole responsibility is to promote our own success. But by continuously exposing characters caught in the maze of self-aggrandizement, the program's ultimate point-of-view teaches the opposite. No character in this sitcom can ever relax, accept anything at face value, or count on continuing friendship. The offering of drugs and wardrobe advice is as likely intended to sabotage as to support you. Being responsible only for the betterment of oneself means that no one else will put aside his or her own self-interest when you need help. Lindsay has no one to save her from Winnipeg. And though he is back as sole anchor, Jim has no one to save him from George.

The Newsroom seems to suggest that we should evaluate ourselves based on our glibness, lip gloss, hair gel, and "whose tits are bigger than whose." Even the outsider intellectual, Daniel Richler, is shown to project this same vanity. But, as in the way dark comedies tend to teach responsibility lessons, The Newsroom's self-evaluate lesson is exactly the opposite. Everyone who relies on such cosmetic verbal and appearance standards is ultimately shown to be foolish and shallow. Similarly, the plot line seems to urge us to evaluate ourselves based on whether we maintain our supremacy over others. But no one here appears happy or content in the winning. Instead, The Newsroom's continual turning of triumph to tragedy suggests that we should evaluate ourselves on the constancy of our convictions rather than on the expediency of the moment. Jim does get his testosterone up--but he is now being charged with sexual harassment.

Nelsons off the hook. I don't blame them for what they did or didn't tell us about the world. *Ozzie and Harriet* was a product of its time, just like we were."[68]

We must understand that a program's lessons are frozen in the context of its era and may be rendered quaint, frivolous, or even irrelevant by the passage of years. In looking back on historic program matter, the lessons of the first two depiction answers (what the physical environment and society are like) may be outmoded. But as in any enduring play, at least some of the portrayed responsibilities and standards for self-evaluation should remain timeless guides to acceptable personal conduct. Insofar as they pertain to human relationships, well-wrought basic consequence lessons are probably eternal as well. Unchecked ambition like that in Shakespeare's *Macbeth* does not cause problems only in medieval Scotland.

Like any play—or, for that matter, any work of art—"Television is a human construct," point out John Fiske and John Hartley, "and the job that it does is the result of human choice, cultural decisions and social pressures. The medium responds to the conditions within which it exists."[69] Advertising analyst Betsy Sharkey adds that "television [as radio before it] has always provided us with a strange sort of validation for our lives. TV fantasy lifts enough from our world to allow us to believe in its world."[70] Depiction analysis subsequently enables us to monitor how these worlds intersect.

ENDNOTES

1. Mary Strom Larson, "Family Communication on Prime-Time Television," *Journal of Broadcasting & Electronic Media* (Summer 1993), 349.
2. Joshua Meyrowitz, "How Television Has Shaped the Social Landscape," *Feedback* (Fall 1989), 17.
3. Reed Hundt, "First Things First," *Broadcasting & Cable* (March 3, 1997), 33.
4. Dennis Lowry and David Towles, "Prime Time TV Portrayals of Sex, Contraception and Venereal Diseases," *Journalism Quarterly* (Summer 1989), 348.
5. Bruce Gronbeck, "Audience Engagement in 'Family,' " in Martin Medhurst and T. W. Benson (eds.), *Rhetorical Dimensions in Media: A Critical Casebook* (Dubuque, IA: Kendall/Hunt, 1984), 10.
6. Conrad Kottak, *Prime-Time Society* (Belmont, CA: Wadsworth, 1990), 52.
7. Barry Sapolsky and Joseph Tabarlet, "Sex in Primetime Television: 1979 Versus 1989," *Journal of Broadcasting & Electronic Media* (Fall 1991), 506.
8. W. James Potter, "Adolescents' Perceptions of the Primary Values of Television Programming," *Journalism Quarterly* (Winter 1990), 843.
9. John Fiske, *Television Culture* (London: Methuen, 1987), 179.
10. "Hollywood Violence Summit: Much Talk, Some Action," *TV Guide* (August 14, 1993), 34.
11. Jon Berry, "Do Marketers Exploit Buying Clout of Drug-Dealing Kids?" *ADWEEK* (February 12, 1990), 35, 38.
12. Ben Stein, *The View from Sunset Boulevard* (New York: Basic Books, 1979), xii.
13. Michael Leahy, "Our Cities Are Big Bad Places—If You Believe Prime-Time TV," *TV Guide* (May 3, 1986), 5–6.
14. Ibid., 7.
15. Stein, 70–71.
16. Ibid., xi.
17. Jeff Jarvis, "Due South," *TV Guide* (December 3, 1994), 10.
18. Denise Kervin, "Gender Ideology in Television Commercials," in Leah Vande Berg and Lawrence Wenner (eds.), *Television Criticism* (New York: Longman, 1991), 235.
19. Fiske, 40.
20. Ronald Lembo and Kenneth Tucker, "Culture, Television, and Opposition: Rethinking Cultural Studies," *Critical Studies in Mass Communication* (June 1990), 99.
21. Joanmarie Kalter and Jane Marion, "The Big Stories TV News Is Missing—and Why," *TV Guide* (July 22, 1989), 3.
22. Richard Blake, "Condominiums in the Global Village," in George Rodman (ed.), *Mass Media Issues*, 3rd ed. (Dubuque, IA: Kendall/Hunt, 1989), 133.
23. Joanmarie Kalter, "Yes, There Are More Blacks on TV—But Mostly to Make Viewers Laugh," *TV Guide* (August 13, 1988), 31.
24. Lauren Tucker, "Was the Revolution Televised?: Professional Criticism about 'The Cosby Show' and the Essentialization of Black Cultural Expression," *Journal of Broadcasting & Electronic Media* (Winter 1997), 91.
25. Kalter, 31.
26. Leonard Maltin, "Why We Love Our Cartoon Characters," *TV Guide* (June 9, 1990), 27.
27. Joanna Elm, "Are the Simpsons America's TV Family of the '90s?" *TV Guide* (March 17, 1990), 8.
28. Mark Dolliver, "No Immediate Peril of Sexless Television," *ADWEEK* (February 22, 1999), 22.

29. Dennis Lowry and David Towles, "Soap Opera Portrayals of Sex, Contraception and Sexually Transmitted Diseases: A Public Health Perspective," *Journal of Communication* (Spring 1989), 81.

30. William Henry, "Is TV Getting Better—Or Worse?" *TV Guide* (March 12, 1988), 5.

31. Janice Kaplan, "Sex on TV '93," *TV Guide* (August 14, 1993), 9.

32. Muriel Cantor and Joel Cantor, "Do Soaps Teach Sex?" *Media & Values* (Spring 1989), 5.

33. Diana Workman, "What You See Is What You Think," *Media & Values* (Spring 1989), 3.

34. Ibid., 3–5.

35. *CBC Guidelines on Sex-Role Portrayal* (August 12, 1991), 3.

36. Mike Oppenheim, "TV Isn't Violent Enough," *TV Guide* (February 11, 1984), 21.

37. Neil Hickey, "The Experts Speak Out," *TV Guide* (August 22, 1992), 17.

38. Jim Calio, "National Television Violence Study," *NATPE Monthly* (June, 1998), 4.

39. Jeff Sagansky, remarks to the International Radio & Television Society Faculty/Industry Seminar, February 9, 1996 (New York).

40. Rhoda Baruch, "Why the Fuss about Television Violence?" *Broadcasting and Cable* (August 29, 1994), 41.

41. Harry Jessell, "Cable Promises to Curb Violence," *Broadcasting* (February 1, 1993), 33.

42. C. Richard Hofstetter and David Dozier, "Useful News, Sensational News: Quality, Sensationalism and Local TV News," *Journalism Quarterly* (Winter 1986), 820.

43. David Rensin, "The Last Safe Neighborhood," *TV Guide* (March 7, 1992), 25.

44. Michael Pacanowsky and James Anderson, "Cop Talk and Media Use," *Journal of Broadcasting* (Fall 1982), 750.

45. Harry Stein, "Where Do They *Get* Those Kids?" *TV Guide* (March 7, 1992), 29.

46. Ian Harris, "Media Myths and the Reality of Men's Work," *Media & Values* (Fall 1989), 12.

47. Joanmarie Kalter, "What Working Women Want from TV," *TV Guide* (January 30, 1988), 7.

48. Gail Belsky, "What's Your Displeasure?," *ADWEEK* (July 11, 1988), W24.

49. Richard Vincent, Dennis Davis, and Lilly Ann Boruszkowski, "Sexism on MTV: The Portrayal of Women in Rock Videos," *Journalism Quarterly* (Winter 1987), 755.

50. R. J. Theberge (ed.), *Crooks, Conmen and Clowns: Businessmen on TV Entertainment* (Washington, DC: The Media Institute, 1981), vi.

51. Ibid., 32.

52. "Television Shows Are Not That Kind to Businessmen," (Mt. Pleasant) *Morning Sun* (June 26, 1997), 4B.

53. Witold Rybczynski, *Taming the Tiger: The Struggle to Control Technology* (New York: Penguin Books, 1985), 27.

54. Henry Perkinson, *Getting Better: Television and Moral Progress* (New Brunswick, NJ: Transaction Publishers, 1991), 225.

55. William Cohen and Gary Hart, "TV's Treatment of Washington—It's Capital Punishment," *TV Guide* (August 24, 1985), 5.

56. Hugh Sidey, "Scowcroft's Concerns," *Time* (May 4, 1987), 17.

57. "Driven by Fear, Drawn by Courage," *Dialogue* (Summer 1994), 4.

58. Jason Robards, "Television So Often Promotes Drinking instead of Combating It," *TV Guide* (May 4, 1985), 39.

59. J. L. McCary, *Human Sexuality* (New York: Van Nostrand, 1973), 106.

60. Nancy Signorielli, Douglas McLeod, and Elaine Healy, "Gender Stereotypes in MTV Commercials: The Beat Goes On," *Journal of Broadcasting & Electronic Media* (Winter 1994), 99.

61. Michael Leahy, "Don"t Mis-Judge Working-Class America," *TV Guide* (December 21, 1985), 12.

62. "Black Programing Called 'Hard Sell,' " *Broadcasting* (February 22, 1988), 168.

63. Joe Schlosser, "Sassa Seeks Role Models," *Broadcasting & Cable* (August 2, 1999), 10.

64. Robert Coles, "What Makes Some Kids More Vulnerable to the Worst of TV?" *TV Guide* (June 21, 1986), 7.

65. Heather Fleming, "TV Debate Moving beyond Ratings," *Broadcasting & Cable* (April 21, 1997), 22.

66. Steve McClellan, "It's Markey v. Industry on V-Chip," *Broadcasting & Cable* (October 30, 1995), 38.

67. Mary Ann Watson, "Women's Lives on the Small Screen," booklet accompanying *Images of Women on Television* exhibit, 1993 (Chicago Museum of Broadcast Communication), 2.

68. David Handler, "Why I Loved, Hated and Now Forgive *Ozzie and Harriet*," *TV Guide* (November 14, 1987), 32.

69. John Fiske and John Hartley, *Reading Television* (London: Methuen, 1978), 17.

70. Betsy Sharkey, "Primetime Women in Their Prime," *ADWEEK* (June 5, 1989), 22.

10

Structural Analysis

Systems theorists assert that electronic media do not really mirror reality but rather, structure and manipulate reality into organized patterns for efficient conveyance. With this perspective in mind, we now examine some of the shaping systems from which these electronic content layouts are derived. As with our depiction analysis in the previous chapter, however, we must recognize at the outset that the structures and meanings assumed by producers may be miscoded or even countercoded by audience members operating from their own frames of reference and perceptual expertise.

SYMBOLS AND ARCHETYPES

The basic building blocks for any codes are the individual units that can be isolated or combined to carry and amalgamate meaning. These units are conventionally referred to as *symbols*. Symbols, state Karyn and Donald Rybacki, "represent a common core of interest, need and experience" among human beings.[1] They are, as Hal Himmelstein adds, "nothing more or less than organizing ideas by which *people* develop perspectives about their relationship with the world."[2] Therefore, any given symbol is "entirely the product of human contrivance," concludes Theodore Meyer Greene. "It has no basis in nature or in logic; the meaning of a pure symbol is arbitrarily attached to it by individual *fiat* or social convention."[3]

Symbols, in short, are humankind's attempt to organize sensations to enable people to deal with objects and concepts that are not immediately present or tangible.

The two most common symbol grammars are the verbal and the pictorial. As Joshua Meyrowitz reminds us:

All human interaction involves these two different types of symbols: language-like [verbal] communication and image-like [pictorial] expressions. . . . Expressions are like pictures without captions. . . . more direct and more ambiguous, more natural yet less precise than linguistic statements. Expressions come directly from a person; they suggest how a person "really feels" and what they are "really like." Yet one cannot base a contract on a smile and a wink. Unless words are used to explain expressions, their meanings are often unclear.[4]

Words are less necessary when a society's breadth of experience is narrow. Sophie Menache notes, for example, that "an ordinary man in tenth-century Normandy probably encountered between 100 and 200 people in his whole life, and his vocabulary contained only some 600 words."[5] Linguistic poverty, then, is a direct reflection of experiential poverty.

This concept did not die with the Middle Ages. It remains tragically relevant today in the urban ghetto and rural backwoods, where lack of direct engagement with the outside world can result in an atrophying of the verbal skills essential to successful participation in the Information Age. That is why universal access to traditional and new electronic media is seen as so important; the media are counted on to stimulate a verbal fluency that is neither modeled nor required within the boundaries of perceptually deprived environments.

Pictorial grammar, conversely, requires less receiver sophistication than does verbal grammar. But it also lacks the assurance of meaning conveyed by most verbal vocabularies. Consequently, for a predominately pictorial medium like television, the likelihood that messages may be misperceived increases. As our profession moves deeper into the global marketplace, careful attention must be devoted to what our camera- or scanner-captured images might convey. We can redub a soundtrack to shift linguistic symbols, but the original pictorial symbols will remain. An image of someone giving flowers to a woman, for instance, may convey a gesture of caring to North American audiences. But as advertising executive Florence Friedman points out, in some Arab countries, that's a metaphor for death. Because of the breadth of pictorial decoding, "television viewing is a complex, multilayered symbolic experience," Professors Lembo and Tucker remind us,[6] and one whose meaning can hardly be taken for granted.

Whether verbal or pictorial, symbols additionally can be categorized into the *personal, social,* or *archetypal* depending on the number of people likely to share the central meaning intended by their user.

Personal symbols are those held in common by a small group of friends, family, and colleagues—or by lodge, sorority, and religious group members. Personal symbols are the province of the secret handshake, computer password, cryptic emblem, or (in the case of an *intra*personal symbol) the flattened and waxed tulip from a seventh-grade sweetheart. They have immense meaning for us as individuals but little utility in communicating with the world at large. Sometimes, however, as with comedienne Carol Burnett's ear-pulling greeting to Grandma, or producer Gary David Goldberg's show-ending salute to his long-dead dog Ubu, the public as a whole is let in on the personal symbol's significance—thereby converting it into a *social symbol.*

Social symbols are commonly understood by many more people, perhaps even by an entire society. Thus, the electronic media can readily exploit them. In some instances, rather than borrowing a preexisting social symbol, the media themselves will construct and market one of their own as a means of more definitively controlling the decoding of the message. In Figure 10-1, for instance, Juan Valdez is created as the Colombian Coffee Growers' metaphor for "100% Colombian Coffee's" quality assurance as "the richest coffee in the world." For U.S. audiences, Senor Valdez is intended to encapsulate and verify the personal and national pride of the growers in any of the several brand names under which their commodity is marketed. His warm and friendly demeanor is also meant to override any association of the adjective *Colombian* with vicious drug-dealing warlords.

Alternatively, electronic media communication may *convert* an existing social symbol into a new construct. The leather-jacketed,

duck-tailed motorcycle rider, for instance, was a media-borrowed and media-amplified symbol of youthful defiance in the 1950s; but this symbol was turned inside out by 'The Fonz' on *Happy Days,* who became the epitome of integrity and humane conscience. Tropical fish were pets for nerds until *NYPD Blue*'s Andy Sipowitz devoted his hard-nosed and angst-ridden virility to their nurturing. And the Energizer Bunny moved beyond being a tacky wind-up toy—or even a battery ad—into a socially symbolic affirmation that, in Barbara Lippert's words, "everything is a commodity; . . . the hip hop Energizer Bunny campaign borrows and samples from other slick or hokey media productions to keep [symbolically] reinventing itself."[7]

While the Energizer Bunny's impact is exceptional, most commercials similarly attempt to refashion existing social symbols in order to register selling concepts in a bare minimum of time. In the following radio spot by copywriter April Winchell, for instance, the cattle-drive metaphor is invoked to quickly crystalize deficiencies endured by customers at Glendale Federal's consolidating Wells Fargo competitor. At the same time, Winchell is co-opting Wells Fargo's historic "stagecoach" symbol by weaving it into her negative analogy:

(MUSIC: AN ORIGINAL CATTLE DRIVING
    SONG)
WOMAN: Merging, merging
    My old bank is merging
    And I'm going out of my mind.
    Every time I go there,
    Things are really slow there,
    Seems I'm always waiting in a
    line.
        It's an uphill battle
    They're treating me like cattle
    And they're simply wastin' my
    time.
    If this is stagecoach banking,
    I'd rather have a spanking,
    I'm waitin' waitin' waitin' in
    line.
        Move them in, hang around,
    check your watch, get annoyed
    stand in line, check your
    nails, look around, stand in
    line!
(SFX: COWS MOOING, WHIPS CRACKING)
ANNCR: If going to your new bank
    feels like a cattle call,

National Federation of Coffee Growers of Colombia

"Supermarket"

Length: 30 Seconds

Comm'l No.: XCSC 7030

FIGURE 10-1
Juan Valdez as positive social symbol. (Courtesy of National Federation of Coffee Growers of Colombia)

MAN: How-how do I know which coffee to get?
WOMAN: Just look for Juan Valdez.
MAN: Right.

(SFX: SUPERMARKET NOISE)
(MUSIC IN)

JUAN: Buenos Dias.

(MUSIC OUT)

MAN: I just saw Juan Valdez.
WOMAN: Of course, he's on every can

of Colombian Coffee. When you see him

you know you're getting the richest coffee in the world.
MAN: Oh.

(MUSIC UP AND UNDER)
ANNCR: (VO) If you want 100% Colombian Coffee

just look for Juan Valdez.

(MUSIC)

100% Colombian Coffee

You can't miss him.

100% Colombian Coffee

maybe it's time to call Glendale Federal Bank. Just give us a ring at 1-800-41-FED UP and we'll switch your account right over the phone. Glendale Federal. The other way to bank. Member FDIC.

(Courtesy of BBDOWest, April Winchell, Writer)

The meaning of social symbols is most stable within their originating culture. But when symbols are able to *cross* cultures and eras and still retain their central signification, they become *archetypes*. Actually, many social symbols are rooted in underlying, enduring archetypes that are then given more specific interpretation by each separate culture.

Take the concept of the comedy, for example. As Northrop Frye points out, an ancient Greek pamphlet, the *Tractatus Coislinianus*, "sets down all the essential facts about comedy in about a page and a half."[8] Frye recounts that the *Tractatus* lists three kinds of comic characters:

1. The *alazons* or imposters who pretend to be more than they are "though it is more frequently a lack of self-knowledge than simply hypocrisy that characterizes them."[9]

2. The *eirons* or self-deprecators who thus make themselves invulnerable because they castigate themselves before others can grab the opportunity. "Central to this group is a hero, who is an *eiron* figure because . . . the dramatist tends to play him down and make him rather neutral and unformed in character."[10]

3. The *bomolochoi* or buffoons, "whose function it is to increase the mood of festivity rather than contribute to the plot . . . with established comic habits like malapropism or foreign accents."[11]

To these three *Tractatus*-specified types, Aristotle added a fourth:

4. The *agroikos*, who can be surly, unsophisticated, or solemn, depending on the comedic context. We find the surly variation "in the miserly, snobbish, or priggish characters whose role is that of the refuser of festivity, the killjoy who tries to stop the fun".[12] Unsophisticated types are the simple, even "hayseed" figures who, in their innocence, often express the uncomplicated ideal. The third (solemn) *agroikos* behavior is "what in vaudeville used to be called the straight man . . . who allows the humor to bounce off him, so to speak."[13]

Humorous commercials mirror these archetypes, as do situation comedies. In the following *Time* magazine spot, for instance, Brad is the classic *eiron* whose self-deprecation becomes the pathetic model for anyone who chooses not to read *Time*. Alazon Phyllis enlarges her own sense of impor-

tance in crowing about how much she is giving up for him by making that very choice. Gradually, Phyllis transforms herself into a surly *agroikos* as she laments the depths to which this literary deprivation has taken her. Through this comedic exaggeration, *Time* can bask in Phyl's overpraise without itself appearing boastful.

(SFX: RESTAURANT CLATTER IN BACK-
GROUND)

BRAD: This is our favorite restaurant, Phyllis, what's the occasion?

PHYL: I have something --- very important to tell you, Brad.

BRAD: Oh, no.

PHYL: This is the hardest thing
I've had to do in my life.

BRAD: Oh, no, Phyl.

PHYL: Believe me, it's the best for
both of us.

BRAD: You met Mom and everything,
hon.

PHYL: You know how you've always
resented me being witty and
bright and urbane, Brad?

BRAD: Oh no, I don't anymore.

PHYL: And how stupid you felt because I was so well-briefed in
the daily events that affect our
lives?

BRAD: I loved it. I love stupid.

PHYL: Well, I know how it must be
resolved.

BRAD: Don't say it, Phyl.

PHYL: Yes. I'm giving up TIME magazine.

BRAD: Ohhhh (utterly blank). What?

PHYL: Yes, Brad. TIME and TIME
alone gave me the je ne sais
quoi that you never ap-
proached.

BRAD: TIME?

PHYL: I flew to it each week and
filled my cup from the depths
of its lively literary basin.

BRAD: TIME magazine?

PHYL: I've been without it a week
already.

BRAD: TIME the weekly newsmaga-
zine?

PHYL: Ask me what's going on in
business, medicine, religion,
art or education.

BRAD: What's going on?

PHYL: I don't know! I haven't the
    faintest idea!
BRAD: Oh, Phyliss, you mean ---
PHYL: Yes. Without TIME, I'm the
    same empty-headed dimwit you are.
BRAD: (In a rush) Oh, I do love
    you.

(Courtesy of Dick Orkin)

These same archetypes can be strikingly apparent in ensemble comedies such as the long-running *Cheers.* Consider, for example, the many vignettes between Cliff, the knowledge-bluffing mailman, and Norm, the tubby accountant who so blatantly embraces his own flaws and failures. As Frye points out, "The multitude of comic scenes in which one character complacently soliloquizes [Cliff] while another makes sarcastic asides to the audience [Norm] show the contest of *eiron* and *alazon* in its purest form, and show too that the audience is sympathetic to the *eiron* side."[14]

In other words, viewers side with *eiron* Norm over *alazon* Cliff. Even though Frye wrote the description of their interaction more than thirty years before *Cheers* was conceived, his observation remains eminently pertinent because both it and the series are based on the same enduring set of archetypal symbols (see Figure 10-2).

Cheers proprietor and hero-figure Sam Malone represents another dimension of the *eiron* role who deprecates himself for his lack of intelligence while his diligently "unformed" character makes him ripe for first barmaid Diane's, and then manager Rebecca's, irritatingly overbearing proddings. Diane and her replacement, Rebecca, play *alazons* to Sam's *eiron* in the same manner that Norm balances Cliff.

For his part, Dr. Frasier Crane, the blithering and pompous psychologist, began as an *agroikos* "killjoy refuser of festivity." But as his character grew, it gradually took on *alazon* importance as his failure to comprehend his own lack of self-knowledge became the subject of more extended comedic plot lines. Fellow psychologist (and subsequent spouse) Lilith then grew to be a regular participant. Lilith took over Frasier's former *agroikos* role, investing it with both 'surly' and 'solemn' dimensions.

Coach, of course, was also an *agroikos*—but of the unsophisticated (second) variety.

FIGURE 10-2
Cheers embodiments of ancient Greek archetypes. (Illustration by Scott Huver)

And on the death of the actor who played him, he was replaced (as bartender) by Woody, who added the "hayseed" ingredient. The feisty waitress Carla is another *agroikos* figure in *Cheers* and, indeed, takes surliness to new heights. However, Carla may be the sitcom's most complicated character because her "fun-stopping" (or stomping) *agroikos* rampages are often balanced by wistful revelations of *eiron*-like self-censure.

Notice, however, that there are no *bomolochoi* among *Cheers* regulars because, by definition, such buffoon figures only function "to increase the mood of festivity rather than contribute to the plot." Instead, *bomo-lochoi* enter and leave the bar as minor or random characters who exist, like Carla's apelike ex-husband, Nick Tortelli, only to incite the regular ensemble's interplay. In fact, when the *Cheers* creators attempted to fashion a spinoff sitcom built around Nick, his inherent buffoon limitations proved a dead weight, as *Chicago Tribune* critic Clifford Terry points out in his review.

In contrast, the subsequently launched series *Frasier* became a solid hit. As mentioned above, its title role character (unlike Nick Tortelli) had been nurtured into a much more robust comedic archetype before the spinoff was attempted. Essentially the same creators who failed with *The Tortellis*

LEADEN <u>CHEERS</u> SPINOFF BARELY RATES A WHIMPER

by Clifford Terry

The premiere episode of <u>The Tortellis</u>, an NBC sitcom that makes its debut at 8:30 P.M. on Channel 5, starts off with Nick Tortelli (played by Dan Hedaya) dreaming that he is in heaven and has been condemned to eternal damnation. "You cheated on both your wives," says a ghostly voice. "You were dishonest in business. You were a terrible father." To which the accused replies, "Don't I get any points for consistency?"

Granting that he might, the same can't be said for the show, a spinoff of "Cheers" that is nothing to shout about.

<u>The Tortellis</u>, whose main characters will be introduced in Thursday's <u>Cheers</u> episode, centers on Nick, the ex-husband of Carla, the barmaid in Sam Malone's Boston saloon played by Rhea Perlman.

In the opener, directed by James Burrows and written by Ken Estin, he has followed his present wife, Loretta (Jean Kasem)—a blond "My Friend Irma"-style airhead with a Marilyn Monroe voice—to Las Vegas. It seems she had fled from New Jersey to the home of her sister, Charlotte (Carlene Watkins), to get away from Nick, an unregenerate "slug," after finding him in the shower with the Avon lady. (His explanation was he was trying out a new brush.)

Before long, Charlotte—the comely, cynical mother of a young boy (Aaron Moffatt)—has agreed to let the Tortellis stay on if they share the rent, and not long after that, they are all joined by Nick and Loretta's son (Timothy Williams) and his new bride (Mandy Ingber). Complications then arise when Nick, who hopes to make it big as a TV repairman, finds that he is strongly attracted to his sister-in-law.

Lacking the sophisticated, off-center humor of <u>Cheers</u>, <u>The Tortellis</u> is filled with leaden lines. When Loretta asks, "Are we the biggest boobs in town or what?", Charlotte answers, "Not in this town." When Charlotte tells Nick she is a substitute schoolteacher, he answers, "What a coincidence. I went to school." When Nick asks Charlotte, "Can't you take a joke?" she answers, "Not when it's married to my sister." Neither are the characters themselves appealing, unless you enjoy watching a neanderthal type swatting his son on the head with a newspaper and pulling his ears.

succeeded with *Frasier* because they began with a much richer symbolic centerpiece.

Archetypal symbols function regardless of whether audiences, producers, or critics are aware of these symbols' presence. Indeed, the most successful show creators may be those who are so artistically sensitive that they comprehend and use archetypes intuitively—without stopping to think about or study them.

The reason some social symbols seem more meaning*ful* and effective often is due to their conformity to humanity's underlying (even subconscious) archetypal expectations. The better that *all* media professionals can learn to recognize broad archetypal patterns, the better chance we have of estimating why a particular project's scenario or set of characters is or is not gelling as we move through production.

When an archetype is abused, either intentionally or unintentionally, the communicative fallout can be devastating. This is a particular danger when the message is allowed to cross cultures without adequate symbolic assessment. For instance, Pepsi-Cola's existence-glorifying slogan "Come Alive—You're in the Pepsi Generation" was translated in Taiwan as the more literal archetypal promise: "Pepsi-Cola Will Bring Your Ancestors Back from the Dead." More tragically, Adolph Hitler's Nazi *swastika* was a social-symbol distortion of an archetypal emblem that represents the mystic life force in the cultures of India and Japan as well as among southwestern Native Americans. When called a *gammadion* (four Greek gamma symbols radiating from a common center), this insignia was also used by the early Christian church to represent Christ as its core. Hence, though the archetype recurs, the social constructs for it can change and even subvert its meaning.

Electronic media professionals, of course, seldom need wrestle with anything of such profundity. Nevertheless, the presence of archetypes as recurring meaning patterns must be acknowledged because, as Frye maintains, "we could almost define popular literature, admittedly in a rather circular way, as literature which affords an unobstructed view of archetypes."[15]

Whether this popular (mass) literature is conveyed in print or via the electronic media is unimportant except that television proba-

bly possesses the more pervasive influence. In fact, states Rose Goldsen:

Television now holds a virtual monopoly on whatever artistic and symbolic forms have a chance to be widely shared throughout the society. All the images, all the tales and ballads and chants and songs and stories that come through that screen, show-and-tell aspects of social reality that then become familiar to all.[16]

RITUAL, MYSTIQUE, AND MYTH

In making her case, Goldsen has led us beyond a discussion of symbols into the larger arena of ritual, mystique, and myth. Even though these three phenomena are interrelated, we discuss each one separately in order to better understand the role each plays in electronic content.

Ritual

We have just explored how social and archetypal symbols carry or suggest meanings to the mass audience. Yet, these symbols are without a storyline until they are immersed in a *ritual*—what Robert Rutherford Smith calls "an act or series of acts, which brings about a satisfactory resolution of the problem with which the program deals."[17] Even though the term *ritual* may seem relevant only to church services, Professor Quentin Schultze points out that

secular television programming shares with religious worship the necessity of public ritual. Both a church service and a television program require prescribed forms of ritual before "participation" is really possible. One could not enjoy or understand a completely innovative show any more than one could really worship a completely unknown god in a foreign church service. Like the mass, television is structured in prescribed ways so that the worshippers may enter into meaningful communion. Television uses its own liturgies to ensure communal experience.[18]

The same observation could apply to radio formats. The aural service's "hot clock" is, in the final analysis, a ritualistic apportioning of an hour that accustoms us to when our 'communal' need for news, weather, musical celebration, traffic reports, or simulated conversation will be fulfilled. The format that successfully pays homage to the life cycles of its target listeners is the format whose ritual thereby possesses what Northrop Frye calls "magic":

If we turn to ritual, we see there an imitation of nature which has a strong element of what we call magic in it. Magic seems to begin as something of a voluntary effort to recapture a lost rapport with the natural cycle. This sense of deliberate recapturing of something no longer possessed is a distinctive mark of human ritual. Ritual constructs a calendar. . . . But the impetus of the magical element in ritual is clearly toward a universe in which a stupid and indifferent nature is no longer the container of human society, but is contained by that society, and must rain or shine at the pleasure of man.[19]

A well-programmed radio station, in other words, gives us the sense that we are in control of our day, not only through the conveyance of coping information, but also via the tension release that flows from life-style-responsive music and feature progressions. Formats are rituals. And "rituals," perceptual psychologist Rudolf Arnheim points out, "not only express what people feel but also help them to feel the way the situation requires"[20]—whether it's the enforced urgency of morning drivetime or the droopy idleness of a Sunday afternoon.

On television, we encounter the ritual of the news anchor who bids us hello, proceeds to unveil all manner of tragedies, and then 'redeems' us at the out-cue with a cheery good-bye. This pattern is matched by the 'reality' ritual of the game show or sports event, which starts with the "natural" challenge of human and situational obstacles to conquer and ends when someone or some team succeeds in its quest and is anointed to participate in a new contest later.

Similarly, the ritual of the soap opera that transports us across the week and then, through a major Friday event, magically suspends time until Monday, is akin to the sitcom that enables us to string together problem revelations and solutions over time in comfortable and comedic half-hour patterns. On the other hand, the *difference* between soap opera and sitcom rituals, Horace Newcomb once suggested, is that "while the situation comedy is doomed to repeat itself in every episode of every series, changing only in the actual 'situation' that precipitates the action, the soap opera will grow and change. . . . The soap opera characters change. They grow older; they marry; they have children; their problems are always appropriate to their situation."[21]

Since Newcomb made this observation a quarter of a century ago, it should be noted that some subsequent sitcoms like *The Cosby Show, Cheers, Murphy Brown*, and *Mad About You* have adopted problem-solving rituals that are fueled by character change. Whether this is the cause or the result of these series longevity is an interesting question. In any case, unlike *Happy Days'* Richie Cunningham, who was the same boy in progressively larger-size slacks, characters in some of our newer sitcoms are engendered by a ritual that allows for psychological as well as character growth. *Cheers'* Sam and Diane/Rebecca did mature through the cross-pollinating ebb-and-flow of their barroom relationships.

Ritual is just as important an element in one-hour action/adventure vehicles. Thus, as John Fiske and John Hartley observed about then-popular crime shows:

A programme like *Ironside* converts abstract ideas about individual relationships between man and man, men and women, individuals and institutions, whites and blacks into concrete dramatic form. It is a ritual condensation of the dominant criteria for survival in modern complex society. Clearly in this condensed form individual relationships can be scrutinized by the society concerned, and any inappropriateness can be dealt with in the form of criticisms of the programme. Hence, *Ironside*'s ritual condensation of relationships is supplanted by *Kojak*'s which is supplanted in turn by *Starsky and Hutch* [and all the shows to follow]. Each of these fictive police series presents a slightly different view of the appropriate way of behaving towards other people.[22]

Whichever series ritualistically wrestles with its problems in the most involving, most engaging way becomes the most esteemed. This is as true of newscasts, and the stories within them, as it is of fictional series. Professor David Altheide, for instance, has isolated what he calls the "Formats for Crisis" ritual. "Any issue that is to be legitimated by extensive media coverage,"

Altheide argues, "must be presented as something new, devastating, with an immediate impact, and as a crisis, but this must be done in a familiar [ritualistic] way." Specifically, Altheide's crisis ritual consists of the following seven stages:

1. A specific event that can be depicted visually is selected.

2. The event will be contrasted with the status quo, indicating a shift.

3. The event or the change it is claimed to represent will be argued to be consequential for a large number of people, perhaps 10 percent of the population.

4. Immediate victims will be shown and often interviewed expressing grief or sorrow.

5. Blame will be placed.

6. A metaphor, such as a wave, will be graphically presented to give symbolic meaning to the whole issue.

7. Prior crises of a similar sort seldom will be assessed for their eventual impact. Each "crisis" is presented as new, without a historical context.[23]

It is striking to see how Altheide's "Formats for Crisis" ritual was adhered to in the coverage of basketball superstar Earvin "Magic" Johnson's revelation that he had tested HIV-positive. Even though a virus and medical diagnosis are not exploitably visual, there was virtually unlimited footage of Johnson's athletic prowess available to illustrate the story (1). The tragedy was contrasted with status quo beliefs that AIDS-related afflictions were chiefly a problem for drug users, homosexuals, and the famous people of the 'artistic' community (2). Now, even virile jocks were shown to be at risk: they and, indirectly, their throngs of loyal fans were discovering that AIDS might impact them or their team (3). Sorrow, remorse, and grief emanated from interviews with Johnson, his basketball colleagues, and his followers (4). Blame bounced from Johnson's promiscuity to the unknown woman who might have infected him to the professional sports establishment for making its stars into irresponsible sex-idols to the government and medical community for failing to do enough to combat the disease (5). The whole issue was metaphorically encapsulated in soaring 'freeze-frames' of the now-grounded athlete's past on-court heroics (6). Yet, previous coverage of the AIDS crisis was seldom brought into play except to imply that earlier stories were all a minor and more disreputable prelude to the "real" crisis now embodied in Magic's affliction (7).

The more recent coverage of President Bill Clinton's encounters with White House intern Monica Lewinsky similarly follow Altheide's crisis-ritual convention. Though visuals of the actual Oval Office gropings do not exist, a single piece of crowd-shot footage showing the President briefly embracing a beret-clad Lewinsky was endlessly enlisted to represent their more private and invasive physical intimacies (1).

As reports of these intimacies grew broader and more specific, the indiscretions were portrayed as a President now out of control. The status quo of the "slick and shifty" politician who used his guile to benefit the underprivileged was replaced by the vision of an arrogant hedonist who would lie to and compromise even his closest associates (2). Before long, the Lewinsky liaison was characterized by White-House-lawn correspondents as a crisis of state that threatened the stock market at home and the credibility of our foreign policy abroad. It was even suggested that the renewed bombing of Iraq was undertaken to deflect attention from the President's indiscretions (3).

As the young intern was revealed to be as much manipulator as prey, the mantle of "victimhood" passed from her to the President's wife and daughter and thence to compromised members of the Clinton administration who had embarrassingly defended the President on the basis of his false assurances to them. When these victims, for personal and political reasons, were reticent in expressing public grief and sorrow, they were superceded by a third wave of victims like Paula Jones, who now had a much broader forum to resurrect previous assertions of sexual mistreatment at the hands of the President (4). Blame, of course, was fundamentally laid at Mr. Clinton's doorstep, but it was later broadened to include Special Prosecutor Kenneth Starr for his zealous and explicit discovery and publication of even the most clinical details of the Clinton/Lewinsky relationship (5).

Despite its judicial complexity, the crisis that led to the President's impeachment (but not conviction) still was encapsulated by the same "snapshot" public embrace with which the whole ritual had begun. Though hardly reflecting the deep constitutional issues that had now been raised, this Clinton/Lewinsky hug remained the visual-of-convenience metaphor for the story as a whole. Some entertainment-packaged coverage did try to advance the cigar as metaphor—but this tangible tool from one Clinton/Lewinsky encounter was much too extreme for the mainstream news media (6). Late in the process, half-hearted attempts were made to compare the Clinton impeachment to that of mid-nineteenth-century chief executive Andrew Johnson. However, the overwhelmingly sexual characterization of the Clinton story made the Johnson comparison seem archaic. Alternate attempts to assess the Clinton situation in terms of President John Kennedy's sexual indiscretions were similarly unenlightening as these only came to light long after Kennedy's death and thus never incited an executive-branch crisis (7).

Victor Turner tells us that a primary function of ritual is to serve as a continuing commentator on society, a dynamic process that must be read as part of a symbolic cultural fabric.[24] So if a news ritual results in faulty coverage, as in the Magic Johnson and Clinton/Lewinsky episodes, perhaps that ritual is simply narrating the cultural fabric's own imperfections.

Mystique

Perfect or imperfect, a ritual acquires a *mystique* if we believe in that ritual's change device. In other words, if an audience has faith that the ritual's problem-solving pattern will succeed, then the ritual is elevated to the status of a mystical experience. "*Stories* do not merely pose problems," Barry Brummett points out,

they suggest ways and means to resolve the problems insofar as they follow discursively a pattern that people might follow in reality. The critic's [or media professional's] task is then to *link* discourse embodying the formal anecdote to an audience's problems, to show how the anecdotal form equips a culture for living in that situation.[25]

In other words, we really want our audiences to believe that they know our world better now than before the newscast began;

that the game show or sportscast has honestly established the better players; that the sitcom 'family' will continue to triumph so appealingly; that the radio station really did make the day brighter than it would otherwise have been. These and other electronic media mystiques are continuously generated and tend to be mutually supportive.

Hence, when we lose faith in one electronic mystique, it can have a negative impact on our total belief perception of media programming. This is why radio's payola scandals of the late 1950s and television's counterpart quiz-show riggings were so damaging, at least in the short term, to the industry. When the mass audience found that the choice of songs they heard was determined by bribes and that their quiz-show champions had cheated to win, all the rituals on the air were suddenly in danger of mystique disintegration. Through public hearings and public firings, broadcasting's damage control efforts did seem to work. Still, some media historians argue that radio/television's mystique has never fully recovered from these seamy revelations.

Commercials have suffered their own mystique losses. Among the most notable came as a result of a 1990 Volvo ad in which a "monster" truck was shown to crush an entire row of cars *except* the Volvo, whose roof remained rigid. Volvo had long enjoyed a well-deserved safety mystique, and this spot, based on an actual occurrence at a New England fairgrounds, was meant as graphic mystical reiteration. Unfortunately, in the Texas shooting of the commercial, someone decided that reinforcing the featured Volvo's roof with extra support beams would be a good idea in case retakes were necessary. This action was never disclosed to the public, however, and when the Texas attorney general's office found out, a national scandal ensued. Volvo fired its advertising agency and began the laborious rebuilding of its legitimate safety mystique that should never have been allowed to be compromised.

In a commercial, the audience must not only understand the portrayed problem-solving ritual, but they must also believe that the depicted solution is best attainable through application of the specific product being advocated. This is the essence of *branding* because, in the words of Ogilvy & Mather executive Robyn Putter, "a brand seeks to persuade by the magnetic pull of what it stands for."[26] For a quarter-century, McDonald's consistently followed a branding strategy of putting "you" at the center of all of its advertising. This was done not only in slogans ("You, you're the one"; "You deserve a break today"; "McDonald's and you") but also through audio and video settings that focused on target customers experiencing positive, even heartwarming experiences with a McDonald's eatery as a backdrop (see the McDonald's script below). This powerful mystique far overshadowed competing chains that, even though they offered very similar services, mistakenly focused more on themselves than on the consumers they were striving to attract.

Long-term, a commercial mystique will flourish only if honest and accurate verbal/visual depictions are used. In the Figure 10-3 Ore-Ida spot, for example, Mom's need to pursue her own activities while still putting a satisfying dinner on the table is serviced by the product that she 'can make with my eyes closed.' Yet, the mystique is more attainable because it does not strive to extend itself beyond the actual product attribute. Somehow, our belief in Ore-Ida is enhanced by the spot's concluding admission that there will still be dishes to do—even in the coziest of families. Ore-Ida's "no big deal" mystique is that it makes a busy household function just a bit more

Video	Audio
SUPER: 'First Order' LOGO: McDonald's OPEN ON MOTHER AND LITTLE DAUGHTER INSIDE MCDONALD'S RESTAURANT SITTING ACROSS FROM EACH OTHER AT TABLE.	MOM: It's your first time. So remember what to say
C/U OF MOTHER.	O.K.?
C/U OF DAUGHTER.	DAUGHTER: O.K.
MOM HANDS HER MONEY	MOM: All right. And you pay with this. O.K.?
DAUGHTER WALKS TOWARDS COUNTER.	SINGER: She's growing up so quickly, I wish she didn't have to do.
DAUGHTER ORDERS.	DAUGHTER: - - -Um, cheeseburger, milk
DAUGHTER TURNS AROUND AND LOOKS AT MOTHER. MOTHER MOUTHS THE WORD, "FRIES".	SINGER: But go ahead and grow, my little one
DAUGHTER TURNS BACK TO COUNTER.	DAUGHTER: - - - and fries.
C/U ON MOM SMILING.	SINGER: It's so beautiful to see.
	DAUGHTER: Thank you.
DAUGHTER TAKES TRAY OF FOOD BACK TO MOTHER.	SINGER: It's a good time
	DAUGHTER: (WHISPERS) Mommy, I got it!
SUPER: It's a good time for the great taste.	MOM: (LAUGHS)
LOGO: McDonald's	SINGER: McDonald's and you.

(Courtesy of Terrence J. O'Malley, Vickers & Benson Advertising Ltd.)

smoothly. The product is not promoted as the American woman's emancipator. She is not forced to swoon over an *au gratin* casserole.

Commercial mystique does not necessarily require a video screen or complicated production. Believability in the following radio spot comes from nothing more than a credibly low-key spokesperson who chats with business travelers about his hostelry's no-hassle temperament. Tom Bodett's neighborly mystique thus epitomizes the homey problem-solving that is portrayed as inherent in the ritual of staying at Motel 6:

BODETT: Motel 6 is in the fast lane again. Hi. Tom Bodett with the highlights. If you've got territory to cover and a route to sell, well time is money. And you don't need to go wastin' either of the two. So make one call to 505-891-6161 and we'll reserve rooms at Motel 6 locations wherever you're goin'. With our wonders of technology you can check in to any darned one without fillin' out a bunch of paperwork. Just enter and

FIGURE 10-3
(Courtesy of Ore-Ida)

TEEN BOY V.O.: It's embarrassing when your mom has more trophies than you do.

But it's neat living with the bowling champ of Wapita Springs.

Even before a tournament, mom's cool.

The night of the State Finals? My mom,

Captain of the "Striking Blondes," made this dinner

with delicious potatoes au gratin. "Wow!" we said.

She said, "No big deal . . . it's one of those new casseroles that Ore-Ida makes.

They have all kinds of fancy new potatoes called Special Recipes.

I can make 'em with my eyes closed."

Dad said, "Is there anything you're not good at?"

"The dishes," mom said.

sign in please. Cause for around 39 bucks, the lowest prices of any national chain, you'll get a clean, comfortable room, free TV, movies and local calls. And long distance ones without a motel service charge. There's over 440 locations coast to coast where you get a good night's sleep and a wake up call. Well, then drop off the key and go. You got people to see and places to be. And we're not here to slow you down. Just remember to keep on the right unless you're passing and don't take any wooden nickels. I'm Tom Bodett for Motel 6 and we'll leave the light on for you.

(Courtesy of John M. Beitter, The Richards Group)

Myth

When a ritual is so meaningful and so believable (mystique-rich) that it can be endlessly retold over time, it becomes a *myth*. Like any conveyance of human discourse, electronic media will inevitably carry these myths. In fact, as Douglas Kellner points out, our media can even contribute myths of their own:

Television images and stories produce new mythologies for problems of everyday life. Myths are simply stories that explain, instruct, and justify practices and institutions; they are lived and shape thought and action. Myths deal with the most significant phenomena in human life and enable people to come to terms with death, violence, love, sex, labor and social conflict. Myths link together symbols, formula, plot and characters in a pattern that is conventional, appealing, and gratifying.[27]

Contemporary use of the term notwithstanding, a myth is not necessarily a falsehood. It is simply a value or faith statement that cannot be scientifically verified. Hence, from the standpoint of our Chapter 4 discussion of the Four Ways of Knowing, myth is the province of the mystic rather than of the scientist. As John Middleton affirms, "The popular notion that a 'myth' is . . . 'un-

true'—indeed that its untruth is its defining characteristic—is not only naive but shows misunderstanding of its very nature. Its 'scientific truth' or otherwise is irrelevant. A myth is a statement about society and man's place in it and the surrounding universe."[28]

Unlike the rigid formulas of science, we can change the symbols comprising a myth at will and still not vary its fundamental substance. Whatever the specific (even personal) referents we substitute in illustrating it, the myth's underlying premise remains more or less stable. As Rollo May testifies:

We find our myths all about us in the unconscious assumptions of our culture; we mold the myths and we use them as images in which we can recognize ourselves, our friends, and our fellows; we use them as guidelines to our ways of life.[29]

Like the symbols from which they are constructed, myths can be divided into three categories, depending on their scope. Structuralist Claude Levi-Strauss[30] labels these categories as universal, cultural-specific, and subcultural myths.

Universal myths are grounded in experiences common to all human beings of every society and era. They include stories of life-cycles and seasons, quests and pilgrimages, destinies and rites of passage.

Culture-specific myths relate to the heroes and evolution of a given society, such as the American myths of uncompromising honesty (young George Washington chopping down the cherry tree) or obligation to tame the frontier (stories of the Old West or the probing of outer space). Very often, Robert Bellah points out, "The mythic hero in American culture must leave society alone or with one or a few others, in order to realize the moral good in the wilderness, at sea, or on the margins of settled society."[31]

Finally, *subcultural* myths encompass the sagas of an individual family or locale. These might include how our own ancestors came 'to America,' or regional/occupational legends like Paul Bunyan (lumbering), Casey Jones (railroading), or Johnny Appleseed (horticulture).

Comparing the development of the United States with its mythic discourses, for instance, anthropologist Conrad Kottak recounts that the American pursuit of the frontier has given us a history replete with travel and encounters with strangers. Growing up in America still entails separation from those who raised us. Issues of venturing out, breaking with home, and creating ties with strangers have been critically important in American history. It is no wonder then that so many American creations express these themes. The joy of the journey and the thrill of the quest continue. One illustration is that for more than two decades American fans have religiously followed a group of fictional characters whose goal is "to boldly go where no one has gone before [*Star Trek*]."[32]

Star Trek, like any media property, is thus the bearer of our myths and of the ideologies (sociopolitical attitudes) that these myths carry. It follows that popular program content is a reflection of our more generally accepted premises. "Every culture reveals itself," observes William Fore, "through its underlying assumptions, the decisions it makes about what's important, how to solve problems, who has the power, what is acceptable and what is forbidden."[33] These decisions are reached through what Michael Real calls *mythic activity*: "the collective reenactment of symbolic archetypes that express the shared emotions and ideals of a given culture."[34]

Mainstream media content resonates these shared emotions and ideals, endlessly repeating these archetypal patterns with which both audiences and advertisers are most comfortable. In 1965, Sprague Vonier, then station manager of WTMJ-TV in Milwaukee, randomly compiled a list of myths he detected in prime-time television. Vonier pointed out that this list was by no means exhaustive but did include many of the mythic attitudes most often conveyed to electronic media audiences. Among the items on Vonier's inventory were:

A person's home is their castle.
Fair play is important.
Everyone has a right to speak their mind.
Everyone is entitled to the best education of which they are capable.
People should be kind to animals and children.
Everyone is created equal.
No person is beyond redemption.
We expect justice at the hands of the law and usually get it. When we don't, we try to correct the situation.
We must strive to be well liked, to please others, to win the acceptance of the community.[35]

We can, without much difficulty, locate these same myths in today's programs because, as Vonier wrote four decades ago,

they find their footings in a heritage of Anglo-Saxon law, of Protestant ethical concepts, of democratic principles of government and a heritage of English literature. They are the same popular philosophical and ethical concepts which have underlain other media of mass entertainment, the movies, popular magazines, radio drama and even the comic strips.[36]

While agreeing that these myths are still prominent in electronic programming of today, contemporary Marxist, feminist, and other critics find them troubling because, they argue, such mythic messages obscure major fissures in our society. Speaking of electronic journalism, for instance, Susan Reilly asserts that "the myths marshalled together on television news tend to reaffirm values that protect the dominant ideology of the culture."[37] Elayne Rapping adds that "as the inequities of class widen, and the real mechanisms, and behaviors that enable the few to 'make it' become increasingly undemocratic and unfit to exemplify the media's supposed values, this kind of mystification and fantasy grows more important."[38]

For their own self-protection, media professionals need to carefully monitor this debate about myths in order to better anticipate the range of possible audience reactions to content. Even if the myths reflected by their messages are entirely noncontroversial, program and commercial creators can only benefit from being more attuned to mythic structures. The more we understand about the assumptions undergirding our messages, the more we may be able to engage target listener/viewer beliefs.

Decoding media messages in this way may seem laborious if not downright impossible. However, as Robert Rutherford Smith advises,

programs are unyielding to analysis only if we insist on dealing with them atomically, one by one. If we look for the underlying rhythms that tie them to one another and to the stories of past cultures, both literate and illiterate, we may find that they lead us into the rich tapestry of the Western tradition. If we can see through the idiosyncrasies of each program to its underlying structure, we may find that it takes on new meaning, or rather, the meaning it has for us becomes clear.[39]

Thus, as novelist Joyce Carol Oates once observed, the cops of *Hill Street Blues* were compelling not because they were crime-fighters like so many others on the air before and since, but because "the Hill Street police are figures of Sisyphus rolling their rocks up the hill and the next day rolling them up again, and again. . . . It is always the next morning, it is always roll call."[40] Though most viewers of the program were probably not familiar with Sisyphus, the deceitful king of ancient mythology, they became very familiar with his recurring myth of futile, Hades-bound endurance. Audiences were enthralled as the hellish rock of anarchy threatened every week to roll back over "The Hill" and crush its defenders, and this mythic progression subsequently was adopted by several other cop and doctor series.

In summary, it is inevitable that the electronic media function as purveyors of myths due to the fact that these media, according to Professor John Cawelti,

communicate to nearly everyone in the culture by depending on an established repertory of basic stories and other artistic patterns in a fashion analogous to the traditional bard's use of epic formulas and a well-known mythology. These conventional patterns guarantee a high degree of accessibility. Of course mere accessibility is no guarantee of artistic interest. How-ever, there is a sense in which the best popular art is not only fairly easy to interpret, but compels audiences to want to understand it, because it deals in an interesting way with stories and themes that seem important.[41]

In other words, muses top commercial creator Jeff Goodby, "you compare the myth with your experience, and put the two together and get something bigger. I think advertising is like that. You use myth from people's lives, popular culture and history to influence people's behavior in the next step in time."[42]

Before leaving this section, let us review the interrelationship of ritual, mystique, and myth by examining the Garfield cartoon strip in Figure 10-4. The (repetitive problem-solving) *ritual*, as reflected in the first panel, is that cats regularly climb things to get where they want without fear of injury. Panel three's associated *mystique* (faith/belief) in this activity is that cats have the capability to land on their feet. As endlessly repeated over time, this mystique underlies the panel two *myth* that cats ALWAYS land on their feet. Unlike most myths, which cannot be scientifically tested, this myth seems to have been empirically and unquivocally *dis*proven by the portly Garfield.

THESIS, ANTITHESIS, AND SYNTHESIS

Another way of analyzing how symbols are manipulated into ritual and mythic structures is to examine how a creator interposes

FIGURE 10-4 (Garfield © 1988 Paws, Inc. Reprinted with permission of Universal Press Syndicate. All rights reserved.)

two opposites to generate a new amalgamation. The concept of these two opposites (the *thesis* and the *antithesis*) and their resulting combination (the *synthesis*) is generally attributed to the philosophical works of Plato, Immanuel Kant, and Georg Hegel. This idea received its most explicit development in Johann Gottlieb Fichte's *Science of Knowledge*. To Fichte, these three entities were interdependent in the science and arrangement of thought. "Just as there can be no antithesis without synthesis, no synthesis without antithesis," he wrote, "so there can be neither without a thesis—an absolute positing."[43]

Even though Fichte's statement of his premise becomes increasingly complex as his writing proceeds, its basic thrust is clearly captured by Karl Popper, who explained its political applications in his *The Open Society and its Enemies*:

First a *thesis* is proffered; but it will produce criticism, it will be contradicted by opponents who assert its opposite, an *antithesis*; and in the conflict of these views, a *synthesis* is attained, that is to say, a kind of unity of the opposites, a compromise or reconciliation on a higher level. The synthesis absorbs, as it were, the two original opposite positions, by superseding them; it reduces them to components of itself, thereby negating, elevating, and preserving them.[44]

Figure 10-5 summarizes this process schematically.

The *artistic* (as opposed to political) manifestation of thesis/antithesis/synthesis is perhaps most noticeable in music, where, beginning in the nineteenth century, composers abandoned the sonata-allegro practice of a simple restatement (recapitulation) of contrasting themes in favor of a *coda* or similar terminal and transformational device. The purpose, explains composer Aaron Copland, "is to create a sense of apotheosis—the material is seen for the last time and in a new light. . . . What sense does it

make to go through all the turmoil and struggle of the development section if only to lead back to the same conclusions from which we started?"[45] The musical coda thus became a distinct destination (synthesis) in which the two contrasting themes introduced earlier in the piece mutually transformed each other to create a new tonal revelation.

Not surprisingly, the process is equally relevant to print and electronic literature. As John Fiske reveals, "traditional narrative begins with a state of equilibrium which is disturbed: the plot traces the effects of this disturbance through the final resolution, which restores a new and possibly different equilibrium."[46]

Cultural criticism often monitors this same pattern in what is called the *social values model*. This model, state Karyn and Donald Rybacki, "assumes that the collective consciousness of a culture is made up of patterns of values in opposition and that a culture deals with its problems either by choosing one value over another or by synthesizing opposing values."[47] The chronic turmoil in the Middle East and the former Yugoslavia illustrates what happens when this social-values model fails. In such instances, opposing and equally powerful culture-based values stalemate each other; no choice of one over the other can be made (even at gun-point), and the resulting enmities make compromising synthesis virtually impossible.

To apply this thesis/antithesis/synthesis structure to our profession, we can turn to its common application in commercials. Consider, as illustration, the following radio spot created by master copywriter Dick Orkin:

COUNSELOR: Bob, Helen, as a trained
    counselor, I believe every
    marriage can be saved.
BOTH: Yeah, sure, we'll see about
    that.
COUNSELOR: Now Bob, what's the
    problem?
HELEN: Cheap jerk here won't buy me
    a new TV.
COUNSELOR: Now Helen, I asked
    Bob.
BOB: There's nothing wrong with the
    old set.
HELEN: Yeah? The vertical hold is
    so bad that I can't tell Greg
    from Karma.

FIGURE 10-5
How synthesis is generated.

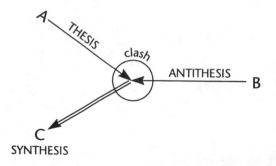

BOB: It's DHAR-ma.

HELEN: Yeah, see he's always ---

COUNSELOR: Now Bob, how about a new set?

HELEN: This cheap jerk?

COUNSELOR: You know, cheap jerk, uh, Bob, what you two need is ---

BOTH: A divorce!

COUNSELOR: No, Granada TV Rental.

BOB: Granada TV Rental?

COUNSELOR: Why put up with a lousy picture? Rent a big brand name color TV for just $19.95 to $39.95 a month.

BOB: No more ghosties?

HELEN: Or fuzzies?

COUNSELOR: Any problems, Granada provides free repairs.

HELEN: Wow!

COUNSELOR: Or Granada gives you a free loaner.

BOB: Wow!

COUNSELOR: Problem solved?

BOTH: Yeah.

COUNSELOR: Next problem, drinking beer and smoking stogies in bed ---

HELEN: I need a brewsky and a stogie to relax me after a hard day.

(Courtesy of Dick Orkin)

In this commercial, Bob articulates the thesis that TV sets with prime-grade picture quality can be costly. Helen's antithesis is that poorly functioning receivers are a major family irritant. The resolving synthesis, as revealed by the Counselor, is Granada—the company that can provide prime picture quality economically. Therefore, there is no longer any financial need to put up with inferior video.

Figure 10-6 illustrates how this same structure can underpin a television spot. In this deliberately sparse treatment, the clash between the optimist's thesis and the pessimist's antithesis is overridden by their unifying love-of-chocolate synthesis that is demonstrably consumed as Yoo-Hoo, 'the cool way to do chocolate.'

For program-length examples of thesis/antithesis/synthesis, read *The Cosby Show* and *The Simpsons* scripts in Appendix A. In *Cosby*'s "Theo's Holiday, " the thesis tells us that asserting one's self-sufficiency is a hallmark of maturity. The ironic antithesis, however, asserts that the working world expects but does not nurture this self-sufficiency. Fortunately, the synthesizing supportive family can promote maturing independence through selective guidance in the ways of the world.

The Simpsons' "Bart Sells His Soul" episode also posits a thesis of self-sufficiency: Bart need only depend on his own wits/behavior to get what he wants. The antithesis counters that one's well-being requires safeguarding of a spiritual dimension, as represented by the concept of the soul. The synthesis is that, while one has to, in Lisa's words, "earn" that spiritual dimension "through suffering and thought and prayer," each person's soul remains a reflection of his or her mortal personality. When they are reunited, both Bart and his soul are still distinctly Bart.

Unlike sitcoms, one-hour dramas, by their very nature, include darker elements. Thus, the thesis is normally the positive/good while the antithesis articulates the negative/evil. Nevertheless, in order to accomplish a synthesis, the good has to be modified in some way as a result of its clash with the bad. It cannot remain unchanged. That is what makes *The Practice* a more comprehensive experience than *Matlock*. *The Practice*'s attorneys grow or atrophy based on what happens to them in their depicted professional and personal lives. Matlock, on the other hand, is the same Andy Griffith week after week.

SEMIOTICS

A much more recent approach to message structure analysis is defined by the inquiries of *semiotics*. Coined by American philosopher Charles Sanders Peirce, the term refers to the study of sign systems. Peirce, as well as Swiss linguist Ferdinand de Saussure, provided much of the basic theory that has deepened scholarly attention to this subject during the last three decades. At the outset, however, it must be said that this interest has not been shared by electronic media professionals. Consequently, semiotics remains largely the tool of university researchers and their graduate students.

Beginning in the 1960s, several European intellectuals began applying semiotic approaches to the discourses of popular cul-

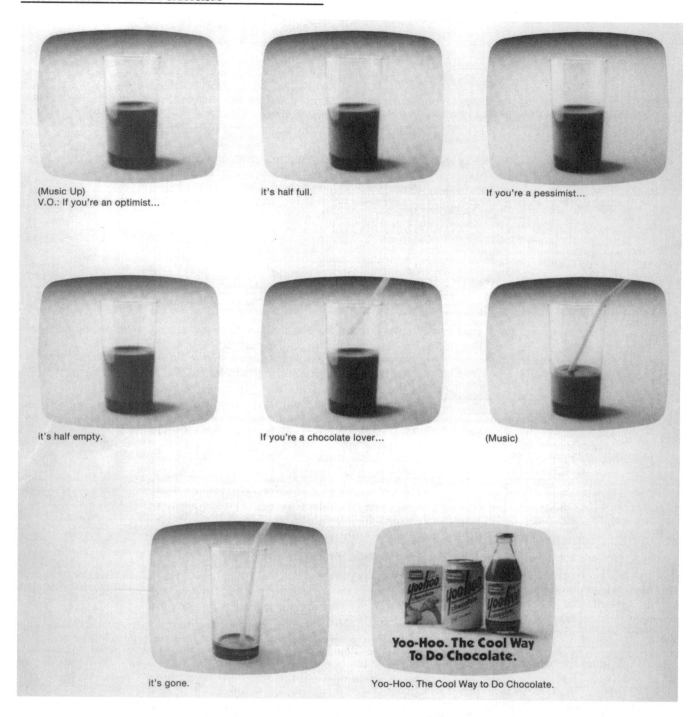

(Music Up)
V.O.: If you're an optimist...

it's half full.

If you're a pessimist...

it's half empty.

If you're a chocolate lover...

(Music)

it's gone.

Yoo-Hoo. The Cool Way to Do Chocolate.

FIGURE 10-6
(Courtesy of Rodney Underwood, Geer DuBois Inc.)

ture. Author Umberto Eco studied James Bond novels and Superman comic strips. Christian Metz attempted to semiotically decode Hollywood movies. Somewhat later, a number of American theorists adapted these efforts to the analysis of television content.

In light of our previous discussion, we might ask whether such scrutiny of semi-

ology's 'sign systems' bears any relationship to the much more conventional study of 'symbols.' While one can indulge in a great deal of metaphysical hairsplitting, Northrop Frye put the sign/symbol distinction in its most comprehensible terms when he wrote that signs are simply those symbolic units "which conventionally and arbitrarily, stand for and point to things outside the place where they occur."[48] Thus, for our purposes, all signs are symbols. But signs are the symbols that possess the greatest utility because they free us from the bonds of our immediate and concrete perceptual environment.

Once we have moved beyond the strictly linguistic purview of Saussure, these signs can be auditory or visual as well as verbal. Semiology, observes Professor Thomas Cooper, "aspires to account for all the levels of coding we ingest, whether in our observation of a photograph or movie, or in our interaction with other human beings. When applying semiology to a television program students discover that they are decoding *several* codes simultaneously such as lighting, costumes, camera movement, editing and acting."[49] Consequently, the semiotic analysis of the electronic media becomes much more complex than that of the printed word. Because television, for instance, uses a number of sign systems simultaneously, a written semiotic analysis of even a 30-second commercial may consume several pages.

In any event, the fundamental unit of semiotic scrutiny can be reduced to this equation:

$$Signifier + Signified = SIGN$$

The *signifier* is the material form; it is the particular sound, object, or image itself. Thus, in the Dow Bathroom Cleaner spot in Figure 10-7, the principal signifier is the 'scrubbing bubble.'

The *signified* is the concept that signifier is meant to represent. In this commercial, the 'bubble' is a visual metaphor for hard scrubbing action.

The *sign*, or resulting associative total, is that the product which harnesses those industrious bubbles will "work hard so you don't have to."

Similarly, in applying semiotic analysis to the following radio spot by copywriter Steve Kessler, we find the signifier to be the back seat, the signified to be the careless technological neglect of other people's comfort, and the amalgamating sign the ministrations of Nissan's 'human engineering' to make the entire car person-compatible.

MALE: I'd like you to turn around
   for a second and look at your

back seat. Come on now, just a quick look at the back seat that follows you everywhere and never complains, even when it has to go out with you for doughnuts at 3 in the morning. You never hear your back seat say:
   'Hey, pal, take the front
   seat, I'm staying here in the
   garage.'
So go ahead, check out your back seat. Does it look comfortable? And when was the last time you even sat in it? I mean, who really even cares about a back seat anyway? Well, anybody who ever sits in your back seat's going to care about it. And so do the designers at Nissan. It's what they call human engineering. Catchy title, huh? It means that Nissan cars are planned around all the people who'll be in them. So even in a performance sedan like the Nissan Maxima you get a back seat that's just as comfortable as the front seats. So when you get home tonight, hop into your back seat. And if you don't like what you find, hop back into your front seat and take your whole car down to a Nissan dealer and see if he can't do better. Thanks.
ANNCR: Nissan --- built for the most
   important race of all: the human
   race.[50]

However derived, signs can be classified as to whether they possess first-, second-, or third-order signification. First-order signs are those for which the specific content is vital. In the above radio commercial, for instance, it is important to the sponsor that listeners understand it is Nissan (not just any auto manufacturer) that builds every part of the car with humanity's needs in mind. By definition, most advertising promotes first-order signs since it is the specific brand, rather than the brand category, that clients are paying to market.

Second-order signs, in contrast, derive their significance, say Fiske and Hartley, "not from the sign itself, but from the way

FIGURE 10-7
(Courtesy of
David C. Latta,
Dow Brands Inc.)

"Sabre Dance"
15 SECOND TV COMMERCIAL

MUSIC: "SABRE DANCE"

MUSIC CONTINUES

MUSIC CONTINUES

MUSIC CONTINUES

MUSIC CONTINUES

Dow Bathroom Cleaner with Scrubbing
Bubbles™. We work hard so you don't have to.

Texize Greenville, S.C. 29602 Division of Dow Consumer Products Inc. ©1987 DCPI
*Trademark of The Dow Chemical Company

the society uses and values both the signifier and the signified. In our society, a car (or a sign for a car) frequently signifies virility or freedom."[51] The car manufacturer and its advertising agency then try to parlay such traditional second-order signification into first-order specificity by convincing you to attribute this virility or freedom only to their model, as is the thrust of the classic Oldsmobile pitch in Figure 10-8. (Obviously, the Nissan radio spot pursues a much different signification, in attempting to stand apart from the historic mainstream.)

Conversely, an industry-wide (generic) promotion to buy American cars, drink Colombian Coffee (as in Figure 10-1), or use

1. MUSIC: (DRAMATIC IN AND UNDER)

2. ...

3. ...

4. ...

5. ...

6. ...

7. ...

8. (Anncr VO): Oldsmobile Cutlass Supreme.

9. The V8...

10. with so much performance.

11. It makes every road...

12. a downhill run.

13. (MUSIC)

14. (Anncr VO): Oldsmobile Quality. (SFX: DOOR SLAM)

15. (Anncr VO): Feel it.

gas appliances remains at the level of second-order signification because it does not reference a specific (first-order) brand. Instead, the benefit/value is attributed to the entire category.

Particularly when teamed up with other signifiers, second-order signs can acquire third-order signification, or what Fiske and Hartley call "a comprehensive cultural picture of the world, a coherent and organized

FIGURE 10-8
(Courtesy of Roger W. Bodo, Leo Burnett Company)

view of reality with which we are faced. It is in this third order that a car can form part of the imagery of an industrial, materialistic, and rootless society."[52] Third-order signs thus cannot be completely controlled by program and commercial creators. Instead, they flow from each consumer's aggregate interpretations of the media's first- and second-order sign usage; these interpretations are influenced, in turn, by how those consumers feel about their 'real world.'

Perceptive electronic media critics are capable of probing possible third-order significations even as they articulate a show's more stable and obvious first- and second-order signs. These reviewers thereby not only convey what the public or colleague media professionals need to know to make basic media-use decisions, but they also (for those interested) divulge the underlying import a program may possess.

In her 1989 critique of the just-premiered *The Simpsons*, for instance, advertising commentator Betsy Sharkey correctly and semiotically predicted the program's success. Sharkey discerned that the Simpson clan (first-order sign) were a perceptive representation of the 1990s U.S. family with its "warts and all" imperfections (second-order sign). Beyond that, the show as a whole exemplified "a growing restlessness in the country. As the individual retains so little control of his work, his environment, his life . . . the '90s are no time for fairy tales." In other words, *The Simpsons* epitomized a coldly realistic environment in which "simply trying to get by" had become the ultimate goal (third-order sign).

Whether they are dealing with first-, second-, or third-order significations, most semioticians who concern themselves with the electronic media tend to treat pictorial and verbal symbols as equals, not only in these signs' import, but also in how they function as meaning conveyances. There is nothing wrong with this practice as long as we respect Robert Rutherford Smith's caution not to

assume that the analogy works more exactly than seems to be the case. For instance, if television pictures sometimes function like words, we may be led to assume that pictures are words, groups of pictures function like sentences, and that they are held together by a "grammar." Such pitfalls are characteristic of analogical thinking. We can avoid them by re-

membering that, although television may yield to structuralist inquiry based on the linguistic model, we have not yet found a visual "language." What we have found is associative groups that sometimes bear structural similarities to languages?[53]

The more electronic media content piles sign upon sign to (often unintentionally) generate greater complexities of meaning, the greater is the scholarly temptation to find some standardized screen through which this meaning can be filtered and interpreted. This procedure, however, may ignore the fact that electronic media content creation is more art than science. As DeWitt Parker reminds us, "in allowing more than one meaning, artistic signs differ from the scientific, where the ideal is always that one sign should have only one meaning."[54] Pictorially no less than linguistically, "the notion that it is possible to reduce language to sign language, to make one word mean one thing," asserts Frye, "is an illusion."[55]

Perhaps the greatest contribution semiology or any other structuralist approach makes to electronic media criticism is to remind industry professionals that the product of our labors is often more significant in more ways to more people than we often stop to consider.

ENDNOTES

1. Karyn and Donald Rybacki, *Communication Criticism: Approaches and Genres* (Belmont, CA: Wadsworth, 1991), 69.
2. Hal Himmelstein, *On the Small Screen* (New York: Praeger, 1981), 97.
3. Theodore Meyer Greene, *The Arts and the Art of Criticism* (Princeton, NJ: Princeton University Press, 1940), 102.
4. Joshua Meyrowitz, "How Television Has Reshaped the Social Landscape," *Feedback* (Fall 1989), 20.
5. Sophie Menache, *The Vox Dei: Communication in the Middle Ages* (New York: Oxford University Press, 1990), 9.
6. Ronald Lembo and Kenneth Tucker, "Culture, Television, and Opposition: Rethinking Cultural Studies," *Critical Studies in Mass Communication* (June 1990), 104.
7. Barbara Lippert, "Rabbit Redux," *ADWEEK* (December 9, 1991), 28.
8. Northrop Frye, *Anatomy of Criticism* (Princeton, NJ: Princeton University Press, 1957), 166.

THE SIMPSONS: TEMPERED CYNICISM AS KNOWING REALITY

by Betsy Sharkey

It's a touching scene—a family trying desperately to connect. All five Simpsons gather round, arms encircling one another. But the moment dissolves into a guerrilla-style hug-fest, with pushing, pinching and at least one strangling.

Welcome to intimacy, Simpson style.

The program is worth a peek because the characters, with their gargoyle eyes, monster overbite, wit and sincere—but failed—attempts at normalcy, are the odds-on favorite to become the Charlie Brown, Linus and Snoopy of the new decade. That the Simpsons seem to work is endemic of what sociologists have identified as a growing need for reality, for roots, for security. Families—warts and all—are suddenly an appealing commodity. In its own way, The Simpsons provides a counterpart to the sanguine Cosby Show. And like Roseanne, The Simpsons offers life with an edge.

Beyond that, creator Matt Groening gives us characters that kids can love and adults can relate to. The Simpsons are for those moments when you quietly concede that you dread a four-hour car trip with the kids—and they agree. The show has the kind of texture and tonality that feels like a conspiratorial wink, one that draws you in and lets you belong. "It's a 'we're hip to the gag' kind of attitude," says Michael Albright, a principal of Albright/Labhardt, L.A., and the agency's creative director. "And clients are just starting to ask for it."

Groening's characters have a tempered cynicism. Occasionally, that attitude has been successfully woven into advertising, such as Hal Riney's early Bartles & Jaymes ads, with their digs at focus groups and MBAs. But Groening's cynicism is not quite a Joe Isuzu, because it has more heart. What the Simpson characters do represent is an intelligent link—that "we-know-you-understand" sentiment—that advertisers will increasingly find goes a long way toward building a bond with the consumer.

The characters are extensions of the mental machinations seen in Groening's Life in Hell comic strip. Filled with rabbits who have nightmares about concepts such as "infotainment," Life in Hell has had an underground following for years. But it is what the Simpsons say about life in these times that is likely to move the series into the mainstream. Their angst is concrete, not esoteric.

That is perhaps why there is so much disagreement over the value the Peanuts characters bring to Metropolitan Life. Charlie Brown remains mired in an introspective debate on the meaning of life in a time when the rest of us are simply trying to get by. While Linus clings to his blanket, Bart Simpson is a kid who's likely to grab it and run. It's the difference between active and passive, and it touches a growing restlessness in the country. As the individual retains so little control of his work, his environment, his life, even muffed attempts at regaining ground, which the Simpsons certainly represent, are very engaging.

The Simpson characters, Groening explains, are "mutated memories of the TV shows I remember as a kid. I tried to live like Beaver—it didn't work." Indeed, the show's core demographics are expected to be an upscale, 18-34-year-old crowd, with a fair measure of kids in there too.

While advertising continues to be chock-full of images of supermoms, precocious kids, futsy fathers and families whose biggest conflict is whether to bake or microwave the brownies, a Simpson-styled reality is such a relief. The Simpsons may use the microwave, but it's reassuring to know they probably won't do it without a fight. It is animation that reminds us that the '90s are no times for fairy tales.

9. Ibid., 172.

10. Ibid., 173.

11. Ibid., 175.

12. Ibid., 176.

13. Ibid., 175–176.

14. Ibid., 172.

15. Ibid., 116.

16. Rose Goldsen, *The Show and Tell Machine* (New York: The Dial Press, 1977), 285.

17. Robert Rutherford Smith, *Beyond the Wasteland: The Criticism of Broadcasting*, rev. ed. (Annandale, VA: Speech Communication Association, 1980), 20.

18. Quentin Schultze, "Television Drama as Sacred Text," in John Ferre (ed.), *Channels of Belief* (Ames: Iowa State University Press, 1990), 21.

19. Frye, 119–120.

20. Rudolf Arnheim, *Toward a Psychology of Art* (Berkeley: University of California Press, 1967), 68.

21. Horace Newcomb, *TV: The Most Popular Art* (Garden City, NY: Anchor Books, 1974), 174.

22. John Fiske and John Hartley, *Reading Television* (London: Methuen, 1978), 90.

23. David Altheide, "The Impact of Television News Formats on Social Policy," *Journal of Broadcasting & Electronic Media* (Winter 1991), 17.

24. Victor Turner, "Process, System, and Symbol: A New Anthropological Synthesis," *Daedalus* (Summer 1977).

25. Barry Brummett, "Burke's Representative Anecdote as a Method in Media Criticism," *Critical Studies in Mass Communication* (June 1984), 164.

26. Drusilla Menaker, "O & M Rightford Establishes a New Harmony," *Advertising Age* (April 15, 1996), S–5.

27. Douglas Kellner, "TV, Ideology, and Emancipatory Popular Culture," *Socialist Review* (May/June 1979), 22.

28. John Middleton, "Introduction," in John Middleton (ed.), *Myth and Cosmos: Readings in Mythology and Symbolism* (Garden City, NY: The Natural History Press, 1967), x.

29. Rollo May, *Existential Psychotherapy* (Toronto: CBC Learning Systems, 1967), 22.

30. Claude Levi-Strauss, "The Structural Study of Myth," in T. A. Seboek (ed.), *Myth: A Symposium* (Bloomington: Indiana University Press, 1958).

31. Robert Bellah et al. *Habits of the Heart: Individualism and Commitment in American Life* (Berkeley: University of California Press, 1985), 144.

32. Conrad Kottak, *Prime-Time Society* (Belmont, CA: Wadsworth, 1990), 101.

33. William Fore, "Escape from Gilligan's Island," *Media & Values* (Summer/Fall 1987), 2.

34. Michael Real, *Mass-Mediated Culture* (Englewood Cliffs, NJ: Prentice-Hall, 1977), 96.

35. Sprague Vonier, "Television: Purveyor of Parables," *Journal of Broadcasting* (Winter 1965/66), 5.

36. Ibid., 6.

37. Susan Reilly, "Utilizing a Critical Pedagogy to Transform U.S. News." Presentation to the Broadcast Education Association Convention, April 14, 1991 (Las Vegas).

38. Elayne Rapping, *The Looking Glass World of Nonfiction TV* (Boston: South End Press, 1987), 130.

39. Smith, 24.

40. Joyce Carol Oates, "For Its Audacity, Its Defiantly Bad Taste and Its Superb Character Studies," *TV Guide* (June 1, 1985), 7.

41. John Cawelti, "With the Benefit of Hindsight: Popular Culture Criticism," *Critical Studies in Mass Communication* (December 1985), 369.

42. Jon Berry, "Jeff Goodby Plays His BMP Power Chord," *ADWEEK* (July 17, 1989), 20.

43. Johann Gottlieb Fichte, *Science of Knowledge*, trans. by Peter Heath and John Lochs (New York: Appleton-Century-Crofts, 1970), 113.

44. Karl R. Popper, *The Open Society and Its Enemies*, Vol. II: *The High Tide of Prophecy: Hegel, Marx. and the Aftermath* (Princeton, NJ: Princeton University Press, 1962), 39.

45. Aaron Copland, *What to Listen for in Music* (New York: Mentor Books, 1957), 118–119.

46. John Fiske, *Television Culture* (London: Methuen, 1987), 180.

47. Rybacki and Rybacki, 139.

48. Frye, 73.

49. Thomas Cooper, "Communication as Corpus Callosum: A Reorganization of Knowledge," *Journalism Educator* (Spring 1993), 87.

50. "ADWEEK's All-Star Creative Team," *Winners* (February 1989), 22.

51. Fiske and Hartley, 41.

52. Ibid.

53. Smith, 32–33.

54. DeWitt Parker, *The Principles of Aesthetics*, 2nd ed. (Westport, CT: Greenwood Press, 1976), 57.

55. Frye, 335.

11 Probing Ethics and Values

Our previous chapter focuses on various mechanisms through which messages are structured and invested with meaning. What we explore now is how people's response to a given message—and to its carrier—is influenced by their interpretation of the "rightness" or "wrongness" of this meaning as they have been led to perceive it. Thus, we now grapple with ethics and values.

For any media professional, the matter of ethics and values is fraught with perils. It is not just a question of having the courage of our own convictions. It is also the necessity to balance those convictions with the variegated standards subscribed to by the listeners and viewers we are striving to reach. How far can we go in presenting programs or positions reflective of our (or our organization's) value system before members of the public feel that these values are being imposed on them? Conversely, how long can we skirt value-laden issues or themes and still strike ratings-building interest in the minds of the audience?

For better or for worse, electronic media practitioners have an economic and social mandate to serve the population via instruments that, like the public schools, are felt to be the property of all. And just like the public schools, everyone assumes they have the unquestioned prerogative to structure the enterprise's curriculum their own way.

ETHICS, VALUES, AND MORALITY DEFINED

People decide how the world should operate based on their own internalized conceptions of right and wrong, good and bad, desirable and undesirable. In very dogmatic individuals, these conceptions can be highly systematized, explicit, and unyielding. For most of us, however, they are quite disorganized and implicit, jumbled together in our minds and behavior patterns like the treasured but unsorted keepsakes in our bottom bureau drawer.

These personal standards may owe as much to Disney as they do to the deity, and may issue as much from incidental (and media-simulated) life experiences as from formal parental or institutional instruction. Nonetheless, for all their seeming inadvertence, these appraising "goggles" (as Marshall McLuhan labeled them), formulate our vision of life and also our expectations for how other people should view life as well.

However assembled, *ethics* constitute the disciplined code of conduct used to guide action and belief. As John Frohnmayer defines the concept, "Ethics is the struggle of man, from the dawn of civilization to the present, to evaluate his actions. It involves putting the immediate situation into a universal context. It is a process that aids in decision-making and in identifying the community to whom the decision is addressed."[1]

As Frohnmayer's comment suggests, each individual does not possess a unique ethical attitude. Instead, writes Professor Louis Day, an ethical system "reflects *a society's notions* about the rightness or wrongness of an act and the distinctions between virtue and vice" [italics added].[2] Because of this social grounding, it is very difficult for an individual to develop (or even conceive of) an ethical system in opposition to that which predominates in his or her "home" culture. Many young Germans cannot understand why their grandparents could have tolerated—much less supported—Nazism, because they fail to comprehend a society in which all the political, social, economic, and artistic institutions were enlisted to promote its tenets. Similarly, young White U.S. southerners cannot grasp why segregation was embraced by their elders because they cannot fathom the dominant and long-standing social ethic then in place.

To the extent that people feel a "belongingness" with a society, they will also subscribe to its ethical teachings. Only when this feeling of belongingness is fractured will they seek either to (1) overturn the system or (2) leave it. The Vietnam conflict, for example, found conscientious Americans pursuing both of these options as their country's ascendant ethical system appeared to be drifting farther and farther from its (and their) traditional moorings.

Values, meanwhile, represent the translation of the ethical code into a procedure for determining and prioritizing objects and actions as worthy or unworthy of pursuit or emulation. Thus, each human society designs a values hierarchy to operationalize its ethical standards. As Eliseo Vivas declares,

man, among the other things which make him unique, is a culture building animal. And he has never been known to create a culture which did not include a more or less well defined hierarchy of values: dramatic conceptions about himself and about the nature on which he depends to survive.[3]

Some theorists, like George Santayana, subdivide values into two constituent parts: moral and aesthetic. "Moral values are generally negative, and always remote," Santayana maintains. "Morality has to do with the avoidance of evil and the pursuit of good: aesthetics only with enjoyment."[4] This definition thus takes the position that *aesthetic* value exists independently of ethical concerns; that the comprehension of beauty is *amoral*, or outside the scope of ethical consideration. Recent controversies involving the display of allegedly obscene exhibits by public art galleries, however, demonstrate how difficult it is to segregate aesthetic concerns from moral ones.

In any case, for most media professionals, this issue is more a theoretical curiosity than a relevant consideration. Due to the immensely public nature of the electronic media, all but a few restricted-access 'pay TV' services must keep mainstream social morality firmly in mind when producing and scheduling programming. Practically speaking, we can never restrict our purview solely to the 'aesthetic enjoyment' to which Santayana refers. As Northrop Frye affirms:

No discussion of beauty can confine itself to the formal relations of the isolated work of art; it must consider, too, the participation of the work of art in the vision of the goal of social

effort; the idea of complete and classless civilization. This idea of complete civilization is also the implicit moral standard to which ethical criticism always refers. . . . The goal of ethical consideration is transvaluation, the ability to look at contemporary social values with the detachment of one who is able to compare them in some degree with the infinite vision of possibilities presented by a culture.[5]

In short, when we attempt to analyze the content of our media projects, we must consider the entire moral spectrum likely to be subscribed to by members of our public. We can no more adopt a very narrow moral viewpoint than we can ignore moral considerations as a whole. We can neither dismiss cultural morality nor presume to dictate it.

Before moving on to a more specific application of all of this to electronic media content, let's review what we have covered so far. Professor David Pfeifer definitionally interrelates our key terms in the following taxonomy:

Ethics is the discipline which studies the rationale for, the principles of, the ideas and theories of morality.
Morality concerns the rightness or wrongness of attitudes and actions within a specific set of moral principles . . .
Moral principles are *value* statements concerning right and wrong [italics added].[6]

If this seems too ponderous and theoretical to have any bearing on programs and commercials, keep in mind that mass media are the inevitable reflectors of their parent society. And, since every society possesses (in Frye's words) its own "contemporary social values," media content inevitably will be read as to how it appears to support or reject those values. For their part, "values are the building blocks of attitudes," Louis Day points out.[7] Therefore, people's attitudes about our electronic messages will be a direct if sometimes subconscious response to the values these messages appear to endorse. "In the very act of telling stories," broadcast executive Sprague Vonier once wrote, "the television industry is conveying a set of values to the audience. In certain instances, the story would not and could not exist except for the cultural values implied in its telling."[8]

Obviously, electronic media practitioners seldom set out with the *primary* goal of promoting a particular ethical construct. In most cases, they are simply trying to develop a (program or advertising) story that will hold an audience. At times, producers even seem unaware of the presence of a particular values statement in their project until they are met with a barrage of objections from a special interest group or network standards and practices department. Such clashes tend to make creators even more wary of constructing messages that may be perceived as heavily value-laden. As actor/producer Alan Alda observed:

On the whole I would say that most of what appears to be values on television is the result of not wanting to offend the people who are watching and not wanting to offend the advertisers. The censorship department at the network probably has more effect on promoting what seem to be a set of values than anybody's conscious design.[9]

As we explore in the previous chapter, however, television is so "symbol rich" that even network standards and practices departments often fail to detect a controversial values discourse that has come to be embedded in a given audio/visual narrative.

THE MEDIA AS VALUES SUPPLIERS

Even though programmers and advertisers are becoming more 'values shy,' the electronic media's involuntary role as values conveyor nonetheless is being enlarged. This is occurring because of two simultaneous trends: the electronic media's increasing pervasiveness and portability within our society and the declining prominence of traditional values-teaching institutions. "Schools don't dare impose values, parents are busy and confused themselves, and organized religion plays a smaller part in many people's lives," declares Rabbi Neil Kurshan. "There's been an erosion among the traditional suppliers of values. There's a vacuum, and so for many young people, television and their peers play a greater role."[10]

Successful sitcoms warmed to this role, asserts Father Andrew Greeley, once it was understood "that implicit ethics and religion in a matrix of humor are highly commercial in a country where meaning and belonging are as important as they have ever been and where those institutions charged with meaning and belonging—churches and schools—are failing to deliver sufficient amounts of either. So ministers of religion condemn television; and television does the work they are not doing."[11] Less positively and more mythologically, English professor Harold Schechter proposes a classicist theory for why so much values instruction has 'descended' to the electronic realm: "In a secular age such as ours, spiritual values must disguise themselves to survive. When the established forms of religion cease to function in any meaningful way in a culture, the gods are driven underground and take up residence in despised and subterranean regions."[12]

As Greeley and Schechter have suggested, clerics and teachers often seem more concerned with castigating the electronic media's values carriage than with reasserting their own responsibility for values integration. Or, by refusing to discuss media impact with their classes and congregations, they feel such impact somehow will diminish.

It won't, of course! So as a media professional, you will unavoidably function as a cultural and social interpreter. Therefore, you must become fully aware of the 'forces and values' to which your industry and your audiences are subject.

Even though merely a by-product of their primarily commercial intent, the electronic media's implicit values presentations can have a number of positive outcomes. Henry Perkinson cites one such outcome in this upbeat retrospective:

I do not say that people became more moral in the 1960s and 1970s, but only that at this time they began to view the existing social arrangements from a moral point of view. Television created this new moral sensitivity. It did this because television, like all media, encodes the culture and thereby distances it from people, which allows them to criticize it. But unlike print, television is a participatory medium; . . . it educes an affective response from viewers. People like or dislike what the medium presents. . . . The social relationships presented on their television screens distressed many people. Women, blacks, the young, the old, the homosexuals—all saw themselves depicted in relationships that were unfair, discriminatory, unjust.[13]

By becoming a presence in virtually every early 1960s U.S. household, television thus was positioned to function as an unprecedented vehicle for collective consciousness-raising.

Even (or especially) when an audio or video portrayal disturbs an audience member's implicit value system, that person is thereby afforded the opportunity to clarify or solidify his or her internalized sense of priority. As John Fisk once pointed out in referencing a long-running prime-time soap opera,

The extent by which *Dallas* exceeds the moral and economic norms of its viewers may just as well put those norms under question as reinforce them; indeed, it may do both simultaneously. The desire for material wealth may be stimulated at the same time as the realization that it will not bring the happiness or satisfaction it promises. The norms of family morality may be upheld as the pleasure and necessity of breaking them is experienced.[14]

In a more calculated way, advertisers are finding that projecting rather than obscuring a values position may not only be accepted but also appreciated by target consumers. Advertising executive Robert Black submits that

people want to feel good about people. They need to feel they can trust who they do business with. There are a lot of choices today on who you can buy products and services from. If a company has a point of view, a value system, it's a link to the audience. It makes people like you. It makes them feel you respect them. It provides them with an emotional reason to believe what you're saying. And pragmatically, it sells.[15]

Thus, from the very beginning, GM's Saturn Division promoted its economy car as the creation of a caring group of hometown folks for whom the vehicle was an expression of personal pride and craftsmanship. Saturn purchasers were encouraged to share this pride and feeling of community through trips to the Tennessee plant, company-promoted Saturn-owner picnics, and "just-drop-in-for-a-donut" visits to dealer service departments. By buying a Saturn, a person was affiliating himself or herself, not just with personal transportation, but with Main Street friendliness and neighborly trust as well.

Due to their faceless and monopolistic image, utility companies long have contended with the perception that they are callous and dictatorial. In an effort to combat this image, the GTE corporate commercial in Figure 11-1 redefines the concept of "power." Instead of domination, GTE "power" is positioned as a tool for illumination, brightening and nurturing the "warm glow" of home and family values that the company appears firmly to embrace.

Sponsors, like all corporate organizations, are interesting values laboratories in and of themselves because they reflect their society's broad cultural norms while also creating their own internal standards. Sometimes, these two values systems may conflict, putting corporate employees in a quandary. This happens in *media* companies just as it does in any bureaucratic environment, of course. Little wonder, then, that program creators frequently use such values clashes as an important plot device.

In their study of *Organizational Life on Television*, Leah Vande Berg and Nick Trujillo isolated six value pairings that are often portrayed in fictional programming's corporate settings. Through exposure to these value depictions and collisions, viewers are given multiple opportunities to reflect on their own standards as well as on those of the employer for whom they or a member of their family work. In brief, Vande Berg and Trujillo's six value pairings are as follows:

1. *Work/play.* Both hard work and leisure pursuits are now glorified as important to productivity.

2. *Success/failure.* This pairing is explored in human as well as economic terms—with sometimes diametrically opposed results. (Corporate success causes human failure or vice versa.)

3. *Individualism/community.* Many character conflicts surface between people who value solitary working and decision-making and those who prize their ability to function as "members of the team."

4. *Reason/emotion.* Organizations revere rationality—but many business triumphs are sparked by an intuitive, emotional element.

5. *Youth/experience.* Eagerness and idealism are often tempered or even sabotaged by the elder voices of maturity or cynicism.

6. *Conformity/deviance.* There is always the choice between compliance and rule-break-

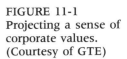

FIGURE 11-1
Projecting a sense of
corporate values.
(Courtesy of GTE)

ANNCR: Light. It is magical, powerful, essential.

AT GTE we place that power at the touch of your hand.

The power to open any darkness, to illuminate the facts of science,

brighten the arenas of sports and business,

create the warm glow that means home.

At GTE, we give you power of light in 6,000 ways,

none of them small.

At GTE, the power is on.

ing; a choice that is muddied when the organization's rules (official policy) and norms (actual practices) conflict.[16]

Television's more or less constant probing of these dichotomies (in news as well as fictional contexts) lets viewer-employees and employers wrestle with core values issues in the nonthreatening arena of 'someone else's shop.' Along the way, it is just possible that values confusions in the viewers' own organizations may be mitigated and their corporate environments thereby improved.

All enterprises benefit from such values clarification. As researchers Thomas Peters and Robert Waterman discovered, "Every excellent company we studied is clear on what it stands for and takes the process of value shaping seriously. In fact, we wonder whether it is possible to be an excellent company without clarity on values and without having the right sort of values."[17] Of course, if the consulted media programs project negative or counterproductive values portraits, they will be of little help in this pursuit.

Another possible drawback to the electronic media's involuntary assignment as corporate or personal values arbiter flows from the fact that these media have become much more fragmented. It is not just that cable, DBS, and the Internet offer new alternatives to broadcast television—but that each of these newer media is itself splintered into dozens (in the case of cable) or even millions (in the case of the Internet) of competing program services and sites. As a consequence, the fractured electronic landscape now tends to accentuate potentially disruptive values *differences* rather than to promote broad and tolerant consensus. Advertising commentator Debra Goldman poses the problem this way:

In case you haven't heard, the networks' monopoly on viewer attention is dead. As *Washington Post* critic Tom Shales observed in a recent obituary for the Big Three, "For 40 years we were one nation, indivisible, under television. That's what's ending. Television is turning into something else, and so are we. We're different. We're splintered. We're not as much of a 'we' as the 'we' we were. We're divisible."

That's the other side of the melting pot meltdown. . . . If, in the schools, the American consensus is now contested by battling ethnic tribes, the consumer consensus has broken into the agendas of life-style tribes, each with its own totems and taboos.[18]

Thus, it is not only that our marketing messages (and their implicit value pronouncements) are now separately directed to dozens of discrete consumer cells. The media themselves are more and more segmented along a variety of socioeconomic lines and values affinities. The "traditional" values orientation of rural and older-skewing CBS is more conservative than that of Fox—which is more conservative than that of Comedy Central—which is more conservative than that of HBO—which is more conservative than that of the Playboy Channel. According to the World Future Society's Howard Didsbury, the explosion of electronic choice, which he labels *telepower*, "may further accelerate the ideological and value fragmentation of American society. The vast increase in cable channels and other means of communication may mean a rapidly increasing loss of shared assumptions, values, and attitudes throughout the nation."[19]

This vast array of choice is not universally available, however, because Didsbury's "telepower" is unevenly distributed. The old days of everyone with a receiving set having access to democratically identical programming are gone forever. That *was broad*casting. But broadcasting is now subject to ever-increasing *narrow*cast competition from

newer technologies that are much more adept at segregating people based on ability to pay and value-distinct life-style. As marketing executive Peter Eder admits,

Unfortunately, the same options aren't available to everyone, and the gap between the media-recipient "have-nots" is widening. Several factors can create dramatically different levels of access to or assimilation of information: the degree of computer access, income and educational levels, geographic location, and ethnic and language barriers. These variations can lead to serious distortions of information, knowledge, and power, and they can ultimately affect our degree of control over our own lives.[20]

If we cannot fully control our own lives, then it follows that we cannot fully shape or exercise our own values system. "Values must be *freely chosen* to be valued by an individual," writes counseling professor Donald Bertsch.[21] But when full access to the values-potent electronic media is more a function of status than a universal experience, exposure to the total range of values choices becomes a luxury for the knowledge-rich and an illusion for the knowledge-poor.

MEDIA ACCESS AND FREEDOM OF EXPRESSION

Actually, this concept of *media access* is comprised of two separate components: (1) a person's right, as we have just mentioned, to receive a full range of media services; and (2) the right of an individual to place *personal messages* on those services so that he or she can freely communicate with others.

The 1934 Communications Act's guarantee of equal-time rights for political candidates is one example of two-pronged access legislation. It attempts (1) to assure public access to the full range of political opinion by (2) ensuring individual media access to the people running for public office. This guarantee was further strengthened in 1971 by the Federal Election Campaign Act that *required* broadcasters to provide "reasonable access" to candidates for federal office. Thus, the responsibility to feature a full spectrum of political expression could no longer be avoided simply by a uniform refusal to carry all candidate-supplied material. The implication, of course, is that broadcasters' own freedom of expression must be curtailed somewhat by compelling them to air the messages of this special class of citizens.

Because other provisions of the Communications Act forbid broadcasters from censoring what a legally qualified candidate chooses to say over the airwaves, politicians (particularly those running for national office) enjoy a unique access privilege.

Soon after the passage of the "reasonable access" legislation, the vast dimensions of this privilege were demonstrated by J. B. Stoner. An avowed white supremacist, Mr. Stoner was a candidate for a U.S. Senate seat in the 1972 Georgia Democratic primary. He purchased time on several radio and television stations for the following spot that no station wanted to air but that none, under pain of license revocation, could reject:

I am J. B. Stoner. I am the only candidate for United States Senator who is for the white people. I am the only candidate who is against integration. All other candidates are race mixers to one degree or another. I say we must repeal [Georgia Senator] Gambrell's civil rights law. Gambrell's law takes jobs away from us whites and gives these jobs to the niggers. The main reason why niggers want integration is because the niggers want our white women. I am for law and order with the knowledge that you cannot have law and order and niggers too. Vote white. This time vote your convictions by voting white racist J. B. Stoner into the run-off election for United States Senator. I thank you.[22]

That Stoner did not win the election goes without saying. But that seven radio and television outlets in Georgia and another in neighboring Tennessee were forced to transmit this message over their own objections and those of the National Association for the Advancement of Colored People, the Anti-Defamation League, and the mayor of Atlanta shows just how complex the ethics of access and free expression can become.

As in most access situations, the Stoner episode involved a balancing of two laudable but often conflicting values structures: libertarianism and social responsibility.

Libertarianism accords preeminence to the rights of the individual. Nineteenth-century Scottish philosopher John Stuart Mill demonstrated the full flowering of this orientation when he wrote in Chapter 2 of his treatise *On Liberty*:

If all mankind minus one, were of one opinion, and only one person were of the contrary opinion, mankind would be no more justified in silencing that one person, than he, if he had the power, would be justified in silencing mankind.[23]

In the United States, such unequivocal libertarianism would later be moderated by comments such as that by Justice Oliver Wendell Holmes, who argued that freedom of speech does not extend to the right to yell "fire" in a crowded theater when there is no fire. Still, there remains immense respect for an unrestricted right of expression as articulated in the First Amendment—and as demonstrated in the Stoner situation.

Social responsibility takes the sometimes contrary position that libertarian actions cannot be condoned without regard for the social good. As in the Holmes example above, the safety of that 'society' of theater-goers is of greater value than the individual prankster's right to free speech. Society, this theory argues, must be protected from patently destructive expression.

Electronic media professionals are often whipsawed between these two philosophies and the laws and regulations that are grounded in each. The Stoner episode clearly demonstrates that in the case of political candidates, libertarianism is accorded a higher valuation than is social responsibility. Conversely, when Congress passed a 1970 law banning cigarette advertising from the airwaves, that action constituted the triumph of social responsibility over libertarianism. A product, it was argued, that was "hazardous to (the public's) health" should not be promoted over the public spectrum. This virtually unprecedented U.S. example of prior restraint was justified on the basis of empirical medical data rather than normative ethical belief. (A San Francisco peace group subsequently tried to have military recruitment commercials banned because military service could also be "hazardous to your health," but this attempt was not successful.)

Much more recently, FCC Commissioner James Quello asserted that a social responsibility approach should take precedence over libertarianism in the case of both electronic indecency (which is not illegal *per se*) and obscenity (which is a criminal offense). In a 1992 speech to the Morality in Media convention, Quello declared:

The sex trash, vileness and excessive violence flooding TV and radio today could, in egregious cases, be considered a violation of the public trust. . . . The FCC has broad discretionary power to regulate broadcasting in the public interest. I believe we have an obligation to encourage constructive social values and to maintain reasonable decency on the airwaves.[24]

Yet, the various efforts by Congress and the FCC to fashion Constitutionally permissible indecency restrictions unavoidably imperil the entire libertarian tradition. As communications attorney Erwin Krasnow has argued,

most liberals and conservatives believe in some degree of regulation for radio and television programs. . . . The activists on the left and the right both want content control, they simply want it in different places. The philosophical schizophrenia at the FCC is a slice of a larger war over who wields the censor's knife. . . . Those who advocate the "indecency decision" and who would expand it to cover "dirty ads" for sugar products or "balanced" comments on controversial issues ignore other values: the cultural values in having unregulated media of expression, the political values in having a free broadcast press, the societal values in keeping the lines of communication free of government coercion. Until the courts step in and declare that broadcasting has the *same* First Amendment rights as all other media, both liberals and conservatives will carve away at content, in ways they could never do with books, movies—or the magazine in which I write.[25]

The First Amendment prohibits "abridging the freedom of speech, or of the press." It mentions nothing about radio and television. Because the First Amendment was crafted in pre-electronic 1789, and because the media that were born more than a century later use the "public" airwaves, broadcasting is thus subject to greater limitations, and broadcast professionals must deal with more pervasive values conflicts.

With the advent of new technologies, different shadings of these same issues are coming to the fore. Questions of what telephone companies may or may not do in delivering video and broadband content—and closing their lines to competitors—raise the spectre of antilibertarian prior restraint. Attempts at regulating Internet expression or reception (particularly in the case of children) trigger international values conflicts.

The V-chip's selective blocking of the more 'adult' television content is seen as a parental aide by some people and as a parental abdication by others. "The V-chip is saying you don't have to take responsibility for your choices any more," charges veteran television executive John von Soosten. "Let someone else do it for you."[26]

Meanwhile, the continuation of a variety of other content restrictions that apply to broadcasters but not to cable or DBS operators are as much an abridgement of broadcasters' rights as are the longstanding discrepancies between what newspapers and stations are allowed to carry. (A newspaper, for example, requires no license, need give no access to a political candidate, may sell or donate space to one candidate and ignore another, and can carry as many cigarette advertisements as it chooses.) This inequality has not gone unchallenged by some policy makers. "We have deemed broadcasters uniquely unworthy of complete First Amendment protection, allowing greater intrusion on broadcast content," charges FCC Commissioner Michael Powell. "Yet, equally powerful communications media such as newspapers and magazines, cable television, satellite television and the Internet all enjoy the full shield of the First Amendment. . . . It is simply intellectually dishonest to say that the First Amendment changes as you surf through the channels of your modern television set."[27]

In these and many other regulatory areas, the question of reach raises as many values issues as does the question of content. "At issue is not so much what we will be allowed to say," suggests Media Institute President Patrick Maines, "but how and where we will be allowed to say it."[28] "There's so much technology around the globe that being able to start your own printing press will not be enough in the twenty-first century," observes Black Entertainment Television Chairman Robert Johnson. "So I see a danger in losing your First Amendment right because you simply become the tree that falls in the woods that nobody's there to hear. You can't get on a satellite, you control no radio or television, you control no cable, and your voice is effectively not heard. And therefore your First Amendment rights, if not eliminated, are certainly eroded."[29]

To explore the values complexities that the access issue raises, examine the PSA in Figure 11-2. Some health advocates asked

SFX: (Dance music)
V/O: When it came to sex, Cindy was
the life of the party.

She went from one partner...

to another,

until one day she met a partner who'd
stay with her for the rest of her life.

AIDS. Don't experiment with sex. If
you do, at least use a condom.

Or being the life of the party could be
the death of you.

Confidential help and information
1·800·872·AIDS
MICHIGAN DEPARTMENT OF PUBLIC HEALTH
AIDS PREVENTION PROGRAM

AIDS. What you don't know can
hurt you.

that every television station air it frequently throughout the program day. Some viewers objected to the spot running at times when children were likely to be in the audience. Other viewers wanted it banned from the airwaves entirely. What are the conflicting values here? What libertarian and social responsibility issues are involved? If you were a station program director, what would you do with this PSA—and why?

Former CBS/Broadcast Group President Richard Jencks once tried to draw a defensi-

FIGURE 11-2
(Courtesy of Marcie
Brogan, Brogan &
Partners)

ble access position for media outlets when he declared "The concept of free speech means that everyone has a right to speak to whatever audience he can command. It does not, however, mean that he has a right to an audience."[30] Legally dictated access, in Jencks's view, is unjust. It tries to stretch an individual's right of expression into entitlement to a whole audience, an audience that would not even exist without its assemblage by the station, system, or website.

On the other hand, Howard Symons, then chief counsel of the House telecommunications subcommittee, wrote that the need for broad public access to the electronic media was essential if the country is to maintain a socially responsible and unmonopolized exchange of views. To Symons's way of thinking:

Ultimately, citizen access validates the notion of the marketplace of ideas. We do not tolerate economic concentration in the commercial marketplace, and Congress has passed laws to prevent it. By the same token, competition in the marketplace of ideas requires many spokespersons putting forward many opinions. Concentrated control of the outlets for expression discourages competition. A citizen (or a citizen group) must have the freedom to present his views in whatever forum he chooses.[31]

Thus, with Jencks and Symons, we again find reasonable, ethical authorities staking out reasonable, ethical positions that, from a practical standpoint, would result in contradictory procedures. To some media professionals, the only answer is to throw up their hands and do whatever their corporate lawyers tell them to do. However, as Professor Edwin Diamond points out,

First Amendment issues can't be settled solely by the tortsmen. For all of us in the television audience, the way these issues are settled will go a long way toward determining the kind of TV [and other electronic media] we have in this country, from the presentation of news and public affairs to the content of popular entertainment shows. Broadcasting law may well be too important to be left to the lawyers alone.[32]

As electronic media are expected more and more to assume the social responsibility tasks that used to be the province of schools and churches, the media's own libertarian privileges may be neglected. Libertarian ideals, at least as far as the media themselves are concerned, may be viewed as expendable by a citizenry increasingly preoccupied more with society's problems than with a station's or system's free expression rights. As former NBC correspondent Bill Monroe lamented,

Why in the 1990s do we still have laws abridging the freedom of the electronic press? Why does nobody give a damn about it? What difference does it make?

Only part of the answer goes back to the early history. A more important factor today is current public opinion. The First Amendment was written in the fading glow of revolutionary campfires. King George III was a living memory. Most Americans today have no memory of being oppressed by their own government.[33]

In the absence of such a memory, the public may be quite willing to allow government to inhibit free electronic expression in order to pursue some presumably greater social good. In 1974, for example, a well-meaning FCC chairman was prodded by Congress to "sanitize" evening television so that it could be more appropriate for children. In response, he persuaded the networks and other key broadcasters to adopt a so-called Family Viewing plan. Basically, the scheme set aside 7 to 9 P.M. as a time in which aired television programming would be of a type suitable to be watched by all members of the family unit.

The plan was killed, however, when a federal court upheld the assertion by producers whose shows subsequently had been moved or canceled that Family Viewing constituted illegal coercion by the FCC and abridgement of producers' First Amendment rights. This was not a question of network prime-time content being obscene or even indecent. Rather, it was a case of an industry accommodating its regulator, which was itself under pressure from a Congress besieged by citizen interest groups who wanted television content further 'cleaned up.' When the particular value structure of the special interests was allowed to permeate the political process, a libertarian defense had to be mounted that seemed to pit the First Amendment against the cause of child welfare.

The Family Viewing episode was not the last example of such values dilemmas. In 1988, spurred on by Harvard's Center for Health Communications, the three major networks, the Writers Guild of America West, and thirteen major studios joined forces to promote the "designated driver" concept. Specifically, the studios agreed "to ask their writers and producers to add dialogue to their shows in the upcoming season conveying a new social norm: the driver doesn't drink," applauded Jay Winsten, the Harvard Center's director. As he further explained,

Our intention is to add tremendous momentum to changes already under way in society. Hollywood is in a powerful position to reinforce these emerging trends by writing occasional script lines that model a new form of social behavior. The shift from previous practice can be in a line or two of dialogue as a person arrives at a party and says: "No thanks, I'm driving," or as several young people decide to share a taxi. The impact will be gradual and ultimately far-reaching.[34]

While no one can argue with the social responsibility of encouraging sober people to chauffeur their inebriated friends, there is the underlying concern that such behind-the-scenes collusion by scriptwriters constitutes unethical persuasion. No matter how laudable the goal, should programming be *secretly* coordinated to further a particular social policy? Is traffic safety to be valued over content honesty? And how have writers' free expression rights been compromised in the process? Producer and former NBC program head Grant Tinker scoffed at such worries:

There are people who have a problem with the project, people who cite artistic integrity; well, I have a problem with those people. They can talk about artistic integrity all they want, but people are getting killed, and if this can save lives then I don't mind giving up some of that integrity.

Is Tinker right? Is this project another case in which social responsibility should take precedence over unbridled libertarianism? Or, should program creators be freed from any compulsion to engage in specific social advocacy, no matter how meritorious the cause?

A much more recent and even more troubling example of behind-the-scenes 'social engineering' came to light in early 2000, when it was revealed that the federal government used financial incentives to get television networks to work antidrug messages into some popular prime-time shows, such as

ER, Chicago Hope, The Drew Carey Show, and *Beverly Hills 90210*. By persuading producers to inject material into their scripts that discouraged the use of illegal substances, the networks were absolved by the federal government from having to air as many antidrug PSAs. Networks formerly had agreed to run these PSAs in exchange for the government's placement of *paid* antidrug commercials on their broadcasts. By submitting advance scripts or tapes to the White House Office of National Drug Control Policy, the networks received 'credits' that lessened their PSA requirements. If the content was not originally eligible for a "credit," the drug office could make suggestions for script changes that would be considered worthy of PSA equivalency.

The networks and producers involved claimed the script changes were very minor and did not compromise the artistic integrity of the episodes involved. But if creators believe such subtle and brief allusion has enough impact on the audience that it can substitute for self-standing, 30-second PSAs, isn't it their social responsibility to take much greater care in choosing the images actually *featured* in their program? As film critic Michael Medved argues:

Industry leaders take great pride, for example, in their positive plugs for condom use, or saving the rain forests, which they insert (often incongruously) into television shows, movies, and popular songs.

Such efforts highlight the schizophrenic attitude of show business professionals toward the larger significance of what they do. On the one hand, they believe they can influence the audience on behalf of worthy causes such as safe sex and recycling; on the other hand, they continue to insist that the violence, hedonism and selfishness so often featured in their work will have no real-world consequences whatever.[36]

Ethical quandaries such as these constantly challenge media professionals and compel us to engage in continuous values reassessment.

PREDOMINANT VALUES SYSTEMS

Given the multiplicity of complementary, overlapping, and competing values systems present in our society, it is impossible for a media outlet—or even a single program—to mirror exactly any one person's values hierarchy. In fact, due to the group effort required to create and administer the simplest media creation, program producers themselves are largely unable to sculpt shows to their own preferences—even on rare occasions when they seek to do so. The "designated driver" campaign involved only a few seconds of the running time of its participating programs—and was anything but the central focus of their storylines.

Despite the many and diverse symbolic threads interwoven into a program, its overall pattern will tend to be tailored the same way as the rest of a society's common values wardrobe. As major and publicly licensed or franchised operations, broadcasting and cable especially cannot afford to dress in extremist program garb for fear of losing advertiser, institutional, or consumer approval. Consequently, radio/television, which Fiske and Hartley refer to as the *bardic mediator*,

tends to articulate the negotiated central concerns of its culture, with only limited and often over-mediated references to ideologies, beliefs, habits or thought and definitions of the situation which obtain in groups which are for one reason or another peripheral. Since one of the characteristics of western culture is that the societies concerned are class-divided, television responds with a predominance of messages which propagate and re-present the dominant class ideology.[37]

This is as true for news programming as it is for entertainment. In their study of news organizations, for example, researchers Ognianova and Endersby found that "mass media organizations, and in particular television news organizations represented by anchors, are positioned in the middle of the ideological spectrum of their audience. The placement where the median news consumer stands is interpretable . . . as an attempt to attract larger audiences."[38]

It is impossible within the confines of this discussion to explore the totality of values from which this predominant ideology is constructed. But we can, as primary examples, explore two somewhat parallel belief structures deeply embedded in the U.S. attitude and, therefore, embedded also in the bulk of electronic media programming. Both largely economic in impact, the *Protestant ethic* and *social Darwinism* were values orientations that vibrated in consonance with the aspirations and needs of the New World's immigrants. It is natural, then, that the new communications media that grew up in this world automatically (if often inadvertently) came to project the tenets of these two philosophies.

The Protestant Ethic

As identified by German sociologist Max Weber in *The Protestant Ethic and the Spirit of Capitalism*, this Pilgrim-imported belief consists of a three-pronged commitment to hard work, frugality, and self-denial.

Through *hard work*, a person developed character and aided God in the attainment of His plan for the universe. "The Church's constant attempt to curb the 'pleasures' of the flesh," recalls John Fiske, "was eagerly taken up by capitalism and transformed into the Protestant work ethic with its acceptance of only that pleasure which had been 'earned' and which was used responsibly (i.e., to prepare the worker for more work)."[39]

Through *frugality*, the fruits of hard work were conserved in order to achieve prosperity. This prosperity consisted of much more than the material wealth that signified it, however. It was also a sign from God as to whether the afterlife would be spent in a heavenly or overheated environment. People who prospered in this world were predestined to succeed in the next. Thus, the associated theory of *predestination* constituted a vital motivator in this entire ethical construct.

Many of today's game shows subtly echo this predestination belief. Mary Rose Williams and Enrique Rigsby observe that "Prizes are not cheap, moderate, or conservative; rather they are grandiose, luxurious and extravagant. The prizes represent the good life—the life that clearly identifies a person who has achieved a level of high status and wealth."[40] Those who win the game (and vicariously, the viewers who cheer them on) thus exude the hallmark of "having it made."

Frugality (and the predestination it strives to radiate) is positive—what people must do to sustain their success. On the other hand, *self-denial*, the Protestant ethic's third element, is negative and stresses what one must *not* do. Through self-denial, one avoids squandering attained resources on unproductive (formerly 'sinful') pursuits.

Wasteful practices undermine not only prosperity but also the image of earthly and afterlife success that such prosperity cultivates. When game show contestants lose assured treasures by gambling on additional cash or prizes, there is the subtle feeling that they have been punished for their greed.

Notice how the Protestant ethic was perfectly attuned to the development of Europe's post-Reformation middle class. What better philosophy than this for a group that lacked the upper-class birthright of the nobility and their co-ruling Roman Catholic or Anglican church hierarchies? Not having been born to wealth or privilege, the aspiring tradesmen, craftsmen, and merchants had to rely on their own hard work and financial acumen to accumulate the capital that was replacing inherited land as the basis of power. Instead of putting their faith in a fixed and exclusive elite, in which counts and cardinals shared the same family names, these middle-class followers of Martin Luther and John Calvin identified much more comfortably with an ideology that prized and identified individual merit rather than royal prerogative.

Especially when transplanted to the New World, the Protestant ethic soon lost its exclusively Protestant character. In this land, virtually everyone had the chance—in fact, the necessity—to start afresh in building a new society. The persecuted Catholics who settled in Lord Baltimore's Maryland, for example, mirrored the tenets of the now secularized Protestant ethic with as much zeal as had the Pilgrims of Plymouth; and so the vital American middle-class took root.

Maccoby and Terzi have asserted that what began as a religious force has subsequently progressed through four stages, with each stage stressing somewhat different values shadings:

(1) the "Protestant" phase that emphasizes self-discipline and rugged individualism;

(2) the "craft" stage stressing moderation and humility (and thus bolstering the elements of frugality and self-denial);

(3) the "entrepreneurial" stage focusing on risk-taking and opportunism; and

(4) the "career" stage that prizes specialization and professionalism.[41]

The common core of these stages is individual hard work, of course, which has been the defining value of the middle class since private enterprise's rebirth in post–medieval Europe. A 1997 poll in *USA Weekend*, for instance, found that 79 percent of respondents agreed that "people who work hard in this nation are likely to succeed."[42] Not surprisingly then, the Protestant ethic remains robust in the U.S. media system, which is itself both the creator and creation of private enterprises.

Unfortunately, however, the Protestant ethic also displays an inherently discriminatory character. Its differentiation between seeming negatively and positively predestined individuals leads to programmatic portrayals that can be warped, antisocial, and cruel. Thus, when it comes to the poor, ill, or elderly, charged broadcast critic Robert Lewis Shayon,

the media generally ignore them; but when they are admitted to the mirror-image of national life, they are usually portrayed in negative terms: the poor are lazy; the mentally ill are violent, unpredictable; and the elderly are burdens on the economy. Their conditions, therefore, are also self-inflicted, for if they deserved their proper share of the good life, they would undoubtedly possess it (Calvin, meet television!)[43]

Social Darwinism

Ironically, the exceptional staying power of the Protestant ethic, with both its positive and negative residues, was heightened in the late nineteenth century by the secular philosophy of social Darwinism. Inspired by the research of English naturalist Charles Darwin, who originated the theory of species evolution via natural selection, social Darwinism applied the scientist's ideas about survival of the fittest to the workings of human society. Fundamentally, social Darwinism maintains that advancement in human society (as measured by the accumulation of wealth and power) is the result of conflict and competition among people. Those who win do so because they are biologically and/or behaviorally superior to those who lose. Conversely, the poor and powerless deserve to remain so because of their inherent and demonstrated inferiority.

As with the Protestant ethic, social Darwinism found fertile ground in the rugged individualism of the American frontier and the cut-throat competition of the country's post–Civil War industrial revolution. The naturalistic idea of the strong possessing first right of survival so that the species could prosper was not very different, in effect, from the Protestant ethic's prosperity signified salvation of the industrious elite.

Neither philosophy can be characterized as unequivocally good or evil, of course. Instead, each must be judged on the basis of its impact within a given human situation. Literary critic Carl Grabo, for instance, laments that "survival of the fittest means not the survival of the fittest individual or species by any scale of human values but those forms which have found refuge in their very mediocrity and conformity."[44]

From an electronic media standpoint, this is the assertion raised by those who decry the alleged formulary sameness of television programs and radio formats, where the clones of past success are said to devour meritorious innovations. As Professor Gene Youngblood charges,

commercial entertainment works against art, exploits the alienation and boredom of the public, by perpetuating a system of conditioned responses to formulas. Commercial entertainment not only isn't creative, it actually destroys the audience's ability to appreciate and participate in the creative process. . . . Driven by the profit motive, the commercial entertainer dares not risk alienating us by attempting new language even if he were capable of it. He seeks only to gratify pre-conditioned needs for formula stimulus. He offers nothing we haven't already conceived, nothing we don't already expect.[45]

Media producers, on the other hand, would reply that *every* formula started as a potent innovation that succeeded because it skillfully *evolved* and *adapted itself* (key Darwinian concepts) to the needs of a viewing or listening audience.

That the appeal of social Darwinism depends on the orientation of its beholder is also evidenced by the workings of Chairman Mark Fowler's FCC in the early and mid-1980s. From the time they took office, Fowler and his staff repeatedly spoke of the need to remove all unnecessary regulations so that the marketplace, not the government, would determine which electronic services were to prosper. Initially embraced by broadcasters, this Darwinistic philosophy

soon acquired a sour side when it became clear that, by adopting it, the Commission no longer felt its role to be that of ensuring the survival of any station.

By opening up the spectrum to more stations and whole new services, the Fowler FCC closed the book on the protectionist era in which so-called free broadcasting had been shielded from the direct competition of cable and other forms of "pay" transmission. Broadcasting, in both its individual and aggregate forms, had to adapt to the deregulated marketplace or die. The fact that only a short time later the Big Three commercial television networks all were sold or drastically reconfigured was the most obvious aspect of the accelerated evolution the industry underwent as a consequence of this shift in government philosophy. In 1998, a successor FCC chairman, William Kennard, reaffirmed this stance when he reminded the International Radio and Television Society that "we must trust in the marketplace. Of course, trusting in the marketplace means giving businesses the opportunity to fail, too."[46]

Meanwhile, local outlets, entire station groups, cable MSOs (multiple system operators), production studios, telephone companies, and Internet players have been sold or subjected to highest-bidder takeovers that fundamentally rearrange media operational priorities. Survival often has come to mean that debt service now must take precedence over public service as large media conglomerates seek to control their own destiny by owning the means of both over-the-air and on-line production and distribution. Only the most nimble, streamlined, and multifaceted companies are seen as having evolved the capability to adapt and prosper in today's rapidly changing electronic media landscape.

While all of these Darwinistic forces are at work behind the scenes, social Darwinism, like the Protestant ethic, continues to permeate what goes over the air as well. In terms of media depiction (especially its *What Is Society Like?* question), for instance, William Fore observes that

the social Darwinist theory—that differences between ethnic groups account for their varying rates of material success—is reflected in the TV world. Thus lower-class and non-white characters are especially prone to victimization, are more violent than their middle-class counterparts and pay a high price for violence. . . . The fittest survive, and in the TV world the fittest are not lower-class, non-white Americans.[47]

Meanwhile, on the game shows, John Fiske detects a Darwinistic linkage between sex and triumph:

We like to think of sexual attractiveness as a natural attribute . . . which enables us to relate it to Darwinian ideas of natural selection and the survival of the fittest which, when transferred to the sphere of economics, play a crucial role in legitimating the basis of a free-enterprise market economy. In the physical or sexual sphere, these ideas enable us to relate notions of sexual attractiveness not only to the survival of the species but to its progressive, evolutionary improvement. . . . This may seem a large responsibility to hand on the shoulders of a half-clad model wrapping herself around a motor scooter that is the reward for knowing Buffalo Bill's real name. But I make no apologies for doing so. There is consistent evidence that our culture links economic success with sexual success.[48]

Whether or not you agree with Fore's and Fiske's specific analyses, social Darwinism in general remains an important underpinning for our industry's programming as well as for its operational practices. Given U.S. economic, political, and sociological history, it would be very surprising if this were not the case.

Detecting a Program's Values Systems

By probing for elements of the Protestant ethic, social Darwinism, or any other belief structure, we not only learn to discern these value systems' pervasiveness, but we also acquire the critical skills necessary to illuminate programming's values assumptions. As we have discussed, media producers seldom set out to teach a values system; rather, they reflect the values of their own upbringing and environment. Nevertheless, as media professionals, it is essential that we understand, and are comfortable with, the values statements that our creations inevitably express.

Individuals within or outside our industry who naively argue that values conveyance should not be an aspect of electronic media programming are seeking the impossible. As DeWitt Parker long ago pointed out in reference to all artistic narrative,

We cannot demand of the writer that he have no moral purpose or that be leave morality out of his story. For, since the artist is also a man, he cannot rid himself of an ethical interest in human problems or with good conscience fail to use his art to help toward their solution. His observations of moral experience will inevitably result in beliefs about it, and these will reveal themselves in his work. Yet we should demand that his view of what life ought to be shall not falsify his representation of life as it is. Just as soon as the moral of the tale obtrudes, we begin to suspect that the tale is false.[49]

Shows that sugarcoat reality thus are no more appropriate as artistic enterprises than are shows that try to bludgeon the audience with a producer's own moral code.

As one example of the deciphering of a program's values structure, read the following student critique of *Love and War*. This sitcom revolved around newspaper columnist Jack Stein and a group of compatriots who operated or hung out at a small Manhattan bistro. The analyzed episode centered on the closing of a landmark emporium.

For another view of the Protestant ethic and social Darwinism in programmatic action, consult the "Theo's Holiday" episode of *The Cosby Show* in Appendix A. Here, the Darwinistic world is not pictured as an evil jungle, but neither is it viewed as unequivocally benevolent. With the help of his parents, older sister Denise, and younger sisters Vanessa and Rudy, fifteen-year-old Theo learns that (as father Cliff says): "Once you're out in the real world . . . you have to make it on your own." "I can't feed my family on a promise," Cliff later declares; and Theo, by the end of the show, has found that the real world is "a lot tougher than I thought. But you know what? So am I." Theo, due to the caring and prudent nurturing of his parents, will be a survivor, even if he still has a lot of adapting to do.

The Protestant ethic's deferred gratifications also underpin this *Cosby* script. Going to college to lay "a foundation for the rest of your life" is contrasted with the short-term lure of "five hundred dollars a day." A variety of hard-working occupational roles are acted out, as is the frugal reality that you can't squander "this much [money] on one meal.

LOVE AND WAR:
"THE DEPARTMENT STORE"

by Janel Atwood

America was founded on the ingrained pilgrim principles of hard work, frugality and self-denial. Social Darwinism has been fostered by our capitalist economy with its belief that strong people and businesses evolve and those that are the fittest will survive. Since these two theories are so elemental in American society, it's important to analyze their impact on media content. The situation comedy Love and War contains many affirming and rejecting examples of the Protestant ethic and social Darwinism.

The Protestant ethic of hard work is almost totally unrewarded in this sitcom. The character Jack works very hard on a commentary that criticizes the newspaper he works for because they will start putting ads on the front page. For his efforts, he is disciplined via reassignment to the hated fashion beat. As he labors on his story for the fashion beat, the closing of Berger's Department Store, we see more examples of how hard work is not rewarded. The sales clerks obviously work hard to persuade customers to buy products, but they don't seem to enjoy their work and the viewer notices no tangible rewards for their efforts. Perhaps the best example of the failure of hard work is exhibited by Gus the elevator operator. As he says, "I'm 78 years old and I drive an elevator. What the hell am I going to do now?" The impression given the viewer is that he has dedicated his life to Berger's Department Store that is now closing and leaving him with nothing. The only case in which hard work is rewarded is in the satisfaction Jack feels with the piece he writes about the demise of Berger's. But even this is an intangible gratification and doesn't seem fundamentally to reinforce the importance of hard work.

On the other hand, the episode promotes frugality as a good quality to possess. Jack and his friends only go shopping when everything's on sale. They are rewarded with a blue blazer, batteries, comfy underwear and an afternoon of friendship. We see other characters eagerly pawing through the sales racks as well, searching for a bargain. Everyone ends the day with nice clothes for less money, reinforcing the importance of frugality.

The third lesson we learn is that those who don't practice self-denial will suffer for it. Jack did not deny himself the opportunity to harshly judge his employers in their own newspaper. Therefore, his employers denied him his column and assigned him to a fashion beat they knew he would despise. Likewise, Nadine (the self-absorbed waitress) was very self-indulgent twenty years ago when she stole a lipstick. The first time she set foot in the store since the incident, the security guard embarrassed her in front of all the shoppers in the women's department. Obviously, self-denial is a face-saving virtue for everyone to possess.

Finally, we come to social Darwinism. The entire show revolves around the human side to the theory that good businesses will succeed and bad ones fail. That's just the way it is. We see sales clerks, a security guard, and an elevator operator who are trampled under the evolutionary progress of the Gap. The show makes us feel sympathetic toward the people at Berger's and hatred for the soul-less, characterless mall with the Gap as the symbol of the new business that cares nothing for customer-tailored services or distinctiveness. In a purely economic sense, the social Darwinism theory is reinforced. After all, Berger's is closing and the Gap is thriving. However, the show leaves the audience with the sense that this is not right. Also, Jack's outspoken editorial that touches off the whole episode is about his newspaper putting advertising on the front page. Yes, the newspaper will survive, via this concession to commercialism. But it will lose part of its journalistic soul. This episode of <u>Love and War</u> shows that social Darwinism is a negative force that leaves people and ethics behind in the endless rush for ever-increasing profit.

In summary, we learn from <u>Love and War</u> that hard work largely goes unrewarded while frugality and self-denial remain valuable personal attributes. At the same time, social Darwinism continues to be a powerful, if regretable, force.

(Courtesy of Janel Atwood)

. . . I am on a budget." When self-denial breaks down, one ends up with a stereo and no electricity to power it. Industriousness and frugality, on the other hand, beget a good credit rating and financial "approval" so that, as mother Clair puts it in her role-playing, "we can start planning for our future."

Though perhaps not as pervasive as the Protestant ethic and social Darwinism, many additional values and value structures also interlace the content that electronic media practitioners create, promote, and transmit. As professionals, we must be sensitive to the values implications of our messages and aware of our obligation to illuminate them honestly and in a straightforward manner. Audiences thereby can more easily compare a given program's content with their own value systems and decide whether it is appropriate for themselves and/or their children.

If we are candid in our values portrayals, no critic should have cause for complaint. Instead, "all that the critic has a right to demand of the artist," maintains Theodore Meyer Greene, "is that he exhibit in his art a genuine breadth of outlook and, simultaneously, a genuine depth of understanding which will reveal specific characteristics and values which had previously passed unnoticed."[50] Applying Greene's precept directly to the electronic media, former CBS Broadcast Group President Howard Stringer adds, "If you argue we have no moral responsibility to sustain values, then perhaps we have an artistic responsibility. Death stings, pain hurts, loss devastates, fear terrifies. And if we still insist that television merely mirrors reality, then let us reflect our reality more skillfully and honestly."[51]

This artistic responsibility to which Stringer refers constitutes the intersection of ethics and art. For, as art critic George Boas points out, "If the world were agreed on the most desirable system of ethics, there would be no disagreement upon the most desirable works of art."[52] Because there is no such agreement, however, media professionals must anticipate that all program decisions are a source of potential controversy. But if we are aware of the values issues involved at the outset, then we can better appraise whether a given piece of media content is worth the risks it entails. The worst thing that can happen is that a major battle ensues over a show that is so poorly conceived that it is not worth fighting for in the first place.

THE MEDIA PROFESSIONAL'S MORAL DUTIES

In evaluating the 'rightness' of an on- or off-air action, the true electronic media professional must consider several factors and classes of people. "Ethical dilemmas do not occur in a vacuum," points out philosophy professor Christopher Meyers. "They are always embedded in a context, a context which invariably includes societal, cultural, professional, and organizational factors. And because these factors—which I call the 'structural underpinnings' of ethical decisions—serve to define professional goals, attitudes, and roles, they also serve to generate and shape the profession's dilemmas."[53]

Professor Louis Day crystallizes these dilemmas in terms of the people who will be impacted either by dilemma resolution or by the failure to achieve such resolution. According to Day, we have a set of "moral duties" or loyalties to six different constituencies. "As media practitioners," he asserts, "we must identify those parties that will be most affected by our actions."[54] Day identifies these parties as:

1. Individual conscience
2. Objects of moral judgment

3. Financial supporters
4. The institution
5. Professional colleagues
6. Society[55]

Individual conscience, of course, refers to that most immediate party—ourselves. Of the six constituences, this is the only constant. For, while the other constituencies may fluctuate over the course of our careers and from one decision to the next, our conscience remains the same singular entity. In addition, even though there are a number of often-powerful advocates for the other constituencies, the sole advocate for one's conscience is that conscience itself. Whatever the programmatic or organizational determination that we are called on to make, "we should feel personally comfortable with our decision or at least be able to defend it with some moral principle," Day advises. "Being able to look ourselves in the mirror without wincing from moral embarrassment is a sign of our virtue."[56] Or, as Emmis Broadcasting chief executive Jeff Smulyan puts it, "Never jeopardize your integrity; if we can't win the right way, we'd rather not win."[57]

Objects of moral judgment are the people or groups most likely to be impacted, for better or worse, by the results that flow from our decision. Canceling a popular animated children's program because of the exaggerated claims of the barter advertising that comes with it may, on the one hand, constitute a parentally commendable policy stance. On the other hand, it may infuriate young viewers and drive them to lower quality shows on competing channels. Which scenario is likely to cause the child audience the greater harm?

Financial supporters consist of advertisers, stockholders, subscribers or (in noncommercial broadcasting), donors and underwriters. While money from these interests is essential if the media outlet is to remain in operation, determinations must be made as to how far we will go in pursuit of this money. A case in point is the so-called "value added" news sponsorship. The syndicated recipe feature sponsored by a grocery chain, the gardening series paid for by a local florist, or the colorectal cancer series underwritten by a pharmacy offering cancer test kits are three examples of this phenomenon. As news anchor Jim Mitchell sees it,

none of these stories is evil in itself. . . . The ethical problem is simply this: those stories are on the air because they can be sold, and they will run as scheduled whether the audience wants them or needs them or not. The resulting pressure can be fatal to independent news judgment. Will a producer jeopardize his job by killing the paid feature to make room for a better, breaking story? Will the reporter whose teen-age suicide series is sponsored by a private psychiatric hospital get into the thorny questions of high cost, failure rate, commercial preying on parental fears? Don't bet on it.[58]

By the same token, should requests by advertisers that their spots not run on occasional "adult theme" episodes of a popular prime-time series be ignored simply because the network insists on an every-week-or-nothing commercial schedule? Don't advertisers have the right to negotiate the most favorable (if noncontroversial) spot placements possible?

The institution, Day's fourth affected party, is the station, studio, agency, or network for which we work. Sometimes, there are multiple institutions to satisfy. A program director deciding whether to preempt a sexually provocative network movie-of-the-week must consider her simultaneous responsibilities to her own station, to the station's parent group owner and its relationship with the network, as well as to that network itself. Loyalty to one's employer (however multitiered) and profession is a corporate expectation that is hardly unique to electronic media enterprises. "Don't under-price yourself or your medium," advises Jeff Smulyan, "don't attack the industry, build it up."[59] Nevertheless, Day cautions, "blind loyalty can work to the detriment of the company."[60] The program director who never raises a question about the outmoded promo jingle package that the general manager purchased back in 1994 is an accomplice to the strangulation of the station's image.

Professional colleagues are not only the people with whom we work, but also individuals performing similar tasks in competing organizations. In evaluating our moral duty in this area, Day proposes that "two questions are relevant: How will my actions reflect on my professional peers? Are my actions in keeping with the expectations of my colleagues?"[61] Undercutting your own rate card to ensure that all your "avails" (commercial slots) are filled, for instance, may seriously inhibit you and salespersons at other outlets from obtaining equitable prices in the future. The result is that your entire medium becomes undervalued. Similarly, the perfectionist self-indulgent videographer who is constantly tardy in returning to the station with footage for the 6 o'clock newscast makes show "lock-up" inexcusably frantic for editors, anchors, and news executives. And the news director who pulls a story on dishonest auto financing practices in deference to a major car advertiser makes it that much more difficult for other news executives in the market to resist similar sponsor pressure.

Society, the final, most amorphous, and most all-encompassing party of interest, should be the beneficiary of that "public interest" standard that is so embedded in electronic media regulation. If we pay attention to the needs of our audiences, then moral and economic achievement often follow hand-in-hand. Audience researcher Willis Duff, for example, reveals that "we have found that the station which is perceived to be most involved in contributing to and caring for its community is almost always number one in news ratings or on the way to that position."[62] More broadly, Bonneville International, a highly successful broadcast and media communications firm, lists as a key part of its corporate mission statement: "Serving and improving individuals, communities, and society through providing quality entertainment, information, news, and values-oriented programming."[63]

It is not often easy to satisfy all six of these interested parties within the parameters of a single decision. But in considering all of their legitimate needs and the impact that decision is likely to have on each of them, the media professional is much more likely to make a determination that is both ethically and organizationally sound. In so doing, the positive values of that professional and of his or her organization will be affirmed and reiterated.

To explore how a single decision might involve moral duties to all six of Day's 'affected parties,' examine the well-sculpted commercial in Figure 11-3. Assume you are the sales manager of your town's CBS affiliate charged with making the determination as to whether to accept this legitimate advertisement for running in access time (immediately following your early evening news).

What considerations would have to be made in terms of (1) individual conscience, (2) objects of moral judgment, (3) financial supporters, (4) the institution, (5) professional colleagues, and (6) society? What, ultimately, would *you* decide to do? Would your decision be any different if the time period requested was immediately after a televised Sunday church service for shut-ins? If the spot conclusion pitched a preplanning premium deposit rather than a free booklet?

AN ETHICS AND VALUES POSTSCRIPT

In a variety of ways, this chapter demonstrates (1) the inevitable role of programming in values conveyance, (2) the necessity for media professionals to be sensitive to the particular values statements made by their messages, and (3) the complexity of ethical decision-making in an industry that impacts so many people in so many ways.

"A society's collective consciousness consists of broad values clusters," write Karyn and Donald Rybacki, "which are reflected in images, dreams, and myths. These values exist in a state of tension . . . so the potential for social change always exists."[64] As a prime reflector (and sometime creator) of these images, dreams, and myths, the electronic media play a significant role in value cluster maintenance. Our media can also heighten or lessen the tension arising from cluster clash depending on how we treat the symbols of social stability and cultural change. As mass communication professionals, ignoring the 'ethics and values' implications of anything we do simply is not an option.

ENDNOTES

1. John Frohnmayer, *Out of Tune: Listening to the First Amendment* (Nashville: Freedom Forum First Amendment Center, 1994), 23.
2. Louis Day, *Ethics in Media Communications: Cases and Controversies* (Belmont, CA: Wadsworth, 1991), 2.
3. Eliseo Vivas, *Essays in Criticism and Aesthetics* (New York: The Noonday Press, 1955), 126–127.
4. George Santayana, "The Nature of Beauty," in Melvin Rader (ed.), *A Modern Book of Aesthetics*, 5th ed. (New York: Holt, Rinehart and Winston, 1979), 172.

FIGURE 11-3
(Courtesy of Steven
Hunter, Moss and
Company, Inc.)

(SFX: MUSIC. CROWD SOUNDS.)

HARRIET (VO): Oh Mary, I'm so sorry. John was so loved.

JOE (VO): John took care of everything. He did it with The GUARDIAN PLAN program.

LEWIS (VO): Makes you think. Advance funeral planning makes a lot of sense.

PETER (VO): Yes...I remember John saying something about it.

JOE (VO): He took care of all the details so Mary wouldn't be burdened.

HARRIET (VO): Ummh-huh. The GUARDIAN PLAN program.

LUKE (VO): I have one. Decided on everything in advance...even price.

ANN (VO): My Walter talked about getting one...but he never did.

KAY (VO): Well I'm certainly going to do something about it. I'm alone now too.

SON (VO): Mom.
MOTHER (VO): Your father was a wonderful, loving man.
SON (VO): I know.

ANNCR (VO): Call 1-800-9-CARING for your copy of our booklet. It's yours free from The GUARDIAN PLAN insurance funded prearranged funeral program.

5. Northrop Frye, *Anatomy of Criticism* (Princeton, NJ: Princeton University Press, 1957), 348.

6. David Pfeifer, "Exploration of Moral Issues Leads to Knowledge of Ethics," *Feedback* (Fall 1991), 20.

7. Day, 10.

8. Sprague Vonier, "Television: Purveyor of Parables," *Journal of Broadcasting* (Winter 1965/66) 4.

9. Horace Newcomb and Robert Alley, *The Producer's Medium* (New York: Oxford University Press, 1983), 14.

10. Joanmarie Kalter, "Television as Value Setter: Family," *TV Guide* (July 23, 1988), 5.

11. Andrew Greeley, "Today's Morality Play: The Sitcom," *The New York Times* (May 17, 1987), H40.

12. Nancy Shulins, "Modern-Day Legends," (Mt. Pleasant) *Morning Sun* (August 26, 1990), 8C.

13. Henry Perkinson, *Getting Better: Television and Moral Progress* (New Brunswick, NJ: Transaction Publishers, 1991), 12–13.

14. John Fiske, *Television Culture* (London: Methuen, 1987), 194.

15. Jon Berry, "Tale of Old Friends Pushes Limits of Advertising," *ADWEEK* (September 28, 1987), 43.

16. Leah Vande Berg and Nick Trujillo, *Organizational Life on Television* (Norwood, NJ: Ablex, 1989), 160–189.

17. Thomas Peters and Robert Waterman, *In Search of Excellence: Lessons from America's Best-Run Companies* (New York: Harper and Row, 1982), 280.

18. Debra Goldman, "Melting Pot Meltdown," *ADWEEK* (September 9, 1991), 27.

19. Howard Didsbury, "The Wolf Is Here: The Impact of Telepower," *Phi Kappa Phi Journal* (Spring 1994), 23.

20. Peter Eder, "Advertising and Mass Marketing: The Threat and the Promise," *Broadcast Cable Financial Journal* (March/April 1992), 20.

21. Donald Bertsch, "Inconsistent Values May Cause Confusion," *Central Michigan Life* (April 25, 1990), 5A.

22. "Broadcasters' Hands Tied as Racist Buys Time to Air His Message," *Broadcasting* (August 7, 1972), 14.

23. John Stuart Mill, *On Liberty*, David Spitz (ed.) (New York: W. W. Norton, 1975), 18.

24. Harry Jessell, "Quello Lauds 'Marketplace' Curbs on Indecency," *Broadcasting* (January 27, 1992), 40.

25. Erwin Krasnow, "The Politics of Program Regulation," *Broadcasting* (November 2, 1987), 28.

26. John von Soosten, remarks to the International Radio and Television Society Faculty/Industry Seminar, February 8, 1996 (New York).

27. Paige Albiniak, "Powell Pushes for Equal First Amendment Rights," *Broadcasting & Cable* (October 25, 1999), 92.

28. Patrick Maines, writing in "Monday Memo," *Broadcasting* (September 24, 1990), 10.

29. Robert Johnson, "The First Amendment Speech You've Never Heard," *Broadcasting & Cable* (May 19, 1997), 22.

30. Richard Jencks, "Is Taste Obsolete?" Speech presented to the Conference of CBS Television Network Affiliates, May 20, 1969 (New York).

31. Howard Symons, "Making Yourself Heard (and Seen): The Citizen's Role in Communications," in Robert Atwan, Barry Orton, and William Vesterman (eds.), *American Mass Media: Industries and Issues*, 2nd ed. (New York: Random House, 1982), 35.

32. Edwin Diamond, "The First Amendment Dilemma," *TV Guide* (October 29, 1977), 6.

33. Bill Monroe, "The Slow Poisoning of the First Amendment," *Communicator* (April 1991), 22.

34. "Drinking and Driving Don't Mix in Hollywood," *Broadcasting* (September 12, 1988), 81.

35. Ibid.

36. Michael Medved, "Hollywood Chic: Illegitimacy and Hypocrisy," *The Washington Post* (October 4, 1992), G1.

37. John Fiske and John Hartley, *Reading Television* (London: Methuen, 1978), 89.

38. Ekaterina Ognianova and James Endersby, "Objectivity Revisited: A Spatial Model of Political Ideology and Mass Communication," *Journalism and Mass Communication Monographs* (October 1996), 22.

39. Fiske, *Television Culture*, 227.

40. Mary Rose Williams and Enrique Rigsby, "The Non-Discursive Rhetoric of Television: Spinning the Wheel with Pat and Vanna," in Leah Vande Berg and Lawrence Wenner (eds.), *Television Criticism: Approaches and Applications* (New York: Longman, 1991), 469.

41. M. Maccoby and K. A. Terzi, "What Happened to the Work Ethic?" in W. M. Hoffman and T. J. Wyly (eds.), *The Work Ethic in Business: Proceedings of the Third National Conference on Business Ethics* (Cambridge, MA: Oelgeschlager, Gunn & Hain, 1979), 19–64.

42. Mark Dolliver, "Don't Cramp My Style," *Adweek* (July 14, 1997), 19.

43. Robert Lewis Shayon, *Open to Criticism* (Boston: Beacon Press, 1971), 227.

44. Carl Grabo, *The Creative Critic* (Chicago: The University of Chicago Press, 1948), 30.

45. Gene Youngblood, "Art, Entertainment, Entropy," in John Hanhardt (ed.), *Video Culture: A Critical Investigation* (Rochester, NY: Visual Studies Workshop Press, 1986), 225–226.

46. Harry Jessell, "DTV or Bust, Says Kennard," *Broadcasting & Cable* (September 21, 1998), 22.

47. William Fore, "Escape from Gilligan's Island," *Media & Values* (Summer/Fall 1987), 4.

48. John Fiske, "The Discourse of TV Quiz Shows, or School + Luck = Success + Sex," in Vande Berg and Wenner, 450.

49. DeWitt Parker, *The Principles of Aesthetics*, 2nd ed. (Westport, CT: Greenwood Press, 1976), 200.

50. Theodore Meyer Greene, *The Arts and the Art of Criticism* (Princeton, NJ: Princeton University Press, 1940), 471.

51. "Standards Go Down as Channels Go Up," *Broadcasting & Cable* (May 10, 1993), 65.

52. George Boas, *A Primer for Critics* (New York: Greenwood Press, 1968), 123.

53. Christopher Meyer, "Blueprint of Skills, Concepts for Media Ethics Course," *Journalism Educator* (Autumn 1990), 29.

54. Day, 27.

55. Ibid.

56. Ibid.

57. John Merli, "Do You Have a Visionary Mission Statement?" *NAB RadioWeek* (November 26, 1990), 4.

58. Jim Mitchell, writing in "Monday Memo," *Broadcasting* (October 7, 1991), 12.
59. Merli, 4.
60. Day, 27.
61. Ibid., 28.
62. Jerry Wishnow, "Stand Up and Stand Out with Public Service," *Broadcasting* (May 9, 1988), 21.
63. Merli, 4.
64. Karyn Rybacki and Donald Rybacki, *Communication Criticism: Approaches and Genres* (Belmont, CA: Wadsworth, 1991), 135.

12

Aesthetics and Art

From the beginning of this book, we have considered electronic media content to possess aesthetic potential—to enjoy the capability, in other words, to offer our audiences *art*. In this chapter, we explore this assumption in detail. Then, in Chapter 13, a comprehensive model for the aesthetic analysis of electronic media discourse is presented. For now, as in the previous chapter on ethics and values, it is important to begin with a definition of our subject terms.

INTERPRETING AESTHETICS

The word *aesthetic* derives from the Greek aesthesis, meaning sensuous. The modern spelling of the term is often shortened by dropping the initial (and phonetically undetectable) 'a.' No matter which way it is written, the fundamental definition of *aesthetics/esthetics* revolves around the sensuous appreciation of beauty.

At the beginning of the twentieth century, literary critic F. V. N. Painter identified aesthetics as "the science of beauty in general . . . to which we have to look for some of the principles that are our guide to critical judgment."[1] To Painter's more famous contemporary, poet/philosopher George Santayana, this beauty "is an ultimate good, something that gives satisfaction to a natural function, to some fundamental need or capacity of our minds. Beauty is therefore a positive value that is intrinsic; it is pleasure."[2]

According to Jerome Stolnitz, it follows that *aesthetic activity* is "perception of an object just for the sake of perceiving it. . . . When we approach the work as a sociologist or moralist, we do not grasp its intrinsic value. To do so we must look at the work without any preoccupation with its origins and consequences."[3]

Unfortunately, this "art for art's (or pleasure's) sake" often collides with *American pragmatism*—the belief that something has

merit because it fulfills a concrete, functional need. In an immigrant society being carved from the wilderness, a premium was placed on objects and activities that contributed to building the settlement. The time for the pursuit of purely artistic experiences was seldom available. The historical recency of this American experience means that "What's it good for?" pragmatism reasserts itself whenever resources tighten. Art and music are the first things to go when the local school board can't balance its budget. "To the degree that this pragmatism reigns supreme," writes American Studies professor George Yudice, "art and culture will be left with little legitimacy other than what is socially, politically, and even economically expedient."[4] Any American artist or art critic thus faces the continuing challenge of promoting aesthetic activity as a legitimate enterprise in itself—while reassuring audiences that art also can address functional needs and gratifications (see Chapter 8).

Fortunately for art in general, and electronic media art in particular, such aesthetic legitimacy does not depend on physical access to the original. "The aesthetic experience," Professor M. S. Piccirillo points out, "unites object and perceiver, creating an aura which does not meaningfully distinguish original from copy."[5]

Reproductions of a Renaissance painting, audio recordings of a rock music performance, or video disk duplications of a film thus have the capacity to stimulate a pleasurable (aesthetic) response similar to that evoked by the original—provided that the *fidelity* of the copies is good enough to mask their copy status. Especially "for the perceiver who has not experienced the original *Mona Lisa*," Piccirillo continues, "the perception of a print of the painting will be an authentic aesthetic experience. Similarly, the experience of a repeat broadcast is as authentic for the first-time viewer as the experience of a first broadcast."[6] Were this not the case, most electronic media experiences (which are nothing more than recorded reproductions of previous creations) would bring little pleasure to our audiences. Listeners or viewers must be able to fantasize the authenticity of *live attendance* even though they are only being exposed to *recorded simulation* or, in the case of the Internet, *on-line regeneration*.

Original or copy, one thing must be kept in mind. Given aesthetics' unequivocal emphasis on pleasure, the analysis of electronic media aesthetics takes a much different critical orientation than does the 'ethics and values' approach discussed in Chapter 11. This is due to one fundamental fact:

The study of beauty, of what possesses the capacity to give us sensual pleasure, has its roots in emotion and not in ethics.

Thus, summarizes critic Clive Bell, "the starting point for all systems of esthetics must be the personal experience of a peculiar emotion. The objects that provoke this response we call works of art."[7] Bell's observation notwithstanding, there may not be a single "starting point" for this powerful phenomenon. Instead, as Figure 12-1 suggests,

FIGURE 12-1
The seamless cycle of aesthetic attainment.

we might better conceive of aesthetics as a free-flowing circular experience that may spin in either direction and that can be set into motion by both preplanned and accidental listening/viewing occurrences.

There are many theories as to how we can detect and evaluate these emotive provocations. A discussion of all of them would easily fill this book. For our purposes, therefore, we restrict ourselves to a summary of the five major schools of thought developed by aesthetics philosophers. These schools are listed in approximate reverse order of their usability in electronic media criticism:

1. Absolutism
2. Individualism
3. Objectivism
4. Cultural Relativism
5. Biopyschological Relativism

Absolutism

Absolutism decrees that beauty/pleasure is vested in an object independently of humanity's response to it. In a sense, this is the aesthetic equivalent of the old brain-teaser about whether a tree falling in the woods makes a sound if no one is there to hear it. The Absolutist would say that it *would*—arguing that no human response is necessary for a natural phenomenon to exist. Whether the sound of that tumbling trunk is aesthetic is another matter. The Absolutist probably would beg the question because of this school's view that humanity is simply incapable of understanding beauty's extra-worldly essence. Therefore, no human verification is needed in any case. Beauty can be comprehended only by the gods—if there are gods.

Obviously, Absolutism is of little help in electronic media criticism. In essence, an Absolutist critique could conclude only that "Here is a show I may or may not enjoy and you may or may not enjoy but if it is legitimately enjoyable there is no assurance that you or I would be capable of experiencing this pleasure anyway." (Something akin to this does occur when a commentator laments a long-dead program from radio or television's past by making us feel guilty because audiences back then were too aesthetically insensitive to appreciate it.)

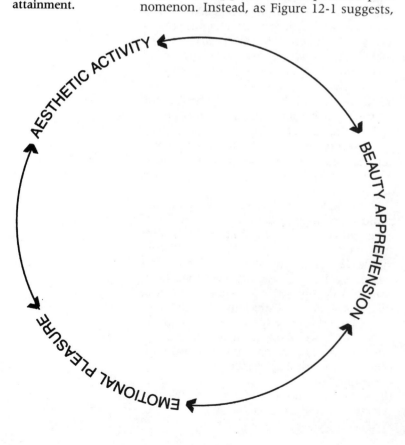

AESTHETIC ACTIVITY

BEAUTY APPREHENSION

EMOTIONAL PLEASURE

Individualism

This school of thought, in contrast, believes that human beings are eminently capable of understanding and ascribing pleasure—so capable, in fact, that one person's determination of beauty is as good as another's. To this way of thinking, no evaluation beyond which each individual makes for himself or herself is appropriate. Therefore, critical disagreements are inevitable and unresolvable.

When film actor George C. Scott, playing General George Patton, overlooks the human carnage littering a battlefield, for example, he confides to his aide, "Lord help me, I do love it so." To the Individualist, Patton's personal ascertainment of beauty in this scene of wartime horror would be entirely appropriate, with no need to apologize. (That the general does apologize to the deity is a moral rather than an aesthetic judgment anyway.) Actor Robert Duvall's gung-ho air cavalry officer in *Apocalypse Now* expresses a similar individualist aesthetic when, after a Viet Cong–sheltering tree line is incinerated, he ecstatically proclaims, "I love the smell of napalm in the morning."

If applied to electronic media criticism, the Individualist school of thought would largely reduce the practice of criticism to that of inventory-taking. "Here are all the things you might like about this program," the Individualist review might say. "But whether you will enjoy any of them or not is entirely up to you and fine with me since your guess is as good as mine." As Individualist C. J. Ducasse would have it:

That a given railroad bridge is a good bridge can be proved or disproved by running over it such trains as we wish it to carry, and observing whether or not it does carry them. But there is no similar test by which the beauty of a landscape would be proved or disproved. Judgments of beauty . . . have to do with the relation of the object judged to the individual's own pleasure experience, of which he himself is the sole possible observer and judge.[8]

By this standard, even a TV test pattern could constitute authentically beautiful programming if, for instance, it reminds you of the past pleasure of making love while a similar graphic was on your screen.

It can be argued that the Internet's explosive growth and personal empowerment will inevitably give a new impetus to Individualism insofar as the electronic media are concerned. "Today, it has become increasingly easy for individuals to 'make' their own culture," asserts *Reason* senior editor Nick Gillespie, "either through actual production or increasingly differentiated patterns of consumption. The upshot of such a situation is that it is and will continue to be increasingly difficult to enforce any single standard of cultural value or practice, whether the enforcer is a government seeking to regulate material it deems indecent, a corporation trying to protect its franchise, or a group of artists or critics interested in cornering the market with its own aesthetic ideology."[9]

Objectivism

This third school of thought takes evaluative primacy away from each individual and bestows it on some stable set of standards through which the 'experts' can advise us as to what constitutes beauty and what does not. Objectivism, therefore, in Jerome Stolnitz's nonendorsing explanation,

makes no reference to the spectator or, indeed, to anything else except the work. It ascribes value to the work as though beauty were something "out there," in some things and not in others. . . . Therefore, when two people disagree about the value of a specific work, only one of them can be right. . . . "Good taste" is the capacity to apprehend the property of aesthetic value, when it occurs in an object. A man has "bad taste" when he lacks this capacity. . . . Therefore, some aesthetic judgments are authoritative, others are not.[10]

As defined by this doctrine, critics and esteemed creators are expected to comprise this body of authorities and to exercise their own 'good taste' in the guidance of other people. There is no tolerance, however, of the notion that consumers' individual backgrounds might modify what, for certain audiences, would constitute a pleasurable experience. Instead, Beethoven is Beethoven, Picasso is Picasso, and PBS is PBS. Even if you are unfamiliar with their works, you had better learn to like them because cultured people do.

In broadcasting's early years, this orientation was common in state-owned entities like the British Broadcasting Corporation (BBC). "Auntie" (as it was affectionately known) decided on the artistically important programming to which the public needed to be exposed and resolutely blanketed that public with it. Enjoying monopoly status and government funding, the BBC could pursue its high-handed, if well-meaning, artistic agenda without regard for popularity ratings or advertiser support.

Once competitors enter the field, however, such electronic media dogmatism proves less and less tenable as audiences with differing tastes go elsewhere. Uncompromising Objectivism can also lead to charges of cultural, racial, and sexual elitism. For the public to be repeatedly told that they should like a given program, format, or service will not cause them to like it if, through premise, context, execution, or scheduling, it fails to tap into the reservoir of listener/viewer experience or expectation.

Cultural Relativism

In the case of the Cultural Relativist school, it is not the gods, individual humans, or the 'experts' who are thought to play the major role in setting aesthetic standards. Rather, the cultural institutions of the society *collectively* are accorded this power. First proposed by anthropologists during the 1930s, this school of thought decrees that we are all members, willingly or unwillingly, of a culture and of one or more subcultures. Therefore, we cannot be immune to the way schools, churches, neighborhoods, occupational settings, and political structures form and shape our concept of the preferable and the pleasurable. John Frohnmayer points out, for example, that "in the Middle Ages, the tri-tone in music was such an anathema that it was called *Diabolus in Musica*—the 'devil in music'—and the composer Thomas Morley said that it was 'against nature.' (The song 'Maria' from *West Side Story* starts with a tri-tone.)"[11]

Neither individual citizen, nor artist, nor media professional can escape these influences, the Cultural Relativist maintains. As film professor Robert Edmonds put it, "the artwork maker grows up in a society, a culture. He cannot avoid being affected by that culture's tastes and values. Thus, from the outset he receives a set of criteria by which to judge the world and his experiences in it."[12] It is inevitable, therefore, continues the

Cultural Relativist, that the aesthetic standards implicitly or explicitly influencing that culture's artists should be recognized and respected as the beauty-defining norm.

At its most manipulative extreme, this orientation results in the enslavement of art, such as happened in Nazi Germany and Stalinist Russia, where the beauty of a work was measured in direct proportion to how closely it mirrored the ideology and goals of the State. The mass-ritual-worshipping films of Hitler's propaganda ministry and the smiling factory workers and happy farmers in Stalinist paintings were much more than voluntary reflections by artists of the indigenous concerns of their cultures. Instead, these were examples of the impressment of art to the servicing of the State's rather than the citizenry's pleasure. Failure to reflect the approved aesthetic meant artistic suppression. As Professor Ellen Harris recounts,

because the music of Paul Hindemith was composed in an atonal idiom, it was officially boycotted by the Nazis in 1934, and Wilhelm Furtwangler, who had dared to schedule a premiere of Hindemith's "Mathis der Maler," was dismissed from his conducting and administrative posts. Neither Hindemith nor Furtwangler was Jewish, but the Nazis condemned them for failing to follow established artistic standards.

Similarly, the Soviet Union banned the music of Sergey Prokofiev and Dmitry Shostakovich in 1948 for "anti-democratic tendencies" and for their adherence to a "cult of atonality, dissonance and discord." More recently, Salman Rushdie was forced to go into hiding because the late Ayatollah Khomeini condemned him to death for inferred criticisms of the Islamic religion in Rushdie's novel, *The Satanic Verses*.[13]

Cultural aesthetics are not always so brutally enforced or manipulated, of course. Indeed, virtually every culture strives to take steps to preserve and promote its own aesthetic heritage and outlook. The French government, for example, recently presented advertising writers with a major challenge by requiring that all commercial copy use only words of French linguistic derivation. This resulted in longer and more contrived phraseology, but preserving the purity of the language was felt to be worth the trouble.

Cultural/artistic preservation becomes a larger issue as economic globalization accelerates. Artistic properties—especially electronic media ones—are increasingly produced by multinational partnerships and marketed on an international basis. Nevertheless, many countries erect quota barriers to the number of foreign programs and musical recordings carried over their airwaves. This has particularly infuriated U.S. studios, who find their products excluded from trade talks and tariff agreements. While countries may be willing to open up their markets to foreign steel, wheat, lumber, and automobiles, they are resistant to lifting restrictions on film and electronic media content that they believe threatens their cultural preservation. Speaking in support of such quotas, Canadian Assistant Deputy Minister of Cultural Affairs Jeremy Kinsman asserts that "others may interpret [our] world, but a national culture needs its own signposts, its own images, its own collective memory."[14]

Over the past several years, the Canadian government therefore has sought to nurture an authentic Canadian aesthetic by requiring its broadcast licensees to feature a gradually escalating percentage of Canadian-origin programming on their schedules. With about 80 percent of their population living within 100 miles of the U.S. border, such action was felt to be necessary—not to enslave the broadcasting industry, but to assist it in achieving cultural independence from the much more massive electronic media presences to the south. This 'Canadianization' policy represents the theory of Cultural Relativism in action.

The problem, however, is that even though an undeniably distinct French-Canadian culture exists and is well served by its own-language radio/television services, some scholars within the country argue that English-speaking Canadian culture, if there ever was such a thing, has long ago melted into an aesthetic outlook that is genuinely and nonnationalistically North American.

Some of the multifaceted programming issues that such Cultural Relativist factors can raise (not just in Canada, but in any country given today's global market) are isolated in the commentary by *Toronto Star* critic Greg Quill.

Every country's electronic media industry is wrestling with similar Cultural Relativist concerns to those Quill raises; these concerns are made much more problematic by the inherently cross-cultural character of the Internet. Attempting politically to regulate and channel art seldom works as expected because the diversity of aesthetic reaction on the part of consumers defies uniform legislative categorization. It is one thing to define and regulate the permissible alcohol level of an adult beverage or the percentage of domestically produced parts required in an automobile. It is quite another to delineate the "pleasure composition" of a piece of art or to quantify the level of its social acceptability.

When powerful business interests are added to the mix (as they inevitably are in electronic media art), cultural classifications become even more blurred. The use of Royal Canadian Mounted Police insignia until recently was licensed by Disney, for instance, and Pokémon frustrates single-culture attribution. Certainly, reaction to art can be culturally shaped. But it is doubtful that it can be successfully dictated in an international media environment.

Biopsychological Relativism

The last of our five schools of thought for how pleasure is determined is the most modern approach and owes the greatest debt to the life sciences. In essence, Biopsychological Relativism takes the position that there is an internalized pattern of likes and dislikes native to the human organism. The organism thus is not as fundamentally dependent on cultural/institutional forces as the Cultural Relativist would suppose. In fact, Professor Edward Wilson, who pioneered the field of sociobiology, asserts that because genes and cultures have co-evolved, culture itself is rooted in biology and "can never have a life entirely on its own."[15]

Therefore, it is argued, fundamental pleasure preferences are found in all men and women because we all share the same neurological characteristics. This position is modified somewhat by *essentialist feminism* that, according to E. Ann Kaplan, "assumes that there is a particular group—'women'—that can be separated from another group—'men'—in terms of an essence that precedes or is outside of culture and that ultimately has to have biological origins. . . . Female values . . . offer an alternative way not only of *seeing* but of *being*."[16] Regardless of whether male and female aesthetic sensibilities are to be considered as similar or distinct, the Bio-

CANADIAN-MADE SHOW PROVES ITS WORTH

by Greg Quill

Not so long ago Canadian broadcasters would have lined up to get their hands on a Canadian-made show that already has a sizeable U.S. audience.

But these days, it seems, the country's commercial TV operators, faced with a plethora of new co-productions made for the ever-fragmenting American TV market, can afford to be choosy.

Why else would Beyond Reality, a decent little 30-minute science-fiction series about a pair of paranormal psychologists investigating assorted inexplicable phenomena, be having such a hard time getting a domestic airing, even though 13 episodes have already been seen on the USA Network specialty service, and another nine ordered for a second run there?

The series co-stars Canada's Carl Marotte and American Shari Belafonte, daughter of veteran actor-singer Harry. It's written by Canadians, shot entirely in Canada by Canadians, features Toronto musician Fred Mollin's music, employs Canadians in all supporting roles, and is produced by Toronto-based Paragon Entertainment.

Moreover, USA Network, with 58 million American viewers, reports Beyond Reality is one of its hottest new shows, with Friday night ratings that prove it's a winner.

"We'd like to see it on the air in Canada," says Richard Borchiver, producer and vice-president of Paragon, headed by Canada's John Slan. "By mid-season, we'll have 22 episodes, a full quota of shows. But we still have no commitment from a Canadian broadcaster, although there's more interest now than there was a month ago. It makes long-term financing of the series very difficult."

"I don't know of any other Canadian producer who has taken the risk we did, financing a $500,000-per-episode series. It more than meets Canadian content requirements, and resulted in millions of dollars being spent in the Toronto film community. Other producers couldn't have afforded it, and the price we're asking for Canadian license fees is hardly out of order."

So how come the series isn't airing in Canada, a full season after its U.S. launch?

Two reasons:

CBC's full-tilt prime-time Canadianization program has pulled the people's network out of the bidding for quality American shows, which, in turn, has lowered the price of those shows for commercial broadcasters in this country, and created a glut of cheap, viewer-friendly foreign material here.

That means prime-time schedules are already stacked with American-made top-raters, and that Canadian shows had better be well above average to compete.

Narrowcasting, the industry's way of rationalizing increased viewer preference for specialized programming, has added to the glut of new shows. It means Canadian and other formerly "foreign" producers who can deliver quality shows cheaply, can get a start on American TV, which, because of its sheer size, is still the engine that drives international production.

But there's a hidden cost. Americans like shows about America. And Canadians, more and more, want shows about Canada.

And to all intents and purposes, Beyond Reality could be set in any American city, even though its protagonists work out of the University of Toronto.

Cultural specificity, and recognizable plots and characters, are new elements in the production-broadcast equation. What works for American TV doesn't have to work for Canadians any more.

Beyond Reality may have been lost, albeit temporarily, in a new broadcast industry shuffle. It can't survive on either an American specialty service or on a solely domestic [Canadian] audience. It needs both.

It has already proven its worth in the biggest TV market in the world. Someone here should take the risk.

(Reprinted with permission—The Toronto Star Syndicate)

psychological Relativist believes that one work can be judged as superior to another based on psychological laws that grow out of common human (and perhaps female as distinguished from male) sensory system factors.

Any organism, for instance, strives primarily to achieve a feeling of equilibrium, or *homeostasis*. Thus, works that radiate this quality give us pleasure, are predictable sources of beauty, and seem to serve a therapeutic function. French painter Henri Matisse regularly took his own paintings to the bedside of sick friends because he was convinced that exposure to vibrant colors enhanced their health. More precisely, "Rectangles have a stability and wholeness that seem comfortable," graphic design scholar Kevin Barnhurst points out. "Even the most vertical of rectangles seems tranquil compared to shapes with more sides."[17] Conversely, a room with a black ceiling is psychologically perceived as the antithesis of tranquil equilibrium because it seems to press down on us and throw our sense of environmental balance out of kilter.

As another example, clinical psychologist and design consultant Carlton Wagner reports that "blue causes the brain to produce measurable amounts of tranquilizing hormones. Saturated pink walls calm agitated or angry people by encouraging the secretion of the brain chemical norepinephrine. These genetic responses are thought to be stable and unaffected by upbringing or by learned likes and dislikes."[18] Thus, drunk tanks and visiting-team locker rooms are often painted pink. Wagner also contends, as do the essentialist feminists, that there are sex-based differences to color perception: "Women, for example, have an inborn preference for blue-based reds, like raspberry, while men prefer yellow-based 'tomato soup' red from infancy. The ironic result can be a closet full of clothes or drawer full of makeup bought in vain to attract the opposite sex."[19]

A knowledge of neurological processes is also valuable in deciding what symbol sets to use on the television screen or on the Website page. As marketers know, *words* are processed voluntarily by the left brain. The consumer makes a calculated decision whether to read them. *Graphics*, however, are immediately and involuntarily processed by the right brain—so graphics usually take the lead in attracting people to the message.

Further, reports the direct-marketing newsletter *Response*: "The brain also registers numbers as graphics. That's why prospects perceive $24.95 as so much less than $25. The right brain involuntarily processes the $24.95 and, whereas the left brain—the logical hemisphere—would have noodled out the difference of only 5 cents, the right brain perceives it as being less. Much less."[20]

Turning to the sense of sound, random shrieks and whistles predictably repel most human beings and lower animal lifeforms as well. Their unstable aural dissonances and unpredictable beats do not convey a calming or enticing sense of symmetry in either pitch or rhythmical progression.

While conceding that cultural institutions may help shape our sensory preferences, the Biopsychological Relativist argues that these preferences can be broadened and shifted through formal or experiential education about additional neurologically palatable stimuli. Thus, Westerners can learn to appreciate the quarter-tone music of the East, and Easterners can learn to enjoy the diatonic (half- and whole-tone) scale of Bach and Beethoven because both tonal systems have an internal equilibrium that one can be taught to detect. This does not mean that tambura or koto music could suddenly supplant the rock group's guitars or the jazz band's saxophones in American media music. The cultural ratification of these instruments and their stylings are too widely established (and broadcast) for such a radical shift to take place.

What the Biopsychological Relativist would claim, however, is that there is no long-term psychological barrier to the acceptance of even radically different systems for pleasure production so long as they do not ignore fundamental perceptual laws. The synthesizer, for example, is now breaking down culturally derived tonal partitions and paving the way for new musical genres that owe their existence to no single cultural tradition.

A Schools-of-Thought-Conclusion

We can summarize our exploration of the various theories for aesthetic determination by specifying to whom or to what each school assigns the power for making this determination.

School	Determining Agent
Absolutism	"the gods"
Individualism	each person independently
Objectivism	the experts
Cultural Relativism	a society's institutions
Biopyschological Relativism	our neurological make-up

Whoever or whatever is the ultimate aesthetic arbiter, we must never forget that it is experienced *pleasure* that fastens an audience's attention to a work of art. This holds true whether that work is a symphony or a radio format hour, a tapestry or a TV sitcom. Though our audiences may not be able specifically to articulate the sense of beauty they are deriving from a program's characteristics, their enjoyment is not dependent on their ability to verbalize its cause.

As media professionals, our job is to create and present aesthetic expressions in such a manner that our public is offered rich pleasure options. We compromise our role and our success when we attempt to force listeners or viewers to conform to some narrow and predetermined taste mandate.

DEFINING ART AND ITS TASKS

If *aesthetics* refers to pleasure-igniting beauty experiences, then *art* is:

that *collection of elements* in which the potential for achieving pleasure through beauty resides.

Art is, as Clive Bell stated earlier, the 'provoker' of "peculiar emotion." In the words of Theodore Meyer Greene, any piece of art is "an object of delight, a vehicle of communication, and, at least potentially, a record of significant insight."[21]

The importance of this *communication* function is also stressed by DeWitt Parker, who believes art to be "man's considered dream; experience remodeled into an image of desire and prepared for communication."[22] Thus, to Parker, art is "the putting forth of purpose, feeling, or thought into a sensuous medium, where they can be experienced again by the one who expresses himself and communicated to others."[23] Ultimately, marvels photographer Minor White, "art is a communication of ecstasy, it is one of the faiths of man."[24]

Given these experts' unanimous emphasis on communication, it could be argued that, because the electronic media are the quickest and most efficient vehicles for widespread communication, these media constitute the richest of all art forms. Such a contention, of course, ignores all the evaluative questions as to the *depth* of delight, insight, desire, feeling, thought, or ecstasy found in a given artistic product. The point is simply that the electronic media possess at least as much *potential* to formulate and communicate aesthetic experiences (and therefore to constitute art) as do more historic and less compound artistic vehicles. As Elayne Rapping asserts,

it is particularly important to remind ourselves that television [and radio before it] is an art form because it is so much more socially powerful than previous forms. It has made dramatic art a universal experience for the first time in human history. This is the first civilization in which people of all classes, ages and educational levels have constant access to dramatic art in the privacy of their homes.[25]

A number of the great performing artists who came to prominence in the midtwentieth century were from areas and families that had no such artistic tradition. But as youngsters, broadcasting brought these aesthetic endeavors to their attention and stimulated the development of their talent. It is sad to speculate on how many other stellar musicians, actors, dramatists, and authors might have arisen from earlier generations had they only had the electronic media to transport these possibilities into their lives.

In any event, the communication-cognizant definitions of art presented above equip us with at least a general conception of art in both its traditional and electronic forms. But a more specific and functional way of defining art is to examine the *tasks* for which art is recruited. By distilling the insights of a number of aesthetics scholars, practitioners, and critics, we arrive at a list of six artistic missions. Three of these are outer-directed toward one's environment; the other three are inner-directed toward one's self:

Outer-Directed Tasks of Art

1. Refine society and culture by offering the ideal.
2. See into the present to reveal our world.
3. Cope with the labors of life.

Inner-Directed Tasks of Art

4. Liberate the imagination and put oneself in the place of others.

5. Lessen tension and internal conflict as an aid to mental health.

6. Inspire fear, disgust, and indignation.

Outer-Directed Tasks of Art

Art's first mission, to *refine society and culture by offering the ideal*, is the most noble of the six purposes and the one most often thought of in traditional conceptions of artistic merit. "What does improve in the arts is the comprehension of them, and the refining of society which results from it," writes Northrop Frye.[26] "Art *creates* culture: it creates the values and meanings by which a society fulfills its destiny," adds Eliseo Vivas.[27] And Monroe Beardsley concludes that "aesthetic experience offers an ideal of human life."[28]

This artistic task thus is tailor-made to the lofty goals of public and state-run broadcasting systems. But commercial media also have embraced this objective in their programming codes, mission statements, and public pronouncements. At the beginning of RCA/NBC's consumer-oriented telecasts during the 1939 World's Fair, for instance, company chairman David Sarnoff entoned:

It is with a feeling of humbleness that I come to the moment of announcing the birth in this country of a new art so important in its implications that it is bound to affect all society. It is an art which shines like a torch of hope in a troubled world. It is a creative force which we must learn to utilize for the benefit of all mankind.[29]

The Hollywood "happy ending" is a long-standing vehicle for serving up the ideal, and Walt Disney built a giant corporation on stories and theme parks that unwaveringly celebrate such idealism. (Conversely, in distributing its darker stories and lessons, the Disney company now uses its Touchstone or Miramax label so as not to sully the upbeat cachet of its centerpiece brand.) But even for Disney, broad-based consensus as to just what constitutes "ideal" or universally beneficial programming is becoming more difficult to achieve in an increasingly multicultural marketplace. Even when they can be agreed on, such artistic refinements are ex-

tremely difficult to execute within the time and fiscal pressures common to the electronic media. As veteran network executive Jeff Sagansky admits, "There's no way that TV can live up to expectations, because there's only so much that inspires. It happens very occasionally in art and literature as well as in video."[30] Still, as poet Robert Browning encourages, "Ah, but a man's reach should exceed his grasp or what's a heaven for?"

Art's second task, the function of *seeing into the present to reveal our world*, most obviously references news programs. However, it has much broader electronic media applications when construed in terms of Theodore Meyer Greene's amplification of this artistic role:

A work of art is expressive in proportion as the artist succeeds in "telling us something," in *revealing* something about human experience and the reality of which we are a part. . . . Sheer prosaic statement of fact in its unrelieved particularity is, in every universe of discourse, wholly unilluminating and uninteresting. What we crave as intelligent human beings is a commentary on our human experience and on the world around us. [See Figure 12-2.] We want to escape the boredom of sheer particularity by discovering the inner nature of things, their relation to one another, and their larger meaning and significance.[31]

When viewed in this light, an insightful drama, sitcom, soap opera, or even commercial may have just as much if not more chance than the "unrelieved particularity" of a bland and superficial newscast to accomplish our world revelation task and thus to constitute art.

Artistic *style*, in fact, is simply "a way of identifying something novel by referencing something well known," says philosophy professor David Carrier.[32] Applying this specifically to our profession, Professor Judine Mayerle reminds us that "the goal of the television producer is to create a program with sufficient references to the known and recognized, but containing enough differences to make the show distinctive."[33] The best programs, adds German arts entrepreneur Reiner Moritz, "persuade people, take them by the hand without being academic and give them something they don't know about and [are] entertaining at the same time."[34]

FIGURE 12-2
Reveling in our world—
and in our human
experience. An interna-
tionally award-winning
commercial for the
Los Angeles Museum
of Contemporary Art.
Courtesy of Melanie
Otay and John Stein,
Stein Robaire Helm)

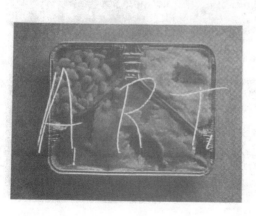

Clearly, this 'seeing into the present' task is much more multifaceted than at first it might appear. That is why it requires the artistic practitioner's special skills. Media theorist Marshall McLuhan has pointed out, in this connection, that only the artist "has the courage or the sensory training to look directly into the present. [Writer/painter] Wyndham Lewis said years ago, 'The artist is engaged in writing a detailed history of the future because he alone is capable of seeing the present.' "[35]

During his unsuccessful 1992 campaign to retain the U.S. presidency, George Bush remarked of television that "We need more of *The Waltons* and less of *The Simpsons*." Yet, in expressing a preference for a highly idealized Depression-era retrospective over an animated commentary on contemporary imperfections, Bush seemed only to confirm the charge that he was out of touch with the reality of life in the United States. A candidate may seek the ideal (Artistic Task #1), but not at the expense of being cognizant of the present (Artistic Task #2). Bush didn't appreciate the principle that, as Professor Anne Bernays expresses it, "Lasting art is neither polite nor charming; it achieves its effect by taking reality to its limits, by agitating the calm."[36]

Showing us our present is just one way art helps us *cope with the labors of life*, the third and final outer-directed artistic task. At its most functional, art can show us what to do, how to do it, and, most important, the way we can *feel* about this doing. According to perceptual psychologist Rudolf Arnheim, "Art is not the hobby of making reproductions, a game quite independent of other aims and needs, but is rather the expression of an attitude toward life and an indispensable tool in dealing with the tasks of life."[37]

In the electronic media, commercials are especially adept in fulfilling this assignment. Philosophy professor John Kavanaugh charges, in fact, that ads are the *only* program content to consistently showcase coping success:

The only times that persons are presented as uniformly happy and ecstatically fulfilled are in commercials: purchasing, collecting or consuming products that resolve problems, deliver self-assurance, win friends.[38]

Therefore, the most successful commercials are usually those that move beyond the mere promotion of product as problem-solver in order to convey the agreeable feeling that such solution-attainment bestows.

The Sealtest TV spot in Figure 12-3, for instance, does not restrict itself to the mere consumption of ice cream as food. Instead, it concentrates on the homey glow that results from experiencing this all-natural product. Even in today's fast-paced, glitzy world (as epitomized by the sports car in frame 1), one can still cope by "returning home" to simpler, nonartificial endeavors. All you have to do is pry open a Sealtest carton.

Inner-Directed Tasks of Art

The inner-directed counterpart of coping with life's external tasks is our need to *liberate the imagination and put oneself in the place of others* (Artistic Task #4). Art can uniquely set free our imagination whether or not the art object has an externally functional purpose. To DeWitt Parker's way of thinking,

it must be insisted that the beauty even of useful things exists for the imagination and for it alone. This is true not only of whatever free beauty we may suppose them to possess, but of their functional beauty as well. . . . In either case the work of art becomes the focus of an activity of the imagination, and the values generated by it are realized there. The beauty of utility, therefore, like the beauty of poetry or song, is a beauty for the imagination.[39]

That radio listening, television viewing, or Internet surfing does not always lead to the accomplishment of some "useful" chore, then, does not automatically render these activities artistically unproductive. To the extent that media experiences further our audience's active imagining, Parker would argue that beauty has been savored.

Often, the liberation of imagination is most easily accomplished through sympathetic (feeling for) or empathetic (feeling as) reactions to depicted characters. For instance, "women who have followed a soap opera for a considerable time," theologian Ross Snyder once asserted, "have experienced more self-revelation from the chief character of the program than they have from their neighbors or their husband all their life."[40]

Referring more generally to all art, Monroe Beardsley writes that the apprehension of any artwork inherently "develops the imagination, and along with it the ability to put oneself in the place of others."[41] As Russian novelist Leo Tolstoy put it, "Art is a human activity consisting in this, that one man

FIGURE 12-3
One way to cope
with modern life.
(Courtesy of Barry
Base, Base Brown &
Partners Limited)

(MUSIC & SINGERS)
HE: You're a natural woman

SHE: And you're

a natural man

HE: We've found a fabulous
ice cream

Full of good things from
the land

SPOKEN: People are going
natural, discovering

the taste of Sealtest All
Natural Ice Cream.

No artificial flavours...

just all natural ingredients.

HE: All natural woman

SHE: All natural man

HE: Yeah...All Natural.....

consciously, by means of certain external signs, hands on to others feelings he has lived through, and that other people are infected by these feelings and also experience them."[42] And Hugh Duncan would add:

Art forms determine the interpretation of the social experience; without them we could not share experience because we could not take the roles of others, or even bring much of our unconscious fantasy into conscious form. Through art we bring private reveries into public mean-

ing, and depict ends in conduct which deepen and enlarge shared experience.[43]

The apparently widespread acceptance of this artistic influence is what motivates public interest group insistence that radio/television portrayals, particularly in programs to which children are regularly exposed, offer characterizations that feature positive role models.

However, when art puts us in the place of other people, there is no requirement that this *placement* must always be positive. Sometimes, the aesthetic experience flows from consummate relief that we ourselves need no longer remain in the depicted predicament. This is akin to the joy of waking up from a bad dream and celebrating our de-tachment. In the Figure 12-4 commercial, for instance, a brewer advocates moderation in the use of its product by encouraging the viewer to temporarily change places with someone in whom that moderation had been sadly lacking.

FIGURE 12-4
(Courtesy of Brian Howlett, Axmith McIntyre Wicht)

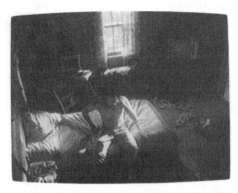

SFX: PHONE RINGS. ANSWERING MACHINE PICKS UP.
MACHINE: You know what to do.
CALLER: Wild party last night, huh?

So what happened to you? Last I heard you were headed for some body piercing place.

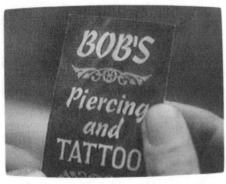

Man that stuff's too weird for me.

Anyway, I'm sure you didn't do anything too stupid.

Cause hey, you're the man, cool guy.
See you at the beach.

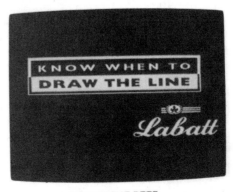

KNOW WHEN TO DRAW THE LINE

Labatt

SFX: PHONE BEEP.

By imagining negative consequences, we often learn positive lessons. Nevertheless, some people seek to protect society in general (and children in particular) from "disturbing" motifs by limiting certain intense subject matter—especially subjects of a violent or sexual nature. The V-chip is no more than an electronic device to make this limiting process more efficient. Yet, many program creators argue that such courses of action deprive their art of much of its ability to liberate the imagination. As Steven Bochco (creator of such series as *L.A. Law* and *NYPD Blue*) declares:

I'm just terrified at the concept of cutting off people's imaginations, because I think underneath a lot of this stuff is a fear of what imagination does to us. There's always a segment of the population . . . that feels they ought to be the arbiters of public taste. . . . That if they can just control everything, everything will be okay and everything will be safe. It's a terribly naive and ignorant point of view. I shudder to think what kind of world we'd live in if we didn't excite people's imagination, and that's what art does."[44]

Our fifth artistic task, to *lessen tension and internal conflict as an aid to mental health*, is recognized by Beardsley as a mechanism that functions "perhaps more as a preventative than as cure."[45] Art, in other words, cannot preclude mental anguish, but it can provide consoling release from stress and anxiety-producing situations. In commenting on television drama, for example, public opinion expert Leo Bogart postulates that "by constantly diverting us from the unpleasant realities of the human condition, it restrains us from dealing with them too closely at the same time that it protects us from feeling their full force."[46] Thus, this artistic task sometimes functions in direct contradiction to task #4's 'putting oneself in the place of others.'

Even though, within the context of our discussion in Chapter 8, artistic tension-lessening therefore may be viewed as escapist, it is also a therapeutic aspect of art that has been recognized for centuries. Thus, as art historian Arnold Hauser observes of the role of literary art in the outwardly prudish medieval court:

There is hardly an epoch of Western history whose literature so revels in descriptions of the beauty of the naked body, of dressing and undressing, bathing and washing of the heroes by girls and women, of wedding nights and copulation, of visits to and invitations into bed, as does the chivalric poetry of the rigidly moral Middle Ages. . . . The whole age lives in a state of constant erotic tension.[47]

Only through art could people relieve this tension without taking the highest of personal risks. (In the Camelot legend, Queen Guenevere would have been burned at the stake for her dalliance with Lancelot were King Arthur not willing to allow her the alternative of spending the rest of her life in a convent!)

Perhaps our own sexually tense era, riddled as it is with the pitched battles over abortion, the deadly spectre of AIDS, and the political fallout from the Clinton/Lewinsky revelations, is similarly compelled to seek this type of anxiety release through its interwoven electronic artforms. The following cross-media commentary by *ADWEEK*'s Barbara Lippert fashions a variation on this theme by suggesting, among other things, the positive correlation between breast obsession and political repression.

The tension-release feature of traditional or electronic art need not, of course, be limited to the alleged pursuit of psychosexual catharsis. In our media, it also can be found in such diverse material as "easy listening" or "New Age" radio that mitigates the staccato stresses of a working day; in the sports broadcast that Professor Walter Gantz says "provides an acceptable outlet for exhibiting emotions and feelings";[48] and also in the soap opera that allows viewers vicariously to settle domestic conflict in a flagrantly self-absorbed manner rather than by alienating—in real life—their own family members.

Creations that primarily or exclusively service tension release may not constitute the richest or most enduring artworks. This is because, by its very nature, tension release comes from acquired passivity; we shouldn't have to concentrate too hard on the work before it succeeds in relaxing us. Nevertheless, such easily digestible artistic experiences help us conserve our aesthetic attention for the more comprehensive artworks that fully demand it. As *Washington Post* critic Tom Shales comments about television programming: "I've always said that if it was all great, we'd all be exhausted; we just couldn't watch great art three hours a night, every day."[49]

INDECENT EXPOSURE

by Barbara Lippert

Geesh. From the hubbub surrounding the Victoria's Secret Super Bowl TV and Internet event, you'd think no one had ever seen a set of hooters before. The old media commercial, the one that appeared on Super Sunday, consisted of footage of supermodels like Tyra Banks, Laetitia Casta and Stephanie Seymour bouncing on the runway in last year's "fashion show," wearing only their Victoria's Secret dainties.

But here's the really innovative part: last year's cleavage was used to promote this year's new media cleavage - - -which was just 72 hours away on the Web. (This was a show about "fashion" the way the Miss Hawaiian Tropic contest is about suntans.)

Yes, the Victoria's Secret Super Bowl media event was really the Bud Bowl of Breasts, made even more user friendly by the techno-innovation of streaming video.

Afterward, when the winning team was interviewed, the most valuable player was asked, "Tyra Banks, you've just had your lifted, rounded, magnificent cleavage displayed on TV and the Internet to a billion people! What are you going to do now?"

Her answer, according to reliable sources, was "I'm going to take this *&%!* miracle bra off! The underwire and pusher-upper pads are killing me!"

The video, however didn't always stream according to plan, unable to accommodate all those millions of attempted users. That's because technology hasn't caught up yet with the number of people who'd like to see supermodels in push-up bras.

Indeed, it could have been part of the smart marketing plan, sort of The Rules version of a bra ad---don't be too available, play hard to get and then put your timer on.

Casta was one of the bouncing models this year and last. She was also the model in the old Tommy Hilfiger ads, with smiling boys in wet trunks at the old swimming hole. She's the lone girl in the group, but she more than holds her own in her wet trunks and bra. The explanation for her fabulous body, which includes very long legs and large, firm, seemingly unaugmented breasts, is: "She's French."

Shortly after the post-Super Bowl pandemonium, Casta kept the Victoria's Secret multimedia momentum going by appearing on The Late Show With David Letterman. Even Dave joked about the history-making, bust-based event: "Computers blew up all over the world," he said. "Everything crashed. A lot of people were killed."

The point is, nobody dies from excess media exposure to cleavage. And Victoria's Secret, which sells underwear (as I like to call it), has a perfect right to show the product. This was made quite clear to me by Ed Razek, president of brand and creative services for Intimate Brands, the parent company. He's steamed the company "got knocked" for the titillating quality of the entertainment.

"It's astonishing to me how far off they were," he said of critics who found the visuals objectifying or exploitative. "They didn't get it. We're not using lingerie to sell trucks. We're not using lingerie to sell tortilla chips or beer. If anybody has a right to use lingerie to sell lingerie, it's us. It would be criminal if we didn't." He's got a point.

We are living at a particularly breast-obsessed time - - -when even teenage girls on television show their cleavage. (It's empowering if she chooses the low-cut sweater.) Breast implant surgery has not only recovered from the silicone scare of the 1980s but has increased 275 percent in the last five years, according to the American Society for Plastic and Reconstructive Surgery.

In an Esquire cover story, "Triumph of Cleavage Culture," writer Mim Udovitch suggests that the mega-coniferous nature of our current breast aesthetic might also point to a new culture of falseness. Later, she quotes a radio talk-show caller giving his theory of breasts: "in politically conservative, repressive times, big breasts on women become very popular, and in liberal, freewheeling times, small breasts become popular." (This is borne out in comparing the small-breasted flappers of the 1920s to the B-52 wearers of the 1950s, and again to the small, perky, no-bra breasts of the 1970s.)

True, we are in a time of backlash; we're having a national nervous breakdown over sex. We have to explain what "oral sex" is to 6-year-olds, all the media are saturated with it, but we don't seem any more at ease or liberated with the physiology of it. A piece in last week's New York Post reported on a recent survey conducted among 3,400 adults by University of Chicago researchers. It showed that 32 percent of women of all ages report a "profound lack of interest in sex," and younger women have more problems than older ones.

Still, the level of exposure in promoting Victoria's Secret's media stunt was genius. After the spot ran on the Super Bowl, Razek told me that "a million people left their sets and turned on their computers and went to our site. That's the largest collective behavior shift in the history of entertainment programming." He also said that "one in five people on the planet will see some part of the show." It's just sad that this kind of marketing and technological breakthrough in the global village had to occur on behalf of bras and thongs.

Indeed, it was the polarization effect of the video and the media plan that upset me. Sure, the stock is up and it makes sense to appeal to men before Valentine's Day. And I understand the company has a "responsibility to its shareholders," says Razek, which is the '90s financial equivalent of reading Playboy for the fiction. But what I objected to was the high-class, phone-sex aesthetic: making Seymour ring the opening bell on Wall Street, advertising in Barron's and giving Bloomberg subscribers a "special desktop show," as if men and women exist on separate planets where men have the power and women wear merry widows.

Show all the satiny, sexy underwear you want, but do it in a way that doesn't alienate women. Don't sell a lap dance on your laptop as a breakthrough for mankind.

The final artistic task, *to inspire fear, disgust, and indignation*, seems, when compared to the other five functions, both counterproductive and antisocial. Yet, this artistic purpose, more than any of the others, distances art's true vibrancy from the frail and fragile nature ascribed to it by the prissy. This function most clearly epitomizes art's labors in the service of individual humanity. As De Witt Parker testifies,

despite their painfulness, man has a need for anger, fear, horror, hate and pity—for all the emotions that are his natural reactions to the evil in the world. Man is an organism predestined to life in a difficult, hazardous, and largely hostile environment; he possesses therefore, partly by inborn constitution, and partly as a result of habit and tradition, tendencies to reaction appropriate to such a world. Like all others, these tendencies demand stimulation and expression, and provide their modicum of pleasure when not too strong. Man has a need to hate as well as to love, to fear as well as to feel safe, to be angry as well as to be friendly, to destroy as well as to construct, even to experience pain itself . . . to give vent to hot anger and indignation and, in the imagination at least, to destroy things that one hates and loathes.[50]

Anyone who has cheered as an evildoer is gunned down by his or her favorite 'private eye' or skewered by a barb out of Jay Leno's mouth has a referent for what Parker is saying. The same dynamic is present when conniving seducers get their comeuppance in a TV soap opera or radio song lyric. And the robustness of this artistic task is also readily apparent in war art, where an enemy people or leader are aesthetically vanquished in order to rally the nation to physically vanquish them on the battlefield.

Conversely, when carefully crafted by the artist/producer, indignation-inspiring expressions can further a very positive objective because, as Parker stated in 1926, "there is the intention to inspire fear or disgust for the evils portrayed, in the hope that men may be persuaded to relinquish them. Such works of art are like the 'scare' advertisements that have begun to compete with the older type that appealed through attraction."[51]

In today's electronic media, a 'scare' commercial itself can be considered art—unless, of course, critical analysis determines it to be too aesthetically deficient to merit that label. In the television script in Figure 12-5, fear, disgust, and indignation are all artfully blended to persuade viewers that the seductive evil of cocaine must, to quote Parker, be "relinquished."

In recent years, the ability of art to engender fear, disgust, and indignation has motivated the use of music in attempts to modify undesirable behavior. In 1990, Vancouver-area 7–11 stores successfully rid themselves of loitering teenagers by piping the signal from an "easy listening" radio station into all their locations.[52] A few years later, a Salt Lake City mall played classical music at its entrances to achieve a similar effect.[53] Minneapolis Police Inspector Sharon Lubinski conceived a strategy of playing loud operatic arias throughout the downtown area in 1998 to disperse milling crowds that often congregated around bars after the 1 A.M. "last call."[54] And the following year, a judge in Fort Lupton, Colorado, compelled people whose loud rock or rap music disturbed the peace to attend sessions at which they were subjected to loud doses of music they disliked—such as Yanni and John Denver.[55]

Different people fear different devils, it would seem, but art possesses the capacity to deal with all of them. In fact, as humanities professor Camille Paglia recounts,

the first artist was a tribal priest casting a spell, fixing nature's daemonic energy in a moment of perceptual stillness. . . . The modern artist who merely draws a line across a page is still trying to tame some uncontrollable aspect of reality.[56]

Artistic Task Clustering

Any piece of media content can be analyzed as to how many of art's six purposes it ad-

VIDEO	AUDIO
OPEN ON LONG SHOT OF LINE OF PEOPLE	WOMAN (SEDUCTIVE, ALLURING VO): Will you lie, cheat, and steal for me?
DISSOLVE TO CU OF TEEN BOY	BOY: Sure.
CU OF BLACK MAN	VO: Will you give up your job?
	MAN: Okay.
CU OF CAREER WOMAN	VO: Will you risk prison?
	WOMAN: Yes.
CU OF FAMILY MAN	VO: Will you abandon your family?
MAN NODS HEAD 'YES'	
CU OF YOUNG MAN	VO: Will you die for me, if I ask?
	MAN: I'll die.
	VO: I knew you would.
DISSOLVE TO TITLE CARD SUPER: Careunit. Nobody cares the way we do.	MALE ANNCR VO: If you, or someone you love, loves cocaine, call CareUnit. We can help.

FIGURE 12-5
(Courtesy of Mark Frazier, DDB Needham Worldwide)

dresses and the pleasurable expressiveness of this coverage. Even though a given program, format, or commercial will seldom evidence more than one or two of these artistic tasks, the beauty of treatment depends not on task spread but on task depth.

Nevertheless, there are some creations that somehow manage to cover most if not all of these six functions without causing our perception of the piece's beauty to fragment. Such is the case with *The Cosby Show*'s "Theo's Holiday," in Appendix A. Reread this script and you will find that the show in some way touches on each task of art we have described:

1. We are offered the ideal of a family that goes out of its way to help each other; the ideal of parents who work to refine society by the living instruction they provide to make their children responsible citizens.

2. The present world of high rents, financial rebuffs, and job-search complexities is also revealed to be the future world which *The Cosby Show* kids, and the viewing kids, must learn to face.

3. Through #1 and #2 endeavors, coping with life's labors is skillfully revealed as the central focus of the entire episode.

4. Theo was given the opportunity to put his present self in the place of his future self and, along with the younger members of the audience, imagine what it will be like to have to function as a self-sufficient adult. Through the same parent-contrived game, Theo's younger sisters, Vanessa and Rudy, were also able to imagine themselves as other people in a similarly instructive yet pleasurable way—a pleasure in which the viewer could easily share.

5. *The Cosby Show* is generically a sitcom. Therefore, it can explore the tensions of growing up and of parenting in a comedic, stress-lessening manner. This same premise could be treated in the drama of a teen-age runaway, but with much more anxiety build than tension release.

6. As a "family" program as well as a sitcom, this show soft-pedals fear, disgust, and indignation. Nevertheless, the fear of being destitute, of not being able to make it on one's own, is a constant prod to Theo to succeed—and to his caring parents to nudge him toward success.

"The activity of art," Jerome Stolnitz concludes, "is the skilled, deliberate manipulation of a medium for the achievement of some purpose."[57] As we demonstrate in this section, that purpose can be both multifaceted and fully achievable if we become critically attuned media 'artists.'

Notice that the six artistic "purposes" we have just discussed also dovetail with the audience gratifications that we explore in Chapter 8. Table 12-1 summarizes the primary relationships. Thus, all art is inherently purposeful. However, it does not matter whether perceivers are cognizant of the purposes being served by the artistic piece to which they are being exposed. Instead, what is important is that the piece, through its form and content, contains the capability to generate such aesthetic activity.

TABLE 12-1
The Relationships between Artistic Task and Audience Gratification(s)

Artistic Task	Audience Gratification(s)
Redefine society/culture by offering the ideal	Personal enrichment/development Escapism/nostalgia
See present to reveal world	Information/surveillance Entertainment/time punctuation
Cope with labors of life	Problem solving Information/surveillance
Liberate imagination/put oneself in place of others	Companionship/conversation building Entertainment/time punctuation
Lessen tension/internal conflict	Catharsis/tension release Escapism/nostalgia
Inspire fear/disgust indignation	Catharsis/tension release

THE THREE SOURCES OF ART

We can best conclude our attempt to define art by briefly examining the three categories into which many theorists subdivide it. It must be admitted at the outset, however, that these distinctions may have less relevance to electronic media professionals than to people working in other potentially artistic enterprises. This is because the three categories, to a great extent, are determined by a work's heritage instead of by the more industry-relevant question of the pleasure the work might engender for the listening or viewing audience.

Fine Art

Sometimes also referred to as *elite*, fine art is described by D. W. Gotshalk as "the production by man of objects intrinsically interesting to perceive; and any object so skillfully produced by man that it has intrinsic perceptual interest has fineness of art."[58] If we subscribe to this definition, the art of the electronic media has as much chance as any painting, sculpture, poem, or symphony to be designated as "fine" because skillful production and intrinsic interest are certainly to be found in the more competent audio/video creations.

In the more conventional sense, however, fine art is thought of as the art of high culture, which, in its technical and thematic complexity, can be produced only by the most rigorously trained and aesthetically sensitive individuals. *It is art that sets out to be art* at every stage of its conception. Further, fine art is seen as possessing several levels of meaning that may be ambiguous or conflicting but are always, as a package, complex.

Typically, a piece of fine art is prized for its unique, one-of-a-kind character in which how the materials are arranged is just as important as the final product or statement the artwork makes. In this context, rock historian Carl Belz believes that "fine art declares itself as being different in kind from life. This is not to say that fine art ignores life or is irrelevant to the concerns of reality. Rather, any fine art expression confronts life, and has meaning in terms of it. . . . Fine art is conscious of its own being, and more generally, conscious of art."[59] Thus, as Kenneth Benoit points out, Sting and Billy Joel have no uneasiness about using the music of Prokofiev and Beethoven in realizing their own artistic aspirations.[60]

As an unequivocally aesthetic enterprise, fine art impacts an international public made up of those who love its form (be it rock music or rococo painting) as much as its content. This public also affords the artist immense (if often belated) recognition. How many painters like van Gogh and composers like Mozart produced today's near-priceless works for mere subsistence return during their lifetimes? Similarly, observes Quentin Schultze, "many upper-middle-class jazz fanatics now scrutinize the forms and structures of the music, elevating jazz into a fine art according to their criteria. In the 1930s, jazz was 'merely' the music of a minority and was criticized on moral and aesthetic grounds."[61]

However long it might take to be accepted, fine art is art for art's sake—it needs no rationale for existence other than its own aesthetic richness. At best, it is treated with pleasure-filled awe by those who seek to appreciate/enjoy it more comprehensively. At worst, it becomes the captive plaything of the snobbish and the pretentious.

Folk Art

Folk art, conversely, is not at all "different in kind from life." Instead, it is obviously functional, like the shepherd songs to quiet the sheep and the patterned wall tapestry that keeps drafts out of the hut. Therefore, it projects a single, highly accessible, and unequivocal meaning. Folk art is often produced by anonymous and formally untrained consumers for their own use or barter. It might later, like jazz, be accorded the status of a fine art by subsequent audiences who assign greater complexities to its structure. But this does not change folk art's historical roots as a local and "ordinary people's" creation.

"Saying 'folk art,' " Professor Henry Glassie declares, "we bring into association some sense of the commonplace and some sense of the exalted. It is humbling and exhilarating to recognize that something so marvelous as art can be produced by people so plain as to be called folk. . . . It is one message of folk art that creativity is not the special right of the rare individual. It is the common property of the human race."[62] Finally, be-

Characteristic	Fine Art	Folk Art
1. Artist identity	Usually famous	Usually anonymous
2. Artist/consumer connection	Separate people	Often same person
3. Meanings	Multiple/complex	Single/unequivocal
4. Artist training	Highly formalized	Informal/self-taught
5. Transferability	International; crosses cultures	Region-bound
6. Utility	Art for art's sake	Functional/practical

TABLE 12-2
Comparing Fine and Folk Art

cause it has its genesis in the life-styles and traditions of a single people, folk art is usually unknown or uncomprehended outside the boundaries of its own geographic region—unless it becomes repackaged as one of the other two art categories by forces beyond its control.

Table 12-2 summarizes the key fine art/folk art distinctions that we have just touched on.

Popular Art

This is a much more controversial category. Some theorists charge that it is not a discrete source of art at all but rather the plagiarized debasing of fine art and folk art properties. For our purposes, we address this controversy by subdividing the term *popular art* into two separate tendencies: *pop art* and *public art*.

Particularly when referred to as *kitsch* (the German term for mass culture) *pop art* is viewed as a mass-media-created pseudo-art that parasitically feeds off and ultimately devours both fine and folk art. It is usually negatively linked with the term *mass culture* to suggest an entirely superficial and fake phenomenon. More than forty years ago, for instance, Dwight Macdonald charged that

mass culture is imposed from above. It is fabricated by technicians hired by businessmen; its audiences are passive consumers, their participation limited to buying and not buying. The Lords of *kitsch*, in short, exploit the cultural needs of the masses in order to make a profit and/or to maintain their class rule. . . . Folk Art was the people's own institution, their private little garden walled off from the great formal park of their master's High Culture. But Mass Culture breaks down the wall, integrating the masses into a debased form of High Culture and thus becoming an instrument of political domination.[63]

Hence, for Macdonald and like-minded theorists, *kitsch* has three broad-ranging negative effects: (1) it economically exploits the masses; (2) it trivializes both fine and folk art; and (3) by blurring the distinctions between fine and folk art, it contaminates the training grounds for both fine and folk artists.

However, despite the overall perceptiveness of his comment, the "wall" between the fine and the folk of which Macdonald speaks was not always as rigid as he suggests. Shakespeare, for instance, used both classic Greek tales and old English folk narratives to weave multileveled drama for a primarily lower-class public. Beethoven freely borrowed from German peasant dances to create the third movement of his Pastoral Symphony. These borrowings did not debase their fine and folk roots but refined, deepened, and preserved them. However, when pop art reduces that same Beethoven creation to a ninety-second "hooked-on classic" with a disco beat, "fabrication" rather than enrichment has clearly occurred and the pleasure potential of the work has been pulverized, just as Macdonald predicted. Similarly, warns advertising psychologist Carol Moog, using fine art in an ad "can really be a turnoff because it's a bastardization of something that's meaningful to people culturally."[64]

Conversely, even through rock-and-roll was likewise disparaged as *kitsch* by some 1950s critics, musicologists have subsequently pointed out that it parlayed a rich blending of the folk traditions of Black rhythm-and-blues and White country/hillbilly music into a new popular authenticity that radio carried but did not contrive. In its genuineness and structural legitimacy, rock-and-roll thus constituted a *public art*—a widely popular amalgamation that reconfigured but did not trivialize its twin sources.

Unfortunately, rock-and-roll was itself subsequently trivialized as the authentic contributions of Little Richard, Carl Perkins, and Hank Williams were mimicked by the plastic and overpackaged performances of people like Pat Boone and Fabian. In like manner, the achievements of the Beatles, the first modern musicians to really capture the lower-class British idiom in their compositions, were subsequently vandalized by such market-manufactured commodities as The Monkees.

In contrast to pop art, *public* arts, from Shakespeare's own productions at London's Globe Theatre to those 1950s broadcasts of seminal rock-and-roll, broaden the base for subsequent aesthetic understanding of their origins. *Pop* art (*kitsch*) functions only to pass off sensuous trivia as artistic authenticity. In other words, the public arts serve an ADDITIVE function to their sources of inspiration—whereas pop art's effect is distortively SUBTRACTIVE. Coined by pioneering broadcast critic Gilbert Seldes, the term *public arts* thus suggests that the electronic media can play a profound role in reshaping and promoting art—rather than in falsifying or trashing it. Indeed, Seldes delineated a comprehensive aesthetic rationale for the electronic media when he wrote:

The fine arts, it can be said, express the soul of a people (the eternal), and the folk arts reflect earthly experience over the centuries (the past). The popular arts express the present moment, the instant mood. . . . I am now trying not to isolate, but to connect them, and the essential connection is this: they [the public arts] are a cross-section of the classic, the folk, and the fine arts, and you may think of this cross-section as fanning out from a narrow base in the classics, widening in the folk arts, and almost as broad in the field of the popular arts as the field itself. . . . Whenever any art, because of specific circumstances, takes on the quality of a public art, it has an effect on us and, in principle, invites or requires an action on our part—acceptance, criticism, rejection.[65]

Made possible primarily by the scope and reach-efficiency of the electronic media, the "cross-sectional" public arts thus constitute unparalleled opportunities for more people to experience aesthetic pleasure. The number of available electronic media choices has mushroomed since Seldes made his case for the public arts. As media professionals, our "invited or required actions" to public arts ministration are therefore now more perplexing—because they are much more numerous.

What is most important is that we do not allow the simple fact of our programming's popularity to be used as an artistic indictment against us. *Popular* does not automatically mean *kitsch*. It is merely, explain Professors Turner and Sprague, that popular art "seeks to be comprehended by and gratifying to as wide an audience as possible. Thus, in contradistinction to fine art, popular art thrives on the cliché or the expected, in which materials are manipulated in such a way as to limit doubt about their meaning."[66]

The popular arts, in other words, attempt meaning clarity in order to minimize mass audience confusion. In unapologetically seeking this wider audience, however, it is to the positive ("public") rather than the negative ("pop") class of popular arts that Russel Nye encourages us:

That the mass audience exists, and that the popular artist must create for it, are simply the primary facts of life for the popular arts. Popular art can depend on no subsidy, state or patron; it has to pay its way by giving the public what it wants, which may not always agree with what the artist may feel to be the most aesthetically apt. Satisfying a large audience involves no less skill than pleasing a smaller or more sophisticated one; popular artists can and do develop tremendous expertise and real talent. A best-selling paperback is not *ipso facto* bad; a song is not necessarily worthless because people hum it; a painting is neither bad because many look at it with pleasure nor good because few do.[67]

"People who automatically think that profit-making culture is bad, need to rethink," agrees John Fiske, "because they can arrive at that conclusion only from an extremely elitist and . . . untenable position."[68]

Northrop Frye makes a further and evolutionary case for the legitimacy of public/popular art when he observes that

popular art is normally decried as vulgar by the cultivated people of its time; then it loses favor with its original audience as a new generation grows up; then it begins to merge into the softer lighting of "quaint," and cultivated people become interested in it, and finally, it begins to take on the archaic dignity of the primitive.[69]

Television's return to *The Honeymooners* and *I Love Lucy*, just like radio's renewed attention to swing and mid-1950s rock music, are a few electronic examples of this aesthetic progression in our own field.

OUR ARTISTIC PROSPECTS

The core definitions of *aesthetics* and *art* were not changed by the invention of radio and television. Nor will they be transformed by the emergence of the Internet. This is true because the essence of art flows from aesthetic communication rather than from the particular technology used to convey it. As television writer/producer Rick Weiss reminds us, "Why do we pick up a brush, a chisel or a camera in the first place? Look at architecture, painting, photography and filmmaking. In any public art form, aesthetic trends emerge only when the mind masters the technology. The first clue of this emergence is when we become blasé about the tools but passionate about the expression."[70]

What has been changed by the staged introduction of the various electronic media is the sheer number of works that are now potentially embraceable by these art and aesthetics definitions. Clearly, the opportunities to create, exhibit, and experience such works have increased exponentially in the telectronic age. Unfortunately, electronic media criticism has not kept up with the cross-pollinating public arts. But it must. As Moses Hadas reminds us, "The larger and more indiscriminate the audience, the greater the need to safeguard and purify standards of quality and taste."[71]

We cannot berate our audiences for lack of keen aesthetic judgment if we fail to cultivate such a judgment in ourselves and reflect it in the programming decisions we make. As Professor Louis Day concludes, "Our artistic tastes often tell us a great deal about our individual character and the kind of society we really are."[72]

ENDNOTES

1. F. V. N. Painter, *Elementary Guide to Literary Criticism* (Boston: Ginn and Company, 1903), 34.
2. George Santayana, "The Nature of Beauty," in Melvin Rader (ed.), *A Modern Book of Esthetics*, 5th ed. (New York: Holt, Rinehart and Winston, 1979), 172.
3. Jerome Stolnitz, *Aesthetics and Philosophy of Art Criticism* (Boston: Houghton Mifflin, 1960), 30–31.
4. George Yudice, quoted in *Daily Report from The Chronicle of Higher Education* (July 15, 1999), 2.
5. M. S. Piccirillo, "On the Authenticity of Televisual Experience: A Critical Exploration of Para-Social Closure," *Critical Studies in Mass Communication* (September 1986), 343.
6. Ibid.
7. Clive Bell, "Significant Form," in Rader, 287.
8. C. J. Ducasse, *The Philosophy of Art* (New York: The Dial Press, 1929), 286.
9. Nick Gillespie, "All Culture, All the Time," *Reason Online* (April 1999), 11.
10. Stolnitz, 390–392.
11. John Frohnmayer, *Out of Tune: Listening to the First Amendment* (Nashville, TN: Freedom Forum First Amendment Center, 1994), 39.
12. Robert Edmonds, *The Sights and Sounds of Cinema and Television* (New York: Teachers College Press, 1982), 157.
13. Ellen Harris, "It Takes Practice and Serious Thought to Learn How to Dislike Art Properly," *The Chronicle of Higher Education* (September 9, 1990), A56.
14. "Disputing the 'Iron Law,' " *Broadcasting* (November 9, 1987), 91.
15. Edward Wilson, quoted in *Daily Report from The Chronicle of Higher Education* (January 27, 1998), 2.
16. E. Ann Kaplan, "Feminist Criticism and Television," in Robert Allen (ed.), *Channels of Discourse* (Chapel Hill: University of North Carolina Press, 1987), 217.
17. Kevin Barnhurst, "News as Art," *Journalism Monographs* (December 1991), 33.
18. "The Language of Color," *ASAP* (September/October 1989), 24.
19. Ibid.
20. *DMAD (Direct Marketing Association of Detroit) Response* (February 1999), 3.
21. Theodore Meyer Greene, *The Arts and the Art of Criticism* (Princeton, NJ: Princeton University Press, 1952), vii.
22. DeWitt Parker, *The Analysis of Art* (New Haven, CT: Yale University Press, 1926), 180–181.
23. DeWitt Parker, *The Principles of Aesthetics*, 2nd ed. (Westport, CT: Greenwood Press, 1976), 13.
24. Minor White, quoted in "End Paper," *The Chronicle of Higher Education* (May 24, 1989), B48.
25. Elayne Rapping, *The Looking Glass World of Nonfiction TV* (Boston: South End Press, 1987), 23–24.
26. Northrop Frye, *Anatomy of Criticism* (Princeton, NJ: Princeton University Press, 1957), 344.
27. Eliseo Vivas, *Creation and Discovery* (New York: The Noonday Press, 1955), x.
28. Monroe Beardsley, *Aesthetics: Problems in Philosophy of Criticism* (New York: Harcourt, Brace and World, 1958), 574.
29. Allison Simmons, "Television and Art: A Historical Primer for an Improbable Alliance," in Douglas Davis and Allison Simmons (eds.), *The New Television: A Public/Private Art* (Cambridge, MA: M.I.T. Press, 1977), 3.

30. Bill Kirtz, "Top Execs Take Hard Look at TV's Future," *Broadcasting* (February 15, 1993), 12.

31. Greene, 43.

32. David Carrier, "Panofsky, Leo Steinberg, David Carrier: The Problem of Objectivity in Art Historical Interpretation." Talk given at Central Michigan University, September 23, 1988 (Mt. Pleasant).

33. Judine Mayerle, "Character Shaping Genre in 'Cagney and Lacey,' " *Journal of Broadcasting & Electronic Media* (Spring 1987), 147.

34. "West Germany's Reiner Moritz: Television's Patron of the Arts," *Broadcasting* (February 19, 1990), 72.

35. Marshall McLuhan, "Great Change-Overs for You," in Harry Skornia and Jack Kitson (eds.), *Problems and Controversies in Television and Radio* (Palo Alto, CA: Pacific Books, 1968), 26.

36. Anne Bernays, "Separating a Work of Art from the Morality of the Artist," *The Chronicle of Higher Education* (January 20, 1993), B2.

37. Rudolf Arnheim, *Toward a Psychology of Art* (Berkeley: University of California Press, 1966), 41.

38. John Kavanaugh, "Idols of the Marketplace," *Media & Values* (Fall 1986), 4.

39. Parker, *Analysis*, 131–132.

40. Ross Snyder, "Architects of Contemporary Man's Consciousness," *Journal of Broadcasting* (Fall 1966), 310.

41. Beardsley, 574.

42. Leo Tolstoy, *What Is Art?*, trans. Aylmer Maude (New York: Liberal Arts Press, 1960), 51.

43. Hugh Duncan, *Symbols in Society* (New York: Oxford University Press, 1968), 223.

44. "Laying Down the Law in Prime Time," *Broadcasting & Cable* (September 4, 1995), 18.

45. Beardsley, 574.

46. Leo Bogart, quoted in "Melange," *The Chronicle of Higher Education* (October 16, 1991), B2.

47. Arnold Hauser, *The Social History of Art*, Vol. 1 (New York: Vintage Books, 1951), 219.

48. Walter Gantz, "An Exploration of Viewing Motives and Behaviors Associated with Television Sports," *Journal of Broadcasting* (Summer 1981), 264.

49. Don West, "A Fan's Notes (and Comment)," *Broadcasting & Cable* (September 26, 1994), 36.

50. Parker, *Analysis*, 118–119.

51. Ibid., 114.

52. Canadian Broadcasting Corporation, *The Journal*, broadcast of September 3, 1990.

53. Reported on *NPR Morning Edition* (November 13, 1997).

54. "Who's Insky, Who's Outsky in 1998," *TV Guide* (December 19, 1998), 24

55. "Cheers and Jeers," *TV Guide* (April 3, 1999), 14.

56. Camille Paglia, quoted in "Melange," *The Chronicle of Higher Education* (May 23, 1990), B2.

57. Stolnitz, 93.

58. D. W. Gotshalk, *Art and the Social Order* (Chicago: The University of Chicago Press, 1947), 29.

59. Carl Belz, *The Story of Rock*, 2nd ed. (New York: Harper and Row, 1972), 5–6.

60. Kenneth Benoit, letter to the editor, *The Chronicle of Higher Education* (May 17, 1989), B5.

61. Quentin Schultze, "Television Drama as a Sacred Text," in John Ferre (ed.), *Channels of Belief* (Ames: Iowa State University Press, 1990), 10.

62. Henry Glassie, quoted in "End Paper," *The Chronicle of Higher Education* (November 15, 1989), B72.

63. Dwight Macdonald, "A Theory of Mass Culture," in Bernard Rosenberg and David White (eds.), *Mass Culture* (New York: The Free Press, 1957), 60.

64. Karen Singer, "Art for Advertising's Sake: The Classics Get Repackaged," *ADWEEK* (January 23, 1989), 34.

65. Gilbert Seldes, *The Public Arts* (New York: Simon & Schuster, 1956), 286–287.

66. Kathleen Turner and Raymond Sprague, "Musical and Visual Invention in *Miami Vice*: Old Genre, New Form," in Leah Vande Berg and Lawrence Wenner (eds.), *Television Culture: Approaches and Applications* (New York: Longman, 1991), 279.

67. Russel Nye, *The Unembarrassed Muse* (New York: The Dial Press, 1970), 6–7.

68. John Fiske, "Popular Television and Commercial Culture: Beyond Political Economy," in Gary Burns and Robert Thompson (eds.), *Television Studies: Textual Analysis* (New York: Praeger, 1989), 22.

69. Frye, 108.

70. Rick Weiss, "Today's Trends Suggest Tomorrow's Reality," *Video Systems* (December 1992), 41.

71. Moses Hadas, "Climate of Criticism," in Robert Lewis Shayon (ed.), *The Eighth Art* (New York: Holt, Rinehart and Winston, 1962), 16.

72. Louis Day, *Ethics in Media Communication: Cases and Controversies* (Belmont, CA: Wadsworth, 1991), 324.

13 The Logic of Aesthetic Form

As we discuss in Chapter 12, electronic media content possesses the potential to serve as art and thus to satisfy us aesthetically. We now examine one system by which we can estimate and evaluate this artistic potential.

Of the myriad standards that attempt to judge art, many can be applied only to a single art form or were developed exclusively to serve the appraisal needs of fine/elite art. Fortunately for our profession, other benchmarks exist. One of the most eclectic and thus most adaptable to the multiple components from which electronic media content is derived is DeWitt Parker's *Logic of Aesthetic Form*. Consisting of six elements, this *logic* coalesces the insights of philosophers and aestheticians dating back to the ancient Greeks and fashions these insights in such a way that they do no art a disservice. With such a heritage and utility, Parker's *logic* can be supremely useful in the aesthetic critiquing of the multifaceted electronic arts.

As delineated in his 1926 book, *The Analysis of Art*, Parker's Logic of Aesthetic Form derives from the presence in a work of:

1. Organic Unity
2. Theme
3. Thematic Variation
4. Balance
5. Evolution
6. Hierarchy

The following sections examine each element in turn by defining its scope and illuminating some of its possible manifestations in electronic media material.

Keep in mind that like any set of artistic standards, the Logic of Aesthetic Form is a qualitative measuring device. It seeks to appraise whether or not a work is well made by its creator(s). As we mention in Chapter 11, such an orientation does not consider the morality of the piece. Instead, aesthetic criticism—via the Logic or any other schema—is primarily concerned with the work's 'beauty potential' and with how the artist was able to encapsulate it. It is up to Depiction Analysis (Chapter 9) to determine what lessons this art "taught" and; it is the responsibility of an Ethics and Values inquiry (Chapter 11) to ascertain whether these lessons are proper or improper.

ORGANIC UNITY

This concept, which dates back at least to Aristotle, decrees that in the construction of an art object, the whole must be greater than the sum of its parts. Further, as Theodore Meyer Greene instructs, "No whole can exist without its parts, and the more organized the whole, the more essential the contribution of each constituent."[1] Thus, whole and parts are mutually *interdependent*, resulting in what Greene characterizes as a work of art that "has an artistic vitality of its own. Its parts derive their artistic significance from the larger whole of which they are constituent members, and its artistic unity, in turn, depends upon the contributions of its several parts and aspects."[2]

Professor Gerald Herbener provides a specific example of this phenomenon when he observes that "for instance, we may think of the point in the creation of a painting in which the final dot of paint has been applied. Before that moment the picture was not yet 'complete.' A speck more, however, will be too much."[3]

Organic unity is what is sought in a solid debate case or a brilliant legal brief. In both, every part of the argument presented is relevant and necessary to winning the issue. Part also dovetails with part in such a way that one cannot isolate and attack any link in the chain of reasoning and therefore must surrender to the supremacy of the interlocked case. So it is in a work of art, where, as philosopher/educator John Dewey realized, different acts, episodes, occurrences melt and fuse into unity, and yet do not disappear and lose their own character as they do so—just as in a genial conversation there is a continuous interchange and blending, and yet each speaker not only retains his own character but manifests it more clearly than is his wont. . . . The existence of this unity is constituted by a single *quality* that pervades the entire experience in spite of the variation of its constituent parts.[4]

Modern Gestalt psychology, which stresses the primacy of the collective wholeness of experiences and behaviors, is simply the *organic unity* of art applied within a scientific context. French cinema historian Jean Mitry interrelates the two approaches this way:

Every feeling is "global." We perceive the relationship and their terms both at the same time, that is, a "whole" which determines the meaning of the parts. This "spontaneous structure" is the "form" of the perceived things, their "Gestalt." . . . The whole art of painting is based on the harmony of shapes and colors, that is, on the meaning that they take relatively amongst themselves. On the level of language, the meaning isn't in the words but in the phrase, that is to say, in the relational process implied by their organization within the phrase. On the level of film, the meaning is not in the images but in the relationship between them. Changing a part transforms the whole, gives it *another meaning*.[5]

An alternative way of visualizing organic unity is to conceive of it as the perfect middle ground between singular boredom and multiple disorder. (See Figure 13-1.) In the words of Professor Thomas Olson, organic unity "avoids monotony (too few materials) with variety through design and avoids confusion (too many materials) with unity through pattern."[6] Thus, marvels Theodore Meyer Greene, organic unity is "the product of a happy resolution of the dynamic tension between the extremes of empty simplicity and unorganized complexity."[7]

In television, a frequently cited example of 'monotony' or 'empty simplicity' is the so-called talking head, in which an on-camera speaker addresses the viewer for an extended period without benefit of shot changes or interest-enhancing visual embellishments. There are too few materials here to retain audience interest because, unlike a real-life conversation, the viewer cannot break the monotony by talking back. At the other extreme is the video kaleidoscope that shows the speaker from so many rapidly shifting perspectives that the meaning of his or her words is pictorially overwhelmed. The middle ground between these two extremes, however, constitutes a pleasing productional unity, employed by the director who functions as an artist rather than a technician.

Organic unity is an especially important consideration in newscast development. As Professor Larry Burriss discovered in his research into viewer reaction to television news:

First, as story complexity (in terms of production elements) increased, the overall recall scores decreased significantly. Thus, it appears that stories using a variety of audio and video elements will tend to result in less comprehension and recall. . . .

The second conclusion is that as story complexity decreased, positive evaluations of the story increased, a conclusion that has implications not so much in terms of the news itself, but in terms of story esthetics and audience appreciation.[8]

While this does not mean we should return to the days of the single desk-bound news reader, it does suggest that the tendency to add productional glitz for the sake of glitz should be held in check if the news is to be understandable and remembered.

To satisfy organic unity's requirements, not only must the right *number* of pictorial elements be chosen, but all elements that are selected must also be directly *relevant* to the subject at hand. In their study of television news retention, for example, German researchers Brosius, Donsbach, and Birk found that

Correspondence of text and pictures enhances the communication of information in television news. Pictures that either exemplify or describe the news text contribute to the retention of the

| Singular Boredom
Monotony
Empty Simplicity | **ORGANIC**
—————
UNITY | Multiple Disorder
Confusion
Unorganized Complexity | FIGURE 13-1
Organic unity as the
ideal moderation. |

news text. In contrast to this, standard news pictures, which suggest actuality and authenticity but do not directly support the news text, have no positive effect on retention compared with the performance of listeners hearing the same text. It may be concluded that if no pictures are available to illustrate a text, one may dispense with pictures altogether, since the resulting information transfer and evaluation of news items will be no different from a radio bulletin without the pictures.[9]

The same principle is likely to apply to entertainment programs and commercials that use extraneous location shots to 'lubricate eyeballs' without regard for the negative impact of these visual irrelevancies on viewer comprehension.

Television's rigid time segmentation poses additional organic unity dangers for news as well as for entertainment and advertising content. "Unlike oral, literary, or film narratives, which are much more likely to last as long as their story requires—television narratives have to fit their assigned Procrustean bed," points out Professor Sarah Ruth Kozloff. "This frequently means that two-hour television movies and miniseries are 'padded' with insignificant events, whereas certain commercials and news stories don't have enough time to develop their stories before they must conclude."[10] In the first instance, organic unity is violated by the presence of extraneous elements; in the second, it is defeated by the absence of needed ones.

On radio, meanwhile, the organic unity of the format is of preeminent importance. Too few elements, and listener attention will wane; too many elements, and an unsettling fragmentation sets in; add extraneous elements, and the station's formatic image becomes dangerously blurred. The artistic task is to feature format events that can be individually enjoyed and yet collectively clustered.

"Unity and multiplicity—these are not disparate but complementary aims," Carl Grabo affirms.[11] That such a complement is difficult to assemble only attests to the fact that the creation of art is not an effortless task. This is as true for electronic media programming as it is for any other artistic endeavor.

In every case, however, the artistic effect is diminished when the audience is made aware of the creator's struggles to achieve unity. The intricate jazz textures of the great Duke Ellington Band, for instance, are so pleasing because they seem so effortless. Yet, as the Duke himself once admitted, "Simplicity is, you understand, really complicated." Similarly, in explaining his company's success in technological innovation, award-winning Sony engineer Masahiko Morizono reveals that his approach to any project is the same: "By analyzing one by one, breaking it down to each individual, critical path, you find that complexity is accumulation of simplicity."[12]

Ultimately, this simplicity is the product of one unifying factor that creates an exact totality. If a piece truly possesses organic unity, that factor should be discernible. Setting alone won't provide organic unity because any setting can be easily populated with extraneous elements. In the sitcom *Spin City*'s first year, creator Gary David Goldberg used a female reporter as a love interest for Michael J. Fox's vice-mayor character. Yet, as Goldberg discovered, this reporter was an outsider incapable of continuous interaction with the rest of the City Hall ensemble. "So we were writing two stories in one each week, we were up to 5 A.M., and it was killing us."[13] The reporter role was written out of the sitcom because the City Hall setting alone couldn't provide the organic unity to make her relevant to the series' essence.

THEME

Theme is the fundamental statement that a work of art constructs. It is the foundation of the piece that the audience should be able to examine or overlook as it prefers. Theme undergirds the work, but it must not be so apparent that the perceiver is forever stumbling over its exposed pillars. As George Boas reminds us, "One of the things of which no one approves—except a professor—is to see the bare bones of structure and formula protruding through the substance and flesh."[14]

Theme amalgamates conflicting elements, whether these elements are of color, shape, tone, value, attitude, or design. The *conflict* (which in drama and literature intertwines the *plot line*) tests and judges the validity of the theme. But conflict and plot should never be mistaken for the underlying theme itself (see Figure 13-2). Because of its determinant role,

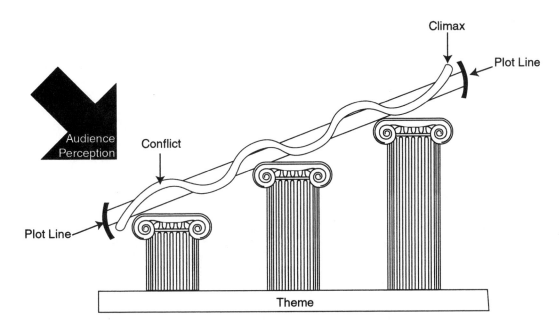

FIGURE 13-2
The structural relationship of theme, plot line, conflict, and climax.

THEME IS ALWAYS A DECLARATIVE STATEMENT—
"We all must come to terms with our heritage."
IT IS NEVER A QUESTION—
"Should you have to come to terms with your heritage?"
NOR AN EQUIVOCATION—
"Sometimes you may be able to avoid coming to terms with your heritage."

The escalating struggle to affirm or reject a focused theme statement comprises the motive force for the entire work, with the final decision constituting its *climax* (look again at Figure 13-2). More than any other factor, theme is the work's value-carrier, even though in some artistic disciplines (such as music, dance, and architecture) this value may just as likely express a tonal, emotive, design, or spatial statement as it does an attitudinal stand.

Finally, a validated theme endures because it contains within itself a declaration not limited to a certain time or culture. Other ages or peoples may interpret this theme differently, but it remains powerful in the sense that it strikes a chord of expressive recognition (if not agreement) and strikes it in a distinctive manner. "Basic human situations like love, death, celebration, and illness constantly recur as the themes of art," writes art authority Edmund Feldman, "but they can be saved from banality by the uniquely personal comment the artist seems to make about them."[15]

Obviously, any electronic media drama, action/adventure, sitcom, or soap opera encases a theme. It is up to the media professionals involved to decide whether that theme is sturdy enough and socially acceptable enough to propel its show successfully to and through the airwaves. Newscasts, game shows, and sports broadcasts can be said to possess themes, too: the recurring theme of the news anchor as your omniscient sentry; the game show's repeated statement about the supremacy of cute and perky; the sportscast-asserted triumph of the outclassed cellar-dweller's eternal hope and spirit. Such themes structure these programs to conform to our expectations as, week after week, they fulfill their own prophecies.

Whatever the show, and given what we discuss in previous chapters about media adherence to mainstream values, it should not be surprising that most sponsor-supported television themes are clustered within a relatively narrow and noncontroversial spectrum. As a case in point, Professor Gary Selnow examined 222 subplots in prime-time television in order to ascertain their thematic structure. He discovered that seven themes keep recurring, with the following four especially common:

"Truth wins out in the end; honesty is the best policy."

"Hard work yields rewards." [The Protestant ethic lives!]

"Ingenuity finds a solution."

"Good wins out over evil."

The three additional subplot themes are:

"Bad wins over good."

"Might makes right."

"Luck is important."[16]

Not surprisingly, Selnow found the last three to be much less pervasive than the first four. They are also much more likely to be rejected by the time of the story's conclusion.

Taken as a whole, these seven themes accounted for 96 percent of the subplots Selnow analyzed and remain the predominant underpinnings of today's programming. As Selnow discovered, "a relatively few moral lessons govern the vast majority of television program resolutions. Television script writers rarely stray from a few narrow themes that have been espoused by mainstream religious cultures and over the centuries have become woven inextricably into the American moral fabric."[17] The core value structures we explore in Chapter 11 thus seem to have served to narrow television's thematic richness—at least as far as prime-time advertiser-supported broadcasting is concerned.

Commercials articulate their own themes, of course. These themes tend to be much more pointed because spots exist *solely* to sell a thematic concept within a bare minimum of time. Unlike other media content, the commercial's theme usually cannot afford to be subtle infrastructure. Instead, it must function as overt message and audience motivator. This is especially true as more and shorter ads create an increasingly cluttered environment in which any single message can easily be buried.

Thus, in the Sealtest spot in the previous chapter (Figure 12-3), the commercial theme (*Sealtest ice cream restores traditional, 'all-natural' goodness to our modern existence*) comes through in every frame. Ice cream is also sold in Figure 13-3. But here, the theme is based on the *un*-natural: *Klondike Bars are so magically desirable that people will do 'anything'*

abnormal to obtain one. Would either theme work as well for either product? The answer to this question involves key product positioning issues and demonstrates how marketing and aesthetic considerations are frequently interrelated.

In less congested commercial environments than those found in U.S. broadcasting, spot themes can afford to be more subtle, and even ironic, as in the British advertisement showcased in Figure 13-4. Even though our man Arkwright's memories of past anniversaries seem limited to recalling what part of the pub he occupied, they apparently are eternalized by his continuous consumption of John Smith's Yorkshire Bitter. The tongue-in-cheek expression of the commercial theme is withheld until the last frame. There, the viewer is politely invited to chuckle at the theme's caustic expression—and thereby inadvertently to accept it.

Whatever the type of artistic work being analyzed, keep in mind that its theme is not what the piece is "about," but rather it is the underlying premise that the work advances.

THEMATIC VARIATION

This third element in DeWitt Parker's *logic* serves to showcase or illuminate the theme from several different angles, thereby investing it with additional shadings and perspectives. To aesthetician Eliseo Vivas, "the variation of the theme aids it in providing the striking quality required to shock attention, to surprise it, and to present it with some degree of difficulty, without which it would become lax through boredom."[18] Parker himself added:

It is not sufficient to state the theme of a work of art; it must be elaborated and embroidered. One of the prominent ways of doing this is to make it echo and re-echo in our minds. . . . Yet to find the same thing barely repeated is monotonous; hence what we want is the same, to be sure, but the same with a difference; thematic variation.[19]

Parker lists the four main techniques by which the variation can be accomplished: recurrence, transposition, alternation, and inversion.

FIGURE 13-3
(Courtesy of David
R. Sackey, W. B.
Doner and Company
Advertising)

MUSIC: What would you do for a
Klondike Bar?

V/O: Would you honk like a goose?
MAN: Hey, she'll do anything.
WOMAN: No, not me, not anything.

MAN: Yes, she will.
WOMAN: Honk? No, that's asking
too much, really.
MAN: She'll do it.

V/O: Klondike's got rich chocolate
... over thick vanilla ice cream ...
WOMAN: Honk.

V/O: Pardon me?
WOMAN: (LOUDER) Honk! Honk!

V/O: Very nice.

SONG: For that chocolate-coated,
ice-cream loaded,

big and thick, no room for a stick ...

What would you do for a
Klondike Bar?

MAN: Little bite, sweetness?

I gotta honk, huh?

Recurrence

Recurrence is the simplest thematic variation device. It involves the mere repetition of the theme, such as the wallpaper pattern that uniformly reproduces itself from one corner of the room to the other, or the musical round in which you *Row, Row, Row Your Boat* to a melodic theme varied only in terms of the moment at which each of its expressions begins.

In radio, we find recurrence most clearly in the short-playlist CHR (Contemporary Hit Radio) or older Top-40 format, in which the same few tunes are constantly recycled throughout the day. *CNN Headline News*, meanwhile, is recurrence in video journalism; in each newscast we encounter like modules, in like order, every thirty minutes.

FIGURE 13-4
(Courtesy of Bill
Gallacher, Boase
Massimi Pollitt)

WIFE: A fine way to spend our 30th
wedding anniversary. (PAUSE)

WIFE: We came here for our 20th
anniversary.

ARKWRIGHT: No we didn't. We stood
at the bar.

ANNCR (VO): John Smith's Yorkshire
Bitter. It's what memories
are made of.

The presence of this pattern also is readily apparent in the construction of episodes of many game shows or action/adventure series. Here, nearly identical activities (be they the wheel spin, the move into 'double jeopardy,' or the car/plane/boat chase) sequentially push along the program's premise at recurring times in each succeeding show.

Transposition

Transposition, conversely, takes the same thematic element and shifts it into another key, tonality, color, design, shape, brightness, or character articulation. We experience the thematic idea higher or lower, darker or lighter, more straight or more curved, or more happy or sad. It is always the same theme, of course, but in a succession of new dressings.

Thus, a radio music format typically will feature more "down" than "up" tempo tunes in afternoon as compared to morning drive-time—but the thematic type of music conveyed (country, urban contemporary, 'classic gold,' etc.) remains consistent. Similarly, a noon TV newscast may emphasize a softer and more hints/helps packaging than does the station's late-evening effort. But the central concept of "Eyewitness News," "Looking Out for You," "News with the Hard Edge," or "Facts without Chatter" is maintained across all dayparts.

Further, in the case of network news, David Altheide has found that the potential in a story for what he calls *thematic encapsulation* is a key factor in that story's being chosen for airing. Altheide defines thematic encapsulation as "the ease with which an event can be briefly stated, summarized, and joined to a similar event or a series of reports over a period of time or within the same newscast."[20] By transposing such thematic subjects as 'the crime next door,' 'people who help,' or 'pocket-book panic' into a number of specific instances, news producers can offer predictability even within the uniqueness of each day's news docket.

Alternation

This third thematic variation category is more complex. In order to function properly, alternation requires the presence of two themes—or, at least, two significantly diverse versions of the same theme. Because of this intricacy, alternation is relatively rare in most formulary electronic media endeavors where but a single thematic approach is adopted so as not to confuse the audience. Alternation is especially difficult to develop within the sitcom's half-hour time constraints—but it also tends to be avoided in one-hour dramas as well. A unique exception

to this rule is producer Dick Wolf's award-winning *Law & Order*, which manages to juxtapose crime and punishment thematic alternations within its innovatively crafted two-part structure.

In radio, the block-programmed station, which features fundamentally different kinds of content during different dayparts, faces a difficult problem in handling alternation. Even though it may try to thematically link its divergencies with a slogan like, "what you want, when you want it," an outlet that, for example, splits itself into classical and jazz, or 'lite' music paired with talk blocks, lacks an authentic thematic consistency. The more extreme the alternations, the more likely they will be perceived not as variations but as digressions.

In local television, a similar difficulty is presented by prime-time access (early evening) *checkerboarding* as opposed to program *stripping*. With checkerboarding, a different show appears in a given time slot each day of the week. In the case of stripping, conversely, five installments of the same series fill the time period. Even if the five checkerboarded programs are of a like genre (all sitcoms or all game shows), this alternation still forces viewer expectations to be more thematically flexible than a program strip demands. Unfortunately for checkerboarding programmers, many consumers do not seek the complications of prime-time's night-to-night variation in a pre-prime-time period. In fact, even prime-time television is moving away from alternation-based scheduling. Many cable networks now strip the same prime-time series across the week, and NBC brought stripping to broadcast prime-time with its multi-evening *Dateline NBC*.

Inversion

Inversion, finally, is thematic *reversal* in which we view the theme from the completely opposite perspective. Black is now white, good is now bad, light is now dark, and high is now low. Such radical shifts of perspective can be accommodated in the fine and folk arts, whose attentive clienteles are familiar with their respective inversion devices. But, to the more casual and heterogeneous popular arts audience, inversion can be more confusing than revealing.

A personality-heavy radio format cannot, at the same time, claim "more platters, less chatter." Similarly, a lovable sitcom or soap opera character cannot be permitted to engage in anything perverse lest we lose mass audience recognition and approval. Longer forms, such as the made-for-TV-movie and the miniseries, can more easily employ inversion, of course, but still with the risk of losing by confusing an often distracted viewership.

Nevertheless, if the inversion clearly and accurately represents the theme subject's reverse image, this variation can set up a defini-tive parallel. In the Figure 13-5 Kikkoman sauce commercial, for instance, the ridicu-lous frame 9 inversion (a city whose prime dish the product clearly will make *worse*) only helps to validate its transpositional 'make better' variations in all the other cities as showcased in the first eight frames.

Whatever thematic variation a creator chooses to use, it can only be as effective as the theme being amplified. It is impossible to attain aesthetically pleasing variation if the central theme is itself deficient.

FIGURE 13-5
An advertising example of thematic variation through inversion. (Courtesy of K. R. Ingalls, Saatchi & Saatchi DFS/Pacific)

Lite Soy Sauce and Lite Teriyaki Marinade & Sauce.

CITIES AND TOWNS ALL OVER THE COUNTRY WILL BE SEEING KIKKOMAN LITES.

BOSTON BAKED BEANS
(SFX: MUSIC THROUGHOUT)

SANTA FE FAJITAS

HONOLULU SPARERIBS
(V/O): Cities and towns all over the country are using less salt, and...

CHICAGO-STYLE PIZZA
still holding on to their local flavors.

KEY WEST SWORDFISH
They're cooking with Kikkoman Lites.

BUFFALO CHICKEN WINGS
Lowest in sodium of the major brands.

SAN FRANCISCO CIOPPINO
Naturally brewed Kikkoman Lite Soy...

NEW YORK STRIP
and Lite Teriyaki sauces.

ATLANTA PEACH PIE
They make every dish better. Well, almost.

KIKKOMAN LITES

BALANCE

Balance, the fourth component of Parker's *logic*, is defined by Edmund Feldman as "the resolution of all forces in a structure leading to equilibrium or equipoise. It is evident in nature, in man, and in the man-made world."[21] "Balance not only adds clarity and vividness to a work," Thomas Olson submits, "it is intrinsically satisfying."[22] For his part, Parker testifies that balance "is *equality* of opposing or contrasting elements."[23] This aesthetically satisfying equality or stability results because balance is *the skilled exploitation of contrast.*

Contrast, in turn, writes Jerome Stolnitz, entails "setting against each other *unlike* elements which nonetheless harmonize with each other. The distinctive character of each element calls attention to that of its opposite, e.g., a 'warm' and a 'cold' color. Yet together their dissimilarities become unified; so the juxtaposition of 'warm' and 'cold' colors constitute a sensuously pleasing pattern."[24]

The two balancing agents may be collectively and equally pleasurable when they are either simultaneously or consecutively perceived. As a *consecutive* illustration of the 'sensuously pleasing' color balance to which Stolnitz has just referred, Robert Edmunds provides this intriguing theatrical anecdote:

In the eighteenth century in the theaters, where the illumination on the stage was by candlelight and other kinds of reflected lamps, actors relieved their eyes when they were not on stage by going to a room painted a kind of apple green. This was a cool color that rested the eyes, and the greenroom exists to this day as the name of the room where actors can go between their appearances on stage.

It was not until more than a hundred years later . . . that full comprehension of the relationships between colors was reached. Only then did people understand the nature of complementary relationships between colors, and their theatrical forbearers of a hundred years earlier would have been delighted to learn that there was a sound theoretical basis for making a greenroom green. The color of the lights on stage was orange or close to being orange. The complement of that color is indeed pale green. Such colors, therefore, are reciprocal, so that green compensates for the "hot" lights on stage. The greenroom was "cool" and restful.[25]

Aesthetic balancing is not just limited to colors, of course. It is also derived from coupled shapes, sounds, movements, and characters. In all cases, however, each half of the pair must contribute equal "weight."

And regardless of whether our perception of these pairings is simultaneous or consecutive, we cannot achieve true balance unless a marked contrast exists between our chosen dualities.

In a very rudimentary sense, this principle can be observed in any well-fashioned dialogue commercial. Effective dialogue spots craft a consistent balance between a "seller" (who is knowledgeable about the product) and a "buyer" (who is ignorant of the product or harbors misconceptions about it). To be both credible and palatable, the commercial's seller and buyer must make distinct and equal contributions to the persuasive progression. A domineering seller will alienate listeners, while a preponderance of questions from the buyer won't allow time for product amplification. In the following U.S. Health Care spot from master copywriter Dick Orkin, however, both characters' points-of-view are presented in equally brief and balanced speeches that give the argument a pleasing equilibrium. Balance is further strengthened by the humorous counter-contrast of two kinds of 'protection.'

```
JEROME:   Um, Mom.
MOTHER:   Yes, Jerome?
JEROME:   Since you and Ernie are
   about to get married ---
MOTHER:   Yes?
JEROME:   I suppose you and I
   should have a little chat.
MOTHER:   What about?
JEROME:   You know, ahem, protec-
   tion.
MOTHER:   Jerome, I was married
   to your father for over 35
   years.
JEROME:   But, Mom, you're 65 now.
   What if there's an accident?
MOTHER:   How do you think we got
   you?
JEROME:   Mom, I'm talking about in-
   surance protection.
MOTHER:   Oh. I thought you were
   talking about, you know ---
JEROME:   What?
MOTHER:   You know.
JEROME:   Mom! Really!
MOTHER:   Ernie and I have the U.S.
   Health Care Medicare Plan.
```

JEROME: Well, Medicare is never enough, you know.
MOTHER: That's why we have U.S. Health Care Medicare.
JEROME: Medicare doesn't cover routine physicals, hearing tests, or eye exams.
MOTHER: But U.S. Health Care will. Plus there's $2 doctor's visits, 365 days of hospital care, skilled nursing care with no prior hospital stay. Oh, and most important, no claim forms to fill out.
JEROME: Why is that so important?
MOTHER: That means Ernie and I have more time for, you know ---
JEROME: What?
MOTHER: You know.
JEROME: Ahem, maybe I'll have a little chat with Ernie.
ANNCR: If you are Medicare eligible, and live in or around the Philadelphia area, call 1-800-323-9930. Ask about U.S. Health Care's Medicare plan.

(Courtesy of Dick Orkin)

Of course, character balance is also of prime importance in the aesthetic realization of *programs*. Once again, if the personae are merely clones of one another, or if positive/promoted roles far 'outweigh' the negative/demeaned ones, then the relationships between these two types of characters will be weak and aesthetically uninformative. Even when, as is the case in most sitcoms, all of the major characters tend to be *likeable*, we still must erect conspicuous contrasts between them in order to fuel audience interest and character interaction.

As one example of such character balancing, notice the multiple and major points of difference that cartoonist Charles Schultz constructed between Charlie Brown and his nemesis Lucy:

Charlie Brown	**Lucy**
male	female
blonde	brunette
unpretentious	vain
conciliatory	belligerent
acquiescent	opportunistic
contemplative	impulsive
sentimental	pragmatic

questioning	opinionated
world-oriented	self-oriented

We can easily construct similar balance/contrast inventories among other characters from the *Peanuts* TV episodes and their parent comic strip, and we can do the same for those of other acclaimed programs as well.

Furthermore, when a given character is capable of being assigned to *multiple* pairings (such as comparing Charlie Brown to sister Sally, friend Linus, and dog Snoopy), the show's interrelationships will prove more aesthetically interesting. Conversely, aesthetically unsatisfying programs tend to support fewer significant points of contrast between fewer characters.

In an even more literal sense, balance is equally important in news programming. Not only must the newscast 'balance' its coverage of issues in adhering to journalistic ethics and overall fairness, but it must also provide an equilibrium between heavy and light (or hard and soft) stories, between sports and weather, and even between one anchorperson and another. Today, twin anchors are seen as necessities—not just to even out the workload and provide pictorial symmetry, but also to represent an equal opportunity equipoise among the population groups who make up the market's viewership.

Once again, in anchor selection or in any other programmatic endeavor, we cannot lose sight of the fact that balance results not merely from the pairing of two entities, but from the pairing of two *equivalent* entities. If one anchor is clearly no match for the other, the newscast can be unstable and uncomfortable to watch.

The term *balance* has its technical ramifications as well. In audio, balance refers to the comparative volume afforded each of the sound sources that comprise the production. Especially in music, this involves sensitive collaboration between performers and recording/mixing engineers. Jack Renner, Telarc's award-winning chief recording engineer and chairman, maintains that his productions have succeeded "because I'm not sitting there [over]mixing the whole performance and constantly overriding the balance decisions that the conductor has so carefully worked out with the orchestra."[26]

On the video side of technical balance, Robert Edmunds reminds us that television's electronically generated contrast is not as keen as that offered by the chemical medium of film:

High contrast images on TV are not as successful as they are in the movies because there isn't a real black or the possibility of a real white in TV. These tones appear in films, however, and when films that were made before television are shown on the television screen, high contrast scenes are not very successful. Too much detail is lost, both in the darkest parts of the image and in the brightest. . . . Because the blackest the TV screen gets is when the set is turned off, it follows that anything that appears on film that is blacker than that gets lost to view.[27]

Most digital television systems narrow this film/television contrast difference, but they do not eliminate it.

Whether technical or dramatic, color or character, the importance and key nature of balance should not be lost on the electronic media professional. As Parker reminds us,

just as only equal weights will balance in a scale pan, so only elements that are somehow equal in value, despite their opposition, will balance aesthetically. . . . The essential thing about balance is equality of opposed values, however unlike be the things that embody or carry the values.[28]

Balance is so crucial to our valuation of an object because more than any other component of the Logic of Aesthetic Form it serves a deep-seated human need that the Biopsychological Relativist (see Chapter 12) would especially appreciate. Parker himself best articulates this need when he observes that

our entire emotional life is constructed on the principle of polarity; stimulation, repose; joy, sadness; love, hate; tension, relaxation. Not only is the organism bilaterally symmetrical, and the muscles built in pairs of balancing antagonists; the inner life has a similar plan. Furthermore, each polar element *demands* its antagonist; it contains within itself already a desire and a premonition of its opposite. Joy contains an impulse to sorrow, and vice versa; hate to love; love to hate. . . . This principle is of the greatest value in explaining the presence of evil and pain in art; for in the long run man prefers a world in which there is the night side as well as the daylight side of life.[29]

This, after all, is why many Christians take such diabolical pleasure in Halloween—but follow it with All Saints' Day.

True balance, true equilibrium, may be impossible to achieve in real life no matter how much we yearn for it. That is why we take so much pleasure in the balance with which the artist provides us. As Otto Bettmann, founder of the famous Bettmann picture archive, said of composer Johann Sebastian Bach, "His music sets in order what life cannot."[30]

EVOLUTION

For art, the term *evolution* is not used in the Darwinian sense (see Chapter 11) to chart species adaptation. Instead, aesthetic evolution decrees that the parts we perceive first in examining an art object should pleasingly determine those we encounter later.

As compared to the frozen quality of *balance, evolution* is fluid. As Parker puts it, "the static character of balance is opposed to the dynamic character of evolution; indeed, all movement depends upon the upsetting of an established equilibrium."[31] When we have nothing but balance, nothing but equilibrium, we can have no such thing as a plot progression. Conflict would always be rigid—like pieces standing on an unplayed chess board. Therefore, in our dramatic experiences (whether these experiences arise from a soap opera, sitcom, news story, sporting event, or commercial), we seek a more flowing kind of balance—what Herbert Langfeld called a balance between the strain of complication and the relief of unraveling.[32] This type of balance constitutes evolution.

The sense of motivating tension that artistic evolution provides does parallel the progenitive tension of *biological* evolution. As biophysicist Stuart Kauffman explains, "Biological evolution proceeds at the boundary between order and chaos. If there is too much order, the system becomes frozen and cannot change. But if there is too much chaos, the system retains no memory of what went on before."[33] Both artistic and biological evolution therefore entail a pulsating premonition of the possibilities and perils of change.

Some people mistake artistic evolution to be the rhythm of a piece. But rhythm lacks evolution's progressive expressiveness. "Rhythm never really gets anywhere," Thomas Olson maintains, "unless joined with evolution, as for example when time rhythm is joined with harmonic evolution in music. On the other hand, evolution as accumulation of meaning need not be rhythmic."[34] Rhythm, in fact, has a different genesis altogether, continues Olson, since "a combination of balance and thematic variation creates rhythm which is a pattern of repeated [not *evolving*] emphasis and pause."[35]

Event Sequencing

In probing evolution, then, we are initially concerned with either a temporal or a cause-and-effect succession of units in the same sense that a line has a beginning, middle, and end, and that a well-wrought painting has a visual flow. In the case of radio formatting, we can examine the sequencing of one element to the next in the actualizing of the hot-clock schematic that is supposed to govern and motivate each programming hour. (See Figure 13-6.) We can also scrutinize succeeding hours and entire dayparts to determine whether these build one on the other or diverge at certain points in pursuit of a different audience.

The virtual demise of network radio in the 1960s and its gradual rebirth in the 1980s were, to a significant degree, evolution-driven phenomena. When the networks' offerings broke the programming flow for their increasingly tightly formatted affiliates, the old networks were abandoned. When they learned how to enhance local station flow through format-specific drop-in features, the new network designs were embraced. Thus, ABC Radio divided itself into four separate services in 1967 in order to provide subject-and-flow matched drop-ins for differently formatted affiliates. Other networks subsequently engaged in similar segmentation. Meanwhile, in the 1980s, new radio syndicators arose whose satellite-delivered products offered entire, evolution-complete programming packages to like-formatted stations around the country.

Turning to television, we likewise see evolution as governing how program units are linked together to build the daily schedule. We can attempt to "age" our afternoon audience, for example, by moving from cartoons to "kiddult" (children and adult) appeal sit-

coms to a daily syndicated talk show and then into our local early-evening newscast. We might also try to 'feminize' our appeal by moving out of evening news into an entertainment-news magazine followed by a game show followed by a sitcom or drama with a strong female lead. In any event, the programmer must develop an evolutionary rationale for what comes before and what comes after—and a rationale that takes into account the schedule evolutions proceeding on competing outlets.

In the case of the Internet, evolutionary power substantially has passed from the programmer to the consumer. In the world of the Web, the consumer has unprecedented authority not only to select a site (a channel) but also to determine how deeply to burrow into that site's various click-through offerings—and in what order. Sequential jumping from site to site with or without the evolutionary intervention of a search engine is also solely determined by the consumer, whose progressive on-line experiences become uniquely individualized. Each 'net' user thus has the capacity to create everything from aesthetically enveloping to unaesthetically jumbled evolutionary experiences.

Returning to the more traditional mass media, evolution obviously is a key factor *within* individual programs as well. The segue from one news story to another or the involvement-heightening interlock of one sitcom scene to the next are just as much evolutionary concerns as is the creation of whole program blocks calculated to attract and nurture an 8 to 11 P.M. viewership. Star producer Steven Bochco describes how he designed the opening evolution of the very first *L.A. Law* episode to (1) overcome perceptions that a 'law show' would be stodgy and (2) 'freeze the viewer's thumb' before he or she could punch another button on the remote control:

You have a cold opening in which this incredibly handsome guy, Arnie Becker, comes into an empty office very early in the morning and a secretary's there and she's already on the phone with some screaming client, divorced woman, and we're no sooner past that than a guy walks in and pulls a gun on Becker and says: "You son of a bitch, I'm gonna kill you because of my divorce," and he pulls the trigger and out comes a flag that says "Bang" on it. And Becker's just freaked out. Now . . . as

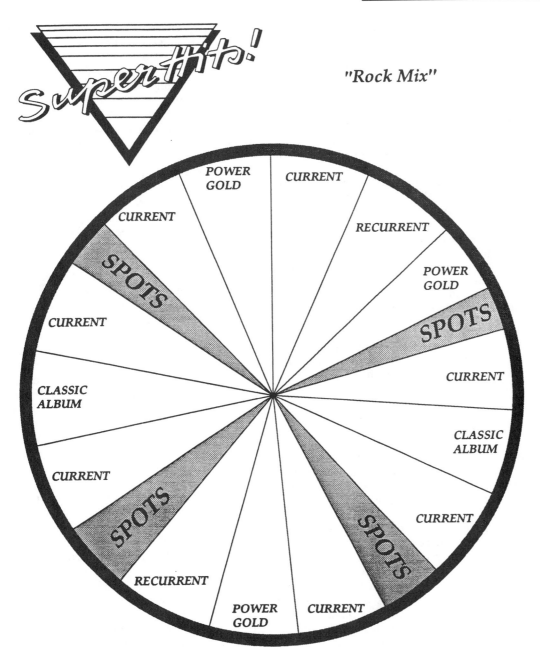

FIGURE 13-6
Hot clock developed by Broadcast Programming, Inc., for its *SuperHits!* format. (Courtesy of Dennis Soapes, Broadcast Programming)

"Rock Mix"

the guy leaves, the secretary comes in and says, "I think you better come quick." And they go into the next office and this lawyer is dead, face down in his franks and beans. And the last line of that opening scene, which in toto could not have been more than two minutes, two and a half minutes of filled time. Becker says, "If he's dead, I got dibs on his office."

Hah! I got 'em. Up goes their thumb. Two minutes, two and a half minutes. Now they say to themselves . . . "I think I'm going to

stick around and see what happens for another five minutes." Now I've already gotten you committed.[36]

Evolutionary theory would maintain that the aesthetic impact of these two minutes would be substantively different if the mini-events were arranged in any other way. The closer the final progression approaches the 'pleasure-full' ideal (which Bochco believes he has achieved here), the closer we come to evolutionary perfection.

Where to Begin

As the Bochco example also indicates, a second evolutionary decision to be made by electronic media artists (with event sequencing being the first) is where to *begin* the work. Unlike a novel, stage play, or movie-house presentation, we cannot depend on our audience being either seated or particularly attentive to what we have to offer. So from the start, we must grab and hold their grazing eyes and ears. Radio writers learned this as far back as the 1920s. In response, observes Robert Edmunds,

they began their radio plays *in medias res*, in the middle of a piece of action. This would certainly catch the attention of the audience; the credits could come later on.

In television the same technique is used for beginning dramatic presentations. The program . . . begins in the middle of action, and this serves as a kind of exposition. It isn't the old-fashioned kind of exposition that took place in a fairly leisurely way, but it serves to set out a situation from which the drama develops.[37]

Duration

Along with where we choose to begin and the order in which we arrange our segments, evolution is also shaped by *duration*—the length of time the perceiver is allowed to spend with each portion of the art work. In the visual arts, our eye scan is not only encouraged to proceed in a certain direction but also to linger at certain points along the way. In music, it is not just that tones follow each other in a certain order, but also that some consume more beats than others and thus remain longer on the aural stage. The melodic progression is deliberately retarded or accelerated depending on whether the tones in question are whole notes, half notes, quarter notes, and so on.

Duration is likewise important to optimal evolution in the literary and dramatic arts. This is true whether we are scripting a single scene or an entire show. Thus, in constructing a media program, Seymour Chatman submits that five basic duration devices can be used: summary, ellipsis, scene, stretch, and pause.[38]

With *summary*, verbal or visual condensation allows us to compress into a single, brief encapsulation separate events that may have occurred over days, weeks, or even years. Old filmic clichés such as the fast-moving hands of a clock, the flipping of calendar pages, or the (pre–Surgeon General's Report) ashtray that rapidly fills with cigarette butts are crude illustrations of this technique. A more sophisticated example is the opening of *The Wonder Years*, in which home-movie snippets of the Arnold family's past reestablish key interrelationships and background for the episode to follow. Depending on from which network season the episode comes, anywhere from a few months to several years may have elapsed between segments of the opening and/or between the opening sequence and the episode in question. Kevin Arnold's twenty-years-later voiceover additionally serves to quickly abstract key clusters of events or attitude progressions.

Ellipsis, Chatman's second duration device, is the complete omission of aesthetically unimportant elements. Instead of summarizing the event or action, we simply skip over it. A doctor is shown leaving the front door of her home—and then wielding a scalpel in an operating room. The meaningless travel time in between is obliterated. This may not be "natural," but as TV critic Robert MacKenzie once wrote, "That's why we read novels and watch television series instead of eavesdropping down at the Greyhound bus station."[39]

On the other hand, in what Chatman calls *scene*, the events evolve in real time without summarization or deletion. The *L.A. Law* sequence described above is, in this sense, a scene—it unfolds as unbroken actuality. Scenes are the key revealers of character-in-action, of course, and are often separated from each other by summary or ellipsis.

As its designation implies, *stretch* causes the event to develop more slowly than it would in actuality. Slow motion is the most obvious application of stretch. It elongates certain happenings or pronouncements to give them greater evolutionary prominence. The commercial that prolongs the glass of wine's free-fall toward the new carpet uses stretch to magnify our horror—or to motivate our relief as we discover that the carpet has been treated with Stainguard.

Pause, Chatman's last duration device, completely freezes the action to further enlarge its importance. In that same Stainguard spot, we might pause just as the wine is splashing out of its glass and hold that shot while a voice-over emphasizes the danger and its product preventive.

Essentially, then, these five means for controlling dramatic duration all relate to *time*. As Figure 13-7 illustrates, they can be placed on a temporal continuum based on how much or how little time they expend as compared to the actual manifestation of the event.

Most people would love to possess the ability to use these duration devices in their real lives. Imagine how wonderful it would be to gloss over or entirely skip unpleasant events, how pleasurable the effect of elongating or freezing our moments of sublime happiness or elation. We have no such power, of course, so we turn to art, where such things can be accomplished.

Special Evolution Issues

Before leaving this fifth component of the Logic of Aesthetic Form, three specific applications of electronic media evolution deserve special attention. Specifically, we need to examine serials, sports, and advertising contexts.

In program *series*, each episode is complete in itself. We can rearrange their order of airing with little or no restrictions because the characters do not grow or change from one episode to the next. Each episode is rather like an independent short story, and nothing seems to happen to the characters between these stories. Therefore, we can easily inspect the evolution within each episode without much reference to or concern for the series as a whole.

A *serial*, on the other hand, is ongoing. In the miniseries, or in daytime or evening soap opera, characters and their interrelationships do change and evolve across the boundaries of the individual episodes. The characters seem to have a life that carries on between serial segments in the same way that the characters in a conventional novel continue to grow between chapters. So in evaluating the serial, we must not only be concerned with how each episode evolves, but we must also pay heed to the evolution of the entire program package.

Optimal attention to evolution can also elevate one sports broadcast over another. A sportscast never simply reproduces a game. It adds, deletes, and rearranges elements to create a more continuous scenario. A television viewer, for instance, points out Sarah Ruth Kozloff,

sees the events filtered through the control room, which switches from crowd shots, to the cheerleaders, to the coaches, to the action; which flashes back to pregame interviews; which forsakes real time for slow motion and freeze frames; and which repeats the same play over and over. The viewer is no longer simply watching the game, but rather a narration of the game in which various choices have been made concerning temporal order, duration, and frequency.[40]

As the game proceeds, the skilled producer or commentator begins to see a storyline emerge and arranges between-plays elements to enhance that storyline's evolution. In this way, even a lopsided contest can retain viewer interest because of the additional narrative that the production crew is weaving.

Thus, reveals football commentator John Madden, "the storyline develops during the game. If, say, John Elway of the Broncos gets hurt in the second quarter, that's the end of that storyline. Now his backup is the storyline. Or if Lawrence Taylor can't do much for the Giants because he's double-teamed or triple-teamed, Carl Banks might emerge as the storyline. The idea is to recognize the storyline when it appears, not try to insist on what the storyline is supposed to be."[41]

Whereas they used to keep such storylines to themselves as underlying thematic motivators for their commentary, sportscasters more recently have explicitly referenced the game's 'storyline(s)' and even spelled it/them out on graphic inserts. The aim may be to make the game more comprehensible for less expert fans or to make it easier to quickly orient latecomers or channel grazers

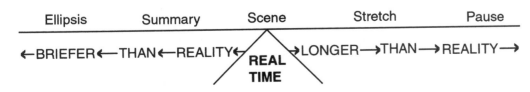

FIGURE 13-7
The duration continuum.

to how the contest has already evolved. This approach certainly increases attention to game evolution, but it may do so at the expense of organic unity when subsequent elements of the coverage obviously lack a close relationship to the storyline that has been displayed so prominently.

Finally, we must also recognize that a further storyline sometimes evolves from how commercials and program elements are interspersed. Occasionally, this is purposeful, as when Visine paid a premium to secure a specific slot on the network premiere of *The Godfather*. Its "Get the Red Out" theme consequently broke forth immediately after gangster Moe Green was shot in the eye and the blood spurted out.[42]

Most of the time, however, advertisement/program segment juxtapositions create an inadvertent evolution that might generate a counterproductive storyline. The "for a healthier pet" dog food commercial running immediately after a news item on pit bull savaging of a child, or the "spirit of California" perfume spot that precedes a talk show segment on prostitution in San Jose are two examples of how 'schedule flow' evolution implies a meaning all its own. (Recall our Chapter 7 discussion of scheduling and flow analysis.) When such back-to-back items are construed as subject-related, audience perception of their evolution can construct a new organic unity that the media outlet never intended.

Evolution as Destination

As program creators, electronic media professionals cannot always control the context in which their work will be displayed. But they should be in command of how the work itself evolves. In evaluating the evolution of any piece of art (media or otherwise) we ultimately need to ask two closely related questions:

1. What was our narrative's intended destination?
2. Does that narrative get there by the most appropriate route?

Audiences need not understand our evolutionary pattern at the beginning of their perception of the work. But they should have been able to appreciate and enjoy that itinerary by the time the work concludes.

HIERARCHY

This final Logic of Aesthetic Form component pertains to the selection and positioning of a work's aspects *in terms of their relative intensity and importance*. Hierarchy is not just how many high-tension and low-tension units are included in the work, but also how the artist alternates between them.

The placement of commercials, for instance, is a hierarchical as well as an evolutionary concern because the spots momentarily postpone plot development (evolution) due to their presumably lesser tension and lower importance to the show (hierarchy). Nevertheless, when carefully preplanned, the scheduling of commercial breaks actually can support the program's hierarchy. This is true, aesthetics professor Stanley Cavell suggests, because

the aesthetic position of commercials, what you might call their possibility—what makes them aesthetically possible rather than merely intolerable—is not their inherent aesthetic interest . . . but the fact that they are readable, not as interruptions, but as interludes.[43]

Sarah Ruth Kozloff agrees by adding that television programs "build their stories to a high point of interest before each break to insure that the audience will stay tuned. . . . Shows frequently time the placement of commercials to coincide with a temporal ellipsis so that while the viewer's attention has been diverted, the story can gracefully leap ahead several hours or days."[44]

In the case of sponsor-supported television, then, one reason that made-for-TV movies often are more pleasurable than theatrical feature films—and usually command higher ratings—is that 'made-fors' are hierarchically constructed with commercial breaks in mind. Plot action is designed to occur in a way that will actually be helped by the injection of commercial clusters. This predetermined pattern also takes into account the need to lock in viewer patronage. So a bare minimum of advertising time is docketed in the movie's first half-hour. Once the audience has become hooked on the uninterrupted storyline, longer and longer spot interludes are tolerated and can be hierarchically anticipated in the script's development.

On the other hand, because they were created initially for uninterrupted movie house (and/or pay cable) exhibition, feature films have not been 'written to breaks.' When a commercial outlet inserts spots in the film, these often come at dramatically inopportune moments and sever hierarchy's ideal stair-step pattern of rising tension.

Perceptual psychologist Rudolf Arnheim further delineates this stair-step arrangement in these terms:

In order to hold our attention, the dominant masses, which determine the basic "plot" of the work at the top level of structure, are made up of secondary units, whose interrelations represent an enriching refinement of, or counter-point to, the top structure.[45]

However, if a secondary (less intense) unit of the show is followed, not by a primary unit, but by a commercial break (another secondary if not tertiary unit), there is high potential for *un*aesthetic boredom to set in.

It must be reemphasized that hierarchy springs from the alternation of more and less *important* components within a work—not from more and less *relevant* ones. To the extent that their entrance is so ill-timed as to disrupt rather than assist audience experiencing of artful build, commercial pods become not just *non*hierarchical but *anti*hierarchical.

Another name for hierarchy is *dominance*, but this term can be misleading. Hierarchy, as we have established, is the intermixing of both dominant and subordinate elements. Dominance alone will not create hierarchy—only fatigue. As an example of this distinction, let us examine schematically the 'build' of a well-structured storyline. Be it sitcom, action/adventure, drama, soap, or documentary, a tale of any appreciable length should possess a gradual but perceptible rising of tension/involvement in which, as shown in Figure 13-8, momentary relaxants help set up the next climb.

Without the interposition of subordinate (tension-relieving) units, without those momentary lulls, the increasing points of intensity would not seem so interesting because there is nothing to set them off, one from the other. Such a structure, illustrated in Figure

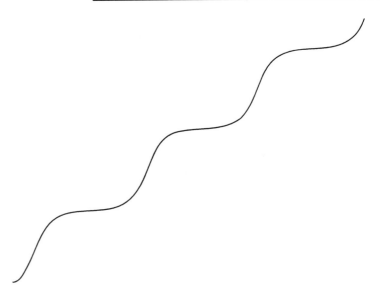

13-9, not only blurs the rising highs into undistinguishable togetherness, but also tires and even exhausts us because there is no place to pause and catch our breath.

A small hill whose side goes straight up is more fatiguing to climb than is a mountainside interspersed with tiered plateaus. Similarly, a dramatic plot-action that gives us no moment of reprieve or a frantic sitcom in which every succeeding event is a more lunatic verbal gag or visual slapstick invites the audience to tune away in order to avoid exhaustion. And a series of web pages that build bursting graphic upon bursting graphic overload the senses without intriguing the mind.

Certainly, hierarchy requires an overall intensity build. But this build should be gradual, with brief, periodic resting places (less important events) to punctuate our progres-

FIGURE 13-8
True hierarchy.

FIGURE 13-9
The absence of hierarchy.

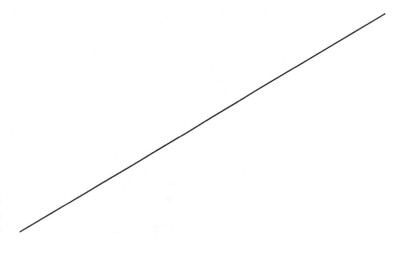

FIGURE 13-10
False hierarchy.

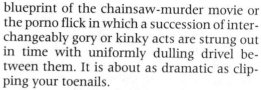

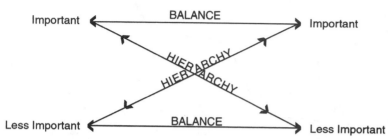

FIGURE 13-11
Balance and hierarchy
compared.

FIGURE 13-12
How would you
expand this moment
into a hierarchical
unit?

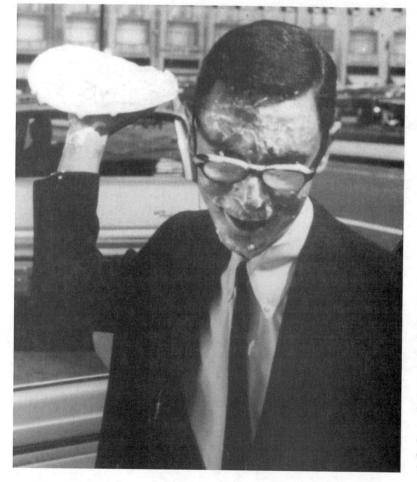

sive advancement through ever more important happenings. However, if these rest stops are too extended or too uniformly low-key—or if the highs are of all the same level—then we experience an emotional drum-beat that is cumulatively unsatisfying because of its repetitiveness. Figure 13-10 graphically suggests this defective pattern. This figure is the blueprint of the chainsaw-murder movie or the porno flick in which a succession of interchangeably gory or kinky acts are strung out in time with uniformly dulling drivel between them. It is about as dramatic as clipping your toenails.

Do not confuse hierarchy with balance. Balance pairs up equally weighted opposites—be they characters, events, or attitudes. Hierarchy intersperses these pairings so that all the major and all the minor dualities are not clustered together (see Figure 13-11).

True hierarchy taps into our psyches because it conforms to the most desirable pattern for the passage of our lives. As DeWitt Parker points out:

The concerns of life fall naturally into focus and fringe, vocation and avocation, important and less important [not less relevant]. Matters of high interest are salient against a background of things of less moment. There is never a dead level of value in life. No life is satisfactory without its hours of intense significance, which give it luster, yet man cannot always 'burn with a gemlike flame'; he must fall back, for rest and refreshment, on the little things. These latter are just as important in their way as the great moments. Some of them function as recreation, others are stage or preparation for the high moments. Yet when life is most satisfactory, these moments of preparation or repose are never merely means to ends; they possess charm of their own as well. When life is so lived it becomes an art, and when a work of art is so constructed, it is an image of life at its best.[46]

Overdoses and suicides by well-known rock stars, actors, and athletes may, in part, be explained by the absence of hierarchical "moments of repose" in their lives. Instead, their managers and agents propel them from one high-intensity performance to the next with such unbroken (albeit successful) intensity that their 'gemlike flame' becomes fused as an explosive, self-consuming firework.

As a mini-exercise in hierarchical development, Figure 13-12 pictures a moment of obvious (if comic) intensity. To generate optimal hierarchy, what would you have immediately precede this event? What would you place immediately after it?

THE COMPLETE LOGIC APPLIED

To demonstrate how *all six* of the Parker-specified elements can coalesce as a critical methodology, we now examine a student-written critique that uses the Logic of Aesthetic Form to estimate the aesthetic worth of a classic episode of the innovative sitcom *WKRP in Cincinnati*. In this two-part story, aging rock-and-roll disc jockey Dr. Johnny Fever is offered the opportunity to upgrade what a colleague calls his "miserable excuse for a career" by hosting a television dance show. The dance show, however, is disco—the *kitsch* antithesis of Fever's lifelong alle-

WKRP AND THE LOGIC OF AESTHETIC FORM

by Mark Wesley Fassett

This particular episode of WKRP in Cincinnati is a solid example of DeWitt Parker's Logic of Aesthetic Form. This episode allows for an interesting illumination of each of Parker's six components.

In discussing organic unity, it is clear that everything in the show revolved around, or was geared toward, Johnny Fever and his bout with schizophrenia. The writer easily could have let the other continuing characters play marginal or irrelevant roles. But instead, each contributed to the show's premise in a very strong way, so that all became interdependent in the helping/hurting of Johnny through their own theme-focusing attitudes.

The theme of this episode was an attempt at a universal statement of moral values. It basically reminds us that superficial wealth and fame are unimportant, when compared to personal peace-of-mind and friendship. In other words, You ultimately must be true to yourself. In the beginning of the episode, Johnny decides to go for the easy money. Overcoming his initial reluctance, he is swept into a fantasy world that causes his own personality and values to progressively deteriorate.

While it is true that the theme revolves around Johnny, the manner in which the other characters react to Johnny's problem accomplishes a good sense of thematic variation. TV producer Avis and radio colleagues Herb and Les all encouraged Johnny's 'Rip' charade for various reasons. They therefore express the theme's antithe-

sis. True radio friends Jennifer, Venus, and Bailey, on the other hand, affirm the theme by denouncing Johnny's contrived alter-ego, Rip Tide. Radio program director Andy and dithering manager Mr. Carlson remain oblivious to Johnny's difficulty, until the business issue of using "the Ripper" on WKRP forces them to face up to his mental anguish. Thematic variation is well accomplished by the various character perspectives, all of which challenge and probe the theme's validity.

This episode included many graphic examples of balance. One way the show provided balance was, again, through its characters. Balance was attained by having different characters relate to Johnny differently—either seriously or with humor. On one side we have radio sales manager Herb, news director Les, and the inept Carlson all encouraging Johnny, in a humorous way, to "go for it." Conversely, radio producer Bailey and fellow deejay Venus give Johnny continuous opposition in a primarily serious fashion. Finally, radio receptionist Jennifer provides Johnny with a harsh, honest awakening to balance the manipulation of TV producer Avis's devious sexual come-ons. Overall, the contrast between humor and drama is well accomplished as is the pairing of the real and the fraudulent.

Another way the show achieves balance is through setting. The changes of locale, from darkened, evil TV studio to bright, upright radio station keep the show stabilized.

In relating the concept of evolution to this production, it is easy to see that the progression of events is well motivated, as it follows Johnny's deepening plight. An interesting note is that, as Johnny goes deeper and deeper into his schizoid Rip Tide, the other characters' reactions to him become stronger. Bailey and Venus grow more and more disgusted with Johnny, until they no longer even speak to him. Les and Herb become more and more enthralled by his superficial success as the show progresses, so that the thematic variation parallels the plot's evolution.

In terms of hierarchy, the most important moments of the show are eas-ily detected. Basically, the less important moments were those lightened by humor, and the most important were the most serious, dramatic occasions. The less and more important elements were strung together very nicely by interjecting the comedic bits at times when it was essential to lighten the mood (such as Herb clumsily burning himself with coffee just before Johnny's climactic explosion in Carlson's office).

In summary, it is evident that this episode of WKRP was very effective aesthetically because it made skilled use of all six of the Logic's components.

(Courtesy of Mark Wesley Fassett)

giance to the folk-art purity of classic rock-and-roll. In an attempt to bridge this chasm, Fever puts on a sequin-clad persona called Rip Tide for his television performances. But the schizophrenia that gradually overtakes him as he tries to be a radio rocker in the morning and a TV disco dynamo at night ultimately reaches a flash point.

This is all merely plot summation, of course. Read one student's view about how show producer Hugh Wilson and writer Steve Marshall sculpted this plot into authentic aesthetic experience.

For another opportunity to apply Parker's schema, we turn to the "Bart Sells His Soul" episode of *The Simpsons* found in Appendix A. Reread that script and then read our Logic of Aesthetic Form critique that dissects it.

AN AESTHETIC ADDENDUM

As we discuss in this and in the previous chapter, art packages and conveys pleasures

THE SIMPSONS AND THE LOGIC OF AESTHETIC FORM

The "Bart Sells His Soul" episode of The Simpsons is artistically crafted and conveyed. The primacy of the soul as the carrier and representation of one's essence is the motivating topic—the organic unity—from which everything in the program springs. Clearly, the primary focus is on Bart's title-signaled selling of his soul and the consequent loss of his impish significance. However, the attempted transformation of Moe and his bar are also a facet of the program's organic unity. Bart and Moe both encounter great unhappiness when they attempt to sell out their true spirits in exchange for financial gain. Bart may be obnoxious and Moe may be seedy—but these are the genuine qualities of their character that cannot be bartered away with impunity.

The show's theme demonstrates that however flawed, one's essential nature is priceless. Bart and Moe both affirm this theme through their separate misfortunes and ultimate recoveries. Moe, in fact, provides a thematic variation to Bart's core validation of the episode's premise. Bart's sister Lisa expresses another variation of the message with her observation that this essential nature or 'soul' has to be earned "through suffering and thought." She also mentions "prayer"—but this part of the equation was ratified only by Bart's experience—not by Moe's. This variance suggests that, though the program's theme is philosophical, it is not necessarily theistic.

Despite its wildly satiric quality, the episode includes a number of balancing forces that create a sense of disciplined stability. The foibles of organized religion as represented by the punitive and superficial Reverend Lovejoy are contrasted with the humane and reflective philosophies that Lisa expresses. Similarly, Milhouse's cold-hearted capitalism is checkmated by Lisa's caring philanthropy. And the broad farce that takes place in Moe's refurbished tavern is a counterweight to Bart's tortuous soul-seeking quest. Even more explicitly, the dream-sequence pairings of children and their souls illustrate the dualities of the physical and the spiritual.

The basic evolutionary progression of this episode is quite straightforward. It begins with Bart's liturgical practical joke that sets the stage for his initial punishment, the questioning of the soul's existence, and the selling of this allegedly fictitious commodity to his friend Milhouse. The scene then shifts to the netherworld of Moe's Tavern to set up the parallel abandoning of Moe's substance for the promise of theme-restaurant riches. Bart then begins to experience problems with the bargain he made while Moe is still at the stage of putting his trade into action. The episode then alternates between deepening soul-loss problems for both Bart and Moe. The two issues intersect at the end of Act Two. Lisa saying grace during the Simpsons' visit to Moe's triggers a now-believing Bart's rush to retrieve his 'soul certificate'

from Milhouse. The start of Act Three finds Bart at the first step in his odyssey—contending with the phantasmagoric pest exterminator. The scene then shifts back and forth between Moe's and Bart's successive soul-less failures. Moe then remakes the tavern and, sadder but wiser, reassumes his true nature. But Bart's more profound epiphany is realized only after he turns, as a last resort, to prayer and accepts the salvation that Lisa provides. At the end of the show, we see the resurrection of the old Bart. He has reunited with his true self, however imperfect that true self might be.

For a prime-time cartoon, this episode is built on a very profound theme; therefore, an effective use of hierarchy is essential to avoid extended and audience-alienating preachiness. In the main, the hierarchy flows from the alternation of Bart's choice and predicament with the choice and predicament experienced by Moe. We begin and end with Bart, but, the body of the show intersperses Bart's escalating crisis with the many more zany disasters that Moe encounters. The six tavern scenes provide often riotous comic relief from the increasing dark and foreboding struggle that Bart is experiencing. Each time Bart's difficulties move to a more fearful level, a segment at Moe's helps relax the tension before it is allowed to escalate once more toward the final affirmation of the show's theme and the 'real' Bart's reemergence. In addition, the episode's subversively funny opening, in which Bart's hymn substitution hijacks the church service, grabs viewer attention but at a tension-free level from which ample and extended dramatic build can compellingly proceed.

and purposes that are largely unattainable in real life. The Logic of Aesthetic Form is one of the most comprehensive structures for accomplishing this packaging. In a statement that encompasses all Logic-employing aesthetic experience, Monroe Beardsley concludes of art, and of life in general:

What is the good of life itself, except to be as fully alive as we can become—to burn with a hard gemlike flame, to choose one crowded hour of glorious life, to seize experience at its greatest magnitude? And this is precisely our experience of art; it is living the best way we know how. Far from being a handmaiden to other goals, art gives us immediately, and richly, the best there is in life, intense aware-ness—it gives us what life itself aims at be-coming, but seldom achieves outside of art.[47]

This is not a bad prescription for elec-tronic media creators to follow as we at-tempt to fashion our own life-intensive pro-gram arts.

ENDNOTES

1. Theodore Meyer Greene, *The Arts and the Art of Criticism* (Princeton, NJ: Princeton University Press, 1952), 137.
2. Ibid., 29.
3. Gerald Herbener, "The Idea of Aesthetics." Speech presented to the Broadcast Education Association Convention, April 7, 1978 (Las Vegas).
4. John Dewey, "Having an Experience," in Melvin Rader (ed.), *A Modern Book of Esthetics*, 5th ed. (New York: Holt, Rinehart and Winston, 1979), 138.
5. Jean Mitry, *Aesthetic and Philosophy of Film*, Vol. 2, trans. Robert Edmunds (Paris: Editions Universitaires, 1965), 197.
6. Thomas Olson, "Lectures on Aesthetic Form," presented at Wayne State University, February 1964 (Detroit).
7. Greene, 403.
8. Larry Burriss, "How Anchors, Reporters and Newsmakers Affect Recall and Evaluation of Stories," *Journalism Quarterly* (Summer/Autumn 1987), 519.
9. Hans-Bernd Brosius, Wolfgang Donsbach, and Monika Birk, "How Do Text-Picture Relations Affect the Informational Effectiveness of Television Newscasts?" *Journal of Broadcasting & Electronic Media* (Spring 1996), 191.
10. Sarah Ruth Kozloff, "Narrative Theory and Television," in Robert Allen (ed.), *Channels of Discourse* (Chapel Hill: University of North Carolina Press, 1987), 67.
11. Carl Grabo, *The Creative Critic* (Chicago: The University of Chicago Press, 1948), 18.
12. "Masahiko Morizono: Sony's Tele-Visionary," *Broadcasting* (September 30, 1991), 45.
13. Gary David Goldberg, remarks to the National Association of Television Program Executives Convention, January 14, 1997 (New Orleans).
14. George Boas, *A Primer for Critics* (New York: Greenwood Press, 1968), 58.
15. Edmund Feldman, *Art as an Image and Idea* (Englewood Cliffs, NJ: Prentice-Hall, 1967), 4.
16. Gary Selnow, "Solving Problems on Prime-Time Television," *Journal of Communication*, 36:(1986), 63–72.
17. Ibid., 71.
18. Eliseo Vivas, *Creation and Discovery* (New York: The Noonday Press, 1955), 98.
19. DeWitt Parker, *The Analysis of Art* (New Haven, CT: Yale University Press, 1926), 37.
20. David Altheide, "The Impact of Television News Formats on Social Policy," *Journal of Broadcasting & Electronic Media* (Winter 1991), 8.
21. Feldman, 263.
22. Thomas Olson, "A Basis for Criticism of the Visual Esthetic Elements of Television," Ph.D. diss., Wayne State University, 1966, 134.
23. Parker, 38.
24. Jerome Stolnitz, *Aesthetics and Philosophy of Art Criticism* (Boston: Houghton Mifflin, 1960), 235.
25. Robert Edmunds, *The Sights and Sounds of Cinema and Television* (New York: Teachers College Press, 1982), 107.
26. Dan Levitin, "Jack Renner," *Recording Engineer Producer* (January 1991), 32.
27. Edmunds, 165.
28. Parker, 38–39.
29. Ibid., 57–58.
30. Zoe Ingalls, "The Lifelong Passion of 'the Picture Man,'" *The Chronicle of Higher Education* (March 24, 1993), B5.
31. Parker, 45.
32. Herbert Langfeld, *The Aesthetic Attitude* (New York: Harcourt, Brace, 1920), 241.
33. Michael Lemonick, "Life, the Universe and Everything," *Time* (February 22, 1993), 63.
34. Olson, "Basis for Criticism," 132.
35. Ibid., 130.
36. "Steven Bochco: Taking Risks with Television," *Broadcasting* (May 6, 1991), 28, 53.
37. Edmunds, 179–180.
38. Seymour Chatman, *Story and Discourse: Narrative Structure in Fiction and Film* (Ithaca, NY: Cornell University Press, 1978), 68.
39. Robert MacKenzie, "WIOU," *TV Guide* (December 1, 1990), 48.
40. Kozloff, 63.
41. John Madden, "The Day I Knocked Pat Summerall's Headset Off," *TV Guide* (August 20, 1988), 13.
42. Paul Schulman, remarks to the International Radio & Television Society Faculty/Industry Conference, February 7, 1991 (New York).
43. Stanley Cavell, "The Fact of Television," in John Hanhardt (ed.), *Video Culture* (Rochester, NY: Visual Studies Workshop Press, 1986), 206–207.
44. Kozloff, 67–68.
45. Rudolf Arnheim, *Toward a Psychology of Art* (Berkeley: University of California Press, 1967), 174.
46. Parker, 61–62.
47. Monroe Beardsley, *Aesthetics: Problems in Philosophy of Criticism* (New York: Harcourt, Brace & World, 1958), 563.

14

Reality Programming

Historically, media critics and responsible broadcasters tried to make and communicate clear and careful distinctions between entertainment and information programming. But in recent years, these distinctions have become blurred, particularly in the hybrid category known as *reality programming*. Because this category has been the focus of such intense critical debate, we devote a separate chapter to its definition and analysis.

A TERMINOLOGY MAZE

Reality programming signifies many different things to many different people. Unfortunately, many of these things are negative. Among the sins attributed to the category are cheapness, sleaziness, distortion, and even downright dishonesty. If we are to come to grips with the issue in a critically competent manner, we first must derive some workable definitions for what we are talking about. We cannot begin to fashion evaluations if there is no agreement as to the essential characteristics of what we are evaluating.

Our task is complicated by the wide spectrum of labels that have been applied to reality vehicles. Among the more prominent are Infotainment, Tabloid TV, Trash TV, Crash TV, Shock TV, and Keyhole Television. Rather than initially trying to define or defuse these largely derisive subcategories, let us begin with a general and neutral definition of the reality genre. We can then proceed to analyze its subsidiaries and their comparative purposes and attributes.

Defining Reality

For the moment, let us say that reality programming refers to

Comparatively inexpensive, nonfiction, recorded programs, whether prescripted or not, that purport to show real people in actual life situations for at least partially entertainment purposes.

This operational definition makes it clear that the *inexpensive* qualification is a comparative one. As we discuss in more detail later in this chapter, a hallmark of even the higher-priced reality genres is that they can be produced for significantly less money than can fictional/scripted entertainment programs such as half-hour sitcoms and one-hour dramas or action/adventure series. Reality offerings are also much less costly than are the rights fees and production expenditures associated with mainstream sporting events, which are not conventionally thought of as reality properties.

Nonfiction, of course, means that the show is characterized as a true-life event rather than as the product of an author's imagination. Just how true-to life it actually is constitutes a variable worth exploring in each program's case, of course. But the fact remains that the key promise of a reality program is that viewers will be exposed to *actuality* (albeit mediated) rather than to scriptwriters' fantasies.

Productionally, all shows conceded to come under the reality heading are *prerecorded*. This again eliminates live sports coverage as well as conventional newscasts. (It does not, however, automatically exclude some of the prepackaged segments that may be included within the fabric of those newscasts.)

Meanwhile, whether a program is *prescripted* is irrelevant in trying to separate reality genres from other kinds of series. Talk and game shows are, for the most part, unscripted. Some court and all magazine series, on the other hand, use significant amounts of prior-written material. Yet all of these formats are generally conceded to be reality properties.

Showing *real people* in *actual life situations*, on the other hand, are essential conditions of and audience expectations connected with any reality series. Whether it is the heavily ritualized environment of the game show, the architectural parameters of a talk studio, or the seemingly random and boundaryless settings of a *Cops* or *World's Most Amazing Videos*, reality program consumers want to believe that they are participating in a genuine occurrence—not just observing a theatrical play.

These consumers choose reality programs because they want to be *entertained*. Although there may be informational elements to the reality show (or to *any* program fare, for that matter), its primary, gratification is a (sometimes catharsis-tinged) entertainment one. In contrast, so-called hard-news programs may be entertainingly packaged, but they are promoted and endorsed as conveyors of serious information.

Individually, these several distinctions may be somewhat imprecise. When taken as a whole, however, they reflect at least a general industry consensus as to whether a given project fits within the "reality" construct. From a critical perspective, it then becomes a more straightforward matter of ascertaining if an individual show and its components are what they purport to be.

News and Entertainment

Having defined the broad field of reality programming, we must next decode the 'catch words' used in referring to the news and nonnews aspects of this field. Certainly, the electronic media industry as a whole has been slow to provide such definitions. Thus, critically perceptive professionals must undertake the task for themselves—lest outside critics do it for (or to) us.

Let us begin with the term *infotainment*. Even though, as Arthur Greenwald points out, "the line between news and infotainment continues to blur,"[1] the term essentially means the packaging of *soft news* items in a way calculated to maximize these items' perceived entertainment value to viewers. A former field producer for the now defunct *PM Magazine*, Greenwald sees that syndicated show as a pioneer of the infotainment approach. Launched in the late 1970s from the Westinghouse stations, *PM* influenced many later series. "*Real People, That's Incredible*, and dozens of others were more earnest

copies," Greenwald asserts. "Although frequent format adjustments kept *PM*'s ratings high for years, the show gradually drowned in a sea of imitators."[2]

But what is this "soft news" that *PM* and its descendents packaged? According to NBC News producer Brett Holey, *soft* news conveys "items of interest but which have less direct affect on you than *hard* news which is something you should know because it affects your world."[3] Looking at the question from another angle, Robert Priddy, then chairman of the RTNDA (Radio Television News Directors Association), stated that "news can be entertaining but it is never entertainment."[4] Thus, infotainment shows embrace 'softer' news pieces with the primary aim to *be* entertaining. 'Hard news' programs and features, conversely, pre-eminently strive to be informative—with entertainment as an optional (though always subordinate) goal.

The difference between news and entertainment therefore is as much one of priorities as of content. Priddy's comment seems to validate media scholar John Fiske's observation that

news professionals in particular and broadcasters in general are keen to separate news from fiction. . . . Generic distinctions between information and entertainment or fact and fiction are crucial for the producers, for they describe different sorts of ethics, different definitions of responsible programming.[5]

Richard Salant would certainly endorse Fiske's statement. The president of CBS News for most of the 1960s and 1970s, Salant was one of the most tireless and articulate advocates for keeping broadcast journalism uncompromisingly distinct from entertainment considerations and devices. In the preface to his division's 1976 book of news guidelines, Salant cited,

the overriding importance peculiar to our form of journalism of drawing the sharpest possible line—sharp perhaps to the point of eccentricity—between our line of broadcast business, which is dealing with fact, and that in which our associates on the entertainment side of the business are generally engaged, which is dealing with fiction and drama. Because it all comes out sequentially on the same point of the dial and on the same tube, and because, then, there are no pages to be turned or column lines to be drawn in our journalistic matrix, it is particularly important that we recognize that we are not in show business and should not use any of the dramatic licenses, the "fiction-which-represents-truth" rationales, or the underscoring and the punctuations which entertainment and fiction may, and do, properly use. This may make us a little less interesting to some—but that is the price we pay for dealing with fact and truth, which may often be duller—and with more loose ends—than fiction and drama.[6]

Infotainment, however, blurs Salant's distinction between entertainment and news by conjoining elements from each category in a single package. Therefore, a crucial critical consideration is whether the infotainment program in question accurately defines for prospective viewers its content ingredients and particular approach to information/entertainment blending.

Tabloid Characteristics

Tabloid programs, for their part, are generally conceded to be shows that occupy the more sensationalized side of the infotainment continuum. *Sensationalism*, in turn, has been defined by William Adams as coverage of "crime, violence, natural disasters, accidents and fires, along with amusing, heartwarming, shocking or curious vignettes about people."[7] Or, as Professors Hofstetter and Dozier dissect it, "First, sensational news is coverage of unexpected events. Second, these events have some inherent entertainment value."[8]

In their studies, Grabe, Zhou, and Barnett isolated "three popular concerns about sensational journalism: it violates notions of social decency, displaces socially significant stories, and is seen as a new-sprung drift into excessiveness." However, the three scholars also discovered other research that blunts these concerns. "One view of sensationalism is that it plays an important role in *maintaining* a society's commonly shared notions of decency and morality by publicly showcasing what is unacceptable. . . . Stories about family conflicts, substance abuse, violence, disaster, and other disruptions of everyday life are regarded as more significant to the lives of ordinary people than the meaty and timely political and economic is-

sues that elites prescribe as important information for the masses."[9]

Sensationalism, then, and the tabloid programs that use it, are not inherently evil or distortive and arguably meet an important need. Standard tabloid techniques, such as flashy graphics, more energetic editing, and the use of music beds, don't necessarily undercut fairness and accuracy. In fact, veteran network news executive Av Westin argues that 'tabloid' is merely "another way of saying, highly popular, fast-paced, full of emotion. All of that is fine, that is what television is about."[10] Notice, however, that what is *not* identified as an acceptable variable is the *truth* of the story. The subject matter and packaging of tabloid pieces may be different from 'hard news,' but both should be expected to treat their respective types of topics honestly. "Tabloid journalism has a long and honorable tradition, going back a couple of hundred years," says television programming executive Richard Kurlander. "Usually the journalism itself is sound; it's only the style that some people object to."[11] Critic Jeff Jarvis puts the style versus substance issue this way: "As any tabloid reporter can tell you, a good story tells itself. It's the second-rate story that needs a reporter's artificial injections of neon."[12]

Nevertheless, one contentious item that may further separate tabloid from conventional 'hard news' presentations is the concept of *balance*. Traditional journalists are taught that, even though objectivity is probably impossible, the balancing of a story to present opposing sides of an issue fairly is an ethical necessity. In the case of tabloid coverage, however, a different standard often applies. Though she is referring to print rather than electronic tabloids, sociologist S. Elizabeth Bird characterizes both when she observes that

invoking as usual their belief that entertainment is their primary goal, the tabloid writers argue that they can afford to neglect such journalistic concepts as "balance." After all, the best and most vivid stories are consistent and clear in their point of view; competing interpretations are anathema to a good tabloid tale.[13]

One can argue that a lack of balance may increase the *danger* that a story will be "untrue"—but this does not mean it inevitably will be false. Therefore, tabloid journalism should be considered *news without a safety net*.

Trash, Shock, and Keyhole

Although tabloid presentations have the capability to convey significant information in a legitimate manner, few authorities would credit *trash TV* with this virtue. To producer Av Westin, the hallmark of trash TV is "prurient, salacious dominance."[14] In other words, this type of program is not informative at all. Its content may shock or grab but has neither 'hard' nor 'soft' news value as we have defined these terms. Indeed, there is absolutely nothing "new" in trash except the ways it finds to distort the truth.

Nor is trash TV reputable entertainment since its appeal is primarily mired in the Three L's: lewdness, lust, and lechery. Such content is difficult enough to justify in print vehicles that are voluntarily brought into the home. But when conveyed via electronic media that directly or indirectly rely on the public spectrum or right-of-way, trash-type content raises major public policy and corporate responsibility issues.

Trash is not a synonym for *tabloid*. Rather, it exists completely beyond the parameters of infotainment. Trash is exclusively entertainment—but entertainment that relies entirely on human debasement rather than human insight. When a program *exploits* rather than *covers* the person(s) on which it is focusing, it is no longer tabloid. It has degenerated into trash.

Consequently, when we as professionals encounter programming to which the *tabloid* or *trash* label has been applied, we have to ask two questions:

1. Is this label an accurate signifier of the show's content and thrust?
2. Do those who have applied the label understand the precise implications of it?

Another way of distinguishing between tabloid and trash is to apply the benchmark of *significance*. As S. Elizabeth Bird asserts, "tabloids may provide a great deal of 'trivia' that is regarded by their audiences as 'important information,' such as human interest and celebrity stories that have *relevant lessons for their lives*" [italics added].[15] Trash, conversely, is nothing more than calculated glimpses into the pathetic deviancies of other people. There is no lesson here—only grotesque caricature. There is no enduring usefulness to trash TV—only a temporary voyeuristic thrill.

Talk TV star Oprah Winfrey has long-term experience with both tabloid and trash. As she recalls and confesses:

We grew up in a society that for years denied dysfunction. TV brought some of this to the surface, but the problem, as I see it now, is that it didn't evolve from there. We needed to be *solving* these problems. Instead, TV got stuck *thriving* on them, and for the worst possible reasons—exploitation, voyeurism, and entertainment. . . . People should not be surprised and humiliated on national television for the purpose of entertainment. I was ashamed of myself for creating the opportunity that allowed it to happen.[16]

Proving that shows can upgrade their orientation and still succeed, Winfrey changed her format from exploitative trash to problem-solving infotainment and became the top-rated talk show in daytime syndication.

The line between 'infotaining' tabloid and debilitating trash, therefore, can be best envisioned in terms of *result*. If the audience has learned something from and about real people or situations that they can apply to their own lives, we are dealing with infotainment. If the style is sensationalized, this is infotainment of the tabloid variety. Conversely, if viewers have been exposed only to the on-camera exploitation of human basket-cases with whom they feel no affinity, the program constitutes trash.

Shock TV is simply the most extreme mutation of the 'trash' phenomenon. It moves beyond any pretense of mainstream entertainment to grab attention by the sheer offensiveness of its subject or by how that subject is portrayed. Consequently, shock programming is anathema to major advertisers and their agencies and remains a fringe enterprise usually limited to off-hours on marginal stations and limited-access cable channels. Some of shock TV's market has also been usurped by the Internet. Because there are virtually no economic or governmental barriers to operating a website, the purveyors of shock have ample opportunities to offer this content on line without worrying about attracting mainstream advertisers or offending federal regulators.

Finally, *keyhole television* signifies those 'hidden camera' or 'personal camera' shows that catch famous or 'ordinary' people in personal or occupational situations that can be revealing, embarrassing, intimate, or downright ludicrous. As a result of the camcorder revolution, many consumers now have ample opportunity to capture family, friends, and themselves on videotape and submit the quirky results for telecast. Obviously, then, much of keyhole reality programming is strictly diversionary entertainment. It can seldom be labeled as trash, because these slice-of-life tableaus are usually lighthearted and innocuous.

However, some keyhole varieties, particularly the *docusoaps*, possess the potential to provide deft mini-insights into the human condition. In fact, when such insights are pronounced, the category takes on the characteristics of infotainment. In her review below, critic Antonia Zerbisias surveys a variety of docu-soaps and the range of revelations of which they are capable.

As a means of graphically summarizing our dissection of reality programming, Figure 14-1 spatially orients and compares its various components. Do not, however, interpret the structure of this continuum to mean that *Information* is "better than" or "preferable to" *Entertainment*. As we mention in Chapter 8, these are merely different gratifications—and gratifications that are addressed by reality programming in a variety of ways. But as Figure 14-1 does indicate, when the alleged 'entertainment' consists of material that exploits and demeans its sub-

---

THE DOCU-SOAP'S BUSTIN' OUT ALL OVER

by Antonia Zerbisias

Say bye-bye to The Young And The Restless, hello to docu-soap.

No, your favorite daily wallow-fest has not been canceled. It's just that the trumped-up, pumped-up travails of Victor and Nikki have nothing on real-life melodrama. Which is why the docu-soap is busting out all over the dial this season.

These continuing documentary series, which combine narrative with reality, make up the hottest new genre on the tube, marrying voyeurism, information and pure emotional juice for your complete viewing experience.

At least five are scheduled for this season, and you can be sure more will follow.

Don't miss the BBC's Airport, 16 high anxiety half-hours tracking life behind the scenes of the multi-ring circus which is Heathrow.

Join paparazzo Dennis as he stalks Hugh Grant and Liz Hurley, Melanie Griffith and Antonio Banderas, Paul McCartney, Mick Jagger and all the other celebs that take off and land at the world's busiest international airport.

Follow flight dispatcher Viv as she deals with plane delays and wandering passengers. Sweat it out with customs inspectors Garth and Cath as they interrogate suspected drug smugglers.

Accompany former salesclerk Claire as she attempts to pass the rigourous safety training course for cabin crew members, and learn a thing or two about getting out alive in the process. This is highly addictive stuff.

And, for programmers looking to cut costs, it's tailor-made TV without the expense and bother of actors, agents, scriptwriters, makeup artists, prop people, production designers or set builders. Just make sure you have agile, fleet-footed camera crews and plenty of tape to capture all the action and reaction.

There's 10 hours of that on Jennifer Fox's An American Love Story. While this stunning cinema verité series, which has the viewer spending five years in the lives and home of Bill Sims, Karen Wilson and their daughters Cicily and Chaney of Flushing, New York, is not quite the "landmark" program many claim it is - - - PBS' The Farmer's Wife last year and the groundbreaking 1973 An American Family are the real stand-outs in that context - - - An American Love Story brings much to the table with its compelling story of a bi-racial couple and their trial and triumphs.

Says Karen in the last installment, which goes back to the beginning of their 32-year relationship, "We were never Ozzie and Harriet."

Ain't that the truth: He's a hard-drinking blues musician while she's a hyperkinetic, chain-smoking corporate personnel manager who defied her friends and community by taking up with him.

Both grew up in the small towns of Ohio where racism flourished. Indeed, when they started dating, the local sheriff visited Karen's mother, demanding that the relationship end. A childhood pal recalls at least one male friend who was so outraged he "talked about maybe trying to pick Bill off with a gun." The couple was constantly hassled by the police, Bill regularly tossed in jail, his dog was killed, his car set on fire.

But An American Love Story isn't just about race. Far from it. Film maker Fox virtually moved in with the Sims-Wilson clan, sleeping on the girls' bedroom floor. Consequently, she captured plenty, maybe too much, including Bill's attempts to quit boozing after his career nosedived, Karen's emergency hysterectomy, Cicily's less than pleasant adventures (with both white and black kids!) at an ultra-white university, Chaney's first dating experiences, the good times and the bad. Life, as we all learn eventually, is an emotional roller-coaster and this is one hell of a thrill ride.

But don't think you must catch every episode to enjoy it. The camera gets so intimate with the Sims-Wilson family that you'll feel you really know these people as soon as you meet them, whenever that is.

Next month, Discovery is launching yet another docu-soap, Downtown Angel Of Medicine, a not-for-the-squeamish look at life and death at Toronto's St. Michael's Hospital. Boasting breathtaking access to the E.R., intensive care units and operating theatres, it kicks off with a moving interplay between a dying woman and the doctor who cares for her.

Later this year, watch for CBC's Little Miracles, which hangs out with the staff and patients at Toronto's Hospital For Sick Children. And next season, CBC will have yet another docu-soap, Niagara Falls, which eavesdrops on the tacky tourist trade in the resort town.

Of course, you have to figure that, while docu-soaps are considered to be reality TV, the presence of cameras must have a mitigating effect on the behaviours of their targets. For example, there's a scene in An American Love Story that has Cicily and a friend discussing a bigoted sales clerk who suddenly become sweet as tupelo honey when she spotted the camera.

Still, it's mindblowing what people reveal of themselves on screen - - - especially Americans who are much less reserved than Canadians or British. After watching a few hours of these series, you begin to believe it really is a Jerry Springer kind of world out there after all - - - only it's not faked.

And, unlike General Hospital and Days Of Our Lives, docu-soap characters don't brush out their big hair and hang up their designer duds in the wardrobe department at the end of their days.

This is real life: What you get is what you see.

(Reprinted with permission—The Toronto Star Syndicate)

ject and audience, it progressively slides below the level of legitimate entertainment and becomes debasement.

REALITY ON RADIO

To this point in the chapter, we have focused mainly on television programming. That is because video reality vehicles have been much more numerous and have drawn much more critical commentary than have counterpart offerings on the audio band. Nonetheless, the roots of reality programming are in radio. They were germinated in *The March of Time's* 1930s journalistic re-creations as well as in Norman Corwin's epic 1940s docudramas, and they later evolved

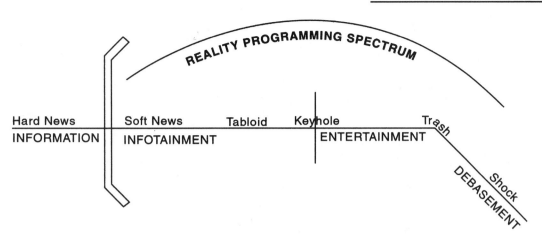

FIGURE 14-1
Mapping reality
programming.

into network and syndicated soft news and tabloid featurettes. In other reality segments today, some disc jockeys still tease listeners with "keyhole" telephone put-ons, and a few others have become well known for "shock" tactics and commentaries that have sometimes drawn FCC sanctions.

Given the overwhelmingly musical nature of modem radio formats, however, aural reality programming is largely a matter of enhancement snippets rather than full-length shows. The major exception is the *talk* format, which can modulate up and down the reality spectrum depending on the topic and how it is approached. The fact that radio offers no visual (exception in the listener's mind's-eye) does not alter the basic distinctions among *soft news, tabloid, keyhole, trash*, and *shock* that we draw in our examination of television. Thus, for example, "topless radio" is merely "shock television" without a picture tube.

Because of a radio format's flow, however, reality excesses can be much more dangerous in that they can catch a listener unawares. There is no *TV Guide* to characterize individual audio segments and provide guidance broken into thirty-minute modules. It is therefore not surprising that the 1978 Supreme Court ruling giving the Federal Communications Commission the power to regulate electronic media indecency came as the result of a radio transmission. This *Pacifica* case drew its name from the Pacffica Foundation, which owned a station that broadcast a George Carlin monologue called "Filthy Words." A parent on an afternoon drive with his son heard the segment and complained to the FCC, which took it from there. Though probably mild by today's

standards, the sudden appearance of the Carlin monologue illustrates the "exposure without warning" nature of radio.

Much more recently, a Midwest disc jockey aired a bogus nuclear attack announcement to make a point about emergency preparedness. But, because of radio's immediacy and visual implicitness, several citizens were unnecessarily panicked by this pseudoreality stunt. (Orson Welles *inadvertently* triggered a similar result in his 1938 dramatization of H. G. Wells's *War of the Worlds*, when an object of pure entertainment was misconstrued as 'hard' information.)

The ultimate difference between radio and television reality programming, then, is that radio ventures have fewer tools that clearly identify and qualify what they are doing. There is no program listing or supered graphic to give a prior warning or device disclaimer. Thus, radio reality features must be much more carefully packaged to avoid accidental distortions and offensiveness that can drive away listeners and the advertisers seeking to reach them.

BUSINESS GRATIFICATIONS

Scaring off advertisers is bad business, of course. And when improperly conceived reality programming does that, it negates its inherent production cost advantage. Remember, as we point out in our "reality" definition: Reality projects are comparatively inexpensive to produce, costing anywhere from 50 percent to 70 percent less than a comparable-length sitcom or drama. Of course, low production outlays are not, by themselves, an assurance of business success. What must also be factored in is the return on investment in the form of audience numbers *that translate into advertising revenues*.

In many instances, syndicated reality shows garner very acceptable ratings. For instance, "daytime talk shows still deliver more GRPs [gross rating points] in key women's demographics than does any other program genre," states industry reporter Cynthia Littleton.[17] For the networks, too, reality can be appealing. In fact, recounts industry analyst Stephen Battaglio, "the birth of the networks' reality binge can be traced to the fall of 1988, when the writers' strike delayed the start of the new TV season. In an effort to put first-run programming on the air, NBC turned to a Geraldo Rivera special called *Devil Worship: Exposing Satan's Underground*. It pulled a 33 percent share and sent a signal to the networks that viewers had an appetite for the stuff."[18]

Nonetheless, regardless of the 'audience numbers' being posted, advertiser reluctance to support reality programming increases the farther to the right of our Figure 14-1 Spectrum the show is located. Furthermore, as studio executive Rich Frank points out, while " 'shock TV' programs virtually guarantee audience delivery at first, they eventually fail when advertisers blanche at the increasing shock value . . . needed to keep audiences."[19] Producer Stephen Cannell states the business downside to the more extreme reality programs even more bluntly:

The advertisers don't seem to be too interested in those shows. . . . Everything I'm hearing from the networks that are programming them is that they don't sell them out. The "bottom tickers" are all over those shows, the guys who wait until it's unsold and then buy units for nothing. And so they're not good business for the networks.[20]

Advertising agency media buyer Mike Drexler adds his own caution: "It has to be demonstrated that the advertiser will not get letters."[21]

Conversely, the more midspectrum reality ventures are unlikely to encounter such advertiser animosity and they still constitute, says Stephen Battaglio, "the pattern for the way networks now use reality shows—as low-cost programs for time periods that seem hopeless."[22] *Dateline NBC* was initiated to serve such a strategy. But when it began to attract a saleable audience, the show was expanded to multiple evenings, producing substantial revenues at production costs much lower than the sitcoms and dramas that formerly filled those time slots. This success, in turn, freed up more program development dollars for the sitcoms, dramas, and other nonreality vehicles in the remainder of the schedule. ABC's *20/20* and CBS's *60 Minutes* and *60 Minutes II* are further manifestations of the same fiscal approach. Infotainment thus has become good business even in broadcast network prime time, proving the inherent appeal and expandability of nonexploitative reality.

There is a limit to how much production costs can be cut, of course, before "on-screen values" are noticeably compromised. As a category, reality TV is less expensive to produce than is fiction TV. But regardless of genre, a show still must be well-crafted to attract and hold a saleable audience. "I don't believe the answer to the economic woes is just to produce shows for less," asserts studio executive Kerry McCluggage. "The challenge is to find ways to deliver production values that make shows valuable in all markets of the world. To do otherwise will result in creating programming that is more disposable. And I'm more interested in finding ways to create programming that is not disposable."[23]

Like most electronic media considerations, reality program production and scheduling choices are business assessments that must take both short- and long-range goals into account. Today's profits and cost efficiencies are valuable only insofar as they contribute to tomorrow's enhanced viability for our company's products and services. Featuring a preponderance of cheap, disposable programming now may result in our studio, station, or channel becoming fully expendable later.

KEY REALITY GENRES

We have examined the broad gratifications sectors into which reality programs can be grouped. And we have explored some business factors that have motivated reality's use. At this point, then, we can catalog specific reality vehicles with greater precision. Most reality shows fit into one of the following and sometimes overlapping genres:

1. News Featurettes
2. Network Magazines
3. Daily Syndicated News Magazines
4. Talk Shows
5. Game Shows
6. Court Shows
7. Criminal Posters
8. Video Verité
9. Keyhole Shows
10. Pseudosports

News Featurettes

Many station newscasts now round out their coverage of local breaking stories with pre-packaged segments covering such areas as health, personal finance, cooking, and gardening. Some of these segments may be categorized as "hard news"; but most, due to their subject matter and lack of immediacy, are infotainment pieces designed to enhance the viewability of the newscast while filling some of its time in a very economical manner. The stories arrive at the station either entirely preproduced or as "unsweetened" visual footage with a script that can be narrated by each station's reporter.

Some featurettes are syndicated properties for which the station pays a fee or agrees to air a 'barter' commercial that is packaged with the story. Others are VNRs—*video news releases*—that have been provided by a corporation, trade association, or similar enterprise. VNRs have become increasingly popular with news directors because they are free and usually are well-produced by former radio/television correspondents who know a local newscast's formatic requirements.

The potential problem with VNRs, however, is that they are sometimes unattributed. In other words, the audience is unaware that a traffic safety story on air bags was contributed by an auto manufacturer who is marketing the devices as standard equipment on all its vehicles. Or, viewers don't realize that a personal finance segment on the value of prearranged funerals was prepared by a mortician's association whose members are likely to benefit from an increase in prearrangement traffic.

Such featurettes are not, in themselves, bad. But as we indicate early in this chapter, the critical issue is whether they are presented for what they are—whether, in this case, the consumer is properly informed of the source of the piece. The credibility of the local news organization can be severely compromised if what has been represented as one of its own stories later causes problems because of inaccuracies.

Should the use of all outside-produced news featurettes—whether VNR or not—be eliminated? Probably no more than newspapers should abandon their syndicated soft news columns and reworked press releases. As former TV news executive Reese Schonfeld once shot back at two prominent newspaper critics: "Until *The New York Times* decides to drop its B and C sections or the *Washington Post* drops its Metro and Style sections, I think Peter Boyer and Tom Shales ought to leave us alone."[24]

Light or heavy, straight information or applied infotainment, the featurette can be a valuable enhancement for both show producers and consumers. Honesty, however, compels that audiences be made aware of the source of these clips so they can make up their own minds about the segments' validity.

Network Magazines

Also known as "soft documentaries" ('soft docs'), these vehicles may expend an entire hour on a story (such as A & E's *Biography*) or, more often, break themselves up into three or four stories. A series such as the long-running *60 Minutes* still sees itself as a hard-news enterprise. However, most network magazines (and, arguably, some *60 Minutes* stories) are very much infotainment enterprises as we define that term. Magazines have almost completely replaced their more serious 'hard documentary' ancestors that cost more money to produce and drew much smaller audiences. "The word *documentary* has taken on a pejorative meaning," argues Av Westin. "If it sounds too much like a long trek through TV land, it won't attract anyone." Contemporary viewers, he adds, "expect a payoff every ten or twelve minutes because of the way cop shows and sitcoms work: the public is now 'video- educated.' . . . Too many of the old-style documentaries expected the viewer to wait around for a payoff at the last ten minutes, with a couple of talking heads."[25]

So the 'soft doc' avoids the "d" word at all costs as a means of better competing in the entertainment-oriented environment of network prime time. Author Ken Auletta chronicled this shift in 1991:

Back in 1970, the three networks premiered a total of 79 prime-time documentaries. By 1986, this number had shrunk to 15. Today, with some notable exceptions, the traditional documentary has been replaced by such ratings grabbers as NBC's "Scared Sexless" and "Bad Girls," which probed in a sensational way the subjects of sex and young women behind bars.[26]

It is argued that this continuing trend simply reflects changing audience preferences, which must be respected in a still-tonnage delivery system. In their research, however, Diamond and Mahony isolated other factors of greater influence:

[As] our group found, the changing nature of the television documentary has less to do with the alleged mindlessness of the public than it does with radical shifts in the thinking of the three old-line networks' new proprietors who are impatient for "payoffs." The old documentary form is still alive at the fringes of the networks' schedules; it also flourishes on public broadcasting, cable TV and other competitors of the Big Three. Classic documentaries are not dead, merely displaced, and the story of their migration tells a great deal about the state of television today.[27]

These alternative sources for 'hard docs' make it unlikely that the broadcast networks could hope to replicate even the modest audience levels of the past if they were to continue the form. The network magazine thus seems destined to be the documentary's permanent replacement as far as the major commercial broadcast networks are concerned.

Daily Syndicated News Magazines

Unlike the network 'soft docs,' daily syndicated news magazines are sold directly to stations for daily stripping. Often referred to as "the tabloids," daily syndicated news magazines have included such vehicles as *Inside Edition, Hard Copy,* and *National Enquirer TV.* Some, like *Entertainment Tonight* and *Access Hollywood,* focus on the people and happenings in the entertainment industry. Stories on these shows are much briefer than on the network 'mags,' with three, four, or more fitting easily into a half-hour program. Tabloid pieces are more in the na-

ture of individual news items—but all with a decidedly sensational bent.

Tabloids do not claim to be newscast substitutes but pride themselves on "getting you behind the headlines" into stories that are provocative, titillating, and less time-sensitive. As with network soft docs, tabloid reporters typically inject themselves into the story rather than maintaining the studied detachment practiced by conventional journalists. In fact, observes TV columnist Monica Collins, these syndicated news magazines "rely heavily on the anchors to wink at viewers about the more outrageous stories, or to provide a helpful dose of anchor-desk bromide when the going gets tough during the tragic tales."[28]

Tragedy of a highly personalized nature is certainly a hallmark of television tabloids—as has historically been the case for their print media predecessors. Most of the time, Collins recites, "the programs bank on an infinite supply of material—mankind's bottomless well of sorrow, pathos and gut-grabbing emotion: murder, mayhem, madness, corruption, greed. Better yet if celebrities are involved."[29] In short, through the studied involvement of their reporters and the intrusive focus on their personalized subjects, the syndicated news magazines, declares critic Robert MacKenzie, "use news to make television, which is not quite the same thing as using television to report news."[30]

As a program genre, there is certainly a place for tabloid-style infotainment—as the popularity of these series manifests. The two main critical concerns with the form are simply that sensational subject matter does not excuse the producer from being honest and accurate, and that tabloids should be exploited by programming executives primarily as entertainment vehicles—not promoted or packaged as *substitutes* for 'hard' newscasts. "Constant exposure to tabloid-style journalism," warns Professor Louis Day, "desensitizes society to the real problems of human existence and elevates such content to a position of respectability."[31]

The question, then, is one of overall schedule balance so that a given outlet does not restrict its news offerings solely to tabloid infotainment. Tabloid newspapers can indulge in such an exclusionary practice, but a more broadly informative performance is expected of a licensed or franchised electronic medium.

In their own way, the TV tabloids may serve an important function by broadening the range of subjects and treatments to which the viewing public is exposed. Former Fox News president Van Gordon Sauter makes this case by arguing that

what these people do is a form of journalism. Not the capital J variety, that's for sure. But it's a journalism that would have been recognized and appreciated by some of the great editors and publishers of the popular press that thrived in this country before journalism became hopelessly corporate, upper-middle-class, complacent and condescending.[32]

Talk Shows

Depending on their subject preferences, talk shows can range from the 'hardest' of news and even newsmaking (such as NBC's eternal *Meet the Press*) to the trashiest of interchanges among combative people who *really love* their dachshunds. Because this chapter focuses on reality programming, we do not discuss hard-news interviews here. Instead, this section concentrates on infotainment talk shows as well as on those shows located farther to the right on our Figure 14-1 reality spectrum. Sometimes, these series have been polished on radio or local stations before making the jump to higher-stakes national television syndication.

When they succeed in illuminating a broadly substantive topic, infotainment talk shows "are even—brace yourself—good journalism," Van Gordon Sauter submits.

With the correct topic and motivated guests, a talk master can reveal the dimensions of significant human issues with a clarity and reality beyond the grasp of print journalists. Anyone who caught the recent programs in which Oprah extracted from her guests gripping personal dramas of racism and aging . . . had a true learning experience. She revealed universal truths and lessons of relevance and immediacy to her audience.[33]

"The purpose of reality programming," adds Professor Wende Dumble, "is to make personal and accessible the mysterious influences that pervade our lives."[34] If we are led to identify *with* (rather than merely leer *at*) the participants in the conversation, then talk shows certainly have the potential to fulfill this purpose.

Conversely, in so-called hot talk, insight tends to be shattered by confrontation. At its worst, this has paved the way for homicide when one guest on *The Jenny Jones Show* killed another three days after the victim had revealed on the program a homosexual attraction for his subsequent slayer. At the very least, hot-talk properties "are exploitative in that they achieve humor or entertainment at the expense of someone on the stage laughing at them," says Disney executive Randy Reiss.[35] When a host depends on ridicule or on heated personal disputation to fuel audience interest, topic revelation is subordinated to the dynamics of derision or individual conflict. And when a guest is set up to be conquered (either by the host or other guests), the program descends into cannibalistic trash.

'Hot' or not, audience-participation talk shows also can convey a distortive sense that all opinions expressed are equally valid and authoritative. Such an interpretation may lead viewers to act on a totally erroneous opinion simply because they "heard it from several people on TV." In addition, the frequently advanced presumption that all the participants are motivated by the desire to 'help' may not, in fact, be accurate. There may, instead, be a calculated desire to hurt that, while contributing to dynamic discord, ravages the guest who is the focus of the discussion. In such cases, argue Professors Vicki Abt and Mel Seesholtz:

The studio audience participation keeps the action going and also contributes to the narrative that all opinions count equally in this democratic global village, and that we're all "plain folks" interested in helping our fellow man. In other words, all "hierarchies of credibility" that exist in society are obliterated. The facsimile of a "town meeting" or "the people's right to know" and the fraudulent egalitarian theme of the global village are part of the dynamics of the television talk show. . . . The absurdity of the situation is analogous to dialing a number randomly and proceeding to explain the most intimate details of your life to whoever answered the phone.[36]

In summary, talk shows are at their best when they illuminate the human condition in a way that is generalizable (perhaps even inspiring) to many people's lives and does not demean the participants involved. Talk shows do no harm when they offer lighthearted and/or lightweight infotainment that

THE ROSIE O'DONNELL SHOW
by Jeff Jarvis

It feels so good when it stops hurting. Finally, someone has come along to rescue daytime TV from America's trash caste, from the sex-obsessed, from the idiot exhibitionists who squatted on our airwaves for too long. They were a cultural fungus. But at long last, they are disappearing, thanks to the deserved death of so many talk shows recently. And I have to say: I told you so. I've long argued that in the end, America's good taste will prevail. The horrid trends that consume the tube - - - tabloids, bloopers, diseases-of-the-week, trash - - - inevitably go overboard until they can shock us no more. Audiences tire of those shows. TV execs lose money on them. Then they slink away, making room for good TV to return.

And good TV has returned to daytime, thanks to Rosie O'Donnell. On her new talk show, I haven't yet seen one dive-bar denizen confessing to new frontiers in adultery. Rosie's show isn't about freaks. It's about fun. It's a nighttime talk show brought to daytime, complete with show-biz guests, music, and a happy studio audience. And it's funny because Rosie has a hailstorm sense of humor and because she has the simple ability to enjoy her guests. When her costar in those Kmart commercials, Penny Marshall, visits, she imitates Marshall, who protests, "I don't tawwwwk like dat!" They're having a party and we got invited. Rosie shows Donnie Osmond her own Donny doll and demands that he sing duets. I sometimes think Rosie borrowed Casey Kasem's record collection; she has an amazing memory for kitsch songs. She has Fran Drescher on - - - but better yet, Drescher's parents, reviewing Florida restaurants from a sofa that surely was slipcovered until their daughter hit it big. She makes them laugh; they make her laugh; it's catching.

Rosie avoids other's pitfalls. She doesn't try to be sly, as David Letterman does (it was Dave's smirk that kept him from succeeding in daytime). She doesn't try to please everyone, as Jay Leno desperately does. She doesn't try to save the world with her smile, as Kathie Lee Gifford does. And Rosie doesn't try to sling sleaze, as every other daytime talk show does.

Instead, Rosie just wants to be more like Johnny Carson - - - how smart of her. She has a standard <u>Tonight</u>-like set and a bandleader, and she even pays tribute to Johnny with a variation on his "Stump the Band," in which Rosie takes audience challenges to sing TV theme songs.

Rosie has Johnny's ability to entertain her guests, her audience, and herself at the same time. She has Johnny's knack for rolling her eyes at the state of the world without whining about it. She may just be the first person to take the night out of <u>Tonight</u>. And in the process, she's making the daytime a nicer place.

proves a pleasant diversion and provides amicable companionship. But they are at their worst when they exploit and manipulate their guests to achieve heated confrontation and to force embarrassing, voyeuristic, and even fraudulent revelation. In the above review of *The Rosie O'Donnell Show* by critic Jeff Jarvis, what brand of talk program does he ascertain her vehicle to be?

Game Shows

Talk-show-like discourse is a core ingredient of "game talk." In this game-show variant, conversational responses by one contestant are 'right' or 'wrong' depending on their predictability to other participants—while the audience eavesdrops on the proceedings. Usually, the subject of the interchange is romance. Beginning decades ago with the originally demure *The Dating Game*, the genre has broadened to encompass much raunchier fare using suggestive (or blatant) questions from the host as the stimulus for "who said/did what" responses from on-the-prowl males and females.

Such game talk is seldom infotainment. There is no meaningful knowledge base from which the contestants are asked to draw—not even trivia. The answers pertain solely to revelations about a specific set of interpersonal relationships (or failure to, consummate same) and offer no generalizable insights—only specific and largely exploitative admissions about the players involved. The formula of such game talk, in fact, seems calculated to create programmatic trash—or worse.

The more traditional game vehicles—which go back to the earliest days of commercial radio—test contestant knowledge of more objective phenomena. Sometimes this is of the serious book-learning variety. But the more popular series lean more toward the trivia of merchandise pricing or are accompanied by major chance elements such as spinning wheels and hidden wild cards. An important appeal of the genre always flows from viewer interest in the contestants involved—in other words, from the "real people in actual life situations" ingredients that define reality programming in general. According to Elayne Rapping, game shows are so powerful because they constitute

dramatic communication—by our peers, rather than hired commercial actors. . . . The people who come on these shows, like those who buy lottery tickets and fill out the endless forms required to compete in the Publishers' Sweepstakes, are driven by frustration and financial difficulty. They want—just once—to "make it big." . . . Those who openly reveal the sad truth of so many American lives—that indeed a refrigerator-freezer *is* a moment of ecstasy in a gray and troubled world—will be scorned or pitied only by those privileged enough to think otherwise.[37]

The personal identification factor that draws viewers to game shows is a significant part of their appeal. And this appeal is heightened when there is a substantial contrast between the contestants, a difference that motivates cheering for one over the other(s). As with sports coverage, the usual

results are involving entertainment and harmless diversion. Yet, unlike sports, many game shows promote themselves as primarily intellectual exercises when, in fact, their informative component is very minimal. Stuart Kaminsky and Jeffrey Mahan have observed that on these programs

intellect rarely seems to be very important. In spite of the shows' surface-level claims about the importance of intelligence, other qualities are more important in the struggle to triumph over the adversities of fate as they are enacted in the quiz and game shows. A good memory, quick reaction under pressure, or physical abilities are more likely than exceptional intelligence to lead to triumph.[38]

The game show's brand of reality, then, may create a distortive, or at least oversimplified picture of what it takes to win in real life. Further, when the game is misperceived as an informative rather than an entertainment event, audiences may lose sight of the importance of substantive knowledge.

Court Shows

Our judicial system presents gamesmanship of a different sort. Public fascination with the contests taking place in our courts has fueled many fictional series, from the deity-like assurance of *Perry Mason* to the frantic self-doubts of *The Practice*'s attorneys. Reality trials carry this fascination one step further by endeavoring to open up *genuine* legal proceedings to the gaze from the living room couch. As Wende Dumble points out, although game shows and 'reality' trials

both offer cash prizes, the stakes of the former are as often refrigerators and brand new cars, while the stakes of the latter include revenge, freedom, and even life itself. The presence of "real" people in the archetypal conflict places the mystery of the trial into a comprehensible human context.[39]

Through such court shows, then, viewers can eavesdrop on authentic trials (or, at least, authentic reenactments) without the discomfort, bother, boredom, and confusion entailed in actual attendance at a trial downtown.

As Harvard law professor Arthur Miller has written, "We are surrounded by law. There is virtually nothing we do that doesn't have a legal element, whether it's buying or selling, living or dying, marrying or divorcing, breathing or polluting."[40] Because the judiciary thus impinges (or threatens to impinge) on almost everyone's life, viewing other people's wrangles with the law without having to get involved ourselves makes for compelling TV. "Watching the trial is a safe deviancy," suggests writer Patricia Volk. "It allows us to participate in the netherworld without getting hurt."[41]

Now that most states have opened up their courts to television coverage, audiences can even experience genuine trial footage with the ponderous parts edited out. An entire cable network, Court TV, is staking much of its success on its ability to cut back and forth between several proceedings like a sports viewer jumps from live game to live game in search of the most exciting play. (In fact, the metaphors of sport and court are now subject to interchange, as evidenced by the re-election billboard in Figure 14-2.)

Even when the cases are reenactments featuring professional actors, the reality of

the transcript is a potent enough hook for many viewers who want a glimpse of how other people face the setbacks of life. For instance, a show like *Divorce Court*, explains Elayne Rapping

is popular because . . . it presents an arena for resolving commonly experienced, painful, but generally private problems. Many people have few helpful, sincere friends to talk to about these things who won't exploit the anguish of their lives. Many people have no intimate friends at all. For those living out their married lives in quiet desperation, keeping up appearances, putting up with pain and humiliation, *Divorce Court* is a vicariously cathartic show.[42]

By making the law accessible to the ordinary citizen through revelation of interesting cases, most court show formulas are well positioned to service each of the gratifications from which infotainment draws. They are informative to the degree that they make the law more comprehensible and less artifi-

FIGURE 14-2
Intermixing the verbiage and images of two spectator pasttimes. (Courtesy of Marcie Brogan, Brogan and Partners)

cially glamorous. They are entertaining to the extent that the audience is drawn into the judicial contest and comes to care about who wins and loses. But they are also potentially distortive if they lead the viewer to believe that justice is always swift or free of expedient compromise.

Criminal Posters

Court shows observe civil and criminal defendants amidst the rhetorical progressions of a trial. Criminal-poster programs survey justice one step earlier by focusing on recent crimes and the efforts to apprehend alleged perpetrators. In some cases, these series even solicit viewers' help in "making the collar." Either way, the audience is introduced to real criminals (often through mug shots) and then either shown how they were caught or what they did that should motivate viewers to help in the catching.

Many of the selected crimes are quite sensational, of course, because a lead-pipe homicide or massage parlor arson offers much more visual drama than does a white-collar embezzlement. Usually, the criminal act is re-created with periodic intercutting of comments from real victims or law enforcement officials. Sometimes, police and even victims portray themselves in the action sequences. In other programs, actors stand in for the cops as well as for other "real-life" participants. Either way, as in the case of trial reenactments, the dynamism of the show flows mainly from the fact that it is based on a real case and real felon with footage shot at the actual scene. Who portrays the individual characters is of relatively lesser importance.

One potential danger to criminal-poster shows is that in focusing on a single transgression, they may obscure the larger societal crisis and give viewers a false sense of mastery. "It's not so much that the so-called 'reality shows' are helping us confront the problems of drugs and crime in our society—although they do, to a certain extent," states Professor Richard Slotkin. "It's more that they give us a sense of *control* over the uncontrollable. *America's Most Wanted* promises that *you* can participate in bringing criminals to justice."[43] Advertising critic Barbara Lippert takes this analysis one step further when she observes:

I can't remember a time when the culture was as police-blotter based. . . . There's something deeper going on than the sheer reality of competition for viewers by declining networks and proliferating independents. One explanation could be the cultural stasis of the Reagan years, when everything became commercialized and bottom-line-minded and few people took activist social or political roles. An obsession with crime is one way to participate through the passivity.[44]

While recognizing the tendency of criminal poster shows (like the one promoted in Figure 14-3) toward psuedovigilanteism and oversimplification, there is also something positive to be said for the role they do play, however limited, in assisting law enforcement. As a trade magazine editorial testified in support of these programs:

Sensational? Yes, as often are the crimes profiled. But they have also been undeniably effective in locating a host of fugitives who are wanted for major and often violent crimes, and who, in some cases, had eluded capture for years (in the case of one murder suspect, eighteen years). That the programs are entertainment vehicles does not diminish their record of success. According to an FBI spokesman, television has made a "distinct" difference in capturing criminals.[45]

Video Verité

Criminal-poster shows revisit and re-create the past misdeeds of felons. *Video verité* programs, conversely, record actual crimes and disasters *in progress*—or, at least, they visually chronicle the authorities' immediate response to such events. Network and syndicated news magazines also regularly engage in video verité techniques when they swoop down on the subject of an exposé. The typical half-hour verité series, like *Cops*, however, tends to offer shorter 'stories' and without the soft doc's interest in putting the tape-captured event into any sort of larger context.

The jerkiness and graininess of many video verité sequences actually seem to add to their appeal. Watching them is like the excitement of watching events we might have shot with our own camcorder—if we had the chance (or the courage, or the authority) to be on the scene. John Langley, creator of the pioneering video verité series *Cops*, explains that "My ideal segment would

have no cuts. We have very few cuts as it is. We try to be as pure as possible and take viewers through the experience from beginning to end. . . . It's a real-life soap opera in some ways. It's a window on the world the average person will never witness."[46]

Of course, as with most nonfiction television (including local newscasts), the emphasis is on dramatic action rather than on dull routine. Thus, what critic R. C. Smith wrote about *Cops* is true of most video verité projects:

Cops is riveting because it's so selective about the kinds of police work it shows. There are more cowboys than clerks among these cops, including the women. You don't see much of them filling out forms, working the phones or drinking bad coffee in parked cars. Still, *Cops* shows you more of the world beyond the law than you may have ever seen before. Though it's not a pretty sight, you may find you can't take your eyes off it.[47]

A nagging video verité issue yet to be resolved involves the personal rights of the private citizens whose likenesses have been recorded. While release forms are normally obtained from people who are featured on videotape, there is some concern about whether some of these individuals really understand what they are signing or the impact of their consent on their future lives. In addition, the recorded 911 calls frequently used as soundtracks are public record and thus require no consent. "There's a privacy issue here," argues critic Robert MacKenzie. "If you make a 911 call, can your moment of stress be exposed for all to hear?"[48] And legalities aside, when are such tragic taped portraitures unethical assaults on individual human dignity?

Reporters for conventional newscasts face similar determinations all the time, of course. And the taping of breaking news in public places is generally free from any requirement to obtain release forms. Concerns about exploitative invasions of personal privacy, however legal, have increased as ENG (electronic newsgathering) technology provides local news with ever-greater capability for live capture and broadcast of human tragedies. Indeed, the expanded exploitation of video verité stylings is making the distinction between 'news' and 'reality' programming more and more difficult to draw. When the genre becomes part of a newscast, does that automatically convert the newscast from information to reality programming? This question underlies the following Greg Quill review of a local newscast's multipart series. Does *Undercover: The Mobs of Metro* constitute the 'straight' information of "hard local news" as Quill labels it? Or is it actually 'reality' infotainment?

Ultimately, whether a video verité piece is information or entertainment probably hinges, once again, on the aspect of *significance*. If Toronto viewers find that *Mobs of Metro* contains something they should know

because it directly 'affects their world,' it can probably be argued that the series is information. Thus, as with any *polysemic* communication (recall our Chapter 3 discussion), the final assigning of meaning and importance may vary widely from viewer to viewer. In fact, whether *Mobs of Metro's* video verité comprises information or infotainment may depend entirely on the neighborhood in which each viewer lives and/or the ethnic group to which each belongs.

Keyhole Shows

Because we discuss these vehicles in our initial section on terminology, little needs be added here. The genre is not unique to television; it probably began when Allen Funt created *Candid Microphone* in 1947 for ABC Radio. Only one year later, Funt's spin-off *Candid Camera* was on ABC Television and subsequently made the rounds of all three networks.

Today, of course, a professional camera crew is no longer a prerequisite. While the latest syndicated reincarnation of *Candid Camera* and Fox's *Totally Hidden Video* were still shot by the pros, other programs such as *America's Funniest Home Videos* and *America's Funniest People* have been created entirely with 'home-brewed' footage. Also in this category, of course, there are the *TV Bloopers and Practical Jokes* shows that reveal celebrities to be as ludicrously vulnerable as any ordinary folks caught by amateur cameras.

These productions all share a common motivating force. As media theorist John Fiske explains,

The practical jokes played on the stars in *TV Bloopers and Practical Jokes* and on the public in *Candid Camera* work according to the "logic of the inside out." They depend on rules which are inversions of the normal and which the players/spectators know but the "victims" do not. . . .

Allowing the viewer to be "in the know" and to participate in the joke reverses the power relations involved in watching normal television, when it is the viewer who lacks knowledge which those on the screen possess and impart. . . . The pleasure involved is carnivalesque, for it is the pleasure of the subordinate escaping from the rules and conventions that are the agents of social control.[49]

Keyhole programs entertain, according to Fiske, because they empower. Like the crim-

---

CITY-TV'S CRIME SERIES FRIGHTENING

by Greg Quill

CITY-TV has bitten off a big chunk of hard local news with its 10-part series, Undercover: The Mobs of Metro.

But it's unlikely that the feisty Toronto independent station's audience will digest, in five- to seven-minute segments in each night's 6 P.M. newscast, what appears to be frightening evidence of a takeover of our streets by dozens of organized crime gangs with connections as far afield as Hong Kong, Colombia, Jamaica, Italy, Vietnam and China.

Granted, series researchers James Dubro, author of Mob Rule, King of the Mob, Mob Mistress, and Undercover: Cases of the RCMP's Most Secret Operative, seems to have curbed a natural instinct for hyperbole and sensationalism in the background, interview topics and narrative he provided for The Mobs of Metro, which premiered Monday night on Channel 57 and continues weeknights through the end of the week.

And series hosts Mark Dailey, CITY's news editor and former crime reporter, and anchor Gord Martineau, do their level best not to inflame passions, but to explain some of the difficult realities behind recent headlines that do little more than hint at the existence of the Cosa Nostra, Chinese triads, Vietnamese gangs, Jamaican posses, local cells of cocaine smugglers controlled by Colombian cartels, and outlaw biker gangs that enforce arbitrary street laws for the right price.

Mind you, they push things, too. One alleged Hamilton Mafiosi, who refused an interview, has his muffled words, hurled vindictively from behind a locked door, subtitled as, "Who are ya? See ya later!"

Has Dubro seen GoodFellas too often, or what?

And we see a Jamaican citizen, who claims he earns his living as a recording artist and is demanding refugee status in Canada, demand evidence of his "alleged" crimes, while a Toronto RCMP officer, in juxtaposed shots, lists a string of serious convictions and criminal allegations against him in Canada, Jamaica, and other parts of the world.

This stuff doesn't dig deep. But then, it doesn't have to. A few scoops of this stuff is frightening enough.

(Reprinted with permission—The Toronto Star Syndicate.)

---

inal poster shows, keyhole series compliment viewers by seeming to rely on their 'inside information.' As in court shows, keyhole programs such as *Big Brother* accord the viewer the high status of judge—without any of the worrisome accountability such status entails in real life.

Keyhole shows also can perpetrate the same potential abuses to which other reality genres are prone. In addition to the obvious privacy/personal dignity issue, there is the conspicuous harm associated with how some private citizens go about capturing the shots they submit. For instance, ABC Entertainment president Robert Iger was compelled to respond to reports that some viewers were putting children and animals at risk in pursuit of the tapes being submitted to *America's Funniest Home Videos*. In announcing that ABC's Standards and Practices department would take an active role in footage screening, Iger told a press conference, "We have a responsibility as a network to make sure we don't encourage that kind of behavior. I think if we keep them off the air, we're discouraging that kind of behavior."[50]

Pseudosports

While some keyhole submissions may randomly qualify for this designation, the main body of pseudosports reality fare consists of those prerecorded and inexpensive athletic contests that exist solely *as* television. Alternately labeled "crash TV," this genre has nurtured such boisterous fare as *American Gladiators, WSL Roller Jam*, and *WWF Wrestling*.

Definitionally, pseudosports is not sports; nor is it infotainment. Instead, this genre exclusively services an inherently mass-mediated entertainment gratification. When a pseudosports property is competently handled, this entertainment can be harmless diversion. But when it descends into go-for-the-groin mayhem, it moves beyond trash to debase both the participants and the viewers who watch them.

Some pseudosports does not even qualify as reality programming because the contestants involved are anything but "real people" and the staged circumstances are anything but "actual life situations." When the only thing with which viewers can identify are bludgeonings, audience and advertiser appeal both narrow. For this reason, major pseudosports packagers carefully cultivate a reality image. In introducing his *American Gladiators* to the advertising industry, for example, Samuel Goldwyn Company executive Ray Solley took pains to point out that the project's fighters would be "all-American role models. They're not so much super-heroes out of comic books as the type of people [real people] representing us in the Olympics."[51]

A REALITY RETROSPECTIVE

This chapter defines and inventories the broad field of reality programming and raises key critical issues associated with these vehicles. Although the electronic media have benefited from a number of "reality" successes, our profession has been slow to realize the multidimensionality of the phenomenon.

Paramount syndication executive (and later Twentieth Television chairman) Lucy Salhany once was asked about reality programming. "We love it," she replied. "So do the viewers. Because the fastest growing programs on television right now are reality-based programs."[52] But when, as the head of the unit that distributed *Geraldo!*, she was queried about trash TV, she responded:

We don't know anything about that. We don't accept the term trash TV because we don't believe that television is trash. So if you'd like to talk about what the print media is calling trash TV. I think you should talk to people in the print media. We don't really understand that term.[53]

Salhany took a similar stance in the case of 'tabloid television' when she reiterated, "We don't understand that term either."[54] She did agree to the term *reality-based programming* but would only comment on it by saying "That's a definition that really has no bounds."[55]

As critical professionals, however, it is our responsibility to define what we sell or air as a means of distinguishing it from what we *refuse* to sell or air. If the print media are attacking us with rigged terminology, we must be able to decode it before we can hope to defuse it.

As we have discovered, the reality programming spectrum is a broad and overlapping one that encompasses many comparative terms and divergent genres. By degree, some of these varieties are more praiseworthy and defensible than are others. But just as principled and business-savvy electronic media professionals cannot unequivocally embrace the total reality continuum, neither can we reject it entirely—or allow outside critics to crucify us for refusing to make such a blanket rejection.

Well-produced, accurately labeled, and responsibly packaged reality programs serve an irreplaceable gratifications purpose for many modem consumers. As Elayne Rapping points out,

"Reality programming" is based on the same conventions and principles that have made local news so important in peoples' lives. In fact, its appeal is identical. The people who, in voyeuristic fascination, watch the acting out of personal life in public on these shows are the same people who sit charmed before the spectacle of local newscasters joking around, caring, sharing community trivia and commiserating with local victims. And they do it for the same reasons: they crave a sense of community, of human intimacy and sharing, that modern life has largely eliminated. . . .

In a world in which emotion is repressed and privatized, there is something almost liberating about sharing in such displays of understandable feeling. And they *are* understandable. Who doesn't long to strike it rich in a single blow? Who doesn't crave justice after a difficult, draining hassle with a neighbor or merchant? Who doesn't desire, just once, to be publicly lauded and rewarded for some special trait or ability that has no dollar value?

Participants on these shows act out these very feelings and let us share in them.[56]

Perhaps the essential delineation between good and bad reality programming, then, is whether the show in question:

promotes insightful sharing
or
inflicts viewer or participant abuse.

ENDNOTES

1. Arthur Greenwald, writing in "Monday Memo," *Broadcasting* (December 3, 1990), 12.
2. Ibid.
3. Brett Holey, remarks to Broadcast and Cinematic Arts students, Central Michigan University, October 2, 1989 (Mt. Pleasant).
4. "Bob Priddy: A Public Service Message," *Broadcasting* (November 28, 1988), 151.
5. John Fiske, *Television Culture* (London: Methuen, 1987), 282.
6. Richard Schaefer, "The Development of the CBS News Guidelines during the Salant Years," *Journal of Broadcasting & Electronic Media* (Winter 1998), 8.
7. William Adams, "Local Public Affairs Content of TV News," *Journalism Quarterly* (Winter 1978), 691.
8. C. Richard Hofstetter and David Dozier, "Useful News, Sensational News: Quality, Sensationalism and Local TV News," *Journalism Quarterly* (Winter 1986), 816.
9. Maria Grabe, Shuhua Zhou, and Brooke Barnett, "Exploiting Sensationalism in Television News: Content and the Bells and Whistles of Form." Paper presented to the Association for Education in Journalism and Mass Communication Convention, August 1998, (Baltimore).
10. "Westin Makes Moves at King World," *Broadcasting* (August 7, 1989), 67.
11. James Kaplan, "Cleaning Up TV's Tabs," *TV Guide* (September 9, 1995), 32.
12. Jeff Jarvis, "Day One," *TV Guide* (April 24, 1993), 7.
13. S. Elizabeth Bird, "Storytelling on the Far Side: Journalism and the Weekly Tabloid," *Critical Studies in Mass Communication* (December 1990), 384.
14. "Westin Makes Moves," 67.
15. Bird, 385.
16. Oprah Winfrey, "What We *All* Can Do to Change TV," *TV Guide* (November 11, 1995), 16.
17. Cynthia Littleton, "The Strong Get Stronger," *Broadcasting & Cable* (December 2, 1996), 26.
18. Stephen Battaglio, "A Bigger Dose of Reality," *ADWEEK* (July 1, 1991), 18.
19. "Tabloid TV and Anti-U.S. Program Quotas Top Issues of Programming Panel," *Broadcasting* (June 12, 1989), 65.
20. "Hollywood's Man of the Hours," *Broadcasting* (November 14, 1988), 50.
21. Cathy Taylor, "Tabloid TV Cleans Up, but Buyers are Wary, *ADWEEK* (September 3, 1990), 17.
22. Battaglio, 19.
23. Steve Coe, "McCluggage: Quality Is Paramount," *Broadcasting* (November 11, 1991), 22.
24. Reese Schonfeld, writing in "Monday Memo," *Broadcasting* (January 23, 1989), 66.
25. Edwin Diamond and Alan Mahony, "Once It Was 'Harvest of Shame'—Now We Get 'Scared Sexless,'" *TV Guide* (August 27, 1988), 6–7.
26. Ken Auletta, "Look What They've Done to the News," *TV Guide* (November 9, 1991), 6.
27. Diamond and Mahony, 7.
28. Monica Collins, "Tabloid Clones Invade TV," *TV Guide* (November 18, 1989), 16.
29. Ibid., 14.
30. Robert MacKenzie, "Inside Edition," *TV Guide* (February 17, 1990), 32.
31. Louis Day, *Ethics in Media Communications: Cases and Controversies* (Belmont, CA: Wadsworth, 1991), 331.
32. Van Gordon Sauter, "In Defense of Tabloid TV," *TV Guide* (August 5, 1989), 4.
33. Ibid.
34. Wende Dumble, "And Justice for All: The Messages Behind 'Real' Courtroom Dramas," in Gary Burns and Robert Thompson (eds.), *Television Studies: Textual Analysis* (New York: Praeger, 1989), 104.
35. David Tobenkin, "Has Talk Gone Too Far?" *Broadcasting & Cable* (March 20, 1995), 22.
36. Vicki Abt and Mel Seesholtz, "The Shameless World of Phil, Sally and Oprah: Television Talk Shows and the Deconstructing of Society," *Journal of Popular Culture* (Summer 1994), 182.
37. Elayne Rapping, *The Looking Glass World of Nonfiction TV* (Boston: South End Press, 1987), 64–65.
38. Stuart Kaminsky and Jeffrey Mahan, *American Television Genres* (Chicago: Nelson-Hall, 1985), 52.
39. Dumble, 107.
40. Arthur Miller, *Miller's Court* (Boston: Houghton Mifflin, 1982), 4.
41. Barbara Lippert, "From Out of the Slime," *ADWEEK* (January 23, 1989), 6.
42. Rapping, 69.
43. Judith Newman, "Sock It To Me," *ADWEEK* (October 1, 1990), M.O. 52.
44. Lippert, 6.

45. "The Longer Arm of Broadcasting," *Broadcasting* (November 6, 1989), 114.
46. Cynthia Littleton, "True Blue," *Broadcasting & Cable* (May 20, 1996), 26.
47. R. C. Smith, "Cops," *TV Guide* (June 10, 1989), 47.
48. Robert MacKenzie, "Rescue 911," *TV Guide* (February 10, 1990), 32.
49. Fiske, 242–243.
50. "ABC's Summer Stock," *Broadcasting* (April 16, 1990), 39.
51. John Motavalli, "Beyond Syndication's Crime Wave," *ADWEEK* (January 23, 1989), 5.
52. "First Run for the Roses," *Broadcasting* (June 5, 1989), 42.
53. Ibid., 40.
54. Ibid.
55. Ibid., 42.
56. Rapping, 61–62.

15 Composite Criticism

In this final chapter, it is appropriate to explore an aggregate methodology that encompasses, at least in part, virtually every critical perspective we examine in earlier sections of this book. This four-part schema, which we label *composite criticism*, has its roots in the writings of George Santayana and Jerome Stolnitz. In his university lectures, Professor Thomas Olson then refined the methodology and applied it specifically to the task of electronic media critiquing.

In brief, composite criticism provides an instrument by which we can, within a single operation, examine a work from four different perspectives. These perspectives bear a distinct relationship to the four communication process components described in Chapter 3. Composite criticism thereby appraises the work within the real-world communication context in which we, as media professionals, must function.

INITIAL DEFINITIONS

Composite criticism's quartet of perspectives is divided into *intrinsic* and *extrinsic* pairings and cross-divided into *appreciation* and *evaluation* activities. Therefore, to begin to understand how each composite perspective is oriented, we must first define the terms that collectively identify them:

Intrinsic pertains to the work itself and the properties internal to it. The focus here is on the work in isolation rather than within any particular social or historical context.

Extrinsic, in contrast, places the work within the environment(s) in which it is created and displayed, examining it as an interactive agent with sender(s) and receiver(s).

Appreciation is the process of favorably and sympathetically inventorying the work's merits and 'pleasure potential,' as well as the difficulties that had to be surmounted in its production.

Evaluation determines whether the work's capabilities were fully realized. It systematically compares achievements and failures in the work's form, content, scope, execution, and ultimate impact.

By cross-pollinating these perspectives, we arrive at the four procedures from which composite criticism is germinated:

Intrinsic Appreciation
Extrinsic Appreciation
Intrinsic Evaluation
Extrinsic Evaluation

In examining each of these four procedures in detail, we want to become especially aware of how they collectively contribute to the overall tasks of criticism, as *criticism* is defined in Chapter 1:

knowledgeable comprehension, positive/negative ascertainment, and resulting carefully considered judgment as a means of reasonably estimating the value of the particular work under scrutiny.

INTRINSIC APPRECIATION

To completely understand intrinsic appreciation's focus, it may be necessary to view what is said in Chapter 12 about art as a vehicle for igniting pleasure experiences. Intrinsic appreciation entails the compiling of an inventory of all the perceiver enjoyments that the work might generate. As astute media professionals, we need to become fully aware of our project's materials, how they are organized, and their resulting expressive capabilities. One of many ways to accomplish this is to apply Chapter 13's Logic of Aesthetic Form as a detector of realized beauty.

Whatever our detecting instrument, the purpose of intrinsic appreciation is exclusively the apprehension of the 'pleasure-successes' achieved by the work. Failures are ignored for the time being because they are the province not of *appreciation* but of *evaluation*.

There is no moral imperative, no right and wrong, involved in intrinsic appreciation—only the attempt to identify aesthetic (as we define the term in Chapter 12) accomplishment. As DeWitt Parker reminds us,

the spirit of art is fundamentally non-moral, for the aesthetic attitude is one of sympathy—an attempt at once to express life and to feel at one with it; it demands of us that we take the point of view of the life expressed and, for the moment at any rate, refrain from a merely external judgment. Through art we are compelled to sympathize with the aspiration towards growth, towards happiness, even when it leads to rebellion against our own standards and towards what we call sin. The sympathy, realism, and imagination of art are antagonistic to conformist morality.[1]

In short, intrinsic appreciation leads us to relish the work for itself rather than for any moral or even practical purpose to which the work might be put. Although this concept may be especially difficult for pragmatic Americans to accept, it is absolutely essential to the attainment of thoroughgoing criticism.

Like the shower murder scene in Alfred Hitchcock's movie *Psycho*, we may hate the event but love its treatment. Similarly, argues Professor Ellen Harris, "one can dislike the subject of Titian's magnificent 'Tarquin and Lucretia,' a very realistic and violent rape, and still recognize the painting's aesthetic beauty. . . . Good art moves your emotions or makes you think."[2] Intrinsic appreciation blooms from just such paradoxes.

Yet, some moralistic highbrows have a great deal of trouble accepting this orientation—not only because they see it as unprincipled hedonism, but, more to the point, because they also view its application to the electronic media as an endorsement of the masses' vulgar tastes. It is to these highbrows that legendary CBS commentator Eric Sevareid was referring when he wrote:

There is, and always has been, a broad swatch of professional intellectuals who fear and detest anything new, particularly if it is adaptable to the pleasure of the great mass of ordinary people. This particular type of intellectual neither knows nor likes ordinary people. This is

why they write about "humanity" and not about persons. They are like the English Puritans who hated bear-baiting, not because it gave pain to the bears but because it gave pleasure to the spectators.[3]

Instead of starting from a pinnacle of disdainful intellectualism, former *Washington Post* critic Lawrence Laurent long ago argued that "the complete television critic begins with a respect and a love for the excitement and the impact of the combination of sight and sound—pictures which can be viewed, and words which can be heard, by millions of people at one time."[4] This combination of respect and love is but another facet of intrinsic appreciation, and it allows media professionals to approach their radio, television, or on-line subjects with initial optimism instead of with terminal cynicism or timidity.

EXTRINSIC APPRECIATION

Extrinsic appreciation extends sympathy for the work by attempting to ascertain the situational problems with which it was forced to cope. That is why extrinsic appreciation is the favorite criticism component for some college students. They don't want their instructor to evaluate their report or term paper without the professor's being acutely aware of all the difficulties they had to surmount in getting the assignment submitted on time. It is hoped that this sympathy for their situational problems will help to overshadow the weaknesses in their submission!

Out in the professional world, however, extrinsic appreciation begins with an acknowledgment of the necessity to meet fundamental standards of profitability and popularity. Through this critical procedure, therefore, we examine the project as a creation of the electronic media *business*, keeping in mind the productional and financial constraints inherent in that business, such as those detailed in Chapters 5, 6, and 7. As recording industry executive Paul Atkinson ruefully admits about radio, for instance:

Radio is interested not in breaking new artists, but in generating the maximum amount of advertising income. And the way they're going to do that is by playing the hits. It's a constant headache for the recording industry to find other ways of breaking artists. . . . radio is so ratings driven that it tends to draw away and dry up the creative fringes.[5]

Similarly, in the case of broadcast network newscasts, CBS producer Richard Cohen urges people to take into account that "When you compress the world into 22 minutes, you lose a lot. Twenty-two minutes is just a starting point."[6] And, in the matter of TV entertainment programs, Media Access Project director Andrew Schwartzman appreciates broadcasters' comparative limitations when he observes that

broadcasters are responsible for tailoring programming to community needs. However, PPV [pay-per-view 'closed circuit' service] is a narrowcast medium, targeted to specific segments of the audience who choose to view it. And the Supreme Court has upheld that the private actions of adults in their own homes have much less justification for governmental intrusion.[7]

These are three examples of authorities conscientiously considering the characteristics of the media involved rather than simply lashing out at, or blindly defending, those media's practices.

Extrinsic appreciation also encompasses a sympathetic comprehension of the locational difficulties faced by the work. When has it been scheduled to air and what competition must it therefore face? More than one fine program has met its demise simply because its time period placed it against highly popular, established series on other channels. What station or network is carrying the show? Weak programs on strong outlets have a much better chance of being "sampled" than do strong programs on weak outlets. The carrier of the work also has a substantial impact on the program's audience delivery requirements. A series running on a *tonnage medium* (see Chapter 7) such as prime-time broadcasting must attract much higher numbers than a show placed at mid-day on a niche cable service. Similarly, the budget required to produce the program establishes firm boundaries as to which networks or stations can afford to purchase it for airing. And the amount of available promotion (in both dollars and partnered delivery systems) determines to a large extent whether audiences will find the content. This last point is as relevant to competition among on-line services as it is to traditional broadcasting rivalries,

and it also explains why so many corporate entities have striven to own both "old" and "new" media assets in order to cross-promote their content properties.

Unfortunately, there is a tendency to view the electronic media as vast and mechanistic enterprises that make their own unilateral and unchallenged rules and that can largely do what they want. But as John Fiske and John Hartley remind us, "television [like radio and like the Web] is a human construct, and the job that it does is the result of human choice, cultural decisions and social pressures. The medium responds to the conditions within which it exists."[8] Extrinsic appreciation takes such pressures into account before the more evaluative aspects of composite criticism are allowed to come into play.

Through extrinsic appreciation, media creator and media consumer alike can enhance their delight in a program because, as George Boas points out, "When one is acquainted with the technique involved and knows its problems, one enjoys the artist's victory over its difficulties, his peculiar manner of overcoming them."[9]

If we know, for instance, the intricacies faced by writers and producers of made-for-TV movies in sculpting their scripts around a certain mandated schedule of commercial breaks (recall our Chapter 13 discussion), we acquire a more benevolent understanding of the artistic hurdles these creators face. We better comprehend the formulaic straitjacket they somehow must overcome in shaping their dramatic product. Similarly, by becoming aware of the daunting acoustical-match problems surmounted by recording engineers in blending a contemporary Natalie Cole rendition with one done by her deceased father four decades earlier, we more fully enjoy the "Unforgettable" duet that resulted.

Modular writing and audio recording challenges are, of course, just two of the many considerations with which electronic media professionals must deal on a continuous basis. Whatever the consideration—or whatever the art form—extrinsic appreciation is essential in bringing a realistic sympathy for the work to the critical task. In referring to an analysis of a painting, for example, George Boas reveals that the relevant question "becomes not whether the painter has painted a picture, or even such and such a picture, but whether he has painted within the given restrictions."[10]

Program properties, as we have observed, involve multiple "painters" and multiple sets of "restrictions," so Boas's comment takes on manifold importance for those of us working in the electronic media. In essence, extrinsic appreciation is an exercise that emphasizes what theorists label *contextual criticism*. As Jerome Stolnitz explains it, "Contextualism has placed art in its natural setting. . . . art is not a 'spiritual mystery.' It arises in the circumstances of human living and it answers to human needs. . . . We now see that different kinds of art can all be valuable 'in their own way.' "[11] It is just this sort of wide-ranging, sympathetic recognition that media professionals need to encourage on behalf of the field in which they work.

INTRINSIC EVALUATION

As we suggest at the start of this chapter, evaluation takes appreciation-derived inventory of the work's (intrinsic) pleasures as well of as its (extrinsic) sympathetically modified capabilities and compares this inventory with that work's faults and missed opportunities. Negative as well as positive ascertainments now enter the critical process through application of whatever standards are deemed relevant.

Using *intrinsic evaluation*, we examine the program in isolation. Thus, we attempt to estimate its worth without regard to the way it was scheduled or delivered, or the initial audience reaction to it. In this way, we may be able to derive strategies to inform the audience of pleasure possibilities in the work of which they may not have been initially aware. As DeWitt Parker explains, "the analysis and constant attention to the subtler details demanded by theory may bring to notice aspects of a work of art which do not exist for an unthinking appreciation. As a rule, the appreciations of the average man are very inadequate to the total possibilities offered, extending only to the more obvious features."[12]

Even though we must consider the work within its genre (sitcom, soap opera, talk show, etc.), intrinsic evaluation does not stop there. It also proceeds to judge the project as a completely unique property. To Jerome Stolnitz, all intrinsic evaluation

respects the uniqueness of the particular work. Like aesthetic perception itself, it sees what is distinctive about the work, what sets it off from "similar" works. Criticism by rules, however, presupposes that works can be classified into "kinds" and are therefore subject to the criteria which measure goodness in each "kind."[13]

For the media professional, both genre and individualistic applications of intrinsic evaluation are viable and mutually supportive. If they were not, we would have great difficulty isolating and promoting the specific contributions of such breakthrough programs as *The Simpsons* or *The Sopranos* or such innovative commercials as the Energizer Bunny and the spot reproduced in Figure 15-1. These and other properties enriched their genres by innovatively reconfiguring long-established conventions.

Intrinsic evaluation scrutinizes both the *content* of the work and how that content is *executed*. These two viewpoints do not always lead us to the same conclusion. Industry observers Mark Christensen and Cameron Stauth point out the distinction when they recall a shift that took place in NBC's program philosophy during the early 1980s:

"Quality" had been the watchword at the beginning of the [Grant] Tinker regime; now it seemed more and more to be replaced by "quality of execution." There could be a significant difference between the two. "Quality" meant substance. "Quality of execution" meant only form. An Army training film could exhibit "quality of execution" if the camera work was performed with a little flair. . . . So what did NBC want?[14]

Quality of content and quality of execution issues reduce themselves to two fundamental questions:

Was the thing worth doing?
Was it done well?

We might reach an affirmative or negative conclusion to both questions—or end up with a 'split decision.' Perhaps the subject was a worthy one but the production team was not up to the task of capturing it. Or, the content may have been drivel but it was shot and edited with real pictorial brilliance. All of these determinations are possible, and all

(MUSIC UNDER)

WOMAN: Very bad dog…

(DOG LOOKS AT CAT)

…Bad, bad dog!

(SFX: CLINK)

(DOG WAKES UP AND WATCHES CAT WALK ACROSS COUNTER)

(CAT APPROACHES TRASH CAN…

AND LOOKS SMUGLY AT DOG)

WOMAN: Very bad dog!
(DOG REMEMBERS SCOLDING)

(DOG WATCHING CAT MAKING A MESS)

(DOG THINKING OF WAYS TO GET BACK AT CAT)

(DOG SEES POLAROID…

AND HAS AN IDEA)

Polaroid
See what develops.

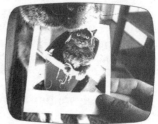

WOMAN: Oh dear…

FIGURE 15-1
(Courtesy of Brian McPherson, Goodby, Silverstein & Partners)

come under the heading of intrinsic evaluation.

As an illustration, read the following preview by *Variety* critic Ray Richmond. Which of Richmond's comments relate to quality of content? Which to quality of execution? What is his ultimate intrinsic evaluation in terms of each question, and how much weight does each of these decisions carry in his overall appraisal of this sitcom?

No single critique, of course, can touch on all elements of a work's execution and content. Instead, the media professional making internal production or programming decisions will tend to focus on those intrinsic evaluative aspects that seem most relevant to audience appeal, advertiser and/or program buyer interest, and the ultimate promise of return on investment. As Fox Television executive Danielle Claman testifies,

even though it's an accomplishment to sell a pilot and get a series order, *keeping* the show on the air is a separate and equally difficult challenge. The network undoubtedly does some creative tinkering with the original concept to sustain an audience. Still, you can take steps to establish a beachhead for the future of the series. Staffing the show with writers capable of constructing storylines and characters that enhance the original concept will help ensure that the network executives stay true to your vision.[15]

Whether it's a movie, a series, a one-shot special, or a commercial, the contributions of writers, technicians, performers, and producers collectively fashion the product about which an intrinsic evaluation must be made.

There are several avenues for such an evaluation. In previous sections, for instance, we address productional ingredients (Chapters 5 and 6), structural analysis (Chapter 10), ethics and values (Chapter 11), and aesthetics (Chapters 12 and 13). These and other vantage points can yield appropriate intrinsic evaluations if we take the time to pursue them. And remember: The more such evaluation takes place *before* the project hits the air, the greater will be our chance of communicative success. Many times, negative commentaries by outside critics are only pointing out flaws that should have been caught before that production was released or placed on the program log.

EXTRINSIC EVALUATION

This final composite criticism component focuses on the *effects of the work on audiences*—and the subsequent *effects of audiences on the work* through their often diverse readings of it. As anthropologist Conrad Kottak reminds us,

there is a reciprocal relationship between television [as well as the other electronic media] and culture. The preexisting culture influences indigenous creations and program choice. Long-term exposure to messages then feeds back on social reality, changing old beliefs, attitudes, and behavior. This process contributes to the development of a new (mass) culture.[16]

Unfortunately, the recognition of this reciprocal relationship is sometimes used to justify pseudocriticism that is devoted to extrinsic evaluation *exclusively*. Thus, we worry about the "effect" of program content without referencing its pleasures, content variables, and system limitations. We become preoccupied with congressional hearings and pressure group crusades—to the neglect of composite criticism's other three aspects.

When used by itself, extrinsic evaluation can be both simplistic and damaging because it fails to consider the work's benefits (intrinsic appreciation) and the complexity of the electronic media's creative/transmission process (extrinsic appreciation). A preoccupation with extrinsic evaluation also ignores the merits and demerits of the work's internal structure, content, and execution (intrinsic evaluation).

Nevertheless, electronic professionals must move beyond a fixation with their own preferences, problems, procedures, and vehicles. We must be concerned with the effects of our enterprises on our audiences—and with their counter-effects on our endeavors. In Horace Newcomb's words, "the intentions of an originator of communication are constantly refracted by the contexts of reception."[17]

In our initial look at intrinsic appreciation, for example, Ellen Harris pointed out that the rape scene in a Titian painting could be beautiful even though we deplore the event. But the reverse is also true. Referring to that same Titian canvas as well as to similar heroically depicted assaults painted by Correggio and Giambologna, art historian Diane Wolfhal argues: "If we simply admire

ACTION

by Ray Richmond

As cable continues to slice away at the over-the-air broadcast audience share in prime, it's inevitable that the free webs fight foul with foul to better compete. Hence, the arrival of Action at 9:30 P.M. Thursdays on Fox. Indeed, exec producers Chris Thompson and Joel Silver originally developed the program for HBO as a replacement for The Larry Sanders Show. What lands on Fox is evidently, virtually the same pilot as was screened at HBO, intact save for the necessary bleeps of several dozen profane words unbecoming a network as, uh, dignified as Fox. Pack away the boys and girls, America. This could get ugly.

While Action is virtually guaranteed to inspire a fresh round of Beltway hyperventilating over program content and screams for network boycotts from the Society of Horrified Midwestern Housewives, all the controversy may be moot, given that Action could be out of action by November thanks to a fairly dreadful time period. All the show must do is find a way to co-exist with NBC's Must See TV Thursday lineup (pitted directly against the new comedy Stark Raving Mad, not to mention opposite a revamped Chicago Hope on CBS, the witchy WB hit Charmed and the steroid freaks of the World Wrestling Federation on UPN).

Still, Action has to be seen as at least a healthy long shot to stick - - - at least in some timeslot - - - thanks to its heavy advance buzz and South Park-like affinity for sophomoric outlandishness.

For all of its ugliness of spirit, Action breaks from the gate sporting a cinema-quality look and a wicked, stylish loopiness that prove instantly irresistible. It stars Jay Mohr (Tom Cruise's arch nemesis in Jerry Maguire) as Peter Dragon, a contemptuous, abusive producer of action-schlock pics whose ego cannot be contained in Earth's present orbit. His idea of light conversation is: "Guess what? I almost just killed grip!"

In Thompson's divertingly immature opening teleplay, Dragon is shown already in midseason form, sniping at his ex (Sara Paxton), insulting every little guy who crosses his path, sparring with agents and sucking up to the stars he needs. In other words, reality is not far afield. Discovering that his studio has just dropped $250,000 on a script from an Adam Rafkin (great work from Jarrad Paul) when he thought it was Alan Rifkin, he wails, "You're telling me we spent a quarter million dollars for the wrong Jew?"

It gets edgier. In the pilot's greatest gag, an agent earnestly pitches a comeback vehicle for his semiretired new client - - - O.J. Simpson.

Action subsequently shifts gears to caper comedy with the arrival of Wendy Ward (superb perf from Illeana Douglas). Wendy is a child star turned high-priced call girl whom Dragon inadvertently befriends on the way to the premiere of his new flop, Slow Torture.

He (feeling ill): "I'm gonna puke on you."

She: "Gee, I don't think I have a price for that."

And so it goes in Action, which promises to feature a string of star cameos (Keanu Reeves gets his privates, uh, massaged in the opener). Buddy Hackett adds a further touch of off-kilter color portraying Dragon's Uncle Lonnie, who also happens to be his chauffeur. Mohr acquits himself splendidly as the ultimate jerk - - - and certainly the most unctuous character in primetime since "Buffalo Bill" Bittinger - - - and his chemistry with the quirky Douglas is right on target.

Producer/director Ted Demme masterfully renders Thompson's warped kickoff tome, with generous assists from Herbert Davis's smooth camera work and Steven J. Wolff's evocative production design. About the worst thing one can say about Action based on its first half-hour is that it's nasty to the core, no doubt too nasty for many tastes. Yet as most readers of this publication would readily attest, that's showbiz.

these works for their incredible beauty and power, ignoring their full range of meanings, then we are gaining only a partial understanding of these important monuments, and we are permitting past misconceptions about rape to live on."[18] In other words, criticism that consists of intrinsic appreciation exclusively is just as deficient as criticism that limits itself to extrinsic evaluation.

This is not to imply that extrinsic evaluation can't comprise a major portion of a critique; it simply shouldn't be the *only* critical component being used. Depiction analysis, as discussed in Chapter 9, is one methodology that obviously emphasizes extrinsic evaluation by focusing on the lessons (meanings) that a work teaches to its perceivers. However, an assessment of business or audience gratifications (Chapters 7 and 8) is just as relevant to extrinsic evaluation. So, too, are analyses of ethics and values (Chapter 11) and message structures (Chapters 4 and 10) insofar as these orientations probe how audience perceptual and belief systems have been engaged or contradicted.

Beyond these aspects, the *timeliness* of a work often deserves special attention. Some program meanings are time-bound whereas others can strike a responsive chord regardless of how many years later the show is apprehended. When viewed today, *Leave It to Beaver* comes across as an anachronistic, impossibly idealized, and exclusively White and paternalistic portrait of '50s family life. *I Love Lucy*, on the other hand, "has become the Mona Lisa of television," writes media historian Christopher Anderson, "a work of art whose fame transcends its origins and its medium. . . . In episode after episode, Lucy rebels against the confinements of domestic life for women. . . . Her acts of rebellion . . . are meant to expose the absurd restrictions placed on women in a male-dominated society."[19]

Another part of timeliness has to do with the technology available to the creator at the time—because audience impact is partially determined by the artistic tools used. In speaking of the new electronic potentials made possible by satellite transmission, for instance, video artist Nam June Paik declares that "just as Mozart mastered the newly invented clarinet, the satellite artist must compose his art from the beginning suitable to physical conditions and grammar."[20] Similarly, industry analysts are now

debating whether HDTV (high-definition television) and on-line programming constitute entirely new media forms or are simply more vibrant and participatory subspecies of traditional television.

Nevertheless, the greater portion of the timeliness effect has to do less with specific instruments than with how the audience interprets the content of the work in relation to other simultaneously available works. Hence, to extend our composer analogy, "Mozart's music may appear serene and cheerful to a modern listener, who perceives it in the temporal context of twentieth century music," writes psychologist Rudolf Arnheim, "whereas it conveyed the expression of violent passion and desperate suffering to his contemporaries in relation to the music they knew."[21]

In a world of *Leave It to Beaver, Father Knows Best*, and *The Adventures of Ozzie and Harriet, I Love Lucy* holds up well as a vehicle for audience involvement and comfortable entertainment. But when placed next to *Seinfeld, Friends*, and *Ally McBeal*, both *Lucy*'s comparatively sparse production tools and quaint life-style assumptions make it easy for some viewers initially to overlook the eternal marital tensions that Lucy and Ricky project. So an astute programmer learns to recognize and spotlight enduring human appeals in both contemporary and 'evergreen' shows. Success may be garnered from even the most aged of reruns if the show has the capacity to generate a pleasing resonance with the target audience—and the programmer knows how to illuminate this resonance through proper scheduling and promotion. As David Handler observes:

Hair styles change. Values change. The way shows look and sound changes. Good acting and writing [intrinsic elements] don't. If we love the people—if they absorb us, make us laugh or cry [an extrinsic evaluation]—then a show isn't dated. It's a classic.[22]

Whether it's a new or vintage property, extrinsic evaluation's determination of a show's current and projected 'meaning impact' for audiences helps us isolate which elements to emphasize in future production or promotion. Careful attention to extrinsic evaluation also lessens the chance that we will be blindsided by unanticipatedly hostile audience reactions.

COMPOSING THE COMPOSITE CRITIQUE

Despite the scope of the task, it is possible for a single analysis to encapsulate all four composite criticism elements in building a comprehensive assessment of a particular program property. In fact, this is not only possible but it also comes close to being *mandatory* if we are fully to meet the terms of criticism's definition repeated earlier in this chapter.

By using composite criticism, we are dutifully retracing the road we or other professionals traveled in creating the work. As Melvin Rader reminds us:

No artist can create without appreciating the values that he wishes to express; without contemplating the expressive medium, elements and forms; and without criticizing the work as it takes shape under his hand. The artist himself is beholder and judge, and the fineness of his art depends largely upon the quality of his appreciation and judgment.[23]

Thus, by replicating this creative process via composite criticism, we are much more likely to place the work in an accurate and realistic perspective, both for ourselves and for our intended audiences.

Written by Howard Reich, the following critique of the ninety-minute special, *Swingin' With Duke*, is an appropriate illustration of composite criticism. Read the review in its entirety before we isolate and discuss its intrinsic/extrinsic elements.

From the standpoint of *intrinsic appreciation*, Reich tells us that *Swingin' With Duke*'s central appeal flows from its exuberance and ebullience. Its range of pleasurable emotions extends from the heart-beat-stimulating effect of hot jump numbers to the tender melancholy generated by its romantic ballads. The musical performances are sumptuous and elegant, capped by one of "the most searing blues performances" of Ella Fitzgerald's career.

Reich displays his *extrinsic appreciation* by pointing out the unique challenge Ellington presents for television producers: "Find a way to feature Ellington without demeaning a music that emerged long before the era of quick cuts, loopy camera angles and other hallmarks of the MTV age." Reich also expresses sympathy for the fact that "Ellington's legacy of compositions, performances and recordings, as well as his impact as a cultural icon, is too large and multidimensional to be covered in a single program." Thus, the critic commiserates with the producers that they faced an impossible task from the beginning.

Having benevolently taken these factors into consideration, Reich's *intrinsic evaluation* can proceed with fairness. The producers found a "clever solution" to the problem of blending today's music-television styling with Ellington's historic jazz: they focused on dancers in front of the band. The music itself was performed sensitively and authentically by artists who learned under the Duke himself. Many of their verbal comments are "even more moving" than the

---

ELLINGTON'S ELOQUENCE

by Howard Reich

Though jazz has enjoyed resurgent interest and recognition in the '90s, the music still turns up infrequently on television. And in American life, if you're not on TV you're simply not on the pop-culture radar.

So jazz fans will applaud Swingin' With Duke: Lincoln Center Jazz Orchestra with Wynton Marsalis, a Duke Ellington celebration that airs at 9 P.M. Wednesday on WTTW-Ch 11. Even with its editing and production flaws, the program (part of the "Great Performances" series) presents the music

with a dignity it's not often accorded in popular media.

The occasion, of course, is the centennial of Ellington's birth, which is being celebrated this year by every jazz organization and ensemble worthy of the name. For television producers, however, the challenge is unique: Find a way to feature Ellington without demeaning a music that emerged long before the era of quick cuts, loopy camera angles and other hallmarks of the MTV age.

Swingin' With Duke offers a clever solution: While the orchestra plays a variety of Ellington classics, an ensemble of swing dancers bound gleefully across a dance floor in front of the band. As in Ellington's heyday, the musicmaking here is not simply about sound but also about movement. To see these exuberant couples bounce, swing and occasionally slow-dance in front of the band is to understand anew much of the meaning and purpose of Ellington's work.

And because so many of these dancers are young, their ebullience points up the timeless quality of Ellington's scores. Ellington, the program is saying, is for listeners young and old whose hearts beat faster during a hot jump number or whose moods turn tender during a melancholy romantic ballad.

Not surprisingly, the orchestra plays Ellington's music sumptuously and with undeniable sensitivity to various facets of the composer's legacy. Few working bands today could bring as much blues atmosphere to "Black and Tan Fantasy," such elegant swing rhythm to "Second Line" and so much pictorial detail to "Daybreak Express." Guest appearances by the saxophonist Illinois Jacquet, who offers a characteristically big and brawny tone in "Cottontail," and singer Dianne Reeves, who revels in the deep blues of "Rocks in My Bed," further distinguish the show. Between the musical numbers, the program includes rare historical footage of Johnny Hodges, Ella Fitzgerald, Sidney Bechet and other Ellington acolytes who long ago set the standard for performance of this music. The sequence in which Fitzgerald sings "Imagine My Frustration" stands out among the most searing blues performances of her career.

The program also includes interview segments with Ellington, who proves as articulate in speech as he is eloquent in song. Even more moving, however are some of the artists' comments about the Duke.

"Duke Ellington was our teacher - - - the way he dressed, the way he looked, how to present ourselves, how to present jazz music," says Jacquet.

"This music is a gift from God. We had to play it to survive," he adds, referring to the inspirational quality it held for African-Americans in an era of pervasive racial discrimination.

But the producers of the film, listed as David Horn and Jac Venza, ran into the same difficulty every Ellington chronicler encounters when dealing with the man's life and music: Ellington's legacy of compositions, performances and recordings, as well as his impact as a cultural icon, is too large and multidimensional to be covered in a single program. By packing this show with live performances, historic footage, running commentary, archival interviews and what-not, the show loses any sense of continuity or flow.

The constant cutting from one source of material to another renders the program too frenetic for the music it attempts to honor. Too often, the splendid orchestral performances are obscured by unnecessary vocal overdubs.

Ultimately, by simultaneously trying to be a performance film for the orchestra, a documentary about Ellington's life and times and a cinematic look at Harlem past and present, Swingin' With Duke falls a little short on all counts. Simply presenting the orchestra's performance in alternation with the archival would have made for a much more powerful 90 minutes.

Nevertheless, the quality of the performances and the repertoire are beyond question, and for these alone Swingin' With Duke is worth watching. The mere fact that the Lincoln Center Jazz Orchestra has succeeded in bringing this music to TV represents a cultural triumph that does not happen often for jazz. It should be savored.

melodies. But though all of these elements are praiseworthy, the producers failed to be selective. "By packing this show with live performances, historic footage, running commentary, archival interviews and what-not, the show loses any sense of continuity or flow." From a technical standpoint, "The constant cutting from one source of material to another renders the program too frenetic for the music it attempts to honor. Too often, the splendid orchestra performances are obscured by unnecessary vocal overdubs." Instead, Reich makes this rectifying suggestion: "Simply presenting the or-chestra's performance in alternation with the archival would have made for a much more powerful 90 minutes."

The overall *extrinsic evaluation* result is that, for the viewer, the show "falls a little short on all counts." "Nevertheless, the quality of the performances and the repertoire" alone make *Swingin' With Duke* worth watching. African-Americans especially may find special meaning in the "inspirational quality" that this music provided "in an era of pervasive racial discrimination." For all viewers, the program brings together elements calculated to evidence the appeal of 'Duke's' music to "lis-

---

FEMALE FITNESS COMMERCIAL DROPS THE WEIGHTS ON MEN

by Barbara Lippert

Way back when, we could count on detergent commercials to offend women. They showed homemakers so bug-eyed at the prospect of a brighter-whiter peak experience that with a few more interests they'd measure up to Stepford status. Boy, did those gals have a great time with the measuring cups and those front-loaders. But the detergent people have wised up. Lately, those kinds of soap commercials are becoming a regular feminist oasis.

These days, strangely enough, the gender offenders in advertising are in the health and fitness area. Because of this new boom, advertisers think they have permission to show a lot more women in bathing suits. While ostensibly showing off strong, lean bodies, they also somehow manage to get in the new cleavage (the sides of breasts) and the new, super-duper, ever revealing triangulated groin area.

This is a commercial for Marcy Fitness Products' "serious" home-fitness equipment, one of the first in the category aimed at women. It shows a woman going through your average day in a rough, male-dominated urban jungle. A man almost runs her over with his cab, some toughs shove her around in the subway, a manly arm dumps a new pile of work on her office desk, and when she gets home, the elevator isn't working (another male screw-up, no doubt). She climbs the stairs to her apartment, gets in the door, leans back and sighs with relief. Then, in the general direction of the living room, she says in a sultry voice, "Boy, do I need you tonight."

She's speaking, of course, to her Marcy home gym, an imposing piece of gleaming steel and black vinyl.

At earlier points in the spot, we get some foreshadowing of the nature of her relationship: After each bad experience with males, we see cuts of this woman working out with her machine, showing the butterfly station, leg extension and the weights slamming down on the stack. This probably satisfied the manufacturer, as it gets in more shots of the product. But it dulls the impact of the shocker, "I need you tonight." And the cuts are too quick.

More power to Marcy for acknowledging the economic strength of women. The resulting spot is intelligent and says a lot in 30 seconds. And doubtless there are many women who use working out as a therapy for a bad day (it's one way to gain personal control) and even as sexual stimulation. But there are plenty of men doing that, too. Does a commercial have to play on anti-male feelings in order to show a strong woman?

(Reprinted with permission of *ADWEEK*)

teners young and old" and "points up the timeless quality of Ellington's scores." In summary, viewers should "savor" this cultural triumph of bringing jazz to television.

For another example of composite criticism in action, read the Barbara Lippert review of a Marcy Fitness Products commercial reprinted above. As Lippert's piece demonstrates, composite criticism is not a tool for assessing only program-length vehicles. It is just as applicable to the judgment of our 30-second projects.

This spot, declares Lippert, "is intelligent and says a lot in 30 seconds" with ample demonstration of the product's therapeutic pleasures and its "gleaming steel and black vinyl" (*intrinsic appreciation*). Despite their potential weakening of the commercial's climax, these multiple demonstrations probably had to be worked in to satisfy "the manufacturer, as it gets in more shots of the product" and to respect the product-inherent necessity "to show a strong woman" (*extrinsic appreciation*).

But while the viewer absorbs compelling examples of the woman's frustrations as well as multiple product-in-use vignettes, "the cuts are too quick." In addition, the earlier interspersal of the woman's "male-dominated" hassles with glimpses of her

Marcy workout "dulls the impact of the shocker, 'I need you tonight.'" (*intrinsic evaluation*). Ultimately, although the commercial makers are to be congratulated "for acknowledging the economic strength of women," they shouldn't "have to play on anti-male feelings" to get across their point of view (*extrinsic evaluation*).

For a final exercise in composite criticism, let us dissect *The Newsroom* episode script found in Appendix A. Even though some of the production values can be ascertained only by actually watching the program, we still can meaningfully apply composite criticism to analysis of its motivating text. This is, after all, what literary criticism does when it dissects a novel, short story, or nonfiction volume.

COMPOSITE CONCLUSIONS

We now have applied the tenets of composite criticism to the critiquing of a 90-minute special, a half-minute commercial, and a half-hour situation comedy. These three sample exercises demonstrate that composite criticism offers a cluster of approaches that collectively and equitably takes into ac-

---

THE NEWSROOM: A COMPOSITE CRITICISM

Much of our intrinsic appreciation of this show comes from its wickedly biting satire. The duplicity and venality of the characters is pleasurable to watch because it is so easy to feel morally superior to them. Clever ironies abound that amplify these duplicities even in a single character speech. In her very first newscast in her new market, for instance, anchorwoman Lindsay does not miss a beat in seguing from her self-serving praise of Toronto as "a competitive world-class city, with amazing opportunities for everyone" to "Good evening. Four homeless men froze to death last night in Toronto's east end." Only moments later, assistant producer Jeremy has no self-consciousness in affirming during a production meeting that "we're dropping the Mother Teresa item and going with the peep-

ing tom in the public washroom." The viewer also enjoys being admitted to a behind-the-scenes media environment. That the entire show takes place within the confines of *Toronto News'* cubicles and studios enhances the feeling of immersion in this phony yet glamorous enterprise.

From an extrinsic appreciation standpoint, there are a number of challenges this production faced. Though it is not apparent from the script alone, Ken Finkleman (see Figure 15-2) not only wrote the episode but also is the series' creator/executive producer/director/star who plays the manipulative news director George Findlay. Filling so many simultaneous roles presents great challenges for one person and for the production. This is television without a safety net because all critical aspects of the show demand the simultaneous attention of a single individual. Finkleman also faced the daunting task of preserving the program's dark, adult humor despite the fact that it ran at 9 P.M. on national broadcast television (CBC-TV). Though the Canadian Broadcasting Corporation is a publicly funded network, sustaining such biting material in the middle of prime time is still a struggle. The Newsroom's caustic satire is much more at home in the intimate theater than in the tonnage world of network prime time. In addition, as a CBC-funded production, the series (like many such Canadian properties) had to be fashioned to attract Canadian audiences - - - while still appealing to foreign viewers in its subsequent syndication. Thus, the characters and situations are expected to resonate far beyond the specific geographic referents used in the script.

The theme of unchecked pride leading to self-destruction is a sturdy underpinning to this episode and an important asset from an intrinsic evaluation standpoint. That this pride is both male and female, both physical and intellectual, is amply demonstrated by competing anchors Jim and Lindsay. Hovering over them, news director George functions as a conniving Mephistopheles, a crafty devil who still survives despite sometimes becoming too entangled in his own schemes. However, a downside to this dramatic conception of George is that his character is totally lacking in redeeming social value.

In fact, it is difficult to find any character in The Newsroom with whom a viewer could positively identify. Such manipulating, completely self-serving individuals do make for potent satire—but at the expense of audience involvement. We enjoy the situations, but we can never feel comfortable relating to the people. In a similar way, it is arguable that some of the dialogue expletives are there more for situational shock-value than for character revelation. The use of the same vulgarities by different players may blur rather than contribute to those characters' distinctiveness.

Finally, the program's portrayal of the print medium as both manipulator of - - - and shill for - - - broadcasting raises some important issues and proves a deft motivator for the quick "who's in, who's out" juxtapositions at the episode's conclusion. However, in its multiple mentions of real-life columnists like the Toronto Star's Sid Adilman, the program may be bending over backwards to appeal to the critics in Canada's entertainment capital while making it less accessible to non-Canadian audiences.

Aired and promoted as a mid-prime-time sitcom, The Newsroom inevitably must answer to extrinsic evaluation-related concerns about its impact on young people. It could be argued that, in depicting the glamorous media world in this manner, the program advances negative role models in the same way as do glitzy, hedonistic MTV videos. On the other hand, the contention can be made that the negative consequences of many of The Newsroom characters' self-indulgent acts teach the errors of such ways. Similarly, the blatant use of alcohol and drugs can be deplored - - - but such use is shown to contribute to those characters' downfall. George's exploitation of these substances to dominate both Jim and Lindsay might be the most searing possible indictment of their dependency-producing side effects.

In a larger sense, The Newsroom's cynicism could be faulted for making viewers totally distrustful of electronic journalism in general. While some people may say this is a positive result, those of us committed to this profession would not concede the universal truth of, or benefit from, such a characterization. This blanket dismissal of broadcast journalism (and also of the print journalists who monitor it) for the sake of edgy humor oversimplifies the enterprise and may make it more difficult for genuine journalism to function as protective watchdog for its public.

count the interests and perspectives of everyone involved in the packaging and communication of electronic media meaning. Professor Quentin Schultze, in fact, equates this critical multi-process to the practice of biblical interpretation. In both, asserts Schultze,

we gain an understanding of a culture by appealing to its sacred narratives, locating the significant context for those stories, and examining how the narratives and people define each other. More specifically, we move from an examination of the text (the program, series or genre),

[INTRINSIC APPRECIATION AND EVALUATION]

to an elucidation of its context (the cultural and historical setting of the people for whom the program is meaningful, as well as the material conditions of its creation and financing),

[EXTRINSIC APPRECIATION]

and finally to the application (the informed meaning of the text for humankind today).[24]

[EXTRINSIC EVALUATION]

When criticism is restricted to a single, myopic perspective, on the other hand, both biblical and electronic texts can be grossly misinterpreted.

Imagine, for example, an interchange between an extremist, self-indulgent videographer and a straitlaced, self-proclaimed protector of community morals. In analyzing her production called "Nude in a Seven-Course Cantonese Dinner," the videographer evidences an exclusionary concern with the sensual pleasure of the work's imagery. The community protector, in contrast, is willing to discuss only how this 'taped depravity' will corrupt the behavior of the community's youth.

These two viewpoints certainly will engender argument. But they will not promote dialogue. The videographer is engaging solely in intrinsic appreciation while the protector is restricting his purview to extrinsic evaluation. The failure of each party to consider the other's process (and their mutual ignoring of intrinsic evaluation and extrinsic appreciation) inevitably will result in a nonproductive standoff.

However, even though it is important to look at both intrinsic and extrinsic factors, one need not always derive a uniformly posi-

tive or negative *conclusion* in regards to those internal and external perspectives. For instance, in the reviews of ABC's courageous *Something about Amelia*, which dealt unblinkingly with incest, some critics lauded the show's acting and storyline (positive intrinsic evaluation) while nonetheless reproaching it for a vagueness that might cause children to misconstrue normal parental shows of affection as acts of evil perversion (negative extrinsic evaluation).

The reverse also can legitimately occur. Several years ago, the students at a Black inner-city high school staged a performance of *Fiddler on the Roof*, the musical portrayal of the triumphs and tragedies of a village of Russian Jews. The students' performance was simultaneously taped for cable access exposure. Even though television reviewers found the result to be theatrically rough and productionally primitive (negative intrinsic evaluation), they still praised the production's powerful impact as a statement of one ghettoized people's sensitive empathy for a different group of ghetto dwellers (positive extrinsic evaluation). This validates Northrop Frye's contention that

> no discussion of beauty can confine itself to the formal relations of the isolated work of art; it must consider too, the participation of the work of art in the vision of the goal of social effort.[25]

In summary, composite criticism comprehensively fulfills criticism's requirements because it intersects all four of the communication process components we discuss at length in Chapter 3. We can, in fact, refine that chapter's diagram of criticism and the communication process (Figure 3-1) by substituting composite criticism's individual elements for what we refer to there simply as *critic*. Figure 15-3 graphically depicts this substitution.

Thus, in examining Figure 15-3, we are reminded that extrinsic appreciation focuses mainly on the *originator* and the *medium* by illuminating and sympathizing with the difficulties both entities face. Extrinsic appreciation also takes into account the problems one of these functions might cause the other (such as the incompetent originator abusing the medium or the deadline-fixated medium providing insufficient time for originator preparation.)

Extrinsic evaluation, meanwhile, is concerned with the effects of the transmission on the *receiver* as well as with the flow-through effects of receiver reaction on long-term *message* shaping (polysemic negotiation).

Finally, for the reason that they *are* intrinsic, intrinsic appreciation and intrinsic evaluation concentrate on the pleasure potential of the *message* itself. These two perspectives thus scrutinize both the content and executional factors that help or hinder the realization of this potential.

Invoking the basic term *criticism* to encompass the four-faceted process we label *composite criticism*, Jerome Stolnitz aptly encapsulates its dimensions and benefits by concluding:

> Criticism calls our attention to the sparkle or charm of the sensory matter, the subtlety of form and the way in which its formal expression unifies the work, the meaning of symbols, and the expressive mood of the entire work. Criticism gives us a sense of the work's "aesthetic intention," so that we do not make illegitimate demands upon it. Criticism also develops aesthetic "sympathy" by breaking down the prejudices and confusions which get in the way of appreciation. It explains the artistic conventions and social beliefs of the artist's time. It relates the work of art to the great

FIGURE 15-3
Composite criticism and the communication process.

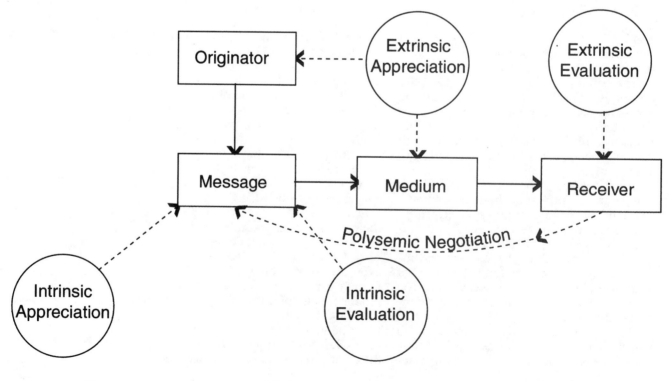

world and shows its relevance to our own experience.[26]

A FINAL CONVICTION

Composite criticism clearly is the most eclectic of the many critical approaches we explore in these fifteen chapters. There are more complex procedures, particularly in the arena of quantitative research, that we lack the space to investigate. Instead, our attempt has been to construct a critical frame of reference that makes sense in the pragmatic world of every electronic media practitioner.

As we indicate at the beginning of this book, criticism is a constructive tool rather than a destructive weapon. Its use as such a tool requires that the critiques we fashion are used to stimulate rather than inhibit our profession. In the ever-changing electronic media environment, we cannot always claim to possess the right answers. But it may not be too much to expect that, over time, we at least learn to ask the right questions.

ENDNOTES

1. DeWitt Parker, *The Principles of Aesthetics*, 2nd ed. (Westport, CT: Greenwood Press, 1976), 272.
2. Ellen Harris, "It Takes Practice and Serious Thought to Learn How to Dislike Art Properly," *The Chronicle of Higher Education* (September 19, 1990), A56.
3. Eric Sevareid, "A Little Less Hypocrisy, Please," (New York: Television Information Office, 1968), 2.
4. Lawrence Laurent, "Wanted: The Complete Television Critic," in Robert Lewis Shayon (ed.), *The Eighth Art* (New York: Holt, Rinehart and Winston, 1962), 156.
5. Steve Pond, "What's Wrong with Radio," in George Rodman (ed.), *Mass Media Issues*, 3rd. ed. (Dubuque, IA: Kendall/Hunt, 1989), 90.
6. "Straight from the Hart: Assailing the Media Filter," *Broadcasting* (January 4, 1988), 124.
7. Bill Lichtenstein, "The Censor," *Channels* (November 5, 1990), 18.
8. John Fiske and John Hartley, *Reading Television* (London: Methuen, 1978), 17.
9. George Boas, *A Primer for Critics* (New York: Greenwood Press, 1968), 81.
10. Ibid., 33.
11. Jerome Stolnitz, *Aesthetics and Philosophy of Art Criticism* (Boston: Houghton Mifflin, 1960), 474–475.
12. Parker, 11.
13. Stolnitz, 482.
14. Mark Christensen and Cameron Stauth, *The Sweeps* (New York: Bantam Books, 1985), 136.
15. Danielle Claman, writing in Peter Orlik (ed.), *The Electronic Media: An Introduction to the Profession* (Boston: Allyn and Bacon, 1992), 381.
16. Conrad Kottak, *Prime-Time Society* (Belmont, CA: Wadsworth, 1990), 14–15.
17. Horace Newcomb, "On the Dialogic Aspects of Mass Communication," *Critical Studies in Mass Communication* (March 1984), 40.
18. Peter Monaghan, "Casting a Critical Eye on Canonized Works, a Scholar Reinterprets Images of Rape in Art," *The Chronicle of Higher Education* (March 12, 1999), A13.
19. Christopher Anderson, "I Love Lucy," *Encyclopedia of Television*, Horace Newcomb (ed.), (Chicago: Fitzroy Dearborn, 1997), 814–816.
20. Nam June Paik, "La Vie, Satellites, One Meeting—One Life," in John Hanhardt (ed.), *Video Culture* (Rochester, NY: Visual Studies Workshop Press, 1986), 219.
21. Rudolf Arnheim, *Toward a Psychology of Art* (Berkeley: University of California Press, 1967), 67.
22. David Handler, "Which Old Favorites Are Still Choice—and Which Aren't," *TV Guide* (April 4, 1987), 20.
23. Melvin Rader, *A Modern Book of Esthetics*, 5th ed. (New York: Holt, Rinehart and Winston, 1979), 16.
24. Quentin Schultze, "Television Drama as a Sacred Text," in John Ferre (ed.), *Channels of Belief* (Ames: Iowa State University Press, 1990), 17.
25. Northrop Frye, *Anatomy of Criticism* (Princeton, NJ: Princeton University Press, 1957), 348.
26. Stolnitz, 494.

Specimen Scripts

THE COSBY SHOW

"Theo's Holiday"

THE COSBY SHOW
"Theo's Holiday"
Show #0221-22

Written by
John Markus
Carmen Finestra
Matt Williams

DR. WILLIAM H. COSBY, JR.
CARSEY-WERNER CO.

(Script provided courtesy of Kim Tinsley, Director of Public Affairs, *The Cosby Show*)

THE COSBY SHOW
"Theo's Holiday"
SHOW #0221-22

CAST

Cliff Huxtable · Bill Cosby
Clair Huxtable · Phylicia Rashad
Denise Huxtable · Lisa Bonet
Theo Huxtable · Malcolm-Jamal Warner
Vanessa Huxtable · Tempestt Bledsoe
Rudy Huxtable · Keshia Knight Pulliam
Cockroach · Carl Payne

SET

ACT ONE

Scene 1

FADE IN:

INT. KITCHEN—EVENING (DAY 1)

(Cliff, Clair, Denise, Theo, Vanessa, Rudy)

(THERE IS A SUMPTUOUS MEAL ON THE TABLE. THE HUXTABLE FAMILY IS EATING DINNER. ALL THE CHILDREN EXCEPT THEO ARE LAUGHING)

THEO: No, really. I could do it.

VANESSA: Could you see Theo up on a billboard?

(THE KIDS LAUGH)

THEO: Hey, it won't be just billboards. It'll be
           catalogues, magazines, TV . . .

DENISE: Hah!

CLAIR: If your brother is serious about a career, I think
           we should encourage him.

DENISE: But, Mom, a model.

THEO: Why not?

RUDY: Because you're Theo.

(THE GIRLS LAUGH)

CLIFF: Wait a minute. I can't just sit back and watch my
           man take all this abuse.

THEO: Thanks, Dad.

CLIFF: I happen to think you're a very handsome fellow,
           and could make a go at modeling.

THEO: I know I could. You see, most of these guys in the
           magazines, when they pose, look like this . . .

(THEO STRIKES A MODEL-LIKE POSE)

THEO
(CONT'D): That's not natural. If I were doing it. I'd stand
           like this . . .

(THEO SHOWS HIS VERSION OF A NATURAL POSE. IT LOOKS PRETTY
GOOD)

GIRLS: Oooooo.

CLIFF: Son, you're a natural.

THEO: Dad, I read that a model, even one who's starting
           out, can make five hundred dollars a day. And the
           great thing is, I could start when I'm eighteen.

CLIFF: What about college?

THEO: I could go, but that's four years out of my
           modeling career.

CLAIR: Theo, your father and I have never said you had to
           go to college. But we do feel that it can help you
           lay a foundation for the rest of your life.

THEO: Mom, at five hundred dollars a day, I don't need a foundation.

CLIFF: You think you'd be ready to go out on your own at eighteen?

THEO: I could do it. I know it's going to be hard, but I could do it.

DENISE: Uh-huh, sure.

THEO: I could.

CLIFF: I don't think you really know how hard it is.

THEO: I know I'd have to find my own place, pay bills, and all that stuff. But I could do it.

CLIFF: You say you can do it, but you don't really know because you haven't tried it.

THEO: I manage my life pretty well right now.

CLIFF: Theo, right now you are going through life on the Doctor and Mrs. Huxtable Scholarship Fund.

(THE CHILDREN AD LIB 'YEAH,' 'RIGHT')

THEO:
(TO HIS SISTERS) Hey, you're on it, too.

(TO CLIFF) I don't need that much. If I get one day's work as a model, I'll have enough to live on for a month. And I figure if I get in a bind, you and Mom . . .

CLIFF/CLAIR: No.

THEO: But you could . . .

CLIFF/CLAIR: No.

THEO: You wouldn't help me at all?

CLIFF: Once you're out in the real world, you can't rely on your mother and me. You have to make it on your own.

CLAIR: But, of course, we'd be happy to help you get started.

CLIFF: No.

CLAIR: C'mon, Cliff. Theo, how much do you think you'd need?

THEO: Oh, five hundred dollars.

DENISE: Theo, get real.

CLIFF: You'll need more than that.

THEO: All right. A thousand.

CLIFF: Tell you what. We'll give you two thousand dollars to get you started.

THEO: Hey, with two "G's" in my pocket, there'd be no looking back.

CLIFF: You sound confident.

THEO: I am.

(GETTING UP AND PICKING UP HIS OVERNIGHT BAG)

            Can I be excused?

VANESSA: Where are you going?

THEO: I'm spending the night at Cockroach's.

CLAIR: You're coming back, aren't you? You're not going out into the real world so soon?

THEO: No, Mom. I'll be back tomorrow.

CLIFF: What time?

THEO: Around ten.

CLIFF: Ten. Got it. See you then.

(THEO STARTS TO EXT)

RUDY: Bye Mr. Model.

(THEY ALL LAUGH AND <u>AD LIB</u> 'GOODBYES' TO THEO. THEO EXITS)

CLIFF: Is everyone going to be here around ten tomorrow?

(THE KIDS <u>AD LIB</u> 'YES')

DENISE: Why?

CLIFF: I need all of you for a project.

CLAIR: What project?

CLIFF:

(SMILING AS HE GETS UP)

            Let's just say we're going to be helping Theo get ready for the real world.

DENISE/
VANESSA/
RUDY: Oooooo.

(CLIFF STRIDES OUT AS WE:)

DISSOLVE TO:

ACT ONE

Scene 2

EXT. HUXTABLE'S FRONT STOOP—THE NEXT MORNING (DAY 2)
(Cliff, Theo, Vanessa)

(VANESSA SITS ON THE STOOP. THEO ENTERS, CARRYING HIS
OVERNIGHT BAG)

THEO: Hey, Vanessa.

(VANESSA LOOKS AT HIM, PUZZLED)

THEO:
(CONT'D):   What's wrong?

VANESSA: You must be mistaking me for someone else. My
            name's not Vanessa.

THEO: Huh?

VANESSA: My name is Margo Farnsworth.

THEO: What are you talking about?

VANESSA: I'm Margo Farnsworth. I have an apartment in this
            building.

THEO: Whatever you say, Margo.

(THEO STARTS UP THE STAIRS)

VANESSA: Wait, I know who you are. The landlord told me
            that a young man who's eighteen and on his own is
            coming here to rent an apartment,

(A BEAT)

THEO: Oh, I get it. Very funny.

VANESSA: What's so funny?

THEO: I'm eighteen and I'm on my own.

VANESSA: That's right. And you're here to rent an apartment.

THEO: Fine. Okay. I'll rent an apartment. Who do I talk to?

VANESSA: The landlord. Just ring the doorbell. I hope you
            get into the building. Some very nice people live
            here.

5.

THEO: Right. Okay, Vanessa.

VANESSA: Who?

THEO: Never mind.

(THEO WALKS UP TO THE DOOR AND RINGS THE BELL)

SFX: DOORBELL

(A BEAT. CLIFF ANSWERS THE DOOR)

CLIFF: Hello.

THEO: Hi, Dad.

CLIFF: Who?

THEO: Oh. I mean, Mr. Landlord.

CLIFF: You must be here for the apartment. I'm Harley.

(EXTENDING HIS HAND)

             Harley Weemax.

THEO: Theodore Huxtable.

CLIFF: Oh, yes. Huxtable. Your parents were here a little
             earlier. They left an envelope for you.

(HE HANDS THE ENVELOPE TO THEO)

CLIFF
(CONT'D):   You got nice folks.

(THEO OPENS THE ENVELOPE AND PULLS OUT A STACK OF FAKE MONEY)

THEO: This is play money.

CLIFF: It's good here.

THEO:
(FINDING A NOTE AND READING IT)

             "Dear Theo, here's your two thousand dollars to get
             started. Good luck. We love you very much. Mom and
             Dad."

CLIFF: Beautiful people. C'mon, I'll show you the
             apartment.

CUT TO:

ACT ONE

Scene 3

INT. LIVING ROOM—CONTINUOUS ACTION (DAY 2)
(Cliff, Clair, Theo, Rudy)

(CLIFF ESCORTS THEO IN)

CLIFF: Welcome to the Real World Apartments. As you can
            see, we have a beautiful lobby. All the woodwork
            is original.

(CLAIR ENTERS FROM THE KITCHEN)

CLAIR:
(TO CLIFF) Hi, Harley.

CLIFF: Hi, Millie.

THEO: Millie?

CLIFF: Yeah, this is Millie Farquar. She owns the Wagon
            Wheel Restaurant here.

CLAIR: Howdy, You'll have to stop by for some grub. We're
            right off the lobby. Open twenty-four hours.

THEO: Good one, Mom.

CLAIR: Who?

THEO: I mean, 'Mrs. Farquar.'

CLAIR: It's 'Miss.' Hope to see you real soon.

(CLAIR EXITS BACK INTO KITCHEN)

CLIFF: You'll like eating at the Wagon Wheel. I recommend
            the Bacon Burger Dog.

(CLIFF AND THEO HEAD TOWARD THE STAIRS)

CLIFF (CONT'D): We have a few rules here at Real World
            Apartments. Rent is due on the first of every
            month, no exceptions. No loud music after ten
            o'clock. No pets and no children.

(RUDY ENTERS DOWN THE STAIRS IN A VERY NICE BUT CONSERVATIVE
OUTFIT. SHE'S CARRYING A BRIEFCASE)

RUDY: Hi, Harley.

CLIFF: Hi, Mrs Griswald.

THEO: Oh, no.

(RUDY CROSSES TO THE KITCHEN AS CLIFF AND THEO HEAD UP THE STAIRS)

CLIFF: Let's go see the apartment.

CUT TO:

ACT ONE

Scene 4

INT. THEO'S ROOM—CONTINUOUS ACTION (DAY 2)
(Cliff, Theo)

(THEO'S ROOM IS TOTALLY STRIPPED AND EMPTY. CLIFF AND THEO ENTER. THEO IS STUNNED)

THEO: Dad!

CLIFF: Who?

THEO: Where's my stuff? My stereo? My posters? My bed?

CLIFF: It's an unfurnished apartment.

THEO: I don't believe this.

CLIFF: Believe what? I'm just showing you an unfurnished
            apartment. And this is not a dream.

THEO:
(CALMING DOWN) Okay. Unfurnished. I got it.

CLIFF: Good.

THEO: So how much is it?

CLIFF: Six hundred dollars a month.

THEO: For one room?

CLIFF: Hey, that's what they go for nowadays.

THEO: I guess I'll have to take it.

CLIFF: Not so fast. How old are you?

THEO: Eighteen.

CLIFF: Sorry.

THEO: What?

CLIFF: I don't rent to people that age. All they want to do is party.

THEO: Did I say I was eighteen? I'm sorry. I meant I've been on my own since I was eighteen. I'm actually twenty-three.

CLIFF: Good.

(THEO STARTS TO TAKE MONEY OUT OF THE ENVELOPE)

THEO: I've got the six hundred dollars for the rent.

CLIFF: Wait. I'll need the first month's rent and the last month's rent.

THEO: Why?

CLIFF: I need the last month's rent in case you try to move out early without paying.

THEO: That's twelve hundred dollars.

CLIFF: And I need another month's rent as security to cover damages.

THEO: That's eighteen hundred dollars!

CLIFF: You add like a twenty-three year old.

THEO: All right. It's a lot of money, but I need a place to live. Here you go.

(THEO STARTS TO HAND CLIFF THE MONEY)

CLIFF:
(MOVING HIS HAND AWAY)

            I can't take it.

THEO: Why not?

CLIFF: I'll need references.

THEO: References?

CLIFF: Yes. Someone to vouch for your character, like your employer. You do have a job, don't you?

THEO: Uh . . . not now. But I'm going to get one. I'm a model.

CLIFF: A model, huh? I'm going to need proof that you'll be able to pay your rent.

THEO: I'll pay it. I promise.

CLIFF: I can't feed my family on a promise. I need a letter stating that you have a steady income.

THEO: Where am I going to get that?

CLIFF: From your modeling agency.

THEO: I don't have one.

CLIFF: If you want to work as a model, you have to have
             an agent. But you're in luck. There happens to be
             a modeling agency right here in the lobby. Ask for
             Kitty La Rue.

THEO: Kitty La Rue. Thanks.

(THEO EXITS)

CUT TO:

ACT ONE

Scene 5

INT. LIVING ROOM—A MOMENT LATER (DAY 2)
(Cliff, Denise, Theo, Vanessa, Rudy)

(DENISE AND VANESSA ARE QUICKLY REARRANGING THE ROOM. THEY'RE
PLACING THE COFFEE TABLE IN FRONT OF ONE OF THE CHAIRS TO
LOOK LIKE A DESK)

CLIFF (O.S.):
(LOUDLY)

             You can't miss it. The modeling agency is right at
             the bottom of the stairs.

DENISE: Hurry.

(VANESSA CROSSES TO THE CORRESPONDENCE DESK AND TURNS THE
CHAIR AROUND AND SITS IN IT. THEO ENTERS DOWN THE STAIRS)

VANESSA: Welcome to the Firestone Modeling Agency.

THEO: This is the modeling agency?

VANESSA: Yes it is. I'm the receptionist, Kitty La Rue.

THEO: I thought you were Margo Farnsworth.

VANESSA: You must have me mistaken for someone else. Do you
             have an appointment?

THEO: No. The landlord sent me. I'm a model and I need
             an agent.

VANESSA: Well, we're always looking for new faces. I'll ask
             Ms. Firestone if she'll see you.

(VANESSA CROSSES AROUND THE COUCH TO DENISE)

VANESSA
(CONT'D): Excuse me, Ms. Firestone.

DENISE: Yes, Kitty?

VANESSA: There's a gentleman here who needs an agent.

DENISE: How does he look?

VANESSA: Not bad.

DENISE: Send him in.

(VANESSA CROSSES TO THEO)

VANESSA: Ms. Firestone will see you.

(THEO CROSSES AROUND THE COUCH TO DENISE. VANESSA EXITS)

THEO: Hi.

(WITHOUT RESPONDING, DENISE GETS UP AND STUDIES THEO'S FACE.
SHE THEN CIRCLES HIM, CHECKING HIM OUT)

DENISE: Do you always stand like that?

(THEO STRAIGHTENS UP)

DENISE
(CONT'D): Would you mind walking across the room for me?

THEO: Huh?

DENISE: Just walk over and back.
(THEO, VERY SELF-CONSCIOUSLY, WALKS ACROSS THE ROOM AND BACK)

DENISE
(CONT'D):
(WATCHING) Uh-huh . . . hmm . . . Uhhh . . . Um-hmm . . .
           Do you have any experience?

THEO: No. But I look good.

DENISE:
(CHUCKLES TO HERSELF, THEN)

           Darling, come with me.

(DENISE ESCORTS THEO TO THE FRONT DOOR. AND OPENS IT)

DENISE
(CONT'D): Take a look. That's New York City. I could throw a
           stick out there and hit twenty guys who look just
           like you. What makes you think you're special
           enough to be a Firestone model?

THEO: I'm a natural. I'm sure if I get that first job,
           I'll never stop working.

11.

DENISE: I like your attitude. Let me see your pictures.

THEO: I don't have any.

DENISE: You're not going to get work without pictures. You need to go to a good photographer and get a full set of prints done. It will cost you eight to twelve hundred dollars.

THEO: Look. Could you do me a favor? I'm trying to get an apartment. Could you just write me a letter saying I'm working as a model?

DENISE: You don't have an apartment?

THEO: No.

DENISE: How am I going to get in touch with you if I ever want to hire you?

THEO: Write the letter, then I'll have the apartment and you'll know where to find me.

DENISE: That would be dishonest. Now if you'll excuse me, I have to call Paris.

(DENISE EXITS. THEO THINKS A BEAT, THEN CROSSES TO THE FRONT DOOR AS CLIFF ENTERS)

CLIFF
(CONT'D): Where are you going?

THEO: To get a reference. Don't let anyone take that apartment.

CLIFF: I can't promise anything, but I'll try.

(THEO EXITS OUT THE FRONT DOOR. RUDY ENTERS FROM THE KITCHEN, NIBBLING ON A COOKIE)

CLIFF
(CONT'D): Mrs. Griswald, where did you get that?

RUDY: Millie made it.

(RUDY EXITS UP THE STAIRS AS WE:)

FADE OUT:

END OF ACT ONE

ACT TWO

Scene 1

FADE IN:

INT. THEO'S ROOM—LATER THAT AFTERNOON (DAY 2)
(Cliff, Theo, Cockroach)

(THEO ENTERS WITH COCKROACH WHO'S WEARING A SUIT AND TIE)

COCKROACH: Man, you weren't kidding. There's nothing in here.

THEO: I know, Cockroach. They're going all out for this. That's why you've got to be good.

COCKROACH: You have nothing to worry about.

CLIFF (O.S.): Hello.

THEO: In here.

(CLIFF ENTERS)

CLIFF: Mrs. Griswald told me you were back.

COCKROACH:
(EXTENDING HIS HAND)

            Hi, Mr. Weemax. I'm Horton W. Dansberry.

THEO: Instead of a letter, I decided to bring my employer.

CLIFF:
(TO COCKROACH)

            You're his employer?

COCKROACH: Yes.

CLIFF: What line of business are you in?

COCKROACH: I'm in oil.

CLIFF: Oil?

COCKROACH: Yes. Let me give you one of my cards.

(COCKROACH HANDS CLIFF A CARD)

CLIFF:
(READING) 'Cockroach Oil.' Very nice card. Isn't it expensive to have them hand-drawn like this?

COCKROACH: Only the best for my company.

CLIFF:
(TO THEO) You work for this man?

13.

THEO: Yes I do.

CLIFF: I thought you said you were a model.

THEO: I am. I'm the spokesman for Cockroach Oil.

COCKROACH: Let me tell you something about this man, Mr.
             Weemax. He's a fine spokesman. Responsible,
             dependable, and hard-working. He's the reason
             Cockroach Oil is what it is today.

CLIFF: That's all I have to hear. Mr. Huxtable, welcome to
             your new apartment.

THEO: Awright. Here you go.

(THEO PULLS OUT HIS MONEY AND GIVES CLIFF A STACK OF IT)

THEO
(CONT'D):   I did it, Dad.

CLIFF: Who?

THEO: Come on, Dad, isn't this what it was all about?
             Getting an apartment on my own? I showed you I
             could do it. Now, let's get my furniture back
             in here.

CLIFF: I don't know what you're talking about.

THEO: Hold it, time out, time out. I have to talk to
             my Dad. Could you find him for me?

CLIFF: I'll see if he's here.

(CLIFF EXITS)

COCKROACH: Who's playing your Dad?

(CLIFF ENTERS)

THEO: My Dad.

CLIFF: Hey, Son. Mr. Weemax said you were looking for me.

THEO: Dad, how much longer will this go on?

CLIFF: Son, the real world stops for no man. But in your
             case, twenty-four hours.

THEO: Twenty-four hours? What am I supposed to do?

CLIFF: In the real world, you'd have to get furniture for
             your apartment, towels, sheets, pillowcases, food.
             You'd have to get a phone, contact the electric
             company . . . I told you it wasn't going to be
             easy.

THEO: That's okay. I can do it.

CLIFF: My boy.

THEO: How do I get my furniture?

CLIFF: I'll ask Mr. Weemax.

(CLIFF EXITS)

COCKROACH: This is fun.

THEO: That's because it's not happening to you.

(CLIFF ENTERS)

CLIFF: Bye, Doctor Huxtable. Love that guy. Your Dad told
           me you're looking for furniture.

THEO: Yeah. Would you happen to know where I could find
           some?

CLIFF: Yes I would. There's a very nice furniture store
           right next to Millie's restaurant. Come on, I'll
           show you.

(CLIFF EXITS)

COCKROACH: Who's Millie?

THEO: Mom.

COCKROACH: Amazing. I wish we did stuff like this at my
           house.

(THEO AND COCKROACH EXIT)

CUT TO:

ACT TWO

Scene 2

INT. DINING ROOM—MOMENTS LATER (DAY 2)
(Cliff, Clair, Theo, Cockroach)

(THE DINING ROOM HAS BEEN TURNED INTO A USED FURNITURE
SHOWROOM, WITH ALL OF THEO'S THINGS—BED, DESK, STEREO,
BOOKSHELVES, ETC.—ARRANGED WITH PRICE TAGS HANGING FROM THEM.
THE STORE OWNER, CLAIR, TAKES INVENTORY AS CLIFF LEADS THEO
AND COCKROACH INTO THE ROOM)

THEO: My stuff.

COCKROACH: They really cleaned you out.

THEO:
(TO CLIFF)

        Millie runs the furniture store?

CLIFF: That's not Millie. That's Amanda.

CLAIR: Hey, Harley, who you got there?

CLIFF: Couple of customers, Amanda.

CLAIR: Send them over.

(CLIFF NUDGES THEO AND COCKROACH TOWARD CLAIR, THEN EXITS)

CLAIR
(CONT'D):   Gentlemen, welcome to Amanda's Furniture City, where money talks and nobody walks. If you like it, touch it. If you break it, you buy it. If you don't see it, we don't have it. But we'll get it. Now, what can I do for you?

THEO:
(LOOKING AT A PRICE ON THE STEREO)

        A hundred and fifty dollars for my stereo?

CLAIR: It's not yours yet. But tell you what. Because I like your face, for a hundred and thirty-five you can walk out with it.

THEO: That's a lot of money. I only have two hundred dollars to furnish my whole apartment.

CLAIR: Does your friend have any money?

COCKROACH: No.

CLAIR:
(TO THEO) Who's he?

THEO: My boss.

CLAIR: Better get yourself a new boss.

THEO:
(LOOKING AT THE PRICE TAG ON THE BED)

        Two hundred dollars?

CLAIR: That's for both beds.

THEO: Can I buy just one?

CLAIR: No. I can't break the set.

THEO: Why not?

CLAIR: They'll get lonely, okay?

(COCKROACH LAUGHS. THEO GIVES HIM A DIRTY LOOK)

THEO: Everything's so expensive. What am I going to do?

CLAIR: You come here for advice or furniture? Look, time is money. You've got to figure out what you need.

THEO: I need it all.

CLAIR: Well, you're not going to get it with two hundred dollars. But, you're in luck. Here at Furniture City, we accept all major credit cards.

THEO: I don't have any credit cards.

CLAIR: You're in luck. Here at Furniture City we accept personal checks.

THEO: I don't have a checking account.

CLAIR: Then you're about to leave Furniture City.

THEO: Mom . . .

CLAIR: Who? Look, my friend, I really want to help you out. What you need to do is go to the bank and get a loan.

THEO: All right. Where's the bank?

CLAIR: It's very easy to find. Just go through Millie's restaurant and make a left.

THEO: C'mon, Cockroach.

COCKROACH: I can't wait to meet the banker.

CLAIR: When you get everything straightened out, come on back. We never close.

(AS THEO AND COCKROACH START TO EXIT)

COCKROACH: I might be back to buy that stereo.

(THEO PULLS COCKROACH OUT OF THE ROOM)

CUT TO:

17.

ACT TWO

Scene 3

INT. KITCHEN—CONTINUOUS ACTION (DAY 2)
(Cockroach, Theo, Denise)

(DENISE IS RINSING SOME DISHES. THEO AND COCKROACH HAVE
ENTERED AND THEO IS CLOSING THE DINING ROOM DOORS BEHIND
THEM)

COCKROACH: Hi, Denise.

THEO: Wait a minute. She's not Denise.

DENISE: Yes, I am.

THEO: You are?

DENISE: Yes.

THEO: Good.

COCKROACH: Theo, I'm starving. Before we go to the bank, can
           we take a break?

THEO: Sure.

(THEO AND COCKROACH START UNLOADING THE REFRIGERATOR)

DENISE: I'll get you some plates.

THEO: Thanks.

(THEO AND COCKROACH CARRY THE FOOD TO THE TABLE. DENISE
BRINGS PLATES AND SILVERWARE OVER. THEY START TO DIG IN.
DENISE STANDS BEHIND THEM AT THE TABLE)

DENISE: So, what have you got there?

THEO: Chicken . . .

(UNSEEN BY THEO AND COCKROACH, DENISE PULLS OUT A SMALL NOTE
PAD AND STARTS WRITING)

THEO
(CONT'D):   . . . some tuna, carrot salad.

DENISE: Would you like sodas?

THEO/
COCKROACH: Yeah.

(DENISE FINISHES WRITING, RIPS OFF THE SHEET OF PAPER AND
LAYS IT ON THE TABLE)

DENISE: That comes to twenty-four dollars and fifty cents.
            That's without the tip of course.

THEO: Hey, what is this?

DENISE: You're eating in Millie's Restaurant.

THEO: I thought you were Denise.

DENISE: I am. Denise Farquar, Millie's daughter. Now pay up.

COCKROACH: Good one. Unbelievable.

(COCKROACH STARTS TO TAKE A BITE OF CHICKEN)

THEO: Put that chicken down.

COCKROACH: I'm hungry.

THEO: You got the money for it?

COCKROACH: No, but you have enough.

THEO: Cockroach, I can't spend this much on one meal. I still have furniture to buy. I have to get my phone, my utilities. I am on a budget.

COCKROACH: Okay. Denise, how much is an apple?

DENISE: A dollar. But that doesn't include tip.

COCKROACH: We'll take two.

THEO: We'll take one and split it.

DENISE: All right.

(AS COCKROACH CUTS THE APPLE IN HALF:)

DENISE
(CONT'D): There's a fifty cent charge for splitting. That comes to a dollar and a half.

THEO: Fine. Here you go.

COCKROACH: Keep the change.

THEO: Cockroach!

COCKROACH: Hey, she's nice.

DENISE: Thank you. Hope to see you again real soon.

THEO: Not at these prices you won't.

(DENISE EXITS)

19.

ACT TWO

Scene 4

INT. LIVING ROOM CONTINUOUS ACTION (DAY 2)
(Rudy, Vanessa, Clair, Cliff, Theo, Cockroach)

(RUDY SITS AT THE DESK. CLIFF LISTENS AT THE KITCHEN DOOR.
VANESSA SITS IN A CHAIR WITH THE COFFEE TABLE IN FRONT OF
HER. CLAIR STANDS NEXT TO VANESSA, GOING OVER A PIECE OF
PAPER)

CLAIR: Just go right down the checklist.

CLIFF: They're coming.

(CLIFF RUSHES TO THE COUCH. HE AND CLAIR QUICKLY SIT DOWN.
THEO AND COCKROACH ENTER)

VANESSA: Would you two please have a seat? I'll be with you
           as soon as I finish here.

THEO:
(QUIETLY TO COCKROACH)

           Vanessa.

COCKROACH: Just be cool.

VANESSA:
(TO CLIFF AND CLAIR)

           Your application for the loan is in perfect order.
           It looks good. I'm going to recommend approval.

CLIFF: Oh, golly. That is so marvelous.

(TO CLAIR) Honey, we can buy our dream house.

CLAIR: And raise a family.

(THEY KISS)

VANESSA: Now, what we have to do is have the loan approved
           by the president of the bank, Mrs. Griswald.

(VANESSA CROSSES TO RUDY)

VANESSA
(CONT'D): Mrs. Griswald?

RUDY: Yes.

VANESSA: Would you look at this application and tell me what
           you think?

(RUDY LOOKS AT THE PAPER A BEAT AND SAYS:)

RUDY: Approved.

VANESSA: Thank you, Mrs. Griswald.

RUDY: You're welcome.

(VANESSA CROSSES BACK TO CLIFF AND CLAIR)

VANESSA: Congratulations.

CLIFF: Oh, golly. I'm so glad we came to this bank.

CLAIR: Me too. Now we can start planning for our future.

(TO VANESSA)

            Thank you for all your help.

(CLIFF AND CLAIR EXIT UP THE STAIRS)

VANESSA: Next.

(THEO AND COCKROACH CROSS TO VANESSA)

THEO: Who are you now?

VANESSA: I'm Ms. Covington. And would you please not eat
            those apples in my office?

(THEO HANDS HIS APPLE TO COCKROACH. HE SETS THEM DOWN)

VANESSA
(CONT'D):   What can I do for you?

COCKROACH: Theo, let me handle this.

(TO VANESSA)

            This gentleman works for me. My name is Horton W.
            Dansberry. I'm the president and owner of Cockroach
            Oil. I'd give you my card, but I ran out.

VANESSA: I see.

(WRITING ON THE PAD)

            Where's Cockroach Oil located?

COCKROACH: Our headquarters are on the top floor of the
            Cockroach Oil Building. It's a forty-nine story
            building.

VANESSA: And the address?

COCKROACH: Nine-eighty-one East Fifty-fourth Street.

VANESSA: Got it.

(REACHING FOR THE PHONE)

Could you give me the phone number? I need to confirm this information.

COCKROACH: Uh . . . we don't have a phone.

VANESSA: You own a forty-nine story building and you don't have a phone?

COCKROACH: Uh . . . the telephone pole out front blew over.

THEO: Forget him. Look, I really need a loan. I have to buy furniture, food, a portfolio . . .

VANESSA: How much money do you need?

THEO: I'd say, uh, twenty-five hundred dollars.

VANESSA: I see.

(WRITING ON THE PAD)

Have you ever taken out a loan before?

THEO: No.

VANESSA: That's too bad. Mr. Huxtable, you have no credit history, and your boss doesn't own a telephone. It doesn't look good.

THEO: But I really need the money. I'll pay it back. I promise.

VANESSA: Well . . . I do like to give young people who are starting out a break. I'm going to recommend that you get the loan.

THEO: Awright.

VANESSA: Mrs. Griswald, could you come here?

RUDY:
(CROSSING TO VANESSA)

What do you want? I'm busy.

VANESSA: This young man wants a loan. I recommend we give it to him.

(RUDY STUDIES THE NOTEPAD FOR A BEAT, THEN:)

RUDY: No.

VANESSA: But . . .

RUDY: No.

THEO: Why not?

RUDY: You have nothing.

(RUDY CROSSES BACK AND SITS AT HER DESK)

VANESSA: Sorry. I tried. Tell you what. Once you start
            working and have some money, come back and we'll
            be glad to give you a loan.

THEO: But I need it now. Are there any other banks in
            this building?

VANESSA: Yes, but they're all owned by Mrs. Griswald.

RUDY: That's right.

DISSOLVE TO:

                        ACT TWO

                        Scene 5

INT. THEO'S ROOM—THAT EVENING (DAY 2)
(Theo, Cliff, Clair, Rudy)

(THEO'S ROOM IS BARE EXCEPT FOR HIS STEREO, A PILLOW AND A
COUPLE OF BLANKETS. A SINGLE LIT CANDLE, SET IN A DISH ON THE
FLOOR, IS THE ONLY LIGHT IN THE ROOM. THEO SITS ON HIS
BLANKETS MUNCHING CONTENTEDLY ON SOME CRACKERS)

SFX: KNOCK

THEO: Come in.

(CLAIR AND CLIFF ENTER. CLAIR CARRIES A COVERED PLATE)

THEO
(CONT'D):   Hi, Mr. Weemax, Amanda.

CLAIR/CLIFF: Who?

CLIFF
(CONT'D):   Son, it's Mom and Dad. Don't you recognize us?

CLAIR: We thought we'd drop by and see how you're getting
            along in your new apartment.

THEO: Pretty good. I did all right. I got everything I
            need and I still have twenty-three dollars left
            over.

CLIFF: Good for you. So, how do you like the real world?

THEO: Well . . . it's a lot tougher than I thought. But
            you know what? So am I.

CLAIR:
(INDICATING THE CANDLE)

            Don't you have any electricity?

THEO: Not yet. I bought my stereo before I knew I had to pay a fifty dollar deposit to get my utilities turned on.

CLIFF: That's pretty steep.

THEO: Yeah. I found out the electric company is owned by Mrs. Griswald.

CLAIR: Well, Theo, we can't stay long.

(HANDING THEO THE PLATE)

             Here, your father and I fixed you a home-cooked meal.

(THEO UNWRAPS THE PLATE)

THEO: Awright! A Bacon Burger Dog.

(THEO DIGS IN)

CLIFF: Son, we're very proud of you. If there's anything you need just call us.

THEO: Thanks. I could use a chair, but other than that, I've got everything I need.

CLAIR: This is everything you need?

THEO: Sure. In fact, even when I'm a model and making lots of money, I'm going to live like this.

CLIFF: I see. You're willing to live like this on your money, but on our money you want to live like the rich and famous.

THEO: I never thought of it that way.

CLAIR: Then I guess you learned a pretty important lesson today.

THEO: Yes, I did. I learned that when I go out in the real world, I never want to do business with anyone in my family.

FADE OUT:

END OF SHOW

THE NEWSROOM

"Dinner at Eight"

THE NEWSROOM
"Dinner at Eight"

by

KEN FINKLEMAN

(Episode #3)

(Script provided courtesy of Ken Finkleman, *The Newsroom*, CBC Television)

<u>1A. INT. BOARDROOM—NEW DAY—DAY 1</u>

(GEORGE AND DERNHOFF SIT WITH AGENTS, CAROLE AND LEONARD ROSS. BOTH IN ARMANI CLOTHES. BOTH IN EARLY 40S. BOTH CONFIDENT, DIRECT, CHARMING. THEY HAVE BROUGHT WITH THEM A NUMBER OF CASSETTES WITH PROSPECTIVE CO-ANCHORS FOR JIM.)

LEONARD: We think your decision to give Jim Walcott a female co-anchor is great. We handle a number of women who can give that spot some real life.

GEORGE: Don't get me wrong. Jim's a great anchor.

CAROLE: We'd love to represent him.

GEORGE: He's no genius, but viewers love him.

CAROLE: Intelligence intimidates. Jim doesn't intimidate.

GEORGE: Exactly. People don't want to come home after a hard day's work and be intimidated by —

LEONARD: By intelligence.

GEORGE: By intelligence.

(DOCUMENTARY CUT TO:
THEY WATCH AN ANCHOR'S AUDITION TAPE.)

LEONARD: Lindsay's out of our Edmonton affiliate. This lady is very, very special.

CAROLE: But she doesn't read "public broadcasting." She reads Alberta, she reads free market.

LEONARD: She has what we call a "go for it" approach to news. She just "does it."

GEORGE: Lindsay's a great name.

CAROLE: We almost named our daughter Lindsay. But we went with Meryl after we saw Meryl Streep in The Bridges of Madison County.

GEORGE: I love that movie.

CAROLE: Lindsay has great eyes. They're expressive and very well placed on her face.

LEONARD: Right now we can put her into any mid-size U.S. market; Cleveland, Baltimore, Kansas City.

GEORGE: The U.S.

LEONARD: The U.S. Also, she has this quirky thing where she cries on a very sad story. But it works.

GEORGE: She cries? Like in Broadcast News.

CAROLE: Exactly like in Broadcast News.

LEONARD: It works.

GEORGE: If it works —

CAROLE: It works.

(DOCUMENTARY CUT TO:
CAROLE SLUGS IN ANOTHER TAPE.)

CAROLE: Monique is also very wonderful. She's got fantastic
            skin, hair and features. Monique doesn't have an
            in-your-face ethnicity.

LEONARD: 74 percent of her audience in Saskatoon thought she
            was white. It's a very subtle ethnicity.

CAROLE: An almost subliminal ethnicity.

GEORGE: Didn't Coke or Pepsi do some advertising like that?
            Subliminal. Does anyone want a Diet Coke?

(DOCUMENTARY CUT TO:
EVERYONE DRINKS GENERIC DIET COLA.)

LEONARD: Color's great but you don't want to hit the viewer
            over the head with it.

DERNHOFF: I'm not sure a black woman works for us right now.

LEONARD/CAROLE: If it doesn't work it doesn't work.

GEORGE: I think what Peter is saying is — (to Dernhoff) —
            and correct me if I'm wrong, a black anchor reads
            equality, equality reads social spending, and a
            social spending message in this deficit reduction
            climate, coming from us, looks like we're taking
            sides and we have to be objective. Which doesn't
            mean that equality isn't a high priority —

CAROLE: We think equality's great.

LEONARD: We've marched for a number of causes.

GEORGE: I'd march too if I didn't have this job where
            objectivity —

(GEORGE DEFERS TO DERNHOFF WHO INDICATES HIS AGREEMENT.)

GEORGE: But a black anchor may be too aggressive a move
            right now. A white anchor, on the other hand, reads
            deficit reduction. Lindsay's blonde, she doesn't
            have that overly blonde-Wendy Mesley-Allison
            Smith-WASP-cut-ALL-social-services-blondeness.

LEONARD: She's a terrific compromise.

CAROLE: I love her name.

2A. INT. NEWS ROOM SET—DAY 1

ON LYNN, THE FLOOR DIRECTOR: "IN FOUR, IN THREE, IN TWO —"

(POV OFF SET, JIM INTROS HIS INTERVIEW WITH DANIEL RICHLER. WE DOLLY BEHIND CREW, HOLING INTERVIEW AT THE FULCRUM IN B.G.)

JIM: My guest is Daniel Richler, writer, critic and one
            of the few intellectual voices to appear regularly
            on Canadian TV and of course son of the very
            prolific Canadian author Mordechai Richler.

(TO DANIEL, LIGHTLY)

            I got the "ch" in Mordechai right this time?

(TO CAMERA)

            MordeCHai, not MordeKai Richler.
            MordeCHai Richler.

(DANIEL STARES AT HIM.
DOLLY GEORGE AND KRIS INTO FRAME IN CLOSE-UP, HOLDING
INTERVIEW IN DEEP B.G. A MONITOR NEXT TO GEORGE AND KRIS,
PLAYS B.G. INTERVIEW.
GEORGE TRIES TO CONCENTRATE ON WHAT KRIS IS SAYING BUT HIS
NATURE PREVENTS IT.)

KRIS: All I'm saying is, Quebec is a distinct society but
            so is Newfoundland. And I think —

(GEORGE CHECKS HIS WATCH.)

GEORGE: Are we on for tonight or is your roommate going to
            be — ?

KRIS: You don't want to hear my thoughts on Quebec, do
            you.

GEORGE: Quebec. Yes. Absolutely I do.

(LOOKS AROUND FURTIVELY)

            But we really shouldn't be talking out here, like
            — is she going to be home or —

KRIS: What's wrong with talking out here about Quebec?

GEORGE: Did I say "out here". I didn't mean "out here".
            You were saying about Quebec —

KRIS: You don't want to hear.

GEORGE: Of course I do. You were saying —

KRIS: I think English Canada doesn't know how to talk to
            Quebec. We really have to learn how to listen to —

GEORGE: I have to —

(POINTING TO MONITOR)

KRIS: What?

GEORGE: — the Daniel Richler interview — I should really
            —

(GEORGE STARTS EDGING AWAY.)

KRIS: See, you don't want to hear —

GEORGE:
(FURTIVE)   I do. Tonight. At your place. What you're saying
            about listening is absolutely correct —

(ON MONITOR, HOLDING KRIS.)

JIM:
(TO A STONE SILENT DANIEL)

            You hear it pronounced MordeKai Richler so often —
            anyway —

(TO CAMERA)

            Daniel was host of the popular TV show on books
            called "Imprint" and has taken another shot at
            fiction himself with his new novel which I haven't
            had a chance to read but which I hear is terrific
            —

(FLIPS THROUGH BOOK)

            What is it? Three hundred and seventy-six pages.

DANIEL:
(NOT HAPPY) That's right.

JIM: Close to four hundred pages. Where do you get all
            your ideas?

3A. INT. NEWSROOM/OFFICE CORRIDOR—DAY 1

(DANIEL, PISSED, WALKS OUT WITH GEORGE. DANIEL PUTTING ON HIS
COAT.)

DANIEL: First, I agreed to come on if my father wasn't
            mentioned. Not only does he mention my father, he
            goes into that MordeKai, MordeCHai shit. Then, all
            he knows about my book is the fucking page count.
            He's a fucking idiot.

GEORGE: I agree he's an idiot, but you were great. Let me
             get that.

(GEORGE OPENS STUDIO DOOR. THEY EXIT INTO OFFICE CORRIDOR.)

DANIEL: And then he says, I'm taking a "shot" at fiction.
             It's not a fucking "shot", it's a fucking novel for
             which I got a fucking substantial advance. The
             reason I did "Imprint" was so I could talk to
             intelligent people on TV not brain-dead anchors,
             more interested in how they look on camera than in
             the entire world of English literature.

(KRIS COMES OUT OF OFFICE CORRIDOR DOORWAY.)

KRIS: Your hair looked great. You were silly to be so
             worried about it.

(DANIEL LOOKS AT GEORGE)

             We didn't have the kind of gel Daniel uses. I lent
             him mine.

DANIEL:
(BACKING OFF): My hair can be very distracting. If it's fucked
             up, people look at my hair and don't listen to
             what I have to say.

GEORGE: I understand.

KRIS: They spent an hour looking for the right gel.

GEORGE: An hour.

DANIEL: It wasn't an hour.

KRIS: It looked great.

GEORGE: The man has the best hair on TV.

DANIEL: Are you ready?

KRIS: Ready.

(TO GEORGE)

             We're going out for a bite. I left your Fiber
             First on your desk and they were out of Metamucil
             but maybe I can stop at a Shopper's —

GEORGE:
(INTERRUPTING) I have to get that stuff for my mother . . .
             One sec.

(TAKES KRIS ASIDE AS DANIEL WAITS)

             I thought WE were getting together tonight.

KRIS: Can we do it another time? He just asked me if —

GEORGE: Is this a sexual thing with him?

KRIS: No. He's written a novel.

GEORGE: Does that make him impotent? I thought we were
           going to talk about Quebec.

KRIS: Can we do that next week?

GEORGE:
(INTENSE WHISPER)

           The country is coming apart and you spent an hour
           looking for gel for his hair and now he's most
           likely going to try to get you into bed. If that's
           the kind of Canada you want, fine!

(TURNS TO DANIEL)

           Daniel, it was great having you on the show. You
           know what I'd love to try; you reviewing the odd
           book for us.

DANIEL: No.

(KRIS AND DANIEL LEAVE GEORGE STANDING.)

GEORGE: No problem. I have to run.

4A. INT. GEORGE'S OFFICE—DAY 2

(GEORGE SITS AT DESK. JIM REFERS TO THE PAPER.)

JIM: I mean, to find out from Sid Adilman's column I've
           lost my spot to some chick.

GEORGE: You're not losing your spot. I don't even know how
           Sid Adilman got that.

JIM: Audrey sent him YOUR press release.

GEORGE: I'm going to tell you the truth. The truth is I
           forgot.

JIM: Seven years we've been together and you forgot you
           sent out a press release cutting off my balls in
           public.

GEORGE: Okay, the truth. I blocked. Certain things are
           tough for me like delivering bad news. I blocked
           because I couldn't deal with your pain over this.

JIM: So I am being phased out.

GEORGE: No! Redefined. This is going to be great for you.

JIM: If it's going to be so fucking great, why did you block over my pain?

GEORGE: Did I say pain? I didn't mean pain. I meant no pain, no gain. A news team is very American. You'll bounce shit off this chick like Johnny did with Ed.

JIM: I'd like to bounce her off.

GEORGE: There! You see. That's the stuff you're capable of with this woman. "I'd like to bounce her off." That's a great ad lib.

JIM:
(SUCKED IN) That shit is second nature to me.

GEORGE: "I'd like to bounce her off" doesn't scan perfectly but it can be rewritten. If you don't like her, she's gone. You have my word.

JIM: Your word.

GEORGE: I don't have final say but this is going to work so my word is irrelevant anyway. You can trust me on that.

4B. INT. COFFEE AREA—DAY 2
(MARK, AUDREY.)

AUDREY: What's a testosterone problem?

MARK: You have one?

AUDREY: Yeah, right! Is that infertility or impotence?

MARK: Impotence. Is this somone I know?

AUDREY: I just wanted to know.

MARK: Come on.

(HE BADGERS HER. SHE REFUSES TO REVEAL. AUDREY, NOT IMMUNE TO GOSSIP IMPULSE, FINALLY GIVES IN.)

AUDREY: Jim asks me to get his voice mail and his doctor called with his testosterone results.

MARK: So what, he can't get it up?

AUDREY: He said he had the results. He's not going to leave that on voice mail. he said to call back. I shouldn't have told you.

MARK: Hey. A guy has a test. No big deal.

AUDREY: This is between us.

MARK: Of course.

5. INT. NEWS ROOM, MARK'S STATION—DAY 2
(MARK WITH JEREMY.)

JEREMY: So he's like a donkey.

MARK: No.

GEORGE: That's sterility and it's mules not donkeys. This
           is impotence.

JEREMY: So he can't get it up.

MARK: I didn't say that. It was a test. But you have to
           figure a good result and the doctor would have left
           the message.

GEORGE: I think he's right.

JEREMY: So you figure —

MARK: This doesn't go past us.

GEORGE/JEREMY: Of course not.

5A. INT. NEWS ROOM, JEREMY'S STATION—DAY 2
(JEREMY ALONE ON PHONE.)

JEREMY: At least a mule can get it up. This is from his doctor.

6. STATION ENTRANCE—NEW DAY—DAY 3
(GEORGE WALKS WITH THE NEW CO-ANCHOR LINDSAY WARD. A
DOCUMENTARY CAMERA FOLLOWS HER.)

LINDSAY: For me news is presenting the story in such a way
           that a housewife in her kitchen peeling potatoes
           for dinner will stop and listen and think, "My god,
           300 people were burned alive in that Bangkok fire!
           Thank god I wasn't in that building." My job is to
           capture the moment and somehow convey that moment
           to the viewer.

GEORGE:
(TO DOC CAMERA)

           She's terrific.

(SHE SPOTS JIM.)

LINDSAY: Jim Walcott.

(SHE SHAKES JIM'S HAND NEXT TO MARK'S WORK STATION. MARK IS
ON PHONE IN B.G.)

LINDSAY: I've always been a huge fan.

JIM:
(TO GEORGE)

            What's the camera?

GEORGE: They're doing a documentary on Lindsay for a
            Witness series on the history of news. Ignore it.

JIM:
(TO GEORGE)

            Do they want something from me?

GEORGE: No. Just stay out of this. If you want to talk
            about your testosterone. My door is open.

JIM: Who told you — ?

GEORGE: I know it's hard, I mean difficult —

(BACKS OFF)

            I have to do this.

(THEY LEAVE JIM BEHIND AS MARK HANGS UP AND RISES WITH PAPER
WORK.)

MARK: Hey, sorry about your testosterone thing.

JIM: Who told you I had a testosterone — ?

MARK: Audrey. I'm not — I shouldn't have — I thought
            she told you —

JIM: What does Audrey know about my testosterone test?

MARK: I'm sorry, I gotta get this upstairs.

JIM: Who else knows about this?

MARK: No one.

(MARK LEAVES. JEREMY CROSSES.)

JEREMY: Hey, Buddy, I heard about the testosterone thing.
            That's a bitch.

JIM: Who told you I had a —

JEREMY: No one. Mark. I was talking to Karen in publicity
            about it. Her cousin had it and apparently they now
            have pills —

(BACKING OFF)

            I have to —

10.

JIM: You told publicity?

JEREMY: No. I mean I told Karen in publicity. She's not
            going to send it to Sid Adilman. I hope. Just
            kidding. Her cousin had the same thing and
            committed suicide but apparently that was before the
            pills came out.

(BACKING OFF)

            I have to get this copy on the frozen homeless
            guys to Bobby.

6A. INT. BOARD ROOM—DAY 3

(LINDSAY POPS A BOTTLE OF WINE AND POURS IT INTO PLASTIC
GLASSES, THE DOC CREW SHOOTING.)

LINDSAY: Toronto's a world-class city. Driving in from the
            airport on the 401 we passed an overturned tanker
            truck that had crushed a car. Evidently three
            people were killed and I was just passing as a
            civilian, not in a news capacity and there were
            three dead. That's a major market.

GEORGE: It's a great city.

LINDSAY: I'd like to propose a little toast. To a great
            city and a great new team.

(THEY DRINK.
DOC CUT TO JIM TALKING TO DOCUMENTARY CAMERA AT A WORK
STATION WITH GEORGE AND LINDSAY. ALL SEATED. AN ODDLY
IMPROBABLE STAGING AS IF THEY ARE NOW ALL SITTING FOR AN
"IN-THE-WORK-SPACE" MOMENT.)

JIM: I have a confession about my first reaction to news
            that I was splitting my duties with this lady.

GEORGE: Water under the bridge. This is going to work.

LINDSAY: And it's going to be fun.

JIM: No, no. I felt threatened. It was part professional
            territoriality and partially a challenge to certain
            masculine impulses. I admit it.

LINDSAY: I've watched you on air and there's no doubt about
            your masculinity.

(TO CAMERA)

            His testosterone is possibly right off the charts.

(GEORGE CLOSES HIS EYES ON "TESTOSTERONE".)

GEORGE: I didn't —

JIM: This is bullshit.

(TO DOC CAMERA)

       I'm sorry. Delete that. I'm a little upset right now. That's not the word. I'm busy. I have to go.

(JIM BACKS AWAY FROM THE CAMERA.)

LINDSAY: What did I say?

(JIM TAKES OFF.)

GEORGE: Jim?

LINDSAY: Is he gay?

GEORGE: Actually that never occured to me. It's possible.

7. INT. COFFEE AREA—LATER—DAY 3

(GEORGE AND JIM. JIM PACES.)

GEORGE: It was a coincidence. She had no idea you even had tests done.

JIM: It's one fucking test. It's not tests. Right in front of a goddamn documentary camera, I lost it.

GEORGE: You didn't lose it.

JIM: I've never lost it like that on camera in my life. I revealed weakness. It's the testosterone. Am I half a man? I'm half an anchor that's for fucking sure.

GEORGE: You're not half an anchor, you're a co-anchor. Calm down. We're on in ten.

JIM: I can't calm down. I can't calm down.

(GEORGE TAKES PILL BOTTLE FROM HIS POCKET.)

GEORGE: I want you to try a Tylenol three with a valium.

8. INT. MAKE-UP AREA—DAY 3

(LINDSAY AND RANI MOVE OUT A DOWN CORRIDOR TO NEWS ROOM SET. WE TRACK THEM AS THEY TALK ABOUT HAIR, MAKE-UP AND CLOTHES.)

RANI: A couple of pointers. Watch out for hair. They'll use a can of spray in one sitting. Tell them only to comb it. And avoid Julia in make-up. She already

put way too much base on you. The woman should be
doing drywall, not make-up.

(HANDS LINDSAY A KLEENEX.)

LINDSAY: Thanks. You're great.

RANI: You'll get it. Most important don't let George
choose your wardrobe. His taste is shit. Good luck.

LINDSAY: Thanks.

(LINDSAY TAKES HER SEAT.)

LINDSAY: Could I get this up an inch or so.

(LYNN HELPS HER WITH HER SEAT ADJUSTMENT.)

LYNN: How's that?

LINDSAY: Perfect. Thanks.

(READING TELEPROMPTER)

Four homeless men froze to death last night in
Toronto's east end when temperatures plummeted to —

(TO FLOOR DIRECTOR)

Do I have too much lip gloss?

LYNN: You're perfect.

LINDSAY:
(READING AGAIN)

Four homeless men froze to death last night in
Toronto's east end when temperatures plummeted to —

(WIGGLES IN SEAT)

That feels great.

(TO DIRECTOR THROUGH MIC)

How's my level.

(READING AGAIN)

Four homeless men froze to death last night in
Toronto's east end —

(GEORGE PASSES.)

GEORGE: Feeling good?

LINDSAY: Great.

GEORGE: How's that chair?

LINDSAY: Great.

GEORGE: Are you going to wear that?

LINDSAY: Yes.

(GEORGE SPOTS SOMETHING.)

GEORGE: Excuse me.

(GEORGE CROSSES TO JIM WHO ENTERS GLAZED, HIS EYES INTENSELY FOCUSED ON NOTHING IN PARTICULAR.)

GEORGE: How do you feel?

JIM: There she is.

GEORGE: Did you take that stuff?

JIM: Oh, yes.

GEORGE: I think this is going to work.

JIM: Oh, yes. There's the anchor - bitch.

(JIM SLIDES INTO HIS SEAT BESIDE LINDSAY AND HOLDS UP A HAND FOR A HI-FIVE. SHE GIVES IT TO HIM. THE FLOOR DIRECTOR STARTS THE COUNT-DOWN.)

LYNN: In five, in four —

(LYNN LEANS INTO JIM AND WHISPERS.)

LINDSAY: I didn't know you were gay. I'm sorry if I said
            anything.

(JIM STARES AT HER.)

LYNN: — in two —

(SHE GIVES THEM THEIR CUE.)

9. INT. STUDIO—DAY 3

(ON GEORGE, MARK, JEREMY WATCHING MONITOR JUST OFF SET.)

JIM: Good evening. Tonight it gives me great pleasure to
        introduce a new addition to the City Hour team,
        Lindsay Ward.

LINDSAY: Thank you, Jim. It's a treat to be in Toronto.
            It's a competitive world-class city with amazing
            opportunities for everyone.

(TO CAMERA)

14.

Good evening. Four homeless men froze to death last
night in Toronto's east end when temperatures
plummeted —

(ON GEORGE AND JEREMY AND MARK WATCHING MONITOR OFF SET.)

GEORGE: They're perfect. He's going to love her.

(CUT TO:

10. INT. STUDIO—DAY 3

(JIM CORNERS GEORGE JUST OFF SET AT THE END OF THE HOUR.)

JIM: That little piece of white Edmonton trash. She
            doesn't know how lucky she is to be sitting next
            to me.

GEORGE: Now THAT'S a healthy attitude.

(DURING FOLLOWING, A DISTRACTED GEORGE PEEKS OVER JIM'S
SHOULDER AT LINDSAY CONGRATULATED BY MARK, JEREMY, RANI.
DERNHOFF KISSES LINDSAY. LINDSAY PRAISES RANI TO DERNHOFF.)

JIM: She takes a goddamn basically cerebral discipline
            like journalism and turns it into whose tits are
            bigger than whose with this little gay trick.

GEORGE: Give her the tits and you take the brains. Our
            audience respects your intellect. She's the body
            you're the mind.

JIM: You think?

GEORGE: I know.

(GEORGE WALKS JIM AWAY.)

JIM: Have you got any more of those pills? Just to cool
            out. Not as a crutch.

GEORGE: Never as a crutch. You don't need that shit but
            also you don't have to be uptight about drugs if
            you can control them.

JIM: If you can control them, if you're an adult, there
            is nothing intrinsically wrong with a stimulant.

GEORGE: Just keep it to yourself.

(GEORGE FURTIVELY HANDS HIM PILLS.)

11. INT. BOARDROOM PRODUCTION MEETING—NEW DAY—DAY 4

JEREMY:
(READING RUNDOWN)

> So we're dropping the Mother Teresa item and going with the peeping tom in the public washroom.

GEORGE: Mother Teresa isn't really local.

MARK: I think the pervert's more relateable.

GEORGE: Done.

(JIM ENTERS. THE ROOMS FALLS SILENT.)

GEORGE: What?

JIM: I thought I'd sit in.

GEORGE: You never sit in.

JIM: Lindsay's here.

RANI: She's observing.

JIM: I won't talk.

(JIM WHISPERS TO GEORGE AS HE SLIDES PAST HIM INTO HIS SEAT.)

JIM:
(WHISPERS) The anchor-bitch is trying to end-run me.

GEORGE:
(BACK TO RUNDOWN) The Raptors, let's settle this, are we going to refer to them as African American or Black?

JIM: Why not African Canadian?

GEORGE: I thought you weren't going to talk. They're not Canadians.

JIM: The team is Canadian.

GEORGE: The players are American!

JIM: How about African American-Canadian.

GEORGE: Get out! Get out! I'm sorry. Sit. Sit.

LINDSAY: Why not just call them by their names.

RANI: Which makes sense.

GEORGE: Is this a loop going here that I'm not in?

RANI: It's not a loop.

GEORGE: Fine, we'll use their names for now.

16.

(TO RUNDOWN)

        Two golfers struck by lightning. Did they die?

JEREMY: Yes.

GEORGE: Good. That's our lead.

12. INT. NEWS ROOM—DAY 4

(PICK UP GEORGE AND JIM.)

JIM: She's in the production meeting. I wasn't even invited.

GEORGE: You're usually at home at this hour, sleeping.

JIM: First I get nailed by a piece of shit testosterone count, then some chick from Edmonton pushes me out of my job.

GEORGE: You're not being pushed out and they have pills for your testosterone.

JIM: Just tell me. Am I out?

(GEORGE HANDS HIM SOME PILLS.)

GEORGE: No. Take these and calm down.

13. INT. GEORGE'S OFFICE—DAY 4

(AUDREY ON COUCH WATCHES GEORGE ON THE PHONE, PACING.)

GEORGE: What kind of pills? Was it a bad reaction? Jesus.

(GEORGE GIVES AUDREY A LOOK, "WHO KNOWS WHERE HE GOT PILLS".)

GEORGE: And testosterone pills too. Five or six days rest? Fine. Tell Jim for me to take it easy, get better, he's our number one guy and we all love him. Bye.

(HANGS UP)

        What a useless asshole. He got into some pills and just went off the goddamn deep end. Tell Lindsay she's on her own tonight and for the rest of the week.

AUDREY: Oh, she'll hate that. Do you still want a muffin?

GEORGE: The dark bran.

(AUDREY RISES AND CROSSES TO THE DOOR.)

17.

AUDREY: What if he only has cranberry left?

GEORGE: I hate cranberry. You know I hate cranberry. Why do you always get cranberry?

AUDREY: He's usually out of bran by now.

GEORGE: Can't he get enough bran so that by eleven in the morning he's not sitting on a bunch of cranberry muffins no one wants!

AUDREY: How about apple cinnamon?

GEORGE: Some places don't even use real apples for apple, they use turnips.

AUDREY: I didn't know that.

GEORGE: The whole muffin business is a goddamn joke.

(SHE SHRUGS AND LEAVES.)

(JUST OFF SET)

14. INT. NEWSROOM/NEWS SET—DAY 4

(MARK AND JEREMY WATCH LINDSAY SOLO ON MONITOR. TEARS ROLL DOWN LINDSAY'S CHEEKS.)

LINDSAY: And when nineteen years later, mother and daughter were finally reunited this week, the final chapter in a long and painful saga turned out to have a very happy ending.

JEREMY: She's crying on the goddamn news?

MARK: She's not crying.

JEREMY: Those are tears. Look.

MARK: She is crying.

(ON GEORGE AND KRIS.)

GEORGE: Is this another Daniel Richler thing?

KRIS: I'm seeing someone else off and on but you can still come over.

GEORGE: Someone else?

(SHE LOOKS AT HIM QUIZZICALLY)

Another novelist?

KRIS: One of the Raptors.

GEORGE: You're seeing a Raptor.

KRIS: Off and on.

GEORGE: Like a guard?

KRIS: A centre. You can still come over.

GEORGE: A centre.

(BACKS OFF, CHECKS WATCH)

           Maybe next week . . .

15. INT. GEORGE'S OFFICE—NEW DAY—DAY 5

(LINDSAY, GEORGE, RANI. LINDSAY POURS A GLASS OF WINE AND PACES SELF-SATISFIED, EXCITED. RANI READS THE GLOBE AND MAIL.)

RANI: Listen to the Globe and Mail.

(READING PAPER)

           John Hasslett Cuff: "Lindsay Warren is a breath of
           fresh air blowing through a stagnant institution
           paralyzed by tired ideas and an old regime
           mentality. Watch for her last solo performance
           tonight before Jim Walcott returns and you'll see
           the generally pusillanimous news administration
           doing something right for once."

LINDSAY: I don't want this to sound self-serving but you
           throw the ball to me in the end zone, and I'll
           catch it. That's a game-winner. Personally I love
           Jim Walcott and respect his work, but run with him
           you're heading for a loss.

GEORGE: Somehow Jim got his hands on some drugs that almost
           killed him. I'm not going to kick him when he's
           down. I will not betray him for my own career when
           he needs me most.

16. INT. NEWS ROOM—DAY 5

(GEORGE STANDS OVER AUDREY AND TALKS QUIETLY AS SHE TYPES INTO HER COMPUTER.)

GEORGE: ". . . and we say good-bye to a talented anchor
           and a loyal co-worker with a heavy heart and a
           sense of great loss." Fax it to Sid Adilman. Don't
           put any name on it.

17. INT. NEWS ROOM—NEW DAY—DAY 6

(JIM COMES THROUGH, TORONTO STAR IN HAND, PAST MARK WHO TURNS OFF SO HE WON'T HAVE TO MAKE EYE CONTACT, PAST JEREMY WHO DOES THE SAME, PAST AUDREY —)

JIM: Is he in?

AUDREY: Yes. Can you give him this muffin? It's low-fat
            carrot.

18. INT. GEORGE'S OFFICE—DAY 6

(CAMERA ON JIM WHO WALKS IN, CATCHING GEORGE ON THE PHONE.
JIM STARTS TO INTERRUPT. GEORGE HOLDS UP A FINGER TO WAIT.)

GEORGE: I don't care how much money has been cut from the
            cafeteria budget! Five more bran a day, it's not
            going to bury them!

(GEORGE HANGS UP.)

JIM: After seven years, I find out in Sid Adilman that
            I'm out on my ass!

GEORGE:
(NOT PAYING ATTENTION TO JIM)

            They can't make five more bran muffins. Fucking
            assholes.

JIM: It's that bitch anchor. She got her claws into you
            didn't she.

GEORGE: Wait, wait. Slow down. What's happening?

JIM: Sid "fucking" Adilman! I'm out on my ass!

GEORGE: I don't know how Sid Adilman got that information.
            I was going to have lunch with you today and
            explain everything.

(SECURITY POKES HIS HEAD IN.)

SECURITY: I'm sorry, sir, I didn't see Mr. Walcott come up.

GEORGE:
(UNCOMPREHENDING)

            I don't understand.

SECURITY: You told us to . . . you know . . .

GEORGE:
(APPEARS CONFUSED)

            I'm sorry, I . . .

SECURITY: You said last night, keep him out of the building.

GEORGE: I can explain.

JIM: Asshole.

(JIM LEAVES GEORGE AND SECURITY STANDING THERE.)

SECURITY: We're still not sure why Mr. Walcott was a security risk.

GEORGE: Oh . . . he had a little drug problem. Who knows what they might do.

SECURITY: I once had to put a guy down on angel dust. I know what you mean.

19. INT. HAIR/MAKEUP ROOM—DAY 6

(LINDSAY, RANI AND GEORGE MEET, IT'S TENSE. LINDSAY IS IN A RED SUIT. SHE POURS HERSELF A GLASS OF WINE.)

GEORGE: I just don't like red. I don't think red reads news. Yellow works on you.

LINDSAY: Red's my favourite color.

(TO RANI)

What do you think?

RANI: Red is energy.

GEORGE: Red "is" energy or red "has" energy?

RANI: Red "is" energy.

LINDSAY: Rani's right.

GEORGE: Rani's not the news director. I'm the news director. I love you in blues, yellow, small prints, not red.

(AUDREY SHOWS DERNHOFF IN.)

GEORGE: Peter, have you seen the numbers? Is she brilliant or is she brilliant?

DERNHOFF: She's wonderful. Everyone's doing a terrific job.

(TO RANI, LINDSAY)

Are you two okay for, 7:30 at Centro?

RANI/LINDSAY: Great.

DERNHOFF:
(TO LINDSAY'S RED DRESS)

I love that color on you. Red has energy. I have to run.

(DERNHOFF LEAVES.)

20. INT. STATION ENTRANCE—NEW DAY—DAY 7

(GEORGE IS RESTRAINED BY SECURITY.)

GEORGE: This is insane. This is a joke.

SECURITY: I'm sorry, Mr. Findlay, but we have orders to keep
           you out off this floor.

GEORGE: This is my show! For Christ sake, Larry, you know
           me!

SECURITY: Those are my orders.

(JEREMY AND MARK PASS WITH FOOD FROM CAFETERIA.)

JEREMY: Buddy, we just read Sid Adilman. Sorry.

MARK: Who would have expected.

GEORGE:
(GRABS THE PAPER)

           You read what in Sid Adilman?!

MARK:
(READS)   Brass shake up at "Toronto News". Lindsay Warren,
           who replaced anchor Jim Walcott, is rumored to have
           orchestrated the move of reporter Rani Sandu into
           the news director job formerly held by George
           Findlay. Sandu said today that the "tired ideas and
           old regime mentality" are a thing of the past.
           Findlay moves into a middle management position,
           where in the words of one industry insider, "he can
           do no more harm".

JEREMY: We've gotta run.

(JEREMY AND MARK EDGE AWAY.)

MARK: You got a shitty deal.

GEORGE: Didn't you guys say something?!

JEREMY: We should say something. That's a good idea.

MARK: We'll say something.

JEREMY: We'll mention this.

(SECURITY MOVES GEORGE OUT.)

21. INT. NEWS ROOM—NEW DAY—DAY 8

(LINDSAY AND RANI AT RANI'S STATION. LINDSAY IS PISSED AND
READING THE STAR.)

22.

LINDSAY: This is a joke. This is impossible. Sid Adilman says they're shipping me out to an anchor job in Winnipeg and you're back on the air. Did you know about this?

RANI: I've already been assigned a story. Winnipeg's supposed to have a great symphony.

LINDSAY: How did this happen?

RANI: It happens.

(BACKING OFF)

I have to get my crew and —

(MARK AND JEREMY WALKING PAST.)

JEREMY: Hey, we read Sid Adilman. You were screwed.

MARK: That was a shocker.

LINDSAY: Did you two have anything to do with this?!

JEREMY: No way.

MARK: We were as shocked as you. But Winnipeg is supposed to have a great ballet.

(JEREMY AND MARK. PASS AUDREY ON THE WAY TO GEORGE'S OFFICE.)

JEREMY: Is he in?

AUDREY: Yeah. Give him this muffin.

(THEY TAKE THE BAGGED MUFFIN AND ENTER.)

22. INT. GEORGE'S OFFICE—DAY 8

(GEORGE, MARK AND JEREMY WATCH A TAPE FROM DOCUMENTARY SHOT FOR WITNESS SHOWING THREE CUTS OF LINDSAY DRINKING WINE.)

GEORGE: I picked off these cuts from the documentary they were shooting of her and sent them upstairs.

JEREMY: Cut together like that she looks like a drunk.

MARK: I didn't know she had a booze problem.

GEORGE: It's a sickness. You can't blame her.

MARK: She's a victim.

GEORGE: She's a victim. Exactly.

JEREMY: So they shipped her out to Winnipeg?

GEORGE: It's a less stressful market.

MARK: I hear they have a good symphony.

JEREMY: You used that tired old regime mentality, right?

GEORGE: Tired and old wins the race.

MARK: She was okay.

GEORGE: She was fantastic and I think this little game of
            musical chairs gave us all pause. I think we're
            going to have to make some changes.

MARK/JEREMY: Changes. Absolutely, changes.

(JEREMY HANDS GEORGE MUFFIN BAG. HE AND MARK HEAD OUT.)

JEREMY: Your muffin from Audrey.

GEORGE: Some new ideas.

MARK/JEREMY: Some new ideas. We'll work on it.

(GEORGE LOOKS DOWN AT MUFFIN.)

GEORGE: This is cranberry.

(THEY HEAD OUT THE DOOR. GEORGE YELLS AFTER THEM.)

GEORGE: I hate cranberry.

(TAG)

23. INT. BOARD ROOM—DAY 8

(GEORGE AND JIM LOOK AT TIES SPREAD OUT ON BOARDROOM TABLE.)

JIM: I think this philosophy of change is a terrific
            idea and I thought these new ties would be in
            keeping —

GEORGE: They're perfect. Except this one and this and this.

JIM: You don't like this?

GEORGE: I hate that. And your little drug problem —?

JIM: I'm clean as a whistle. That was a real scare.

GEORGE: I think we both learned a lot from that little
            incident. And the testosterone —

JIM: The pills seem to work.

GEORGE: The drive is back?

JIM: Big time.

(AUDREY ENTERS.)

24.

AUDREY: Sorry.

GEORGE: It's okay. What?

AUDREY:
(GLANCES AT JIM)

            It should wait. I mean —

GEORGE: Hey, we don't have anymore secrets here. It was our
            inability to be direct with each other that created
            all these problems in the first place. We don't
            want to read what you have to say in Sid Adilman
            tomorrow.

(SMILING TO JIM)

            Am I right?

JIM: Tell me.

AUDREY: You won't have to wait 'til tomorrow. It came out
            in Sid Adilman this afternoon. Jim's being charged
            with sexually harassing two of the wardrobe girls.

                    — THE END —

THE SIMPSONS

"Bart Sells His Soul"

Production No. 3F02

THE SIMPSONS
"Bart Sells His Soul"

Written by
Greg Daniels

Created by
Matt Groening

Developed by
James L. Brooks
Matt Groening
Sam Simon

(Script provided courtesy of Antonia Coffman, 20th Century Fox Television)

BART SELLS HIS SOUL
by
Greg Daniels

ACT ONE

Scene 1

FADE IN:

EXT. ESTABLISHING—SPRINGFIELD CHURCH—SUNDAY MORNING

(THE CHURCH MARQUEE READS: "NO SHOES—NO SHIRT—NO SALVATION."
FAMILIES ENTER WEARING THEIR SUNDAY BEST.)

INT.—SPRINGFIELD CHURCH—VESTIBULE—CONTINUOUS

(BART HOLDS A BASKET LABELLED "TODAY'S HYMNS." EACH PERSON
TAKES A XEROXED HANDOUT FROM IT AS THEY ENTER.)

BART: Hymns here! I got hymns here! Get 'em while
                 they're holy! Fresh from God's brain to your
                 mouth!

(SNEAKY CHUCKLE)

INT. SPRINGFIELD CHURCH—A LITTLE LATER

REV. LOVEJOY: And now please rise for our opening hymn . . .

(CONSULTING HANDOUT)

                 Uh, "In the Garden of Eden" by "I. Ron
                 Butterfly?"

(AT THE ORGAN, MRS. FISCHE PUTS ON HER BIFOCALS AND BEGINS
SIGHT-READING THE SHEET MUSIC.)

(MUSIC: "IN-A-GADDA-DA-VIDA" INTRO)

CONGREGATION:
(SINGING)   In the Garden of Eden, honey / Don't you know
                 that I love you? / In the Garden of Eden, baby
                 / Don't you know that I'll always be true
                 . . . ?

BART:
(GLEEFUL CHUCKLE)

DISSOLVE TO:

INT. CHURCH—TEN MINUTES LATER

(MRS. FISCHE IS ROCKING OUT AT THE ORGAN, BUT SHE DOESN'T
LOOK TOO HAPPY ABOUT IT.)

2.

HOMER:
(ASIDE)

> Hey, Marge, remember when we used to make out to this hymn?

MARGE:
(SHUSHING SOUND)

(REPEAT MRS. FISCHE'S ORGAN MUSIC IN THE BACKGROUND OVER HOMER AND MARGE'S LINE.)

CONGREGATION:
(SINGING)

> Oh, won't you come with me and take my hand?
> Oh, won't you come with me and walk this land?

PRINCIPAL SKINNER:
(BASSO PROFUNDO)

> Please take my ha-a-a-nd!

REV. LOVEJOY:
(TO HIMSELF)

> Wait a minute — This sounds like rock and/or roll.

(A BEACH BALL CAROMS OFF HIS HEAD.)

(DISSOLVE TO:)

INT. CHURCH—A MINUTE LATER

(THE EXHAUSTED CONGREGATION SWAYS AS MRS. FISCHE FINISHES UP WITH THE SPECTACULAR ORGAN ARPEGGIOS. SEVERAL MEMBERS HOLD UP LIT VOTIVE CANDLES.)

(SMASH CUT TO:)

INT. LOVEJOY'S OFFICE—A FEW MINUTES LATER

(REV. LOVEJOY, FURIOUS, HAS ALL THE CHILDREN LINED UP AND IS ANGRILY WAVING THE XEROXED HANDOUT.)

REV. LOVEJOY: I know one of you is responsible for this. So repeat after me: If I withhold the truth, may I go straight to hell, where I will eat naught but burning hot coals and drink naught but burning hot cola . . .

(CUT AROUND THE ROOM TO SEE CHILDREN REPEATING AFTER HIM.)

RALPH:
(SCARED)

> . . . where fiery demons will punch me in the back . . .

KIDS:
(SIMULTANEOUS WITH RALPH)

> . . . where fiery demons will punch me in the back . . .

BART:
(NONCHALANT)

> . . . where my soul will be chopped into confetti and strewn upon a parade of murderers and single mothers . . .

KIDS:
(SIMULTANEOUS WITH BART)

> . . . where my soul will be chopped into confetti and strewn upon a parade of murderers and single mothers . . .

MILHOUSE:
(NERVOUS)

> . . . where my tongue will be torn out by ravenous birds . . .

KIDS:
(SIMULTANEOUS WITH MILHOUSE)

> . . . where my tongue will be torn out by ravenous birds . . .

(MILHOUSE GLANCES NERVOUSLY OUT THE WINDOW TO SEE A CROW SITTING ON A BRANCH. IT SUDDENLY WHIPS ITS HEAD AROUND 180 DEGREES AND STARES DIRECTLY AT MILHOUSE.)

CROW:
(HELLISH SHRIEK)

MILHOUSE:
(CRACKING)

> Bart did it! That Bart right there!

BART:
(BETRAYED)

> Milhouse!

REV. LOVEJOY: Milhouse, you did the right thing. Bart, come with me for punishment.

(TO MILHOUSE)

> You too, Snitchy.

4.

INT. CHURCH - A FEW MINUTES LATER

(REV. LOVEJOY, MILHOUSE, AND BART STAND IN FRONT OF THE
ORGAN.)

REV. LOVEJOY: I want you to clean every one of these organ
                pipes that you have befouled with your "popular
                music."

(HE HANDS THEM A VARIETY OF LONG, THIN BRUSHES AND WALKS OFF.
THEY BEGIN LISTLESSLY SNAKING THE BRUSHES UP INTO THE PIPES.)

BART: You shank. How could you tell on me?

MILHOUSE: Well, I didn't want hungry birds pecking my soul
           forever.

BART: Soul? Come on, Milhouse. There's no such thing
       as a soul. It's just something they made up to
       scare kids, like the Boogeyman or Michael
       Jackson.

MILHOUSE: But every religion says there's a soul, Bart.
           Why would they lie? What would they have to
           gain?

(WE SEE A BUSINESS-LIKE REV. LOVEJOY IN HIS OFFICE EMPTYING
THE COLLECTION PLATE INTO A CHURNING, VEGAS-STYLE MONEY
SORTER.)

REV. LOVEJOY:
(SING-SONG)

       I don't hear scrubbing.

BART: Well, if your soul's real, where is it?

MILHOUSE:
(RUBBING CHEST)

       It's kinda in here.

(THEN BUILDING CONFIDENCE)

       And when you sneeze, that's your soul trying to
       escape. Saying "God bless you" crams it back in.
       And when you die, it squirms out and flies away.

BART: Uh huh. What if you die in a submarine at the
       bottom of the ocean?

MILHOUSE:
(SMUG)

       Oh, it can swim. It's even got wheels, in case
       you die in the desert and it has to drive to
       the cemetery.

BART:
(DISDAINFUL)

> How can someone with glasses that thick be so
> stupid? Listen. You don't have a soul, I don't
> have a soul, there's no such thing as a soul.

(MILHOUSE SIMMERS SILENTLY FOR A BEAT, THEN . . .)

MILHOUSE: Fine.

(CAGEY)

> If you're so sure about that, why don't you sell
> your soul to me.

BART:
(BEAT)

> How much you got?

MILHOUSE: Five bucks.

BART: Deal.

(CLOSE UP ON A SHEET OF CHURCH STATIONERY WITH BART'S HAND
WRITING THE WORDS "BART SIMPSON'S SOUL." PULL BACK TO SEE
BART GIVE IT TO MILHOUSE.)

BART:
(CONT'D)

> There you go: one soul.

(BART SMELLS THE BILL HAPPILY THEN POCKETS IT. SIMULTANEOUSLY,
MILHOUSE CAREFULLY FOLDS THE SOUL, PUTS IT IN HIS SHIRT
POCKET AND PATS IT.)

MILHOUSE: Pleasure doing business with you.

BART: Any time, chummmmm . . . p.

Scene 2

INT. STATION WAGON - THAT AFTERNOON

(DR. HIBBERT AND HIS FAMILY ARE OUT FOR A DRIVE.)

DR. HIBBERT: All right, where would you kids like to eat
             tonight?

PRE-TEEN HIBBERT KID: The Spaghetti Laboratory!

LITTLE HIBBERT GIRL: FaceStuffers!

TEENAGE HIBBERT BOY: Professor V.J. Cornucopia's Fantastic
             Foodmagorium and Great American Steakery!

6.

DR. HIBBERT:
(CHUCKLES)

>   Well, what about this place?

(READING SIGN)

>   "Moe's."

(HIS CAR PULLS UP IN FRONT OF MOE'S.)

INT. MOE'S - A MINUTE LATER

(IT'S A TYPICALLY DISMAL SCENE AS HOMER, BARNEY, CARL, AND THE BARFLIES SLUMP ON THE BAR. ONE SOBS SOFTLY. AS THE HIBBERTS ENTER, A SHAFT OF LIGHT SHOOTS IN FROM THE DOOR AND HITS BARNEY.)

BARNEY:
(FLAILING)

>   Agh! Natural light! Get it off me! Get it off
>   me!

DR. HIBBERT:
(LOOKING AROUND)

>   Oh, I'm sorry. I thought this was a family
>   restaurant.

MOE:
(LYING)

>   Oh, it is. It is. Just, uh, pull them stools up
>   to the pool table.

LITTLE HIBBERT GIRL: Daddy, this place smells like tinkle.

DR. HIBBERT: Mmm-hmm, I think we'll just go to The Texas
>   Cheesecake Depository.

(THE HIBBERTS EXIT.)

MOE: Everybody is goin' to family restaurants these
>   days. Seems nobody wants to hang out in a dank
>   pit no more.

CARL: Ya ain't thinking of gettin' rid of the dank,
>   are ya?

MOE: Uh, maybe I am.

MOE:
(CONT'D)
(LOST IN THOUGHT)

>   Yeah. Family restaurants. That's where the big
>   bucks are.

MOE:
(CONT'D)   I could turn this joint into a place where you wouldn't be ashamed to bring your family, huh?

HOMER: I'm not ashamed.

(HOMER PULLS MAGGIE OUT FROM UNDER HIS STOOL. SHE HAS A COCKTAIL PARASOL STICKING OUT OF HER MOUTH. IT OPENS AND CLOSES AS SHE SUCKS. HE PLOPS HER DOWN ON TOP OF THE BAR.)

MOE: Hey, put a coaster under that.

EXT. SIMPSON HOUSE - DRIVEWAY - DAY

(BART OPENS A PACKAGE LABELLED "DINOSPONGES" WITH A CARTOON DINOSAUR SAYING: "DAMPEN ME FOR DINOSAUR TERROR." HE GINGERLY PULLS OUT A DRIED DINOSAUR SPONGE AS IF IT IS A HIGH EXPLOSIVE. HE SETS IT ON THE DRIVEWAY AND PICKS UP A HOSE.)

BART:
(SNEAKY)

        Oh, Li-sa. There's a little present for you lying in the driveway.

LISA: (O.S.)
(EXCITED)

        Oh boy! Really?

BART'S FANTASY

(BART SPRAYS THE SPONGE WITH A HOSE. IT INSTANTLY GROWS INTO A 70-FOOT T-REX WHICH ROARS AND SEIZES LISA IN ITS JAWS.)

DINOSAUR:
(SPONGY GUMMING SOUNDS)

LISA: Nooooo! It's dripping funny-smelling water all over me!

(BART SNICKERS.)

BACK TO REALITY

(AS LISA APPROACHES, BART SPRAYS THE SPONGE. IT SLOWLY, UNDRAMATICALLY INCREASES IN SIZE BY THIRTY PERCENT AND IS WASHED INTO THE GUTTER.)

BART:
(GROANS)

        I wasted five bucks on these.

LISA: Where'd you get five bucks? I want five bucks.

BART:
(PROUDLY)

        I sold my soul to Milhouse.

LISA: What? How could you do that? Your soul is the most valuable part of you!

BART: You believe in that junk?

LISA: Well, whether or not the soul is physically real, Bart, it's the symbol of everything fine inside us.

BART:
(TSK SOUNDS)

        Poor gullible Lisa. I'll keep my crappy sponges, thanks.

LISA: Bart, your soul is the only part of you that lasts forever. For five dollars, Milhouse could own you for a zillion years.

BART: Well, if you think he got such a good deal, I'll sell you my conscience for four-fifty.

(LISA SHAKES HER HEAD AND STARTS TO LEAVE.)

BART:
(CONT'D)   I'll throw in my sense of decency, too. It's a Bart sales event!

(RE-RECORD:)

        Everything about me must go!

INT. BART'S ROOM - A FEW MINUTES LATER

(SANTA'S LITTLE HELPER IS LYING ON THE FLOOR, PEACEFULLY. BART ENTERS.)

BART: Hey, boy. How ya doin'?

(BART BENDS OVER TO PET THE DOG.)

SANTA'S LITTLE HELPER:
(SUSPICIOUS GROWL)

(BART BACKS AWAY.)

BART:
(CONT'D)   Man, what's gotten into you?

(HE WALKS BY THE CAT.)

SNOWBALL II:
(SUSPICIOUS HISS)

BART: Geez. You're pretty uppity for someone who eats
                   bugs all day.

(THE CAT COUGHS UP A SPIDER, WHICH SKITTERS AWAY.)

EXT. KWIK-E-MART - LATER THAT AFTERNOON

(BART WALKS UP AND SMACKS INTO THE AUTOMATIC DOOR, WHICH
DOESN'T OPEN.)

BART:
(SMUSHED FACE)

                   Stupid automatic door.

(ROD AND TODD WALK UP, AND THE DOOR IMMEDIATELY OPENS FOR
THEM.)

ROD/TODD: Thank you, door.

(BART FROWNS AND SLIPS INSIDE.)

INT. KWIK-E-MART - ICE CREAM FREEZER - CONTINUOUS

(JIMBO, DOLPH AND KEARNEY ARE LEANING ON THE ICE CREAM
FREEZER. BART WALKS UP. JIMBO LEANS OVER AND BREATHES ON THE
FREEZER DOOR UNTIL IT FOGS UP, THEN WRITES "BITE ME.")

DOLPH: Ha! Some ice cream guy's gonna see that and
                   it'll blow his mind.

BART: Let me try.

(BART BREATHES ON THE GLASS, BUT IT WON'T FOG UP.)

JIMBO: Way to breathe, No-Breath.

(BART LOOKS UNEASY. HE TURNS TO LEAVE AND BANGS INTO THE DOOR
AGAIN, LEAVING A SMUDGE.)

BART:
(SMUSHED FACE)

                   This is getting weird.

APU (V.O.):
(INTO MICROPHONE)

                   Sanjay, to the entrance with the Windex.

(MICROPHONE SOUND)

                   Sanjay, to the entrance with the Windex.

Scene 3

EXT. MOE'S - DAY

(A BANNER READS: "COMING SOON — FAMILY RESTAURANT.")

INT. MOE'S - CONTINUOUS

(MOE HAS STARTED TO RENOVATE. SHEETS ARE THROWN OVER THE BAR, ETC. HE IS READING A BOOK CALLED " 'YOUR GIMMICKY RESTAURANT' BY BENNIGAN AND FUDDRUCKER" AND TALKING WITH HOMER AND A BARNEY-SHAPED FORM UNDER ONE OF THE SHEETS.)

MOE: So come on. I need a name that says friendly, all-American cooking.

HOMER: How about Chairman Moe's Magic Wok?

BARNEY-SHAPED FORM: I like it!

MOE: Nah. I want something that says people can have a nice, relaxing time.

HOMER: I got it! Madman Moe's Pressure Cooker!

BARNEY-SHAPED FORM: I like it!

MOE:
(SNAPS FINGERS, INSPIRED)

                  Hey, how about Uncle Moe's Family Feedbag?

BARNEY-SHAPED FORM: I hate it.

(FROM OUTSIDE WE HEAR A TRUCK PULL UP AND HONK.)

MOE: Oh boy. The deep fryer's here.

EXT. MOE'S - CONTINUOUS

(HOMER, MOE, AND BARNEY RUN OUT AND SEE AN ENORMOUS CAST IRON DEEP FRYER RESTING ON A TRUCK BED. STENCILLED ON THE FRYER IS "U.S.S. MISSOURI — C DECK MESS.")

MOE: I got it used from the Navy. You can flash-fry a buffalo in forty seconds.

HOMER: Forty seconds?

(WHINING)
                  But I want it now.

INT. SIMPSON HOUSE - TV ROOM - DAY

(BART AND LISA WATCH TV.)

ON TV

ITCHY AND SCRATCHY

(THE TITLE CARD READS: "ITCHY AND SCRATCHY IN 'SKINLESS IN SEATTLE.' ")

(WE PAN ACROSS A BEAUTIFUL SEATTLE SKYLINE AND DOWN TO SCRATCHY, WHO IS HOLDING A BOUQUET OF FLOWERS AND A NOTE SAYING: "MEET ME AT THE SPACE NEEDLE (SIGNED WITH A HEART)." HE STOPS AT A BIG X, SIGHS LOVINGLY, AND HEARTS FLOAT UPWARD TO THE TOP OF THE SPACE NEEDLE, WHERE WE SEE ITCHY.)

(ITCHY SEES A SIGN THAT SAYS "DO NOT THROW PENNIES FROM THE TOWER," GETS AN IDEA, TAKES A PENNY OUT OF HIS LOAFER AND DROPS IT. LINCOLN SCREAMS IN HORROR AS IT PICKS UP SPEED. THE PENNY MISSES THE LOVE-STRUCK SCRATCHY AND SIZZLES INTO THE SIDEWALK.

ITCHY, FRUSTRATED, RUNS TO A SOUVENIR STAND, SCOOPS UP ARMFULS OF MINI SPACE NEEDLES AND HURLS THEM DOWN. THEY LAND IN A HEART FORMATION AROUND SCRATCHY. SCRATCHY SIGHS CONTENTEDLY AND OOZES MORE HEARTS.

WE HEAR SAWING SOUNDS AND SEE THE ENTIRE TOP OF THE SPACE NEEDLE, INCLUDING THE RESTAURANT, SNAP OFF AS ITCHY SAWS OFF THE LAST SUPPORT. IT STARTS TO FALL TOWARD SCRATCHY, WHO IS OBLIVIOUS AS THE GIANT SHADOW WIDENS OVER HIM. AT THE LAST MOMENT, HE LOOKS UP TO SEE THE NEEDLE HEADING RIGHT TOWARDS HIM. IT IMPALES HIM RIGHT THROUGH THE EYE AND HE RUNS BACK AND FORTH IN PAIN AS A FEW HEARTS OOZE OUT OF HIM. SUPER: SPONSORED BY SEATTLE CHAMBER OF COMMERCE.)

ANGLE ON BART AND LISA

(LISA IS LAUGHING HARD. BART STARES AT THE SCREEN, A LITTLE BEWILDERED.)

BART:
(TAPPING HEAD):

      I know that's funny, but I'm just not laughing.

LISA: Hmmm . . . Pablo Neruda said laughter is the language of the soul.

BART:
(DEFENSIVE)

      I'm familiar with the works of Pablo Neruda.

LISA: I think we should do a test.

(SHE ROLLS HIS SKATEBOARD INTO THE HALL. A BEAT LATER, A SINGING HOMER WALKS BY AND SLIPS ON IT. HE PITCHES FORWARD AND WEDGES HIS HEAD IN BETWEEN THE BANISTERS.)

HOMER:
(YELLS, THEN ANNOYED GRUNT)

LISA:
(STIFLED LAUGH)

       Well?

BART:
(FORCES A WEAK LAUGH; THEN, WORRIED)

       Nope. I don't feel a thing.

LISA: That's creepy, Bart. I think you really did lose
       your soul.

(SANTA'S LITTLE HELPER RUNS UP AND BITES HOMER IN THE ASS.)

HOMER:
(PAINED BEWILDERED GROANS)

(LISA LOOKS AT BART.)

BART: Nothing.

(FADE OUT. OVER BLACK WE HEAR:)

HOMER (O.S.):
(WEAKLY)
       Help me. Why isn't anybody helping me?

FADE OUT:

END OF ACT ONE

ACT TWO

Scene 4

FADE IN:

EXT. VAN HOUTEN HOUSE - FRONT STEPS - LATER THAT DAY

(MRS. VAN HOUTEN HAS ANSWERED THE DOOR.)

BART: Hi, is Milhouse home?

MRS. VAN HOUTEN:
(GESTURES AROUND BACK)

       He's playing in the dirt with his army men . . .

(BART STARTS TO HEAD AROUND TO THE BACK OF THE HOUSE.)

MRS. VAN HOUTEN:
(CONT'D)

       . . . oh, and a white piece of paper, I believe.

BART:
(GASPS)

(HE DASHES TOWARD THE BACK YARD.)

EXT. VAN HOUTEN HOUSE - BACKYARD - CONTINUOUS

(BART RUNS INTO THE BACKYARD TO SEE MILHOUSE PLAYING WITH HIS PLASTIC SOLDIERS AND BART'S SOUL.)

MILHOUSE:
(GRUFF VOICE)

Cover me, Sarge! I'm going after Bart's soul.

(MAKES SHOOTING NOISES, THEN IN ACCENT)

If the Ayatollah can't have it, no one can!

(MILHOUSE, MAKING ENGINE SOUNDS, RUNS A TOY TANK BACK AND FORTH OVER THE SOUL. BART WINCES.)

BART:
(JUMPY)

Ah, you know, Milhouse —

MILHOUSE:
(FRANK NELSON SMUG)

Yeesss?

BART: Bet you're getting tired of that soul, huh?

MILHOUSE:
(FRANK NELSON SMUG)

Nooooo.

BART: Suppose someone wanted to <u>buy</u> it from you?

MILHOUSE: Oh, you want to buy it back, Bart? Sure. No
              problem . . .

(BART LOOKS RELIEVED.)

MILHOUSE:
(CONT'D)
(COLD)

. . . Fifty bucks.

BART: What?!

MILHOUSE: Who's stupid now? Huh?

(STUPID MILHOUSE LAUGH)

(BART WALKS AWAY.)

14.

INT. SIMPSONS - LIVING ROOM - LATER

(HOMER, OBLIVIOUS, IS WATCHING TV.)

ON COMMERCIAL ON TV

(WE SEE MOE'S BAR IS NOW DECORATED IN KOOKY CHILI'S-STYLE MANNER (OLD GAS STATION FIXTURES, TOOLS, AN OLD SLED, LICENSE PLATES, A CIGAR STORE INDIAN, A STUFFED JACKALOPE, A STUFFED ALLIGATOR WITH A COWBOY HAT, A PLAYER PIANO, ETC.) AND IS PACKED WITH HAPPY FAMILIES. MOE APPROACHES THE CAMERA DRESSED IN GAY '90'S ATTIRE, SPORTING A HANDLEBAR MUSTACHE, AND WITH HIS HAIR PARTED IN THE MIDDLE.)

MOE: If you like good food, good fun, and a whole
                lotta crazy crap on the walls, then come on down
                to "Uncle Moe's Family Feedbag."

(A SHOT OF A DELICIOUS, FRESH-LOOKING TURKEY DINNER WITH ALL THE TRIMMINGS (GLASS OF WINE, SALAD, ETC.) ON A TRAY.)

ANNOUNCER (V.O.):
(MASON ADAMS VOICE)

                At Moe's, we serve good old-fashioned home
                cooking . . . deep fried to perfection.

(THE TRAY IS LOWERED INTO THE DEEP FRYER, AND COMES OUT A BROWN, CRISPY MASS. A CUSTOMER BREAKS OFF A PIECE, TRIES IT, AND GIVES MOE A THUMBS UP.)

MOE:
(CONT'D)

                Now that's "Moe" like it.

(WINKS AT CAMERA)

                So bring the whole family - mom, dad, kids. Uh,
                no old people. They're not covered by our
                insurance. It's fun! And remember our guarantee:
                If I'm not smiling when your check comes, your
                meal's on me, Uncle Moe.

(MOE SMILES GROTESQUELY, AND KEEPS SMILING AS WE HEAR THE JINGLE.)

JINGLERS: Come to Uncle Moe's for family fun / It's good,
                good, good, good, good, good, good.

(ANGLE ON)

HOMER: Mmm. Sounds good.

<u>Scene 5</u>

<u>INT. SIMPSON HOUSE - BART'S BEDROOM - THAT NIGHT</u>

(MARGE HUMS AS SHE TUCKS BART IN AND HUGS HIM.)

MARGE: Hmm. Bart, what's wrong? There's something a
                  little off about your hug.

BART:
(STARTING TO CONFESS)

                  Mom, I need to tell you something. I kinda—

MARGE:
(CUTS HIM OFF)

                  Uh, uh, uh, let me guess. A mother can always
                  tell.

(HUGS HIM AGAIN)

                  Hmm, it's not fear of nuclear war.

(BEAT)

                  Hmm, it's not swim test anxiety.

(BEAT)

                  It almost feels like you're missing something.
                  Something important.

BART:
(BRIGHTENING)

                  Like I don't have a soul?

MARGE:
(LAUGHS)

                  Aw, honey, you're not a <u>monster</u>.

<u>ANGLE ON BART</u>

(HE LOOKS CRESTFALLEN.)

<u>DISSOLVE TO:</u>

(BART TOSSING AND TURNING IN BED.)

<u>BART'S DREAM:</u>

<u>EXT. SPRINGFIELD CENTRAL PARK</u>

(AS BART APPROACHES THE PARK, HE WALKS UNDER A BANNER THAT
READS "ME & MY SOUL" DAY AND HEARS SOUNDS OF KIDS HAVING FUN.
AS HE GETS CLOSER, HE SEES THAT EACH CHILD IS PLAYING WITH
THEIR OWN SOUL (A MILKY-WHITE GHOSTLY VERSION OF THEMSELVES).

HE SEES KIDS AND THEIR SOULS ON SEESAWS, PUSHING EACH OTHER
ON SWINGS, RIDING BICYCLES BUILT FOR TWO AND HAVING CHICKEN
FIGHTS.)

(SHERRI AND TERRI'S SOULS ARE SPINNING THE JUMPROPE FOR SHERRI
AND TERRI.)

SHERRI, TERRI, & THEIR SOULS: Bart sold his soul and that's
           just swell / Now he's going straight to Hell-o
           operator, give me number nine / And if you
           disconnect me, I'll . . .

(THEIR SINGING AND LAUGHTER CONTINUE. BART LOOKS HURT. NELSON
RUNS UP.)

NELSON: No soul, huh? Don't worry. I'm still behind you.

(WE SEE NELSON'S SOUL CROUCHED DOWN BEHIND BART. NELSON PUSHES
BART OVER.)

NELSON AND HIS SOUL: Haw-haw!

(MARTIN AND HIS SOUL, IN MATCHING SAILOR OUTFITS, RUN DOWN TO
THE SHORE OF A LAKE AND STAND BY A BUNCH OF ROWBOATS.)

MARTIN: Ahoy there, friends! Everybody find a first mate!

MARTIN'S SOUL:
(CLAPPING WITH PRISSY EXCITEMENT)

           Oh, I choose Martin!

(THEY HOP INTO A ROWBOAT, EACH GRABBING AN OAR, AND ROW OFF.
OTHER KIDS AND THEIR SOULS FOLLOW AND HEAD OFF TOWARD A
GLOWING EMERALD CITY ON THE OTHER SIDE OF THE LAKE. MILHOUSE
RUNS BY, HAND-IN-HAND WITH HIS OWN SOUL AND BART'S SOUL. THE
SOULS GET ON THE BENCH AND DO ALL THE ROWING AS MILHOUSE
RELAXES IN THE BACK OF THE BOAT. BART TRIES TO FOLLOW, BUT
WITHOUT A SOUL TO GRAB THE OTHER OAR, HE CAN ONLY ROW AROUND
AND AROUND IN A CIRCLE.)

BART: Wait! Wait for me!

(SHERRI, TERRI, AND THEIR SOULS ROW BY.)

SHERRI, TERRI, & THEIR SOULS: Bart, it's time to end this
           dream / And don't forget the standard scream.

BACK TO REALITY

(BART SITS UPRIGHT IN BED.)

BART:
(SCREAM)

<u>Scene 6</u>

<u>INT. UNCLE MOE'S FAMILY FEEDBAG - EVENING</u>

The Simpsons enter and survey the crazy decor.

MARGE: An alligator with sunglasses? Now I've seen
            everything!

(MOE GREETS THEM, DRESSED AS IN THE COMMERCIAL, WITHOUT
MUSTACHE.)

MOE: Hiya, folks! Welcome to Uncle Moe's!
(CHUCKING KIDS UNDER THE CHIN)

            Aw, look at all the cute little minors.

HOMER:
(TO MARGE) Wow, that's Moe! The guy from the ad!

MOE: Right this way, Homer.

HOMER:
(PROUDLY)

            And he knows my name.

MARGE:
(LOOKING AROUND)

            Street signs? Indoors?!

("WHEN IN ROME")

            Whatever.

(MOE LEADS THEM OFF, PAST A TABLE WHERE THE FLANDERSES SIT.)

<u>ANGLE ON FLANDERS</u>

(HE GIVES HIS ORDER TO AN UNCTUOUS WAITER.)

FLANDERS: Rod, you order anything you want for your big
            ten-oh.

ROD:
(CONSULTING MENU, HAPPY)

            Million Dollar Birthday Fries!

UNCTUOUS WAITER:
(CUTESY)
            Uh-oh!

<u>AN ALARM GOES OFF.</u>

18.

MAUDE:
(READING MENU)

"Moe gets so excited when you order his Million
Dollar Birthday Fries he just has to celebrate."

(SIRENS WAIL AS MOE RUNS OUT OF THE KITCHEN WAVING SPARKLERS
AND CARRYING THE FRIES IN A FESTIVE BASKET STRAPPED TO HIS
HEAD.)

MOE:
(MANIC)

Here ya go! Here I am! Uncle Moe! 'Thank ya
Ma'am! This'll be a treat! Uncle Moe! Here I am!
While you eat!

(MOE FINISHES HIS DANCE WITH A BIG FLOURISH AND KNEELS DOWN
NEXT TO ROD, WHO BEGINS SLOWLY EATING THE FRIES.)

MOE:
(CONT'D)

(FORCED SMILE)

Please take the fries off my head, kid. The
basket is extremely hot.

DISSOLVE TO:

(MOE, NO BASKET ON HIS HEAD, IS TAKING THE SIMPSONS' ORDER.)

LISA: How're the Southwestern Pizza Fingers?

MOE: They're

(CHECKING MENU)
               awesomely outrageous!

MARGE: Oooh. These look good. Guilt-Free Steakfish
               Filets.

MOE: Nah, nah, nah. Let me level with you, Marge.
               That's just our name for bottom-feeding suction
               eel. You don't want that.

MARGE:
(DISAPPOINTED SOUND)

MOE: Why don't you try Moe's Hobo Chicken Chili? I
               start with the best part — the neck.

(ENTICING)

               And then I add secret hobo spices.

MARGE: Ooo, tres bien.

MOE: Yeah.

(MOE TURNS AROUND AND IS INSTANTLY HIT IN THE HEAD WITH A BARRAGE OF WATER FROM RALPH WIGGUM AND HIS BATTERY-OPERATED SQUIRT GUN.)

RALPH:
(EXCITED LAUGHTER)

MOE:
(ANGRILY)

> Hey, what the hell are ya doin', ya little freak —!

RALPH:
(TERRIFIED WHIMPER)

(RALPH LOOKS SHOCKED. MOE RECOVERS HIS SMILE.)

MOE: I'm sorry, kid. Sorry. I'm not used to the laughter of children. It cuts through me like a dentist's drill.

(DRYING HIS FACE OFF)

> But no, no, that was funny, that was funny, takin' away my dignity like that. Ha ha ha.

INT. MOE'S RESTAURANT - SIMPSONS TABLE - A LITTLE LATER

THE SIMPSONS HAVE RECEIVED THEIR FESTIVE FOOD (COMPLETE WITH LITTLE TOOTHPICK FLAGS, UMBRELLAS, ETC.). BART LOOKS WORRIED.

LISA: I would like to say grace.

(EYES BART)

> Lord, have mercy on my <u>soul</u>, and Mom's <u>soul</u>, and Dad's <u>soul</u>, and Maggie's <u>soul</u>, and let every <u>soul</u> in Christendom! . . .

(GRUNT)

(A ROLL BOUNCES OFF HER HEAD FROM OFF-SCREEN.)

MARGE: Bart!

BART: I can't take this anymore. I want my soul and I want it now!

(HE RUNS OUT.)

HOMER: Bart, you didn't finish your Spaghetti and Moe-Balls!

HOMER'S BRAIN: Silence you fool! It can be ours.

HOMER RE-RECORD
(MOUTH FULL)

(SHOOING BART)

        Run, boy!

(CHEWS)

        Run!

CUT TO:

EXT. STREET - NIGHT

(BART RUNS DOWN THE STREET INTO THE DARKNESS.)

HOMER (O.S.):
(MOUTH FULL) Run for your life! . . .

(CHEWING SOUNDS)

        . . . Boy!

FADE OUT:

                END OF ACT TWO

                 ACT THREE

                 Scene 7

FADE IN:

EXT. VAN HOUTEN HOUSE - EARLY EVENING

(BART POUNDS ON THE FRONT DOOR.)

BART: Milhouse! Milhouse! You win! I want this
               nightmare to end!

(THE DOOR CREAKS OPEN TO REVEAL A SCARY FIGURE IN A SPACE
SUIT.)

FIGURE:
(DEEP FILTERED BREATHING, THEN OMINOUS)

        Leave this place. You are in great danger.

BART:
(SCARED)   Where's Milhouse?

FIGURE: The one you call Milhouse is gone.

(REMOVES HELMET) (WISEGUY VOICE)

        He went to his Gramma's place while we're
        spraying for potato bugs.

(WE PULL BACK. A STRIPED EXTERMINATION TENT IS DRAPED OVER
THE VAN HOUTEN HOUSE.)

BART:
(FRUSTRATED MOAN)

> When Milhouse left, did you notice if he was carrying a piece of paper?

FIGURE: Oh, yeah. You don't forget a thing like that.

INT. MOE'S RESTAURANT - SAME EVENING

(A WEARY, BEDRAGGLED MOE STRUGGLES OUT OF THE KITCHEN WITH A HUGE TRAY OF FOOD. THE BIRTHDAY ALARM GOES OFF AGAIN.)

MOE: Aw, God.

(MOE LABORIOUSLY SETS THE TRAY DOWN AND GOES BACK INTO THE KITCHEN.)

ANGLE ON:

(SHERRI AND TERRI. THEY ARE SITTING AT A TABLE IN PARTY HATS WITH SOME OTHER LITTLE GIRLS AND THEIR MOMS. MOE COMES RUNNING OVER WITH HIS SPARKLERS, FRY HAT, ETC.)

MOE: Here ya go! Here I am! Uncle Moe! Thank ya Ma'am! This'll be a treat! Uncle Moe! Here I am! While you eat!

SHERRI: Yay! Now do it for Terri.

MOE: What, it's _your_ birthday, too?

SHERRI & TERRI: We're twins.

MOE:
(SIGHS, THEN LACKLUSTER)

> Here ya go. Here I am. Eat your fries. Eat 'em.

(HE PLUNKS DOWN THE FRIES IN FRONT OF SHERRI AND TERRI. A LITTLE BOY SHOVES A CRAYONED PLACEMAT AT MOE.)

LITTLE BOY: Here's you.

(THE PICTURE IS OF AN UGLY STICK-FIGURE MOE. WRITTEN ACROSS THE TOP IS "MR. STINKY." MOE LOOKS HURT.)

MOE: Ah geez, and ya got the stink lines and everything.

(STILL UPSET, MOE PLUNKS JAILBIRD'S CHECK DOWN ON HIS TABLE. JAILBIRD POINTS TO A POSTER OF A SMILING MOE WITH A WORD BALLOON SAYING, "IF I DON'T SMILE, YOU EAT FOR FREE.")

JAILBIRD: Uh, dude, you did _not_ smile. We eat for free. Come on Shoshanna, let's roll.

(CHUCKLES)

(JAILBIRD AND HIS BIKER CHICK GIRLFRIEND GET UP TO LEAVE.)

MOE:
(PLEADING)

> But I made you those fried green Moe-matoes, just like you asked! C'mon!

KRUSTY:
(RE: MOE)

> Look at the vein on that guy's forehead. He's gonna blow.

(WE HEAR THE BIRTHDAY ALARM AGAIN. MOE TURNS AND SEES PATTY AND SELMA SITTING AT A TABLE WEARING BIRTHDAY HATS. THEY WAVE LASCIVIOUSLY.)

PATTY AND SELMA:
(ALLURING GRUNTS)

> Ser-vice!

(THERE'S A TUGGING ON MOE'S APRON.)

VERY CUTE LITTLE GIRL: Unky Moe?

MOE:
(TRYING NOT TO LOSE IT)

> What is it, sweetheart?

VERY CUTE LITTLE GIRL: My sodie is too cold — my teef hurt.

MOE: Aw, your "teef" hurt, huh? Your "teef" hurt?

(SNAPPING)

> Well, that's too freakin' bad! You hear me? I'll tell you where you can put your freakin' "sodie, too!"

CUSTOMERS:
(MORTIFIED GASPS)

ANGLE ON THE FLANDERSES

(NED AND MAUDE CLAMP THEIR HANDS OVER ROD AND TODD'S EARS.)

TODD: Ow! My "freakin'" ears!

NED & MAUDE:
(BIG GASP)

MAUDE: Oh, let's go, dear.

(THEY GET UP TO LEAVE.)

NED: Well, I expect that type of language at Denny's, but not here.

(EVERYONE CLEARS OUT OF THE RESTAURANT.)

MOE: Aw, come on folks! Wait! Please, come back! Please! I got a new offer! Whenever Uncle Moe threatens you, you get a free steak . . . fish.

(THE RESTAURANT IS EMPTY. MOE SIGHS.)

Scene 8

EXT. DOWNTOWN STREET - LATE THAT NIGHT

(BART, ON HIS BIKE, HAS STOPPED TO LOOK AT A MAP.)

BART:
(FRANTIC)

Okay, okay. Milhouse's Grandmother lives on 257th Street, and I'm on Third.

(MOANS)

(HE LOWERS THE MAP. SUDDENLY, A STREET CLEANER IS JUST INCHES AWAY, COMING DIRECTLY AT HIM, ITS BRIGHT LIGHTS BLINDING AND ITS HORN BLARING. BART JUMPS OFF HIS BIKE AND TUMBLES ONTO THE CURB. AS HE WATCHES IN HORROR, THE BIKE IS SUCKED UNDER THE STREET CLEANER. THERE'S A HORRIBLE SOUND OF METAL GRINDING AND SHREDDING, THEN THE BIKE POPS OUT COMPLETELY UNHARMED AND SPARKLING CLEAN.)

BART: Well, finally, a little luck.

(BART STARTS TO RIDE AGAIN. THE BIKE SQUEAKS TWICE, THEN FALLS COMPLETELY APART, STILL SPARKLING. THE DRIVER LEANS OUT OF THE STREET CLEANER AND LOOKS BACK AT BART.)

DRIVER:
(EVIL CHUCKLE)

(AS HE'S LOOKING IN THE WRONG DIRECTION, THE STREET CLEANER BUMPS DOWN THE STAIRS INTO A SUBWAY ENTRANCE, WITH HORRIBLE GRINDING AND CLANKING NOISES.)

DRIVER:
(CONT'D)
(EVIL CHUCKLE TURNS INTO BUMPY DISMAYED NOISE, WHICH FADES)

EXT. 181ST STREET - LATER

(CHIEF WIGGUM AND RALPH PULL UP TO THE CURB. THE CHIEF GETS OUT AND LEAVES RALPH BUCKLED IN THE FRONT SEAT.)

WIGGUM: Son, you wait here while daddy tries to talk
             some sense into this raving derelict.

(WIGGUM APPROACHES A RAVING DERELICT.)

RAVING DERELICT:
(RAPID FIRE GIBBERISH)

WIGGUM: Now slow down. Slow down.

RAVING DERELICT:
(RAPID FIRE GIBBERISH)

WIGGUM:
(LISTENS)

             Who's been stealing your thoughts?

(LISTENS)

RAVING DERELICT:
(RAPID FIRE GIBBERISH)

             . . . Curiosity shop . . . I have powers beyond
             your imagination . . .

ANGLE ON RALPH

(HE'S WAITING PATIENTLY IN HIS SEAT. SUDDENLY, A CRAZED-
LOOKING BART POPS UP IN THE WINDOW.)

BART:
(EERILY COMPOSED)

             Hello, Ralph.

RALPH:
(JUMPS)   Hi Bart. I know you from school.

BART:
(COMPLETE DISDAIN)

             Yes. A simple proposition, Ralph: How would you
             like to make a dollar?

RALPH:
(INNOCENTLY) Uh, I don't know.

BART: All you have to do is sign a paper that says I
             can have your soul.

(INTENSELY)

             I need a soul, Ralph. Any soul. Yours.

RALPH:
(WHIMPERS, STARTS TO CRY)

(RALPH SQUIRMS IN HIS SEAT BELT AS BART STARTS TO REACH TOWARD HIM.)

WIGGUM: Hey. What's goin' on over there?!

(WIGGUM SHINES HIS FLASHLIGHT RIGHT IN BART'S EYES. BART SHIELDS HIS FACE AND CRINGES.)

BART:
(DRACULA-STYLE HISS)

(BART LOPES OFF INTO THE NIGHT.)

INT. MOE'S - SAME TIME

(HOMER, BARNEY AND CARL ARE BACK AT THEIR REGULAR POSITIONS AT THE BAR, AS WORKERS REMOVE DECORATIONS FROM THE WALLS, PRY OUT BOOTHS WITH A CROWBAR, ETC.)

MOE: G'on, take it all. Get it all out of here.

BARNEY: You know, Moe, you might want to keep the fire extinguishers.

MOE: Nah. Too many bad memories.

BARNEY: Well, look at the bright side, Moe. You still got us.

MOE:
(CHEERING UP)
     Yeah. Yeah, you know, that actually makes me feel a little better.

HOMER: Why? That was the problem in the first place. You were going broke because we were your only customers. Wasn't that the problem in the first place? That you were going broke . . . Moe?

(MOE DOESN'T REPLY.)

HOMER:
(CONT'D)   Moe? Hey, Moe? Oh, you're thinking about all the money you blew, aren'tcha?

(MOE NODS SADLY.)

HOMER:
(CONT'D)   What was it? 50-60 thousand dollars? . . . Moe? Look, maybe it would help if you went over all the mistakes you made from the beginning . . . Moe?

MOE: What?

HOMER: Let me get a pad. . . .

INT. GRAMMA VAN HOUTEN'S APT. - LATER THAT EVENING

(IT IS A CRAMPED APARTMENT. MILHOUSE'S PARENTS ARE LYING UNCOMFORTABLY ON THE FOLD-OUT COUCH WITH SUITCASES OPEN ON THE FLOOR. MILHOUSE LIES ON A COT. THE DOORBELL RINGS. NANA VAN HOUTEN BUSTLES IN.)

NANA VAN HOUTEN:
(MILHOUSEY VOICE)

> A caller at this hour?

(TO MR. VAN HOUTEN)

> You dial 9-1, then when I say so, dial 1 again.

(SHE OPENS THE DOOR TO REVEAL A HAGGARD-LOOKING BART.)

BART: Milhouse, please.

MILHOUSE: Bart, I can't play now. It's two A.M.

(BART WALKS UP AND GRABS MILHOUSE BY HIS PAJAMAS.)

BART: Milhouse, I gotta have my soul back. I'll do anything you want.

MILHOUSE: Uh . . . well . . .

MR. VAN HOUTEN:
(FROM SOFA-BED)

> Milhouse, give him back his soul! I've got work tomorrow.

MILHOUSE: I'm really sorry. I kinda traded your soul to the guy at the comic book store. But look, I got some cool POGS. Alf POGS. Remember Alf? He's back in POG form.

(HE PULLS OUT A HANDFUL FROM HIS PAJAMA POCKET.)

BART:
(FURIOUS)

> You traded my soul for POGS?!

(DESPAIRING)

> Noooo!!

(BART RUNS OFF DOWN THE HALL. MILHOUSE WATCHES HIM GO.)

NANA VAN HOUTEN:
(O.S.)

> Oh, close that door. You're letting the heat out.

27.

MR. VAN HOUTEN (O.S.):
(EXASPERATED)

Shut up! Shut up! Shut up!

Scene 9

EXT. ESTABLISHING - ANDROID'S DUNGEON - DAWN

(THE SUN'S FIRST LIGHT HITS A LUMP ON THE STOOP. IT'S BART, CURLED UP, ASLEEP. THE COMIC BOOK GUY COMES TO OPEN THE STORE.)

COMIC BOOK GUY: If you are waiting for the "Hi & Lois" signing, it has been moved to the Springfield Coliseum.

BART: Please. You have something of mine on a little piece of paper.

COMIC BOOK GUY: Oh, so you're Bart Simpson, eh?

INT. ANDROID'S DUNGEON - CONTINUOUS

(HE OPENS THE DOOR AND ENTERS.)

COMIC BOOK GUY:
(CONT'D)

Well, since my breakfast burrito is congealing rapidly, I will be blunt. You're too late. I sold your soul last night.

(VOICE GETS EERIE)

Yes, yes, I found a buyer right away for that item.

BART: Who?

COMIC BOOK GUY: I'm not at liberty to divulge the party, but they were most interested in having possession of a little boy's soul.

(BART GROANS AND BANGS HIS HEAD ON A CABINET.)

COMIC BOOK GUY: Excuse me. No banging your head on the display case, please. It contains a very rare "Mary Worth" in which she has advised a friend to commit suicide. Thank you.

EXT. SPRINGFIELD STREET - MORNING

(AS BART WALKS HOME IT STARTS TO RAIN.)

INT. BART'S ROOM - A LITTLE LATER

(BART WALKS INTO HIS ROOM, KNEELS BY HIS BED, AND PRAYS.)

BART: Are you there, God? It's me, Bart Simpson. I know I never paid too much attention in church, but I could really use some of that good stuff now. I'm afraid. I'm afraid some weirdo's got my soul and I don't know what they're doing to it. I just want it back. Please.

(STARTS TO CRY)

   I hope you can hear this . . .

(THE SOUL FLUTTERS DOWN ONTO THE BED, RAGGED AND A LITTLE CRUMPLED.
BART LOOKS UP TO SEE: LISA.)

BART: Lisa! <u>You</u> bought this?

LISA: With the change in my piggy bank.

BART: There's no change in your piggy bank.

LISA: Not in any of the ones you know about.

BART: Oh Lise, thank you.

(BART IS SO HAPPY HE KISSES HER.)

LISA: Happy to do it. But you know, Bart, some philosophers believe that nobody is born with a soul — that you have to earn one through suffering and thought and prayer, like you did last night.

BART:
(NOT LISTENING)

   Uh huh.

(BART IS TOO BUSY CRAMMING THE PAPER INTO HIS MOUTH AND DESPERATELY TRYING TO EAT IT. HE FINALLY SWALLOWS THE LAST BITE WITH A RELIEVED GULP AND CRAWLS INTO BED.)

INT. SIMPSON HOUSE - BART'S BEDROOM - A LITTLE LATER

(BART HAS FALLEN ASLEEP, THE DOG AND CAT CURLED UP ON THE BED NEXT TO HIM.)

BART'S DREAM

(A SMILING BART AND HIS SOUL ROW CONTENTEDLY ACROSS THE LAKE. THEY APPROACH MARTIN'S BOAT AND RAM IT LIKE A BUMPER CAR. MARTIN'S SOUL FALLS OVERBOARD.)

MARTIN'S SOUL:
(YELP)

BART & BART'S SOUL:
(DOUBLE SNEAKY CHUCKLE)

(BART AND HIS SOUL ROW OFF INTO THE DISTANCE.)

FADE OUT:

THE END

APPENDIX B

Suggested Exercises

CHAPTER 1:
THE ESSENCE OF CRITICISM

1. For the next several days, keep a running tally of how many times you hear people use the term *criticism* or its derivatives. In what percentage of these cases was the term used in a negative sense? What are the implications of your finding for the practice of authentic criticism as we define it in this chapter?

2. Watch a thirty-minute television program of your choice and compile parallel columns listing its strengths and weaknesses. How do the lengths of these two columns compare?

3. Repeat exercise #2, but this time, listen to a selected radio station for a one-hour period.

4. Using the 'weaknesses' list compiled for either exercise #2 or #3, derive a series of *rectifications*. In other words, make a suggestion for how each weakness could be corrected.

5. Read Barbara Lippert's Chapter 5 review of the 7-Up "Beautiful Rain" commercial. Then dissect this critique as to its coverage, or lack of coverage, of each of the five steps in S. Stephenson Smith's *critical process*.

6. Estimate the number of assigned book reports/reviews you have completed to this point in your life. Compare this figure to the approximate number of electronic media program reports you have been asked to prepare. What do you conclude from this comparison?

7. In what contemporary periodicals might you still find "science" and "gossip" media criticism? Locate an example of each and analyze these two pieces as to how they meet or fail to meet the tasks encompassed by S. Stephenson Smith's *critical process*.

8. Select an article on electronic media criticism from one of the following academic journals: *Journal of Broadcasting & Electronic Media, Critical Studies in Mass Communication,* or *Journalism & Mass Communication Quarterly*. What key insights does the article offer that would be helpful to media consumers? On the other hand, what barriers to consumer comprehension of these insights are erected by the article's scholarly mode of expression?

CHAPTER 2:
CRITICAL FUNCTIONS

1. Select electronic media reviews prepared by five different critics. Which of these commentators best exemplifies the concept of the critic as *guide*? Which one least exemplifies this concept? In your estimation, is the best reviewer also the best "guide"? Why or why not?

2. Turn to Betsy Sharkey's commentary on *The Simpsons* in Chapter 10. What valuation yardsticks seem most important to this writer?

3. Repeat #2 using Jeff Jarvis's "The Rosie O'Donnell Show" piece in Chapter 14. Are each writer's yardsticks appropriate to his or her subject matter? To their likely readership (an advertising trade magazine for Sharkey and a general circulation television magazine for Jarvis)? Are both writers candid about the yardsticks they are employing?

4. Read Barbara Lippert's "Indecent Exposure" commentary in Chapter 12. How many of our five OTHER CRITIC RESPONSIBILITIES does this piece serve?

5. Repeat #4 in terms of Greg Quill's Chapter 12 critique of *Beyond Reality*.

6. Write your own review of a prime-time television series now in its first year. Make certain to cover all five of these OTHER CRITIC RESPONSIBILITIES in your piece.

7. Using the same show as in #6, assess which of the Ralph Smith-isolated "6 elements that critics value" are present in it. Did you subscribe to any of these values in your own review of the show?

8. Make a list of four reasons for, and four reasons against, the use of re-creation in your local newscast's coverage of a convenience store robbery in which the clerk was severely beaten with a baseball bat. As the news director, would you support or oppose the re-creation? Would your lists and decision be any different if you were doing a 30-minute year-end documentary on violent crime in your city?

9. Watch three continuous hours of programming on the television network of your choice. Compile a list of all of the cases of stereotyping that you observed. Which of these were demeaning, in your opinion? Was there a way in which any or all of these negative stereotypes could have been avoided without significantly (a) changing or (b) weakening the show? Would the modification you derived actually strengthen the program? Why or why not?

10. Repeat #9 with two hours of a music-formatted radio station as your reference point. In this case, ascertain whether the same or similar negative stereotypes recur in featured song lyrics. If so, could anything be done to rectify the situation without compromising the format?

11. Cite at least four current television portrayals that illustrate and support Parker's contention that "the good must know its alternative or it is not good."

CHAPTER 3:
CRITICISM AND THE COMMUNICATION PROCESS

1. Dissect Jim Sollisch's Chapter 2 'TV Ratings' commentary by isolating which, if any, of his discussion relates to (a) originator criticism, (b) message criticism, (C) medium criticism, and (d) receiver criticism.

2. Repeat #1 using a review by one of your local newspaper critics as the focal point.

3. In your opinion, are there any *auteur* executive producers still prominent on today's prime-time schedule? If not—why

not? If so, select your favorite and describe what makes her or his work distinctive.

4. Scrutinize today's top-rated prime-time series in terms of its polysemic character. How many distinct meanings does it seem to project—and to what audiences? Repeat this exercise with one of the lowest-rated programs. Is the more successful show also more polysemic? Or less so?

5. Repeat #4 using the series with the *second*-highest ratings and with a different low-rated show than the one considered in exercise #4. Did you detect the same or a dissimilar relationship of polysemy to ratings success than that found in your completion of the previous exercise?

6. Use a VCR to continuously tape an evening's viewing—including all channel "grazing" activity. Instead of changing the channels by using your receiver's tuner, change them via the tuner on the VCR. (On some VCRs, this will require momentarily stopping the machine.) At a later date, review the entire tape. Does this viewing montage present meanings in addition to those vested in the individual program elements from which you have casually constructed it?

7. Evaluate the accuracy or inaccuracy of Gunter Anders's observation about radio by citing examples from your own experience as to how you use that medium.

8. For the next six television commercials you see, speculate on the identity of their intended viewers. Were these types of viewers successfully appealed to in your estimation? Why or why not?

9. Repeat #8 in terms of the next six radio commercials that you hear.

10. Repeat #8 again, using a television program or an hour of a radio station's drive-time as your subject. Is it more difficult to guess a commercial's target audience or the target audience for a program or format? Why?

CHAPTER 4:
KNOWLEDGE PROCESSING

1. Is Van Gordon Sauter's Chapter 2 "Dangerous Years" critique empirical, normative, or both? Cite specific examples from his piece to support your conclusion.

2. Repeat #1 with Dan Kening's Chapter 3 commentary on "WYTZ's Love Sponge" as your focus.

3. Figure the share, rating, and CPM in the case of a population of 1.5 million with a research sample size of 220, of whom 134 report viewing TV, 56 are tuned to our station, and a 30-second commercial costs $1,750.

4. Because she is a psychologist, you would expect Susan Small-Weil's "A Child's-Eye View" commentary in Chapter 8 to reflect the scientific way of knowing. But does it also contain vestiges of (a) the mystic and/or (b) the rhetorician? If so, what portions of Small-Weil's article evidence these approaches?

5. Examine Debra Goldman's Chapter 3 critique of *Forgive or Forget*. Is this piece primarily scientific, rhetorical, or mystical? What is the rationale for your conclusion?

6. Dissect Ray Richmond's Chapter 15 review of *Action* to isolate the sitcom's perceived *logos, pathos*, and *ethos* elements. How, in turn, does Richmond use these proofs in constructing the review itself?

7. Analyze an episode from your favorite one-hour television series. Can you detect in it aspects of the *forensic/judicial*? the *demonstrative/epideictic*? the *deliberative/political*?

8. Repeat #7 in terms of one of your least favorite one-hour shows. Which series seems to be richer in these rhetorical elements? Does their presence or absence contribute to your liking/disliking of the two programs?

9. Is Betsy Sharkey's Chapter 10 review of *The Simpsons* a good example of "the way of the critic"? To answer this question, examine her review in the same manner that we examined David Remnick's *Playground Pros* piece in this chapter.

10. Listen to one hour of programming on a tightly formatted music radio station. Now, write three brief descriptions of this experience—one from each of the Perceptual Triad perspectives.

11. Repeat #10 using a one-hour television entertainment program as your referent. Was exercise #10 or #11 easier to accomplish? Why?

12. Probe the Antonia Zerbisias commentary in Chapter 14 as to how it reflects, or fails to reflect, each plane of the Perceptual Triad. Does your finding dovetail with how informative or uninformative you perceived this particular critique to be?

13. In the same way that we scrutinized the Friskies commercial (Figure 4-4), perform a Perceptual Triad investigation on the Chapter 2 "Club Med" spot (Figure 2-3).

CHAPTER 5:
TONAL AND TALENT INGREDIENTS

1. Using a one-hour action/adventure program as your subject, analyze the contribution made by, and the appropriateness of, its musical soundtrack. Is the music a programmatic enhancement or is it a crutch for shoddy plot or dialogue? Would the music be missed if omitted? Are its instrumentation, tempo, type, and volume well suited to the program's character?

2. Repeat #1 focusing on a daytime soap opera.

3. Compose a critique that compares an hour's programming on two competing music radio stations as to clarity, execution, continuity, and aptness of task. Which of these four elements was easiest to discuss? Which most difficult? Why?

4. If you can, cite your own experience to illustrate Parker's comment that "In music we get so close to ourselves that at times it is almost frightening."

5. Watch five MTV or VH-1 music videos. In which of these does the video seem to be a "throwaway afterthought"? In which does the video make more of the song than it deserves? In which does the video inhibit enjoyment of the song?

6. Evaluate the use of music in the Chapter 4 "Mr. Turkey" commercial (Figure 4-1) from the twin standpoints of continuity and aptness of task.

7. Analyze the afternoon drive-time personalities on two competing music radio stations using Tim Moore's twin benchmarks of (1) whether the correct amount of talk is used to "lubricate" the format and (2) whether the host seems to bring a sense of control to and through the microphone.

8. Examine the late news shows of two local television stations. In what ways do the on-camera talent try to behave as trustworthy friends? Which station's performers are most successful in this regard? Does this station also offer the more "informative" newscast as you perceive it? How do *you* define *informative*?

9. Watch a game show host other than Pat Sajak and analyze his performance in terms of the following: (a) communication with the viewer; (b) communication with the studio audience; (c) communication with the contestants; (d) techniques of and success in

controlling the pace of the show. Is there anything in your findings that explains or justifies why all game show hosts have been *male*?

10. Analyze the nonverbal communication displayed by actors in a selected sitcom. How much of this nonverbal characterization would be discernible to a theatre audience if the show were performed on stage?

11. Repeat #10 using a different sitcom. Then compare the two shows as to the amount and clarity of their casts' nonverbal communication as captured by the cameras.

12. In the case of #10 (and/or #11), how many of the detected nonverbal portrayals were set up by a directorial shot change? In what percentage of cases was the shot change necessary to audience perception of the behavior?

CHAPTER 6: STAGE-MOLDING INGREDIENTS

1. Listen to sixty minutes of a music-formatted radio station in order to ascertain how aural transitions and volume are used or abused in the hour's various program elements. If you were the program director, what, if anything, would you have done differently to further format cohesion?

2. Examine any half-hour television entertainment program. Try to isolate specific examples of the use of sound to direct audience attention to certain portions of the picture.

3. Perform a lighting analysis of the Subaru commercial in Chapter 4 (Figure 4-3) similar to the way in which we decoded the Philips spot. Also list the type of shot used in each frame. Is there any discernible pattern at work here?

4. Repeat #3 using the Fantastik Swipes commercial (Figure 9-4) as your subject.

5. Watch one episode of a daytime soap opera and compare the number of scenes using Notan to those using Chiaroscuro lighting. In what sorts of contexts was each technique typically used?

6. List and compare the number of separate (horizontal plane) shots in two different sitcoms. Is there a relationship between the number of shots and show pacing? between number of shots and amount of dialogue? between number of shots and the sense of viewer involvement? Which show seemed to use the most effective shot pattern? What

was it about the pattern that made it most effective?

7. Repeat #5 using two action/adventure shows as your subjects.

8. Repeat #5 using episodes from two soap operas as your subjects.

9. Select a one-hour drama. Analyze that production's exploitation of the vertical camera plane. Is this exploitation a help or hinderance to character development? to the sense of character interaction?

10. Repeat #8, this time restricting your investigation to the director's use of spatial mobility techniques.

11. Assuming that you were the director, what specific spatial mobility techniques would you have used in or between each of the frames in Chapter 9's "I Am Michigan" commercial (Figure 9-1)?

12. Repeat #11 using Chapter 10's Colombia Coffee Growers commercial (Figure 10-1) as your subject.

13. Compare two local newscasts by listing the shot transitions each uses to shoot the in-studio news team over the course of the program. Is there a difference in shot number, transition method, and average shot duration between the two newscasts? Repeat this experiment using another night's edition of each of these two programs. Are your findings the same?

14. Repeat #13 using two evening *network* newscasts. What, if any, are the transition/duration distinctions that emerge between network and local shows?

15. Watch as much television as necessary in order to find at least six undesirable montage creations that resulted from unfortunate program matter/commercial linkages.

16. View any sitcom episode. While watching, note the occasions when you do not feel yourself placed at Pepper's "point of optimum receptivity." Were these occasions a help or hinderance to your sense of involvement in the storyline?

17. Repeat #16 using a one-hour drama or action/adventure show as the object of your analysis.

CHAPTER 7: BUSINESS GRATIFICATIONS

1. Define what, in your estimation, constitutes "the public interest." In light of your definition, which current electronic media

offerings seem the *most* effective public interest servants? Which seem the *least* effective in serving this role? How do your *most* and *least* selections compare in terms of their apparent business/financial success?

2. Read the Antonia Zerbisias "Docu-Soap" review in Chapter 14. Given her observations, what do you believe would be Zerbisias's definition of program "quality"?

3. Analyze the radio stations in your locality in terms of the specific audience that each apparently is trying to reach. Which stations seem the most successful in this regard? by what criteria? To what factors would you attribute their success?

4. List the specific business gratifications alluded to in Greg Quill's "Canadian-Made Show" article found in Chapter 12. Which of these gratifications apparently were achieved by *Beyond Reality* and which were not?

5. Repeat #4 using Dan Kening's Chapter 3 "Love Sponge" critique as your focal point. In this case, what business gratifications does WYTZ hope to achieve? Is there any difference between the business gratifications sought by the station and the personal gratifications sought by Bubba the Love Sponge?

6. Look at the day-long program schedule of one of the network-affiliate television stations in your market. Try to decipher the audience flow pattern that this station is attempting to cultivate.

7. Repeat #6 using a cable television network. Isolate and attempt to account for differences between the station's and the cable network's apparent flow strategies.

8. Isolate at least six specific examples of counterprogramming by local television stations. What universe is each station apparently trying to reach via this strategy? Is this counterprogramming maintained or abandoned in preceding and following shows? (Restrict your analysis to times programmed by the station rather than by its network.)

9. As an ABC programming executive, what would you recommend to mitigate John Sias's problems in scheduling the start of *ABC Monday Night Football*? As an outside critic, would your recommendation be any different? Why or why not? Do you think the network's current method of scheduling the telecast is the best one?

10. Listen to an hour of a local radio station's programming and try to sketch out the hot clock it seems to be using. (For a hot clock model, consult Chapter 13's Figure

13-6.) Listen also to the preceding hour and try to ascertain if, or how, the hot clock changes.

11. Repeat #10 focusing on a closely competing station. Do the two outlets' hot clocks seem to mirror each other or do they evidence counterprogramming strategies?

12. Analyze this chapter's five 'schedule and flow analysis' questions in terms of the 9 P.M. programs aired by all the local television outlets in your market.

CHAPTER 8:
AUDIENCE GRATIFICATIONS

1. What, according to Debra Goldman's Chapter 3 critique, are the gratifications that viewers would most likely derive from *Forgive or Forget*? Which of these gratifications would apparently not be shared by Goldman herself?

2. Read Howard Reich's review of *Swingin' with Duke* in Chapter 15. Which of the seven use/gratification factors does the program appear to service?

3. Repeat #2 in terms of *The Simpsons* as described by Betsy Sharkey in her Chapter 10 review.

4. Select a one-hour television series and write your own analysis of the use/gratification factors it seems most likely to provide in every episode. Include in your assessment which of these factors would *not* be appealing to you personally—and why.

5. Watch a vintage ("evergreen") sitcom and compare its gratifications with those provided by a first-run sitcom. In what ways, if any, do the gratification patterns vary between the two shows? What, in your opinion, are the reasons for this variation or lack of it? Would the gratification patterns for the "evergreen" have been different when it was first-run?

6. Read *The Cosby Show* script in Appendix A. To which audience gratifications does it seem to cater? Would these gratifications vary from one demographic group to another?

7. Repeat #6 using the Appendix A's script from *The Simpsons*. In addition to the questions posed above, would this show's gratification patterns be different if the show was 'live action' rather than animation?

8. Research the television coverage of the 1992 Los Angeles riot. Did it create the same

"overmagnification" of reality as occurred in Detroit in 1967? What difference, if any, did the 1992 availability of large numbers of camcorders make?

9. List your personal top four "media best friends" as found in either radio or television programming. What is it about them (and about the programs or outlets on which they appear) that makes these individuals so appealing to you?

10. State the precise problem-solving claims made by each of the next six radio commercials you hear and also by the next six television commercials you see. What devices were used to convey these solutions? Were any other gratifications contained in these commercials?

11. Compare how problems are developed in a sample soap opera installment and in an episode of a selected sitcom. How many problems were present and how many were resolved within each episode's boundaries?

12. Into which of Gans's "taste publics" do you fall? Into which do/did your parents and grandparents fall? How do your personal program choices reflect or contradict your taste-public membership? How do/did your parents' choices reflect or contradict theirs?

13. Select what, in your opinion, is the most violent program series currently on television. Write a position paper on it that addresses the question of whether the series' violence, in whole or in part, would seem to have a socially beneficial catharsis effect. What type of viewer would be most captivated (positively or negatively) by this violence?

14. Repeat #13 in terms of the most violent song lyrics now receiving radio airplay.

15. Repeat #13 using a violence-heavy website or video game.

CHAPTER 9: DEPICTION ANALYSIS

1. Describe, in as detailed a manner as possible, the physical environment in which a selected, locale-specified sitcom or dramatic series is placed. If possible, this should be a locale with which you have direct, real-life experience. Based on your own knowledge, which elements of this *depicted* environment clash most with the physical *reality* of such a locale?

2. Reread David Remnick's Chapter 4 "Playground Pros" piece. According to this

documentary, what is society like (at least in the Black neighborhoods of Washington, DC)? Do we have any clues as to Remnick's own conceptualization of this society or of U.S. society as a whole?

3. How is the ethnic or occupational group to which you belong depicted in the electronic media? Write a brief commentary that cites specific examples of your findings and takes a position on the accuracy or fraudulence of these depictions.

4. Analyze five radio commercials and five television commercials from the standpoint of the consequences predictions they make. Which consequences seem reasonable based on normal product category expectations? Which are outlandish or incredible?

5. Watch a daytime soap opera for three consecutive days. What does it show to be the consequences of sex and love? Does it define or distinguish between these two concepts in any way?

6. Listen to three hours of radio music programming. In terms of the lyrics aired, answer the same questions posed in #5.

7. Select an episode of an action/adventure show and list each act of physical violence (however you define that phenomenon). In how many acts are the consequences of that violence sanitized?

8. Repeat #7 focusing on another action/adventure program. Which program is more violent? Which program is more unrealistic because of the percentage of its violence that is sanitized?

9. Repeat #7 using a law-enforcement-based reality program such as *Cops*. Compare your findings with those flowing from your action/adventure analysis. What conclusions can you draw in comparing how fictional and 'reality' shows depict violence?

10. What are the consequences of actions as depicted in the commercials discussed by Susan Small-Weil in her Chapter 8 "Child's-Eye View" commentary? Which of these consequences lessons were unintended by the advertiser?

11. Select two television series in which parenting is prominently depicted. How are the responsibilities of parenting shown in each program? Are there major differences between the two as to what these responsibilities are? Are there differences as to the methods advocated for carrying out these responsibilities?

12. Study the visual (on-location) stories in a network newscast. In which cases did

the picture seem more important than the subject of the story itself?

13. Repeat #12 by focusing on a local station newscast. Did it appear more or less susceptible than the network to the emphasis on pictorial images over substantive content?

14. Identify the self-evaluative standards taught by the following spots: Church's Chicken (Figure 3-5); Mr. Turkey (Figure 4-1); and Labatt's (Figure 12-4). In each case, do you believe that the standard you detected was the standard intended by the spot's creators?

15. Watch three different sitcoms. How is happiness defined in each? How much importance does the program attach to the pursuit of happiness?

16. Repeat #15 using three game shows as your focal point. As a group, do the sitcoms or the game shows make happiness attainment more important as a self-evaluative standard? Why is this the case?

17. What commercial website has the greatest potential to make you "happy"? Which of its elements contribute most to engendering this feeling?

18. Conduct your own five-part depiction analysis of an hour-long drama or action/adventure program.

19. Repeat #18 using a newscast as your referent.

20. Prepare a complete depiction analysis of *The Cosby Show* script in Appendix A.

21. Repeat #20 using the Appendix A *Simpsons* script as your referent.

22. View one episode of a daytime soap opera. From your perceptions, can it be read hegemonically? Repeat this experiment on another soap and compare the results. Identify the groups most likely to engage in each of the possible hegemonic readings you've uncovered.

23. Repeat #22 using two network prime-time newscasts.

24. Analyze whether a selected action/adventure show handles violence in a responsible manner by applying Louis Day's six questions to it.

25. Repeat #24 using several music videos as your referents.

CHAPTER 10:
STRUCTURAL ANALYSIS

1. Analyze two current sitcoms as to the presence and interaction of *alazons*, *eirons*, *bomolochoi*, and *agroikos*. Is the show that more clearly and extensively features these archetypes the more enjoyable program? Why or why not?

2. Identify and decode the symbols used in the "I Am Michigan" television spot (Figure 9-1). Which of these symbols could as easily be used in the promotion of *any* state? Which seem exclusive to Michigan? Which could be used by some states but not by others?

3. Listen to a selected disc jockey's entire on-air shift. What archetypes does the deejay exploit in facilitating audience communication?

4. Describe the problem-solving progression (ritual) used in episodes of two currently aired sitcoms. Was one show's ritual more believable (more mystique-rich) than the other's? If so, did this believability make it the more enjoyable sitcom? Why or why not?

5. Repeat #4 using two action/adventure programs as your subjects.

6. Analyze the ritual put in place by your favorite radio station's morning drive-time programming. Does this ritual mirror your own morning life cycle? If so, via what devices?

7. What mystique or mystiques does Barbara Lippert allude to in her Chapter 5 review of 7-Up spots? Does she believe these commercials have properly and effectively exploited mystique?

8. Read Debra Goldman's Chapter 3 review of *Forgive or Forget*. What, in her opinion, seems to be the underlying mythic structure of this series?

9. Over a week's viewing, compile a list of myths that were conveyed by the programs you observed. Do any of Sprague Vonier's items appear on your list?

10. Dissect five television news-magazine stories from at least two different shows to determine whether each story follows a thesis/antithesis/synthesis progression. Do the stories that conform to this progression seem more or less complete than other stories? more or less balanced? more or less accurate?

11. Describe how the thesis/antithesis/synthesis structure is exploited in Chapter 4's Subaru commercial (Figure 4-3). Repeat this exercise with Chapter 9's Michelin spot (Figure 9-3). Which advertisement makes the best use of this structure?

12. Identify two other sitcoms that, like *The Cosby Show* and *The Simpsons*, regularly

follow the thesis/antithesis/synthesis pattern. Identify two sitcoms that don't seem to mirror this structure. Does the presence or apparent absence of the pattern relate to the comparative satisfaction you derive from each show?

13. Ascertain the signifier/signified/sign components of the next six television commercials to which you are exposed.

14. Repeat #13 with the next six radio commercials you hear. Is this semiotic structure more difficult or easier to isolate in radio as compared to television? Why?

15. Dissect the semiotic structure of the *Dangerous Years* documentary as described by Van Gordon Sauter in his Chapter 2 review.

16. What are the first, second, and third order signs in the Marcy Fitness commercial described by Barbara Lippert in her Chapter 15 review? What is Lippert's attitude toward the appropriation of these signs and the interrelationship the spot seems to establish between them?

17. Isolate a major, recent news story that seems to have evolved via Altheide's seven-step crisis ritual. Identify each step in the same manner used in the chapter to discuss the Magic Johnson and Clinton/Lewinsky progressions.

CHAPTER 11: PROBING ETHICS AND VALUES

1. Watch three continuous hours of television programming on a single channel. Make a list of all the values that are expressed or implied during these three hours (in the aired commercials as well as the programs).

2. Repeat #1 during the same time of day, but watching a different channel. Do the values displayed vary between the two channels in number or type? What do you believe are the reasons for this similarity or discrepancy?

3. Reread Jim Sollisch's Chapter 2 TV ratings commentary. As evidenced in his writing, what personal values does Sollisch himself seem to hold?

4. Should J. B. Stoner's commercial have been guaranteed broadcast access? Is there any other type of message that should be accorded such a guarantee? Write a brief position paper that sets forth and illustrates your

position. Remember to take into account the rights of the medium operator as well.

5. Try to construct a defense for reimposition of the Family Viewing plan. Your plan should be feasible and constitutional in today's multichannel world.

6. Read Barbara Lippert's Chapter 15 review of the Marcy Fitness commercial. Are elements of the Protestant ethic and social Darwinism present in the spot and/or in Lippert's comments about it?

7. Repeat #6 using Dan Kening's Chapter 3 "Love Sponge" piece as your subject. Does Kening seem to accept or reject the Protestant ethic and social Darwinism? Does the 'Love Sponge' himself mirror either or both these orientations?

8. Select any sitcom, drama, or action/adventure episode and dissect how it supports or contradicts Protestant ethic and social Darwinism tenets.

9. Repeat #8 using a local newscast as your point of reference. Watch the newscast for three succeeding days before drawing your conclusions.

10. Repeat #9 choosing a newscast from a different station or from a network. Are the Protestant ethic and social Darwinism present to the same degree in both newscasts? What is your explanation for this discrepancy or nondiscrepancy?

11. Read the script of *The Newsroom* found in Appendix A and analyze how it embraces or rejects the Protestant ethic and social Darwinism.

12. Repeat #11 using the Appendix A script of *The Simpsons* as your subject.

13. Taking an organization that is prominently depicted in a one-hour drama (such as *ER*'s hospital), discuss its apparent corporate values. Use Vande Berg and Trujillo's six organizational value pairings as the structure for your commentary.

14. Examine Ray Richmond's Chapter 15 review of *Action* from the standpoints of libertarianism and social responsibility. To which of these philosophies does Fox seem to subscribe according to this review? Can you detect Richmond's own philosophical viewpoint from his writing?

15. Repeat #14 with Dan Kening's review in Chapter 3 as your referent. Does the philosophical orientation of the 'Love Sponge' seem to be more libertarian or social responsibility-based?

16. Assume you were a television entertainment series producer asked to participate

in the Center for Health Communications's "designated driver" project. What would *your* response have been and how would you ethically defend your response if questioned about it in a public forum?

17. Try to match each of Maccoby and Terzi's Protestant ethic stages with a program series that seems graphically to epitomize that stage. (Thus, you are looking for four separate programs.)

18. Over the past year, have the federal government's dealings with the electronic media seemed to lean more toward libertarianism or social responsibility? Consult recent trade publications before composing your answer.

19. As a station program director, you have been offered a critically acclaimed outdoors/ecology series for Saturday afternoon airing at no charge to you. The show has a proven track record with males ages twenty-five to forty-nine. The entire license fee will be paid by a firearms manufacturer who, in exchange, wants you to air one sixty-second spot at the end of the show. The commercial promotes the company's new pump-action 22-caliber rifle. Your station has never accepted firearms advertising before, but there is no written or corporate policy about such advertising. You have ascertained that your prime competitor will take the show under these terms if you don't. Using Day's six moral duties/constituences as your framework, write a position paper that outlines the factors involved in your decision making.

CHAPTER 12:
AESTHETICS AND ART

1. Listen to an hour of a given radio station's music programming. Then, write five brief aesthetic analyses of it as seen from the respective orientations of Absolutism, Individualism, Objectivism, Cultural Relativism, and Biopsychological Relativism.

2. Inventory all the possible pleasures delivered by the 'docu-soaps' that Antonia Zerbisias describes in her Chapter 14 column. Which of these pleasures seem to be enjoyed by Zerbisias herself?

3. According to his Chapter 14 review, which of art's six tasks does Jeff Jarvis believe to be served by *The Rosie O'Donnell Show*? Cite specific quotes from Jarvis's piece to document your answer.

4. Repeat #3 using Greg Quill's "CITY-TV's Crime Series" review in Chapter 14 as your subject.

5. View a game show and identify which of art's six tasks it seems to fulfill. Then watch another game show and conduct the same analysis. Are the two shows similar or divergent in the artistic tasks they serve? What do your findings imply about the aesthetic of game shows in general?

6. Repeat #5 using two soap operas. What (if any) artistic task-serving is common to both game show and soap opera genres? Which tasks apparently are not served by either program type?

7. Examine the Wendy's and Club Med television commercials in Chapter 2 (Figures 2-1 and 2-3) and the Check-Up Gum spot in Chapter 9 (Figure 9-2). Ascertain which of the six artistic tasks each spot serves.

8. Choose a reality program that you feel "inspires fear, disgust, and indignation." Describe how this inspiration is realized and whether you believe this show thereby performs a positive service for the audience.

9. Repeat #8 using a current radio-featured song lyric as your referent.

10. Analyze *The Simpsons* script in Appendix A as to how many of the six artistic tasks this episode accommodated and how this accommodation was achieved.

11. Repeat #10 using the Appendix A script from *The Newsroom* as your subject.

12. Select one complete evening's prime-time schedule as listed in *TV Guide*. Attempt to categorize each program as a fine, folk, or popular art (subdividing the last category into "public" and "pop" art).

13. Reread Barbara Lippert's Chapter 5 critique of selected 7-Up commercials. Which school or schools of aesthetic thought are reflected in her commentary?

14. Repeat #13 with Howard Reich's Chapter 15 review of *Swingin' with Duke* as the subject.

CHAPTER 13:
THE LOGIC OF AESTHETIC FORM

1. Write a critique of a local radio station's complete morning drive-time that addresses the question of whether or not, in its totality, the daypart's programming possesses organic unity.

2. Repeat #1 using a different radio station. In comparing the two outlets, does the one reflecting the greater sense of organic unity also seem to be the "better" station overall? By what criteria did you arrive at this determination?

3. Isolate the theme of the next six television commercials you see. Does the theme's articulation rest more on the visual or the aural component of each spot?

4. What, according to David Remnick's Chapter 4 review, seems to be the theme that "Playground Pros" projects? What theme, in contrast, would the critic have liked it to articulate?

5. Watch a made-for-TV movie. Which of the four types of thematic variation did it appear to use? Did each of these variations assist or inhibit your enjoyment of the feature?

6. Analyze the visual balances projected in the way a selected local television newscast is staged. Pay special attention to set design, shot progression, and alternation between news presenters.

7. Repeat #6 using a competing station. Which newscast seemed to project the more pronounced sense of visual equilibrium? Did this feeling carry over into your impression of the show as a whole?

8. Plot the evolution of a daytime soap opera during the course of a selected week. What factors seem to govern the evolutionary pace? Does evolution ever break down? If so, where and why?

9. Repeat #8 with a single episode of a dramatic series (not a *serial*). What were the differences in evolutionary technique between the self-contained dramatic episode and the soap's five serial segments?

10. Compare and critique the evolution of two competing radio stations' afternoon drive-time programming.

11. Graph the hierarchical patterns of episodes from two different action/adventure shows. Is the show with the more skillful hierarchy also the more appealing show overall? Why or why not?

12. Repeat #11 using two sitcoms as your referents.

13. Compose a Logic of Aesthetic Form critique of *The Cosby Show* script found in Appendix A.

14. Repeat #13 with Appendix A's script from *The Newsroom* as your referent.

15. Conduct a Logic of Aesthetic Form analysis of a 'reality' court show.

16. Repeat #14 focusing on a different court show. Is the show that more closely conforms to Parker's Logic also the more enjoyable one for you?

17. Study Barbara Lippert's Chapter 15 review of the Marcy Fitness commercial. How many Logic of Aesthetic Form components does Lippert allude to in this piece?

18. Take another look at the Club Med (Figure 2-3), Subaru (Figure 4-3), and Yoo-Hoo (Figure 10-6) television commercials. What type of thematic variation is employed in each?

19. Using the co-anchors on a local television station newscast, try to structure a balance/contrast inventory similar to the chapter-presented comparison of Charlie Brown and Lucy.

20. Repeat #19 focusing on the co-anchors at a competing station. Is the show with the longest balance/contrast anchor inventory more or less entertaining to watch? Does it seem to be the more or less informative program?

21. Critique the evolution of a sitcom episode from the three standpoints of event sequencing, where it begins, and event duration. Repeat this exercise in the following week to ascertain whether the same evolutionary techniques are used. Be certain to identify which of the five duration devices are being utilized.

22. Repeat #21 with a drama series as your subject.

23. Isolate the storylines that emerge from three different sports broadcasts. In each case, did the storyline seem predetermined or the natural outgrowth of game events?

24. Rent an uncut video copy of a movie scheduled to be shown on broadcast television. Watch the video, plotting out the ideal points for commercial breaks. Compare your hierarchical plan with that subsequently followed in the broadcast of the film.

CHAPTER 14: REALITY PROGRAMMING

1. Reread David Remnick's Chapter 4 review of "Playground Pros." Is this show, in fact, a *reality* program? Why or why not?

2. Observe the early-evening newscast of every television station in your market. Attempt to apportion each segment of their

coverage into either the "information" (hard news) or the "infotainment" category. From a percentage standpoint, which station has the greatest amount of infotainment? Which the least amount? How do these percentages compare with the ratings being garnered by these outlets?

3. Repeat #2 in terms of local stations' midday newscasts. Do the approximate ratios of information to infotainment remain the same? Are the stations heaviest/lightest in infotainment at noon similarly ranked in their early-evening newscasts? Can you draw any broad conclusions from these data?

4. Of the infotainment segments found in #2 and/or #3, how many could be labelled as "tabloid"? Was the station with the highest percentage of infotainment also the outlet with the greatest amount of tabloid material? Are there any stations that entirely avoid tabloid content in their newscasts? In their overall programming?

5. Repeat #2 and #4 with the broadcast networks' evening newscasts as your subject. How do your findings here compare with what you discovered about local stations? As an additional perspective, you may wish to add at least one evening CNN news hour into this analysis—and/or a half-hour of CNN Headline News.

6. Are there any television programs currently running in your market that could be labelled as "Shock"? If so, isolate the precise characteristics of the show(s) that justify this designation.

7. Repeat #6 in terms of locally available radio offerings.

8. Analyze the program schedules of all television stations in your market to compile a list of shows aired by each that fit into one of the ten reality genres. Which reality genre is the most often scheduled in your market? Which genre is most often scheduled on each station? Are reality shows most frequently aired against each other or as counterprogramming to nonreality fare?

9. Divide the current radio and television talk shows running in your market into "regular talk" and "hot talk" categories. Which category is the more numerous? Are there outlets that air only one of these two categories? Can any of these offerings be labelled "trash"? Why or why not?

10. Place each game show running in your market into one of five categories depending on the contestant attribute it seems most to emphasize: (a) intelligence; (b) a good memory; (c) quick reaction under pressure; (d) physical abilities or appearance; (e) sociability/extroversion. Which category is the most prominent? The least prominent? What does this suggest about the audience gratifications catered to by these game shows?

CHAPTER 15: COMPOSITE CRITICISM

1. Isolate all the intrinsic appreciation elements mentioned by Greg Quill in his Chapter 12 commentary on *Beyond Reality* and Betsy Sharkey in her Chapter 10 critique of *The Simpsons*.

2. Watch the television program you dislike the most and write an intrinsic appreciation inventory for it. Make this inventory as extensive as possible.

3. Identify the extrinsic appreciation elements in Ray Richmond's *Action* review in this chapter and in Barbara Lippert's "Indecent Exposure" commentary in Chapter 12.

4. Reread the Clifford Terry preview of *The Tortellis* found in Chapter 10. List all of Terry's intrinsic evaluation comments and, across from them, all of his intrinsic appreciation statements. Are these two lists balanced? If not, what does the imbalance imply about the show and/or about the critic?

5. Find the intrinsic evaluation elements in Tony Scott's *Dead Silence* critique in Chapter 1 and in Van Gordon Sauter's Chapter 2 preview of *Dangerous Years*.

6. Cull out the extrinsic evaluation aspects of these two Chapter 14 critiques: Greg Quill's "Crime Series" preview and Jeff Jarvis's review of *The Rosie O'Donnell Show*.

7. Conduct a composite critique of *The Cosby Show* script in Appendix A.

8. Repeat #7 with *The Simpsons* script as your subject.

9. Prepare a composite criticism of the Figure 11-2 "AIDS" PSA.

10. Repeat #9 using the Figure 11-3 "Guardian Plan" commercial as your subject.

11. Imagine that the "Nude in a Seven-Course Cantonese Dinner" example cited in the chapter was an actual half-hour experimental video, shot entirely in black-and-white, and shown on the Arts & Entertainment cable network. Despite its title, most of the piece is devoted to a nonverbal portrayal

of a Hong Kong orphan boy's rescue from life on the streets by a master chef who then lovingly teaches him the culinary arts. The only soundtrack alternates natural sound effects with soft oriental string music. After many frustrations and failures in his apprenticeship, the novice finally achieves chef status. The climax is a dream sequence in which the form of a graceful female nude, representing the goddess of unselfish sustenance, gradually emerges from a montage of the gourmet dishes that the young chef has prepared. From this description, try to construct a brief composite criticism that overcomes the one-dimensional opinions of the creating videographer on the one hand and those of that chapter-identified protector of community morals on the other.

12. What information was missing from #11 that, if supplied, would have enabled you to compose a more thorough composite critique of this video program?

Index